THIRD EDITION

Public Speaking

An Audience-Centered Approach

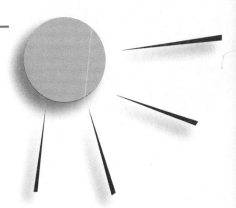

Steven A. Beebe
SOUTHWEST TEXAS STATE UNIVERSITY

Susan J. Beebe
SOUTHWEST TEXAS STATE UNIVERSITY

ALLYN AND BACON

Boston · London · Toronto · Sydney · Tokyo · Singapore

DEDICATED TO OUR PARENTS,
RUSSELL AND MURIEL BEEBE
HERB AND JANE DYE

AND TO OUR SONS,
MARK AND MATTHEW BEEBE

Vice President, Humanities: Joseph Opiela
Series Editor: Carla F. Daves
Senior Developmental Editor: Marlene Ellin
Series Editorial Assistant: Andrea Geanacopoulos
Marketing Manager: Karon Bowers
Production Administrator: Mary Beth Finch
Editorial-Production Service: Thomas E. Dorsaneo
Text Design, Composition, and Illustration: Seventeenth Street Studios
Cover Administrator: Linda Knowles
Composition and Prepress Buyer: Linda Cox
Manufacturing Buyer: Megan Cochran

Copyright © 1997, 1994, 1991 by Allyn & Bacon
A Viacom Company
Needham Heights, MA 02194
http://www.abacon.com
America Online: Keyword: College Online

Library of Congress Cataloging-in -Publication Data
Beebe, Steven A., 1950—
    Public speaking : an audience-centered approach / Steven A. Beebe,
Susan J. Beebe. —3rd ed.
        p. cm.
    Includes bibliographical references and index.
    ISBN 0-205-19847-3
    1. Public speaking. 2. Oral communication. I. Beebe, Susan J.
II. Title.
PN4121.B385 1997
808.5'1--dc20
                                                    96-13684
                                                        CIP

Printed in the United States of America
10 9 8 7 6 5 4 3 2   01 00 99 98 97

Contents

Preface

Speaking is both an art and a science. An effective public speaker artfully crafts a message while also relying upon time-tested principles of human communication. We believe the lynch pin linking the art and the science of speaking well is a focus on audience. The audience, after all, is the reason for delivering any speech.

Public Speaking: An Audience-Centered Approach is intended to be the primary text for a college-level public speaking course. Focusing on the importance of remaining audience-centered throughout the speechmaking process, its key purpose is to help teach students how to become skilled public speakers.

We continue to be grateful to students and teachers for their warm, positive response to our two previous editions. We regard it as the highest of compliments when instructors tell us, "You present information the same way I teach my students." In this new edition, we have retained those elements of the text that users have praised: the audience-centered focus, lively and interesting examples, comprehensive coverage of all aspects of public speaking, a colorful and artfully crafted design, and an engaging writing style that speaks to students—our audience.

We have made some key changes as well. We recognize that increasing numbers of students today are leading double lives, working at jobs as well as earning college degrees. So we have shifted our focus to bridge some of the gaps between the classroom and the workplace. Our central goal, however, is still to provide an accessible practical resource that students can use to improve their speaking skill in any setting.

AN AUDIENCE-CENTERED FOCUS

All public speaking books include information about adapting to an audience. Most, however, discuss audience analysis in one chapter as a single step in the speechmaking process, then proceed to lead students methodically through subsequent steps. In contrast, our approach emphasizes the importance of the audience throughout our entire discussion of the process. We believe that Aristotle was right: The audience is the most important entity in the process. And as audiences in the United States become increasingly diverse, it is all the more important to teach students to focus on the many and varied needs and perspectives of their listeners. Central to this new edition is a recognition that being audience-centered means understanding and appreciating diversity.

Preparing and delivering a speech involves a series of steps in a focused process. Our audience-centered model captures both the step-by-step sequence of speech preparation and the ongoing process of focusing on the speech goal: communicating well with an audience.

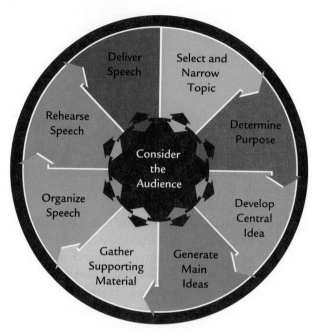

The model shown here, introduced in Chapter 2 along with an overview of the speech making process, reappears throughout the text. Different tasks in the speechmaking process are highlighted each time. Viewing the model as a clock, the speaker begins the process at the "12 o'clock" position with "select and narrow topic" and moves around the model clock-wise to "deliver speech." At each step, however, the speaker is reminded to consider the audience, so the process is also recursive. The arrows that traverse the steps in both directions indicate that a speaker sometimes needs to revise a previous step before continuing on to the next. Visual learners especially appreciate having this clear, easy-to-understand panorama of the public speaking process unfold before their eyes.

 We also use a miniature version of this model, like the icon shown here in the margin, to highlight text discussions that emphasize audience-centered skills and principles.

Presenting our model early in the text gives students some of the essential knowledge they need to begin constructing speeches right away. As they progress through the text, they deepen their understanding of each step in the model as they continue preparing and delivering speeches.

● FEATURES NEW TO THE THIRD EDITION

The praise we received for our previous two editions stems, we believe, from our commitment to developing a book in collaboration with our users—our audience. In this edition we have retained those elements of the book that have been applauded by both teachers and students, but we have also responded to their suggestions for new material and made changes in the order of our treatment of essential public speaking competencies. For example, we have reorganized the sequence of those chapters which teach students to gather supporting materials and then use the materials they find to support their ideas. Our streamlined chapter "Outlining Your Speech" (Chapter 11) now follows our discussion of both organizing the speech and preparing introductions and conclusions. In addition, teachers who like students to conceptualize a persuasive speech based upon a proposition of fact, value, or policy will find a new treatment of this approach in Chapter 16.

Our reviewers asked for more tools to help students become effective public speakers in contemporary society. To that end we have integrated more information about audience diversity, ethics, and technology. We also focus on techniques that bridge theory and practice, emphasizing how to help students provide meaningful feedback to their classmates and themselves.

● NEW MATERIALS ON AUDIENCE DIVERSITY   In our previous editions we emphasized that focusing on audience required a recognition and appreciation of the rich diversity of cultural, ethnic, religious, and socioeconomic backgrounds represented by many contemporary U.S. audiences. In this edition we have strengthened this emphasis, including new examples in every chapter as well as special sections throughout the book. Our goal is to free students from an entrenched egocentric and ethnocentric mind set. Effective communication occurs only when communicators consider and respond to their listeners' preferences and backgrounds. Chapter 1 introduces students to characteristics of diverse audiences they are likely to encounter. Chapter 5, which emphasizes audience analysis and adaptation, includes expanded coverage of culture and diversity, offering suggestions for communicating effectively with a diverse audience. Chapter 9 includes new material on how to organize ideas to adapt to a culturally diverse group of listeners. Expanded treatment of sexist and culturally biased language in Chapter 12 encourages students to increase their sensitivity to the power of language in shaping and reflecting cultural attitudes. A new section in Chapter 13 includes strategies for adapting delivery style to different audiences. Chapter 17 includes expanded coverage about differences in reasoning that stem from cultural preferences in constructing and responding to arguments. In addition, numerous examples throughout the text, as well as our photographic illustrations, enrich students, understanding of different cultural values and distinctions.

● NEW CHAPTER ON ETHICS   As in our two previous editions, we continue to make numerous references to speechmaking ethics throughout the book. In this edition, however, we have strengthened our treatment of ethics with a new chapter (Chapter 3) that reviews the strong tradition of free speech in our democratic society. This addition does more than just heighten student awareness of ethical issues; we suggest practical ways to ensure that students understand the value of being a speaker of integrity. We include explicit discussions of plagiarism, the legitimate use of evidence and reasoning, and the need for tolerance.

At the end of each chapter we have also added a new set of ethical questions to spark student discussion about ethical and free speech issues.

● NEW INFORMATION ON TECHNOLOGY   In this edition, we continue our tradition of introducing students to the latest advances in technology to enhance their speaking skill. We have expanded our discussion of the use of electronic data bases for speechmaking research. A new section about using the Internet and the world wide web suggests ways to connect with discourse communities and search for various forms of data. Chapter 14, Visual Aids, includes expanded treatment of using the latest CD-ROM and computer-generated graphics to enhance speech presentations. Although all students may not have access to state-of-the-art hardware and software during their speech course, some may have such resources available at their workplace, either now or later on. In addition to these explicit suggestions, we have also added a new section at the end of each chapter called "Using Media and Technology"; these activities suggest ways for students to use the latest technology to expand their exposure to public speaking and to improve their speaking skill.

● NEW APPENDIX ON PRESENTATION VISUALS   To help students prepare the kinds of the presentations typically demanded in business and professional settings, we have added a richly illustrated introduction to the planning and design of visual aids. Coverage includes storyboarding, basic principles of layout and design, and type and color selection. A detailed walkthrough provides guidance in using PowerPoint™ and other electronic design packages.

● NEW CASES THAT ILLUSTRATE PUBLIC SPEAKING AS A PRACTICAL ART   To help students make connections between the "laboratory" speeches they deliver in a public speaking class and those they will need to deliver in work and civic situations, we've included a new feature called "Speakers at Work." In six chapters we have included brief case narratives written by people who use public speaking skills successfully in the course of their daily work in business, government, education, and civic circles. Each case focuses on a public speaking occasion that called upon the speaker's ability to analyze and adapt to a special audience situation. By reading about these real-life experiences, students will learn the value of the skills they are mastering as well as tips for translating principles into practice.

● NEW INSTRUCTION ON PEER FEEDBACK   Most instructors invite students to offer comments and feedback about their classmates' speeches, but students sometimes lack the skill required to offer constructive recommendations. In Chapter 4 on listening, we've added a new section to help student audiences provide helpful, constructive feedback to their classmates. We teach them how to offer comments that are specific, descriptive, balanced, and sensitive. We also suggest how student speakers can provide feedback to themselves. The ultimate goal of public speaking instruction, we believe, is to help students learn to be their own best critics.

● NEW CLASSIC AND CONTEMPORARY PUBLIC SPEAKING EXAMPLES   Effective teaching helps students visualize the skills we want them to learn. In this edition, we have incorporated an array of fresh, contemporary examples designed to pique student interest and teach essential public speaking competencies. We've included news items that relate to developments in politics, science, and the arts. We've also incorporated new excerpts from great speeches past and present to illustrate particular skills and to help students understand the role and power of rhetoric in shaping history. Two new speeches in Appendix D show students how to inform and entertain, respectively. Martin Luther King's classic "I Have A Dream" speech is still included as an example of a persuasive speech that inspires and models classic principles.

● OUR PARTNERSHIP WITH INSTRUCTORS: PRACTICAL SUPPLEMENTAL RESOURCES

A text alone cannot do the complex job of building public speaking skill. Students learn best in partnership with an experienced teacher who can instill confidence and impart practical knowledge. Accordingly, we continue to offer a cornucopia of resources to assist instructors in their work.

- *Instructor's Annotated Edition by Diana Ivy, Texas A&M, Corpus Christi.* Continuing the tradition we pioneered with our first edition, we offer a special instructor's edition of the text that includes teaching strategies, suggested videos and supplemental readings, individual and collaborative class activities, suggestions for writing assignments—all printed in the margin along side the student text.

- *Instructor's Resource Manual/Test Bank by Diana Ivy, Texas A&M, Corpus Christi.* You'll find a wealth of support in this exceptional resource: an introduction on "Achieving Gender Equity in the Public Speaking Classroom," sample syllabi, transparency masters, chapter outlines, creative teaching ideas, student activities—plus more than 1,000 objective and essay questions organized by type and level difficulty.

- *Computerized Test Bank.* This computerized (Esatest III) version of the test bank items lets you use your IBM or Macintosh computer to produce tailor-made tests. Every copy comes with a GRADEBOOK disc and an ONLINE TESTING program.

- *Allyn & Bacon Public Speaking Transparency Package.* More than 100 new full-color transparencies created with PowerPoint™ software provide visual support for classroom lectures and discussion on a full range of course topics.

- *Online Transparency Package.* Our transparencies are also available through Allyn & Bacon's World Wide Web site at http://www.abacon.com. A brief User's Guide available in the Communication area explains how to access both PC and Macintosh versions of the PowerPoint™ images. Users can then download either selected portions or the entire package.

- *Contemporary Classic Speeches Video.* This video, available through exclusive agreement with Cable News Network, consists of multiple segments, ranging from under five minutes to half an hour in length. Speakers include Jesse Jackson, Rosa Parks, Ronald Reagan, Bill Clinton, and other well known figures.

- *Allyn & Bacon/AFA Students Speeches Video.* This new two-hour video contains 12 award-winning student speeches available through a special agreement between Allyn & Bacon and American Forensic Association. Recorded at the 1996 AFA National Individual Events Tournament, the speeches cover a wide range of informative and persuasive topics, including auto insurance fraud, the credit card crisis among college students, and a vaccine to treat viruses. The accompanying Video User's Guide contains a full transcript and outline for each speech as well teaching tips and aids for using the speeches in class.

- *Allyn & Bacon Communication Video Library.* * These videotapes, produced by Insight Media, cover such topics as Fearless Public Speaking, Body-Language, The Art of Listening, and Keys to Effective Speaking.

- *Speech Preparation Workbook by Jenifer Dreyer and Gregory H. Patton, both of San Diego State University.* This workbook for student purchase takes the speech preparer through the various stages of speech creation—from audience analysis to writing the speech—and provides guidelines, tips, and easy-to-fill-in pages.

- *Interactive Speechwriter Version 1.1 by Martin R. Cox.* This interactive software for student purchase provides supplemental material and enhances students' understanding of key concepts discussed in the text. Includes tutorials, self test questions, sample speeches, and templates for writing the outline as well as informative, persuasive, and motivated sequence speeches. (Available for Windows and Macintosh)

- *Public Speaking in the Multicultural Environment, 2nd Edition by Devorah Lieberman, Portland State University.* This two-chapter essay for student purchase exposes public speaking students to cultural diversity factors influencing both the speaker and the audience. Comes complete with activities.

- *Simon & Schuster Audio Soundguide for Public Speaking.* Complete with student speeches, vignettes, and self-quizzes, this audio study guide for student purchase helps students understand and master the skills necessary to excel at public speaking.

- *Allyn & Bacon Website.* If you're already connected to the Internet, you can access the new Allyn & Bacon website. Online textbook resources in public speaking are under development at http://www.abacon.com!

ACKNOWLEDGMENTS

We want to thank many people who have helped produce this book. Our partnership as authors has been greatly enhanced by the ideas and support we have received from our friends, colleagues, and students. We are grateful to all of the authors and speakers we have quoted or referenced; their words and wisdom have added depth to our knowledge and richness to our experience.

*Some restrictions may apply.

This is the first edition of the book published by Allyn and Bacon following the transfer of Prentice Hall's speech communication book list to this find publishing house. We want to continue to acknowledge Steve Dalphin, our first editor at Prentice Hall, for encouraging us to write this book. Our editors at Allyn and Bacon have done an outstanding job of providing support and creative suggestions to improve and update this book. We are thankful for the ever-present support we receive from Carla F. Daves, Acquisitions Editor at Allyn and Bacon. Marlene Ellin, Senior Development Editor, has masterfully guided us through the revision process. Her outstanding attention to detail and creative suggestions have given us fresh ideas and insight.

Many reviewers helped us make decisions about what should be included, revised and strengthened in this new edition. We thank the following public speaking instructors for sharing their experience, advice and wisdom with us: Michael W. Kramer of the University of Missouri; Mary Helen Richer of the University of North Dakota; Myra G. Gutin of Rider University; Shane Simon of Central Texas College; Dr. Melanie Anson of Citrus College; Edward J. Streb of Rowan College; Nancy R. Wemm of Glenville State College; Ed Lamoureux of Bradley University; K. David Roach of Texas Tech University; Rhonda Parker of the University of San Francisco; Richard Armstrong of Wichita State University; Denise Vrchota of Iowa State University; and Darla Germeroth of the University of Scranton.

We are again grateful to our friend and colleague Tom Burkholder from Southwest Texas State University, who wrote the outstanding essay in Appendix A. It is one of the finest distillations of the history of classical rhetoric that we have read. Dan Cavanaugh, also of Southwest Texas State University, did an excellent job of authoring Appendix C, "Preparing Visual Aids for Presentations." We also want to thank our friend Diana Ivy from Texas A & M, Corpus Christi, for sharing her wealth of teaching strategies in the revised Instructor's Annotated Edition and Instructor's Resource Manual, and for masterfully revising the test file. Her gifts as a teacher sparkle through every suggestion and test question that she has authored.

We are continually grateful for the support and ideas we have received from our colleagues and students at Southwest Texas State University. Tom Willett at William Jewell College, Dan Curtis at Central Missouri State University, John Masterson at the University of Miami, and Thompson Biggers at mercer University are long-time friends and exemplary teachers who have influenced our work and life. Sue Hall, Department of Speech Communication administrative assistant at Southwest Texas State University, again provided outstanding support and assistance in helping us keep our work on schedule. Manuscript typist Rhonda Brooks and research assistants Rhonda Kellett and Maria Kharcheva were also of considerable help in preparing this revision and keeping us on schedule.

Both of us have been blessed with gifted teachers who have helped us develop as educators. Mary Harper, former speech and drama teacher at Grain Valley High School, Grain Valley, Missouri, and Margaret Dent, retired speech teacher of Hannibal High School, Hannibal, Missouri, provided initial instruction in public speaking that remains with us today. We appreciate the patient encouragement we received from Robert Brewer, our first debate coach at Central Missouri State University, where we first met each other over twenty-five years ago. We both served as student teachers under the unforgettable guidance of the late Louis Banker at Fort Osage High School. We have also benefited from the skilled instruction of Mary Jeanett Smythe of the University of Missouri, Columbia. We also wish to acknowledge Loren Reid, also from the University of Missouri, Columbia; to us, he is the quintessential speech teacher.

Finally, we appreciate the patience, endurance, support, and love of our sons, Mark and Matthew Beebe. They will always be our most important audience.

Steven A. Beebe
Susan J. Beebe
San Marcos, Texas

Public Speaking

Jacob Lawrence
The Migration of the Negro, Panel No. 1, 1940-41
Tempera on masonite
12 x 18" (30.5 x 45.7 cm)
©The Phillips Collection, Washington, D.C.

Introduction to Public Speaking

*A journey of a
thousand miles begins
with a single step.
—Old Chinese Proverb*

● OUTLINE

A unique communication format

The communication process
Communication as action ·
Communication as interaction ·
Communication as transaction ·

Public speaking's rich heritage

Public speaking and diversity

Summary

● OBJECTIVES

**After studying this chapter you
should be able to do the following:**

1. *Explain how public speaking differs from
   casual conversation.*

2. *Sketch and explain a model that illustrates the components and process of
   communication.*

3. *Discuss in brief the history of public
   speaking.*

4. *Explain how becoming an audience-
   centered public speaker can help you
   speak effectively to diverse audiences.*

is eyes were buried in his script. His words in monotone emerged haltingly from behind his mustache, losing volume as they were sifted through hair. Audiences rushed to see and hear him, and after they had satisfied their eyes, they closed their ears. Ultimately, they turned to small talk among themselves while the great man droned on.[1]

Perhaps you think you have heard this speaker—or even taken a class from him. But the speaker described here in such an unflattering way is none other than Albert Einstein. Sadly, although the great physicist could attract an audience with his reputation, he could not sustain their attention and interest because he lacked public speaking skills.

Although you may not be blessed with his intellect, you have at least one distinct advantage over Einstein: the opportunity afforded by this course and this text to study and practice public speaking. Right now, however, the experience may seem less like an opportunity and more like a daunting task. Why undertake it?

First, you will undoubtedly be called upon to speak in public at various times in your life: as a student participating in a classroom seminar; as a businessperson convincing your boss to let you undertake a new project; as a concerned citizen addressing the city council's zoning board. In each of these situations, the ability to speak with competence and confidence will empower you. It will give you an edge that other, less skilled communicators lack—even those who may have superior ideas, training, or experience. It will position you for greater things. Former presidential speechwriter James Humes, who labels public speaking "the language of leadership," says, "Every time you have to speak—whether it's in an auditorium, in a company conference room, or even at your own desk—you are auditioning for leadership."[2]

John H. McConnell, CEO of Worthington Industries, suggests a second and perhaps even more compelling reason to study public speaking. The skills you develop in this class may someday help you get a job. Notes McConnell,

> *Many students who work summers at our plants, then go back to school in the fall, ask me what courses they should take to be best prepared for business. I always say, "Take all the speech courses and communication courses you can because the world turns on communication."*[3]

McConnell's advice is supported by research as well as personal observation. A recent survey of personnel managers revealed that they consider communication skills the top factor in helping graduating college students obtain employment[4] (see Table 1.1).

We recognize, however, that even if you are fully convinced of the need to become a more competent public speaker, the prospect of standing in front of a group of people to deliver a speech may still fill you with panic. If so, take heart:

TABLE 1.1
Top Factors in Helping Graduating College Students Obtain Employment

Rank/Order	Factors/Skills Evaluated
1	Oral (speaking) communication
2	Listening ability
3	Enthusiasm
4	Written communication skills
5	Technical competence
6	Appearance
7	Poise
8	Work experience
9	Resume
10	Specific degree held
11	Grade point average
12	Part-time or summer employment
13	Accreditation of program
14	Leadership in campus/community activity
15	Participation in campus/community activity
16	Recommendations
17	School attended

Dan B. Curtis, Jerry L. Winsor, and Ronald D. Stephens, "National Preferences in Business and Communication Education," *Communication Education* 38 (January 1989), p. 11.

the skills you will learn in this course will help you manage your fears. In Chapter 2, we will offer a number of specific suggestions for managing nervousness and developing confidence. For now, it may reassure you to know that public speaking has much in common with conversation, a form of communication in which you engage every day. Like conversation, public speaking requires that you organize your thoughts and put them into words.

"Alicia, do you ever feel that people here are giving you trouble because you're Hispanic?" asks her roommate Sharon.

Alicia wrinkles her brow in thought, then replies, "I guess once in a while, but not for the reasons you'd expect. Like I notice the Anglos getting all nervous when I stand close to them when we talk. And they don't like to look me in the eye for a long time." Using these two points, Alicia could easily organize a speech about differences between Hispanic and Anglo nonverbal behavior.

Speaking in public is also like conversation because you have to make decisions "on your feet." Most of these decisions will be based on your knowledge of who your listeners are, your role in speaking with them, and their reactions to what you are saying. If they look puzzled or ask questions, you will re-explain your idea. If they look bored, you may tell a funny story. In fact, because we believe that the ability to adapt to your audience is so vital, this book will focus on public speaking as an audience-centered activity.

But public speaking is not exactly like conversation. If it were, surely Albert Einstein's lectures would have been more riveting, there would be no need for this book, and there would be no reason to take a public speaking class. Let's look at some of the ways in which public speaking *differs* from conversation.

A unique communication format

Usually the result of forethought and planning rather than a spontaneous event, *public speaking is more intentional than conversation*. Whereas the person involved in conversation speaks spontaneously, usually motivated by something another speaker says, the public speaker may spend hours or even days planning and practicing his or her speech. Having already worked on his inaugural address for several weeks, President-elect John F. Kennedy rose before 8:00 A.M. on January 20, 1961, to review the speech and make final corrections. He practiced aloud while he took a bath, dressed, walked from room to room, and even while he ate breakfast.[5]

More than thirty years later, another U.S. President, Bill Clinton, went down to the wire rewriting and revising a speech on the economy, to be delivered to a joint session of Congress on February 17, 1993. *New Yorker* columnist Sidney Blumenthal describes the zero-hour scene this way:

> *As late as six that night, only three hours before he was to deliver the speech, it remained in unfinished pieces. The crowding of would-be speechwriters in the Roosevelt Room resembled the stateroom scene from "A Night at the Opera." Riding to the Capitol, Clinton was still revising his text.[6]*

Both Kennedy's painstaking editing and rehearsing and Clinton's relentless revising reflect the intentional nature of public speaking.

Public speaking is also less fluid and interactive than conversation. People in conversation may alternately talk and listen, and perhaps even interrupt one another, but *in public speaking the roles of speaker and audience are clearly defined and remain stable*. Rarely do audience members interrupt or even talk to speakers, although some cultures invite more speaker–audience interaction than do others. Even under these circumstances, however, the roles of speaker and audience are still clearly defined and stable.

Of course, occasionally a speaker is interrupted by applause or a heckler's shout. Clinton was interrupted by applause seventy-seven times when he finally delivered that much-revised 1993 speech on the economy.[7] A less welcome interruption was that created by activists protesting recent cuts in social programs, who tried to drown out Speaker of the House Newt Gingrich's June 5, 1995, speech to the American Booksellers Association Convention. After being delayed for nearly thirty minutes, Gingrich vented his frustration openly, shouting, "This is nonsense!" in indignation at the unexpected interruptions.[8]

Finally, *public speaking is more formal than conversation*. The slang or casual language we often use in conversation is not appropriate for most public speaking. Audiences expect speakers to use standard English grammar and vocabulary. The nonverbal communication of public speakers is also more formal. People engaged in conversation often sit or stand close together, gesture spontaneously, and move about restlessly. The physical distance between public speakers and their audiences is usually greater. And although public speakers may certainly use extemporaneous gestures while speaking, they also plan and rehearse some gestures and movement to emphasize especially important parts of their speeches.

Speaking in public, then, requires that you both sharpen existing communication skills, and learn and apply new ones. To better understand what is involved, let's look now at several models of communication that illustrate the public speaking process and its components.

The communication process

COMMUNICATION AS ACTION

Even the earliest theorists recognized that communication is a process. The models they formulated were linear, suggesting a simple transfer of meaning from a sender to a receiver, as shown in Figure 1.1. Although they were simplistic, these models identified most of the elements of the communication process. We will explain each one as it relates to public speaking.

Source   A public speaker is a *source* of information and ideas for an audience. The job of the source or speaker is to **encode** or translate the ideas and images in his or her mind into a system of symbols that will be recognized by an audi-

encode
The originator of a message translates it into verbal and nonverbal symbols.

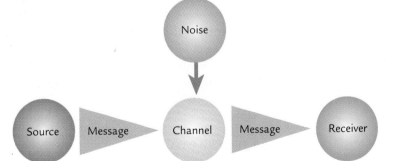

FIGURE 1.1
A linear model of communication

ence. The speaker may encode into words (for example, "The fabric should be two inches square") or into gestures (showing the size with his or her hands).

■ *Message* The *message* in public speaking is the speech itself—both what is said and how it is said. If a speaker has trouble finding words to convey his or her ideas, or sends contradictory nonverbal symbols, listeners may have trouble decoding. In addition, listeners may not interpret the speaker's message as he or she intended because of differences in their frame of reference.

■ *Channels* A message is usually transmitted from sender to receiver via two *channels: visual* and *auditory.* Audience members see the speaker and decode his or her nonverbal symbols—eye contact (or lack of it), facial expressions, posture, gestures, and dress. If the speaker uses any visual aids, such as graphs or models, these too are transmitted along the visual channel. The auditory channel opens as the speaker speaks. Then the audience members hear words and such vocal cues as inflection, rate, and voice quality.

decode
The receiver of a message assigns meaning to the originator's verbal and nonverbal symbols.

codes
Verbal or nonverbal symbols that can be interpreted by another.

■ *Receiver* The *receiver* of the speaker's information or ideas is the individual audience member. The receiver's task is to **decode** the speaker's verbal and nonverbal symbols (or **codes**) back into a message. Of course, the decoded message will never be *exactly* the thought or idea the speaker intended to convey. The receiver's perception of the message will depend on his or her own particular blend of past experiences, attitudes, beliefs, and values. As we have already emphasized, an effective public speaker should be receiver- or audience-centered.

■ *Noise* When something interferes with the communication of a message, we call it *noise.* Noise may be *external,* physical noise. If your 8:00 A.M. public speaking class is frequently interrupted by the roar of a lawn mower running back and forth under the window, it may be difficult to concentrate on what your instructor is saying. A noisy air conditioner, a crying baby, or incessant coughing may also make it difficult for audience members to hear or concentrate on a speech.

Noise may also be *internal.* It may stem from either *physiological* or *psychological* causes and may directly affect either the source or the receiver. A bad cold (physiological noise) may cloud a speaker's memory or subdue his or her delivery. An audience member who is worried about an upcoming exam (psychological noise) is unlikely to remember much of what the speaker says. Regardless of whether it is internal or external, physiological or psychological, or whether it originates with the sender or the receiver, noise interferes with the transmission of a message.

● COMMUNICATION AS INTERACTION

Realizing that linear models were overly simplistic, later communication theorists designed models that depicted communication as a more complex process (see Figure 1.2). These models were circular, or interactive, and added two important new elements: feedback and context.

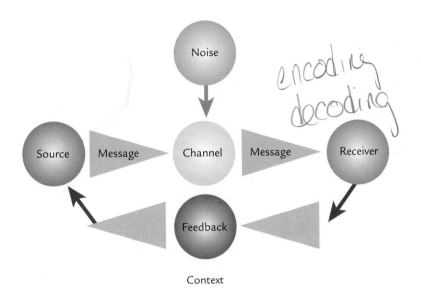

encoding
decoding

FIGURE 1.2
An interactive model of communication

■ *Feedback*   As noted earlier, one way in which public speaking differs from casual conversation is that the public speaker does most or all of the talking. But public speaking is still interactive. Without an audience to hear and provide *feedback,* public speaking serves little purpose. Skillful public speakers are audience-centered. They depend on the nods, facial expressions, and murmurings of the audience to adjust their rate of speaking, volume, vocabulary, type and amount of supporting material, and other variables in order to communicate their message successfully.

■ *Context*   The *context* of a public speaking experience is the environment or situation in which the speech occurs. It includes such elements as the time, the place, and the speaker's and audience's cultural traditions and expectations. To paraphrase John Donne, no *speech* is an island. No speech occurs in a vacuum. Rather, each speech is a blend of circumstances that can never be replicated exactly again.

The person whose job it is to deliver an identical message to a number of different audiences at different times and in different places can attest to the uniqueness of each speaking context. If the room is hot, crowded, or poorly lit, these conditions affect both speaker and audience. The audience who hears a speaker at 10:00 A.M. is likely to be fresher and more receptive than a 4:30 P.M. audience. A speaker who fought rush-hour traffic for ninety minutes to arrive at his or her destination may find it difficult to muster much enthusiasm for delivering the speech.

ELEMENTS OF THE COMMUNICATION PROCESS

Element	Definition
SOURCE	Encodes ideas and images into verbal and nonverbal symbols
RECEIVER	Decodes or translates symbols back into a message
MESSAGE	The meaning the receiver assigns to the symbols; the content of the speech
CHANNELS	The pathways through which messages and symbols pass between a source and receiver
NOISE	External and internal variables that interfere with the communication of a message
FEEDBACK	Response to the message
CONTEXT	Environment or situation in which the speech occurs, including factors such as time, place, and the speaker's and audience's culturally based expectations

COMMUNICATION AS TRANSACTION

The most recent communication models do not label individual components. Transactive models focus instead on communication as a simultaneous process. As the model in Figure 1.3 suggests, we send and receive messages simultaneously, adapting to the context and interpreting the verbal and nonverbal feedback of others as we speak.

FIGURE 1.3
A transactive model of communication

Many of the skills that you will learn from this book relate not only to preparing effective speeches (messages), but also to the elements of feedback and context in the communication process. Our audience-centered approach focuses on "reading" your listeners' responses and adjusting to them as you speak.

Although communication models have been developed only recently, the elements of these models have long been recognized as the keys to successful public speaking. As you study public speaking, you will continue a tradition that goes back to the very beginnings of Western civilization.

Public speaking's rich heritage

Even before people could read, they listened to public speakers. The fourth century B.C. was a golden age for rhetoric in the Greek Republic, where the philosopher Aristotle formulated guidelines for speakers that we still follow today. As politicians and poets attracted large followings in ancient Rome, Cicero and Quintilian sought to define the qualities of the "true" orator. In medieval Europe, the clergy were the most polished public speakers. People gathered eagerly to hear Martin Luther expound his fourteen Articles of Faith. Later, citizens of the New World listened to the town criers and impassioned patriots of colonial America. In the nineteenth century vast audiences heard speakers such as Henry Clay and Daniel Webster debate states' rights; they listened to Frederick Douglass, Angelina Grimke, and Sojourner Truth argue for the abolition of slavery, and to Lucretia Mott plead for women's suffrage; they gathered for an evening's entertainment as Mark Twain traveled the Lyceum and Redpath lecture circuits.

Sojourner Truth, a powerful evangelist and advocate for abolition, had a spellbinding effect on mid-nineteenth-century audiences. [Photo: The Bettmann Archive]

In the first half of the twentieth century, radio made it possible for people around the world to hear King Edward VIII announce that he was abdicating the throne of England to marry an American divorcee, and to listen to Franklin Delano Roosevelt decry December 7, 1941, as "a day which will live in infamy." And in the last half of the century, television provided the medium through which audiences saw and heard the most stirring speeches: Martin Luther King, Jr., declaring "I have a dream" (August 28, 1963); Gerald Ford assuring a nation reeling from Watergate that "Our long national nightmare is over" (presidential inauguration, August 9, 1974); George Bush affirming the American sense of community as "a thousand points of light" (acceptance of the Republican nomination for president, August 18, 1988); and Edward Kennedy eulogizing former First Lady Jacqueline Kennedy as "a lesson to the world on how to do things right" (May 23, 1994).

In short, public speakers through the centuries have provided information, influenced thought and action, entertained, and paid tribute. And in so doing, they have affected both people's daily lives and the course of history.

As people spoke and listened to other speakers, they also studied ways to make speeches better and went on to teach others what they learned. Your own study and practice of public speaking will be built on many of the foundations laid even before Aristotle. If you had been a student of the Greek Protagoras, for example, you would have been required to argue opposing sides of issues in order to discover the merit of each side. If you had studied with Gorgias, you would have toiled to polish and embellish the language and style of your presentations. The influence of these Greek Sophists and others is still reflected in the admonitions of modern speech teachers to their students. Appendix A details the contributions of other early rhetoricians, such as Corax, Plato, Aristotle, Cicero, and Quintilian.

In more recent times, students of nineteenth-century public speaking spent very little time developing their own speeches. Instead they practiced the art of *declamation*—the delivery of an already famous address. Favorite subjects for declamation included speeches by such Americans as Patrick Henry and William Jennings Bryan, and by the British orator Edmund Burke. Collections of speeches, such as Bryan's own ten-volume set of *The World's Famous Orations*, published in 1906, were extremely popular.

Hand in hand with declamation went the study and practice of *elocution*, the expression of emotion through posture, movement, gestures, facial expression, and voice. From the mid-nineteenth to early twentieth centuries, elocution manuals, providing elaborate and specific prescriptions for effective delivery, were standard references not only in schools, but also in nearly every middle-class home in America.[9] Young children (including the mother of one of your authors) took elocution lessons, and elocution became an accepted means of literary study as well as a popular form of entertainment.

As the twentieth century progressed, a more balanced study of speech preparation and speech delivery gradually gained favor. In the United States, audience expectations and preferences changed too, from formal, bombastic oratory to a more conversational, extemporaneous style of speaking.

RECAP

THE RICH HERITAGE OF PUBLIC SPEAKING

Time Period	Event
FOURTH CENTURY B.C.	Greek rhetoric flourishes—Age of Aristotle.
FIFTEENTH CENTURY	European clergy are the primary practitioners of public speaking.
EIGHTEENTH CENTURY	American patriots make impassioned public pleas for independence.
NINETEENTH CENTURY	Abolitionists and suffragettes speak out for change; Lyceum speakers lecture and entertain; public speaking is taught through declamation.
TWENTIETH CENTURY	Elocution gives way to extemporaneous delivery.

Public speaking and diversity

Although the history of public speaking is as old as the history of Western civilization, it has only been during the last half of the twentieth century that attention has been focused on the rhetoric of diversity. We are just beginning to understand that the gender, ethnicity, and culture of both speaker and audience are critical components of the context of a speaking event.

Diverse audiences have different expectations for appropriate and effective speech topics, argument structure, language style, and delivery. For example, a speech that may be quite persuasive to Native Americans may not have the same effect on Anglos who do not share the beliefs and values underlying the message:

> For the Indian audience, Red Power rhetoric is persuasive insofar as it serves . . . purposes prescribed by traditional Indian religious/cultural precepts. White audiences, which do not share these precepts, remain unconvinced. . . [10]

Similarly, a presentation that seems perfectly sensible and acceptable to an American businessperson who is accustomed to straightforward, problem-oriented logic, may seem shockingly rude to a Chinese business counterpart who expects more circuitous, less overtly purposeful rhetoric. And feedback that some speakers might consider disruptive may only signal the audience's enthusiastic reception of the speaker's message. African audiences, as well as some African American ones, "come to participate in a speech event," explains one expert. "They are the secondary creators in the event, containing among them a vital part of the message."[11]

To be effective, then, public speakers need to understand, affirm, and adapt to diverse audiences. And it is with this acknowledgment of the critical role of the audience that we come full circle. Aristotle was right. The audience is the most important component in the communication process. It was true in the fifth century B.C., when students listened to the Greek rhetorician Gorgias. It was true in the nineteenth century, when parents of elocution students attended a school recital. And it was still true in December of 1994, when a culturally diverse twentieth century audience heard the speeches of PLO leader Yasir Arafat and King Hussein of Jordan as they accepted their shared Nobel peace prize. It is the focus on audience that provides a coherent framework for the history of public speaking, from classical rhetoric to the contemporary rhetoric of diversity.

Adapting to diverse audiences also provides the unifying principle of this text. In Chapter 2 we present a model of speech preparation that emphasizes the importance of the audience. Then, throughout the text, we illustrate how this focus on and consideration of audience can guide a speaker effectively through each stage of speech preparation and delivery.

Culture and ethnicity are strong factors in determining an audience's response to both the content of a speech and the speaker's delivery style. These Japanese-Americans are displaying their enthusiasm in a manner that might seem restrained to members of other ethnic groups. [Photo: Starr '92/Stock Boston]

Summary

As you are called upon to speak in public at various times throughout your life, skill in public speaking can empower you. It can help you secure employment, advance your career, and have an impact on public policy.

Although similar in some ways to conversation, public speaking is more intentional, more structured, and more formal. Like other forms of communication, public speaking is a process. As you develop the skills you need to participate effectively in that process, your study will be guided by experience and knowledge gained over the hundreds of years that people have been making and studying speeches. Throughout history, speechmakers have acknowledged that the audience is the most important element in the communication process.

● CRITICAL THINKING QUESTIONS

1. How do you think this course in public speaking can help you with your career goals? With your personal life?

2. Provide an example of internal noise that is affecting you as you read this question.

3. Explain how you think your culture influences your expectations of a public speaker.

● ETHICAL QUESTIONS

1. *Declamation* is defined in this chapter as "the delivery of an already famous address." Is it ethical to deliver a speech written and/or delivered by someone else? Explain your answer.

● SUGGESTED ACTIVITIES

1. Listen to an entire public speech, either on TV or in person. In what ways does this speech seem more intentional, structured, and formal than would a conversation with this same speaker?

2. Write a brief analysis of the speech you listened to for Activity 1, identifying each of the elements of the communication process discussed in this chapter: source, receiver, message, channel, noise, feedback, and context.

1. Rent videos of Shakespeare's *Henry V* starring, first, Laurence Olivier (1945) and later, Kenneth Branagh (1989). Compare the speeches the two actors make to their troops before sending them into battle. How does the context differ in the two films? What do the two actors do that is similar? What is different, and why?

"Martin Luther King, Jr."
Xavier Jones/SuperStock

Overview of the Speechmaking Process

> If all my talents and powers were to be taken from me by some inscrutable Providence, and I had my choice of keeping but one, I would unhesitatingly ask to be allowed to keep the Power of Speaking, for through it, I would quickly recover all the rest.
> —Daniel Webster

● OBJECTIVES

After studying this chapter you should be able to do the following:

1. List and describe the key steps in preparing and presenting a speech.

2. Describe why speakers sometimes feel nervous about speaking in public.

3. Use several techniques to become a confident speaker.

nless you have some prior experience in higher mathematics, you may not have the foggiest notion of what calculus is when you first take a class in that subject. But when you tell people that you are taking a public speaking class, most at least have some idea what a public speaker does. A public speaker talks while others listen. You hear speeches almost every day. Each evening, when you turn on the news, you get a "sound bite" of some politician delivering a speech. Each day when you attend class, an instructor lectures. But even after hearing countless speeches, you may still have questions about how a speaker prepares and presents a speech.

In Chapter 1, we discussed the characteristics and parameters of public speaking and reviewed the elements of human communication. In this chapter, we will preview the preparation and presentation skills that you will learn in this course. This overview will help you with early speaking assignments by giving you a look at the entire process. Then, because most beginning speakers feel nervous about giving speeches, we will end this chapter with some tips for developing your confidence.

Preparing your first speech: A look at the speechmaking process

You have been speaking since before you were two. Speaking has seemed such a natural part of your life that you have probably never stopped to analyze the process. But now you are sitting at your desk, thinking about your first assignment. The assignment may be to introduce yourself to the class. Or your first assignment may be a brief informative talk—to describe something to your audience. Regardless of the specific assignment, however, you may be asking yourself "What do I do first?"

You don't need to read *Public Speaking: An Audience-Centered Approach* from cover to cover before tackling your first speech. There is no better way to learn how to deliver a speech than to start speaking publicly. To help you begin, we will provide a short preview of the major steps that will be discussed in more detail later in this book. This overview will help you with your early speaking assignments and will also give you a scaffolding on which to build your skill in public speaking.

The model in Figure 2.1 diagrams the various tasks involved in the speechmaking process, emphasizing audience as the central concern. We'll refer to this audience-centered model throughout the text. And a smaller version of this model will appear in the margins throughout to indicate blocks of text that deal specifically with the audience-centered approach. (See icon at left.)

We will begin our discussion of the speechmaking process with the central element: considering your audience. We will then discuss each step of the process, starting with selecting and narrowing a topic, and moving clockwise around the model, examining each interrelated step.

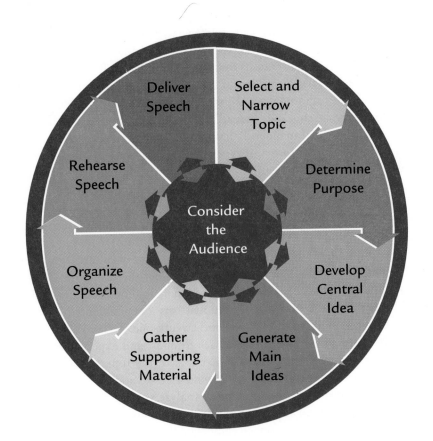

FIGURE 2.1
This model of the speechmaking process emphasizes the importance of considering your audience as you work on each task involved in designing and presenting a speech. As we discuss each task in depth throughout the book, we will also use a smaller image of this model to flag information and advice that remind you to consider your audience.

CONSIDER YOUR AUDIENCE

Why should the central focus of public speaking be the audience? Why is it not topic selection, outlining, or research? The simple truth is, your audience influences the topic you choose and every later step of the public speaking process. Your selection of topic, purpose, and even major ideas should be based on a thorough understanding of your listeners. In a very real sense, your audience "writes" the speech.

As Figure 2.1 shows, considering your audience is an ongoing activity. The needs, attitudes, beliefs, values, and other characteristics of your audience should play a leading role at every step. After you select your topic, you need to consider how the audience will respond to your examples, organization, and delivery. That's why, in the model, arrows connect the center of the diagram with each step of the process. At any point during the process, you may need to revise your thinking or your material if you learn new information about your audience. So the model also has arrows pointing both ways across the boundaries of each step in the process. Chapter 5 contains a comprehensive discussion of the principles and strategies involved in analyzing and considering your audience.

Being audience-centered involves making decisions about the content and style of your speech *before* you speak, based on knowledge of your audience's values and beliefs. It also means being sensitive to your audience's responses *during* the speech so that you can make appropriate adjustments. Different cultures have radically different conventions for public speaking. In Russia, for example, speakers have a "no frills" approach that emphasizes content over delivery. When one of your authors taught public speaking for several semesters in the Bahamas, however, he shocked students by suggesting that they try to achieve a conversational, informal manner. Bahamian audiences, the author quickly discovered, expect formal oratory from their speakers, very much as American audiences in the nineteenth century preferred the grandiloquence of Stephen A. Douglas to the quieter, homespun style of Abraham Lincoln. So your author had to embellish his own style when he taught the class.

You need not teach or give speeches in foreign countries to recognize the importance of adapting to the cultural expectations of different audiences. The population of the United States is highly diverse in terms of culture, age, ethnicity, sexual orientation, and religous tradition. Consider the backgrounds of your classmates. How many different cultural and ethnic traditions do they represent? Several years ago, the typical college student was a newly minted high-school graduate between the ages of eighteen and twenty-one. Today your classmates probably reflect a wide range of ages, backgrounds, and experiences. You will want to adjust not only your delivery style but also your topic, pattern of organization, and even your dress, according to who they are and what subject or subjects they are interested in. If you learn to analyze your audience and adapt to their expectations, you can apply these skills in numerous settings: a job interview, a business presentation, a city council campaign—even a marriage proposal.

● SELECT AND NARROW YOUR TOPIC

If your first speech assignment is to introduce yourself to the class, the topic of your speech has been selected for you—*you* are the topic. It is not uncommon to be asked to speak on a specific subject. But there will be many times when you will be asked to speak and not be given a topic. The task of selecting and narrowing a topic will be yours. Choosing or finding a topic on which to speak can be frustrating. "What should I talk about?" can become a haunting question.

Although there is no definitive answer to what you should talk about, you may discover a topic by asking three standard questions: "Who is the audience?" "What is the occasion?" and "What are my interests, talents, and experiences?"

- *Who is the audience?*   Your topic may grow from basic knowledge about your audience. For example, if you know that your audience members are primarily between the ages of twenty-five and forty, this information should help you select a topic of interest to people who are probably working, and either seeking partners or raising families. An older audience may lead you to other concerns or issues: "Will social security be there when I need it?" or "The advantages of belonging to the American Association of Retired Persons."

- *What is the occasion?*   Besides your audience, you should consider the type of occasion when choosing a topic. A commencement address calls for a different topic than, for example, a speech to a model railroad club.

■ *What are my interests, talents, and experiences?* Rather than racking your brain for exotic topics and far-flung ideas, examine your own background. Your choice of major in college, your hobbies, and your ancestry are sources for topic ideas. What issues do you feel strongly about? Reflect on jobs you've held, news stories that catch your interest, events in your hometown, your career goals, or interesting people that you have met. Chapter 6 contains a discussion of specific strategies for finding topics, and Appendix B provides topic ideas that you can modify to suit your audience and the occasion.

Once you have chosen your topic, you must narrow it to fit the time set for your talk. If you've been asked to deliver a ten-minute speech, the topic, "How to Find Counseling Help on Campus" would be more manageable than the topic, "How to Make the Most of Your College Experience." As our model suggests, your audience should be foremost in your mind when you work on your topic.

● DETERMINE YOUR PURPOSE

You might think that once you have your topic, you are ready to start the research process. Before you do that, however, you need to decide on both a general and a specific purpose. Chapter 6 describes three types of general purposes for giving a speech: to *inform*, to *persuade*, and to *entertain*. Even though we identify each purpose separately, they often overlap. For example, you may want to inform and entertain your audience while suggesting creative ways to avoid long lines during registration. In speech classes, your main purpose will most often be set by your instructor.

Speaking to inform is the primary objective of class lectures, seminars, and workshops. When you inform, you teach, define, illustrate, clarify, or elaborate on a topic. Chapter 15 will show you how to construct an effective speech with an informative purpose.

Ads on TV and radio, sermons, political speeches, and sales presentations are examples of speeches designed to persuade. They seek to change or reinforce attitudes, beliefs, values, or behavior. To be persuasive, you need to be sensitive to your audience's attitudes toward you and your topic. Chapters 16 and 17 will discuss the principles and strategies for persuasive speeches.

The third general purpose for giving a speech is to entertain your audience. After-dinner speeches and comic monologues are mainly intended for entertainment. Often the key to an effective entertaining speech lies in your choice of stories, examples, and illustrations, as well as in your delivery. Appendix D has examples of informative, persuasive, and entertaining speeches.

After making sure you understand your general purpose, you need to formulate a **specific purpose:** a concise statement indicating what you want your listeners to be able to know, do, or feel when you finish your speech. Perhaps you have had the experience of listening to a speaker and wondered, "What's the point? I know he's talking about education, but I'm not sure where he's going with this subject." You may have understood the speaker's general purpose, but the specific one wasn't clear. If you can't figure out what the specific purpose is, it is probably because the speaker does not know either.

■
specific purpose
A concise statement indicating what you want your listeners to be able to do when you finish speaking.

Deciding on a specific purpose is not difficult once you have narrowed your topic: "At the end of my speech, the class will be able to identify three counseling facilities on campus and describe the best way to get help at each one." Notice that this purpose is phrased in terms of what you would like the audience to be able to do by the end of the speech. Your specific purpose should be a fine-tuned, audience-centered goal. For an informative speech, you may simply want your audience to restate an idea, define new words, or identify, describe, or illustrate something. In a persuasive speech, you may try to rouse your listeners to take a class, buy something, or vote for someone.

Once you have formulated your specific purpose, write it down on a piece of paper or note card and keep it before you as you read and gather ideas for your talk. Your specific purpose should guide your research and help you choose members' materials that are related to your audiences. As you continue to work on your speech, you may even decide to modify your purpose. But if you have an objective in mind at all times as you move through the preparation stage, you will stay on track.

RE CAP

DETERMINE YOUR PURPOSE

Decide on Your General Purpose

TO INFORM	To share information by defining, describing, or explaining
TO PERSUADE	To change or reinforce an attitude, belief, value, or behavior
TO ENTERTAIN	To amuse through humor, stories, or other illustrations

Decide on Your Specific Purpose

What do you want your audience to know, do, or feel when you finish your speech?

General Purpose	Specific Purpose
TO INFORM	At the end of my speech, the audience will be able to identify three counseling facilities on campus and describe the best way to get help at each one.
TO PERSUADE	At the end of my speech, the audience will want to take advantage of counseling facilities on campus.
TO ENTERTAIN	At the end of my speech, the audience will be able to relate to the series of misunderstandings I created when I began making inquiries about career advisors on campus.

DEVELOP YOUR CENTRAL IDEA

You should now be able to write the central idea of your speech. Whereas your statement of a specific purpose indicates what you want your audience to do when you have finished your speech, your central idea identifies the essence of your message. Think of it as a one-sentence summary of your speech. Here are two examples:

TOPIC:	Compact discs
GENERAL PURPOSE:	To inform
SPECIFIC PURPOSE:	At the end of my speech, the audience will be able to identify the key reason compact discs have greater sound fidelity.
CENTRAL IDEA:	Compact discs have greater sound quality because they "read" the music information digitally, rather than analogically.
TOPIC:	Kachina dolls
GENERAL PURPOSE:	To inform
SPECIFIC PURPOSE:	At the end of my speech, the audience will be able to describe the significance of kachina dolls to the Hopi Indians.
CENTRAL IDEA:	Kachina dolls, carved wooden figures used in Hopi Indian ceremonies, are believed to represent spirits of the dead which will help produce a good harvest.

● GENERATE THE MAIN IDEAS

"A good many people can make a speech," said H. V. Prochnow, "but saying something is more difficult." Effective speakers are good thinkers; they say something. They know how to play with words and thoughts to develop their main ideas. The Romans called this skill **invention**—the ability to develop or discover ideas that result in new insights or new approaches to old problems. Cicero called this aspect of speaking the process of "finding out what [a speaker] should say."

invention
The ability to develop or discover ideas and new insights.

With an appropriate topic, a specific purpose, and a well-worded central idea on paper, the next task is to identify the major divisions of your speech, or key points that you wish to develop. To determine how to subdivide your central idea into key points, ask these three questions:

1. Does the central idea have logical *divisions*?

2. Can you think of several *reasons* why the central idea is true?

3. Can you support the central idea with a series of *steps*?

Let's look at each of these questions along with examples of how to apply them.

1. *Does the central idea have logical divisions?* If the central idea is "There are three ways to interpret the stock market page of your local newspaper," your speech could be organized into three parts. You will simply identify the three ways to interpret the stock market page and use each as a major point. A speech about the art of applying theatrical makeup could also be organized

into three parts: eye makeup, face makeup, and hair makeup. Looking for logical divisions in your speech topic is the simplest way to determine key points.

2. *Can you think of several reasons the central idea is true?* If your central idea is "Medicare should be expanded to include additional coverage for individuals of all ages," each major point of your speech could be a reason you think Medicare should be extended. For example, Medicare should be expanded because (1) not enough people are being served by the present system, (2) the people currently being served receive inadequate medical attention, and (3) the elderly cannot afford to pay what Medicare does not now cover. If your central idea is a statement that suggests that whatever you are talking about is good or bad, you should focus on the reasons your central idea is true. Use these reasons as the main ideas of the speech.

3. *Can you support the central idea with a series of steps?* Suppose that your central idea is "Running for a campus office is easy to do." Your speech could be developed around a series of steps, telling your listeners what to do first, second, and third to get elected. Speeches describing a personal experience or explaining how to build or make something can usually be organized in a step-by-step progression.

Your time limit and topic will determine how many major ideas will be in your speech. A three- to five-minute speech may have only one major idea. Don't spend time trying to divide a topic that does not need dividing.

● GATHER VERBAL AND VISUAL SUPPORTING MATERIAL

With your main idea or ideas in mind, your next job is to gather material to support them—facts, examples, definitions, and quotations from others that illustrate, amplify, clarify, and provide evidence. Here, as elsewhere in preparing your speech, the importance of being an audience-centered speaker cannot be overemphasized. An old saying has it that an ounce of illustration is worth a ton of talk. If a speech is boring, it is usually because the speaker has not chosen supporting material that is relevant or interesting to the audience.

Supporting material should be personal and concrete, and it should appeal to your listeners' senses. Tell stories based on your own experiences and provide vivid descriptions of things that are tangible so that your audience can visualize what you are talking about. Besides sight, supporting material can appeal to touch, hearing, smell, and taste. The more senses you trigger with words, the more interesting your talk will be. Descriptions such as "rough, splintery surface of weather-beaten wood" or "the sweet, cool, refreshing flavor of cherry Jell-O" evoke sensory images. We will discuss in Chapter 8 the variety of supporting material available to you.

How does a public speaker find interesting and relevant supporting material? By developing good research skills. Woodrow Wilson once admitted, "I use not only all the brains I have, but all that I can borrow." Although it is important to have good ideas, it is equally important to know how to build on existing knowledge. You can probably think of a topic or two about which you consider yourself an expert. Chances are that if you gave a short speech about a sport that you practiced for years or about a recent trip that you took, you would not need to gather much additional information. But sooner or later, you will need to do some research on a topic in order to speak on it intelligently to an audience. If your college classes up to this point have required only brief forays into the library, that experience is about to change shortly. By the time you have given several speeches in this course, you will have learned to use a number of the following resources: your library's computerized card catalog, the *Social Sciences Index*, the *Directory of American Scholars*, *Bartlett's Familiar Quotations*, government document holdings, your library's computerized periodical index, and an assortment of CD-ROM indexes. You would also be wise to spend some time learning to use the Internet and electronic databases such as LEXIS/NEXIS, as well as Netscape and Gopher commands to navigate the World Wide Web.

In addition to becoming a skilled library user, you will also learn to be on the lookout as you read, watch TV, and listen to the radio for ideas, examples, illustrations, and quotations that could be used in a speech. Finally, you will learn how to gather information through interviews and written requests for information on various topics. Chapter 7 will explain more thoroughly how to use all of these resources.

Besides searching for verbal forms of supporting material, you can also seek visual supporting material. For many people, seeing is believing. Almost any presentation can be enhanced by reinforcing key ideas with visual aids. Often, the most effective visual aids are the simplest: an object, a chart, a graph, a poster, a model, a map, or a person—perhaps yourself—to demonstrate a process or skill. The sample speech, "Can You Read My Mind?" on page 30 incorporates simple, yet effective, visual aids. Today there are many technologies for displaying visual aids. One of the most basic is an overhead projector that displays 8 1/2-by-11-inch acetate transparencies. Slide projectors and audio cassette players are also easy to use and readily available. In addition, most classrooms now have video cassette recorders, so you can show brief video segments to introduce or reinforce a point. The latest graphics packages for personal computers can help you generate colorful graphs, charts, signs, and banners. And with today's CD-ROM technology you can project stunning video images with the proper equipment. Of course, using this high-tech equipment requires new skills and often extra rehearsal time.

In Chapter 14 we discuss some basic advice about using visual aids: make your visual aids large enough to be seen and allow plenty of time to prepare them; look at your audience, not your visual aid; control your audience's attention by timing your visual displays; and keep your visual aids simple. Always concentrate on communicating effectively with your audience, not on dazzling your listeners with glitzy visual displays.

The simplest visual aids are often the most effective. The bright, attractive graph this speaker is using enables his audience to understand at a glance the relationships among a collection of complex data. [Photo: Charles Gupton/Stock Boston]

● ORGANIZE YOUR SPEECH

As a wise person once said, "If effort is organized, accomplishment follows." A clearly and logically structured speech helps your audience remember what you say. It also helps you feel more in control of your speech, and greater control will help you feel more comfortable while delivering your message.

disposition
The organization and arrangement of ideas and illustrations.

Ideas, information, examples, illustrations, stories, and statistics need to be presented in a logical order. Classical rhetoricians—early students of speech—called the process of developing an orderly speech **disposition**. Speakers need to present ideas and illustrations in an orderly sequence so that listeners can easily follow what they are saying.

Every speech has three major divisions: the introduction, the body, and the conclusion. The introduction helps capture attention, serves as an overview of the speech, and provides your audience with reasons to listen to you. The body presents the main content of your speech. The conclusion summarizes your key ideas. You may have heard this advice on how to organize your speech: Tell them what you're going to tell them (the introduction), tell them (the body of the speech), and tell them what you told them (the conclusion).

As a student of public speaking, you will study and learn to apply variations of this basic pattern of organization (chronological, topical, cause–effect, problem–solution) that will help your audience understand your meaning. You will learn about previewing and summarizing—methods of oral organization that will help your audience retain your main ideas. In the sample speech below, notice how the introduction catches the listener's attention, the body of the speech identifies the main ideas, and the conclusion summarizes the key ideas.

Since your introduction previews your speech and your conclusion summarizes it, most public speaking teachers recommend that you prepare your introduction and conclusion after you have carefully organized the body of your talk. If you have already generated your major ideas by divisions, reasons, or steps, you are well on your way to developing an outline. Your major ideas should be indicated by Roman numerals. Use capital letters for your supporting points. Use Arabic numerals if you need to subdivide your ideas further. You should *not* write your speech word for word. If you do, your speech will sound stilted and unnatural. It may be useful, however, for you to use brief notes—written cues on note cards—instead of a complete manuscript.

You may want to look in Chapters 9 and 11 for approaches to organizing a message and sample outlines. Chapter 10 provides more detailed suggestions for beginning and ending your speech. For your first speech, you may want to adapt the following sample outline format to your talk.

Description	Example
TOPIC: Could be assigned by your instructor, or selected by you	**TOPIC:** How to invest money
GENERAL PURPOSE: To inform, persuade, or entertain—your instructor will probably assign your general purpose	**GENERAL PURPOSE:** To inform
SPECIFIC PURPOSE: A clear statement indicating what your audience should be able to do after hearing your speech	**SPECIFIC PURPOSE:** At the end of my speech, the audience should be able to identify principles that will help them better invest their money.

Description	**Example**
CENTRAL IDEA: A one-sentence summary of your talk	CENTRAL IDEA: Knowing the source of money, how to invest it, and how money grows can lead to increased income from wise investments.
INTRODUCTION: Attention-catching opening line	INTRODUCTION: Imagine for a moment that it is the year 2050. You are sixty-five years old. You've just picked up your mail and opened an envelope that contains a check for $100,000! No, you didn't win the lottery. You smile as you realize your own modest investment strategy over the last forty years has paid off handsomely.
PREVIEW MAJOR IDEAS	Today I'd like to answer three questions that can help you become a better money manager: First, where does money come from? Second, where do you invest it? And third, how does a little money grow into a lot of money?
TELL YOUR AUDIENCE WHY THEY SHOULD LISTEN TO YOU	Knowing the answers to these three questions can literally pay big dividends for you. With only modest investments and a well-disciplined attitude, you could easily have $100,000.

BODY:
I.   Major Idea
    A. Supporting idea
    B. Supporting idea
 	
II. Major Idea
    A. Supporting idea
    B. Supporting idea
    C. Supporting idea
 	
III. Major Idea
    A. Supporting idea
    B. Supporting idea
	BODY:
	I. There are two sources of money.
	    A. You already have some money.
	    B. You will earn money in the future.
	
	II. There are three things you can do with a dollar.
	    A. You can spend your money.
	    B. You can lend your money to others.
	    C. You can invest your money.
	
	III. There are two principles that can help make you rich.
	    A. The "magic" of compound interest can transform pennies into millions.
	    B. Finding the best rate of return on your money can pay big dividends.

CONCLUSION: Summarize major ideas	CONCLUSION: Today, I've identified three key aspects of effective money management: (1) sources of money, (2) what you can do with money, and (3) money management principles that can make you rich. Now, let's go "back to the future"! Remember the good feeling you had when you received your check for $100,000? Recall that feeling again when you are depositing your first paycheck. Remember this simple secret for accumulating wealth: A part of all I earn is mine to keep. You truly have it within your power to "go for the gold."

In addition to developing a written outline for your use, consider using visual aids to add structure and clarity to your major ideas. Developing simple visual reinforcers of your key ideas can help your audience retain essential points.

In Chapter 14 and Appendix C we will offer tips for designing computer graphics using such software as PowerPoint™ and Persuasion™. For example, in the outline we just presented, the first major idea could be summarized on a visual aid like Figure A.

The second major idea in our speech example could look like Figure B.

The third major idea could be reinforced with a visual like Figure C.

For all of the steps we have discussed so far, your success as a speaker will ultimately be determined by your audience. That is why throughout the text we will refer you to the audience-centered speechmaking model presented in this chapter.

Once you are comfortable with the structure of your talk and you have developed your visual aids, you are ready to rehearse.

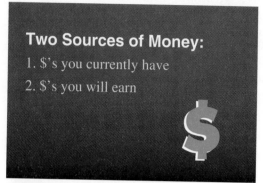

Figure A

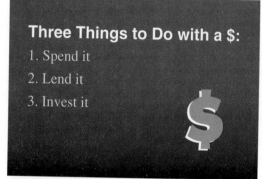

Figure B

Figure C

● REHEARSE YOUR SPEECH

Remember the joke in which one man asks another, "How do you get to Carnegie Hall?" The answer: "Practice, man, practice." The joke may be older than Carnegie Hall itself, but it is still good advice to all beginners, including novice speakers. A speech is a performance. As with any stage presentation, be it music, dance, or theater, you need to rehearse. A sage once said, "The best rule for talking is the one carpenters use: Measure twice, saw once." Rehearsing your speech is a way to measure your message so that you get it right when you present it to your audience.

The best way to practice is to rehearse your speech aloud, standing just as you will when you deliver it to your audience. As you rehearse, try to be comfortable with the way you phrase your ideas, but don't try to memorize your talk. In fact, if you have rehearsed your speech so many times that you are using exactly the same words every time, you have rehearsed long enough. Rehearse just enough so that you can discuss your ideas and supporting material without leaving out major parts of your speech. It is all right to use notes, but most public speaking instructors will limit the number of notes you may use.

As you practice, seek as much eye contact with your audience as you can. Also be certain to speak loudly enough for all in the room to hear. If you are not sure what to do with your hands when you rehearse, just keep them at your side. Focus on your message, rather than worrying about how to gesture. Avoid jingling change with your hand in your pocket or using other gestures that could distract your audience. If you practice your speech as if you were actually delivering it, you will be a more effective speaker when you talk to the audience.

Besides rehearsing your physical delivery, you also will make decisions about the style of your speech. "Style," said Jonathan Swift, "is proper words in proper places." The words you choose and your arrangement of those words make up the style of your speech. As we have seen, some audiences respond to a style that is simple and informal. Others prefer one that is grand and highly poetic. To be a good speaker, you must become familiar with the language that your listeners are used to hearing and know how to select the right word or phrase to communicate an idea. Work to develop an ear for how words will sound to your audience.

● DELIVER YOUR SPEECH

The time has come, and you're ready to present your speech to your audience. Delivery is the final step in the preparation process. Before you walk to the front of the room, look at your listeners to see if the audience that is assembled is the one you were expecting. Are the people out there the same age, race, and gender that you had predicted? Or do you need to make any last-minute changes in your message to adjust to a different distribution?

When you are introduced, walk calmly and confidently to the front of the room, establish eye contact with your audience, smile naturally, and deliver your opening sentence. Concentrate on your message and your audience. Deliver your speech in a conversational style and try to establish rapport with your listeners. Deliver your speech just as you rehearsed it before your imaginary audience: Maintain eye contact, speak loudly enough to be heard, and use some natural variation in pitch. Finally, remember the advice of columnist Ann Landers: "Be sincere, be brief, and be seated."

RECAP

THE BASIC STEPS IN THE SPEECHMAKING PROCESS

Consider your audience	Generate main ideas
Select and narrow your topic	Gather verbal and visual supporting material
Determine your purpose	Organize your speech
Develop your central idea	Rehearse your speech
Deliver your speech	

Now that we've seen what effective speakers must be able to do, let's look at a speech that illustrates these capabilities. The following speech by Christopher Therit models many of the attributes of a well-crafted message that we have discussed.

"Can You Read My Mind?"
Christopher Therit, Millersville University

> **The dog ran into the barn.**

Christopher uses the blackboard to catch the attention of his listeners.

Let me tell you something about myself. ("The dog ran into the barn" is written on the chalkboard.) What's the matter? You look a bit confused. You know nothing more about me now than before I wrote on the board, right? There is something behind those letters other than the chalkboard. Can you see it? Graphology, the study of a person's handwriting.

He tells his audience why his speech may be of interest to them. This helps establish a motivation for his audience to listen to him.

Did you know that over 1500 firms use graphology in order to hire new employees? I'm going to be telling you things today that will better help you understand yourself, as well as others. If you don't know that you can analyze your own handwriting, you may not know the real you.

I'm going to be answering three specific questions for you today: (1) What is graphology? (2) How does it work? (3) How is it used today?

These three questions are an excellent way to provide a preview of the three key ideas he presents in his speech, and they will help the audience follow the flow of his speech.

According to an article entitled "Graphoanalysis—Choosing the 'Write' Person" by Marion Chesney, *graphology* is defined as "the scientific study of the individual strokes of handwriting to determine the character and personality of the writer." The terms *graphoanalysis* and *graphology* are synonymous. "Graphology takes into account over 400 factors, including height and width of letters, the degree the writer has simplified or ornamented those letters, the space between the letters, the slant and slope of the letters, and how connected or disconnected the letters are," says Diane Cole, author of an article called "What Your Handwriting Says about You." Just like your fingerprints, your handwriting is uniquely yours.

Using a definition, especially as quoted from an expert, adds clarity and credibility to his message.

So how does graphology work? As I stated before, over 400 factors go into determining a person's personality. Today I will be showing you just a few of those factors.

He returns to the second rhetorical question to introduce his second major point, and then tells the audience how this question will be answered.

The first one is slanting . . . the way that our writing slants reveals certain characteristics about us. This is a graphometer. If your writing slants less than 5° to the right or left of the center, you are said to be self-reliant. If your handwriting slants to the left more than 5° of this line, you are said to be defiant, or resistant to an opposing authority or force . . . . Finally, if your writing slants more than 5° right of the center line, you are said to be compliant or cooperative. The farther that your writing slants to the (left or) right of the line, the more (self-reliant or) compliant or cooperative you (are).

> *Now is the time*

He uses a visual aid to help make his first subpoint.

Becoming a confident speaker

Even if you carefully follow all of the steps for effective speechmaking and work diligently to polish your content and delivery, you may still feel nervous before you give your speech. This nervousness is not uncommon. In a survey seeking to identify people's phobias, 41 percent of all respondents reported public speaking as their most significant fear; fear of death ranked only sixth![3] Another study found that more than 80 percent of the population feel anxious when they speak to an audience. You may find comfort in knowing that you

The second is T crosses . . . This is a T-chart. The first *T* indicates enthusiasm, follow-through, and a person who will get the job done. This second one is ambition, but a lot of times the ambition is above potential in this T-cross because it's high above the stem. The next one is procrastination. This is indicated when the cross is to the left of the stem . . . . This next one indicates high goals but (lack) of enthusiasm. This is indicated when the cross is very short and still above the stem. The cup on the cross indicates a shallow purpose. The bent-like stem indicates a short-tempered or tight person or someone who is trying to keep something under control. Finally, the tent-like stem of this *T* indicates a person who is stubborn.

Florence Anthony, a teacher at the New York School for Social Research states, "You can never pin down one trait and say it means the same thing in every handwriting, 100% of the time." Ruby Allen, a handwriting expert, says, "Handwriting reveals the inner workings of man, because the hand is guided by the brain. And when you write, that's the way it is. First you think, then you react. You put on the surface of paper an impression of your conscious and your subconscious. We see you, how you feel, what you think, and what you are. Your handwriting forms a tapestry of your personality."

So how is graphology used today? As I mentioned earlier, over 1500 firms use it to hire their new employees. Imagine going for a job interview and being asked to write an essay to be turned in with your résumé, only to have that essay turned over to a graphologist to be read and analyzed. Your acceptance to the position would hinge on your handwriting instead of your résumé. A dermatologist in Hawaii has found graphoanalysis to be beneficial to his practice. He found that emotions are responsible for more than 50% of skin ailments.

As you can see, many professional people use graphology to help people with their jobs and personal problems. The more you know about yourself, the more self-confident you may be in life. Self-confidence brings the world to you, puts it in your hands, and allows you to mold it in any way you wish.

Being the intelligent audience that you are, I'm sure you now know what graphology is . . . how it works, and how [we use it] today. I want to challenge each and every one of you to focus on your own handwriting and see if you notice some of the elements that I talked about today. Do you see anything about yourself that you've never seen before? Do you?

Here he uses another visual aid to make his second subpoint.

Christopher uses quotations from experts to add credibility and help clarify the point he is making.

He introduces his final point by returning to his third rhetorical question, as well as to the information in the introduction. This helps the audience keep track of the information being presented (because it is so clearly organized) and ties the speech together.

To help draw the audience in, he makes a direct reference to his listeners.

In concluding his speech, he summarizes the three key points he has developed.

are not alone in experiencing speech anxiety: Studies suggest that about 20 percent of college students are highly apprehensive about communicating with others.[4]

Even if your anxiety is not acute, you can benefit from learning some positive approaches that will allow your nervousness to work *for* you. The following discussion will provide some tools to help you manage your anxiety. First, we'll try to help you understand it: Knowledge is power. Second, we will make specific suggestions that will help you experience greater comfort and less anxiety when you speak in public.

What causes you to feel nervous about speaking in public? Why do your hands shake and your knees quiver? Why does your voice go up an octave? Why are there butterflies in your stomach? When you are nervous, you may notice that your breathing rate changes, and you may perspire more. What is happening to you? Believe it or not, your brain is signaling your body to help you with a difficult task.

Your view of the speaking assignment, your self-image, and your self-esteem interact to create anxiety. You want to do well, but you are not sure you can or will. Presented with this conflict, your body responds by increasing your breathing rate, pumping more adrenaline, and causing more blood to rush through your veins. In short, you have more energy to deal with the conflict you are facing. To put it more technically, you are experiencing physiological changes because of your psychological state. Increased energy and other physical changes explain why you may have a more rapid heartbeat, shaking knees and hands, a quivering voice, and increased perspiration. You may experience butterflies in your stomach because of changes in your digestive system. Due to your discomfort, you may also make less eye contact with your audience, use more vocalized pauses ("Um," "Ah," "You know"), and speak too rapidly. Though you see these occurrences as hindrances, your body is simply trying to help you with the task at hand. To help you further understand and channel the fear you experience, consider the following observations.

■ *You are going to feel more nervous than you look.*   When he finished his speech, Daryl sank into his seat and muttered, "Ugh, was I shaky up there! Did you see how nervous I was?"

   "Nervous? You were nervous?" asked Larry, surprised. "You looked pretty calm to me."

   You should realize that your audience cannot see everything you feel. If you worry that you are going to appear nervous to others, you may, in fact, increase your anxiety. Your body will exhibit more physical changes to deal with your self-induced state of anxiety.

■ *Almost every speaker experiences some degree of nervousness.*   President Kennedy was noted for his superb public speaking skills. When he spoke, he seemed perfectly at ease. Former Prime Minister Winston Churchill was also hailed as one of this century's great orators. Amazingly, both Kennedy and Churchill were extremely fearful of speaking in public. *Today Show* weatherperson Willard Scott also has confessed that he gets the jitters before every broadcast. Almost everyone experiences some anxiety when speaking. It is unrealistic to try to eliminate speech anxiety. Instead, your goal should be to manage your nervousness so that it does not create so much internal noise that it keeps you from speaking effectively.

■ *Anxiety can be useful.*   Extra adrenaline, increased blood flow, and other physical changes caused by anxiety improve your energy level, and this enables you to function better than you might otherwise. Your heightened state of readiness can actually help you speak better. Don't let your initial fear convince you that you cannot speak effectively.

Perhaps the best way to reduce speaker anxiety is to experience what it's like to deliver a speech successfully. Seek out opportunities to speak at local civic and political events where the audiences are likely to be receptive to your message. [Photo: Robert E. Daemmrich/Tony Stone Images]

DEVELOPING CONFIDENCE

The next instructions provide specific advice to help you cope with anxiety.[5] The first one summarizes a number of suggestions you have already read.

KNOW YOUR AUDIENCE   A key theme throughout this text is to know to whom you are speaking and to learn as much about your audience as you can. The more you can anticipate the kind of reaction your listeners will have to your speech, the more comfortable you will be in delivering your message.

BE PREPARED   The following formula will apply to most speaking situations you experience: The better prepared you are, the less anxiety you will experience. Being prepared means that you have researched your topic and practiced your speech several times before you deliver it. Being prepared also means that you have developed a logically coherent outline rather than one that is disorganized and difficult to follow. Transitional phrases and summaries can help you present a well-structured, easy-to-understand message.

SELECT AN APPROPRIATE TOPIC   You will feel less nervous if you talk about something with which you are familiar or have some personal experience. In the chapters ahead, we will offer more detailed guidance about how to select a topic. Your comfort with the subject of your speech will be reflected in your delivery.

RE-CREATE THE SPEECH ENVIRONMENT WHEN YOU REHEARSE When you rehearse your speech, try to imagine that you are giving the speech to the audience you will actually address. Stand up. Imagine what the room looks like, or consider rehearsing in the room in which you will deliver your speech. What will you be wearing? Practice rising from your seat, walking to the front of the room, and beginning your speech. Practice aloud, rather than just saying the speech to yourself. A realistic rehearsal will increase your confidence when your moment to speak arrives.

● **KNOW YOUR INTRODUCTION AND YOUR CONCLUSION**
You are likely to feel the most anxious during the opening moments of your speech. Therefore, it is a good idea to have a clear idea of how you will start your speech. We aren't suggesting a word-for-word memorization of your introduction, but you should have it well in mind. Being familiar with your introduction will help you feel more comfortable about the entire speech.

If you know how you will end your speech, you will have a safe harbor in case you lose your place. If you need to end your speech prematurely, a well-delivered conclusion can permit you to make a graceful exit.

● **VISUALIZE YOUR SUCCESS** Studies suggest that one of the best ways to control anxiety is to imagine a scene in which you exhibit skill and comfort as a public speaker.[6] As you imagine giving your speech, picture yourself walking confidently to the front and delivering your well-prepared opening remarks. Visualize yourself giving the entire speech as a controlled, confident speaker. Imagine yourself calm and in command.

● **USE DEEP BREATHING TECHNIQUES** One of the symptoms of nervousness is a change in your breathing and heart rates. Nervous speakers tend to take short, shallow breaths. To help break the anxiety-induced breathing pattern, consider taking a few slow deep breaths before you rise to speak. No one will be able to detect that you are taking deep breaths if you just slowly inhale and exhale from your seat before your speech begins. Besides breathing deeply, try to relax your entire body. Combine deep breathing with the visualization just mentioned, to help you relax.

● **ACT CALM TO FEEL CALM** Evidence suggests that you can bring on certain emotions by behaving as if you were feeling them. If you wish to feel greater calmness, behave in a calm way. Give yourself extra time to arrive at your speaking destination so you won't have to rush around hurriedly to find the right building or room. As you are waiting to be introduced, try not to fidget. Walk to the front of the room as though you were calm and collected. Before you present your opening sentence, take a moment to look for a calm, supportive, friendly face. Think calm and act calm to feel calm.

● **FOCUS ON YOUR MESSAGE RATHER THAN YOUR FEAR**
The more you think that you are anxious about speaking, the more you will increase your level of anxiety. Think about what you are going to say instead. In the few minutes before you address your listeners, mentally review your major ideas, your introduction, and your conclusion. Focus on your ideas rather than on your fear.

● **SEEK SPEAKING OPPORTUNITIES** The more experience you gain as a public speaker, the less nervous you will feel. As you develop a track record of successfully delivering speeches, you will have more confidence. This course in public speaking will give you opportunities to enhance both your confidence and your skill through frequent practice.

RECAP

TIPS FOR DEVELOPING CONFIDENCE

THINGS TO DO

Learn as much as possible about your audience.

Be prepared and well organized.

Select a topic you are interested in or know something about.

Rehearse aloud.

Be familiar with how you will begin and end the speech.

Visualize being successful.

Take deep breaths to relax.

Behave calmly before the speech begins.

Focus on the message.

Seek other speaking opportunities to gain experience and confidence.

Summary

In this chapter we presented an overview of the entire speechmaking process. To help you prepare for your first speaking assignment, we introduced the steps involved in preparing and presenting a speech, showing how the audience is the central focus at each step. Our audience-centered model of public speaking suggests that throughout the speech crafting and delivery process, the choices you make about designing and presenting your message should be guided by your knowledge of your audience. Based upon information about your listeners, you then select and narrow your topic, determine your purpose, develop your central idea, and generate the main ideas. These speech preparation steps are followed by gathering and organizing your supporting material, including visual aids. With a draft of your speech outline in hand, you are then ready to rehearse and deliver your speech.

Beginning public speakers sometimes feel nervous just thinking about giving a speech. Don't be surprised if you feel more nervous than you look to others. Remember that almost every speaker experiences some nervousness, and that some anxiety can actually be useful. We offered several specific suggestions to help you manage your apprehension. In addition to following the advice for effective speaking, you can imagine the speech environment when you rehearse and use relaxation techniques such as visualization, deep breathing, and focusing thoughts away from your fears.

CRITICAL THINKING QUESTIONS

1. Jason Reed has just received his assignment for his first speech in his public speaking class. What key skills will he need to master in order to become a competent public speaker?

2. Shara Yobonski is preparing to address the city council in an effort to tell them about the Food for Friendship program she has organized in her neighborhood. What steps should she follow to prepare and deliver an effective speech?

3. Mike Roberts, president of his fraternity, is preparing to address the University Academic Council to persuade them to support a Greek housing zone on campus. This is his first major task as president and he is understandably nervous about his responsibility. What advice would you give to help him manage his nervousness?

ETHICAL QUESTIONS

1. A friend of yours took public speaking last year and still has a file of speech outlines. Even though you will give the speech yourself, is it ethical to use one of her outlines as a basis for your speech?

2. Your first assignment is to give a speech about something interesting that has happened to you. You have decided to talk about the joys and hassles of a train trip you took last year. Your sister recently returned from a cross-country train trip and had several interesting tales to tell. Would it be ethical to tell one of her experiences as if it had happened to you?

3. You read an article in *Reader's Digest* that could serve as the basis for a great speech about the ravages of AIDS. Would it be ethical to paraphrase the article, using most of the same examples and the overall outline as the basis for your speech if you *tell* your listeners that your speech is based upon the article?

SUGGESTED ACTIVITIES

1. Interview someone who gives public presentations as part of his or her job (minister, politician, lawyer, or businessperson, for example). Ask what steps the person follows in preparing a speech.

2. Whom would you nominate as one of the outstanding public speakers in the country? Write a brief paper noting how your nominee exemplifies characteristics of an effective speaker discussed in this chapter.

3. Describe one informative purpose and one persuasive purpose for each of the following topics:

Nuclear power plants   Caffeine   Public speaking

Political parties   Your school   Computer technology

4. For the following central idea sentences, identify possible major divisions in the speech according to one of these questions: Does the central idea have logical *divisions*? Can you think of several *reasons* the central idea is true? Can you support the central idea with a series of *steps*?

The conflict in Bosnia has a long history.

The method of choosing a President in the United States is flawed.

Any one of several diets could help you lose weight.

The 65-mile-per-hour speed limit is a bad idea.

Our national parks need more resources to maintain their beauty.

The Internet has an interesting history.

IQ can be measured in several ways.

There are several ways of ensuring a stress-free lifestyle.

5. Identify at least three tips for helping you become a confident speaker. Write a brief paragraph explaining why you think those techniques will be helpful to you.

6. Deliver a three- to five-minute speech introducing yourself to the class. Use the model presented earlier in this chapter to help you prepare your talk.

USING TECHNOLOGY AND MEDIA

1. Videotape the speech you prepare for Activity 6 in the "Suggested Activities." Save the recording for viewing again in connection with other exercises and at the end of the course. You will be able to note differences between this first speech and the last speech you deliver.

2. If you are not familiar with the electronic databases in your school library, make an appointment with a librarian early in the course to begin learning what electronic resources are available to you for doing research. Learning how to use these databases now will help you in developing speeches throughout this course.

"Hear, See, Speak."
Arnold Rice/SuperStock

Ethics and Free Speech

*An honest tale speeds
best being plainly told.*
—*William Shakespeare*

● OBJECTIVES

**After studying this chapter you
should be able to do the following:**

1. *Define ethics.*

2. *Explain the relationship between ethics
   and free speech.*

3. *List and explain five criteria for ethical
   public speaking.*

4. *Define and discuss how best to avoid
   plagiarism.*

5. *List and explain three criteria for ethical
   listening.*

n May 1995, just days after the bombing of the Alfred P. Murrah Federal Building in Oklahoma City, G. Gordon Liddy, host of a widely syndicated radio talk show, gave his listeners advice on how to shoot federal agents who might invade their homes—aim at the agents' heads. The next day he retracted his advice. Saying the head was too hard to hit, Liddy recommended instead shooting twice at the body. "And if that does not work," he concluded, "then shoot to the groin area."[1] The backlash that followed Liddy's outrageous remarks included criticism from President Bill Clinton, who challenged the motives of the "loud and angry voices in America today . . . They spread hate; they leave the impression, by their very words, that violence is acceptable."[2] Clinton was not questioning Liddy's *right* to free speech, but his *ethics*.

Ethics are the beliefs, values, and moral principles by which we determine what is right or wrong. Ethics serve as criteria for many of the decisions we make in our personal and professional lives, and also for our judgments of others' behavior. The student who refuses to cheat on a test, the employee who will not call in sick to gain an extra day of vacation, and the property owner who does not claim more storm damage than was actually inflicted, have all made choices based on ethics. We read and hear about ethical issues every day in the media: life support systems, surrogate pregnancies, and drug testing have engendered heated ethical debates among medical professionals. Advertising by some attorneys has incensed others, who believe that the current increase in frivolous litigation is tarnishing the profession. And in the political arena, debates about social program reform, fiscal responsibility, and the regulation of business and industry all hinge on ethical issues.

Although you are undoubtedly familiar with many of these issues, you may have given less thought to the ethical issues that affect public speaking. These issues center around one main concern: in a country in which free speech is protected by law, the right to speak freely must be balanced by the responsibility to speak ethically. In fact, ethical considerations should guide every step of the public speaking process we discussed in Chapter 2. As you determine the goal of your speech, outline your arguments, and select your evidence, you should be thinking about the beliefs, values, and morals of your audience, as well as your own. Ethical public speaking is inherently audience-centered, always taking into account the needs and rights of the listeners.

Any discussion of ethical public speaking is complicated by the fact that ethics are not hard-and-fast objective rules. Each person's ethical decisions reflect his or her individual values and religious beliefs, as well as cultural norms. Although we cannot, therefore, offer a universal definition of ethical public speaking, we can offer principles and guidelines that reflect the ethics of contemporary North American society and the legal guarantees granted under the U.S. Constitution, including the right to free speech. And as we offer guidelines for ethical speaking and listening, we will include suggestions for acknowledging and encouraging diversity.

ethics
The beliefs, values, and moral principles by which we determine what is right or wrong.

We will turn first to a discussion of free speech and its protection by law and public policy. Then we will discuss the ethical practice of free speech by both speakers and listeners, providing guidelines to help you balance your right to free speech with your responsibilities as an audience-centered speaker and as a critical listener. Within this framework, we will define and discuss plagiarism, one of the most troublesome violations of ethical public speaking.

Speaking freely

In 1791 the First Amendment to the U.S. Constitution was written to guarantee that "Congress shall make no law . . . abridging the freedom of speech." In the more than 200 years since then, entities as varied as state legislatures, college and university campuses, the American Civil Liberties Union, and the federal courts have sought to define through both law and public policy the phrase "freedom of speech."

Occasionally the government has tried to restrict free speech, but these efforts have been countered by strong protests from both elected officials and private citizens. Only a few years after the ratification of the First Amendment, Congress passed the Sedition Act, providing punishment for those who spoke out against the government. When both Jefferson and Madison declared this act unconstitutional, however, it was allowed to lapse. More than 100 years later, during World War I, the Supreme Court again tried to restrict speech that presented "a clear and present danger" to the nation. This led to the founding, in 1920, of the American Civil Liberties Union, the first organization formed to protect free speech. In 1940, Congress again declared it illegal to urge the violent overthrow of the federal government. However, even as various international organizations sought to restrict the kind of hate speech employed by Hitler and the Nazis, U.S. courts and lawmakers argued that only by *protecting* free speech could the United States protect the rights of minorities and the disenfranchised.

For most of the last half of the twentieth century, the Supreme Court has expanded rather than limited free speech, upholding it as "the core aspect of democracy."[3] For example, during the Vietnam War, the Court directed the Georgia legislature to seat elected member Julian Bond, despite protests from some who were angry that Bond had spoken publicly in support of draft resistance.

Another boost for free speech occurred not in the courts, but on a university campus. In December 1964, more than 1,000 students at U.C. Berkeley took over three floors of Sproul Hall to protest the recent arrest of outspoken student activists. The Berkeley Free Speech Movement, as the incident came to be known, permanently changed the political climate of America's college campuses. In a written statement on the thirty-year anniversary of the protest, Berkeley's vice chancellor Carol Christ wrote, "Today it is difficult to imagine life in a university where there are serious restrictions on the rights of political advocacy."[4]

In 1989, shortly after flag-burning was declared a "speech act" protected by the First Amendment, protestors provoked police into action by testing the new law on the steps of the U.S. Capitol. [Photo: AP/World Wide Photos]

Further strengthening of free speech protection has occurred in the 1980s and 1990s. In 1989 the Supreme Court defended the burning of the U.S. flag as a "speech act" protected by the First Amendment. During the first half of 1995 alone, the U.S. Supreme Court handed down eight rulings on free speech, including one that struck down a law barring civilian federal employees from giving speeches during their free time on topics unrelated to their jobs. As we near the end of the twentieth century, just about the only remaining restrictions on free speech in the United States are those that prohibit libel and slander.

RECAP

HISTORY OF FREE SPEECH IN THE UNITED STATES

1791	First Amendment guarantees that "Congress shall make no law . . . abridging the freedom of speech"
1798	Sedition Act passes
1919	Supreme Court suggests that speech presenting a "clear and present danger" may be restricted
1920	American Civil Liberties Union is formed
1940	Congress declares it illegal to urge the violent overthrow of the federal government
1964	Berkeley Free Speech Movement takes place
1966	Supreme Court forces Georgia to seat Julian Bond, who spoke publicly in support of draft resistance
1989	Supreme Court defends the burning of the U.S. flag as a "speech act"
1995	Supreme Court hands down eight free speech rulings in first six months

Speaking ethically

As the definition of free speech expands, the importance of its ethical practice increases. As we have said, there is no definitive ethical creed for a public speaker. But teachers and practitioners of public speaking generally agree that an ethical speaker is one who has a clear, responsible goal; uses sound evidence and reasoning; is sensitive to and tolerant of differences; is honest; and avoids plagiarism. In the discussion that follows, we will offer suggestions for observing these ethical guidelines.

● HAVE A CLEAR, RESPONSIBLE GOAL

The goal of a public speech should be clear to the audience. For example, if you are trying to convince the audience that your beliefs on abortion are more correct than others', you should say so at some point in your speech. If you keep your true agenda hidden, you may be violating your listeners' rights. In addition, an ethical goal should be socially responsible. A socially responsible goal is one that gives the listener choices, whereas an irresponsible, unethical goal is either physically or psychologically coercive. The brainwashing and physical torture of POWs during the Vietnam War and of captured American fliers during Operation Desert Storm are examples of unethical coercion. Adolf Hitler's speeches, which incited the German people to hatred and genocide, were also coercive, and so were those of Chinese leader Deng Xiaoping, who tried to intimidate Chinese citizens into revealing the whereabouts of leaders of the unsuccessful 1989 student uprising in Tiananmen Square.

If your overall objective is to inform or persuade, it is probably ethical; if your goal is to inflame or coerce, it is probably unethical. But law and ethics do not always agree on this distinction. As we have pointed out, Congress and the Supreme Court have tried at times to limit speech that incites sedition, violence, and riot, but they have also protected free speech rights "for both the ideas that people cherish and the thoughts they hate."[5] Even those who defend a broad legal right to free speech recognize that they are protecting unethical, as well as ethical, speech. The ACLU's controversial decision to support the right of the American Nazi Party to rally in the late 1960s in Skokie, Illinois—a place with a substantial population of Holocaust survivors—exemplifies this dilemma. So, too, does the current controversy regarding the public broadcasts of extremist hate groups. Because these groups' goals are irresponsible, many people consider their messages to be unethical, so they question whether the groups should be allowed to broadcast over federally regulated airwaves.

● USE SOUND EVIDENCE AND REASONING

Ethical speakers use critical thinking skills such as analysis and evaluation to draw conclusions and formulate arguments. Unethical speakers substitute emotion and false claims for evidence and logical arguments.

In the early 1950s, Wisconsin Senator Joseph McCarthy incited national panic by charging that Communists were infiltrating every avenue of American life. Thousands of people came under suspicion, many losing jobs and careers because of the false accusations. Never able to substantiate his claims, McCarthy succeeded in his witch-hunt by exaggerating and distorting the truth. One United Press reporter noted, "The man just talked in circles. Everything was by inference, allusion, never a concrete statement of fact. Most of it didn't make sense."[6] Although today we recognize the flimsiness of McCarthy's accusations, in his time the man wielded incredible power. Like Hitler, McCarthy knew how to manipulate emotions and fears to produce the results he wanted. It is sometimes tempting to resort to false claims to gain power over others, but it is always unethical to do so.

It can also be tempting simply to bypass sound evidence and reasoning. In our current political environment, both media "sound bites" and presidential debates have come under fire as shallow forums. Erik Sorenson, executive producer of the "CBS Evening News," has complained that sound bites range "from cheap shots to clever turns of phrases."[7] And former CBS anchor Walter Cronkite has called the presidential debates "part of the unconscionable fraud that our political campaigns have become," because "substance is to be avoided if possible. Image is to be maximized."[8] Although using clever phrases and emphasizing positive images are not in themselves unethical, if they substitute for sound evidence and reasoning, then these tactics can become unethical practices.

One last, but important, requirement for the ethical use of evidence and reasoning is to share with an audience all information that might help them reach a sound decision, including information that may be potentially damaging to your case. Even if you proceed to refute the opposing evidence and arguments, you have fulfilled your ethical responsibility by presenting the perspective of the other side. And you can actually make your own arguments more convincing by anticipating and answering counterarguments and evidence.

● BE SENSITIVE TO AND TOLERANT OF DIFFERENCES

As we noted in Chapter 1, being audience-centered requires that you become as aware as possible of others' feelings, needs, interests, and backgrounds. New Jersey Senator Bill Bradley has described this ethical dimension as "tolerance, curiosity, civility—precisely the qualities we need to allow us to live side by side in mutual respect."[9] Sometimes called *accommodation,* sensitivity to differences does not mean that speakers must abandon their own convictions for those of either their sources or their audience members. It does mean that speakers should demonstrate a willingness to listen to opposing viewpoints and learn about different beliefs and values. Such willingness not only communicates respect; it can also help a speaker to select a topic, formulate a purpose, and design strategies to motivate an audience.

Your authors are currently involved in an informal educational exchange with a professor from the St. Petersburg Cultural Institute in Russia and recently had a chance to visit the professor and her family in St. Petersburg. In talking with the professor's talented teenage daughter, we inquired as to her plans after she finished her university education. Smiling at us in both amusement and amazement, she replied, "Americans are always planning what they are going to do several years in the future. In Russia, we do not plan beyond two or three weeks. Life is too uncertain here." Having gained this insight into Russian life, we know now that it would raise false hopes to attempt to motivate Russian audiences with promises of benefits far in the future. Our new understanding helps us see that speaking of immediate, deliverable rewards is a more realistic and ethical approach.

Regardless of the audience's ethnicity, gender, or cultural background, sensitivity and tolerance preclude the use of abusive or biased language. We mentioned earlier in this chapter the legal–ethical debate surrounding the use of hate speech. In Chapter 12 we will return to this issue and also look at ways to avoid more subtle discriminatory or offensive language.

Knowingly offering false or misleading information to an audience is an ethical violation. When former Reagan White House spokesman Larry Speakes admitted that he had invented a number of presidential quotes during several highly publicized occasions, his confession sparked a national scandal and widespread censure. In February of 1995, Speaker of the House Newt Gingrich impressed a group of restaurateurs with a shocking speech about government waste.[10] He claimed that a 120-bed federal homeless shelter in Denver cost $8.8 million a year to operate, whereas a privately funded shelter nearby cost only $320,000 a year. The problem was, no such federal shelter existed in Denver; nor did any in the nation receive that much federal money. Further, claimed a *Washington Post* reporter, "Those are far from the only factual errors Gingrich has made recently as he speaks out on almost everything from the inner city to the computer age." Although the results are less devastating than those stemming from Joseph McCarthy's distortions, Gingrich's false claims still represent a serious breach of ethics.

Speakers also have an ethical responsibility to give credit for ideas and information that is not their own. Presenting the words and ideas of others without crediting them is called *plagiarism*. This ethical violation is both serious enough and widespread enough to warrant a separate discussion.

● AVOID PLAGIARISM

Most people are taught from earliest childhood that it is wrong to steal. Yet even those who would never think of stealing money or shoplifting may be tempted to **plagiarize**—present someone else's words or ideas as though they were one's own. Perhaps you can remember copying a grade-school report directly from the encyclopedia, or maybe you've even purchased or "borrowed" a paper to submit for an assignment in high school or college. These are obvious forms of plagiarism. A less obvious form is "patchwork" plagiarism—lacing a speech with compelling phrases you find in a source that you do not credit. Whether your lapse is intentional or due merely to careless or hasty note taking, the offense is equally serious.

plagiarize
Present someone else's words or ideas as though they were one's own.

Most colleges impose stiff penalties on students who plagiarize. Plagiarists almost always fail the assignment in question, frequently fail the course, and are sometimes put on academic probation or even expelled. Why is plagiarism such a big deal? As one college professor put it, "Theft of ideas is the most heinous crime in academics since the ideas are the only products professors have. Since ideas, and the ownership of ideas, are so important to professors, there are great punishments for plagiarism and cheating."[11]

Penalties for plagiarism outside academia are severe as well. A decade ago, it cost a U.S. Senator his bid for the Democratic nomination for president. In August 1987 Delaware Senator Joseph Biden plagiarized the words of former British Labor Party Leader Neil Kennock in a speech in Des Moines, Iowa. When the plagiarism was exposed, along with evidence of a previous plagiarism from a speech by Robert Kennedy, Biden was forced to withdraw from the presidential race. Publicized evidence of plagiarism also haunted Boston University Dean H.

Joachim Maitre, who in 1991 used phrases from a movie critic's essay in a commencement speech without crediting the critic. Both Biden and Maitre violated their ethical responsibilities and paid the price for that violation with their reputations. In Biden's case, it cost him his career.

Now that you understand what plagiarism is and why it carries such severe penalties, we will consider how best to avoid it.

● DO YOUR OWN WORK   The most flagrant cases of plagiarism result from not doing your own work. For example, while you are poking around the library for ideas to use in a speech assignment, you may discover an entire speech or perhaps an article that could easily be made into a speech. However tempting it may be to use this material, and however certain you are that no audience member could possibly have seen it, resist the urge to plagiarize. First, you will be doing yourself a disservice if you do not learn how to compose a speech on your own. After all, you are in college to acquire new skills. In addition, the risk may be much greater than you suspect.

A few years ago one of your authors heard an excellent student speech on the importance of early detection of cancer. The only problem was, she heard the same speech again in the following class period! Upon finding the "speech"— actually a *Reader's Digest* article that was several years old—both students were certain that they had discovered a surefire shortcut to an A. Instead, they failed the assignment, ruined their course grades, and lost your author's trust.

Another way speakers sometimes attempt to shortcut the speech preparation task is to ask another person to edit a speech so extensively that it becomes more that other person's work than their own. This is another form of plagiarism, as well as another way of cheating themselves out of the skills they need to develop.

● ACKNOWLEDGE YOUR SOURCES   Our admonition to do your own work in no way suggests that you should not research your speeches and then share the results with audience members. In fact, as we have said, an ethical speaker is responsible for doing just that. Furthermore, some information is so widely known that you do not have to acknowledge a source for it. For example, you need not credit a source if you say that the HIV virus must be present for a person to develop full-blown AIDS, or that the Treaty of Versailles was signed on June 28, 1919. This information is widely available in a variety of reference sources. However, if you decide to use in your speech any of the following, then you must give credit to the source:

■ Direct quotations, even if they are only brief phrases

■ Opinions, assertions, or ideas of others, even if they are paraphrased rather than quoted verbatim

■ Statistics

■ Any nonoriginal visual materials, including graphs, tables, and pictures

In order to be able to acknowledge your sources, you must first practice careful and systematic note taking. Indicate with quotation marks any phrases or sentences that you copy verbatim from a source, and be sure to record the author, title, publisher, publication date, and page numbers for all sources from which you take quotations, ideas, statistics, or visual materials. Additional suggestions for systematic note taking will be offered in Chapter 7.

In addition to keeping careful records of your sources, you must also know how to cite your sources for your audience, both orally and in writing. Perhaps you have heard a speaker say, "Quote," while holding up both hands with index and middle fingers curved to indicate quotation marks. This is an artificial and distracting way to cite a source; an *oral citation* can be integrated more smoothly into the speech. For example, you might say, "According to Stephen H. Wildstrom, writing in the July 3, 1995, issue of *Business Week* . . . ."—then pause briefly to signal that you are about to begin quoting—" 'For people who divide their computing time between home, office, and the road, the new generation of laptops could be real labor savers.' "[12] Notice that this example provides the author, publication title, and date of publication, which are usually sufficient for oral documentation.

You can also provide a *written citation* for a source. In fact, your public speaking instructor may ask you to provide a bibliography of sources along with the outline or other written materials he or she requires for each speech. Instructors who require such citations will usually assign the format in which they want such material; if they do not, you can use a style guide such as those published by the Modern Language Association (MLA), American Psychological Association (APA), or the University of Chicago Press (Chicago style). You may already have used one of these style guides; if not, you can usually find them in the library, or you can consult a condensed version in a college composition handbook. For written documentation, you should include the article title and page numbers. For example, here is an MLA citation for the same source we cited orally:

Windstrom, Stephen H. "Laptops for the Desktop." *Business Week* 3 July 1995. 18.

Perhaps now you are thinking. What about those "gray areas," those times when I am not certain whether information or ideas I am presenting are "common knowledge"? A good rule of thumb is this: When in doubt, document. You will never be guilty of plagiarism if you document something you didn't need to, but you could be committing plagiarism if you do not document something you really should have.

 RECAP

SPEAKER ETHICS

THE ETHICAL PUBLIC SPEAKER . . .

Has a clear, responsible goal

Uses sound evidence and reasoning

Is sensitive to and tolerant of differences

Is honest

Avoids plagiarism

Listening ethically

Until now, we have been focusing primarily on the ethical exercise of free speech by the speaker. But audience members, too, share responsibility for ethical communication. In the fourth century B.C., Aristotle warned, "Let men be on their guard against those who flatter and mislead the multitude . . . " And contemporary rhetorician Harold Barrett has said that the audience is "the available and necessary source of correction" for the behavior of a speaker.[13] The following sections summarize Barrett's "attributes of the good audience," which can serve as guidelines for ethical listening.

Listeners share responsibility with speakers in maintaining high ethical standards for public speech. If a speaker is spewing messages filled with hatred and bias — or simply hiding or distorting information — don't hesitate to communicate your disapproval by frowning, looking away, or even walking out. [Photo: John Ficara/Woodfin Camp & Associates]

COMMUNICATE YOUR EXPECTATIONS

As an audience member, you have the right—even the responsibility—to enter a communication situation with expectations about both the message and how the speaker will deliver it. Know what information and ideas you want to get out of the communication transaction, and communicate your listening objective honestly, interacting with the speaker through appropriate nonverbal and verbal channels.

Listen attentively. Maintain eye contact with the speaker. Nod in agreement when you support something the speaker says; look puzzled if you do not understand the speaker's point. It is difficult for a speaker to be audience-centered if the audience does not provide feedback.

BE SENSITIVE TO AND TOLERANT OF DIFFERENCES

You have seen this admonition before, when we discussed the importance of being a sensitive and tolerant speaker. But it is equally important for you to exercise social and cultural awareness and tolerance as a member of the audience. Listen attentively and courteously. Making an effort to understand the needs, goals, and interests of both the speaker and other audience members can help you judge how to react appropriately and effectively as a listener.

LISTEN CRITICALLY

Being courteous and tolerant is not the same thing as approving of what Barrett terms "socially detrimental individualism or advantage-seeking." In fact, the necessary counterbalance to the absolute exercise of free speech is the listener who recognizes and refuses to license abusive or dangerous ideas or plans. As University of Chicago professor and ethicist Richard M. Weaver explains, "It is the principle of our society that we can listen to propaganda from all the special interests . . . and do a pretty fair job of sifting the true claims from the false."[14] In other words, it is our job to listen critically.

To listen critically is to hold the speaker to his or her ethical responsibilities. Is the speaker presenting both sides of the issue? Is the speaker disclosing all the information to which he or she has access, or is the speaker trying to hide something? Is the speaker being honest about the purpose of the speech? As already noted, you can communicate to the speaker through nonverbal feedback during a speech. Frowning or looking away can signal to the speaker that you do not approve of his or her message. You can, in extreme cases, walk out of the room. If there is a chance that you may have misunderstood the speaker, take advantage of opportunities after the speech to question him or her. Read more about the topic for yourself, to check the speaker's facts. And if you conclude that the speaker's message or motives are indeed unethical, discuss your opinion with others, and seek out or create a forum through which you can express your dissent. While you can and should refuse to sanction unethical messages and tactics, seek ways to question and refute ideas and arguments without being discourteous or resorting to unethical tactics yourself.

RECAP

LISTENER ETHICS

THE ETHICAL LISTENER . . .

Communicates expectations

Is sensitive to and tolerant of differences

Listens critically

Summary

This chapter focused on the role and importance of ethical speaking and listening in a society that protects free speech. Although Congress and the courts have occasionally limited free speech by law and policy, more often they have protected and broadened its application. The right to free speech has also been upheld in this country by such organizations as the American Civil Liberties Union and by colleges and universities.

Speakers who exercise their right to free speech are responsible for tempering what they say by applying ethics, or moral principles and values. Although there is no definitive standard of ethics, most people agree that public speakers must be responsible, honest, and tolerant in order to be ethical.

We discussed at length plagiarism, one of the most common violations of speech ethics. You can usually avoid plagiarism by understanding what it is, doing your own work, and acknowledging the sources for any quotations, ideas, statistics, or visual materials you use in a speech.

We concluded the chapter with guidelines for ethical listening. Ethical listeners should communicate their expectations; be sensitive to and tolerant of differences; and listen critically, refusing to sanction unethical messages and tactics.

● CRITICAL THINKING QUESTIONS

1. Explain how ethics serve as a balance to free speech.

2. Why do you think the Supreme Court has historically considered flag burning and pornography to be "free speech acts"?

3. The following passage comes from a book entitled, *Abraham Lincoln, Public Speaker,* by Waldo W. Braden:

   The Second Inaugural Address, sometimes called Lincoln's Sermon on the Mount, was a concise, tightly constructed composition that did not waste words on ceremonial niceties or superficial sentiment. The shortest Presidential inaugural address up to that time, it was only 700 words long, compared to 3,700 words for the First, and required from 5 to 7 minutes to deliver.[15]

Now determine which of the following statements should be credited to Braden if you were to use them in a speech:

   A. Lincoln's Second Inaugural is sometimes call Lincoln's Sermon on the Mount.

   B. Because he was elected and sworn in for two terms as President, Abraham Lincoln prepared and delivered two inaugural addresses.

   C. Lincoln's Second Inaugural was 700 words and 5 to 7 minutes long.

● ETHICAL QUESTIONS

1. There is evidence that Franklin D. Roosevelt's long-time aide Louis Howe actually wrote the famous line from Roosevelt's first inaugural address: "The only thing we have to fear is fear itself." More recently, it has been openly acknowledged that Presidential speechwriter Peggy Noonan wrote some of the most memorable and successful speeches of Presidents Ronald Reagan and George Bush, including Reagan's 1986 eulogy to the Challenger astronauts and Bush's 1988 speech accepting the Republican nomination for President. Is the use of such ghostwriters a violation of speech ethics?

2. In his first speech on Watergate, Richard Nixon defended his subordinates as "people whose zeal exceeded their judgment and who may have done wrong in a cause they deeply believed to be right." Nixon's statement implies that people who mean well should not be judged too harshly, even if they commit unethical acts. Do you agree?[16]

1. Photocopy or clip any articles you discover during your public speaking that discuss and/or censure the ethics of public speakers. Determine in each case which of the ethical principles discussed in this chapter were violated.

USING TECHNOLOGY AND MEDIA

1. Watch and take notes on at least five prime-time television commercials. Do you think these commercials are ethical? Why or why not? If not, what are your rights and responsibilities as an ethical listener/consumer?

"The Storyteller."
Adalphe Tidesmond/SuperStock

Listening

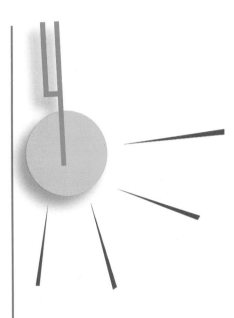

Learn how to listen and you will prosper —even from those who talk badly.
—Plutarch

OBJECTIVES

After studying this chapter you should be able to do the following:

1. Identify the stages in the listening process.

2. List and describe four barriers to effective listening.

3. Discuss strategies to become a better listener.

4. Identify strategies for improving your note-taking skill.

5. Discuss the relationships between listening and critical thinking.

6. Use criteria for evaluating speeches.

re you a good listener? Considerable evidence suggests that your listening skills could be improved. Within twenty-four hours after listening to a lecture or speech, you will recall only about 50 percent of the message. Forty-eight hours later, you are above average if you remember more than 25 percent of the message. (And in a recent survey of adult listeners, only 15 percent reported that they were above-average listeners.)

A psychology professor had dedicated his life to teaching and worked hard to prepare interesting lectures, yet he found his students sitting through his talks with glassy-eyed expressions.[1] To learn what was wrong, and also find out what was on his students' minds if they were not focusing on psychology, he would, without warning, fire a blank from a gun and then ask his students to record their thoughts at the instant they heard the shot. Here is what he found:

20 percent were pursuing erotic thoughts or sexual fantasies.

20 percent were reminiscing about something (they weren't sure what they were thinking about).

20 percent were worrying about something or thinking about lunch.

8 percent were pursuing religious thoughts.

20 percent were reportedly listening.

12 percent were able to recall what the professor was talking about when the gun fired.

You hear over one billion words each year. Yet how much information do you retain? In this chapter, we are going to focus on improving your listening skill. If you apply the principles and suggestions we offer, we believe that you will be not only a better listener but also a better public speaker. In addition, improving your listening skill will strengthen your ability to think critically and evaluate what you hear, and also enhance your one-on-one interpersonal listening. In this chapter, we will discuss how people listen and identify barriers and pitfalls that keep both speakers and audiences from listening effectively. We will also make some suggestions for improving your listening and note-taking skills. Finally, we will discuss how you can enhance your ability to listen critically and evaluate speeches.

Stages in listening

istening is not the same as hearing. Hearing is a physiological process. You hear sounds when sound waves strike the eardrums and cause them to vibrate. These vibrations cause the hammer, anvil, and stirrup of the middle ear to vibrate too, thereby producing sound. Eventually the vibrations reach the auditory nerve, which turns the vibrations into electrical energy. This energy ultimately reaches your brain. Listening, however, is part of the communication process. Although you may have *heard* your geography professor, you may not be able to recall a thing your professor said if you weren't *listening*. You didn't decode the message.

When we listen, we hear words and try to make sense of what we hear. Listening involves *selecting, attending, understanding,* and *remembering.* Let's look at each of these four stages of the listening process in greater detail.

● SELECTING

Stop reading this book for a moment and take note of the sounds you hear. Do you hear the whir of an air conditioner or furnace, the wind, a ticking clock, voices, a car, a train, or a plane? You have the ability to **select** what you will listen to. Instead of listening to the noises around you, you can read this book and concentrate on the ideas in it, or you can focus on your own thoughts. When the time comes to deliver your speech to an audience, keep in mind that your potential listeners have the same choice. Your job as a speaker is to motivate them to select *your* message.

selecting
Singling out a message from several competing messages.

● ATTENDING

The sequel to selecting is attending. When you select a sound, you attend to it; you focus on it. Even though you may pay attention to a sound for only a fraction of a second, your mind must be focused on it for listening to occur. One of your key challenges as a public speaker will be to capture and hold the attention of your audience. What helps an audience listen to a message?

attending
Selecting incoming information for further processing.

■ *Activity and movement.* An audience is more likely to listen to an action-packed message than to one that listlessly lingers on an idea too long. Incorporating meaningful movement into your delivery and using visual aids also help hold an audience's attention.

■ *Concrete words and images.* Effective speakers use words and images that the audience can visualize. Vividly describing a Shinto marriage ceremony will more likely hold an audience's attention than will reciting research conclusions about marriage in Japan.

■ *Issues and events close to an audience.* To make an audience more concerned about the state of medical care, focus on the problems in the audience's own community rather than on those in a large city a thousand miles away. People pay attention to what affects them directly.

■ *Familiar ideas and events.* Listeners can more easily summon up an image of something they have already seen than of something totally foreign. Referring to people, places, and events in the community that the audience has seen and heard can focus a listener's attention.

■ *New, different, or novel ideas, issues, and events.* While this may seem to contradict the previous points, audiences can become intrigued with something new or unseen if you relate it to something that concerns them, their communities, or their families.

■ *Stories that create suspense.*   Everyone likes a good story, especially one that keeps listeners on the edge of their seats. Whether the story is true or hypothetical, a well-told yarn can keep listeners tuned in.

■ *Conflict.*   Stories that pit one side against another, and descriptions of opposing ideas and forces in government, religion, or interpersonal relationships foster attention. The Greeks learned long ago that the essential ingredient for a good play, be it comedy or tragedy, is conflict.

■ *Humor.*   A fisherman went into a sporting goods store. The salesperson offered the man a wonderful lure for trout: It had beautiful colors, eight hooks, and looked just like a rare Buckner bug. Finally, the fisherman asked the salesperson, "Do fish really like this thing?"

   "I don't really know," admitted the salesperson. "I don't sell to fish."

   The speaker using this story could have simply said, "It's important to know your audience." Using a bit of humor makes the point while holding the listener's attention.

All of these factors help an audience pay attention.[2] Your job as a speaker is to make sure that you incorporate these factors into your speech, so your audience will not have to work hard to attend to your message.

● UNDERSTANDING

As you select and attend to a sound, you try to make sense out of what you hear. **Understanding** is the process of assigning meaning to the stimuli to which you attend. Although there is no single theory that explains how people make sense of the world, we do know that you understand what you hear by relating it to something you have already seen or heard. If you are talking about oxymorons (a combination of seemingly contradictory words in the same phrase) and your audience does not know what an oxymoron is, the best way to tell them is with an example that draws on their store of knowledge: "efficient bureaucracy" would probably work. Your job as a speaker is to make sure your audience has the knowledge to understand what you are saying.

● REMEMBERING

How do you know whether someone listened to you or not? Most listening experts believe that you can find out whether someone has listened to you only by testing whether they can **remember** what they heard. Your geography professor determines how well you understand geography by testing you on the content of his or her lecture. But intentionally or not, the professor is testing your listening skill as well as your knowledge of geography.

You have both a *short-term memory* and a *long-term memory*. Most of the information you encounter enters your short-term memory, but it does not stay there for long. Storage space in short-term memory is very limited. If the information is important, you transfer it to long-term memory. Often you need to rehearse or repeat it to make the transfer successful. To help an audience remember your message, you will need to build in redundancy. When learning the basics

understanding
Assigning meaning to the stimuli to which you attend.

remembering
Recalling ideas and information.

of written composition, you may have been taught to avoid repeating yourself. Oral communication, however, needs to be more redundant. An introductory statement announcing your major ideas, a clear presentation of your major points, and a summary of your key thoughts will build redundancy into your message and help your audience remember it. And—to repeat ourselves—audience members will be more likely to remember your message if you relate it to their interests.

RECAP

STAGES IN LISTENING

SELECTING	You sort through both internal and external sources of sound and thought.
ATTENDING	You focus on a specific message.
UNDERSTANDING	You make sense out of words and nonverbal information.
REMEMBERING	You are able to recall messages, especially those that directly affect you.

Barriers to effective listening

Unfortunately, even if you follow all of the advice we have provided on how to keep your audience's attention, some of the people you speak to will not be listening carefully. And when you are part of an audience, your attention *will* wander, even during an interesting speech. Let's look now at the barriers that interfere with the listening process, along with some ways that you, as both speaker and audience member, can overcome them.

● INFORMATION OVERLOAD

We all spend a large part of each day listening. That's good news and bad news. The good news is that because we listen a lot, we have the potential of becoming very effective listeners. The bad news is that instead of getting better at it, we get tired of listening because we hear so much information that we "tune out."

As a public speaker, you can keep your audience from tuning out by delivering a message that is clear and easy to understand. Finally, as mentioned earlier, you will have to build redundancy into your message so that if listeners miss an idea the first time you present it, perhaps they will catch it during your concluding remarks. Remember that listening is hard work. Decide what is important in a speech and focus on that.

● PERSONAL CONCERNS

You are sitting in your African history class on a Friday afternoon. It's a beautiful day. You slump into your seat, open your notebook, and prepare to

No matter how well crafted your speech or how artful your delivery, noise or other distractions can steal your audience's attention. Always try to eliminate potential problems from the environment before beginning to speak. [Photo: Gary Braasch/Tony Stone Images]

take notes on the lecture. As the professor talks about an upcoming assignment, you begin to think about how you are going to spend your Saturday. One thought leads to another as you mentally plan your weekend. Suddenly you hear your professor say, "You will be expected to know the principles I've just reviewed for Monday's test." What principles? What test? Since you were present in class, you heard the professor's lecture, but you're not sure what was said.

Your own thoughts are among the biggest competitors for your attention when you are a member of an audience. Most of us would rather listen to our own inner speech than to the message of a public speaker. As the psychology professor with the gun found, sex, lunch, worries, and daydreams are major distractions for the majority of listeners.

To counteract this problem, as a speaker, you can focus on maintaining your audience's attention, using occasional "wake-up" messages such as, "Now listen carefully because this will affect your future grade (or family or employment)." As a listener, you can learn to recognize when your own agenda is keeping you from listening, then force yourself to focus on the speaker's message. Later in this chapter, we will offer specific suggestions for things to do when you find your attention flagging.

OUTSIDE DISTRACTIONS

While sitting in class, you notice that a fluorescent light is flickering overhead. Two classmates behind you are swapping stories about their favorite soap opera plots. Out the window you see a varsity hero struggling to break into his car to retrieve the keys he left in the ignition. As your history professor drones on about the Bay of Pigs invasion, you find it difficult to focus on his lecture. Most of us don't listen well when physical distractions are competing with the speaker.

When you are the speaker, try to control the physical arrangements of the speaking situation before you begin your speech. Do the best you can to reduce or eliminate distractions (close windows and window shades to limit sight and sound in the room in which you are speaking; turn off blinking fluorescent lights if you can; try to discourage whispering in the audience). Try to empathize with your listeners. Check out the room ahead of time, sit where your audience will be seated, and look for possible distractions.

As a listener, you will also need to do your best to control the listening situation. If you have to, move to another seat. If the speaker has failed to monitor the listening environment, you may need to close the blinds, turn up the heat, turn off the lights, close the door, or do whatever is necessary to minimize distractions.

PREJUDICE

Your buddy is a staunch Democrat. He rarely credits a Republican with any useful ideas. So it's not surprising that when the Republican governor from your state makes a major televised speech outlining suggestions for improving the state's sagging economy, your friend finds the presentation ludicrous. As the speech is broadcast, your buddy constantly argues against each suggestion, mumbling something about Republicans, business interests, and robbing the poor. The next day he is surprised to see editorials in the press praising the governor's speech. "Did they hear the same speech I did?" your friend wonders. Yes, they heard the same speech, but they listened differently. When you prejudge a message, your ability to understand it decreases.

Another way to prejudge a speech is to decide that the topic has little value for you even before you hear the message. Most of us at one time or another have not given our full attention to a speech because we decided beforehand that it was going to bore us.

Sometimes we make snap judgments about a speaker based on his or her appearance, and then fail to listen because we dismissed his or her ideas in advance as inconsequential or irrelevant. Female speakers often complain that males in the audience do not listen as attentively as they would to another male; members of ethnic and racial minorities may feel slighted in a similar way.

On the flip side, some people too readily accept what someone says just because they like the way the person looks, sounds, or dresses. For example, Tex believes that anyone with a Texas drawl must be an honest person. Such positive prejudices can also inhibit your ability to listen accurately to a message.

What can you do as a public speaker to counteract this sort of prejudice? The most effective strategy is to use your opening statements to grab the audience's attention. Focus on your particular listeners' interests, needs, hopes, and wishes. When addressing an audience that may be critical or hostile toward your message, use arguments and evidence that your listeners will find credible. Strong emotional appeals will be less successful than careful language, sound reasoning, and convincing evidence. As a listener, you need to guard against becoming so critical of a message that you don't listen to it or so impressed that you decide *too quickly* that the speaker is trustworthy.

 RE**CAP**

BARRIERS TO EFFECTIVE LISTENING

Barrier	Listener's Tasks	Speaker's Tasks
Information overload	Concentrate harder on the message; identify the most important parts of the message.	Develop a message that is clear and easy to understand. Build in redundancy.
Personal concerns	Focus on the speaker's message rather than on your own self-talk.	Use attention-holding strategies and "wake-up" messages.
Outside distractions	Aggressively attempt to control the listening environment.	Monitor the physical arrangements before you begin your speech. Take action by doing such things as closing the shades if there are distractions outside, or turning up the air conditioner if it's too warm.
Prejudice	Focus on the message, not the messenger.	Use strong opening statements that focus on listeners' interests.

Becoming a better listener

Now that we have examined barriers to effective listening, we will offer some additional suggestions for improving your listening skill.

● STRIVE FOR UNCONSCIOUS COMPETENCE

An overarching strategy to enhance your listening skill is to become increasingly sensitive to those factors that detract from your listening skill. People who are oblivious to their lack of listening skill are *unconsciously incompetent*—they don't know that they have a problem listening effectively. You become *consciously incompetent* when you realize that you have a problem but aren't quite sure what to do about it. When you learn what your bad listening habits are and how to correct them, you can become *consciously competent*.

We want you to become mindful of what you need to do to enhance your listening skill by reading this chapter. The ultimate goal is to become *unconsciously competent*—to become such a good listener that you are not aware of the skills and effective habits that you have cultivated. At that point, you no longer have to remind yourself to concentrate on what you are hearing; incorporating effective listening skills has become second nature to you.

● ADAPT TO THE SPEAKER'S DELIVERY

Good listeners focus on a speaker's message, not on his or her style. To be a good listener, you will have to adapt to the particular idiosyncrasies some speakers have. You will have to ignore or overlook a speaker's tendency to mumble, speak in a monotone, or fail to make eye contact. Perhaps more difficult still, you may even have to forgive a speaker's lack of clarity or coherence. Rather than mentally criticizing an unpolished speaker, you may need to be sympathetic and try harder to concentrate on the message. Good listeners focus on the message, not the messenger.

Poor speakers are not the only challenge to good listening. You also need to guard against glib, well-polished speakers. Just because a speaker may have an attractive style of delivery does not necessarily mean that his or her message is credible. Don't let a smooth-talking salesperson convince you to buy something without carefully considering the content of his or her message.

● LISTEN WITH YOUR EYES AS WELL AS YOUR EARS

Even though we have cautioned you against letting a speaker's style of delivery distract you, don't totally ignore a speaker's body language. Nonverbal clues play a major role in communicating a message. One expert has estimated that as much as 93 percent of the emotional content of a speech is conveyed by nonverbal clues.[3] Even though this statistic does not apply in every situation, emotion is primarily communicated by unspoken messages. For example, facial expressions help identify the emotions being communicated; a speaker's posture and gestures can reinforce the intensity of the emotion.[4] If you have trouble understanding a speaker, either because he or she speaks too softly or because he or she speaks in an unfamiliar dialect, get close enough so that you can see the speaker's mouth. A good view can increase your level of attention and improve your understanding.

● AVOID OVERREACTING TO A MESSAGE

Heightened emotions can affect your ability to understand a message. If you become angered at a word or phrase a speaker uses, your listening comprehension decreases. Because of differing cultural backgrounds, religious convictions, and political views, listeners may become emotionally aroused by certain words. Words that connote negative opinions about a person's ethnic origin, nationality, or religious views can trigger strong emotions. Cursing and obscene language are red flags for some listeners.

Yin Ping is an Asian American who has distinguished himself as a champion debater on the college debate team. One sly opposing team member sought to distract him by quoting a bigoted statement that disparaged Asian Americans for "taking over the country." It was tempting for Yin Ping to respond emotionally to the insult, but he kept his wits, refuted the argument, and went on to win the debate. When someone uses a word or phrase you find offensive, you need to overcome your repugnance and continue to listen. You should not allow the speaker's language to close down your mind.

How can you keep your emotions in check when you hear something that sets you off? First, recognize when your emotional state is affecting your rational thoughts. Second, use the skill of self-talk to calm yourself down. Say to yourself, "I'm not going to let this anger get in the way of listening and understanding." You can also focus on your breathing for a moment to calm down.

● AVOID JUMPING TO CONCLUSIONS

"Not another speech about religion," you groan to yourself as your classmate, Frank Fuller, a divinity student, gets up to speak. "He's always preaching to us." As Fuller begins his slide lecture, you slump down in your seat, prepared to be bored and bothered. Sure enough, his opening line is "The Bible: It's not what you think!" But about halfway through the speech, you start listening to Fuller and realize that he is presenting some fascinating historical evidence connected with Noah's Ark. He's not trying to convert you; he's just describing some of the archaeological evidence related to the Bible. At the end of the speech, your classmates give him a hearty round of applause. Now you're sorry you missed the first part of the speech.

Don't jump to conclusions prematurely. Give a speaker time to develop and support his or her main point before you decide whether you agree or disagree or think the message has any value. As we've already noted, if you mentally criticize a speaker's style or message, your listening efficiency will decline.

● BE A SELFISH LISTENER

Although this suggestion may sound crass, being a selfish listener can help you maintain your powers of concentration. If you find your attention waning, ask yourself questions such as "What's in it for me?" and "How can I use information from this talk?" Granted, you will find more useful information in some presentations than others, but you should be alert to the possibility in all speeches. Find ways to benefit from the information you are listening to, and try to connect it with your own experiences and needs.

● LISTEN FOR MAJOR IDEAS

In a classic study, Ralph Nichols asked both good and poor listeners what their listening strategies were.[5] The poor listeners indicated that they listened for facts such as names and dates. The good listeners reported that they listened for major ideas and principles. Facts are useful only when you can connect them to a principle or concept. In speeches, facts as well as examples are used primarily to support major ideas. You should try to summarize mentally the major idea that the specific facts support.

If you had been present on that brisk March morning in 1933 to hear Franklin Delano Roosevelt deliver his first inaugural address, you would have heard him introduce his key idea in the fourth sentence of the speech: "This great Nation will endure as it has endured, will revive and will prosper. So, first of all, let me assert my firm belief that the only thing we have to fear is fear itself." A good listener would recognize this immediately as the core of the speech.

How can you tell what the major ideas in a speech are? A speaker who is well organized or familiar with good speaking techniques will offer a preview of the major ideas early in the speech. If no preview is provided, listen for the speaker to enumerate major points: "My first point is to talk about the history of Jackson County." Transitional phrases and a speaker's internal summaries are other clues that can help you identify the major points. If your speaker provides few overt indicators, you may have to discover them on your own. In that event, mentally summarize the ideas that are most useful to you. As we suggested earlier, be a selfish listener. Treat a disorganized speech as a gold mine to be scoured. Take your mental mining pan and search for the meaningful nuggets.

● KEEP YOUR FOCUS

If you are a typical student, you spend over 80 percent of your day involved in communication-related activities.[6] You spend about 14 percent of your communication time writing, 17 percent reading, 16 percent speaking, and at least 53 percent listening. You listen a lot. Your challenge is to stay on course and keep your listening focused.

One way to stay focused is to determine your listening purpose. There are at least four major listening goals. First, you listen for pleasure, just for the fun of it. You might watch TV, listen to music, go to a movie, or chitchat with a friend. A second reason you listen is to be supportive of others, to empathize. To have empathy means you attempt to feel what the speaker is feeling. Usually, empathic

Attending dramatic performances is a good way to sharpen your listening skills. If the language is from another era or locale, the experience will be especially enriching. [Photo: Cary Wolinsky/Stock Boston]

listening occurs in one-on-one listening situations with a good friend. Or sometimes in your job you may need to listen empathically to a client, customer, or co-worker. A third reason to listen is to gain information, to learn. You have already spent over a dozen years listening in classrooms to gain information. Finally, you listen to evaluate critically what you hear. When you evaluate a message, you are making a judgment about its content. You are interested in whether the information is reliable, true, or useful. Determining which of these listening objectives apply to a particular situation can help you stay focused.

Knowing your listening goal can also help you develop an appropriate listening strategy. If you are listening for pleasure, you need not take notes. Listening to empathize involves staying with the speaker each step of the message. Empathic listeners will often mentally paraphrase or summarize the speaker's message. If you are listening to learn, you will develop associations for long-term recall. When listening critically, knowing both what the facts are and how they relate to the speaker's arguments and conclusions will be important.

As a speaker, it is also important for you to know your listeners' objectives. If you planned to deliver an educational lecture, but it turns out your listeners are there only for pleasure, you will have to do some quick adjusting to meet your listeners' needs.

 PRACTICE LISTENING

Since we've noted that you spend more than 53 percent of your time listening each day, you may wonder why we suggest that you practice listening. But listening skills do not develop automatically. You learn to swim by getting proper instruction; you don't develop your aquatic skills by just jumping in the water and flailing around. Similarly, you learn to listen by practicing the methods we recommend. Researchers believe that poor listeners avoid challenge. For example, they listen to and watch TV situation comedies rather than documentaries or other informative programs. Skill develops as you practice listening to speeches, music, and programs with demanding content.

An active listener is one who remains alert and mentally re-sorts, rephrases, and repeats key information when listening to a speech. Evidence suggests that you can listen to words much faster than a speaker can speak them. Most speakers talk at about 125 words a minute.[7] You may have the ability to listen to well over 700 words a minute. Therefore, it's natural that your mind may wander. But you can use the extra time instead to focus on interpreting what the speaker says.

First, use your listening time to *re-sort* disorganized or disjointed ideas. If the speaker is rambling off strings of disorganized ideas, seek ways to rearrange them into a new, more logical pattern. You can also *rephrase* or summarize what the speaker is saying. This mental activity will help you stay alert so you can follow the speaker's flow of ideas. Listen for main ideas, and then put them into your own words. You are more likely to remember your mental paraphrase than the speaker's exact words.

Finally, do more than just rephrase the information as you listen to it. Periodically, *repeat* key points that you want to remember. Go back to essential ideas and restate them to yourself. If you follow these steps for active listening, you will find yourself feeling stimulated and engaged instead of tired and bored as you listen to even the dullest of speakers.

RECAP

ACTIVE LISTENING

Steps	Definition	Example
Re-sort	Reorganize jumbled or disorganized information.	What the speaker said: "There are several key dates to remember: 1776, 1492, and 1861."
		You re-sort: 1492, 1776, 1861.
Rephrase	Paraphrase the speaker's ideas, rather than trying to remember his or her exact words.	What the speaker said: "If we don't stop the destructive overspending of the defense budget, our nation will very quickly find itself much deeper in debt and unable to meet the many needs of its citizens."
		You rephrase: "We should spend less on defense, or we will have more problems."
Repeat	Periodically, mentally restate key ideas you want to remember.	Repeat the rephrase above five minutes later into the speech.

BECOMING A BETTER LISTENER

The Good Listener . . .	The Poor Listener . . .
Adapts to the speaker's delivery	Is easily distracted by the delivery of the speech
Looks for nonverbal clues to aid understanding	Focuses only on the words
Controls emotions	Erupts emotionally when listening
Listens before making a judgment about the value of the content	Jumps to conclusions about the value of the message
Mentally asks, "What's in it for me?"	Does not attempt to relate to the information personally
Listens for major ideas	Listens for isolated facts
Remains focused	Does not mentally summarize
Seeks opportunities to practice listening skills	Avoids listening to difficult information

Improving your note-taking skill

What's everyone taking notes for?" wondered Carolyne, scanning the lecture hall during her American history class. "Can't they remember the key points without trying to scribble them in their notebooks?" At the end of the lecture, however, Carolyne found that she was getting confused about the dates and events her professor had mentioned, so she tried to borrow the notes of one of her fellow listeners.

So far in this chapter, we have suggested ways to improve your listening skill. But we also recognize that you will not remember everything you listen to. It is difficult to recall the details of a lengthy speech unless you have taken notes. Coupling improved listening skill with increased skill in taking notes can greatly enhance your ability to retrieve information. Try the following suggestions to improve your note-taking skill.

- *Prepare.* Come prepared to take notes, even if you're not sure you need to. Bring a pencil or pen and paper to every class, lecture, or meeting.

- *Determine whether you need to take notes.* After the presentation has started, decide whether you need to take notes. If you receive a handout that summarizes the content of the message, it may be best to pay attention, concentrate on the message, and take very few notes.

- *Make a decision about the type of notes you need to take.* If notes seem to be necessary, decide whether you need to outline the speech, identify facts and principles, jot down key words, or just record major ideas. Some speakers do not follow organized outline patterns, in which case it will be tricky to outline the message. If you are going to take an objective test on the material, you may need to note only facts and principles. Noting key words may be enough to help you recall what was said if you are going to prepare a report for someone else to read. Or you may want to write down just major ideas. The type of notes you take will depend on how you intend to use the information you get from the speech.

■ *Make your notes meaningful.* Beware of taking too many notes; the goal is to remember the message, not to transcribe it. Instead, use the re-sorting and rephrasing techniques we discussed earlier and write down only what will be meaningful to you later.

RECAP

IMPROVING YOUR NOTE-TAKING SKILL

1. Prepare.

2. Determine whether you need to take notes.

3. Make a decision about the type of notes you need to take.

4. Make your notes meaningful.

Listening and critical thinking

Effective listening also requires a well-developed critical faculty. To listen and think critically, you need to cultivate a variety of skills that we will return to throughout this text. Critical listening includes distinguishing fact from inference, spotting problems in a speaker's reasoning, or identifying weak evidence to support a speaker's point.

The ability to separate facts from inferences is one of the most basic critical listening skills. **Facts** are based on something that has proven to be true by direct observation. For example, it has been directly observed that water boils at 212 degrees Fahrenheit, that the direction of the magnetic north pole can be found by consulting a compass, or that U.S. Presidents have been inaugurated on January 20th every four years for several decades. An **inference** is a conclusion based on partial information, or an evaluation that has not been directly observed. You infer that your favorite sports team will win the championship or that it will rain tomorrow. You can also infer, if more Republicans than Democrats are elected to Congress, that the next President might be a Republican. But you can only know this for a *fact* after the presidential election. Facts are in the realm of certainty; inferences are in the realm of probability and opinion—where most arguments advanced by public speakers reside. A critical listener knows when a politician

facts
Information based on something that has proven to be true by direct observation.

inference
A conclusion based on partial information, or an evaluation that has not been directly observed.

running for office claims, "It's a fact that my opponent is not qualified to be elected" that this statement is *not* a fact, but an inference.

Learning to critically evaluate messages is an important responsibility for each of us. Whether we are listening to the rhetoric of a presidential candidate or hearing someone trying to sell us a used Chevrolet, we need to make distinctions between facts and inferences so that we can base our own actions on sound information.

Analyzing and evaluating speeches

You will no doubt listen to a number of speeches in this course so that you can practice both your listening skill and your skill at analyzing and critically evaluating messages. When you evaluate something, you judge its value and appropriateness. One of the benefits of learning speechmaking skills is that they can help you become a better judge of the speeches you hear. To be effective, a speaker's message must be understandable to listeners, achieve its intended purpose, and be ethical.[8] These three requirements can translate into criteria for evaluating a speech.

The message must be understandable to the audience. If listeners fail to comprehend the ideas, the speech fails. Similarly, if the speech does not achieve its intended purpose—to inform, persuade, or entertain—then the speech has been less than successful. And finally, being understood and achieving the desired goal are for naught if the speaker has unethically twisted facts, plagiarized the message, deceived the audience as to the purpose of the speech, or attempted to hide other choices the listeners could pursue. Note, however, that unethical speeches can be very effective in achieving the speaker's own unethical goals.

GIVING FEEDBACK TO OTHERS

With these three criteria in mind, we turn now to the issues of evaluating speeches, providing feedback to others, and responding to others' feedback to improve your own speeches. The Speech Evaluation Form at the end of this discussion reflects our audience-centered model of the speechmaking process. You can fill it in while you listen to a speech or immediately afterwards. Focusing on the criteria listed in the form will help you listen critically and effectively. Most likely, your public speaking teacher will invite you and your classmates to provide comments about one another's speeches. You can use this form as a starting point.

When you're invited to critique your classmates, your feedback will be more effective if you keep some general principles in mind. *Criticism* comes from a Greek word meaning "to judge or discuss." Therefore, to criticize a speech is to discuss the speech—identifying both strengths and aspects that could be improved. Effective criticism stems from developing a genuine interest in the speaker rather than seeking to find fault. When given the opportunity to critique your classmates, supplement the evaluations you provide on the form with the following kinds of feedback.

1. *Give feedback that describes what the speaker has done.* In a neutral way, describe what you saw the speaker doing. Act as a mirror for the speaker to help him or her become aware of gestures and other nonverbal signals of which he or she may not be aware. (If you are watching a videotape of the speech together, you can help point out behaviors.) Avoid providing a list of only your likes and dislikes; provide descriptive information instead.

   EFFECTIVE: Stan, I noticed that about 50 percent of the time you had direct eye contact with your listeners.

   LESS EFFECTIVE: Your eye contact was lousy.

2. *Give feedback that is specific.* When you describe what you see a speaker doing, also make sure your descriptions are precise enough to give the speaker a clear image of your perceptions. Saying that the speaker had "poor delivery" doesn't give him or her much information—it's only a general, evaluative comment. Be as specific and thoughtful as you can.

   EFFECTIVE: Dawn, your use of color on your overhead transparency helped to keep my attention.

   LESS EFFECTIVE: I liked your visuals.

3. *Begin and end with positive comments.* Some teachers call this approach the feedback sandwich. First, tell the speaker something he or she did well. This will let the speaker know you're not an enemy who's trying to shoot holes in his or her performance. Then, share a suggestion or two that may help the speaker improve the presentation. End your evaluation with another positive comment or restate what you liked best about the presentation. Beginning with negative comments immediately puts the speaker on the defensive and can create so much internal "noise" that he or she will stop listening. Starting and ending with positive comments will engender less defensiveness.

   EFFECTIVE: Gabe, I thought your opening statistical statement was very effective in catching my attention. You also maintained direct eye contact when you delivered it. Your overall organizational pattern would have been clearer to me if you had used more signposts and transition statements. Or, perhaps you could use a visual aid to summarize the main points. You did a good job of summarizing your three points in your conclusion. I also liked the way you ended your speech by making a reference to your opening statistics.

   LESS EFFECTIVE: I got lost when you were in the body of your speech. I couldn't figure out what your major ideas were. I also didn't know when you made the transition between the introduction and the body of your speech. Your intro and conclusion were good but the organization of the speech was weak.

4. *Give the speaker some suggestions or alternatives for improvement.* It's not especially helpful to rattle off a list of things you don't like without providing some suggestions for improvement. As a student of public speaking, your comments should reflect your growing skill and sophistication in the speech-making process.

EFFECTIVE: Jerry, I thought your speech had several good statistics and examples that suggest you spent a lot of time in the library researching your speech. I think you can add credibility to your message if you share your sources with the listener. Your vocal quality was effective and you had considerable variation in your pitch and tone. At times the speech rate was a little fast for me. A slower rate would help me catch some of the details of your message.

LESS EFFECTIVE: You spoke too fast. I had no idea whom you were quoting.

5. *"Own" your feedback by using I-statements rather than you-statements.* An I-statement is a way of phrasing your feedback so that it is clear that your comments reflect your personal point of view. "I found my attention drifting during the body of your speech" is an example of an I-statement. A you-statement is a less sensitive way of describing someone's behavior by implying that the other person did something wrong. "You didn't summarize very well in your conclusion," is an example of a you-statement. A better way to make the same point is, "I wasn't sure I understood the key ideas you mentioned in your conclusion." Here's another example:

EFFECTIVE: Mark, I found myself so distracted by your gestures that I had trouble focusing on the message.

LESS EFFECTIVE: Your gestures were distracting and awkward.

6. *Provide usable information.* Provide feedback about areas in which the speaker can improve rather than about aspects of the presentation that he or she cannot control. Maybe you have heard this advice: "Never try to teach a pig to sing. It wastes your time. It doesn't sound pretty. And it annoys the pig." Saying things such as, "You're too short to be seen over the lectern," "Your lisp doesn't lend itself to public speaking," or "You looked nervous" is not constructive. Concentrate on behaviors over which the speaker has control.

EFFECTIVE: Taka, I thought your closing quote was effective in summarizing your key ideas, but it didn't end your speech on an uplifting note. Another quote from Khalil Gibran that I'll share with you after class would also summarize your key points and provide a positive affirmation of your message. You may want to try it if you give this speech again.

LESS EFFECTIVE: Your voice isn't well suited to public speaking.

As you provide feedback, whether in your public speaking class or to a friend who asks you for a reaction to his speech, remember that the goal of feedback is to offer descriptive and specific information that helps a speaker build confidence and skill.

GIVING FEEDBACK TO YOURSELF

While you are collecting feedback from your instructor, classmates, family, and friends, keep in mind that the most important critic of your speeches is *you*. The ultimate goal of public speaking instruction is to learn principles and skills that enable you to be your own best critic. As you rehearse your speech, use self-talk to comment about the choices you make as a speaker. After your speech, take time to reflect on both the virtues and areas for improvement in your speechmaking skill. As an audience-centered speaker, you must learn to recognize when to make changes on your feet, in the midst of a speech. For example, if you notice that your audience just isn't interested in the facts and statistics that you are sharing, you may decide to support your points with a couple of stories instead. We encourage you to consider the following principles to enhance your own self-critiquing skills.

1. *Look for and reinforce your skills and speaking abilities.* Try to recognize your strengths and skills as a public speaker. Take mental note of how your audience analysis, organization, and delivery were effective in achieving your objectives. Such positive reflection can reinforce the many skills you are learning in this course. Resist the temptation to be too harsh or critical of your speaking skill. After each speaking opportunity, identify what you did right, and add a suggestion or two for ways to improve.

2. *Evaluate your effectiveness based on your specific speaking situation and audience.* Throughout the book we offer many suggestions and tips for improving your speaking skill. We also stress, however, that these prescriptions should be considered in light of your specific audience. Don't be a slave to rules. If you are giving a pep talk to the little league team you are coaching, you might not have to construct an attention-getting opening statement. Be flexible. Speaking is an art as well as a science. Give yourself permission to adapt principles and practices to specific speech situations.

3. *Identify one or two areas for improvement.* You may be tempted to overwhelm yourself with a long list of things you need to do as a speaker. Rather than trying to work on a dozen goals, concentrate on two or three, or maybe even just one key skill that you would like to develop. To help you make your decision, use the audience-centered model of public speaking that we introduced in Chapter 2.

Ultimately, the goal of this course is to teach you how to listen to your own commentary and become your own expert in shaping and polishing your speaking style.

Speech Evaluation Form

Speaker _____

Evaluator _____

Use the following scale to evaluate elements of the speech:

Outstanding	Good	Average	Fair	Poor
1	2	3	4	5

In addition to entering a number on each blank line, provide written comments to identify strengths and suggest ways to improve the speech.

Audience Orientation

The speaker was audience-centered   _____

The speaker adapted to the listeners   _____

Comments:

Introduction

The introduction caught my attention   _____

The introduction provided an overview of the main ideas   _____

The introduction established the speaker's credibility   _____

The introduction established a motivation to listen   _____

Comments:

Topic Selection

The topic was appropriate for the audience   _____

The topic was appropriate for the occasion   _____

The topic was appropriate for the speaker   _____

The topic was appropriate for the time limits   _____

Comments:

Purpose

The purpose was clear   _____

The purpose was appropriate for the audience   _____

The purpose was achieved   _____

Comments:

continued next page

Speech Evaluation Form   continued

Organization

The speech had an introduction, body, and conclusion   _____

The speech was easy to follow   _____

The speaker used transitions and signposts to clarify

    the organization   _____

The main ideas were clear to the audience   _____

Comments:

Supporting Information

The supporting information was credible   _____

The supporting information was varied and interesting   _____

Comments:

Visual Aids

The visual aids were attractive and understandable   _____

The visual aids were introduced at appropriate points

    in the speech   _____

Comments:

Delivery

The speaker made eye contact with the audience   _____

The speaker varied his voice and tone   _____

The speaker used appropriate gestures   _____

The speaker had good posture and seemed confident   _____

Comments:

Conclusion

The speaker summarized the key points   _____

The speaker ended the speech in a memorable,

    effective way   _____

Comments:

Ethics

The speaker cited sources for information and ideas

    appropriately   _____

The speaker presented viewpoints other than his or her own   _____

The speaker was clear about the true purpose of the speech   _____

Comments:

Summary

In this chapter, we described the listening process, identified barriers to good listening, and suggested methods for improving your listening habits. Listening is a process that involves selecting, attending, understanding, and remembering. Some of the barriers that keep us from listening at peak efficiency include information overload, personal concerns, outside distractions, and prejudice. We offered several suggestions to overcome these barriers and improve your listening skill:

Adapt to the speaker's delivery.

Listen with your eyes as well as your ears.

Avoid overreacting to a message.

Avoid jumping to conclusions.

Be a selfish listener.

Listen for major ideas.

Practice listening.

Become an active listener.

We also provided suggestions for taking effective notes to help you retain information that you hear. We concluded the chapter with an examination of the criteria for a good speech, and suggestions for ways to give and receive evaluative feedback on speeches in exchanges with your peers and instructors. We also discussed the goal of this text: to develop your self-evaluation skills so that you can support your own growth as a speechmaker.

● CRITICAL THINKING QUESTIONS

1. You are heading for your least favorite class: British Literature of the 1800s. You know you are in for another boring lecture delivered by a professor who does nothing but read in a monotone from yellowed notes. What are some strategies you can use to increase your listening effectiveness in this challenging situation?

2. For some reason, when Alberto hears the President speak, he just tunes out. What are some of the barriers that may keep Alberto from focusing on the message he is hearing?

3. Jackie aspires to be a broadcast journalist, following in the footsteps of well-known announcers such as Connie Chung and Diane Sawyer. Although she is a pretty good listener, she often has difficulty taking accurate notes on what she hears. What strategies do effective note takers use to capture messages accurately?

1. Margo discovered that one of her classmates who had taken world history the previous semester was selling the lecture notes. Margo studied the notes and found she could pass the exams without attending class. Is this kind of "listening" behavior ethical? Why or why not?

2. Chester was going to hear a congressional candidate speak at a benefit. Chester decided he would bring a book to read during the speech because the speaker was from a political party different from Chester's. Was Chester being fair to the speaker?

3. Janice was assigned the task of critiquing one of her classmate's speeches. Although she thought the speech was pretty good, she gave the speaker low marks because she strongly disagreed with what the speaker was saying. Was this an appropriate evaluation? Why or why not?

● SUGGESTED ACTIVITIES

1. Rank from most significant to least significant the barriers to effective listening discussed in this chapter as they apply to your own listening habits.

   Information overload

   Personal concerns

   Outside distractions

   Prejudice

   Describe your plan to help manage your three most troublesome listening barriers.

2. While you are listening to a speech by one of your classmates, try to listen for major ideas and construct a rough outline of the speech. If your classmate worked from an outline, compare your notes with that outline. If your outline is markedly different from your classmate's, try to analyze why.

3. Watch a documentary on TV. Every four or five minutes, mentally summarize key ideas presented in the program. When the program is over, write down the key ideas and summarize as much of the information as you can. The next day, without looking at what you wrote, try again to summarize the program's content. Note differences between your immediate recall and your twenty-four-hour recall. Two weeks after viewing the program, write another summary and note the differences among your immediate response, your twenty-four-hour recall, and your two-week memory.

4. Listen to a televised or videotaped speech and use the form on p.71 to evaluate it. In addition, decide whether it meets our criteria for a "good" speech: Was the message understandable? Did the speaker achieve his or her intended purpose? Was the speech ethical?

1. Use an audiotape recorder to record one of your professor's lectures as you also take notes. Replay the lecture as you reexamine your notes to determine whether they captured the important points of the lecture.

2. Replay the videotape you made of yourself delivering the speech you wrote in Chapter 2. Use the evaluation form in this chapter to note your own strengths and weaknesses. What skills would you like to target for improvement?

"Audience Two."
Diana Ong/SuperStock

Analyzing Your Audience

For of the three elements in speechmaking—speaker, subject, and person addressed—it is the last one, the hearer, that determines the speech's end and object.
—Aristotle

● OBJECTIVES

After studying this chapter you should be able to do the following:

1. Describe informal and formal methods of analyzing your audience.

2. Discuss the importance of audience analysis.

3. Explain how to gather demographic, attitudinal, and environmental information about your audience and the speaking occasion.

4. Identify methods of assessing your audience's reactions to your speech while it is in progress.

5. Identify methods of assessing audience reactions after you have concluded your speech.

t seemed harmless enough. Charles Williams was asked to speak to the Cub Scout pack about his experience as a young cowboy in Texas. The boys were learning to tie knots, and Williams, a retired rancher, could tell them how to make a lariat and how to make and use other knots.

His speech started out well. He seemed to be adapting to his young audience. However, for some reason, Williams thought the boys might also enjoy learning how to exterminate the screw worm, a pesky parasite of cattle. In the middle of his talk about roping cattle, he launched into a presentation about the techniques for sterilizing male screw worms. The parents in the audience fidgeted in their seats. The seven- and eight-year-olds didn't have the foggiest idea what a screw worm was, what sterilization was, or how male and female screw worms mate.

It got worse; his audience analysis skills deteriorated even more. Williams next talked about castrating cattle. Twenty-five minutes later he finally finished the screw worm–castration speech. The parents were relieved. Fortunately, the boys hadn't understood it.

Williams' downfall resulted from his failure to analyze his audience. He may have had a clear objective in mind, but he hadn't considered the background or knowledge of his listeners. Audience analysis is essential for any successful speech.

Becoming an audience-centered speaker

Chapter 1 identified the key elements in communication: source, receiver, message, channel. All four elements are important, but perhaps the most important is the receiver. In public speaking, the receiver is the audience, and the audience is the reason for a speech event.

In Chapter 2, we presented a model that provides an overview of the entire process of speech preparation and delivery (see Figure 5.1). We stressed there and reemphasize here the concept of public speaking as an audience-centered activity. At each stage in crafting your speech, you must be mindful of your audience. The audience analysis skills and techniques that we present in this chapter will help you throughout the public speaking process. Consciousness of your audience will be important as you select a topic, determine the purpose of your speech, develop your central idea, generate main ideas, gather supporting material, firm up your organization, rehearse, and deliver your speech.

When you think of your audience, don't think of some undifferentiated mass of people waiting to hear your message. Instead, think of individuals. Public speaking is the process of speaking to a group of individuals, each with a unique point of view. Your challenge as an audience-centered public speaker is to find out as much as you can about these individuals. From your knowledge of the individuals, you can then develop a general profile of your listeners.

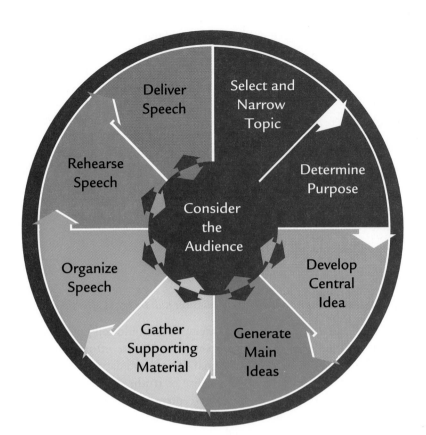

FIGURE 5.1
Audience analysis is central to to the speechmaking process.

What is audience analysis?

Audience analysis is the process of examining information about the listeners whom you expect to hear your speech. That analysis helps you adapt your message so that your listeners will respond as you wish. You analyze audiences every day as you speak to others or join in group conversations. Most of us do not deliberately make offensive comments to our family and friends. Rather, we adapt our message to the individuals with whom we are speaking.

For example, Mike spent a glorious spring break at Daytona Beach. He and three close friends piled in a car and headed for a week of adventure. When he returned from the beach, sunburned and fatigued from merrymaking, people asked how his holiday went. He described his escapades to his best friend, his mother, and his communication professor.

To his best friend, he bragged: "We partied all night and slept on the beach all day. It was great!" He informed his mother, "It was good to relax after the hectic pace of college." And he told his professor, "It was mentally invigorating to have time to think things out." It was the same vacation—but how different the messages were! Mike adapted his message to the people he addressed; he had analyzed his audiences.

audience analysis
The process of examining information about the expected listeners to a speech.

When you are speaking in public, you should use the same process. The principle is simple, yet powerful: An effective public speaker is audience-centered. Several key questions can help you formulate an effective approach to your audience:

To whom am I speaking?

What does my audience expect from me?

What topic would be most suitable to my audience?

What is my objective?

What kind of information should I share with my audience?

How should I present the information to them?

How can I gain and hold their attention?

What kind of examples would work best?

What method of organizing information will be most effective?

Being audience-centered does not mean you should tell your listeners only what they want to hear, or that you should fabricate information simply to please your audience or achieve your goal. If you try adapting to your audience by abandoning your own values and sense of truth, then you will become an unethical speaker rather than an audience-centered one. It was President Truman who pondered, "I wonder how far Moses would have gone if he'd taken a poll in Egypt?" The audience-centered speaker adjusts his or her topic, purpose, central idea, main ideas, supporting materials, organization, and even delivery of the speech in such a way that encourages the audience to listen to his or her ideas. The goal is to make the audience come away from the speaking situation, if not persuaded, then at least feeling thoughtful rather than offended or hostile.

In this chapter, you will learn both formal and informal strategies for gathering information about your audience. You will examine ways to analyze and adapt to your audience before, during, and after your speech. You will also learn to use the information you gather to achieve your purpose.

Analyzing your audience before you speak

t is unlikely that audience members for the speeches you give in class will have similar backgrounds. In most colleges and universities, the range of students' cultural backgrounds, ethnic ties, and religious traditions is rapidly expanding. Learning about your audience members' backgrounds and attitudes can help you in selecting a topic, defining a purpose, and developing an outline, and in other speech-related activities. It is important to analyze your audience before doing anything else. We will discuss three basic dimensions you can use for prespeech analysis:

1. Demographic audience analysis

2. Attitudinal audience analysis

3. Environmental audience analysis

● DEMOGRAPHIC ANALYSIS

A basic approach to analyzing an audience is to identify its demographic makeup. **Demographics** involve population data, including such characteristics as age, race, gender, educational level, and religious views. Let's consider how demographic information can help you better understand your audience.

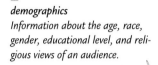

demographics
Information about the age, race, gender, educational level, and religious views of an audience.

● AGE   Knowing the age of your audience can be very helpful in choosing your topic and approach. Although you must use caution in generalizing from only one factor such as age, that information can suggest the kinds of examples, humor, illustrations, and other types of supporting material to use in your speech.

For example, many of the students in your public speaking class will probably be in their late teens or early twenties. Some, however, may be older. The younger students may know the latest rap performers or musicians, for example, but the older ones may not be familiar with Coolio, Ice-T, or The Notorious B.I.G. If you are going to give a talk on rap music, you will have to explain who the performers are and describe or demonstrate their style if you wish to have all the members of your class understand what you are talking about.

● GENDER   Josh began his speech by thanking his predominantly female audience for taking time from their busy schedules to attend his presentation on managing personal finances. Not a bad way to begin a talk. He continued, however, by noting that their job of raising children, keeping their homes clean and their families fed was among the most important tasks in America. Josh thought he was paying his audience a compliment. He did not consider that today, most women work outside the home as well as in it. Many of his listeners were insulted. Many of his listeners stopped being listeners.

A key question to ask when considering your audience is, "What is the ratio of males to females?" No matter what the mix may be, you should avoid making sweeping judgments based on gender stereotypes. Although you can certainly make some legitimate assumptions about topics that might interest each sex, it would be as inappropriate to assume that all men are sports fanatics as to conclude that all women enjoy an evening at the ballet. Instead, try to ensure that your remarks reflect sensitivity to diversity in your listeners' points of view.

One goal of an audience-centered speaker is to avoid sexist language or remarks. A sexist perspective is one that stereotypes or prejudges how someone will react based on his or her gender. Take time to educate yourself about what words, phrases, or perspectives are likely to offend or create psychological noise for your listeners. This may require thinking carefully about the implications of words or phrases you take for granted. For example, many people still use the words *ladies* or *matrons* without thinking about the connotations they carry in U.S. culture. Be especially wary about jokes. Many are derogatory to one sex or the other. Avoid stereotypes in your stories and examples as well.

Contrary to early findings on gender differences in listening, current research indicates that women are just as critical as men in evaluating persuasive messages. [Photo: Bob Daemmrich/Stock Boston]

In addition, you should try to make your language, and your message, as inclusive as possible. If you are speaking to a mixed-gender audience, make sure that your speech relates to all of your listeners, not just to one gender. If, for example, you decided to discuss breast cancer, you could note how this disease affects the lives of husbands, fathers, and brothers as well as those of women.

Finally, be cautious about assuming that men and women will respond differently to your message. Early social science research found some evidence that females were more susceptible to efforts to persuade them than males.[1] For many years textbooks and communication teachers presented this conclusion to students. More contemporary research, however, suggests that there may be no major differences between how susceptible men and women are to persuasive messages.[2]

In addition, although some research suggests that women are socialized to be more emotional and empathic than men, additional evidence suggests that men can be equally sensitive.[3] Whereas it is clear that there are learned sex differences in language usage and nonverbal behavior, we caution against making sweeping gender-based assumptions about your audience.

● CULTURE, ETHNICITY, AND RACE   Culture is a learned system of knowledge, behavior, attitudes, beliefs, values, and norms that is shared by a group of people. Ethnicity refers to that portion of a person's cultural background that relates to a national or religious heritage. A person's race is his or her biological heritage, such as Caucasian or Hispanic. The cultural, ethnic, or racial background of your audience will influence the way they perceive your message.

You need not have international students in your class to have a culturally diverse audience. Special ethnic and cultural traditions thrive among people who

■
culture
A learned system of knowledge, behavior, attitudes, beliefs, values, and norms that is shared by a group of people.

■
ethnicity
That portion of a person's cultural background that relates to a national or religious heritage.

■
race
A person's biological heritage.

have lived in the United States all of their lives. A student from a Polish family in Chicago, a German family in Texas, or a Haitian family in Brooklyn may be a native U.S. citizen with cultural traditions different from your own. Effective public speakers seek to learn as much as possible about the special cultural values and knowledge of their audience so that they can understand the best way to deliver their message.

Researchers classify or describe cultural differences along several lines.[4] Understanding these classifications may provide clues to help you adapt your message when you speak before diverse audiences.

■ *Individualistic and Collectivistic Cultures*   Some cultures place greater emphasis on individual achievement, while others place more value on group or collective achievement. Among the countries that tend to value individual accomplishment are Australia, Great Britain, the United States, Canada, Belgium, and Denmark. Japan, Thailand, Columbia, Taiwan, and Venezuela are among those that have more collectivist cultures. Audience members from individualistic cultures tend to value and respond to appeals that encourage personal accomplishment and single out individual achievement. Audience members from collectivistic cultures may be more likely to value group or team rewards and achievement.

■ *High-Context and Low-Context Cultures*   *Context* refers to the importance of unspoken or nonverbal messages. In high-context cultures, people place considerable importance on such contextual factors as tone of voice, gestures, facial expression, movement, and other implied aspects of communication. People from low-context traditions are just the opposite. They place greater emphasis on the words themselves; the surrounding context has a relatively low impact on the meaning of the message. The Arab culture is a high-context culture as are those of Japan, Asia, and Southern Europe. Low-context cultures, which place a high value on words, include those of Switzerland, Germany, the United States, and Australia. Listeners from low-context cultures will need and expect more detailed and explicit information from you as a speaker. Subtle and indirect messages are less likely to be effective. People from high-context cultures will pay particular attention to your delivery and to the communication environment when they try to interpret your meaning. These people will be less impressed by a speaker who boasts about his or her own accomplishments; such an audience will expect and value more indirect ways of establishing credibility.

■ *Tolerance of Uncertainty and Need for Certainty*   Some cultures are more comfortable with ambiguity and uncertainty than others. Those cultures in which people need to have details "nailed down" tend to develop very specific regulations and rules. People from cultures with a greater tolerance of uncertainty are more comfortable with vagueness and are not upset when all the details aren't spelled out. Cultures with a high need for certainty include those of Russia, Japan, France, and Costa Rica. Cultures that have a higher tolerance for uncertainty include those of Great Britain and Indonesia. If you are speaking to an audience with many people who have a high need for certainty, make sure you provide concrete details when you present ideas.

■ *High-Power and Low-Power Cultures*   Power refers to the ability to influence or control others. Some cultures prefer clearly defined lines of authority and responsibility; these are said to be high-power cultures. Low-power cultures are more comfortable with blurred lines of authority and less formal titles. Austria, Israel, Denmark, Norway, Switzerland, and Great Britain typically have an equitable approach to power distribution. Higher power cultures include those of the Philippines, Mexico, Venezuela, India, Brazil, and France; when you speak, people from these cultural traditions will respond positively to clearly defined power roles and structures. Those from low-power cultures will favor more egalitarian approaches to leadership and governance.

RECAP

DESCRIBING CULTURAL DIFFERENCES

INDIVIDUALISTIC CULTURES	Individual achievement is emphasized more than group achievement.
COLLECTIVISTIC CULTURES	Group or team achievement is emphasized more than individual achievement.
HIGH-CONTEXT CULTURES	The context of a message—including nonverbal cues, tone of voice, posture, and facial expression—is often emphasized more than the words.
LOW-CONTEXT CULTURES	The words in a message are emphasized more than the surrounding context.
TOLERANCE OF UNCERTAINTY	People can accept ambiguity and are not bothered if they do not know all the details.
NEED FOR CERTAINTY	People dislike ambiguous messages and want to know what their future holds.
HIGH-POWER CULTURES	Status and power differences are emphasized; roles and chains of command are clearly defined.
LOW-POWER CULTURES	Status and power differences receive less emphasis; people strive for equality rather than exalting those in positions of leadership.

● ADAPTING TO DIVERSE AUDIENCES   Keep in mind that cultural and ethnic traditions affect the way people process messages. If you have been educated in the United States, you will probably be inclined to develop highly structured speeches that follow an outlined pattern. But if you were addressing a Russian or Eastern European audience, they would have difficulty processing such a speech. They are more comfortable with less structure. One study suggests that members of some cultures prefer formal oratory rather than the conversational speech style that is usually taught in American speech classes. As we noted in Chapter 2, Bahamian audiences expect a public speaker to address an audience with formal phrases, such as, "Mr. Chairperson, honored guests, ladies, and gentlemen . . . " Bahamian audiences also expect speakers to use formal gestures and intonation, even when speaking to a class. [5] Japanese speakers addressing a predominantly Japanese audience also are expected to begin a speech by making respectful references to their listeners. When you think about adapting to your listeners, you should consider the form in which they are used to receiving information, and ways that you can overcome difficulties they might experience in understanding your message. We will discuss these issues in more detail in Chapter 15 when we review principles of informing others.

Although you may not have immediate plans to deliver a speech in Moscow, Nassau, Mexico City, or Tokyo, it will not be unusual for you to face audience members who hail from one of these cities when you speak on campus or in your hometown. In all probability, some of your audience will represent a mix of cultures and backgrounds.

Even though we have identified ways to describe cultural and ethnic differences among your audience members, we want to caution you again against making sweeping generalizations about your audience. Within every cultural group there are many variations and preferences. If you find that you are addressing an audience of Native Americans, for example, you cannot assume that they will all appreciate an anecdote about bow hunting. Always guard against making ethnic or racial assumptions that might offend your listeners.

What then are the best strategies to consider when you address a diverse audience?[6] First, consider using a variety of supporting materials to appeal to people with different backgrounds. Pictures and images can communicate universal messages—especially emotional ones. Showing a picture of a war-ravaged Bosnian village can clearly and dramatically illustrate the devastation of armed conflict, regardless of audience members' cultural backgrounds. Words alone would not have as powerful an impact. The more varied your listeners' cultural experiences, the more effective it will be to use visual materials to illustrate your ideas. Another approach is to use supporting materials that have broad appeal to many audience members. Most audiences, for example, value a good story with a point or moral that is relevant to the point you want to make. Humorist Mark Twain's novels are internationally loved because of the universal themes of friendship and adversity that Twain used in his stories; during both his U.S. and international speaking tours, he delighted audiences with tales from his boyhood days in Hannibal, Missouri. Another strategy is to consider whom you most want to reach or which audience members are your primary listeners. Even if you use specific strategies to influence this target audience, you can probably trust that other audience members will also respond positively if you speak effectively.

ADAPTING TO A CULTURALLY DIVERSE AUDIENCE

BEFORE YOU SPEAK . . .	Assess your listeners' cultural backgrounds and expectations about the speaking process.
	Assess your own cultural background, expectations, and biases about the speaking process.
	Assess the level of formality your listeners expect.
	Assess whether your listeners will respond to a linear, step-by-step structure.
DURING YOUR SPEECH . . .	Beware of developing a message that would be effective only to people just like you; be audience-centered.
	Avoid making sweeping generalizations about your audience's culture or ethnicity.
	Consider using a mix of supporting materials to make your points clear and memorable.
	Consider using visual aids that have universal appeal.
	Consider using stories, illustrations, and narratives with messages that span cultural backgrounds.
	Consider tailoring your speech to a set of target or primary listeners in your audience.

● **RELIGION**   Marsha is a follower of Scientology, and she believes that *Dianetics* is as important as the Bible. Planning to speak before a Bible-belt college audience, many of whose members view Scientology as a cult, Marsha would be wise to consider how her listeners will respond to her message. This is not to suggest that she should refuse the speaking invitation. She should, however, be aware of her audience's religious beliefs as she prepares and presents her speech.

When touching on religious beliefs or an audiences values, you must use great care in what you say and how you say it. Again, remind yourself that some members of your audience will undoubtedly not share your own beliefs, and that few beliefs are held with the same intensity as religious ones. If you do not wish to offend your listeners, you must plan and deliver your speech with much thought and sensitivity.

● **EDUCATION**   Knowing the educational background of your listeners can help you select and narrow your topic and also determine the purpose of your speech. Mary White Eagle, a Native American from Roswell, New Mexico, was invited to speak to her daughter's grade school class. Although she could have talked about the oppression of her ancestors, she instead spoke about the houses that had to be built and rebuilt to follow the herds of buffalo that roamed the Southwest. Knowing the educational background of your audience can also help you make decisions about your choice of vocabulary, your language style, and your use of examples and illustrations.

If your audience consists of your classmates, it is easy to identify their educational level. Outside the classroom, assessing the audience's level of education can sometimes be difficult. You can, however, make certain inferences from the speaking situation. It is easier to make guesses about the level of education of your audience if their ages range from five to eighteen. When speaking to adult audiences, you may need to ask whoever invited you to brief you about the audience's educational background.

ATTITUDINAL ANALYSIS

Demographic information allows you to make some useful inferences about your audience and to predict likely responses. Learning how the members of your audience feel about your topic and purpose may provide specific clues about possible reactions. Attitudinal analysis explores an audience's attitudes toward a topic, purpose, and speaker, while probing the underlying beliefs and values that might affect these attitudes.

It is important for a speaker to distinguish among *attitudes, beliefs,* and *values.* The attitudes, beliefs, and values of an audience may greatly influence a speaker's selection of a topic and specific purpose, as well as various other aspects of speech preparation and delivery.

An **attitude** reflects likes or dislikes. Do you like health food? Are you for or against capital punishment? Do you think that it is important to learn cardiopulmonary resuscitation (CPR)? Should movies be censored? What are your views on nuclear energy? Your answers to these widely varied questions reflect your attitudes.

attitude
An individual's likes or dislikes.

A **belief** is what you hold to be true or false. Beliefs underlie attitudes. Why do you like health food? You may *believe* that natural products are better for your health. That belief explains your positive attitude. Why are you against capital punishment? You may *believe* that it is wrong to kill people for any reason. Again, your belief explains your attitude. It is useful for a speaker to probe audience beliefs. If the speaker can understand why audience members feel the way they do about a topic, he or she may be able to address that underlying belief, whether trying to change an attitude or reinforce one.

belief
The way an individual structures reality to determine what is true or false.

Values are enduring concepts of good and bad, right and wrong. More deeply ingrained than either attitudes or beliefs, they are therefore more resistant to change. Values support both attitudes and beliefs. For example, you like health food because you believe that natural products are more healthful. And you *value* good health. You are against capital punishment because you believe that it is wrong to kill people. You *value* human life. As with beliefs, a speaker who has some understanding of an audience's values will be better able to adapt a speech to them.

value
Enduring concepts of good and bad, right and wrong.

ANALYZING ATTITUDES TOWARD THE TOPIC
The topic of a speech provides one focus for an audience's attitudes, beliefs, and values. It is useful to know how the members of an audience feel about your topic. Are they interested or apathetic? How much do they already know about the topic? If the

topic is controversial, are they for it or against it? Knowing the answers to these questions from the outset allows you to adjust your message accordingly. For example, if you plan to talk about increasing taxes to improve education in your state, you may want to know how your listeners feel about taxes and education.

When you are attempting to analyze your audience, it may help you to categorize it along three dimensions: interested–disinterested, favorable–unfavorable, and captive–voluntary. With an *interested* audience, your task is simply to hold and amplify their interest throughout the speech. If your audience is *uninterested* you will need to find ways to "hook" them. In Chapter 16 we will describe ways to motivate an audience by addressing issues related to their needs and interests. In our visually-oriented culture, consider using visual aids to gain and maintain the attention of apathetic listeners

You may also want to gauge how *favorable* or *unfavorable* your audience may feel toward you and your message before you begin to speak. Some audiences, of course, are neutral, apathetic, or simply uninformed about what you plan to say. We will provide explicit suggestions for approaching favorable, neutral, and unfavorable audiences in Chapter 17 when we discuss persuasive speaking. But even if your objective is simply to inform, it is useful to know whether your audience is predisposed to respond positively or negatively toward you or your message. Giving an informative talk about classical music would be quite challenging, for example, if you were addressing an audience full of die-hard funk fans. You might decide to show the connections between classical music and funk in order to arouse their interest.

Your speech class is a *captive* audience rather than a *voluntary* one. Class members have to show up in order to earn credit for class, so you need not worry that they will get up and leave during your speech. But your goal is to keep them from leaving mentally as well. Your speech class audience is similar to other captive audiences you may face later in professional and community settings. Your goal is to make your speech just as interesting and effective as one designed for a voluntary audience. You still have an obligation to address your audience members' needs and interests and to keep them engaged in what you have to say.

 RE CAP

TYPES OF AUDIENCES

CAPTIVE

An audience that has an external reason for attending a speech.

EXAMPLE

Students in a public speaking class.

Employees at a speech presented by the company's chief executive officer.

VOLUNTARY

An audience that chooses to attend the speech because of an innate interest and personal desire to listen.

Parents attending a lecture by the new principal at their children's school.

Students who attend a rally to lower tuition costs on campus.

INTERESTED	EXAMPLE
Listeners who choose to attend a speech or who find the speech immediately relevant to their needs and goals.	Mayors who attend a talk by the governor about increasing government services to cities.

Students planning a trip to Washington, D.C., who attend a lecture by the tour guide about how to prepare for the trip. |
UNINTERESTED	
Listeners who see little relevance in the speech topic or little reason to listen to the speech.	Junior high students attending a lecture about retirement benefits.
FAVORABLE	
Listeners who are predisposed to agree with the issue or ideas presented by the speaker.	A religious group that meets to hear a group leader talk about the importance of their beliefs.
NEUTRAL	
Listeners who have no strong feelings about the issues or ideas presentedby the speaker.	Members of a school cafeteria staff who attend a lecture about the new school bus schedule.
UNDECIDED	
Listeners who have heard the pros and cons about an idea or issue but who have not yet decided whether they agree or disagree.	Members of the community who have heard both candidates running for school board president, yet can't decide how they will vote.
UNFAVORABLE	
Listeners who are predisposed to disagree with the issue or ideas presented by the speaker.	Students who attend a lecture by the university president explaining why tuition and fees will increase 15 percent next year.

● ANALYZING ATTITUDES TOWARD YOU, THE SPEAKER
The audience's attitude toward you in your role as speaker is another factor that can influence their reaction to your speech. Regardless of how they feel about your topic or purpose, if members of an audience regard you as credible, they will be much more likely to be interested in, and supportive of, what you have to say. Credibility—being perceived as trustworthy, knowledgeable, and interesting—is one of the main factors that will shape your audience's attitude toward you. If you establish your credibility before you begin to discuss your topic, your listeners will be more likely to believe what you say, and to think that you are knowledgeable, interesting, and dynamic.

When a high school health teacher asks a former drug addict to speak to a class about the dangers of cocaine addiction, he recognizes that the speaker's experiences make him credible, and that his message will be far more convincing than if the teacher himself lectured on the perils of cocaine use.

An audience's positive attitude toward you as a speaker can overcome negative or apathetic attitudes they may have toward your topic or purpose. If your analysis reveals that your audience does not recognize you as an authority on your subject, you will need to build your credibility into the speech. If you have had personal experience with your topic, be sure to let the audience know. You will gain credibility instantly. We will provide additional strategies for enhancing your credibility in Chapter 17.

The speaking environment should reflect the speech's subject matter, purpose, and tone. Here the seating arrangement allows the audience to view the surrounding paintings during the lecture. Even if the speaker's topic does not relate directly to these works of art, the spacious, elegant environment will encourage listeners to focus on higher-order aesthetic or intellectual concerns. [Photo: Richard Pasley/Stock Boston]

● ENVIRONMENTAL ANALYSIS

In addition to learning about your audience, it is useful to find out as much as you can about the environment in which you will be speaking. In your speech class, you have the advantage of knowing what the room looks like, but in a new speaking situation, you may not have that advantage. If at all possible, visit the place in which you will speak to examine the physical setting and find out, for example, how far the audience will be from the lectern. Physical conditions can have an impact on your performance, the audience's response, and the overall success of the speech.

Room arrangement and decor may affect the way an audience responds. You should be aware of the arrangement and appearance of the room in which you will speak. If your speaking environment is less than ideal, you may need to work especially hard to hold your audience's attention. Although it is unlikely that you would be able to make major changes in the speaking environment, it is ultimately up to you to obtain the best speaking environment you can. The arrangement of chairs, the placement of audiovisual materials, and the opening or closing of drapes should all be within your control.

In preparing for a speaking assignment, keep the following environmental questions in mind:

1. How many people are expected to attend the speech?

2. How will the audience seating be arranged?

3. How close will I be to the audience?

4. Will I speak from a lectern?

5. Will I be expected to use a microphone?

6. Will I be on a stage or a raised platform?

7. What is the room lighting like? Will the audience seating area be darkened beyond a lighted stage?

8. Will I have adequate equipment for my visual aids?

9. Where will I appear on the program?

10. Will there be noise or distractions outside the room?

Try to avoid last-minute surprises about the speaking environment and the physical arrangements for your speech. A well-prepared speaker adapts his or her message not only to the audience but also to the speaking environment.

Also keep in mind that when you arrive to give your speech, you can make changes in the previous speaker's room arrangements. The purpose of the speaker who spoke immediately before Yue Hong was to generate interest in a memorial for Asian Americans who fought in Vietnam. Since he wanted to make sure the audience felt free to ask questions, he asked to have the chairs arranged in a semi-circle and made sure the lights were turned on. But Yue Hong was giving a more formal presentation on the future of the Vietnamese population in his talk, which included a brief slide show. So he realleged the chairs in realigned rows and darkened the room when the preceding speaker had finished his session.

RECAP

ELEMENTS OF AUDIENCE ANALYSIS

DEMOGRAPHIC CHARACTERISTICS	Age
	Gender
	Cultural, ethnic, or racial background
	Religion
	Education
ATTITUDINAL CHARACTERISTICS	Attitudes
	Beliefs
	Values
ENVIRONMENTAL CHARACTERISTICS	Furniture arrangement
	Seating arrangement
	Microphone availability
	Number of people present
	Room lighting and decor

Now that we have discussed *why* you should do a demographic, attitudinal, and environmental analysis of your audience, you may wonder, "*How* do I go about researching all of this information about my audience?" As an audience-centered speaker, you should try to find out as much as you can about the audience *before* planning the speech. There are two approaches you can take: informal and formal. Let's look at these two approaches in detail.

To analyze your audience informally, you can simply observe them and ask questions before you speak. Informal observations can be especially important in helping you assess obvious demographic characteristics. For example, you can observe how many members of your audience are male or female, and you can also make some inferences from their appearance about their educational level, ethnic or cultural traits, and approximate age.

You should also talk with people who know something about the audience you will be addressing. If you are invited to speak to a group you have not seen before, ask the person who invited you some general questions about the audience members: What is their average age? What are their political affiliations? What are their religious beliefs? What are their attitudes toward your topic? Try to get as much information as possible about your audience before you give your speech.

Or, rather than relying only on inferences drawn from such conversations, if time and resources permit, you may want to conduct a more formal survey of your listeners to gather both demographic data and information about their attitudes, beliefs, and values. How do you go about developing a formal survey? First, decide what you want to know about your audience that you don't already know. Let your topic and the speaking occasion help you determine the kinds of questions you should pose. Once you have an idea of what you would like to know, you can ask your potential audience straightforward questions about such demographic information as age, sex, occupation, and memberships in professional organizations. Here is a sample questionnaire:

Demographic audience analysis questionnaire

1. Name (optional):_____
2. Sex: Male ❏ Female ❏
3. Occupation:_____
4. Religious affiliation:_____
5. Marital status: Married ❏ Single ❏ Divorced ❏
6. Major in school:_____
7. Years of schooling beyond high school:_____
8. Annual income:_____
9. Age:_____
10. Ethnic background:_____
11. Hometown and state:_____
12. Political affiliation: Republican ❏ Democrat ❏ Other ❏ None ❏
13. Membership in professional or fraternal organizations:_____

You can modify this questionnaire according to your audience and topic. If your topic concerns the best approach to finding a rental apartment and you are speaking in a suburban area, find out how many members of your audience own a home and how many are presently living in an apartment. You may also want to ask how they found their current apartment, how many are now searching for an apartment, and how many anticipate searching for one. Answers to these questions can give you useful information about your audience and may also provide examples to use in your presentation.

Although knowing your audience's demographics can be helpful, again, we caution you that inferences based on generalized information may lead to faulty conclusions. For example, it might seem reasonable to infer that if your audience consists mainly of eighteen- to twenty-two-year-olds, they will not be deeply interested in retirement programs. But unless you have talked to them specifically about these topics, your inference may be incorrect. Whenever possible, ask specific questions about audience members' attitudes.

To gather useful information about audience members' attitudes, beliefs, and values, you can ask two basic types of questions. **Open-ended questions** allow for unrestricted answers, without limiting answers to choices or alternatives. Use open-ended questions when you want more detailed information from your audience. Essay questions, for example, are open-ended. **Closed-ended questions** offer several alternatives from which to choose. Multiple-choice, true-false, and agree-disagree questions are examples of closed-ended questions.

open-ended questions
Questions that allow for unrestricted answers, without limiting answers to choices or alternatives.

closed-ended questions
Questions that offer an alternative for an answer, such as true-false, agree-disagree, or multiple-choice questions.

After you develop the questions, it is wise to test them on a small group of people to make sure that they are clear and will encourage meaningful answers. Suppose that you plan to address an audience about school-based health clinics that dispense birth control pills in high schools. The following sample questions illustrate various open and closed formats.

SAMPLE QUESTIONS

Open-Ended Questions

1. What are your feelings about having high school health clinics that dispense birth control pills?

2. What are your reactions to the current rate of teenage pregnancy?

3. What would you do if you discovered your child was receiving birth control pills from your high school health clinic?

Closed-Ended Questions

1. Are you in favor of dispensing birth control pills to high school students in school-based health clinics?

   Yes ❏ No ❏

2. Birth control pills should be given to high school students who ask for them in school-based health clinics. (Circle the statement that best describes your feeling.)

   Agree strongly   Agree   Undecided   Disagree   Disagree strongly

   continued next page

---

3. Check the statement that most closely reflects your feelings about school-based health clinics and birth control pills.

❏ Students should receive birth control pills in school-based health clinics whenever they want them, without their parents' knowledge.

❏ Students should receive birth control pills in school-based health clinics whenever they want them, as long as they have their parents' permission.

❏ I am not certain whether students should receive birth control pills in school-based health clinics.

❏ Students should not receive birth control pills in school-based health clinics.

4. Rank the following statements about school-based health clinics and birth control pills, from most desirable (1) to least desirable (5).

❏ Birth control pills should be available to all high school students in school-based health clinics, whenever students want them, and even if their parents are not aware that they are taking the pills.

❏ Birth control pills should be available to all high school students in school-based health clinics, but only if their parents have given their permission.

❏ Birth control pills should be available to high school students without their parents' knowledge, but not in school-based health clinics.

❏ Birth control pills should be available to high school students, but not in school-based health clinics, and only with their parents' permission.

❏ Birth control pills should not be available to high school students.

What are some of the pitfalls of developing an attitudinal questionnaire? According to experts, some of the common problems in designing effective surveys are (1) developing clear and unbiased questions, (2) selecting a large enough sample to be representative of the entire audience if you are speaking to a large group, (3) writing questions that are both clear to the reader and easy for you to interpret, and (4) making sure that the questions will give you the information you need.[7] Simply being aware of these problems may help you avoid them as you plan your formal attitudinal analysis.

Adapting to your audience as you speak

So far, we have focused on discovering as much as possible about an audience before the speaking event. Prespeech analyses help with each step of the public speaking process: selecting a topic, formulating a specific purpose, gathering supporting material, identifying major ideas, organizing the speech, and planning its delivery. Each of these components of your speech is

Watching and listening to your audience as you speak can be challenging. Yet audience-centered speakers are able to monitor spoken and unspoken responses from their audience and adapt accordingly. In this narrative, Dr. Ben Morse, Manager of Merchandising for Burger King Corporation, describes how his listening skill and sensitivity to nonverbal cues helped him adapt to his audience by transforming a product introduction into an interactive problem-solving session.

Shortly after I assumed my position at Burger King, I was asked to update an audience of franchisees on a new menu board that we were considering. I was enthusiastic about this product, and based on conversations with my colleagues, I assumed that the franchisees would be as well.

As I began my update, however, I noticed that the audience was listening but seemed somewhat skeptical. When I completed my fifteen-minute update, I learned why. One of the franchisees raised his hand and proceeded to grill me not about the new menu board, but about another board that we had introduced some time ago. Because I was new at my job, I was definitely at a disadvantage; my knowledge about the item in question was pretty limited. However, I knew it was my job to address all of the franchisees' problems, so I listened carefully.

As I observed the rest of my audience, it was obvious that the problems this franchisee had raised were very troubling to them: their voices grew loud and agitated; their fists were clenched; and their body positions were tightly closed. Nonetheless, they also seemed ready to listen to what the "new guy" could do to help them.

At that point I did a major about-face, shelving the idea of selling the new menu board concept and switching over to demonstrating concern and understanding for my audience's situation. I opened up the session to let them speak, doing my best to listen actively and not to use a defensive tone or body posture. As I took notes, I nodded to acknowledge that I understood the issues they were speaking about and simultaneously scanned back through my notes on a briefing I'd had concerning the board in question.

After listening to a number of speakers, I isolated three major problems that kept cropping up and wrote them on a whiteboard, inviting the franchisees to amend my statements of them. Then I systematically went through the list and told them what I would do to resolve each problem. Fortunately, I had already spoken with the suppliers for the product, so I knew what means I had at my disposal.

At the end of the session, the franchisees asked me to make another presentation the next day to confirm the actions I outlined on the whiteboard. So that evening I called the suppliers, talked with my boss, and then prepared overhead transparencies to show the franchisees exactly what we could do for them. At the next day's presentation, the skepticism had disappeared; my audience was now agreeable, supportive, and finally ready to focus on my original product introduction.

After this experience, I began doing "trial ballooning" before all of my presentations. I prepare an outline or a set of transparencies to show in advance to a few audience members or to my colleagues, and their feedback helps me identify any additional issues or potential trouble spots that I should address. This practice has helped me avoid getting hit with curveballs on the day of my delivery.

dependent on understanding your audience. But audience analysis and adaptation do not end when you have crafted your speech. They continue as you deliver your speech.

Generally, a public speaker does not have an exchange with the audience unless the event is set in a question-and-answer or discussion format. Once the speech is in progress, the speaker must rely on nonverbal clues from the audience to judge how people are responding to the message. Let's look at some types of audience behavior that may yield clues to your listeners' responses as you are giving your speech.

● IDENTIFYING NONVERBAL AUDIENCE CUES

● EYE CONTACT   Perhaps the best way to determine whether your listeners are maintaining interest in your speech is to note the amount of eye contact they have with you. The more contact they have, the more likely it is that they are listening to your message. If you find them looking down at the program (or, worse yet, closing their eyes), you can reasonably guess that they have lost interest in what you're talking about.

● FACIAL EXPRESSION   Another clue as to whether an audience is "with you" is facial expression. An attentive audience not only makes direct eye contact but also wears an attentive facial expression. Beware of a frozen, unresponsive face. This sort of expression we call the "in-a-stupor" look. The classic in-a-stupor expression consists of a slightly tilted head, a faint, frozen smile, and often a hand holding up the chin. This expression may have the appearance of interest, but it more often means that the person is daydreaming or thinking of something other than your topic.

● RESTLESS MOVEMENT   An attentive audience doesn't move much. An early sign of inattentiveness is fidgeting fingers, which may escalate to pencil wagging, leg jiggling, and arm wiggling. Seat squirming, feet shuffling, and general body movement often indicate that members of the audience have lost interest in your message.

● NONVERBAL RESPONSIVENESS   An interested audience is one in which members verbally and nonverbally respond when encouraged or invited by the speaker. When you ask for a show of hands and audience members sheepishly look at one another and eventually raise a finger or two, you can reasonably infer lack of interest and enthusiasm. Frequent applause and head nods of agreement with your message are indicators of interest and support.

● VERBAL RESPONSIVENESS   Not only will some audiences indicate agreement nonverbally, but some will also indicate their interests verbally. Audience members may shout out a response or more quietly express agreement or disagreement to people seated next to them. A sensitive public speaker is constantly listening for verbal reinforcement or disagreement.

● RESPONDING TO NONVERBAL CUES

The value in recognizing nonverbal clues from your listeners is that you can respond to them appropriately. If your audience seems interested, supportive, and attentive, your prespeech analysis has clearly guided you to make proper choices in preparing and delivering your speech.

If your audience becomes inattentive, however, you may need to make some changes while delivering your message. If you think audience members are drifting off into their own thoughts or disagreeing with what you say, or if you suspect that they don't understand what you are saying, then a few spontaneous changes may help. Consider the following tips for adapting to your listeners.[8]

If your audience seems inattentive or bored:

- Tell a story.

- Use an example to which the audience can relate.

- Use a personal example.

- Remind your listeners why your message should be of interest to them.

- Eliminate some abstract facts and statistics.

- Use appropriate humor.

- Make direct references to the audience, using members' names or mentioning something about them.

- Ask the audience to participate by asking questions or asking them for an example.

- Ask for a direct response, such as a show of hands, to see whether they agree or disagree with you.

- Pick up the pace of your delivery.

- Pause for dramatic effect.

If your audience seems confused and doesn't understand your point:

- Be more redundant.

- Try phrasing your information in another way, or think of an example you can use to illustrate your point.

- Use a handy visual aid such as a chalkboard or flip chart to clarify your point.

- Slow your speaking rate if you have been speaking rapidly.

- Clarify the overall organization of your message to your listeners.

- Ask for feedback from an audience member to help you discover what is unclear.

- Ask someone in the audience to summarize the key point you are making.

If your audience seems to be disagreeing with your message:

- Provide data and evidence to support your point.

- Remind your listeners of your credibility, credentials or background.

- Rely less on anecdotes and more on facts to present your case.

- Write facts and data on a chalkboard, overhead transparency, or flip chart if one is handy.

- Identify the major points of disagreement.

- If you don't have the answer and data you need, tell listeners you will provide more information by mail, telephone, or e-mail (and make sure you get back in touch with them).

Remember that it is not enough to note your listeners' characteristics and attitudes. You must also *respond* to the information you gather by adapting your speech to retain their interest and attention. Moreover, you have a responsibility to ensure that your audience understands your message. If your approach to the content of your speech is not working, you should alter it and note whether your audience's responses change. If all else fails, you may need to abandon a formal speaker–listener relationship with your audience and open up your topic for discussion. Later chapters on supporting material, speech organization, and speech delivery will discuss other techniques for adjusting your style while delivering your message.

RECAP

ASSESSING YOUR AUDIENCE AS YOU SPEAK

Observe audience eye contact. Are they looking back at you?

Monitor audience facial expression. Are they responsive to your message?

Monitor audience movement. Are they restless? Is there a lot of fidgeting, shuffling, and general body movement?

Assess whether the audience is responsive to you. Do they respond to your requests? Do they laugh and applaud when appropriate?

Assess audience verbal response. Do they respond verbally when appropriate?

Analyzing your audience after you speak

After you have given your speech, you should indulge in a little Monday-morning quarterbacking. It is important to evaluate your audience's response. Why? Because it can help you prepare your next speech. Postspeech analysis helps you polish your speaking skill, regardless of whether you will face the same audience again. From that analysis you can learn whether your examples were clear and your message was accepted by your listeners. Let's look at some specific methods for assessing your audience's response to your speech.

NONVERBAL RESPONSES

The most obvious nonverbal response is applause. Is the audience simply clapping politely, or is the applause robust and enthusiastic, indicating pleasure and acceptance? Responsive facial expressions, smiles, and nods are other nonverbal signs that the speech has been well received.

Realize, however, that audience members from different cultures respond to speeches in different ways. Japanese audience members, for example, are likely to be restrained in their response to a speech and show little expression. Some Eastern European listeners may not maintain eye contact with you; they may look down at the floor when listening. In some contexts, African American listeners may enthusiastically voice their agreement or disagreement with something you say during your presentation.[9]

Nonverbal responses at the end of the speech may provide some the general feeling of the audience, but they are not much help in identifying which strategies were the most effective. You should also consider what the members of the audience say, both to you and to others, after your speech.

VERBAL RESPONSES

What might members of the audience say to you about your speech? General comments, such as "I enjoyed your talk" or "Great speech," are good for the ego—which is important—but are not of much analytic help. Specific comments can indicate where you succeeded and where you failed. If you have the chance, try to ask audience members how they responded to the speech in general as well as to specific points in which you have a particular interest.

SURVEY RESPONSES

You are already aware of the value of conducting audience surveys before speaking publicly. You may also want to survey your audience after you speak. You can then assess how well you accomplished your objective. Use the same survey techniques that we discussed earlier. Develop survey questions that will help you determine the general reactions to you and your speech, as well as specific responses to your ideas and supporting materials. Professional speakers and public officials often conduct such surveys. Postspeech surveys are especially useful when you are trying to persuade an audience. Comparing prespeech and postspeech attitudes can give you a clear idea of your effectiveness. A significant portion of most political campaign budgets goes toward evaluating how a candidate is received by his or her constituents. Politicians want to know what portions of their messages are acceptable to their audiences so that they can use this information in the future.

If your objective was to teach your audience about some new idea, a posttest can assess whether you expressed your ideas clearly. Actually, classroom exams are posttests that determine whether your instructor presented information clearly.

BEHAVIORAL RESPONSES

If the purpose of your speech was to persuade your listeners to do something, you will want to learn whether they ultimately behave as you intended. If you wanted them to vote in an upcoming election, you might survey your listeners to find out how many did vote. If you wanted to win support for a particular cause or organization, you might ask them to sign a petition after your speech. The number of signatures would be a clear measure of your speech's success. Some religious speakers judge the success of their ministry by the amount of contributions they receive. Your listeners' actions are the best indicators of your speaking success.

Summary

This chapter emphasized the importance of being an audience-centered speaker. To be an effective speaker, it is essential to learn as much as you can about your listeners before, during, and after your speech. Before your speech, you can perform three kinds of analysis: demographic, attitudinal, and environmental. You can use informal and formal approaches to gather information about your listeners for your analyses.

While speaking, it is important to look for feedback from your listeners. Audience eye contact, facial expression, movement, and general verbal and nonverbal responsiveness provide clues as to how well you are doing. Finally, you should evaluate audience reaction after your speech. Again, nonverbal clues as well as verbal ones will help you judge your speaking skill. The best indicator of your speaking success is whether your audience is actually able or willing to follow your advice or remembers what you have told them.

● CRITICAL THINKING QUESTIONS

1. Dr. Cassandra Ruiz has been invited to speak on birth control to a women's group. She thought her audience would be women of child-bearing age. After writing her speech, however, she found out that all the women to whom she will be speaking are at least twenty years older than she expected. What changes, if any, should she make?

2. Phil Owens is running for a seat on the school board. He has agreed to speak to the Chamber of Commerce about his views, but he wants to know what his audience believes about a number of issues. How can he gather this information?

3. You are in the middle of your presentation attempting to persuade a group of investors to build a new shopping mall in your community. You notice that a few of the audience members are losing eye contact with you, shifting in their seats, and looking at their watches. What do you do to regain their attention?

● ETHICAL QUESTIONS

1. Maria strongly believes that the drinking age should be increased to twenty-two years of age in her state. Yet when she surveyed her classmates, the overwhelming majority thought the drinking age should be lowered to eighteen. Should Maria change her speech topic and her purpose to avoid facing a hostile audience?

2. Dan knows that most of the women in his audience will be startled and probably offended if he begins his speech by saying, "Most of you broads in this audience are too sensitive about sexist language." This is how Dan really feels. Should he alter his language just to appease his audience?

3. Do most politicians place too much emphasis on the results of political opinion polls to shape their stand on political issues?

4. Has political correctness gotten out of hand on college campuses today? Are we becoming too sensitive to cultural, ethnic, and gender issues in our public dialogue?

● SUGGESTED ACTIVITIES

1. Conduct a demographic analysis of your speech class. Identify as much information as you can by observing (informal method). Then, using a formal method, construct a survey to assess other demographic characteristics of your audience. Compare the formal and informal methods of gathering information for accuracy and completeness.

2. Conduct a formal attitudinal analysis of your speech class, assessing their attitudes about one of the following topics:

The federal budget deficit	The arms race
Children of divorce	Open adoption
Abortion and birth control	Preventing minority student dropouts
Financing a college education	Student politics
Criteria for choosing a career	Opening student credit accounts
Nursing home care	

3. Design a survey to evaluate attitudes about the quality of education on your campus. Include both open-ended questions and closed-ended questions in your survey.

4. Conduct an environmental analysis of your speech classroom. What positive and negative features of your classroom make it appropriate or inappropriate as a lecture hall? What changes would you make in the speaking environment to enhance speaking success?

5. Each class member should be given a white card, a red card, and a green card. While a student is rehearsing a speech, the class members should hold up the green card if they agree with what the speaker is saying, the red card if they disagree, and the white card if they are neutral or indifferent about the speech content. The speaker should attempt to adapt to the audience feedback.

6. Make a list of the nonverbal clues that let you know that your audience is enjoying your speech or agreeing with your message. Make a second list identifying the nonverbal clues that communicate audience disagreement or boredom.

1. If you have an Internet address and several of your classmates also have access to the Internet, conduct a survey for your next speech via e-mail or the Internet. Either send your audience-analysis survey on the Internet or provide each class member with a hard copy of the survey and invite those with Internet access to respond to your survey via e-mail.

2. Watch a televised presidential address and compare your own reaction to the speech with the instant postspeech audience analysis available through e-mail or phone surveys immediately following the speech.

3. Videotape your audience while you are giving a speech. When you watch the video later, note whether you adapted or adjusted to your audience's nonverbal cues.

"Les Constructeurs."
Fernand Leger/Bridgeman/Art Resources

Developing Your Speech

In all matters, before beginning, a diligent preparation should be made.
—*Cicero*

● OBJECTIVES

After studying this chapter you
should be able to do the following:

1. *Select a topic for a classroom speech that
   is appropriate to the audience, the
   occasion, and yourself.*

2. *Narrow a topic so that it can be thoroughly discussed within the time limits
   allotted for a specific assignment.*

3. *Write an audience-centered specific-purpose statement for an assigned topic.*

4. *Explain three ways of generating a skeleton outline from a central idea.*

5. *Apply to a speaking assignment the four
   steps for getting from a blank sheet of
   paper to a preliminary outline for the
   speech.*

d Garcia has arranged the books and papers on his desk into neat, even piles. He has sharpened his pencils and laid them out parallel to one another. He has even dusted his desktop and cleaned the computer monitor's screen. Ed can think of no other task to delay writing his speech. He loads his word processing program, carefully centers the words *Informative Speech*, and then slouches in his chair, staring glumly at the blank expanse that threatens his well-being. Finally, he types the words *College Football* under the *Informative Speech* heading. Another long pause. Hesitantly, he begins his first sentence: "Today I want to talk to you about college football." Rereading his first ten words, Ed decides that they sound moronic. He deletes the sentence and tries again. This time the screen looks even blanker than before. He writes-deletes-writes-deletes. Half an hour later, Ed is exhausted and still mocked by a blank screen. And he is frantic— this speech *has* to be ready by 9:00 A.M.

Getting from a blank screen or sheet of paper to a speech outline is often the biggest hurdle you will face as a public speaker. Fortunately, however, it is one that you can learn to clear. If your earlier efforts at speech writing have been like Ed Garcia's, take heart. Just as you learned to read, do long division, drive a car, and get through college registration, so too, can you learn to prepare a speech.

The first steps in preparing a speech are as follows:

1. Select and narrow your topic.

2. Determine your purpose.

3. Develop your central idea.

4. Generate your main ideas.

At the end of step 4, you will have a rough outline of the speech and will be ready to develop and polish your ideas further.

As we observed in Chapter 5, audience-centered speakers consider the needs, interests, and expectations of their audience during the entire speech preparation process. As you move from topic selection to outlining, remember that you are preparing a message for your listeners. Always keep the audience as your central focus.

Select and narrow your topic

Your first task, illustrated by Figure 6.1, is to choose a topic on which to speak. You will need to narrow this topic to fit your time limits. Sometimes you can eliminate one or both of these steps; the topic has been chosen and properly defined for you. For example, because you visited England's Lake District on your tour of Great Britain last summer, your English literature teacher asks you to speak about the mountainous landscape of that region before your class studies the poetry of Wordsworth and Coleridge. Or imagine a future day in which the Lion's Club asks you to speak at their weekly gathering about the goals of the local drug abuse task force, which you chair. In both cases, your topic and its scope have been decided for you.

In other instances, the choice of topic may be left entirely to you. In your public speaking class, your instructor may provide such guidelines as time limits and type of speech (informative, persuasive, or entertaining) but allow you to choose your topic freely. In this event, you should realize that the success of your speech may rest on this decision. But how do you go about choosing an appropriate, interesting topic?

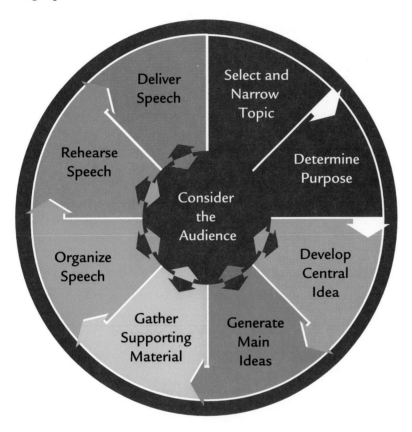

FIGURE 6.1
Selecting and narrowing the topic and determining the general and specific purpose of the speech are early speech-making tasks.

● GUIDELINES FOR SELECTING A TOPIC

Davy Crockett was scheduled to speak first on a platform with a political opponent known always to deliver the same standard speech. So Davy memorized that speech, gave it, and left the opponent speechless.[1]

● **CONSIDER THE AUDIENCE** The downfall of Crockett's literally speechless opponent was that he relied on a standard spiel, rather than tailoring his speeches to each specific audience. In Chapter 5 we discussed the reasons and methods for finding out about your audience. "What interests and needs do the members of this audience have in common?" and "Why did they ask me to speak?" are important questions to ask yourself as you search for potential speech topics. Keeping in mind their audiences' interests and expectations, a university president invited to speak to a civic organization should talk about some new university program or recent accomplishment; a police officer speaking to an elementary school's PTA should address the audience's concern for the safety of their young children.

Not only should a speaker's choice of topic be relevant to the *interests* and *expectations* of his or her listeners; it should also take into account the *knowledge* listeners already have about the subject. A student giving a visual aid speech several semesters ago forgot or ignored this requirement when she chose to speak on "how to pop popcorn." Although the listeners were interested in popcorn (and, in fact, eagerly awaited samples), they had trouble focusing on the speech because it bored them. Few college students do not know how to pop corn in an electric popper! The speech offered no new information.

Finally, speakers should choose topics that are *important*—that matter to their listeners, as well as to themselves. It was a poignant moment when Mary Fisher, single mother of two young children, herself infected with HIV by her ex-husband, addressed the Republican National Convention in August 1992 to plead for compassion and assistance for persons with AIDS. In your public speaking class, too, you should offer speeches on topics of real or potential importance to your audience. In November 1994, Bruce Gronbeck, then-president of the Speech Communication Association, reminded an audience of communication instructors that the kinds of speeches students need to give "have nothing to do with macramé, perfect fudge every time, or how to set up a functional study area in a dorm room."[2] At least by the end of the semester, Gronbeck maintained, students should be giving "the important kinds of . . . speeches that show . . . people how to confront the issues that divide them . . . ."

RECAP

SAMPLE AUDIENCE-CENTERED TOPICS

AUDIENCE	TOPIC
Retirees	Preserving social security benefits
Civic organization	The Special Olympics
Church members	Starting a community food bank
First graders	What to do in case of a fire at home
Teachers	Building children's self-concepts
College fraternity	The designated-driver program

● CONSIDER THE OCCASION   Several years ago, the guest speaker at a graduate school commencement failed miserably in his assignment. The topic he chose—how a graduate degree prepares one for the challenges of life—showed that he had given a good deal of thought to the interests, needs, expectations, and knowledge of his audience. Still, his speech both stunned and angered the graduates, friends, and relatives gathered in that auditorium. For more than an hour, the speaker argued that there are no jobs for people with graduate degrees and that those degrees are not of much value in one's personal life.

Was this speaker's topic of *interest* to his listeners? Undoubtedly. Did they *expect* to hear someone talk about life after graduation? Yes. Could he *add to their knowledge* of the subject? Probably. Was his topic *appropriate to the occasion?* Definitely not! A commencement address calls for praise of hard-earned accomplishments and an optimistic sending forth of the graduates. The unrelenting pessimism of the speaker was *not* appropriate to this occasion. Neither was the length of this speech appropriate to a ceremony in which the focus should be on the graduates. Even though this speaker had thought of his audience, his speech showed that he had not considered the occasion. He therefore failed. To be successful, a topic must be appropriate to both audience *and* occasion.

● CONSIDER YOURSELF What do you talk about with good friends? You probably discuss school, mutual friends, political or social issues, hobbies or leisure-time activities, or other topics of interest and importance to you. As with most people, your liveliest, most animated conversations revolve around topics of personal concern and conviction.

The best public speaking topics are also ones that reflect your personal experience or especially interest you. Where have you lived? Where have you traveled? Describe your family or your ancestors. Have you held any part-time jobs? Describe your first days at college. What are your favorite classes? What are your hobbies or interests? What is your favorite sport? What social issues especially concern you? Here is one list of topics that was generated by such questions:

Kansas City blues music

"Yankee, go home": the American tourist in France

Why most diets fail

Behind the counter at McDonald's

My first day at college

Maintaining family ties while living a long distance from home

Getting involved in political campaigns

The impact of the Beatles on twentieth-century music

An alternative to selecting a topic with which you are already familiar is to select one you would like to know more about. Your interest will motivate both your research and your eventual delivery of the speech.

● TECHNIQUES FOR SELECTING A TOPIC

All successful topics reflect audience, occasion, and speaker. But just contemplating those guidelines does not automatically produce a good topic. Sooner or later, we all face a speech for which we cannot think of a good topic, whether it is the first speech of the semester, that all-important final speech, or a speaking engagement long after your school years are over. Nothing is so frustrating to a public speaker as floundering for something to talk about!

Fortunately, there are several techniques that can help generate speech topics. They are somewhat more artificial than thinking of audience, occasion, and self to produce a "natural" topic choice. Nevertheless, they can yield good topics.

● B R A I N S T O R M I N G   A problem-solving technique widely used in such diverse fields as business, advertising, writing, and science, **brainstorming** can easily generate ideas for speech topics as well.[3] To brainstorm a list of potential topics, get a sheet of paper and a pencil or pen. Set a minimum time limit of, say, three to five minutes. Write down the first topic that comes to mind. Do not allow yourself to evaluate it. Just write it down, as a simple word or a phrase, a vague idea or a well-focused one. Now jot down a second idea—again, anything that comes to mind. The first topic may remind you of a second possibility. Such "piggybacking" of ideas is perfectly OK. Continue without any restraints until your time is up. At this stage, anything goes. Your goal is quantity—as long a list as you can think up in the time you have.

The following list of twenty-two possible topics came from a brainstorming session of about three minutes:

Antiques

Where to find antiques

Decorating with antiques

Quilts

Quilt patterns and their history

Cats

Wild animals

The problem of keeping wild animals as pets

Zoos

Natural-habitat zoos

Breeding endangered species

Holidays

Children's birthday parties

Schools

School volunteer programs

Job hunting

Preparing an effective résumé

Public relations as a career

Plants

How to care for common houseplants

Poisonous plants native to this region

Wildlife native to this region

If your brainstorming yields several good topics, so much the better. Set aside a page or two in your class notebook for topic ideas, and list the extra topics there. You can then consider them when you get your next assignment.

RECAP

HOW TO BRAINSTORM FOR A TOPIC

1. Get a blank sheet of paper.

2. Set a time limit for brainstorming.

3. Begin writing as many possible topics for a speech as you can.

4. Do not stop to evaluate your topics; just write them down.

5. Let one idea lead to another—free-associate; piggyback off your own ideas.

6. Keep writing until your time is up.

● **LISTENING AND READING FOR TOPIC IDEAS**   Very often something you see, hear, or read triggers an idea for a speech. A current story on the evening TV news or in your local paper may suggest a topic. The following list of topics was brought to mind by recent headline stories in a large daily newspaper:

How to read and interpret stock market indicators

Prison overcrowding

Health codes and restaurants

The Nobel Prize

How record prices for art and artifacts are affecting museum acquisitions

Television evangelism

Deteriorating interstate highways

Mothers Against Drunk Driving

In addition to discovering topics in news stories, you might find them in an interesting segment of *60 Minutes, 20/20,* or *Maury Povich.* Chances are that a topic covered in one medium will have been covered in another as well, making extended research on the topic possible. For example, Oprah Winfrey's interview of a surrogate mother may be paralleled by *Newsweek's* report on a much publicized court case concerning surrogacy.

You may also find speech topics in one of your other classes. A lecture in an economics or political science class may arouse your interest and provide a good topic for your next speech. The instructor of that class could probably suggest additional references on the subject you choose.

Sometimes even a subject that you discuss casually with friends can be developed into a good speech topic. You have probably talked with classmates about such campus issues as dormitory regulations, inadequate parking, or frustrations with registration and advisers. Campuswide concerns would be relevant to the student audience in your speech class, as would such matters as how to find a summer job or the pros and cons of living on or off campus. The college work-study program provided the topic for this recent student speech:

> One day not long ago, a freshman in this university entered the office of the Economics Department, hoping she was in the right place. There she stood, shaking in front of the secretary's desk, holding the assignment for her first job.
>
> Let me tell you that that person was me! Currently I work for the Economics Department in the Business School as a member of the College Work-Study Program.
>
> The College Work-Study Program is a federal financial aid program that combines the benefits of financial assistance with valuable work experience. In the next few minutes I will talk about this program, outlining the requirements, responsibilities, and pay plan it involves.[4]

Just as you jotted down possible topics generated by brainstorming sessions, remember to write down topic ideas that you get from the media, class lectures, or informal conversations. What seems like a great topic today may be only a frustrating blank tomorrow if you rely on memory alone.

● SCANNING LISTS AND INDEXES   By now, you probably have a list of topics from which to choose. But if all your efforts have failed to produce any ideas that satisfy you, try this technique. Turn to a reference work such as a dictionary, an encyclopedia, or the *Reader's Guide to Periodical Literature* to stimulate your thinking. Open one of these books at random and look down the lists of words and phrases they contain. If you read them long enough, some idea will probably strike you as a possible speech topic.

The following topics were suggested by a portion of the *S* listings in a popular dictionary:

The Salvation Army

Saccharin and other artificial sweeteners

The role of sacrifice in religion

Seat belts

The Salk vaccine

Salt and blood pressure

Margaret Sanger and the modern birth control movement

Saturn

Theater scenery

Year-round schools

Sects and cults

Of course, you still need to think of your audience, your occasion, and your-self when considering any topic as a possibility and continuing to add to your list of potential topics.

A final word of caution before moving forward in the speech preparation process. For most brief classroom speeches (under ten minutes), you should allow at least one week from topic selection to speech delivery. A week gives you enough time to develop your ideas. Many habitual procrastinators (like Ed Garcia, the speaker who opened this chapter), who reluctantly agree to begin their assignments a week in advance, learn to their surprise that the whole process is far easier than when they delay work until the night before they are supposed to deliver their speech.

RECAP

SELECTING A TOPIC

GUIDELINES	TECHNIQUES
Consider the audience.	Brainstorm.
Consider the occasion.	Listen and read.
Consider yourself.	Scan lists and indexes.

NARROWING THE TOPIC

After brainstorming, reading the newspaper, watching TV, and talking to friends, you have come up with a topic. For some students, the toughest part of the assignment is over at this point. But others soon experience additional frustration because their topic is so broad that they find themselves overwhelmed with information. How can you cover all aspects of a topic as large as "television" in three to five minutes? Even if you trained yourself to speak as rapidly as an auctioneer, it would take days to get it all in!

The solution is to narrow your topic so that it fits within the time limits set by your assignment. The challenge lies in *how* to do this. One of the following methods will work well for most students.

If you have a broad, unmanageable topic, you might first try narrowing it by constructing a *ladder*. A ladder can be as simple as a vertical list of words connected by arrows. The general topic is at the top, with each succeeding word a more specific or concrete topic.

Megan used a ladder to help her narrow her general topic, music. Writing *Music* at the top of a sheet of paper, she constructed a ladder that looked like this:

Music

Folk music

Irish folk music

The popularity of Irish folk music in the United States

Megan decided to work on a speech about the popularity of Irish folk music in the United States. If that topic is still too broad, she can continue adding rungs to the ladder, focusing, for example, on the reasons for the success in the United States of such Irish groups as the Cranberries and the Chieftains.

A second method begins with a tabular form, such as the one shown here, on a blank sheet of paper.

At the top of the table, write your original topic idea.

Television

Now divide your topic into two or three more specific categories. You may decide that different types of entertainment are logical subdivisions of television. So you write in the next spaces *Comedy, Drama,* and *Variety.*

Television

Comedy	Drama	Variety

You are most interested in television comedy, so you choose to focus on that category. Now ask yourself, "Do I have enough to give a speech on television comedy?" Your answer would be no, for you realize that the topic is still too broad. So you must subdivide further.

How can you logically divide the subject of television comedy? You could talk about famous comic actors. So you scrawl *Actors* under *Comedy.* You could also talk about the subjects of television comedies. You write *Subjects* beside *Actors.* Or you could talk about comic techniques. So you add *Techniques* to the other two components of television comedy.

Television

Comedy			Drama	Variety
Actors	Subjects	Techniques		

Again you consider the possibilities. Can one of these comic elements be turned into a topic for a good three- to five-minute speech? Success is certainly closer than it was when your topic was "television." You find the *subjects* of television comedies especially interesting but realize that the topic is still rather broad. Around what subjects do most television comedies center? Under *Subjects* you write *Family life, Friendship,* and *Work.*

Can you prepare a good three- to five-minute speech on how today's television comedies reflect modern family life? You remember reading an interview with Bill Cosby in which he discussed that very topic. You have some knowledge of the subject yourself, being a fan of *Cybil*, *Grace Under Fire* and *Home Improvement*. Moreover, you know that most of your class will also have seen these programs, at least occasionally. And you feel confident that the subject can be covered fairly thoroughly in three to five minutes. Your original idea has been narrowed to a workable topic for the assignment.

You may find later that your topic is still a bit too broad. Too many family comedies reflect the wide diversity of family arrangements for a talk of no more than five minutes. So you choose one comedy, *Grace Under Fire* let's say, and you decide to talk about how this show treats the role of modern mothers. It is also possible that you may find yourself in the very rare situation of having narrowed your topic so much that you cannot find enough information to talk for even three minutes. In that case, you go back a step. To stay with our example, you return to how family comedies reflect modern family life.

Determine your purpose

Now that you have selected and narrowed your topic, you need to decide on a purpose (as shown in Figure 6.1). If you do not know what you want your speech to achieve, chances are your audience won't either. Ask yourself, "What is really important for the audience to hear?" and "How do I want the audience to respond?" Clarifying your objectives at this stage will ensure a more interesting speech and a more successful outcome.

To construct a speech about a visit to Yellowstone National Park, you would probably begin with a broad conception of your topic, like the panoramic image on the left. Then, using either a ladder or a tabular diagram, you would begin to pinpoint what interested you most during the visit. Finally, you might recall the day your car was stuck behind a wandering herd of bison. A ranger told you that this was an increasingly perplexing park management problem. Voila! This specific aspect of your visit would be a perfect topic to research and transform into a speech. [Photo: left, A & L Siniboldi/Tony Stone Images; right, John Warden/ Tony Stone Images]

Virtually all speeches have one of three general purposes: to inform, persuade, or entertain. The speeches you give in class will generally be either informative or persuasive. It is important that you fully understand what constitutes each type of speech so that you do not confuse them and fail to fulfill an assignment. You certainly do not want to deliver a first-rate persuasive speech when an informative one was assigned! Although Chapters 15 through 18 will discuss the three general purposes at length, let's summarize them here so that you can understand the basic principles of each.

● SPEAKING TO INFORM   An informative speaker is a teacher. Informative speakers give listeners information. They define, describe, or explain a thing, person, place, concept, process, or function. In this excerpt from a student's informative speech on anorexia nervosa, the student describes the disorder for her audience:

> *Anorexia nervosa is an eating disorder that affects one out of every two hundred American women. It is a self-induced starvation that can waste its victims to the point that they resemble victims of Nazi concentration camps.*
>
> *Who gets anorexia nervosa? Ninety-five percent of its victims are females between the ages of twelve and eighteen. Men are only rarely afflicted with the disease. Anorexia nervosa patients are usually profiled as "good" or "model" children who have not caused their parents any undue concern or grief over other behavior problems. Anorexia nervosa is perhaps a desperate bid for attention by these young women.[5]*

Most of the lectures you hear in college are informative. The university president's annual "state of the university" speech is informative, as is the Colonial Williamsburg tour guide's talk. Such speakers are all trying to increase the knowledge of their listeners. They may use an occasional bit of humor in their presentations, but their main objective is not to entertain but to inform. Chapter 15 provides specific suggestions for preparing an informative speech.

● SPEAKING TO PERSUADE   Persuasive speakers may also offer information, but they use the information to try to change or reinforce an audience's convictions and often to urge some sort of action. Jennifer offered compelling statistics to persuade her audience that interracial adoption should be encouraged:

> *According to the Oklahoma State Adoption Agency ... on January 25, 1995, there are 1,000 minority children waiting for a family in my state alone every single day. In addition, there are 30 to 40 families waiting for a child every day.[6]*

The representative from Mothers Against Drunk Driving (MADD) who spoke at your high school assembly urged you not to drink and drive and to help others realize the inherent dangers of the practice. The fraternity president talking to your group of rushees tried to convince you to join his fraternity. Appearing on television during the last election, the candidates for president of the United States asked for your vote. All of these speakers gave you information, but they used that information to try to get you to believe or do something. Chapters 16 and 17 will focus in more detail on persuasive speaking.

● SPEAKING TO ENTERTAIN   The entertaining speaker tries to get the members of an audience to relax, smile, perhaps laugh, and generally enjoy themselves. Storyteller Garrison Keillor spins tales of the town and residents of Lake Wobegon, Minnesota, to amuse his listeners. Comedian Whoopi Goldberg delivers a comic patter to make her audience laugh. Most after-dinner speakers talk to entertain their banquet guests. Like persuasive speakers, entertaining speakers may inform their listeners, but providing knowledge is not their main goal. Rather, their objective is to produce a smile at least and a belly laugh at best. Appendix D includes the Speech "Schadenfreude" which is an example of a speech to entertain.

You need to decide at the beginning which of the three general purposes your speech is to have. This decision will keep you on track throughout the development of your speech. The way you organize, support, and deliver your speech will depend, in part, on your general purpose.

 CAP

GENERAL PURPOSES FOR SPEECHES

To inform	To share information by defining, describing, or explaining a thing, person, place, concept, process, or function
To persuade	To change or reinforce a listener's attitude, belief, value, or behavior
To entertain	To help an audience have a good time by getting listeners to relax, smile, and laugh

● SPECIFIC PURPOSE

Now that you have a topic and you know generally whether your speech should inform, persuade, or entertain, it is time you decided on its specific purpose. Unlike the general purpose, which can be assigned by your instructor, the specific purpose of your speech must be decided by you alone, because it depends directly on the topic you choose.

To arrive at a specific purpose for your speech, you have to think in precise terms of what you want your audience to *do* at the end of your speech. This kind of goal or purpose is called a **behavioral objective** because you will specify the behavior you seek from the audience. For the speech on how television comedy represents the modern family, you might write, "At the end of my speech, the audience will be able to explain how comedy portrays American family life

behavioral objective
What you want your audience to do after listening to your speech.

today." The specific-purpose statement for a how-to speech using visual aids might read, "At the end of my speech, the audience will be able to use Microsoft Word 6.1 word processing software." For a persuasive speech on universal health care, your specific-purpose statement could say, "At the end of my speech, the audience will be able to explain why the United States should adopt a plan of national health insurance." A speech to entertain will have a specific purpose, too. A stand-up comic may have a simple specific purpose: "At the end of my speech, the audience will laugh and applaud." An after-dinner speaker whose entertaining message has more informative value than that of the stand-up comic may say: "At the end of my speech, the audience will list four characteristics that distinguish journalists from the rest of the human race."

● FORMULATING THE SPECIFIC PURPOSE Note that all of our sample specific-purpose statements begin with the same twelve words: "At the end of my speech, the audience will be able to . . . " The next word should call for an observable, measurable action that the audience should be able to take by the end of the speech. Use verbs such as *list, explain, describe,* or *write.* Do not use vague words such as *know, understand,* or *believe.* You can discover what your listeners know, understand, or believe only by having them show their increased capability in some measurable way.

A statement of purpose does not say what you, the *speaker,* will do. The techniques of public speaking help you achieve your goals, but they are not themselves goals. To say, "In my speech, I will talk about the benefits of studying classical dance" emphasizes your performance as a speaker. The goal of the speech is centered on you, rather than on the audience. Other than restating your topic, this statement of purpose provides little direction for the speech. But to say, "At the end of my speech, the audience will be able to list three ways in which studying classical dance can benefit them" places the audience and its behavior at the center of your concern. This latter statement provides a tangible goal to guide your preparation and by which you can measure the success of your speech.

The following guidelines will help you prepare your statement of purpose.

■ *Use precise language in wording the specific purpose.*

IMPRECISE: At the end of my speech, the audience will be able to explain some things about Hannibal, Missouri.

PRECISE: At the end of my speech, the audience will be able to list five points of interest in the town of Hannibal, Missouri.

■ *Limit the specific purpose to a single idea.* If your statement of purpose has more than one idea, you will have trouble covering the extra ideas in your speech. You will also run the risk of having your speech "come apart at the seams." Both unity of ideas and coherence of expression will suffer.

TWO IDEAS: At the end of my speech, the audience will be able to write a simple computer program in BASIC and play the CD-ROM game MYST.

ONE IDEA: At the end of my speech, the audience will be able to write a simple computer program in BASIC.

 Be sure that your specific purpose meets the interests, expectations, and levels of knowledge of your audience.   Also be sure that it is important. Earlier in this chapter, we discussed these criteria as guidelines for selecting a speech topic. Consider them again as you word your purpose statement.

Behavioral statements of purpose help remind you that the aim of public speaking is to win a response from the audience. In addition, using a specific purpose to guide the development of your speech will help you focus on the audience during the entire preparation process.

RECAP

CRITERIA FOR A SPECIFIC PURPOSE

YOUR SPECIFIC PURPOSE SHOULD . . .

Be written in precise language

Be limited to a single idea

Meet the needs, interests, expectations, and level of knowledge of your audience

● USING THE SPECIFIC PURPOSE   Everything you do while preparing and delivering the speech should contribute to your specific purpose. The specific purpose can help in assessing the information you are gathering for your speech. For example, you may find that an interesting statistic, although related to your topic, will not help achieve your specific purpose. In that case, you can substitute material that will directly advance your purpose.

The specific purpose can also help you make decisions about the best use of visual aids. Let's say that your statement of purpose reads, "At the end of my speech, the audience will be able to recane old wicker chairs." In this instance, you will probably want a set of drawings to illustrate the process of recaning. The set, you may decide, will need at least two different kinds of drawing: one, rather realistic, to show the position of hands and tools when doing the lacing or interweaving, and a second that would diagrammatically illustrate the patterns of weaving for the various types of cane and wicker furniture. You will also have to decide whether to have reproductions of the drawings available for the audience after the lecture is over. As in all other aspects of preparing your speech, your specific purpose determines your decisions regarding visual aids.

As soon as you have decided on it, write the specific purpose on a three-by-five-inch note card. That way you can refer to it as often as necessary while developing your speech.

Develop your central idea

Having stated the specific purpose of your speech, you are ready to develop your central idea, the first step shown in Figure 6.2. Closely related to the purpose statement, the central idea (also called the *thesis*) is worded differently and functions differently during the speech-writing process. Like a purpose statement, a central idea restates the speech topic. But, whereas a purpose statement guides the speaker in preparing and delivering the speech, the central idea will eventually guide the audience in their understanding of the speech. Put another way, the purpose statement is what the speaker hopes to accomplish; the central idea is what he or she expects to say.

PURPOSE STATEMENT: At the end of my speech, the audience will be able to explain how censorship of school textbooks harms children.

CENTRAL IDEA: Censorship of school textbooks threatens the rights of school children.

FIGURE 6.2
State your central idea as a one-sentence summary of your speech, and then generate major ideas by looking for natural divisions, reasons, or steps to support your central idea.

As a speaker, you rarely put your purpose statement into words for the audience. However, you usually state your central idea at least twice: in the introduction and again in the conclusion of your speech. If, after a speech, an audience member is asked, "What was the speech about?" the answer is likely to be the central idea.

● FORMULATING THE CENTRAL IDEA

Unlike the purpose statement, which focuses on audience behavior, the central idea focuses on the content of the speech. The central idea is usually a one-sentence summary. From it the audience can tell what the speaker is going to discuss. The following guidelines will help you put your central idea into words.

■ *The central idea should not be a question; rather, it should be a declarative statement.*

QUESTION: Are Caesarean births unnecessary?

DECLARATIVE STATEMENT: Caesarean births are often unnecessary.

■ A question provides little direction for the speech and does not even suggest whether the speaker is going to support the affirmative or the negative answer. Imperative statements, or commands, are only rarely used as central ideas. One of your authors recently delivered a commencement address in which he used an imperative central idea, "Stop, look, and listen," for the sake of memorability. But such instances are rare. Similarly, a persuasive central idea might occasionally be worded as an exclamation if it is a surprising idea or a position the speaker holds strongly: "The death penalty should be banned in all states!" But in most cases, a declarative statement makes a speaker's position clear.

■ *The central idea should be a complete sentence rather than a phrase or clause.*

PHRASE: car maintenance

COMPLETE SENTENCE: Maintaining your car regularly can ensure that it provides reliable transportation.

The phrase "car maintenance" is really not a central idea but a topic. By the time you word your central idea, you should be ready to summarize your speech in a single sentence. The second example is a clear summary of the speech.

■ *The central idea should use specific language rather than vague generalities.*

VAGUE: Hurricane Andrew caused extensive damage to Miami for a number of reasons.

SPECIFIC: Hurricane Andrew caused extensive damage to Miami because of the increasing coastal population, the inadequacy of building codes, and the proliferation of non-native vegetation.

The specific wording provides not only the central idea of the speech but also a blueprint for the three main points of the speech: increasing coastal population, inadequacy of building codes, and proliferation of non-native vegetation.

■ *The central idea should be a single idea.*

TWO IDEAS:	Deforestation by lumber interests and toxic waste dumping are major environmental problems in the United States today.
ONE IDEA:	Toxic waste dumping is a major environmental problem in the United States today.

More than one central idea, like more than one idea in the purpose statement, will lead only to confusion and lack of cohesion in the speech.

■ *The central idea should reflect consideration of the audience.*   Just as you considered your audience when selecting and narrowing your topic and when composing your purpose statement, so should you consider your audience's needs, interests, expectations, and knowledge when stating your central idea. If you do not consider your listeners, you run the risk of losing their attention before you even begin developing the speech. If your audience consists mainly of college juniors and seniors, the second of the following central ideas would be better suited to your listeners than the first.

INAPPROPRIATE:	Whether or not you decide to go to college should be based on two important considerations: career goals and personal goals.
APPROPRIATE:	Deciding whether to go to graduate school should be based on three factors: career goals, personal goals, and program availability.

RE**CAP**

CRITERIA FOR A CENTRAL IDEA

THE CENTRAL IDEA SHOULD . . .

Be a declarative statement

Be a complete sentence

Be written in specific language

Be limited to a single idea

Reflect consideration of the audience

As mentioned earlier, central ideas are stated at least twice in most speeches. Speakers first present their central idea near the end of their introductions, when making a *preview statement* that includes the central idea and an outline of the main points of the speech. The following introduction, from a student's speech on sudden infant death syndrome, overtly states the central idea in its last sentence.

> *Sudden infant death syndrome is known by many names. It is called crib death or SIDS. It is the leading cause of death in infants under a year old. SIDS is responsible for about 10,000 infants' lives per year. These infants usually range in age from two to four months. The reason SIDS is such a problem is because, after twenty years of research, SIDS still remains a mystery.* **Today I would like to talk to you about the three major theories about sudden infant death syndrome.**[7]

In his conclusion, the speaker states his central idea again, this time naming the three theories.

> **In review, the three main theories of SIDS are the theory of maturation, the theory of dopamine, and the theory of asbestos in the lungs.** *All SIDS deaths involve apnea. This is the stoppage of air flow to the lungs, either temporarily or permanently. The real answer to why apnea occurs may be in one of the theories discussed today, or it could be something nobody has yet considered.*

Although such overt repetition might be considered poor writing, it makes for good public speaking. Writers have an advantage over public speakers. Readers can reread a sentence or passage they missed the first time around. Listeners cannot do that. However, a listener who misses the central idea when it is stated in the introduction may be able to arrive at it from the main points in the speech. But if that is not possible for one reason or another, surely the central idea will be made clear when the speaker repeats it in the speech's conclusion.

The central idea performs one other important function. You can use it to guide the division of your speech into main ideas. Such a preliminary outline can be constructed after you have written your central idea.

RE CAP

PURPOSE STATEMENT VERSUS CENTRAL IDEA

THE PURPOSE STATEMENT	THE CENTRAL IDEA
Indicates what the speaker hopes to accomplish	Summarizes the speech
Guides the preparation of the speech	Guides the audience in their understanding of the speech

Generate your main ideas

Next to topic selection, probably the most common stumbling block in developing speeches is the preliminary outline. Trying to decide how to subdivide your central idea into two, three, or four main points can make you chew your pencil, scratch your head, and end up as you began, with a blank sheet of paper. The task will be much easier if you use the following strategy.

Write the central idea at the top of a clean sheet of paper. Then ask these three questions:

- Does the central idea have *logical divisions?* (These may be indicated by such phrases as "three types" or "four means.")

- Can you think of several *reasons* the central idea is true?

- Can you support your central idea with a series of *steps* or a chronological progression?

You should be able to answer yes to one of these three questions. With your answer in mind, write down the divisions, reasons, or steps you thought of. Let's see this technique at work with several central idea statements.

● FINDING LOGICAL DIVISIONS

Suppose that your central idea is "A liberal arts education benefits the student in many ways." You now turn to the three questions. But for this example, you needn't go beyond the first one. Does the central idea have logical divisions? The phrase "many ways" indicates that it does. You can logically divide your speech into the many ways in which the student benefits. A brief brainstorming session then helps you come up with five main ways in which a liberal arts education benefits students:

1. Job opportunities

2. Appreciation of culture

3. Broad base of knowledge

4. Understanding history

5. Concern for humankind

At this stage, you needn't worry about Roman numerals, parallel form, or even the order in which the main ideas are listed. We will discuss these and the other features of outlining in Chapter 11. Your goal now is simply to generate ideas. Moreover, just because you write them down, don't think that the ideas you come up with now are engraved in stone. They can—and probably will—change. After all, this is a *preliminary* outline. It may undergo many revisions before you actually deliver your speech. In the case of our example, five points may well prove to be too many to develop in the brief time allowed for most classroom speeches. But since it is much easier to eliminate ideas than to invent them, list them all for now.

● ESTABLISHING REASONS

Suppose that your central idea is "Marriage is an endangered institution." Asking whether there are logical divisions of this idea will be no help at all. There are no key phrases indicating logical divisions—no "ways," "means," "types," or "methods" appear in the wording. The second question, however, is more productive: You can think of *reasons* this central idea is true. Simply ask yourself, "Why?" after the statement "Marriage is an endangered institution." You can then list these three answers:

1. There are fewer marriages each year.

2. More men and women are living together outside of marriage.

3. More couples are getting divorced each year.

Notice that these main ideas are expressed in complete sentences, while the ones in the preceding example were in phrases. At this stage, it doesn't matter. What does matter is getting your ideas down on paper. You can rewrite and reorganize them later.

● IDENTIFYING SPECIFIC STEPS

"U.S. involvement in Latin American politics has increased tremendously since 1980." You stare glumly at the central idea you so carefully formulated yesterday. Now what? You know a lot about the subject; your political science professor has covered it thoroughly this semester. But how can you organize all the information you have? Again, you turn to the three-question method.

Are there logical divisions of the main idea? You scan the sentence hopefully, but you can find no key phrases suggesting logical divisions.

Can you think of several *reasons* the thesis is true? You read the central idea again and add "Why?" to the end of it. Answering that question may lead you to talk about the reasons for U.S. involvement in Latin America. But your purpose statement reads, "At the end of my speech, the audience will be able to trace the evolution of United States involvement in Latin American politics since 1980." Giving reasons for that involvement would not directly contribute to your goal. So you turn to the third question.

Can you support your central idea with a series of steps? Almost any historical topic, or any topic requiring a chronological progression (for example, topics of how-to speeches), can be subdivided by answering the third question. You therefore decide that your main points will be the chronological sequence of events from 1980 to the present that led to increased U.S. involvement in Latin America. Jotting down the four or five most important events, you know that you can add, replace, or eliminate some ideas later. You have a start.

Notice that you consulted your purpose statement when you chose your main ideas in that last example. Although you needn't worry about form while constructing your tentative outline, you do need to refer to the purpose statement when deciding on your main points. If your outline will not help achieve your purpose, you need to rethink your speech. You may finally change either your purpose or your main ideas, but whichever you do, you need to synchronize them. Remember, it is much easier to make changes at this point than after you have done the research and produced a detailed outline.

RECAP

GENERATING MAIN IDEAS

ASK WHETHER YOUR CENTRAL IDEA . . .

Has *logical divisions*

Is true for a number of *reasons*

Can be supported by *steps*

Meanwhile, back at the word processor . . .

It's much too long since we abandoned Ed Garcia, the student in the opening paragraphs of this chapter who was struggling to write a speech on college football. Even though he has procrastinated, if he follows the steps we have discussed he should be able to outline a successful informative speech.

Ed has already chosen his topic. His audience is likely to be interested in his subject. Since he is a varsity defensive tackle, they probably expect him to talk about college football. And he himself is passionately interested in and knowledgeable about the subject. It meets all the requirements of a successful topic.

But "college football" is too broad for a three- to five-minute talk. Ed needs to narrow his topic to a manageable size. He adjusts his monitor and begins.

College Football

What could he cover under *College Football*? Ed's school has recently been reprimanded by the NCAA for violating recruiting regulations. The audience might be interested in that subject. So he types *Recruiting* under *College Football*. Since he himself is a player, his audience might also like to hear about the game from a player's point of view. He adds *Playing* beside *Recruiting*.

College Football

Recruiting	Playing

The more he thinks about it, the more Ed feels he would like to talk about what happens on the playing field. But he realizes that his topic is still too broad. He decides to focus on either the *Benefits* or the *Disadvantages* of playing football. He types these terms under *Playing*.

College Football

Recruiting	Playing	
	Benefits	Disadvantages

Ed knows that most of his classmates view football players as privileged, pampered students. To balance this view, he thinks that maybe he should talk about the disadvantages. In his three years on the team, Ed has encountered two major disadvantages: the demands made on a player's time, and the threat and reality of physical injury.

Ed himself has suffered several injuries and feels qualified to talk about this aspect of football. The topic "injuries in college football" should work.

Once he has worked out the topic, Ed needs a purpose statement. He decides that his audience may know something about how players are injured, but they probably do not know how these injuries are treated. He types, "The audience will be able to explain how the three most common injuries suffered by college football players are treated."

A few minutes later, Ed derives his central idea from his purpose: "Sports medicine specialists have developed specific courses of treatment for the three most common kinds of injuries suffered by college football players."

Deciding on a tentative outline is also fairly easy now. Since his central idea mentions three kinds of injuries, he can organize his speech according to those three ideas (logical divisions). Under the central idea Ed lists:

1. Bruises

2. Broken bones

3. Ligament and cartilage damage

Now Ed has a preliminary outline and is well on his way to developing a successful three- to five-minute informative speech.

Summary

This chapter presented a logical way of getting from a blank piece of paper to a tentative speech outline. Four main steps are involved:

1. Select and narrow your topic.

2. Determine your purpose.

3. Develop your central idea.

4. Generate your main ideas.

The difficulty of selecting a topic varies greatly from speech to speech. Sometimes speakers are asked to address a specific topic. At other times they may be given only such broad guidelines as time limits and occasion. As speakers ponder their topics, they must consider the interests, expectations, and knowledge levels of their audiences. They should select topics of importance and consider the special demands of the occasion. Finally, all speakers must take into account their own interests, abilities, and experiences. Usually these "boundaries" will help them select appropriate topics. If they are still undecided, they may try such techniques as brainstorming, consulting the media, or scanning lists and indexes that might contain potential topics.

After choosing a broad topic area, a speaker may need to narrow the topic. This chapter provided two methods for narrowing a topic so that it fits within the time limits that have been set.

The next task a speaker faces is deciding on general and specific purposes. He or she must consider whether a speech is going to be informative, persuasive, or entertaining. With a general purpose in mind, the speaker can write a specific-purpose statement. A specific purpose should be worded behaviorally, in terms of what the speaker wants the audience to be able to do at the end of the speech. The specific purpose serves as a yardstick by which the speaker can measure the relevance of ideas and supporting materials while developing the speech.

Specific-purpose statements indicate what speakers hope to accomplish; central ideas, by contrast, summarize what will be said. The central idea should be worded as a simple declarative sentence. It is usually stated in both the introduction and the conclusion of a speech. From the central idea, the speaker can derive a preliminary outline.

One method for producing this outline is to determine whether the central idea has logical divisions, can be supported by a group of reasons, or can be achieved through a series of steps. These divisions, reasons, or steps will produce an outline from which the speaker can work while moving on to support and develop the speech.

1. Your public speaking class invites a gubernatorial candidate to address the class. The candidate accepts the invitation and speaks for thirty minutes on the topic, "Why the state should increase its funding of public transportation." Analyze the candidate's choice of topic according to the guidelines presented in this chapter.

2. Below are several specific-purpose statements. Analyze each according to the criteria presented in this chapter for formulating a specific purpose. Rewrite the statements to correct any problems.

   At the end of my speech, the audience will know more about the Mexican Free-Tailed Bat.

   I will explain some differences in nonverbal communication between Asian and Western cultures.

   At the end of my speech, the audience will be able to list some reasons for xeriscaping one's yard.

   To describe the reasons I enjoy spelunking as a hobby.

   At the end of my speech, the audience will be able to prepare a realistic monthly budget.

   The advantages and disadvantages of living in a college dormitory.

3. Below are the topic, general purpose, and specific purpose Marylin has chosen for her persuasive speech. Write an appropriate central idea and main points for the speech. Be prepared to explain how you derived the main points from the central idea.

TOPIC:	National Presidential Primary
GENERAL PURPOSE:	Persuasive
SPECIFIC PURPOSE:	At the end of my speech, the audience will be able to list and explain three reasons the United States should adopt a national presidential primary.
CENTRAL IDEA:	
MAIN POINTS:	

ETHICAL QUESTIONS

1. Like Davy Crockett's crestfallen opponent, many speakers prepare a stock speech and proceed to deliver it to a variety of audiences and on a variety of occasions. Is this practice ethical? Explain your answer.

2. While eating lunch in the student center cafeteria, you overhear a stranger at the next table describing a paper she is writing for her political science class. She mentions a book she used to support her argument that the death sentence should not be abolished. Would it be ethical for you to "borrow" her topic and consult the book she mentioned to prepare a speech for a public speaking course assignment?

● SUGGESTED ACTIVITIES

1. Brainstorm a list of at least fifteen potential topics for an informative classroom speech. Applying the criteria discussed in this chapter, select the topics best suited to your audience, the occasion, and yourself. If you wish, use one of these topics for an assigned informative speech.

2. Browse through a current newspaper, news magazine, or *TV Guide*. See how many potential speech topics you can discover in the stories your source contains. Write them down. File or copy your list into your speech notebook or computer file.

3. Using one of the techniques described in this chapter, narrow each of the following general categories into a workable topic for a three- to five-minute informative speech:

The ocean

Technology

Money

● USING TECHNOLOGY AND MEDIA

1. Watch a television news magazine such as *60 Minutes*, *20/20*, or *Primetime Live*. Keep a scratch pad and pen at hand, and jot down potential speech topics as they come to mind during the program. Don't forget the commercials—they often raise questions or issues that would make good topics.

2. If you have access to an on-line network, browse through the offerings and "listen in" on a few chatrooms and special interest group exchanges. Again, jot down any speech topic ideas that come to mind; then transfer them to your speech notebook or computer file. When you decide on a topic, you may want to return to one of the chatrooms to discuss your idea or gather more information.

"Market Place, Guatemala."
John Hollis Kaufmann/SuperStock

Gathering Supporting Material

Learn, compare, collect the facts! . . . Always have the courage to say to yourself—I am ignorant.
—Ivan Petrovich Pavlov

OBJECTIVES

After studying this chapter you should be able to do the following:

1. List five potential sources of supporting material for a speech.

2. Describe at least three types of electronic resources.

3. Briefly describe five types of traditional library resources.

4. List five information items a researcher should record for all supporting material, including potential visual aids.

pple pie is your specialty. Your family and friends relish your flaky crust, spicy filling, and crunchy crumb topping. Fortunately, not only do you have a never-fail recipe and technique, but you also know where to go for the best ingredients. Fette's Orchard has the tangiest pie apples in town. For your crust, you use only Premier shortening, which you buy at Meyer's Specialty Market. And your crumb topping requires both stone-ground whole-wheat flour and fresh creamery butter, available on Tuesdays at the farmer's market on the courthouse square.

Just as making your apple pie requires that you know where to find specific ingredients, so does a successful speech require knowledge of both sources and types of supporting material that speechmakers typically use. Chapters 7 and 8 together comprise the speech development step illustrated by Figure 7.1: Gather Supporting Material. In this chapter we will identify various sources of information and discuss ways to access them. In Chapter 8 we will focus on recognizing and effectively using various types of supporting material.

FIGURE 7.1
Finding, identifying, and effectively using supporting material are activities that comprise an essential step of the speech preparation process.

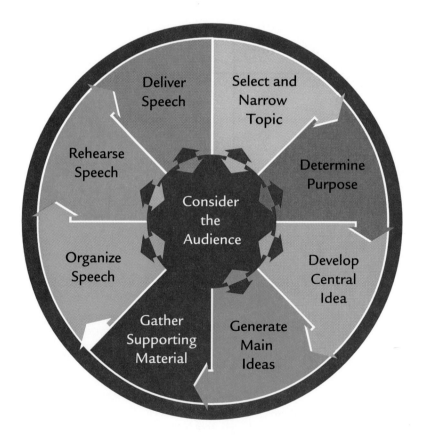

Personal knowledge and experience

Because you will probably give speeches on topics in which you have a special interest, you may find that *you* are your own best source. Your speech may be on a skill or hobby in which you are expert, such as tropical fish, stenciling, or stamp collecting. Or you may talk on a subject with which you have had some personal experience, such as buying a used car, deciding whether to join a club, or seeking nursing home care for an elderly relative. Don't automatically run to the library to try to find every piece of supporting material for every topic on which you speak. It is true that most well-researched speeches will include some objective material gathered from outside sources. But you may also be able to provide an effective illustration, explanation, definition, or other type of support from your own knowledge and experience. As an audience-centered speaker, you should realize, too, that personal knowledge often has the additional advantage of heightening your credibility in the minds of your listeners. They will accord you more respect as an authority when they realize that you have firsthand knowledge of a topic.

Interviews

If you don't know the answers to some of the important questions raised by your topic, but you can think of someone who might, consider seeking an interview as a means of gaining material for your speech. For example, if you are preparing a speech on the quality of food in the school cafeteria, who better to ask about the subject than the director of food services? If you want to discuss the pros and cons of building a new prison in an urban area, you might interview an official of the correctional services, a representative of the city administration, and a resident of the area. Or if you want to explain why the United States has retained the electoral college, you might consult your professor of political science or American history. A topic of local concern can almost always be supported by information from individuals who are involved directly. And often college or university faculty members can provide expert testimony on a wide variety of social, economic, and political topics.

A word of caution, however, before you decide that an interview is necessary: Be sure that your questions cannot be answered easily by reading a newspaper article or a book. Do some preliminary reading on your subject before you decide to take up someone's valuable time in an interview. If you decide that only an interview can give you the material you need, you should prepare for it in advance.

● DETERMINING THE PURPOSE OF THE INTERVIEW

The first step in preparing for an interview is to establish a purpose or objective for it. Specifically, what do you need to find out? Do you need hard facts that you cannot obtain from other sources? Do you need the interviewee's expert testimony on your subject? Does the person you are going to interview have a particularly significant personal experience that you wish to hear described firsthand? Or do you need an explanation of some of the information you found in print sources? Before you begin preparing for the interview, decide just what you want to have or know when the interview is over.

For example, Lee plans to give a persuasive speech on reducing the health threat of asbestos. His interest was piqued by an article in *Time,* which provided some background on the magnitude of the problem and some of the current measures being taken to control it. But Lee also remembers reading a recent article in the local newspaper regarding the discovery of asbestos in a local middle school. He decides to interview the principal of that school to hear the perspective of someone who works in the building and is responsible for the health and safety of others. Lee has determined the purpose of his interview.

● SETTING UP THE INTERVIEW

Once you have a specific purpose for the interview and have decided with whom you are going to talk, arrange a meeting. It is unwise to arrive unannounced at the office of a businessperson, public official, educator, or other professional and expect an on-the-spot interview. Even Mike Wallace has been refused under such circumstances! Instead, several days in advance, telephone the office of the person you hope to interview, explain briefly who you are and why you are calling, and ask for a meeting. It is reasonable to request a certain date and time for the interview, but realize that it will have to be scheduled at the convenience of the person granting the interview. Try to be flexible. Most people are flattered to have their authority and knowledge recognized and willingly grant interviews to serious students if schedules permit.

Lee calls the middle school office and asks for the name of the principal. Upon being told that it is Mrs. Saladin, Lee asks to speak with her. When she comes on the line, he explains briefly his purpose for the interview and requests an appointment sometime late Tuesday afternoon. Mrs. Saladin, however, has a staff meeting scheduled for that time and suggests Wednesday morning at 10:00 A.M. instead. Lee agrees.

If there is any possibility that you may want to record or videotape the interview, ask for the interviewee's OK during this initial contact. If permission is refused, you will need to be prepared to gather your information without electronic assistance.

Lee asks Mrs. Saladin whether she would mind being audio taped during the interview. She hesitates, then replies that due to the potentially controversial nature of the issue, she would prefer not to be taped. Lee hastens to assure her that he will be happy just to take written notes.

● PLANNING THE INTERVIEW

Now that you know what you need to find out, whom you will see, and when the meeting will take place, your next step is to prepare for the interview itself. Do not try to "wing it" and let the interviewee ramble at will. As a rule, this approach will not get the information you need. If you don't ask specific questions, you may end up with only a few minutes of awkward silence, or the interviewee may stray far from your topic. Even if the person you are interviewing does stay on track and talk freely about your topic, chances are that he or she won't provide exactly the information you need. To ensure the results you want, you need to plan a set of questions. A few suggestions can help you do so.

● GATHER BACKGROUND INFORMATION   First, do your homework. Experienced interviewers are successful largely because they prepare so thoroughly for their interviews. Likewise, before you interview someone, find out as much as you can about your subject, the person you are interviewing, and the field of knowledge. Prepare questions that take full advantage of the interviewee's specific knowledge of your subject. You can do this only if *you* already know a good deal about your subject. Build your line of questioning on facts, statements the interviewee has made, or positions he or she has taken publicly.

Lee decides that prior to Wednesday he will reread the *Time* article that originally aroused his interest in the topic of asbestos and also do some additional reading on the topic. Because he did not attend the local public schools, he does not know Mrs. Saladin, but he has read the statements she made to the local newspaper reporter. In addition, Lee's friend, Carmen, has a daughter who attends the local middle school. He asks Carmen about Mrs. Saladin and discovers that she is respected as a competent administrator.

● PLAN SPECIFIC QUESTIONS   In addition to learning something about your subject and the person you are going to interview, it is helpful to think about how you should combine the two basic types of interview questions: closed-ended and open-ended.

As we discussed in Chapter 5, closed-ended questions call for a yes or no answer or some brief statement of fact. "How many years have you served in the job?" and "Do you think that next month's tax referendum will pass?" are examples of closed-ended questions. Lee needs to ask Mrs. Saladin several closed-ended questions. For example, he will want to ask, "How long have you been principal at this school?" and "When did you first become aware that the school contained asbestos?"

If you ask only closed-ended questions, however, you will limit and possibly frustrate your interviewee. You may also frustrate yourself. Open-ended questions allow the interviewee to express a personal point of view more fully. They may also give you more of the kind of information you probably want: expert testimony and personal experience. "Why do you think the asbestos should not be removed?" and "What, in your opinion, are the most serious potential consequences if it is removed?" are examples of open-ended questions. Open-ended questions often follow closed-ended questions. If the person you are interviewing answers a closed-ended question with a simple yes or no, you may wish to follow up on the answer by asking, "Why?"

● PLAN A SEQUENCE OF QUESTIONS   Once you have designed your questions to yield the answers you want, you need to consider the order in which to ask them. You may want to organize questions according to subject categories, with three or four questions on one subject followed by three or four on another. Or you may want to arrange them according to complexity of information, with the easiest questions first, in part to ensure that you understand the subject. Or you may want to order them by content sensitivity. Questions about your interviewee's participation in some covert or suspicious activity or about an unpopular stand on an issue should probably come last. Your organization of questions should be designed to build some rapport with your interviewee and to ensure that you get at least some information, should he or she decline to answer the more sensitive or difficult questions. Early in the interview, Lee plans to ask Mrs. Saladin such questions as, "You seem to have the trust of your staff and the community as a whole. What do you think has contributed the most to your earning that trust?" Not until later in the interview will he ask her, "How do you plan to deal with those parents who say they will keep their children home and picket the school if the asbestos has not been removed by March 1?"

● PLAN A RECORDING STRATEGY   Although at Mrs. Saladin's request Lee did not use a tape recorder for his interview, if the person you will see agrees to be electronically recorded, you will need to decide whether or not to tape the interview. Audio and video recorders have both advantages and disadvantages. They can free you from having to take copious notes. You can concentrate instead on processing and analyzing the ideas and information being presented. Another advantage is that your record of the interview is complete. You will not have to decipher hastily scribbled notes a day or two after the interview.

The main disadvantage of using an electronic recorder is that it makes some people more self-conscious and nervous than if you were scribbling notes. You want the person being interviewed to concentrate on your questions and not on vocal inflection. If you use an audio or video recorder, be prepared to turn it off and switch to manual note taking if you sense at any time that the interviewee is distracted by the device.

When taping an interview, there are a number of questions that you should ask yourself. What kind of recorder should you use? Would a simple tape recorder with a built-in mike be less intimidating than a video camera on a tripod? Although the person you are interviewing is aware that you are taping the interview, would he or she be more comfortable if the machine were out of sight? Ask the interviewee. You might also want to ask some casual questions before turning on the recorder so that both of you can ease into the interview proper.

CONDUCTING THE INTERVIEW

● ON YOUR MARK   Dress for the interview. For most interviews, conservative, businesslike clothes show that you are serious about the interview and that you respect the norms of your interviewee's world. Lee selects a pair of neatly pressed khaki slacks and a shirt and tie for his interview with Mrs. Saladin.

Take a pad and pen or pencil for note taking. Even if you are planning to use a tape recorder, you may want to turn it off at some point during the interview. Or Murphy's Law may snarl your tape or break your recorder. Lee even takes along an extra pen, avoiding the potential embarrassment of having to ask for one should his first one run out of ink. Ensure that the interview can continue, in spite of any mishaps.

● GET SET   Arrive for the interview a few minutes ahead of the scheduled hour. Lee arrives at the school office at 9:50 A.M. for his 10:00 A.M. appointment. Be prepared, however, to wait patiently, if necessary. While the interview may be a high priority for you, the person you will interview has granted it as a courtesy and may need to complete something before speaking with you.

Once you are settled with the person you will interview, remind him or her of your purpose. In Lee's case, he shakes Mrs. Saladin's hand and then briefly repeats that he is interested in her perspective on the topic of the asbestos threat because she works in, and is responsible for the health of others who work in, a school known to contain asbestos. If you are familiar with and admire the work the interviewee has done or published, don't hesitate to say so. Sincere flattery can help set a positive tone for the exchange. If you have decided to use a recorder, set it up. You may keep it out of sight once the interviewee has seen it, but never try to hide a recorder at the outset—such a ploy is unethical. If you are going to take written notes, get out your paper and pen. Now you are ready to begin asking your prepared questions.

● GO!   As you conduct the interview, use the questions you have prepared as a guide but not a rigid schedule. If the person you are interviewing mentions an interesting angle you did not think of, don't be afraid to pursue the point. Listen carefully to the person's answers, and ask for clarification of any ideas you don't understand. For example, at one point Mrs. Saladin tells Lee that the local Physical Facilities Committee endorsed the closing of the middle school three years earlier. Before she can continue, Lee, who is not familiar with the makeup or mission of that committee, asks Mrs. Saladin to explain those factors, as well as to elaborate on the committee's reasons for recommending closing the campus. Again, be sensitive to your interviewee's reaction to being recorded; turn off the recorder if he or she seems overly aware of it or hesitant to talk freely because of it.

Do not prolong the interview beyond the time limits of your appointment. The person you are interviewing is probably very busy and has been courteous enough to fit you into a tight schedule. Ending the interview on time is simply to return the courtesy. Thank your interviewee for his or her contribution, and leave.

● FOLLOWING UP THE INTERVIEW

As soon as possible after the interview, read through your notes carefully and copy over any portion that may be illegible. If you recorded the interview, label the tape with the date and the interviewee's name. You will soon want to transfer any significant facts, opinions, or anecdotes from either notes or tape to four-by-six-inch index cards or to a word processor's notepad or document. You will find a format for transcribing information later in this chapter. Lee transfers his notes to his computer's electronic notepad, from which he can later paste them into his speech outline.

Mail-order materials

The federal government, business and industrial groups, nonprofit organizations, and professional societies produce pamphlets, books, fact sheets, or other information about an extraordinarily wide variety of subjects. This information is usually available at little or no cost and is a fertile source of supporting materials.

How do you find out about these materials? One well-known listing is the U.S. Government Printing Office's *Monthly Catalog of U.S. Government Publications*. Since the government publishes information about almost every subject imaginable, the *Monthly Catalog* can lead to a number of excellent sources.

The reference section of your library will probably have the *Encyclopedia of Associations* and the *Directory of Nonprofit Organizations*. Though these reference works do not indicate specific publications, they can give you an idea of some of the businesses and organizations that may have a special interest in your topic. These references include the addresses and telephone numbers of the businesses and organizations they list, so you can write, call, or send a fax requesting the information you need. For example, your authors were recently involved in organizing a parent volunteer program in a local elementary school. Upon checking the *Directory of Nonprofit Organizations,* we found a listing for the National Association of Partners in Education, headquartered in Alexandria, Virginia. A call to its office revealed that the association provides booklets, pamphlets, and other information to schools considering volunteer programs and business partnerships. The office mailed us a kit immediately, and we had it within a week.

The time between your request for information and its arrival may be too long for you to use the information in your speech. Many students do not choose speech topics far enough in advance to make mail-order sources practical for classroom assignments. At least a week, and sometimes as much as a month, may go by before the materials arrive. However, even if their value for use in class is limited, mail-order materials may prove very useful when you have been invited well in advance of the speaking date to make a presentation.

One other drawback to mail-order information needs to be mentioned here. Private companies and organizations produce printed materials only because they have a vested interest in the field. Without saying that all such materials are inaccurate, it is probably fair to say that they are by nature one-sided. You can expect oil companies, for example, to minimize the harm oil spills can do to an environment. Therefore, you need to consider these sources carefully before using the information they provide. Ideally, you should have independent sources of information, which may mean writing to several organizations for information.

Electronic resources

The question has been raised," says University of Texas Professor of Library and Information Science Francis Miksa, "whether it is possible to have an all-electronic library, with no books on the shelves."[1] Difficult as it may be to imagine, a library with no books is a distinct possibility for the near future. As both the capacity and accessibility of electronic resources continue to grow at an explosive rate, researchers find themselves working with far different tools, and needing far different skills, than they did just a few years—or even a few months—ago.

Although no single chapter can provide a comprehensive guide to electronic resources, we can introduce you here to some of the more commonly available ones and give you an idea of how they can help you find supporting materials for your speeches.

● THE INTERNET

Science fiction author William Gibson first used the term *Cyberspace* to describe an environment in which computers and people coexisted in virtual reality. Today, we use the term *Cyberspace* to describe a real phenomenon, which is called the Internet.[2] Originating as a modest network of four computers in 1969, the Internet today is a vast collection of thousands of smaller electronic networks used by millions of people all over the world.[3]

In spite of—or perhaps because of—its size and success, the Internet is not easy to describe. Its resources are so vast that

> Users can find information on such things as the most recent Supreme Court decisions, hourly updates on earthquake activity around the world, search university libraries all over the world, view satellite weather photos, read press releases from the White House, leave personal messages at NASA, find out about food recipes, baseball scores, pruning apple trees, raising ostriches, and thousands of other topics.[4]

In addition to finding and retrieving information, Internet users can access games and programs from other computers, and they can communicate with other users through e-mail. But it is the information function of Internet that is of primary interest to those of us searching for supporting materials for a speech.

With the proper equipment, it is not hard to "get on" the Internet. You need a computer (either a Mac or a PC), a communications software package, and a modem connected to a telephone line. In addition, you must have an Internet connection. Although you can purchase a permanent direct link by subscription, it is not financially or technologically feasible for most of us to do so. It is possible to access some functions of the Internet through subscription servers such as America Online, which we will discuss shortly. But while you are a college or university student, you may be able to get an account (often available without charge) that will allow you to dial into your college's computer, which is in turn connected to the Internet. When you get your account, you will also receive instructions for the prompts you will need to type into your computer to access the Internet, and to download and print documents from it.

Now for the bad news—or at least the challenge. Remarkable tool that it is, the Internet has also been described as "electronic anarchy." Because it is not owned or regulated by any single entity, it has no single organizational system. Instead, you must become familiar with several different systems to access information on the Internet. First, all Internet users have an e-mail address. You will be assigned one, too, when you get your account. If you know the addresses for the people and organizations you want, you can access them directly. Many individuals now include their e-mail addresses on their business cards. Addresses of organizations are also available from published directories found in both libraries and bookstores.

If you do not have the specific e-mail address for the information you want, you will need to search a specific database through an index or menu. Archie indexes the files of a number of Internet servers to create a single searchable database. Gopher is another menu-driven database, which is supplemented by Veronica, a service that searches Gopher materials through the use of key words. WAIS (Wide Area Information Server) and the WWW (World Wide Web) are still other databases. Similar to the way in which Veronica supplements Gopher, Mosaic and Netscape enhance the World Wide Web. Netscape, with its user-friendly icons, is perhaps the single most popular Internet access system currently in use. Although we do not have space here to discuss in detail the specific advantages, limitations, and instructions for all these various access systems, you can read more about them in books written for that express purpose (for example, the best-selling *Navigating the Internet,* by Richard J. Smith and Mark Gibbs). Or, better yet, you can log on to the Internet and browse its offerings for yourself. Allow plenty of time—you are bound to discover irresistible distractions! And you may find some of your most valuable supporting material by accidentally stumbling onto it.

Both the Internet's databases and the indexes to those databases continue to grow at a phenomenal rate. You will need to allow yourself time to "surf" the Internet to become familiar with even a small portion of its offerings.

COMMERCIAL SERVERS

Whether or not you have direct access to the Internet, you may find it useful to subscribe to one or more commercial servers. Those designed for home use include CompuServe, America Online, Delphi, and Prodigy, among others. For a monthly fee, currently around $10 for basic services, subscribers can use e-mail; access various on-line reference materials; get instant updates on news, weather, sports, and the stock market; play games; shop; and make travel reservations. In addition, customer service includes such support as printed guides and both telephone and on-line assistance. File managers make it easy to access materials and services, especially for the novice who may find the Internet a bit overwhelming.

Other commercial servers target business, professional, and academic users. LEXIS/NEXIS, for example, is an extensive database of full-text government documents, law journals, and newspapers and periodicals, which expands at the rate of a phenomenal 2.5 million documents each week.[5] Although a subscription to LEXIS/NEXIS is quite expensive, you can pay by the search, or access it through a code if your university library subscribes to it.

One disadvantage of using a commercial server is that a number of databases may be available only as "extended services," subject to hourly connect charges and various surcharges. But if you are prepared to pay for the convenience, commercial servers can be a good source of supporting materials for your speeches.

ELECTRONIC INDEXES

In addition to full-text document databases, electronic resources include numerous indexes that list both materials available on electronic servers and traditional library holdings, such as books and periodicals. Developing a bibliography by electronic index can save you time; if they are hooked up to printers, most indexes allow you to print out citations as you find them, eliminating the need to record bibliographic information by hand.

A number of traditional indexes are now available on laser disc scanners or on-line databases. These include the *Reader's Guide to Periodical Literature,* the *Humanities Index,* the *Social Sciences Index,* and various individual newspaper indexes. We will discuss these indexes in more detail later in the chapter.

Other indexes have been developed especially for electronic use. CARL UnCover, for example, is a database consisting of tens of thousands of journals from a variety of disciplines. You can search UnCover for a particular journal title, if you know it, or by key word. You can also order documents, which can

```
Database:    General Periodicals Index-A
Subject:     Freedom of speech
Library:     S.W.T. Library

   Shaky freedoms: the U.S. Supreme Court challenges liberalism. Carl
   Mollins. Maclean's, July 17, 1995  v108  n29  p22 (1).
   Holdings:  Your library subscribes to the journal, but detailed informa-
   tion about holdings is not available.

   Free at last. (free speech rights upheld by U.S. Supreme Court protection
   of Boston St. Patrick's Day parade exclusion of gay marchers) (Editorial)
   (Brief Article) The New Republic, July 10, 1995  v213  n2  p8(1). Mag.
   Coll. : 79L0097
   Holdings:  Your library subscribes to the journal, but detailed informa-
   tion about holdings is not available.
```

FIGURE 7.2

Two articles indexed by the electronic General Periodicals Index under the subject heading "Freedom of Speech."

then be delivered to you by fax within twenty-four hours. Expect to pay both a service fee and a copyright fee for this service, which will probably run about $10 to $20 per article.

The *General Periodicals Index* (See Figure 7.2) is similar to the *Reader's Guide,* covering a wide range of topics appearing in popular magazines. The *National Newspaper Index* indexes five major newspapers: the *New York Times,* the *Wall Street Journal,* the *Christian Science Monitor,* the *Washington Post,* and the *Los Angeles Times.* Similarly, *NewsBank* both indexes and provides text or articles from more than 450 U.S. and Canadian newspapers (See Figure 7.3).

Find out which electronic indexes are available in your library. They can be invaluable as you research your speeches. Realize, however, that your library will not necessarily own copies of all articles and materials listed in its electronic indexes. You will need to consult a periodicals list or card catalogue to determine which resources are readily available.

RE CAP

ELECTRONIC RESOURCES

Resource	Usefulness	Disadvantages
The Internet	A collection of thousands of smaller databases	Complex organization can be confusing, inefficient
Commercial Servers	Offer on-line reference materials and full-text articles and documents	Hourly fees can add up
Electronic Indexes	Contain vast bibliographies; usually offer printout capabilities	List numerous references your library may not carry

```
          CD NewsBank Comprehensive (December 01 1994 - September 05 1995)

  Use the up and down arrows or PgUp and PgDn to move through the list. To
  display the article for a highlighted headline, press the Enter key.
  To mark/unmark the article for later printing or downloading, press F3.
  To print or download the article, press F4.

                                                  [ LIST SCREEN: 1 of 124 ]

  Date                         Headline

    September 3, 1995          China approves women's conference newspaper
    August 29, 1995            China limits free speech at U.N. women's form
    August 22, 1995            ABC libel pact bodes ill for journalism. exp
    August 16, 1995            Canada's 'right to fair trial' clashes with
    August 14, 1995            Publishers Arrested In Germany The American p
    August 10, 1995            Transcript of a Press Conference by the Pres
    August 4, 1995             WE ARE IN THE PROCESS OF THE REMAKING


  F2 Help     Enter    Continue    Esc    Cancel
```

```
          CD NewsBank Comprehensive (December 01 1994 - September 05 1995)

  For more of this article, press up and down arrows or PgUp and PgDn. For
  the next article, press → key. To print or download the article, press F4.
  To mark/unmark the article for later printing or downloading, press F3.

                                        [ DISPLAY SCREEN: 1 of 124 ]

  Source: Reuters
    Headline:                  China approves women's conference newspaper

    Date: September 3, 1995
    Dateline: Hauirou

    Index Terms:               newspaper
                               freedom of speech
                               China
                               U.N. Conference on women (1995)
  Text:
  Chinese authorities have told the Earth Times it has approved to
  publish, a day after editors threatened to pull the newspaper out of


  F2 Help     Enter    Continue    Esc    Cancel
```

FIGURE 7.3
A number of headlines and a single article entry from Newsbank. The full text of the article is available as well.

Just a few years ago, a student working on a five- to seven-minute speech might have worried about not finding enough supporting material. Today a student who uses electronic resources might with good reason worry about being overwhelmed with far more information than he or she needs for a short speech. How can you decide what resources have the highest potential value among the hundreds of titles you may discover in your searches of various electronic databases?

First, keep in mind that most electronic searches will yield some material that is only marginally relevant. In searching for sample eulogies for Chapter 18 of this text, for example, one of your authors did a key-word search of *NewsBank*, using the word *funeral*. Although the search yielded some good illustrations, it also produced dozens of obituaries and articles about the funeral industry. Fortunately, it is often possible to tell at a glance when material is irrelevant to the specific purpose at hand, so you can easily skip over it and scroll on.

Even so, you may still find yourself overwhelmed by documents and articles that seem relevant and promising. At that point, you will need to use the same criteria for effectiveness that you would apply to supporting material gathered from any type of resource. In Chapter 8 we will discuss in detail guidelines for selecting the best supporting material.

Traditional library resources

Despite the rapid development of electronic resources, the more traditional holdings of libraries remain rich sources of supporting materials. Although your college or university library may seem a forbidding maze, all libraries, from the smallest village library to the huge Library of Congress, house the same sorts of materials and are organized in a similar way.

Unless you have already done so, spend some time becoming familiar with your library's layout and services. Some libraries offer staff-guided tours; most others will at least have floor plans and location guides available. Before you have to do research under pressure, explore the library at a leisurely pace. Find out what electronic resources are available and where they are located. In addition, find the location of the following five types of holdings:

- Books

- Periodicals

- Newspapers

- Government documents

- Reference materials

● BOOKS

When you think of libraries, you generally think of books. And with good reason: Most of the floor space of a library is devoted to books.

● STACKS   Libraries' collections of books are called the **stacks.** Stacks may be either open or closed, depending on library policy. An open-stack library means that the collections are on open shelves and available to anyone who wishes to browse through them. Open stacks give researchers the chance of making lucky finds, since books on a particular subject are shelved next to one another. For example, if you are looking for a specific book on play therapy, you may, on the same shelf, find two or three other books on the same subject. The main drawback to open stacks is that they are vulnerable to both loss of materials and the misplacement of books by careless users.

The closed-stack library is one in which only persons granted certain privileges are allowed in the stacks—most generally, librarians, library aides, faculty, and graduate students. Undergraduates and others must consult the card catalog and copy onto a retrieval card or call slip the title, author, and call number of the book they want. This card or slip is then given to a librarian at the circulation desk, who sends it to the appropriate area of the stacks. A library worker there will find the desired book and send it to circulation, where the borrower can either check it out or use it in the study area of the library.

The advantages of the closed-stack library are that users are saved some legwork, and the stacks generally stay more orderly than in an open-stack system. The chief disadvantages are the length of time it can sometimes take to get materials and the impossibility of making a lucky find. Whatever the setup, you will have to adapt to the particular method your library uses.

● CARD CATALOG   Just how do you find what you want from among those several floors in your college library? You probably have used a **card catalog** in a smaller public or school library. University libraries are no different. Even though their holdings are much larger than those of the average public library, university libraries also contain card catalogs.

Card catalogs may be either traditional or computerized. Today even very small community and school libraries are likely to have computerized card catalogs. Instead of running around a huge number of filing cabinets, trying to find the drawers you need, you go to a screen or monitor, turn it on, and follow the directions given. If you type in a subject, an author, or a title, the screen will display the library's holding for that category. Figure 7.4 illustrates a sample entry from a computerized card catalog.

The books you find in your library will be important sources as you prepare your speeches. Books can provide in-depth coverage of topics, which is simply not possible in shorter publications. However, books are inherently outdated. Most books are written two or three years before they are published. If your speech addresses a current topic or if you want to use current examples, you will probably not find these in books. For up-to-date information, you should turn to periodicals and newspapers.

stacks
The collection of books in a library.

card catalog
A file of information about the books in a library; may use an index card filling system or a computerized system.

FIGURE 7.4

An entry from a computerized card catalog. The same entry appears on the screen regardless of whether the book is accessed through title, author, or subject.

MATERIAL:	Book [Author]
CALL NUMBER:	Z657 .F5 1994
AUTHOR:	Fish, Stanley Eugene. [Title]
TITLE:	There's no such thing as free speech, and it's a good thing, too / Stanley Fish.
PUBLICATION:	New York : Oxford University Press, 1994.
DESCRIPTION:	xii, 332 p.; 24 cm.
NOTES:	Includes bibliographical references (p. 309–317) and index.
SUBJECT:	Freedom of speech. [Subject]
SUBJECT:	Freedom of speech—United States.
SUBJECT:	Academic freedom.
SUBJECT:	Academic freedom—United States.

● PERIODICALS

The term *periodicals* refers to both general-interest magazines; such as *Newsweek, Consumer Reports,* and *Sports Illustrated;* and trade and professional journals, such as *Communication Monographs,* the *Quarterly Journal of Economics,* and *American Psychologist.* Both types of periodicals are useful to researchers. As we just observed, periodicals are more timely than books. Current magazines may be only a few days old.

Just as you need a card catalog to help you find books, you need similar help to decide what periodicals might be useful. Several indexes can provide such assistance.

● PERIODICAL INDEXES   A large number of indexes are published, covering a large number of general subject areas and listing most of the thousands of periodicals published on a regular basis.

■ The *Reader's Guide to Periodical Literature* is the oldest and most frequently consulted periodical index. It lists both popular magazines and a few trade and professional journals. Articles are alphabetized according to both subject and author. Figure 7.5 illustrates a typical subject entry in the *Reader's Guide.* The *Reader's Guide* is a cumulative index, published every two weeks. The volumes are combined into quarterly and annual volumes. Its cumulative structure allows the *Reader's Guide* to be available for very current materials, as well as in bound volumes for easy reference to past years. In addition, as noted earlier, many libraries now subscribe to the *Reader's Guide* in electronic form.

■ The *Social Sciences Index* and the *Humanities Index* list professional, trade, and specialty publications dealing with the social sciences and the humanities, for the most part. Originally published as the *Reader's Guide Supplement,* the *Social Sciences Index* and the *Humanities Index* are organized and cumulated like the *Reader's Guide.* Also like the *Reader's Guide,* these indexes are now available in electronic form, although older volumes may be available only in bound form.

FREEDOM OF SPEECH
See also
Freedom of the press
Libel and slander
Privileged communications. L Winner. il *Technology Review* v 98 p 70 My/Je '95
Street corners in cyberspace. A. L. Shapiro. il *The Nation* v261 p10–12+ Jl 3 '95

Title

Author

Periodical

■ The *Education Index* lists articles not only about education but also on various subjects that are taught (think about the wide range of departments within a university, and you will have some idea of the scope). Its format is similar to that of the other periodical indexes.

■ The *Public Affairs Information Service Bulletin* indexes both periodicals and books in such subject areas as sociology, political science, and economics. Entries are listed alphabetically by subject, in much the same format as the other indexes. An electronic P.A.I.S. is also available.

Other specialized indexes may also prove valuable, depending on your topic and purpose. The *Business Periodicals Index,* the *Psychology Index,* the *Music Index,* the *Art Index,* and the *Applied Science and Technology Index* are a few of these specialized publications that you may wish to explore at one time or another.

NEWSPAPERS

Just as periodicals are more up-to-date than books, so newspapers are more current than periodicals. You may be able to find information that is only hours old by reading the latest edition of a daily newspaper. Newspapers also offer more detailed coverage of events and special stories than do periodicals, simply because they are published more often. Finally, newspapers usually cover stories of local significance that most often would not appear in national news magazines.

Generally, libraries have only the latest newspapers in their racks. Back issues are quickly transferred to microfilm for more efficient and permanent storage. Don't let microfilm intimidate you. Microfilm readers are easy to use, and most librarians or aides working in the newspaper section will be glad to show you how to set up the reader with the film you need.

■ *Newspaper Indexes.* As with any research, before you can consult a newspaper, you have to know where to look. To find relevant information on your subject, you need to consult a newspaper index. In addition to the electronic National Newspaper Index and NewsBank, a number of medium-to-large newspapers publish their own indexes; your library may carry several of these, particularly if one such newspaper is published nearby.

When doing newspaper research, keep this tip in mind: If you need information about a specific event and you know the date on which it occurred, you can simply locate a newspaper from that or the following day and probably find a news story on the event.

All major libraries contain a specialized group of published works called reference materials. Reference materials are indexed in the card catalog. Their call numbers usually have a *ref* prefix or suffix to show that they are housed in the reference section of the library. Like periodicals, newspapers, and microfilms, they are usually available only for in-house research and cannot be checked out.

Reference materials include encyclopedias, dictionaries, directories, atlases, almanacs, yearbooks, books of quotations, and biographical dictionaries. All may, at one time or another, prove useful to the speaker. Let's examine a few of the most frequently consulted reference works.

■ *Encyclopedias.* The standard for general encyclopedias has for many years been the *Encyclopaedia Britannica.* Nearly every library will have a fairly recent set of *Britannica,* as well as several other general encyclopedias, such as the *Encyclopedia Americana* and the *World Book Encyclopedia.* Your library may provide access to electronic encyclopedias, as well as bound sets.

In addition, there are a number of specialized encyclopedias. Art, philosophy, psychology, and music are just a few of the fields covered by specialty encyclopedias.

■ *Dictionaries.* The foremost dictionary of the English language is the *Oxford English Dictionary,* or *OED.* Published in twelve large volumes, the *OED* provides definitions, pronunciations, etymologies, and usage histories for every word in the dictionary. No other dictionary is this comprehensive. In all likelihood, you will rarely need as much information about a word as the *OED* provides. Therefore, the unabridged *Random House Dictionary of the English Language* or a desktop *Webster's Collegiate Dictionary* will probably serve your purposes.

There are also specialty dictionaries. *Black's Law Dictionary,* which provides legal definitions, is one example. Such diverse fields as geography, music, and economics also have their own special dictionaries.

■ *Directories.* The *Encyclopedia of Associations,* the *Directory of Nonprofit Organizations,* and other directories, including telephone directories, are usually available in the reference section.

■ *Atlases.* An atlas is a geographical tool that provides maps, tables, pictures, and facts about the people and resources of various regions. Frequently used atlases include *Good's World Atlas,* the *Rand McNally College World Atlas,* and the *Township Atlas of the United States.* There are also specialized atlases of history and politics.

■ *Almanacs and yearbooks.* Almanacs and yearbooks are compilations of facts. The *Statistical Abstract of the United States* is published annually by the Census Bureau and contains statistics on nearly every facet of life in the United States, including birth and mortality rates, income, education, and religion. The *World Almanac* contains factual information about almost every subject imaginable. Its content ranges from facts about ruling monarchs of the eighteenth century to a list of every winner of the Kentucky Derby.

■ *Books of quotations.*   These are compilations of quotes on almost every conceivable subject. Most of these books are arranged alphabetically by subject; a few are arranged according to author, with the subject entered in an index. The *Oxford Dictionary of Quotations* and *Bartlett's Familiar Quotations* are two widely consulted works.

■ *Biographical dictionaries.*   These are reference works that contain biographical articles—some short, others not—on persons who have achieved some recognition. Usually, biographical dictionaries are organized alphabetically. Probably the best-known general works in this area are the *Who's Who* series, which include brief biographies of international, national, and regional figures of note. The *Dictionary of National Biography* provides biographies of famous British subjects who are no longer living; the *Dictionary of American Biography* does the same for deceased Americans of note. The *Dictionary of American Scholars* provides information about American academicians (you can probably find profiles of some of your current professors in this work). And if none of those just mentioned has the biography you are seeking, you might try the *Biography Index,* a quarterly publication that lists current articles and books containing biographical sketches. One of these directories or indexes might be especially useful to the speaker who wants to quote a reputed expert but does not know anything about the expert's credentials.

Reference librarians are specialists in the field of library science. They are often able to suggest additional resources that you might otherwise overlook. A suggestion here: If you plan to use the reference section, visit the library during daytime working hours. A full-time reference librarian is more likely to be on hand and available to help you at that time than in the evenings or on weekends.

GOVERNMENT DOCUMENTS

Government documents can be a rich source of materials. The federal government researches and publishes information on almost every conceivable subject, as well as keeping exhaustive records of almost all official federal proceedings. Documents published by the government are usually housed together in a special area of the library called the government document section.

The most important index of government documents is the *Monthly Catalog of U.S. Government Publications.* Also useful to speakers is the *American Statistics Index,* which indexes government statistical publications exclusively.

The huge mass of government pamphlets, reports, and other publications presents a challenge to both library archivists and to researchers. Your best ally in learning to use this vast wealth of material is a good government documents librarian, who will point out the major features and holdings of his or her unique domain.

In addition to the materials just described, most libraries offer a number of special services. These include interlibrary loans and area library privileges.

The interlibrary loan is one way to obtain materials that you have found listed but are not owned by your library. You might, for example, discover in an article you are reading, a reference to a book that you might also want to read. But your library does not have the book in its collection. An interlibrary loan can locate the book at another library and get it to you, usually within a few days. Some libraries charge a small fee for this service.

Many libraries also have exchange arrangements with libraries of neighboring colleges and universities. You may find that in addition to your own college library, there are two or three others within a fairly convenient radius available for your use.

Generally, the libraries of public colleges and universities are open to all, although you may not be able to check out materials unless you are a student there.

Becoming a well-organized researcher

You have toured the library and have a location guide in hand for future reference. You know the kinds of materials and services your library offers and how to use them. In short, you're ready to begin researching your speech. But unless you approach this next phase of speech preparation carefully and systematically, you may find yourself wasting a good deal of time and energy retracing steps to copy bits of information you forgot the first time. Approaching research logically can make your efforts easier and more efficient. You need to develop a preliminary bibliography, locate and evaluate materials, take notes, and sketch or photocopy possible visual aids.

● DEVELOP A PRELIMINARY BIBLIOGRAPHY

A preliminary bibliography, or list of potentially useful sources, should be your first research goal. The preliminary bibliography may include electronic resources, as well as references to any or all of the print materials we just discussed: books, periodicals, newspapers, reference materials, or government documents. You will probably list more sources than you actually look at or refer to in your speech; at this stage, the bibliography simply serves as a menu of possibilities.

You will have to develop a system for recording your list of sources. If an electronic index is connected to a printer, you may be able to print out the references you discover. If not, or if you are using more traditional resources, you will need to copy down all necessary bibliographical information, which we will discuss shortly. Using three-by-five-inch note cards will give you the greatest flexibility. Later you can omit some of them, add others, write comments on the cards, or alphabetize them much more easily than if you had made a list on a sheet of paper. Let's see what bibliographical information needs to appear on the cards.

For a book, you will need to record the author's name, title of the book, publisher and date of publication, and the library's call number. Figure 7.6 illustrates how to transfer information from an electronic catalog entry to a bibliography card.

You may wish to include in your bibliography a government publication, pamphlet, newsletter, fact sheet, or some other specialized information format. As long as you record the title, author, publisher, date, and page number, you will probably have at hand the information you need to locate any print material. For a government document, you will also need to record the Superintendent of Documents classification number, available in the *Monthly Catalog of U.S. Government Publications*.

The key to making a useful bibliography is to establish a consistent form so that you can find the page number, title, publisher, or some other vital fact about a publication at a glance. Following a consistent form will also help ensure that you do not accidentally leave out a crucial piece of information about the source.

MATERIAL: Book
CALL NUMBER: KF4772 .H343 1993

AUTHOR: Haiman, Franklyn Saul.

TITLE: "Speech acts" and the First Amendment / Franklyn S. Haiman; with a foreword by Abner J. Mikva.

PUBLICATION: Carbondale : Southern Illinois University Press, c1993.
DESCRIPTION: x, 103 p. ; 23 cm.

NOTES: Includes bibliographical references (p. 89–97) and index.

SUBJECT: Freedom of speech--United States.
SUBJECT: Hate speech--United States.

KF4772
.H343
1993
Haiman, Franklyn Saul.
    "Speech Acts" and the
First Amendment
(Carbondale : Southern
Illinois University Press,
    1993.)

FIGURE 7.6
Transferring information from an electronic catalog entry to a bibliography card.

How many sources should you have in a preliminary bibliography for, say, a ten-minute speech? A reasonable number might be ten or twelve that look promising. If you have many more than that, you may feel overwhelmed by material. If you have fewer, you may have too little information. Out of a list of three books, seven articles, and two pamphlets, you might find that your library does not have a couple of them, several others are checked out, and still others are not as useful as you had hoped. If you are left with three or four good sources, you will be doing well.

● LOCATE MATERIALS

Electronic full-text servers will provide you with the actual text of an article. But for all of the other items in your preliminary bibliography, you will need to locate the texts yourself. Let's suppose that you decide to look first for the books you want. In a closed-stack library, you fill out a request card to get the books you're interested in. Take the card to the circulation desk and wait nearby for your books to arrive.

In an open-stack library, you look for books yourself. To find them, you must understand the library's shelving system. Library books are shelved according to either a Library of Congress or a Dewey Decimal call number, depending on the system your particular library uses. Most larger libraries have adopted the Library of Congress system because it represents more subdivisions of subject categories. At any rate, the first letter or number of a call number indicates the general type of book—literature, social science, religion, and so on. Letters or numbers following the initial designation indicate a subcategory. Your location guide will tell you the floor or section of the stacks that houses books carrying the call numbers in which you are interested.

Once you know where to find a book you want, go to that area and check the call number guides on the ends of the bookcases to find exactly where on the shelves your book should be. Like dictionary guide words, the call number guides indicate the call numbers of the first and last book in each bookcase. All books with call numbers between the two guide numbers will be located in that bookcase.

If the title you want is not where it should be and you think it will be an important resource for your speech, you can go to the circulation desk and ask to place a hold on the book. The book will then be reserved for you when it is returned by its current borrower.

Before searching for an article in a periodical, you will need to determine whether your library does in fact subscribe to the periodical you need. You can find out by consulting a periodicals list or checking with a librarian. Once you know what periodicals are available, your library's location guide will tell you where they are housed. Some libraries devote a floor or section just to periodicals. All the bound periodicals will be arranged on shelves there, in alphabetical order. Current issues may be displayed on magazine racks, or they may be located in a reading room or other special area of the library.

Other libraries shelve their periodicals in the stacks, according to subject matter. You look up the title of the periodical in the card catalog, copy the call number, and proceed as if you were looking for a book. As a rule, periodicals cannot be checked out, so you will need to take notes at the library or photocopy the articles you want for further reference.

Newspapers are usually housed together in their own section of the library, although current newspapers, like current magazines, may be in a separate reading room. As mentioned earlier, older issues of newspapers are usually on microfilm. You will need to present the name of the newspaper and the date of the issue you want to the librarian in charge of newspaper microfilms. The librarian will find the film and bring it to you. When you receive the microfilm, you load it into a reader and look for the article you are interested in. Inserting the film into the reader may be a little tricky, so don't hesitate to ask for help from a librarian if you are inexperienced.

The government documents section usually arranges materials according to the Superintendent of Documents classification number, which, as noted earlier, can be found in the *Monthly Catalog of U.S. Government Publications*. Government document sections may have other ways of organizing their information as well, including vertical files of materials. Again, if you do not have much experience using government documents, the librarian in that section can be very helpful.

Reference materials are usually housed together in the reference section of the library and cannot be removed from the area. You will either have to take notes or make photocopies to get the information you want.

● EVALUATE MATERIALS

As you find the materials listed in your preliminary bibliography, think critically about which ones are likely to be useful for your speech. For a book, this may involve glancing over the table of contents; flipping quickly through the book to note any charts, graphs, or other visual materials that might be useful; and perhaps skimming a key chapter or two. Shorter articles, pamphlets, and fact sheets should be skimmed as well. The purpose of this quick preview is to evaluate the usefulness of the sources before you begin reading more closely and taking notes.

You may wish to devise a number or letter system to rank your materials according to their potential usefulness. The ranking code will make it easier to remember and concentrate on the materials that are most likely to yield the information you need. If you find any other useful information in the material you are previewing, note that on your card as well. It may be hard to remember after a hectic weekend which book had those great charts you could reproduce for your speech.

If none of the materials you find look particularly good, you may need to return to the bibliography-building stage to try to locate more potential sources.

Ideas for supporting a speech can pop up in unexpected settings. Even if you're going to spend an hour people-watching in the park, carry your note cards with you. Something you observe may spark a thought worth recording and pursuing later in the library. [Photo: Sylvain Grandadam/ Tony Stone Images]

TAKE NOTES

Read carefully, but selectively. Once you have located, previewed, and ranked materials, you are ready to begin more careful reading and note taking. Start with the sources that you thought would be the most helpful. If you are looking at an article, a pamphlet, an encyclopedia entry, or another kind of short work, you can read the whole thing. But you probably do not have time to read entire books, so read only those chapters or sections that seem particularly relevant and potentially useful to your speech.

Record information. When you find an example, a statistic, an opinion, or other material that might be useful to your speech, write it down, or enter it into a computer file if you are lucky enough to have a portable computer. You can also photocopy the page at the library and take it home to record or highlight the information later. Be sure to add the source information to the photocopy before you leave the library.

Don't create extra work for yourself by scribbling notes on scratch paper, the inside of a book over, a checkbook, or the latest letter from Mom. Instead, keep a speech notebook or computer file, or use note cards that you can easily carry with you. Even if you plan to photocopy or enter most of your information into a computer file, it is a good idea to carry a few cards with you whenever you are working on a speech. You can jot down an idea that comes to mind while you are sipping coffee or note a fact you discover in a magazine article you read in a doctor's office or at a friend's house. You can also use note cards during an interview and even to jot down original ideas or information you already know from firsthand experience. Use the same format as you do for notes you take from printed material. When you return to your desk, store the cards in a file box. Then, when you begin to organize your speech, you can arrange your note cards in the order of your outline, simplifying the integration of your supporting material into your speech.

What should you include in your notes? First, you will want to put only one item of supporting material or one idea on each card or each page of your speech notebook or computer file. If you are photocopying your sources and find a single page with several pieces of supporting material, you may wish to "cut and paste"—literally cut the page apart and paste the separate items onto separate note cards. There is no rule as to how many note cards or pages you will have for each source. You may write only one note card or page from one article you read, five from another, and twenty from a third. The amount of useful supporting material you find will vary widely from source to source.

If you copy a phrase, sentence, or paragraph verbatim from a source, be sure to put quotation marks around it when you write it down or enter it. You may need to know later in the preparation process whether it was a direct quote or a paraphrase.

In addition to copying the information itself, you need to indicate the source from which it came. In Chapter 3 we discussed the ethical importance of crediting sources of ideas and information. If you consistently record your sources when you take notes, you will avoid the possibility of committing unintentional plagiarism later. You may wish to number the entries in your bibliography and then place the source number at the top of each note card or page on which you copy information or quotes from that source. Then you will need to add only the page number of each note. A somewhat more extended option is to use only the author's last name, title, and page number on the note card. Or you may wish to write a complete bibliographical reference on each card or page. This procedure takes more time but ensures that you will have vital reference information immediately at hand as you work on your speech later.

Finally, leave enough space at the top of each note card or page to add a heading, which should summarize the idea expressed in the note. Such headings will make it easier to find a particular bit of material quickly when you are ready to assemble the speech. Figure 7.7 illustrates two note cards—one with a paraphrased note and one with a direct quotation.

● SKETCH OR PHOTOCOPY POSSIBLE VISUAL AIDS

As we noted earlier in this chapter, in addition to discovering verbal supporting material in your sources, you may also find charts, graphs, photographs, or other potentially valuable visual material. You may think you will later be able to remember what visuals were in which sources. But many speakers have experienced frustrating searches for the "perfect" visual aid they remember seeing *somewhere* while they were taking notes for their speech. Even if you are not certain at this point that you will even use visual aids in the speech, sketch or photocopy any good possibilities on note cards, recording source information just as you did for your written materials. Then, when the time comes to consider if and where visual aids might enhance the speech, you will have some readily at hand.

Paraphrased Note

Influence of Audience on Invention

Barrett, Harold. Rhetoric and Civility:
    Human Development, Narcissism, and
    The Good Audience (Albany: SUNY Press,
    1991), p.40.

Audience = most important influence
in invention

Direct Quotation

Hate Speech Protected

Walker, Samuel. Hate Speech: The History
    of an American Controversy (Lincoln:
    University of Nebraska Press, 1994), p.3.

"As a matter of law and national
policy, hate speech is protected by the
First Amendment."

RE CAP

BECOMING A WELL-ORGANIZED RESEARCHER

1. Develop a preliminary bibliography.

2. Locate materials.

3. Evaluate materials.

4. Take notes.

5. Sketch or photocopy possible visual aids.

Summary

Public speakers need to know where and how to find supporting materials to use in their speeches. This chapter discussed five sources of supporting materials: personal knowledge and experience, interviews, mail-order materials, electronic resources, and traditional library resources.

Most speakers can provide some illustrations, explanations, definitions, or other supporting material from their own knowledge and experience. Such material has the advantage of increasing the audience's respect for the speaker's authority.

Interviewing someone who is an expert on the subject of the speech or who has a unique point of view about the subject is a second way to gather supporting materials. Interviewers may take written notes or tape their interviews; later, they can transcribe the information they have gathered onto note cards.

Information about many topics is available by mail from various sources. Directories available in the reference sections of most libraries can suggest names and addresses of government agencies, businesses, and organizations that may publish relevant information. Researchers must allow ample time to order and receive such information.

Both the capacity and availability of electronic resources have increased dramatically over the last few years. The Internet provides a vast collection of resources to anyone with a computer, modem, and account number. In addition, a number of commercial servers provide convenient access to some Internet databases and to specialized services and resources. Electronic indexes can provide a bibliography of sources that a researcher can then explore either electronically or via more traditional research methods.

Even with the advent of electronic resources, most speakers still rely heavily on library materials—books, periodicals, newspapers, reference materials, and government documents—as sources of supporting material. This chapter discussed how to locate these sources in libraries and also suggested several special services that speakers can consider as they search for relevant material to include in their speeches.

Once a speaker knows where to look for materials, he or she should develop a preliminary bibliography of sources, locate those sources, skim and evaluate materials as to their potential value for the speech, take useful notes, including bibliographical information, and sketch or photocopy possible visual aids.

● CRITICAL THINKING QUESTIONS

1. Imagine that you are preparing an informative speech on buying a new computer. Specifically, you want your audience to be able to make informed choices about makes, models, power, speed, and various available options. Explain how you might use each of the five key sources of supporting material in developing this speech.

2. For each of the following topics, list at least two library resources likely to yield relevant information:

The Russian mafia

The weather phenomenon known as El Niño

The use of voucher systems in education

The Devil's Triangle

How HMOs operate

The Battle of San Jacinto

The trial of Julius and Ethel Rosenberg

3. In what reference works would you look first for the following information?

All the vice presidents of the United States

Biographical information on Anne Brontë

The history of opera

The origin of the term *spoonerism*

The ten most popular names for newborn boys in America in 1996

The name of the person who said, "Democracy becomes a government of bullies tempered by editors."

● ETHICAL QUESTIONS

1. As the Internet increases in both scope and popular use, so too, does electronic pornography. According to one source, users accessed *Playboy*'s electronic headquarters nearly five million times in a single week.[6] Legislative attempts to curb the availability of porn offerings have been attacked as a violation of free speech, yet parents feel helpless to control their children's ready access to electronic pornography. What do you see as a viable solution to this problem?

2. While in the library gathering material for a speech on endangered species in your region, you find a wonderful, quotable magazine article from which you take copious notes. However, in your excitement, you neglect to record bibliographical information for this source on your note cards. You discover your omission as you begin composing your speech the night before you must deliver it; you have no time to return to the library. How can you solve your problem in an ethical way?

SUGGESTED ACTIVITIES

Use library resources to discover the answers to the following questions.

1. Does your library have the following periodicals? Indicate whether each is available in bound volumes or on microfilm.

   American Art Journal

   Consumers Research Magazine

   Physics Teacher

   Western Political Quarterly

   Ecological Monographs

2. The front page of the *New York Times,* November 20, 1952, had a story about the financial condition of U.S. colleges. What was the headline of that story? Who wrote the story?

3. What is the primary difference between the *Statistical Abstract of the United States* and the *American Statistics Index?*

4. Copy the entries you find under the heading "Philosophy, Jewish" in the *Education Index* for July 1988–June 1989.

5. Use a quotation dictionary to find a quotation about enthusiasm. Write down the quotation and its source. Which dictionary did you use?

6. Who won the Academy Award for Best Actor in 1962? For what film? Where did you find the information?

7. What is the call number for Herman Melville's *Moby Dick?*

USING TECHNOLOGY AND MEDIA

1. Which of the following computer services does your library offer?

   LEXIS/NEXIS

   Magazine Index

   Newsbank

   Business Index

2. Obtain or create as comprehensive a list as possible of additional electronic databases and indexes to which your library subscribes.

Supporting Your Speech

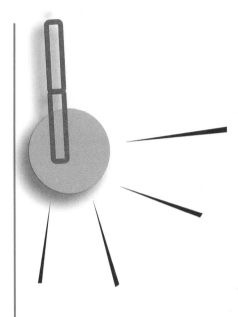

*I use not only all
the brains I have, but
all I can borrow.*
—Woodrow Wilson

OBJECTIVES

**After studying this chapter you
should be able to do the following:**

1. *Explain the importance of supporting
materials to a speech.*

2. *List the six main types of supporting
materials.*

3. *Explain at least one guideline for using
each of the six types of supporting
materials.*

4. *List and explain seven criteria for determining which supporting materials to
use in a speech.*

orty-six-year-old tobacco heir Patrick Reynolds speaks frequently at universities, youth assemblies, and corporate seminars around the country.[1] He has appeared on most of the major network and cable news and talk shows, including "Good Morning, America" and "Oprah." Reynolds' objective is not, as one might suppose, to defend the tobacco industry, but to campaign aggressively *against* it.

Citing information from the American Cancer Society, the American Lung Association, and the federal government, Reynolds points out that one out of every five deaths in the United States is due to smoking, making it the leading killer in this country. He tells his audiences that 60 percent of all smokers start by age fourteen, with 90 percent becoming addicted by the age of nineteen. And then Reynolds adds his own personal, tragic, and ironic illustrations: his father, mother, aunt, and half-brother have all died of smoking-related causes.

Patrick Reynolds has been described as a "compelling" speaker. Why? At least in part, because of the skill with which he combines facts, statistics, and illustrations to capture and maintain the attention of his audiences. Without effective supporting material, a speaker like Reynolds would find his plea dismissed as only so much hot air.

As we saw in the previous chapter, gathering appropriate supporting material is an essential step in the speech preparation process. And once you have gathered a variety of materials, you will need to make decisions about how to use them to best advantage. You will need to look at your speech from your audience's perspective and decide where an explanation might help them understand a point, where statistics might convince them of the significance of a problem, and where an illustration might stir their emotions. In this chapter, we will discuss these and other types of supporting material, and present guidelines for using them effectively.

Illustrations

he young woman walked to the front of the public speaking class and turned to face her classmates. She was about to deliver her final speech of the semester. Her audience prepared to listen politely, but without much enthusiasm, to yet another speech. In a low, soft voice, the speaker began:

Four years ago a little girl was born in a hospital in this city. Her parents' excitement quickly turned to anguish as doctors quietly and sympathetically told them that their baby was suffering from several birth defects, the most severe a heart problem that would result in the baby's death if not repaired immediately. Less critical, but nevertheless disturbing, were a cleft lip and cleft palate that disfigured the baby's face and left her unable to suck normally.

The parents' worry was multiplied by the fact that their medical insurance did not cover newborns. They despaired of being able to take care of their baby. Then an angel appeared—in the form of a representative from the March of Dimes. That organization, she explained, was prepared to help in emergencies just such as theirs. (Speaker holds up an eleven-by-fourteen-inch picture of a beautiful, smiling four-year-old girl.) Thanks to the efforts of the March of Dimes, here is that same little girl today. They truly made her life possible—I know, because she is my little sister.[2]

By this point in the speech, the room was silent. Eyes were tearing and attention was riveted on the speaker, who went on to talk about the work of the March of Dimes and to encourage support of that organization—and to earn an A on her final speech.

The reason for the success of that speech? *Everybody likes to hear a story.* If you remember nothing else from this chapter, remember that one principle. An illustration almost always ensures audience interest.

Now that we recognize the value of illustrations, let's look more closely at different kinds of illustrations. As we examine the examples, we will also look at some guidelines for using them.

● BRIEF ILLUSTRATIONS

Brief illustrations are often no longer than a sentence or two. To drive home a point during her speech on recycling, Sonia offered the following brief illustration:

Our family used to fill two big trash cans every week. Now that we recycle, we barely fill one.

Sometimes a series of brief illustrations can have more impact than either a single illustration or a more detailed extended illustration. In his remarks on the one-year anniversary of the Brady Law, Bill Clinton offered this string of brief illustrations:

In March of 1994, the Brady Law stopped a handgun purchase by a man in Kansas under a restraining order for allegedly stalking his wife and threatening to kill her. In April, the law led to the arrest of a suspected drug dealer in Texas, with standing warrants for possession of cocaine and heroin, with intent to distribute. In November it helped to catch two gang members, both convicted felons, who traveled all the way from California to Nevada to purchase weapons.[3]

The impact of this series of illustrations is greater than the impact of any one of the illustrations by itself. An audience could dismiss a single example as atypical, but three strongly suggest that there is a trend toward success for the Brady Law.

EXTENDED ILLUSTRATIONS

Longer and more detailed than the brief illustration is the extended illustration. The student who told about her baby sister used an extended illustration. It resembles a story. It is more vividly descriptive than a brief illustration, and it has a plot—which includes an opening, complications, a climax, and a resolution.

Glen offered this extended personal illustration in his speech on what he called the "Tragic Trilogy"—gangs, drugs, and guns:

> *I, like most of us, had become desensitized to the violence, the shootings, the mindless, motiveless drive-bys with which we are bombarded every day. At least, I was until that fumble rolled to my feet. It happened when Jason died. He was my friend.*
>
> *We grew up together, played high school football together. He pursued his only dream, which was to play in the NFL. He was a prize recruit, receiving a full scholarship to the University of Houston to play middle linebacker. Halfway through his freshman year, he was playing. He was living his dream.*
>
> *His dream came to an end as he walked down a Houston street wearing a red Kansas City Chief's hat. He was in the wrong part of town, wearing the wrong color, and he was shot and killed from the window of a moving car.*[4]

To use an extended illustration takes more time than to cite a brief example, but longer stories can be more dramatic and emotionally compelling. As we will discuss in Chapter 10, extended illustrations can work well as speech introductions. And Chapter 15 will discuss further the use of extended illustrations in informative speeches.

HYPOTHETICAL ILLUSTRATIONS

Hypothetical illustrations may be either brief or extended. They are different from the illustrations we have discussed so far, because they have not actually occurred. Rather, they are scenarios that *might* happen. Plausible hypothetical illustrations may serve your purpose better than any real examples by enabling your audience to identify with someone in a particular situation. The following hypothetical illustration was used to introduce a speech on protecting the rain forests:

> *Imagine yourself exploring the deep, undiscovered regions of the Amazon jungle. It's hot, and it's wet, and you're tired. You've been there for some time now. You trample through the thick vegetation and you come across an animal you've never ever seen before.*[5]

Notice the word *imagine* in the preceding illustration. The purpose of a hypothetical illustration is not to trick your listeners into believing a bogus story. They should be aware from the beginning that the illustration is hypothetical. In his January 8, 1992, "State of the State" address, California Governor Pete Wilson related several encounters with citizens hard hit by the recession. Unfortunately, he did not make clear that these illustrations were hypothetical, prompting his own press office to spend four days trying to track down the fictitious citizens.

● USING ILLUSTRATIONS EFFECTIVELY

Illustrations are almost guaranteed attention getters, as well as a way to support your statements. But even this excellent form of support can be ineffective if not used to its best advantage. The following suggestions should help you use illustrations more effectively in your speeches.

- *Be certain that your illustrations are directly relevant to the idea or point they are supposed to support.* As obvious as this principle seems, many student speakers, learning of the value of illustrations, go to great lengths to use as many of them as they can in their speeches. They are so eager, in fact, that some of their illustrations have little bearing on the specific point they are trying to make. Their listeners become confused. Never leave your audience in doubt as to why you used a certain illustration. Be sure that illustrations are obviously related to the idea they support.

- *The illustrations you choose should represent a trend.* It is not ethical to find one or two isolated illustrations and use them as though they were typical. If your illustrations are rare instances, you owe it to your listeners to tell them so.

- *Make your illustrations vivid and specific.* You probably know people who cannot tell a joke. They just can't relate a story or deliver a punch line. Or they lack the sense of timing needed to make a joke funny. Unfortunately, some speakers bumble their best illustrations in a similar way. Some years ago, a speech professor was fascinated to discover that one of his students had been on the last voyage of the Italian ship, the ill-fated *Andrea Doria*. Early in the semester, he urged the young man to relate his experience as part of an informative speech on how humans respond to danger. The professor expected a speech with great dramatic impact. Instead, much to his surprise, the student's narrative went something like this: "Well, there was a loud noise and then the sirens went off and we all got in lifeboats and the ship sank."[6] Hardly the stuff great drama is made of! If you have chosen to tell a poignant story, give it enough detail to make it come alive in the minds of your listeners. Paint a mental picture of the people, places, and things involved.

- *Use illustrations with which your listeners can identify.* Just as you want to use illustrations that are typical, so too do you want to use audience-centered illustrations—ones with which the members of your audience can relate.

If, upon hearing your illustration, your listeners mentally shrug and think, "That could never happen to me," the power of your story is considerably lessened. The best illustrations are the ones that your listeners can imagine happening to themselves. Other compelling stories, like the sinking of the *Andrea Doria*, can illustrate such great human drama that everyone listening will be immediately interested and attentive. If you cannot find a plausible example, you may want to invent a hypothetical one, which you can gear specifically to your audience. You can then be sure of its pertinence to your listeners.

■ *Remember that the best illustrations are personal ones.* Speakers gain conviction and enthusiasm when they talk about personal experiences. Patrick Reynolds, for example, with whom we opened this chapter, is a compelling speaker in large part because he shares his own tragic personal experiences that resulted from smoking. Of course, you will not have had personal experience with every topic on which you may speak. In a speech on the conflict between the legislative and executive branches of government, a good illustration might be the working relationship between Newt Gingrich and Bill Clinton. The best illustrations for a speech on American military strategy during the Revolutionary War might come from the letters of George Washington. But if you *have* had personal experience with the subject on which you are speaking, be sure to describe that experience to the audience.

Explanations and descriptions

Probably the most commonly used forms of support are explanations and descriptions. An **explanation** is a statement that makes clear how something is done or why it exists in its present or past form. A **description** tells you what something is like. Descriptions provide the details that allow audience members to develop mental pictures of what their speakers are talking about.

explanation
A statement that makes clear how something is done or why it exists in its present or past form.

description
Identifying facts, information, and details about something.

● EXPLAINING HOW

Heidi had already discussed the significance of the problem of "huffing," or sniffing inhalants. She had traced the history of the problem and had offered a brief illustration of a fifteen-year-old who died from sniffing. Her next step was to explain *how* inhalants act on the body:

> *Yes, inhalants damage the body, but how? Karen Krom from the West Central Region School Psychologists Conference in April stated that inhalants are not water soluble. If they were water soluble, the blood would carry them to the kidneys where they would be prepared for excretion, but they are fat soluble. This causes the huffed product to stay in the brain longer because the brain is mostly composed of fat, resulting in memory loss, loss of motor functions, and numerous neurological effects.[7]*

Speakers who discuss or demonstrate processes of any kind will rely at least in part on explanations of *how* those processes work.

EXPLAINING WHY

Explaining *why* involves giving causes or reasons for a policy, principle, or event. As part of her speech on Gulf War Syndrome, Amy explained three possible causes of it:

> No one is entirely sure what caused Gulf War Syndrome, but three possibilities are often discussed. One theory contained in the November 22, 1993, issue of Time *magazine suggests that American soldiers may have been exposed to chemical or biological weapons—not because Iraq attempted to use them but rather because the American military bombed known chemical weapons sites and then proceeded to send ground troops into those areas. A second theory advanced in the March 7, 1994, issue of the* Nation *indicates that Gulf War Syndrome may be caused by the negative side effects of experimental drugs. These drugs were given without benefit of informed consent to several thousand people who were not monitored for side effects or complications. The final theory is outlined in the June 28, 1993, issue of* Newsweek. *Gulf War Syndrome may be caused by a combination of environmental pollutants including depleted uranium, a by-product of the fuel used in nuclear power plants.*[8]

Often, once the causes or reasons are explained, the speaker can then tailor a solution to those specific causes. A student seeking to reverse a university policy against freshmen having cars on campus can first explain *why* that policy was adopted and then point out *why* it is no longer needed. In short, explaining *why* some condition or event exists provides an analysis that often leads to better solutions.

DESCRIBING

To describe is to produce **word pictures**—detailed sensory information that allows an audience mentally to see, hear, smell, touch, or taste the object of your description. The more senses you appeal to with your word pictures, the better. Good descriptions are vivid, accurate, and specific; they make people, places, and events come alive for the audience. More specific instructions for constructing word pictures are given in Chapter 15.

Description may be used in a brief example, an extended illustration, a hypothetical instance, or by itself. In a speech on the endangered African elephant, a student vividly describes the animal's behavior:

> As the sun rises in Kenya, an elephant crosses the savannah to the edge of a water hole, its trunk raised to catch the first scent of danger. Satisfied that the way is clear, it signals and is joined by a companion. In greeting, the two twist their trunks together, flap their ears and hit tusk against tusk, sending a sharp cracking sound across the hills.[9]

word picture
Detailed description that allows a listener mentally to see, hear, smell, touch, or taste the object of your description.

USING EXPLANATIONS AND DESCRIPTIONS EFFECTIVELY

Perhaps because they are the most commonly used forms of support, explanation and description are also among the most frequently abused. When large sections of a speech contain long, nonspecific explanations, audience eyelids are apt to fall. The following suggestions will help you use explanation and description effectively in your speeches.

■ *Keep your explanations and descriptions brief.* Length alone is often the reason for boredom with many explanations and descriptions. An explanation should supply only enough details for an audience to understand how or why something works or exists. Too many details may make your listeners say your speech was "everything I *never* wanted to know about the subject."

■ *Use language that is as specific and concrete as possible.* Explanations tend to be general and thereby somewhat deadly. Vivid and specific language will bring your explanations alive. Liveliness will help you hold the audience's attention and paint in your listeners' minds the image that you are trying to communicate. Chapter 12 will provide more tips on making your language specific.

■ *Avoid too much explanation and description.* Even brief, specific explanations are boring if they are used alone, without other kinds of support. You will hold your audience's attention more effectively if you alternate explanations and descriptions with other types of supporting material, such as brief examples or statistics.

Definitions

Steve thought and thought but couldn't come up with a good opening for his speech. In desperation, he turned to the dictionary. To introduce his speech on modern legal training in the United States, he decided to define *lawyer*. Much to Steve's disappointment, his introduction only succeeded in putting his 8:00 A.M. class soundly back to sleep. Steve's problem? He had misused a perfectly legitimate form of support. He did not need to define *lawyer* for a college class—or for any class beyond elementary school, for that matter. Steve had resorted to an unnecessary definition as a crutch, and it didn't hold up.

Definitions have two justifiable uses in speeches. First, a speaker should be sure to define any and all specialized, technical, or little-known terms in his or her speech. If Steve had discussed "tort reform," he would have needed to define that phrase early in his speech. Such definitions are usually achieved by *classification,* the kind of definition you would find in a dictionary. At other times, a speaker may define a term by showing how it works or how it is applied in a specific instance—what we call an *operational definition*. Let's look at examples of both types of definitions.

● DEFINITION BY CLASSIFICATION

If you have to explain the meaning of a term, you may use a standard dictionary definition from the *Oxford English Dictionary,* a desktop *Webster's,* or another reputable general dictionary, or you may turn to a specialized dictionary, such as *Black's Law Dictionary*. Any of these references will define words by classification—that is, by first placing a term in the general class, group, or family to which it belongs and then differentiating it from all the other members of that class. A dictionary definition also has authority. This can be an important advantage, especially when you are discussing a controversial subject. If you quote a reputable dictionary, the audience will usually accept without question at least the definition you are using.

In simpler or less controversial instances, it is also possible to define by classification in your own words, such as Shannon did in her speech on the dangers of vaccines: "A vaccine is basically a dead viral cell that is injected into the patient's body."[10] Note how this definition fits our explanation of how to define by classification: generally speaking, a vaccine is a "dead viral cell," but it differs from other dead viruses by being "injected into the patient's body."

OPERATIONAL DEFINITIONS

As noted earlier, there are times when a word or phrase may not be totally unfamiliar to an audience, but you as a speaker may be applying it in a unique or specific way that needs to be clarified. At other times, defining a word by classification may result only in an abstract notion that does not particularly clarify the word's meaning. In such cases, you would be better off to provide a more concrete *operational definition,* explaining how a word or phrase works or what it does. The phrase "child abuse" is defined operationally in the following example:

> *When we hear of child abuse, we think of children physically battered. Yet there is a kind of abuse just as crippling, just as horrifying: emotional abuse. It leaves no scars on the body, but breaks a child's heart and spirit.*[11]

Operational definitions are usually original; they are not found in dictionaries. Although they may lack the credibility of dictionary definitions by classification, they can be specifically tailored to a speech.

USING DEFINITIONS EFFECTIVELY

These suggestions can help you use definitions more effectively in your speeches.

■ *Use a definition only when needed.* As we mentioned, novice speakers too often use a definition as an easy introduction or a time filler. Resist the temptation to provide a definition unless you are using a relatively obscure term or one with several definitions. Unnecessary definitions are boring and, more serious still, insulting to the audience's intelligence.

■ *Be certain that your definition is understandable.* You probably have had the frustrating experience of looking up a word in the dictionary, only to find that the full definition is as confusing as the word itself. The word *dogmatic,* for example, may be defined as "characterized by or given to the use of dogmatism." To find a more satisfactory definition, you have to look down the column until you find *dogmatism.* Your listeners do not have that capability, so make certain that you give them definitions that are immediately and easily understandable—or you will have wasted your time and perhaps even lost your audience.

■ *Be certain that your definition and your use of the term throughout a speech are synonymous.* Even seemingly simple words can create confusion if not defined and used consistently. For example, Roy opened his speech on the potential hazards of abusing nonprescription painkillers by defining *drugs* as nonprescription painkillers. A few minutes later, he confused his audience by using the word *drug* to refer to cocaine. Once he had defined the term, he should have used it only in that context throughout the speech.

Analogies

An **analogy** is a Comparison. Like a definition, it increases understanding; unlike a definition, it deals with relationships and comparisons—the new to the old, the unknown to the known. In her speech to the 1990 graduating class of Wellesley College, Barbara Bush found the concept of color a unifying analogy for the speaker, the occasion, and school tradition:

analogy
A comparison.

> *Now I know your first choice for today was Alice Walker, known for* The Color Purple. *Instead you got me—known for the color of my hair! Of course, Alice Walker's book has a special resonance here. At Wellesley, each class is known by a special color, and for four years the class of '90 has worn the color purple. Today you meet on Severance Green to say goodbye to all that, to begin a new and very personal journey, a search for your own true colors.*[12]

Analogies can help your listeners understand unfamiliar ideas, things, and situations by showing how these matters are similar to something they already know.

There are two types of analogies. A *literal* analogy compares things that are actually similar (two sports, two cities, two events). A *figurative* analogy may take the form of a literary simile or metaphor. It compares things that at first seem to have little in common (the West Wind and revolution)[13] but share some vital feature (a fierce impetus for change).

LITERAL ANALOGIES

Laial opened her speech on violence in the schools by comparing the most troublesome disciplinary problems of 1940 with those of 1990:

> *In 1940, some of the top-rated disciplinary problems faced by public school teachers were:*
>
> *talking out of turn*
>
> *chewing gum in class and*
>
> *running in the halls*
>
> *In 1990, school officials cited a different breed of problems:*
>
> *drug and alcohol abuse*
>
> *suicide and*
>
> *robbery*[14]

Laial's comparison of the disciplinary challenges of the two decades is a literal analogy—a comparison between two similar things. The literal analogy is often employed by people who wish to influence public policy. For example, proponents of trade restrictions argue that since Japan maintains its trade balance through stringent import controls, so should the United States. If Columbia, Missouri, solved both ecological and financial woes by successfully instituting an aluminum can tax, why not try the same approach in litter-plagued, budget-troubled Lawrence, Kansas? The more similarities a policymaker can show between the items being compared, the better his or her chances of being persuasive.

FIGURATIVE ANALOGIES

On a warm July afternoon in 1848, feminist Elizabeth Cady Stanton delivered the keynote address to the first women's rights convention in Seneca Falls, New York. Near the end of her speech, she offered this impassioned analogy:

> *Voices were the visitors and advisers of Joan of Arc. Do not "voices" come to us daily from the haunts of poverty, sorrow, degradation, and despair, already too long unheeded? Now is the time for the women of this country, if they would save our free institutions, to defend the right, to buckle on the armor that can best resist the keenest weapons of the enemy—contempt and ridicule.*[15]

A literal analogy might have compared the status of women in medieval France to that of women in nineteenth-century America. But the figurative analogy Stanton employed compared the voices that moved Joan of Arc to the social causes motivating nineteenth-century women.

Because it does not rely on facts or statistics but rather on imaginative insights, the figurative analogy is not considered a form of "hard" evidence. But because it is creative, it is inherently interesting and should help grab an audience's attention. Speakers often employ figurative analogies in their introductions and conclusions. Eric opened his speech on the National Flood Insurance Program with this figurative analogy between gambling on horse races and gambling with nature:

> *If someone were to lose thousands of dollars gambling on horse races, would you want your tax dollars to bail them out? Probably not. What if they lost those thousands of dollars without having any knowledge they were even gambling? What if I told you sooner or later you might find yourself or someone you know in a similar predicament? Currently in the United States there are millions of people gambling not on horse races, but on Mother Nature by living on flood plains or coasts. When these people lose, they lose big: beach houses, farm houses, and apartment houses go out to sea, down the river, or simply soak up catastrophic damages.*[16]

USING ANALOGIES EFFECTIVELY

These suggestions should help you to use literal and figurative analogies more effectively.

■ *Be certain that the two things you compare in a literal analogy are very similar.* If you base your speech on a literal analogy, it is vital that the two things you compare be very much alike. In an informative speech, a literal analogy that doesn't quite work may hamper rather than help an audience's understanding of the thing or idea you are trying to explain. In a persuasive speech, few things give your adversaries as much joy as being able to point up a major dissimilarity in a literal analogy. For example, the two cities being compared are in actuality more different than alike, the opponent may argue. One is relatively poor; the other is wealthy. One has an elected mayor and a city council; the other has an elected board of commissioners and an appointed city manager. What worked in one will not work in the other. One reason socialized medicine has not been adopted in the United States is that critics of the idea have pointed out how dissimilar the United States is to most of the countries that have adopted such programs. What works in those nations would not work here, they argue. The more alike the two things being compared are, the more likely it is that the analogy will stand up under attack.

■ *The essential similarity between the two objects of a figurative analogy should be readily apparent.* When you use a figurative analogy, it is crucial to make clear the similarity on which it is based. If you do not, your audience will end up wondering what in the world you are talking about. And you will only confuse your listeners further if you try to draw on that same analogy later in your speech. It may be a good idea to try out a figurative analogy on an honest friend before using it during a speech. Then you can be certain that your point is clear.

Statistics

Many of us live in awe of **statistics.** Perhaps nowhere is our respect for statistics so evident—and so exploited—as in advertising. If three out of four doctors surveyed recommend Pain Away aspirin, it must be the best. If Sudsy Soap is 99.9 percent pure (whatever that means), surely it will help our complexions. And if nine out of ten people like Sloppy Catsup in the taste test, we will certainly buy some for this weekend's barbecue. How can the statistics be wrong? Some people, on the other hand, are suspicious of *all* statistics. They have witnessed too many erroneous weather forecasts and election predictions.

In reality, the truth about statistics lies somewhere between unconditional faith in numbers and the wry observation that "there are three kinds of lies: lies, damned lies, and statistics."

■
statistics
Numerical data that summarize facts and examples.

● USING STATISTICS AS SUPPORT

Just as three or four brief examples may be more effective than just one, a statistic that represents hundreds or thousands of individuals may be more persuasive still.

Statistics can help a speaker express the magnitude or seriousness of a situation:

> *The National Center for Health Statistics estimates that by the end of this year 50,000 teenagers, in the U.S. alone, will attempt suicide; at least 5,000 will succeed.*[17]

Or statistics can express the relationship of a part to the whole:

Fully 80 percent of all completed suicides gave advance warnings of their intentions.[18]

Whatever their purpose, statistics are considered by most people to be the ultimate "hard" evidence—firm, convincing fact. The following discussion will help you analyze and use statistics effectively and correctly.

● USING STATISTICS EFFECTIVELY

▪ *Use reliable sources.* It has been said that figures don't lie, but liars figure! And indeed, statistics can be produced to support almost any conclusion desired. Your goal is to cite *reputable, authoritative,* and *unbiased* sources.

The most reputable sources of statistics are usually government agencies, independent survey organizations, scholarly research reports, and such statistical reference works as the *World Almanac* and the *Statistical Abstract of the United States.* Private businesses may also be reputable, but their statistics must be viewed with a bit more caution. The data collection methods of these organizations may be questionable, or their data may be biased by special interests.

Statistical sources should also be authoritative. No source is an authority on everything and thus cannot be credible on all subjects. For example, we expect the U.S. surgeon general's office to gather and release statistics on smokers' risks of developing lung cancer. But we would look askance at statistics from that same office that deal with the numbers of scud missiles deployed by Iraq in 1991 during Operation Desert Storm. The most authoritative sources are also original sources—the data collectors themselves. If you find an interesting statistic in a newspaper or magazine article, look closely to see if a source is cited. If it is, try to find that source and the original reporting of the statistic. Do not just assume that the secondhand account has reported the statistic accurately and fairly. As often as possible, go to the original source.

As well as being reputable and authoritative, sources should be as unbiased as possible. We usually extend to government research and various independent sources of statistics the courtesy of thinking them unbiased. Because they are, for the most part, supposed to be unaffiliated with any special interest, their statistics are presumed to be less biased than those coming from such organizations as the American Tobacco Institute, the AFL-CIO, or the Burger King Corporation. All three organizations have some special interest at stake and are more likely to reflect their biases when gathering and reporting data.

As you evaluate your sources, try to find out how the statistics were gathered. For example, if a statistic relies on a sample, how was the sample taken? A Thursday afternoon telephone poll of twenty registered voters in Brooklyn is not an adequate sample of New York City voters. The sample is too small and too geographically limited. In addition, it excludes anyone without a telephone or anyone unlikely to be at home when the survey was conducted. Sample sizes and survey methods do vary widely, but most well-known polls involve samples of 500 to 2,000 people, selected at random from a larger population. In the speech that opened with the literal analogy between school discipline problems in 1940 and those in 1990, Laial went on to cite the results of a 1993 Harris poll of 2,508 schoolchildren. This is a respectable sample size. Of course, finding out about the statistical methodology may be more difficult than discovering the source of the statistic, but if you can find it, the information will help you to analyze the value of the statistic.

■ *Interpret statistics accurately.* People are often swayed by statistics that sound good but have in fact been misinterpreted. Urging medical schools to add courses in geriatrics (care of the elderly) to their curriculum, a student speaker pointed out such a misinterpretation. She noted:

> *According to a Report on Education and Training in Geriatrics and Geron-tology released in 1984, courses of this type (geriatrics) have more than dou-bled in the last five years. This looks very promising, but what the statistics don't say is that the majority of these courses are electives with shockingly low enrollments.[19]*

As the student went on to explain, doubling the number of geriatric courses does not by itself mean that there is a corresponding increase in the numbers of doctors being trained in that specialized field.

Another student pointed out a misleading interpretation of data regarding research spending for Alzheimer's disease:

> *While federal research spending on Alzheimer's has increased almost tenfold since 1976, only $37.1 million was spent in 1984.[20]*

In this case, a tenfold increase in spending seems significant until one knows the meager total budget. One set of statistics often takes on meaning only in relation to other sets.

A misinterpretation of day care statistics was the focus of a third student's criticism:

> Newsweek *estimates that 2 million children receive formalized day care in the United States today. Unfortunately, this still leaves out the 5 ½ million children left alone, along with countless others under the care of unreliable relatives or neigh-bors . . . . And even if these children were in licensed day care, the facilities for most centers are wholly inadequate.[21]*

The large number of children in formalized day care—two million—would seem to indicate that the problem of child care is under control. However, as the student speaker pointed out, that figure is not a measure of success at all. If anything, it is an indicator of the huge size of the problem.

All three speakers pointed out statistics that did not mean what they seemed to mean. In each of these cases, the speaker's skillful analysis helped listeners understand the true situation. Unfortunately, in other cases, the speaker may be the culprit in mis-interpreting the statistics. Both as a user of statistics in your own speeches and as a consumer of statistics in articles, books, and speeches, you need to be constantly alert to what the statistics actually mean.

■ *Make your statistics understandable and memorable.* You can make your statistics easier to understand and more memorable in several ways. First, you can *compact* a statistic, or express it in limits that are more meaningful or more easily understandable to your audience. Ann Landers printed this letter to help her readers better grasp the enormity of the almost unimaginable sum of a trillion dollars:

> *If you were to count a trillion one-dollar bills, one per second, 24 hours a day, it would take 32 years.*
>
> *Or, to put it differently, it has been figured that with 1 trillion dollars, you could buy a $100,000 house for every family in Kansas, Missouri, Nebraska, Oklahoma, and Iowa.*
>
> *Then you could put a $10,000 car in the garage of each one of those houses. There would be enough left to build 10 million-dollar libraries and 10 million-dollar hospitals for 250 cities in those states. There would be enough left over to build 10 million-dollar schools for 500 communities.*
>
> *And there would still be enough left to put in the bank and, from the interest alone, pay 10,000 nurses and teachers, plus give a $5,000 bonus for every family in those states.*[22]

You might also make your statistics more memorable by *exploding* them. Exploded statistics are created by adding or multiplying related numbers—for example, cost per unit times number of units. Because it is larger, the exploded statistic seems more significant than the original figures from which it was derived. "Doonesbury" cartoonist Garry Trudeau used an exploded statistic to good advantage in this commencement speech at Vassar College:

> *Now, the average comic strip only takes about 10 seconds to digest, but if you read every strip published in the* Washington Post, *as the President of the United States (Ronald Reagan) claims to, it takes roughly 8 minutes a day, which means, a quick computation reveals, that the Leader of the Free World has spent a total of 11 days, 3 hours and 40 minutes of his presidency reading the comics.*[23]

Finally, you can *compare* your statistic with another that heightens its impact. Talking about telephone sales frauds, one student pointed out that such solicitations net over $50 million a year. To heighten the impact of that figure, he went on to say,

> *Comparatively speaking, this amounts to 15 percent of the overall cost of $373 million taken in all robberies in the United States in 1983.*[24]

■ *Round off numbers whenever you can do so without distorting or falsifying the statistic.* It is much easier to grasp and remember "two million" than 2,223,147. Percentages, too, are more easily remembered if they are rounded off. And most people seem to remember percentages even better if they are expressed as fractions. "About 30 percent" is a better way to express "31.69 percent," and "about one third" is even easier to understand and remember.

■ *Use visual aids to present your statistics.* Most audience members have difficulty remembering a barrage of numbers thrown at them during a speech. But if the

	America Online	CompuServe	prodigy	Microsoft
Members	5 million	4.3 million	2 million	850,000
Monthly cost	$9.95 first five hours; $2.95 each additional hour	$9.95 first five hours; $2.95 each additional hour	$9.95 first five hours; $2.95 each additional hour	$4.95 first five hours; $2.50 each additional hour

FIGURE 8.1
Charts can help your audience understand a series of statistics

numbers are placed on a chart or graph in front of your listeners, they can more easily grasp the statistics. Figure 8.1 illustrates how a speaker could lay out a chart of statistics regarding membership and costs of various on-line providers. Using such a chart, you would still need to explain what the numbers mean, but you wouldn't have to recite them. We will discuss visual aids in Chapter 14.

Opinions

Two types of **opinions** may be used as supporting materials in speeches: the testimonies of expert authorities, and quotations from literary works. If the person you quote is a recognized authority in the area of your topic, citing his or her opinion may add credibility to your own arguments. Or the person you quote may have "said it in a nutshell"—phrased an argument or observation clearly, succinctly, and memorably. Let's look at the specific purposes and advantages of both expert testimonies and literary quotations.

opinion
Testimony or quotation that expresses the attitudes, beliefs, or values of someone else.

EXPERT TESTIMONY

Having already presented compelling examples and statistics on the ways in which captive dolphins are endangered, Tara underscored her final point using expert testimony from famed oceanographer Jacques Cousteau:

> *One of the biggest problems of holding a dolphin in captivity has to do with their sonar system. You have heard the beeps and clicking noises that they make. These are methods of communication and sonar. They tell the dolphin where he is and most importantly, where the surface is. In an enclosed area, these noises bounce off of the walls and echo back to the dolphin. Jacques Cousteau, in his 1986 book,* Dolphins, *says that this echo causes the dolphin to "live in a total state of disorientation."*[26]

If your topic is controversial or if it is not currently the object of widespread concern, the testimony of a recognized authority such as Cousteau can add a great deal of weight to your own arguments. Or if your topic requires that you make predictions—thought processes that can be supported only in a marginal way by statistics or examples—the statements of expert authorities may prove to be your most convincing support. Experts may be quoted directly or paraphrased, as long as you are careful not to alter the intent of their remarks.

LITERARY QUOTATIONS

If you want to summarize your ideas or make a point in a memorable way, you may wish to include a literary quotation in your speech. A student speaking on the deterioration of the nation's library holdings quoted Joseph Addison on the significance of books:

> *Books are the legacies left to mankind, delivered down from generation to generation, as presents to the posterity of those yet unborn.*[27]

Addison's words express the speaker's point in a poetic and memorable way. Note too that the quotation is short. Brief, pointed quotations usually have greater audience impact than longer, more rambling ones. As Shakespeare said, "Brevity is the soul of wit" (*Hamlet,* II:2).

Literary quotations have the additional advantage of being easily accessible. A number of quotation dictionaries exist in the reference sections of most libraries. Arranged alphabetically by subject, these compilations are easy to use.

USING OPINIONS EFFECTIVELY

Here are a few suggestions for using opinions effectively in your speeches.

- *Be certain that your authority is an expert in the subject you are discussing.* Unless the authority you are calling on has expertise in the subject on which he or she is expressing an opinion, your quote will have little value. Quoting the opinions of an atomic scientist about works of art, for example, is to do little more than accept the opinions of the average person. Be sure, then, that the sources you quote are not merely recognized authorities but recognized in the particular subject area they are talking about. Advertisements, especially, ignore this rule when they use sports figures to endorse such items as flashlight batteries, breakfast cereals, and cars. Sports figures may indeed be experts on athletic shoes, tennis rackets, or stopwatches, but they lack any specific qualifications to talk about most of the products they endorse.

- *Identify your sources.* Perhaps you chose an eminently qualified authority on your subject. Unless the audience, too, is aware of the qualifications of your authority, they may not grant him or her any credibility. If a student who quotes the director of the Literacy Services of Wisconsin identifies that person only as Vyvyan Harding, no one will recognize the name, let alone acknowledge her authority.

- *Cite unbiased sources.* Just as the most reliable sources of statistics are unbiased, so too are the most reliable sources of opinion. The chairman of General Motors may offer an expert opinion that the Chevrolet Lumina is the best mid-sized car on the market today. His expertise is unquestionable, but his bias is obvious and makes him a less than trustworthy source of opinion on the subject. A better source would be the *Consumer Reports* analyses of the reliability and repair records of midsized cars.

■ *The opinion cited should be representative of prevailing opinion.* Perhaps you have found a bona fide expert who supports your conclusions. Unless his or her opinion is shared by most of the experts in the field, its value is limited. Citing such opinion only leaves your conclusions open to easy rebuttal.

■ *Quote your sources accurately.* If you quote or paraphrase someone, be certain that your quote or paraphrase is accurate and within the context in which the remarks were originally made. Major misunderstandings may result from someone's being quoted inaccurately. "Letters to the Editor" columns in major news publications often include letters from irate readers who have found themselves misquoted in recent articles. The gentleman who wrote the following letter, for example, was upset because a misquoted word implied heartlessness on his part:

You quote me as "defending holiday layoffs at companies already rife with cutback rumors" by saying, "They're going to have a lousy Christmas anyway." . . . All I meant was that the disadvantages of pre- and postholiday cutbacks at the two companies under discussion tended to balance each other out, since the impending layoffs were a known fact and uncertainty regarding one's own job increases stress. I said, "They are going to have a lousy Christmas either way."[28]

■ *Use literary quotations sparingly.* Even though a relevant literary quote may be just right for a speech, use it with caution. Overuse of quotations often bores an audience and causes them to doubt your creativity and research ability and to view you as somewhat pretentious. It is sometimes better not to use any quotation than to use literary quotations out of desperation, just because you can't find anything better. Be sure that you have a valid reason for citing a literary quotation, and then use only one or two at the most in a speech.

RECAP

TYPES OF SUPPORTING MATERIALS FOR A SPEECH

ILLUSTRATIONS	Relevant stories
EXPLANATIONS	Statements that make clear how something is done or why it exists in its present or past form
DESCRIPTIONS	Word pictures
DEFINITIONS	Concise explications of a word or concept
ANALOGIES	Comparisons of one thing to another
STATISTICS	Numbers that summarize data or examples
OPINIONS	Testimony or quotations from someone else

Judicious use of supporting materials is often the key to maintaining your audience's interest and attention. In the following narrative, Henry Sweets, Director of the Mark Twain Boyhood Home and Museum in Hannibal, Missouri, tells of a speaking engagement that challenged him to adapt to an unexpected turn of events by drawing on his understanding of how audiences of different ages respond to different types of supporting materials.

As an expert on Mark Twain, I'm frequently asked to speak to audiences ranging from elementary school children to college students, to civic and church groups. These engagements have taken me all across the Midwest and up and down the East Coast.

When I received a request from a St. Louis area prep school, I was told that the upper-level students were studying Mark Twain, and I was to speak at an assembly preceding a schoolwide party with a Twain theme. For such presentations I usually mix Twain's own stories with biographical details, so for this occasion I mapped out a forty-five-minute speech that was about half stories and half biography. I figured that teenagers would have an appreciation for both of these elements.

When I arrived at the school, however, I soon discovered that I would be stepping onto the stage in front of the entire school, kindergartners included. I had to think quickly to find a way to hold the attention of an audience with such a wide range of ages. Clearly, the biographical material would not go over well for children in the lowest grades. Then I remembered that I had a remarkable resource at my disposal. Mark Twain's stories, I knew, appeal to people of all ages—that's one of the reasons they've remained so popular for such a long time. So, quickly I decided that during most of my allotted time I would play the storyteller and keep the facts to a minimum.

Therefore, aside from explaining who I was, where Hannibal was, and tossing in a few biographical facts before each story, I let Mr. Twain do most of the presenting that day. And together we managed to keep the whole audience tuned in. In fact, following the speech, a reporter for the school newspaper wanted to interview me about the sources for the stories I had told.

Now when I go to a speaking engagement, I always have enough stories and factual information on hand to be prepared for similar spur-of-the-moment demands. I'm prepared to speak anywhere from ten minutes to an hour on several subjects without any notes. I'm always able to adapt to the audience I find, even if it's not the audience I expected.

Selecting the best supporting material

Particularly if you have accumulated a wealth of supporting material, you will need to decide what to use and what to eliminate. In addition to considering the guidelines for using each of the six types of supporting material effectively, use the following criteria to help you make your final decision.

■ *Recency*   Especially if you are searching for illustrations, statistics, or expert testimony, the more recent the supporting material, the better. At one time, daily newspapers yielded the most recent information a researcher was likely to find; today, continuously updated electronic resources can yield materials that are literally only minutes old—vital if you need, for example, stock market figures or currency exchange rates.

■ *Significance*   The larger the numbers you cite, the stronger your illustrations.

The more experts who support your point of view, the more your supporting material will command your audience's attention.

■ *Proximity*   The best supporting material is that which is the most relevant to your listeners, or "closest to home." If an illustration describes an incident that could affect the audience members themselves, that illustration will have far greater impact than one that is more remote.

■ *Concreteness*   Abstract assertions and explanations by themselves will bore an audience. If you need to discuss principles and theories, explain them with concrete examples and statistics.

■ *Variety*   Even if your supporting material meets the first four requirements, if it is all of the same type, your audience may lose interest or question your research. A mix of illustrations, opinions, definitions, and statistics is much more interesting and convincing than the exclusive use of any one type of supporting material.

■ *Humor*   Audiences usually appreciate a touch of humor in an example or opinion. Only if your speech is on a *very* somber and serious topic is humor not appropriate.

■ *Suitability*   Your final decision on whether or not to use a certain piece of supporting material will depend on its suitability to you, your speech, the occasion, and—as we continue to stress throughout the book—your audience. For example, you would probably use more statistics in a speech to a group of scientists than in an after-luncheon talk to the local Rotary Club.

Summary

Interesting, convincing supporting material is essential to a successful speech. You may choose from various types of supporting material, including illustrations, explanations and descriptions, definitions, analogies, statistics, and opinions.

Once you find material to support your ideas, you should follow the suggestions presented in this chapter to gauge the validity and reliability of your evidence. Seven additional criteria—recency, significance, proximity, concreteness, variety, humor, and suitability—can help you choose the most effective support for your speech.

● CRITICAL THINKING QUESTIONS

The following excerpts from student speeches contain various types of supporting material discussed in this chapter. Read each excerpt and then identify the type of supporting material it contains. (Some may contain more than one type. In that case, identify the *primary* type of supporting material contained in the excerpt.)

_____ 1. It was another beautiful day at the amusement park. Warm sunshine, the smell of cotton candy, the kids, and the rides. The roller coaster's whooshing 60-miles-per-hour speed was accompanied by the familiar screams of delight from kids of all ages. Another ride, the comet, was flying gracefully through the heavens when suddenly a chain broke, flinging one of the gondolas 75 feet into the air before it crashed, killing a man and seriously injuring his son.[29]

_____ 2. In 1983 the Consumer Product Safety Commission reported nearly 10,000 hospital emergency rooms treated injuries from amusement rides.[30]

_____ 3. "The bottom line," says former CPSC Chairperson Nancy Steorts, "is that the American consumer has no way of knowing the level of safety on a particular ride at a particular location. In effect, we are forcing the consumer to play amusement ride roulette with his or her family's safety."[31]

_____ 4. Maryland has one of the best safety records in the country, and it is essential that all states adopt and consistently enforce the same thorough regulations.[32]

_____ 5. Do you remember what the weather was like a few months ago? Recall when it was cold; when you would shiver getting out of bed, getting out of the shower, walking outside, when it was most wise to stay inside, wrap yourself in a warm blanket, and turn up the heat.[33]

_____ 6. Imagine you are poor, according to a wide variety of government standards. It is nearly impossible for you to pay your heating bills. So you would be eligible for a portion of the . . . [money] allocated for this program for fiscal year 1985.[34]

_____ 7. leptophos, a chemical pesticide which is not registered with the EPA[35]

● ETHICAL QUESTIONS

1. Go back through the chapter and reread each of the "Using _____ Effectively" guidelines for each type of supporting material. Which of these guidelines for *effective* use of supporting material might also be considered a guideline for *ethical* use of supporting material? Explain your choices.

2. Is it ever ethical to invent supporting material if you have been unable to find what you need for your speech? Explain.

● SUGGESTED ACTIVITIES

1. Read an investigative story in a newspaper or a national news magazine. See how many different types of supporting materials you can identify in the story.

2. From the same story you used for Activity 1, select three different types of supporting materials. Apply to each one the relevant "Using _____ Effectively" suggestions found in this chapter. Determine whether you think the author used each piece of supporting material effectively. If not, which suggestion(s) did he or she not follow?

1. Videotape a minimum of five sixty-second television commercials aired during evening prime time. Create a log such as the one below, in which you briefly identify each commercial and the types of supporting material it incorporates. Place a mark in the appropriate box every time each type of supporting material is used. What was the most frequently used type of supporting material in these five television commercials?

Sample Log

Type(s) of Supporting Material Used						
Brief Description of Commercial	Illustrations	Explanations/ Descriptions	Definitions	Analogies	Statistics	Opinions
1.						
2.						
3.						
4.						
5.						

2. Was your sample size for question 1 large enough to allow you to generalize your findings (that is, to say that _____ is the most frequently used type of supporting material in *all* television advertising)? Explain your answer.

"Star Heart Series #2."
Marilee Whitehouse-Holm/SuperStock

Organizing
Your Speech

*Organized thought is the
basis of organized action.
—Alfred North
Whitehead*

● OUTLINE

Organizing your main points
*Arranging Ideas Chronologically ·
Organizing Ideas Topically · Ordering Ideas
Spatially · Arranging Ideas to Show Cause
and Effect · Organizing Ideas by Problem
and Solution · Acknowledging Cultural
Differences in Organization*

Subdividing your main points

Integrating your supporting materials

Organizing your supporting materials
*Primacy or Recency · Specificity · Complexity
· "Soft" to "Hard" Evidence*

Developing signposts
Transitions · Previews · Summaries

**Developing visual support for
signposts**

Summary

● OBJECTIVES

**After studying this chapter you
should be able to do the following:**

1. *List and describe five patterns for
   organizing the main points of a speech.*

2. *Explain how organizational strategies
   vary according to culture.*

3. *List five patterns of organization
   applicable to subpoints.*

4. *Describe how to integrate supporting
   materials into a speech.*

5. *List and explain four organizational
   strategies specifically adapted to
   supporting materials.*

6. *List and define three types of verbal and
   nonverbal speech signposts.*

7. *Explain how visual aids can supplement
   signposts.*

aria went into the lecture hall feeling exhilarated. After all, Dr. Anderson was a Nobel laureate in literature. He would be teaching and lecturing on campus for at least a year. What an opportunity!

Maria took a seat in the middle of the fourth row, where she had a clear view of the podium. She opened the notebook she had bought just for this lecture series, took out one of the three pens she had brought with her, and waited impatiently for Dr. Anderson's appearance. She didn't have to wait long. Dr. Anderson was greeted by thunderous applause when he walked out onto the stage. Maria was aware of an almost electric sense of expectation among the audience members. Pen poised, she awaited his first words.

Five minutes later, Maria still had her pen poised. He had gotten off to a slow start. Ten minutes later, she laid her pen down and decided to concentrate just on listening. Twenty minutes later, she still had no idea what point Dr. Anderson was trying to make. And by the time the lecture was over, Maria was practically asleep. Disappointed, she gathered her pens and her notebook (which now contained one page of lazy doodles) and promised herself she would skip the remaining lectures in the series.

Dr. Anderson was not a dynamic speaker. But his motivated audience of young would-be authors and admirers might have forgiven that shortcoming. What they were unable to do was to unravel his hour's worth of seemingly pointless rambling—to get some sense of direction or some pattern of ideas from his talk. Dr. Anderson had simply failed to organize his thoughts.

This scenario actually happened. Dr. Anderson (not his real name) disappointed many who had looked forward to his lectures. His inability to organize his ideas made him an ineffectual speaker. You, too, may have had an experience with a teacher who possessed awesome knowledge and ability in his or her field but could not organize his or her thoughts well enough to lecture effectively. No matter how knowledgeable speakers may be, they must organize their ideas in logical patterns to ensure that their audience can follow, understand, and remember what is said. Our diagram of audience-centered communication shows that speeches are organized *for* audiences, with decisions about organization being based in large part on an analysis of the audience.

In the first eight chapters of this book, you learned how to plan and research a speech based on audience needs, interests, and expectations. The planning and research process has taken you through five stages of speech preparation:

- Select and narrow a topic

- Determine your purpose

- Develop your central idea

- Generate main ideas

- Gather supporting material

As the arrows on the model in Figure 9.1 suggest, you may have moved *recursively* through these first stages, returning at times to earlier steps to make changes and revisions based on your consideration of the audience. Now, with the results of your audience-centered planning and researching in hand, it is time to begin to put the speech together—in other words, to organize your ideas and information. The next stage in the audience-centered public speaking process is simply that:

■ Organize your speech

First, we will discuss the patterns of organization commonly used to arrange or structure the main ideas of a speech. Then we will discuss how to organize subpoints and supporting materials. Finally, we will talk about transitions, previews, and summaries. Chapter 10 will discuss introductions and conclusions, and Chapter 11 will deal with outlining, the final two components of the organizational stage of the preparation process.

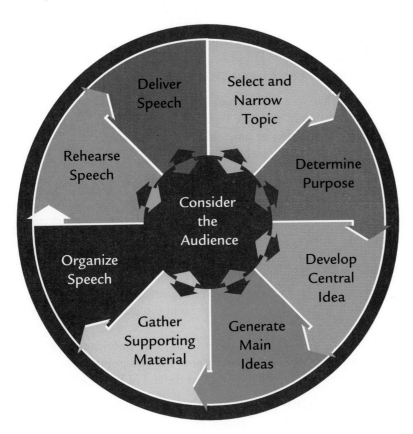

FIGURE 9.1
Organize your speech to help your audience remember your key ideas and to give your speech clarity and structure.

Organizing your main points

n Chapter 6, we discussed how to generate a preliminary "skeleton outline" by determining whether your central idea had *logical divisions,* could be supported by several *reasons,* or could be explained by identifying specific *steps.* The divisions, reasons, or steps became the main points of the body of your speech and the first stage in the organization task highlighted in Figure 9.1.

Now you are ready to consider how best to order your main ideas. You will have to make choices from among five organizational patterns: (1) chronological, (2) topical, (3) spatial, (4) causal, and (5) problem–solution. While organizing your speech, you will also have to make decisions about combining several of these patterns. One additional pattern of organization, the motivated sequence, is actually a variation of the problem–solution pattern. Because it is used almost exclusively in persuasive speeches, a detailed discussion of the motivated sequence will appear in Chapter 17.

ARRANGING IDEAS CHRONOLOGICALLY

If you decide that your central idea could be explained best by a number of steps, you will probably organize those steps chronologically. Chronological organization is organization by time; that is, your steps are ordered according to when each step occurred or should occur. Historical speeches and how-to speeches are the two kinds of speeches usually organized chronologically.

Examples of topics for historical speeches might include the history of the women's movement in the United States, the sequence of events that led to the 1974 resignation of President Richard Nixon, or the development of the modern Olympic Games. You may wish to organize your main points either from earliest to most recent (forward in time) or from recent events back into history (backward in time). The progression you choose depends on your personal preference and on whether you want to emphasize the beginning or the end of the sequence. According to the principle of **recency,** the event discussed *last* is usually the one the audience will remember best.

recency
Placing the most important information last.

In the following speech on the crisis facing the American family farm, the speaker moves forward in time, developing his last point in detail so that it remains fresh in the minds of his audience at the end of his speech.

PURPOSE STATEMENT: At the end of my speech, the audience will be able to explain how the current farm crisis has developed.

CENTRAL IDEA: American family farms are facing a great crisis.

I. The 1970s were flourishing economic times. Interest rates were low, and machinery was relatively inexpensive.

II. In the early 1980s, farmers began to over-produce; at the same time, agricultural exports dropped.

III. By the mid-1980s, crop and land prices fell, while interest rates soared.

IV. In the mid-1990s, farming is experiencing its worst days since the Great Depression.[1]

In another historical speech, this one discussing the factors that led to the literary renaissance in England, the speaker believes the introduction of the printing press to be the most important influence and organizes the speech backward in time.

PURPOSE STATEMENT: At the end of my speech, the audience will be able to list and explain the two forces that prompted the English literary renaissance.

CENTRAL IDEA: Two powerful forces for change led to the English literary renaissance, which began late in the fifteenth century:

I. 1485—Henry VII defeated Richard III at the Battle of Bosworth Field, ascended the throne, and began the Tudor dynasty.

II. 1476—William Caxton brought the printing press to England.

By discussing the printing press last, the speaker gives it the greater emphasis in the speech. Chronological organization, then, refers to either forward or backward progression, depending on which end of a set of events the speaker intends to emphasize. The element common to both movements is that dates and events are discussed in sequence rather than in random order.

How-to explanations usually follow a sequence or series of steps arranged from beginning to end, from the first step to the last—forward in time. A speech explaining how to strip painted furniture might be organized as follows:

PURPOSE STATEMENT: At the end of my speech, the audience will be able to list the four steps involved in stripping old paint from furniture.

CENTRAL IDEA: Stripping old paint from furniture requires four steps:

I. Prepare work area and gather materials.

II. Apply chemical stripper.

III. Remove stripper with scrapers and steel wool.

IV. Clean and sand stripped surfaces.

● ORGANIZING IDEAS TOPICALLY

If your central idea has natural divisions, your speech can often be organized topically. Speeches on such diverse topics as factors to consider when selecting a mountain bike, types of infertility treatments, and the various classes of ham radio licenses all could be organized topically.

Natural divisions are often fairly equal in importance. It may not matter which point is discussed first, second, or third. The order in which you arrange your main points will be a matter of personal preference. At other times, you may wish to emphasize one point more than the others. If so, you will again need to consider the principle of *recency*. As we observed a moment ago, audiences tend to remember best what they hear last. For example, if your speech is on the various living arrangements available to college students, you may decide to discuss living at home, rooming in a dorm, joining a fraternity or sorority, and renting an apartment. If you want your audience of fellow students to consider living at home because of the savings involved, you would probably discuss that possibility as the fourth and last option. Your speech might have the following structure:

PURPOSE STATEMENT: At the end of my speech, the audience will be able to discuss the pros and cons of the four lifestyle options for college students.

CENTRAL IDEA: College students have at least four living arrangements available to them:

    I. Living in a dormitory

    II. Renting an apartment

    III. Joining a fraternity or sorority

    IV. Living at home

By contrast, if your topic is controversial and you know or suspect that your audience will be skeptical or hostile toward your ideas, you may want to organize your main points according to the principle of **primacy,** or putting the most important idea first. That way you do not risk losing or alienating your audience before you can reach your most significant idea. Further, your strongest idea may so influence their attitudes that they will be more receptive to the rest of your speech.

primacy
Placing the most important information first.

PURPOSE STATEMENT: At the end of my speech, the audience will be able to explain the advantages of federal funding for abortions.

CENTRAL IDEA: Federal funding for abortions has three advantages:

    I. It prevents the birth of unwanted, potentially abused children.

    II. It eliminates the monetary barrier to equal rights.

    III. In the long run, it actually saves welfare money.

In this example, the speaker realized that advocacy of federal funding for abortions would be controversial. The three main points of the speech were therefore arranged according to primacy, advancing the most persuasive argument first.

One other set of circumstances may dictate a particular order of the main points in your speech. If your main points range from simple to complicated, it makes sense to arrange them in order of **complexity**, progressing from the simple to the more complex. If, for example, you were to explain to your audience how to compile a family health profile and history, you might begin with the most easily accessible source and proceed to the more involved.

complexity
Arranging ideas from the simple to the more complex.

PURPOSE STATEMENT: At the end of my speech, the audience will be able to compile a family health profile and history.

CENTRAL IDEA: Compiling a family health profile and history can be accomplished with the help of three sources:

    I. Elderly relatives

    II. Old hospital records and death certificates

    III. National heath registries[2]

Teachers from the very early elementary grades on, use order of complexity to organize their courses and individual lessons. The kindergartner is taught to trace circles before learning to print a lowercase *a*. The young piano student practices scales and arpeggios before playing Beethoven sonatas. The college freshman practices writing 500-word essays before attempting a major research paper. Most of the skills you have learned have been taught by order of complexity.

● ORDERING IDEAS SPATIALLY

When you say, "As you enter the room, the table is to your right, the easy chair to your left, and the kitchen door straight ahead," you are organizing your ideas spatially. Spatial organization is arranging items according to their location and direction. It does not usually matter whether the speaker chooses to progress up or down, east or west, front or back, as long as ideas are developed in a logical order. If the speaker skips up, down, over, and back, he or she will only confuse the audience rather than paint a distinct word picture for them.

Speeches on such diverse subjects as the Heard Museum in Phoenix, the travels of Robert Louis Stevenson, and the makeup of an atom, may all be organized spatially. Here is a sample outline for the first of those topics:

PURPOSE STATEMENT: At the end of my speech, the audience will be able to list and describe the four permanent exhibits of the Heard Museum.

CENTRAL IDEA:	The Heard Museum in Phoenix has four large permanent exhibits on Native American anthropology and culture:

    I. Ethnological and historical materials of southwestern Native Americans

    II. Basketry

    III. Jewelry and pottery

    IV Kachina dolls

The organization of this outline is spatial, progressing from the front entrance through the Heard Museum.

● ARRANGING IDEAS TO SHOW CAUSE AND EFFECT

cause and effect
Discussion of a situation and its causes, or of a situation and its effects.

A speech organized to show **cause and effect** may first identify a situation and then seek its causes. Or the speech may present a cause and then describe its effects. What you want the audience to remember will dictate which of these strategies you choose. If you wish to emphasize the causes, you will discuss the effect first and then examine its causes. For example, Laurel Johnson explains the causes of *not* writing wills:

PURPOSE STATEMENT:	At the end of my speech, the audience will be able to explain and refute the reasons people don't write wills.
CENTRAL IDEA:	There are many reasons people don't write wills:

    I. Unwillingness to face death

    II. Fear that writing a will may cause us to die

    III. Ignorance of how to prepare a will[3]

Note that here the effect is presented as the central idea. The causes will be developed as the three main ideas of the speech.

If, by contrast, you wish to emphasize the effects of a situation, you generally present the situation as your central idea and then examine its effects. The following outline of a student speech on adult illiteracy examines the effects of that problem:

PURPOSE STATEMENT:	At the end of my speech, the audience will be able to discuss three effects of adult illiteracy.
CENTRAL IDEA:	Adult illiteracy is a major problem for America today.

    I. High cost to society

    II. Poverty for the illiterates

III. Decline in readership of newspapers and public notices[4]

The causes or effects presented as main points may themselves be organized according to the principles of recency, primacy, or complexity that we discussed earlier in this chapter.

● ORGANIZING IDEAS BY PROBLEM AND SOLUTION

Although you may organize your ideas according to a pattern of cause and effect to discuss how a problem developed or what its results are, if you want to emphasize how best to *solve* the problem, you will probably use a **problem—solution** pattern.

In discussing cause–effect organization, we observed that you may either deal with an effect first and then causes, or with a cause first and then effects. The problem–solution pattern can likewise be used in either order. You may sometimes wish to present a solution or a proposal and then note the problems that it will solve. An example of that approach is this outline for a speech on business-school partnership programs.

problem-solution
Discussion of a problem and its various solutions, or of a solution and the problems it would solve.

PURPOSE STATEMENT: At the end of my speech, the audience will be able to explain how business-school partnership programs can help solve three of the major problems facing our public schools today.

CENTRAL IDEA: Business-school partnership programs can help alleviate many of the problems faced by public schools today:

I. Staffing special programs which schools with budget cuts can no longer afford

II. Offering assistance in understaffed classes in the arts

III. Providing in-kind services and materials

In other instances, you may want to present a problem and then offer several possible solutions. The next outline is an example of this approach.

PURPOSE STATEMENT: At the end of my speech, the audience will be able to list and explain four ways in which the increase in crime on university campuses can be solved.

CENTRAL IDEA: The overwhelming increase in crimes on university campuses can be reduced through implementation of a variety of safety measures:

I. Stricter enforcement of the Student Right to Know and Campus Security Acts

II. Assignment of student identification numbers that are different from students' social security numbers

III. Implementation of improved safety standards for off-campus student housing

IV. Conversion of campus buildings to an integrated security system requiring key cards for admittance[5]

Deciding what to emphasize can help you organize your problem–solution speech, again according to the principles of primacy and recency. If you wish to emphasize problems, you should present the solution first and then discuss the problems as your main ideas. If you want to emphasize the solutions, you should discuss the problem first and then present your solutions.

ACKNOWLEDGING CULTURAL DIFFERENCES IN ORGANIZATION

Although the five patterns just discussed are typical of the way in which speakers in the United States are expected to organize and process information, they are not necessarily typical of all cultures.[6] In fact, each culture teaches its members patterns of thought and organization that are considered appropriate for various occasions and audiences. On the whole, U.S. speakers tend to be more linear and direct than do Semitic, Asian, Romance, or Russian speakers. Semitic speakers support their main points by pursuing tangents that might seem "off-topic" to many U.S. speakers. Asians may only allude to a main point through a circuitous route of illustration and parable. And speakers from Romance and Russian cultures tend to begin with a basic principle and then move to facts and illustrations that only gradually are related to a main point. The models in Figure 9.2 illustrate these culturally diverse patterns of organization.

FIGURE 9.2
Organizational patterns by culture (From D.A. Lieberman, Public Speaking in the Multicultural Environment. *Copyright © 1994. All rights reserved. Reprinted by permission of Allyn & Bacon.)*

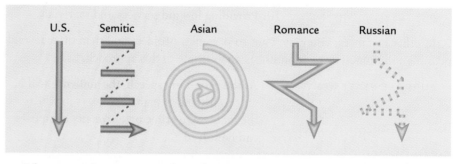

Of course, these are very broad generalizations. As an audience-centered speaker, you should investigate and adapt to the customary organizational strategy of your particular audience. In addition, when you are listening to a speech, recognizing the existence of cultural differences can help you appreciate and understand the organization of a speaker from a culture other than your own.

Pattern	Description
Chronological	Organization by time or sequence
Topical	Organization according to the speaker's discretion, recency, primacy, or complexity
Spatial	Organization according to location or position
Cause—effect	Organization by discussing a situation and its causes, or a situation and its effects
Problem—solution	Discussion of a problem and then various solutions, or of a solution and then the problems it would solve

Subdividing your main points

Once you decide how to organize your main points, you may need to subdivide them. For example, if you give a how-to speech on dog grooming, your first main point may be

I. Gather your supplies.

"Supplies" indicates that you need more than one piece of equipment, so you add subpoints that describe the specific supplies needed:

I. Gather your supplies.

   A. Soft brush

   B. Firm brush

   C. Wide-toothed comb

   D. Fine-toothed comb

   E. Scissors

   F. Spray-on detangler

While your overall organization is chronological, the subpoints in this example are arranged topically. Any of the five organizational patterns that apply to main points can apply to subpoints as well. It is also possible that your main points may be arranged according to one pattern and your subpoints according to another.

Another example of using different patterns to organize main points and subpoints can be found in this speech on "superbugs," antibiotic-resistant bacteria.

PURPOSE STATEMENT:	At the end of my speech, the audience will be able to explain a new offensive strategy for combating the proliferation of dangerous antibiotic-resistant "superbugs."
CENTRAL IDEA:	A new offensive strategy is needed to combat antibiotic-resistant "superbugs."

    I. Antibiotic-resistant forms of infections are proving increasingly deadly.

    II. "Superbugs" are proliferating for several reasons.

    III. Defenses against "superbugs" should and can be strengthened.[7]

The overall design of this speech combines the cause–effect and problem–solution patterns, moving from a discussion of the problem, to an analysis of its causes, to a consideration of potential solutions. But within this pattern are various subpatterns. For example, the subpoints of point I are organized topically:

I. Antibiotic-resistant forms of infections are proving increasingly deadly.

    A. Tuberculosis

    B. Streptococcus

    C. Staphylococcus aureus

The third infection, *staphylococcus aureus,* is the most dangerous strain, with 95% of all staph infections resistant to the antibiotic once used against them. Applying the principle of recency, the speaker opted to discuss this infection last.

Right now, don't worry too much about such outlining details as Roman numerals, letters, and margins. They will be covered in Chapter 11. Your goal at this time is to get your ideas and information on paper. Keep in mind, too, that until you've delivered your speech, none of your decisions are etched in stone. You may need to add, regroup, or eliminate points or subpoints at any stage in the preparation process, as you consider the needs, interests, and expectations of your audience. The Nobel prizewinning author Isaac Bashevis Singer has observed, "The wastebasket is a writer's best friend." He could just as accurately have said "speaker" instead of "writer." Many drafts indicate that you are working and reworking ideas to improve your product and make it the best you can. It does *not* mean that you are a poor writer or speaker.

Integrating your supporting materials

Once you have organized your points and subpoints, you are ready to flesh out the speech by inserting your supporting materials. If you have entered your supporting materials into a word processor, you can, of course, organize and re-organize them at will. If you have written or pasted supporting materials on note cards, the process of incorporating them should also be fairly easy. One good method is to write each main point and subpoint on a separate note card of the same size as the ones on which you recorded your supporting materials. Arrange these note cards in the order in which you have organized your speech. Then go through your supporting-material note cards, one by one, and decide where in the speech you will use each one. The headings you wrote at the top of each card should help in this procedure. Place each supporting-material card behind the appropriate main point or subpoint.

Once your supporting materials are logically placed into your outline, your next goal is to incorporate them smoothly into your speech so as not to interrupt the flow of ideas. Notice how skillfully this goal is met by the speaker in the following example, who is talking about generic drugs:

> *What you are getting when you buy a generic drug is a copy of a copy. It was on this basis that Janny Scott reported in the August 3, 1992, Los Angeles Times, "Just because two drugs are bioequivalent, does not mean they will have the same therapeutic effects because of changes in filler ingredients."*
> *... when a generic company comes along and copies the drug, they substitute anything they wish for the missing listed ingredients to round out the drug. It is the substituting of filler ingredients that causes many generic drugs to take on properties and characteristics that the name brand drug does not possess.[8]*

In this example, the speaker follows four steps in integrating the supporting material into the speech:

1. State the point.

2. Cite the source of the supporting material.

3. Present the supporting material.

4. Explain how the supporting material substantiates or develops the point.

Let's examine briefly each of these steps.

1. *State the point.* This statement should be concise and clear so that the audience can grasp it immediately. In our example, the speaker's point is "What you are getting when you buy a generic drug is a copy of a copy."

2. *Cite the source of the supporting material.* This does not mean that you have to give complete bibliographical information. It is unlikely that your listeners will either remember or copy down the volume number of a periodical. But, as we discussed in Chapter 3 when we talked about using oral citations to

prevent suspicion of plagiarism, you will want to provide the author's name (if available) and the title and date of the publication. The speaker in our example mentions all three. He might also have offered an additional bit of information: the qualifications of the author. Chances are that none of his audience will recognize as an authority the name Janny Scott. If Ms. Scott's credentials are simply that she is the reporter under whose byline the article appears, or if the speaker could not identify her, he might have chosen to omit her name altogether in the oral citations.

3. *Present the supporting material.* State the statistic, opinion, illustration, or other form of supporting material you have chosen to substantiate your idea. In the example, the speaker uses the quote from the *Los Angeles Times* to prove his point.

4. *Explain how the supporting material substantiates or develops the point.* Do not assume that audience members will automatically understand the connection. Our example concludes with an explanation of why a drug that is "a copy of a copy" may not have the same effect as the original product:

> *. . . when a generic company comes along and copies the drug, they substitute anything they wish for the missing listed ingredients to round out the drug. It is the substituting of filler ingredients that causes many generic drugs to take on properties and characteristics that the name brand drug does not possess.*

Your listeners will not remember too many specific facts and statistics after a speech, but they should remember the main points. Connecting ideas and supporting materials makes it more likely that they will.

Organizing your supporting materials

Suppose you have decided what supporting materials to use and pinpointed the spots in your speech that require support. But in support of your second main point you have an illustration, two statistics, and an opinion. In what order should you present these items?

You can sometimes use the five standard organizational patterns to arrange your supporting materials, as well as your main points and subpoints. Illustrations, for instance, may be organized chronologically. In the following excerpt from a speech on Boy Scouting, a student arranges several brief examples in a chronological sequence:

> *Since the days of Teddy Roosevelt [every one] of our nation's Presidents have been involved in Boy Scouting. President John F. Kennedy expressed his sincere belief in Boy Scouting when he said, "In a very real sense, the principles learned and practiced as Boy Scouts add to the strength of America and*

her ideals." President Gerald Ford shared with the American public, "I am the first Eagle Scout to become President, and I thank scouting for the three great principles: Self-Discipline, Teamwork, and Moral Values, which are the basic building blocks of great leadership."[9]

At other times, however, none of the five patterns may seem suited to the supporting materials you have. In those instances, you may need to turn to an organizational strategy more specifically adapted to your supporting materials. These strategies include (1) primacy or recency, (2) specificity, (3) complexity, and (4) "soft" to "hard" evidence.

● PRIMACY OR RECENCY

We have already discussed how the principles of primacy and recency determine whether you may want to put material at the beginning or end of your speech. Those patterns are used so frequently to arrange supporting materials that we mention them again here. Suppose that you have several statistics to support a main point. All are relevant and significant, but one is especially gripping. In his speech on inflated car insurance premiums, Chris opts to present his most dramatic statistic first, to shock audience members to attention:

> *An August, 1993,* Consumer Reports *article illustrates the dollar dilemma car owners have experienced. A Pontiac Firebird Trans Am costs about $18,000 to buy, but if you are a young man in Detroit, you could spend another $10,000 a year just to insure it. A married couple with a teenage son could spend more than $7,500 a year to insure a Honda Accord or a Toyota Corolla in Philadelphia. A retired couple driving a nine-year-old Oldsmobile Delta 88 in San Francisco could pay more than $1,300 a year, though the car itself is worth no more than $3,700.*[10]

Chris applies the principle of primacy to catch the attention of his audience members by presenting his most dramatic statistic first. Another speaker might opt to organize supporting materials according to the principle of recency, saving the most significant support for last. While our example is of statistics, the principles involved can also apply to groups of examples, opinions, or any combination of supporting materials.

Seasoned politicians like Senator Carol Moseley Braun (Democrat, Illinois) reserve speeches based on the primacy principle for their toughest audiences. In a speech to supporters enumerating her accomplishments, Braun would most likely use recency as the organizing principle, citing her latest, most significant achievements last. [Photo: Bob Daemmerich/ Stock Boston]

As we mentioned earlier, only if your topic is extremely controversial and your audience is likely to be neutral or hostile should you present your most powerful supporting material first.

SPECIFICITY

Sometimes your supporting materials will range from very specific examples to more general overviews of a situation. You may either offer your specific information first and end with your general statement, or make the general statement first and support it with specific evidence.

In her speech on drinking water contamination, Athena presents a specific instance first and then moves to a national statistic on the problem:

> . . . *according to the January, 1994, issue of* Discover, *last year in Milwaukee over 370,000 people became ill, 4,000 were hospitalized, and 54 people died from drinking water contaminated by cryptosporidium. Frighteningly, Kathleen Fessler, an epidemiologist for the Milwaukee Health Department, explains, "Some people got sick from a single sip of water at an airport fountain." And at best, the statistics are conservative . . . .The* ABC Evening News *of September 27, 1993, reports that the EPA estimates that on average each year nearly one million people become infected and at least 900 die from poorly purified water.*[11]

COMPLEXITY

We have already discussed moving from the simple to the complex as a way to organize subtopics. The same method of organization may also determine how you order your supporting materials. In many situations, it makes sense to start with the simplest ideas that are easy to understand and work up to more complex ones. When describing how the sun causes skin cancer, the next speaker first explains the simplest effect of sun—rapid aging of the skin—and then goes on to the more complex effect—molecular alteration:

> *First, the sun can dry skin and make it less elastic. The result is premature wrinkles. Second, the sun can actually affect the molecular structure of the body, deranging DNA molecules. An immediate result is damage to our immune system and loss of our ability to fight off disease. A second, potentially more significant effect of such genetic mutation is that it may be passed on to our children and their children.*[12]

"SOFT" TO "HARD" EVIDENCE

Supporting materials can also be arranged from "soft" to "hard." Soft supporting materials are based mainly on opinion or inference. Hypothetical illustrations, explanations and descriptions, definitions, analogies, and opinions are usually considered soft. Hard evidence includes factual examples and statistics. Actually, it would be more accurate to think of soft and hard as two ends of a continuum, with various supporting materials falling somewhere between. The surgeon general's analysis of the AIDS crisis, for example, would be placed nearer the hard end of the continuum than would someone's experience seeing the NAMES Project AIDS Memorial Quilt, even though both are opinions. The surgeon general is a more credible speaker whose analysis is the result of his or her extensive knowledge of and research into the subject.

Soft-to-hard organization of supporting materials relies chiefly on the principle of recency—that the last statement will be remembered best. Notice how the following speaker moves from an illustration to a simple statistic and finally to a more complex statistic, in a speech on sleep deprivation:

> *Dr. James Walsh, Director of the Sleep Disorders and Research Center in St. Louis, reports that the Exxon Valdez oil spill in 1989 occurred when the ship's intoxicated captain left the control of the oil freighter in the hands of the severely fatigued third mate. . . . A March, 1993,* Journal of the American Medical Association *reports that sleepiness is second only to the common cold in the number of complaints we make to our doctors every year. And the San Diego Department of Veterans Affairs Medical Center noted in the June, 1993, study that giving up just three hours of sleep in a single night can reduce our immune system's ability to ward off disease by as much as 50 percent.*[13]

The speaker has arranged her supporting material from soft to hard.

RECAP

ORGANIZING YOUR SUPPORTING MATERIALS

Strategy	Description
Primacy	Most important material first
Recency	Most important material last
Specificity from	From specific information to general overview or general overview to specific information
Complexity	From simple materials to more complex ones
Soft to hard evidence	From opinion or example to fact or statistic

Developing signposts

Once you have arranged your note cards, you have a logically organized, fairly complete outline of your speech. But if you tried to deliver the speech at this point, you would find yourself often groping for some way to get from one point to the next. Your audience might become frustrated or even confused by your hesitations and awkwardness. Your next organizational task is to develop signposts—words and gestures that allow you to move smoothly from one idea to the next throughout your speech, showing relationships between ideas and emphasizing important points. Three types of signposts can serve as glue to hold your speech together: transitions, previews, and summaries.

● TRANSITIONS

Transitions indicate that a speaker has finished an idea and is moving to another. Transitions may be either verbal or nonverbal. Let's consider some examples of each type.

● **VERBAL TRANSITIONS** A speaker can sometimes make a verbal transition simply by repeating a key word from an earlier statement or by using a synonym or a pronoun that refers to an earlier key word or idea. This type of transition is often used to make one sentence flow smoothly into the next (this sentence itself is an example: "This type of transition" refers to the sentence that precedes it). Other verbal transitions are words or phrases that show relationships between ideas. Note the italicized transitional phrases in the following examples:

- *In addition to* transitions, previews and summaries are *also* considered to be signposts.

- *Not only* does plastic packaging use up our scarce resources, it contaminates them *as well*.

- *In other words,* as women's roles have changed, they have *also* contributed to this effect.

- *In summary,* Fanny Brice is probably the best remembered star of Ziegfeld's Follies.

- *Therefore,* I recommend that you sign the grievance petition.

Simple enumeration (*first, second, third*) can also point up relationships between ideas and provide transitions

One type of transitional phrase that can occasionally backfire and do more harm than good is one that signals the end of a speech. *Finally* and *in conclusion* give the audience implicit permission to stop listening, and they often do. If the speech has been too long or has otherwise not gone well, the audience may even audibly express relief. Better strategies for moving into a conclusion include repeating a key word or phrase, using a synonym or pronoun that refers to a previous idea, offering a final summary, or referring to the introduction of the speech. We will discuss the final summary in more detail later in this chapter. Both of the last two strategies will be covered as well in Chapter 10.

Internal previews and summaries, which will be discussed shortly, are yet another way to provide a verbal transition from one point to the next in your speech. They have the additional advantage of summarizing your main ideas, thereby enabling audience members to understand and remember them.

Repetition of key words or ideas, the use of transitional words or phrases, enumeration, and internal previews and summaries all provide verbal transitions from one idea to the next. You may need to experiment with several alternatives before you find one that will give you the smooth transition you seek in a given instance. If none of these alternatives seems to work well, you might consider a nonverbal transition.

RECAP

VERBAL TRANSITIONS

Strategy	Example
Repeating a key word, or using a synonym or pronoun that refers to a key word	*"These problems* cannot be allowed to continue."
Using a transitional word or phrase	*"In addition to* the facts that I've mentioned, we need to consider one additional problem."
Enumerating	*"Second,* there has been a rapid increase in the number of accidents reported."
Using internal summaries and previews	*"Now that we have discussed the problems* caused by illiteracy, *let's look at some of the possible solutions."*

● NONVERBAL TRANSITIONS   Nonverbal transitions can occur in several ways, sometimes alone and sometimes in combination with verbal transitions. A change in facial expression, a pause, an altered vocal pitch or speaking rate, or a movement all may indicate a transition.

For example, a speaker talking about the value of cardiopulmonary resuscitation began his speech with a powerful anecdote of a man suffering a heart attack at a party. No one knew how to help, and the man died. The speaker then looked up from his notes and paused, while maintaining eye contact with his audience. His next words were: "The real tragedy of Bill Jorgen's death was that it should not have happened." His pause, as well as the words that followed, indicated a transition into the body of the speech.

Like this speaker, most good speakers will use a combination of verbal and nonverbal transitions to move from one point to another through their speeches. You will study more about nonverbal communication in Chapter 13.

● PREVIEWS

In Chapter 12, we will discuss the differences between writing and speaking styles. One significant difference which we will note here is that public speaking is more repetitive. Audience-centered speakers need to remember that the members of their audiences, unlike readers, cannot go back to review a missed point. The maxim often quoted by public speaking teachers is "Tell them what you're going to tell them; tell them; then tell them what you've told them." A preview fulfills the first third of that formula: "Tell them what you're going to tell them." As its name indicates, a preview is a statement of what is to come. Previews help to ensure that audience members will first anticipate and later remember the important points of a speech. Like transitions, previews also help to provide coherence.

Two types of previews are usually used in speeches: the preview statement or initial preview, and the internal preview. The preview statement usually occurs at or near the end of the introduction. It is a statement of what the main points of the speech will be. In other words, it is a blueprint of the speech, revealed to the audience for the first time. Speaking on green marketing, Rachel offers this preview statement at the end of her introduction:

> We'll start looking at this murky topic by examining what green marketing is and the problems associated with it. Next, we'll talk about specific cases of deception in environmental advertising. And finally, we'll discuss some solutions that help to separate the trash from the trees.[14]

Rachel's main ideas are clearly defined. Sometimes speakers will enumerate their main points to identify them even more clearly:

> In the next few minutes I'd first like to look at the new problem of farm suicides and how it is sweeping across the wheat and cornfields of America. Secondly, I would like to look at why the problem is occurring and finally, offer solutions for the dislocated farmer, the farmer who has had his farm foreclosed on.[15]

Notice that the first preview statement consists of three sentences; the second consists of two sentences. The word *statement* does not necessarily mean one long, rambling sentence.

In addition to outlining the main points of the speech, a preview statement will usually contain a speaker's central idea. It may even include a modified purpose statement. Melody states her central idea as part of her preview statement:

> Illiteracy among athletes must be stopped. In order to fully grasp the significance of this problem, we will look at the root of it, and then move to (its) effects, and finally, we will look at the solution.[16]

Another speaker includes an overt statement of purpose with her preview statement:

> My purpose today is to convince each of you that having a will is important by discussing why people avoid writing a will; what a will is and why we need one; and finally, how can we obtain a will.[17]

To summarize, the preview statement reveals the main ideas of the speech to the audience for the first time. It may also include the central idea or the speaker's purpose. Finally, the preview statement provides a smooth connection between the introduction and the body of the speech.

In addition to using previews near the beginning of their speeches, speakers also use them at various points throughout. These internal previews introduce and outline ideas that will be developed as the speech progresses. As has been noted, internal previews can serve as transitions. The following speaker, for example, has just discussed what radon gas is and how many people are exposed to it. She then provides this transitional preview into her next point:

> To truly comprehend the significance of the problem, we need an understanding of how radon works.[18]

Her listeners then expect her to discuss how radon works, which, of course, she does. Their anticipation increases the likelihood that they will later remember the information.

Sometimes speakers couch internal previews in the form of questions that they plan to answer. Note how the question in this example provides an internal preview:

> Now that we know about the problem of hotel security and some of its causes and impacts, the question remains, what can we do, as potential travelers and potential victims, to protect ourselves?[19]

Just as anticipating an idea will help audience members remember it, so will mentally answering a question help them plant the answer firmly in their minds.

SUMMARIES

"Tell them what you've told them"—the final portion of the public speaking teacher's advice—justifies the use of summaries. Like previews, summaries provide additional exposure to a speaker's ideas and can help ensure that audience members will grasp and remember them. Most speakers use two types of summaries: the final summary and the internal summary.

A final summary occurs in or just before the end of a speech. Sometimes, as was mentioned earlier, the final summary serves as a transition between the body and the conclusion; at other times, the summary *is* the conclusion.

The final summary is the opposite of the preview statement. The preview statement gives an audience their first exposure to a speaker's main ideas; the final summary gives them their *last* exposure to those ideas. Here is an example of a final summary from a speech on U.S. Customs:

> Today, we have focused on the failing U.S. Customs Service. We have asked several important questions, such as, "Why is Customs having such a hard time doing its job?" and "What can we do to remedy this situation?" When the cause of a serious problem is unknown, the continuation of the dilemma is understandable. However, the cause for the failure of the U.S. Customs Service is known: a lack of personnel. Given that fact and our understanding that Customs is vital to America's interests, it would be foolish not to rectify this situation.[20]

This final summary leaves no doubt as to the important points of the speech. We will discuss the use of final summaries in more detail in Chapter 10.

Pat phrases at the end of your speech may set your audience to daydreaming. Instead, refer back to an important idea or summarize key points to sustain their attention. [Photo: Bob Daemmerich/ Stock Boston]

Internal summaries, as the name suggests, occur within and throughout a speech. They are often used after two or three points have been discussed, to keep those points fresh in the minds of the audience as the speech progresses. Susan uses this internal summary in her speech on the teacher shortage:

> *So let's review for just a moment. One, we are endeavoring to implement educational reforms; but two, we are in the first years of a dramatic increase in enrollment; and three, fewer quality students are opting for education; while four, many good teachers want out of teaching; plus five, large numbers will soon be retiring.[21]*

Like internal previews, internal summaries can help provide transitions. In fact, internal summaries are often used in combination with internal previews to form transitions between major points and ideas. Each of the following examples makes clear what has just been discussed in the speech as well as what will be discussed next:

> *Now that we've seen how radon can get into our homes, let's take a look at some of the effects that it can have on our health once it begins to build.[22]*

> *We have looked at the great need. Americans are dying now. You and I can help.[23]*

> *It seems as though everyone is saying that something should be done about NutraSweet. It should be retested. Well, now that it is here on the market, what can we do to see that it does get investigated further?[24]*

Developing visual support for signposts

Transitions, summaries, and previews are the "glue" that holds a speech together. Such signposts can help you achieve a coherent flow of ideas and help your audience remember those ideas. Unfortunately, however, you cannot guarantee your audience's attentiveness to your signposts. In Chapter 1 we discussed the concept of noise as it affects the public speaking process. It is possible for your listeners to be so distracted by internal or external noise that they fail to hear or process even your most carefully planned verbal signposts.

One way in which you can increase the likelihood of your listeners' attending to your signposting is to prepare and use visual aids to supplement your signposts. For example, you could display on an overhead transparency a bulleted or numbered outline of your main ideas as you initially preview them in your introduction, and again as you summarize them in your conclusion. In Chapter 14 and Appendix D we will discuss guidelines for developing and using such visual aids. Especially if your speech is long or its organization complex, you can help your audience remember your organization if you provide visual support for your signposts.

Summary

In this chapter, we examined the process of organizing your speech in a logical way so that audience members can follow, understand, and remember your ideas. We pointed out early in the chapter that the process of organization is by nature audience-centered. Speeches are organized for audiences, with the speaker keeping in mind at all times the unique needs, interests, and expectations of the particular audience.

A speaker must first consider how best to organize the main points of the speech. We discussed five patterns and noted that any combination of them is possible. The patterns are chronological, topical, spatial, causal, and problem–solution. We also discussed the fact that yet other organizational patterns may be dictated by culture.

Next we talked about subdividing main points and organizing those subpoints so that audience members could most readily grasp, understand, and remember them. The five patterns for organizing main points can apply to subpoints as well.

We then discussed how to integrate supporting materials into a speech. We described a process of putting all main points, subpoints, and supporting materials on note cards and then organizing those cards. We also suggested a strategy of (1) stating the main point, (2) citing the source, (3) presenting the supporting material, and (4) explaining how the supporting material substantiates or develops the point.

The next task we analyzed was the arrangement of supporting materials. We observed that supporting materials may sometimes be organized according to one of the five patterns we discussed but that other organizational strategies might be primacy, recency, specificity, complexity, or soft to hard evidence.

Finally, we discussed the importance of developing various types of signposts that communicate the organization to the audience. Signposts include verbal and nonverbal transitions, previews, and summaries, as well as possible visual aids.

Chapters 10 and 11 will cover the two remaining parts of the organizational task: preparing your introduction and conclusion and outlining the speech.

CRITICAL THINKING QUESTIONS

Here are some examples of central ideas and outlines of main points. Identify the organizational pattern used in each group of main points. If the pattern is topical, do you think the speaker also applied the principle of primacy, recency, or complexity? If so, identify which one.

1. **Purpose Statement:** At the end of my speech, the audience will be able to list and explain the three factors to consider in buying or renting a home.
   Central Idea: The prospective home buyer or renter should consider three factors in selecting a home:

I. Interior decorating

II. Layout

III. Location

2. **Purpose Statement:** At the end of my speech, the audience will be able to explain three theories about what happened to the dinosaurs.
Central Idea: There are at least three distinct theories about what happened to the dinosaurs.

I. A large asteroid hit the earth.

II. There was a gradual climate shift.

III. There was a gradual change in the level of oxygen in the atmosphere.

3. **Purpose Statement:** At the end of my speech, the audience will be able to explain why provision for the mentally ill is inadequate in the United States.
Central Idea: The process of caring for the mentally ill has broken down in the United States.

I. Less than half of the needed number of community-based "halfway houses" exist.

II. Funding is inadequate.

III. Involuntary commitment is rare.[25]

4. **Purpose Statement:** At the end of my speech, the audience will be able to describe the layout and features of the new university multipurpose sports center.

5. **Central Idea:** The new university multipurpose sports center will serve the activity needs of the students.

I. The south wing will house an Olympic-size pool.

II. The center of the building will be a large coliseum.

III. The north wing will include handball and indoor tennis facilities as well as rooms for weight lifting and aerobic workouts.

ETHICAL QUESTIONS

1. On page 200 we suggest that in an oral citation a speaker might omit the name of the author of the supporting material, if the speaker is unable to discover the credentials of that author. Does this seem like an ethical strategy? Why or why not?

2. Several times in this chapter we discuss the principles of primacy and recency. If a speaker has a statistic that offers overwhelming evidence of the severity of a given problem, is it ethical for the speaker to save that statistic for last, or should the speaker reveal immediately to the audience how severe the problem really is? In other words, is there an ethical distinction between primacy and recency? Discuss your answer.

● SUGGESTED ACTIVITIES

1. Read one of the speeches in Appendix C. Answer the following questions:

   a. According to what pattern are the main points organized?

   b. Identify any subpoints of the main points, and describe how they are organized.

   c. Look at the supporting materials. If two or more are used to support any one main point or subpoint, what strategy do you think the speaker used to organize them?

   d. Is there a preview statement? If so, what is it?

   e. Is there a final summary? If so, what is it?

   f. Find at least one example of each of the following:

   A transition word or phrase

   An internal preview

   An internal summary

2. Select three topics from the following list. For each topic, write a purpose statement, a central idea, and two to five main points. Identify the organizational strategy you would use to organize those main points.

   Protecting endangered species

   Responsible pet ownership

   Three well-known fad diets

   Solving the problem of world hunger

   The electoral college

   History of the Panama Canal

   The funding of health care research

High adventure in our national parks

Being an organ donor

History of motion pictures

How to grow a successful vegetable garden

Great blues guitarists

USING TECHNOLOGY AND MEDIA

1. Watch a single report on one of the television prime-time news magazine programs, such as *20/20* or *Primetime Live*. Take notes on the types of supporting materials offered during the segment. Then identify the strategy or strategies by which those supporting materials are organized.

2. If you have access to a computer lab, find out whether any of the available software has a special outlining feature. If so, use it to prepare an outline for a speech topic you chose for Suggested Activity 2. Then evaluate the software. Did it make outlining easier or harder for you than doing it on your own?

"Woman Seated at a Table by a Window."
Carl Holsoe/Christies's, London/SuperStock

Introducing and Concluding Your Speech

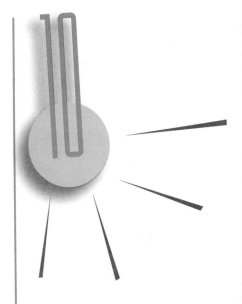

The average man thinks about what he has said; the above average man about what he is going to say.
—Anonymous

● OBJECTIVES

After studying this chapter you should be able to do the following:

1. Discuss why introductions and conclusions are important to the overall success of a speech.

2. Explain the five purposes of the introduction to a speech.

3. List and describe ten methods of introducing a speech.

4. Explain the four purposes of the conclusion to a speech.

5. List and describe three methods of concluding a speech.

ome TV advertisers have less than fifteen seconds to present their messages. Yet the opening of any commercial is carefully crafted to get your attention. That same brief commercial message usually ends with a summary and perhaps a phone number or address of a place where you can purchase what is being sold. The person who designed that message knows something that you should know, too: the introduction and conclusion of a message are vital to achieving your communication goal. Just as a trumpet fanfare signals the appearance of someone important, your speech introduction signals the arrival of your message to your listeners. And just as most fireworks displays end with a grand finale, your speech should end, not necessarily with fireworks, but with a conclusion that signals the end of your well-crafted message.

While making up only about 20 percent of the total speech you deliver, the introduction and conclusion provide audiences with important first and final impressions of speaker and speech. These elements are too important to the overall success of your speech to be left to chance or last-minute preparation.

Many speakers think the first task in preparing a speech is to start drafting your introduction. Actually, the introduction is more often the last part of the speech you develop. One of the key purposes of your introduction is to provide an overview of your message. How can you do that until you know what the message is going to be? In Chapter 9, we discussed patterns and strategies for organizing the body of your speech, and we explained how to use appropriate transitions, previews, and summaries. Those tasks should precede the crafting of both the introduction and conclusion to your speech. In this chapter, we will further our exploration of organization with a discussion of introductions and conclusions.

Purposes of introductions

Within a few seconds of meeting a person, you form a first impression that is often quite lasting. So, too, do you form a first impression of a speaker and his or her message within the opening seconds of a speech. The introduction may convince you to listen carefully to a credible speaker presenting a well-prepared speech, or it may send the message that the speaker is ill prepared and the message not worth your time. In a ten-minute speech, the introduction will probably last no more than a minute and a half. To suggest that the introduction needs to be well planned is an understatement, considering how important and yet how brief it is.

As a speaker, your task is to ensure that the message you send in your introduction convinces your audience to listen to you. Specifically, a good introduction serves five important functions:

- Get the audience's attention.

- Introduce the subject.

- Give the audience a reason to listen.

- Establish your credibility.

- Preview your main ideas.

Let's examine each of these five functions in more detail.

GET THE AUDIENCE'S ATTENTION

You are exposed to countless verbal messages every day, both from the media and from other people. For you to focus on any one message, it must have something to grab your attention and put you in a receptive mood. A key purpose of the introduction is to gain favorable attention for your speech. Because listeners form their first impressions of the speech quickly, if the introduction does not capture their attention and cast the speech in a favorable light, the rest of the speech may be wasted on them. The speaker who walks to the podium and drones, "Today I am going to talk to you about . . . " has probably lost most of the audience in those first few boring words. Some of the ways to gain the attention of audiences will be discussed later in this chapter. Most people can be "hooked" by a good illustration, humor, a startling fact or statistic, or one of the other methods we will discuss.

Why do we emphasize *favorable* attention? For one very good reason. It is possible to grab an audience's attention but in so doing to alienate them or disgust them so that they become irritated instead of interested in what you have to say. For example, a student began an antiabortion speech with a graphic description of the abortion process. She caught her audience's attention but made them so uncomfortable that they could hardly concentrate on the rest of her speech.

Another student gave a speech on the importance of donating blood. Without a word, he began by savagely slashing his wrists in front of his stunned audience. As blood spurted, audience members screamed, and one fainted. It was real blood, but not his. The speaker worked at a blood bank. Using the bank's blood, he had placed a device under each arm that allowed him to pump out the blood as if from his wrists. He certainly grabbed his audience's attention! But they never heard his message. The shock and disgust of seeing such a display made that impossible. He did not gain favorable attention.

The moral of our two tales: By all means, be creative in your speech introductions. But also use common sense in deciding how best to gain the favorable attention of your audience. Alienating them is even worse than boring them.

INTRODUCE THE SUBJECT

Perhaps the most obvious purpose of an introduction is to introduce the subject of a speech. Within a few seconds after you begin your speech, the audience should have a pretty good idea of what you are going to talk about. Do not get so carried away with jokes or illustrations that you forget this basic purpose. Few things will frustrate your audience more than having to wait through half your speech before figuring out what you are talking about! The best way to ensure that your introduction does indeed introduce the subject of your speech is to include a statement of your central idea in the introduction.

In the introduction to a speech on geriatric medicine, Kathryn left little room for doubt about the subject of her speech: After opening the speech with an illustration about her grandfather's poor health care at the hands of a doctor who misdiagnosed the disease, Kathryn said that doctors

> *have simply not been provided with proper medical training in the care of the elderly.*[1]

In a speech on the importance of listening, Amy offered this statement of her central idea near the end of her introduction:

> *Listening is the interpretation and evaluation of what we hear. Today I'd like to talk about listening.*[2]

In both cases, the speakers made certain that the subjects of their speeches were announced in the introductions.

GIVE THE AUDIENCE A REASON TO LISTEN

Even after you have captured the attention of your audience and introduced the topic, you have to give the audience some reason to want to listen to the rest of your speech. An unmotivated listener quickly tunes out. You can help establish listening motivation by showing the members of your audience how the topic affects them directly.

In Chapter 8, we presented seven criteria for determining the effectiveness of your supporting material. One of those criteria was *proximity,* the idea that listeners will be most attentive to information that affects them directly. Just as proximity is important to supporting materials, it is also important to speech introductions. "This concerns *me*" is a powerful reason to listen. Notice how Mary involves her audience with the problem of toxic silver dental fillings:

> *It's estimated that 90 percent of the American population has silver fillings. That's some 225 million Americans with mercury in their teeth. Because this number is so large and many of us are counted in this number, I'd like to tell you about mercury, the toxic poison, and show you why we must escape its contamination.*[3]

The significance of the statistics is attention-getting, but the speaker motivates her audience to listen further by pointing out their personal susceptibility to the potential dangers.

Andy also uses proximity to motivate his audience to listen, in his introduction to a speech on antibiotic-resistant "superbugs":

> *It always happens when you're the busiest. Your body gives out on you. Like any forensicator [a student involved in competitive intercollegiate speech events], you don't have time to get sick. So you see a doctor, grab an antibiotic, and feel better. Problem solved . . . or created.*[4]

While Mary begins with a statistic and then points out that individual audience members are included in that number, Andy begins by constructing a hypothetical example that could happen to any member of his audience. It does not matter so much *how* or *when* you demonstrate proximity, as that you *do* at some point establish that your topic is of vital personal concern to your listeners.

● ESTABLISH YOUR CREDIBILITY

Credibility is the attitude listeners hold toward a speaker. A credible speaker is one whom the audience judges to be a believable authority and a competent speaker. A credible speaker is also someone the audience believes in and can trust. Even though we will discuss credibility in greater detail in Chapter 17, we stress here that as you begin your speech, you should be mindful of your listeners' attitudes toward you. When thinking of your listeners, ask yourself, "Why should they listen to me? What is my background with respect to the topic? Am I personally committed to the issues about which I am going to speak?"

Many people have so much admiration for a political or religious figure, an athlete, or an entertainer that they sacrifice time, energy, and money to hear these celebrities speak. When Pope John Paul II travels abroad, people travel great distances and stand for hours in extreme heat or cold to celebrate Mass with him.

Nelson Mandela, speaking here to a capacity crowd in Los Angeles, earned his credibility through a lifetime of unwavering courage and leadership. When you speak, you will need to establish your own credibility by being well-prepared, exuding confidence, and telling listeners why you're qualified to speak on your topic. [Photo: Alan Levenson/Tony Stone Images]

But most people cannot take their own credibility for granted when they speak. If you can establish your credibility early in a speech, it will help motivate your audience to listen. One way to build credibility in the introduction is to be well prepared and to appear confident. Speaking fluently while maintaining eye contact does much to convey a sense of confidence. If you seem to have confidence in yourself, your audience will have confidence in you.

A second way to establish credibility is to tell the audience of your personal experience with your topic. If you are an expert on your topic, don't let modesty keep you from letting the audience know. Instead of considering you as boastful, most audience members will listen to you with respect. Notice how Loren opened his speech on Boy Scouting:

> *I come before you today representing one out of 15 million people in over 67 countries throughout the world who belong to a very special organization, an organization designed to help prepare youth for their future life. The organization is Boy Scouting, the world's best known youth movement.*[5]

Learning that the speaker was someone who was actively involved in scouting undoubtedly helped motivate the audience to listen to his point of view.

● PREVIEW YOUR MAIN IDEAS

A final purpose of the introduction is to preview the main ideas of your speech. As you saw in Chapter 9, the preview statement usually comes near the end of the introduction, often immediately following a statement of the central idea. The preview statement "tells them what you're going to tell them." It allows your listeners to anticipate the main ideas of your speech, which in turn helps ensure that they will remember those ideas after the speech.

As also noted in Chapter 9, a preview statement is one of several organizational strategies called signposts. Just as signs posted along a highway tell you what is coming up, a signpost in your speech tells the listeners what to expect by enumerating the ideas or points that you plan to present. If, for example, you were giving a speech about audience analysis, you could say,

> *Today I'd like to cover the three approaches to analyzing an audience for a speech. First, I'll discuss how to gather demographic information. Second, I will teach you how to conduct an attitudinal analysis of your listeners. And finally, I will review principles of environmental analysis.*[6]

Identifying your main ideas will help organize the message and enhance listeners' learning.

The introduction to your speech, then, should get your audience's attention, introduce the subject, give the audience a reason to listen, establish your credibility, and preview your main ideas. All this—and brevity too—may seem impossible to achieve. But it isn't!

PURPOSES OF YOUR INTRODUCTION

PURPOSE	METHOD
Get the audience's attention.	Use an illustration, a startling fact or statistic, quotation, humor, a question, a reference to a historical event, a reference to a recent event, a personal reference, a reference to the occasion, a reference to a preceding speech.
Introduce the subject.	Present your central idea to your audience.
Give the audience a reason to listen.	Tell your listeners how the topic directly affects them.
Establish your credibility.	Offer your credentials. Tell your listeners about your commitment to your topic.
Preview your main ideas.	Tell your audience what you are going to tell them.

Effective introductions

With a little practice, you will be able to write satisfactory central ideas and preview statements. It may be more difficult to gain your audience's attention and give them a reason to listen to you. Fortunately, there are several methods for developing effective introductions to your speeches. Not every method is appropriate for every speech, but chances are that you can discover among these alternatives at least one type of introduction to fit the topic and purpose of your speech, whatever they might be.

Specifically, we will discuss ten ways of introducing a speech:

- Illustrations
- Startling facts or statistics
- Quotations
- Humor
- Questions
- References to historical events
- References to recent events
- Personal references
- References to the occasion
- References to preceding speeches

ILLUSTRATIONS

Not surprisingly, since it is the most inherently interesting type of supporting material, an illustration can provide the basis for an effective speech introduction. In fact, if you have an especially compelling anecdote that you had planned to use in the body of the speech, you might do well to use it instead in your introduction. A relevant story often effectively introduces a subject. An interesting illustration invariably gains an audience's attention. And a personal anecdote can help establish your credibility.

Patricia opened her speech on playground hazards with this personal illustration:

> *I can remember as a child the excitement of swinging high on the swings, walking on the teeter totter to balance it, and playing squeeze the lemon on the slide at recess. I can also remember breaking my nose because I was standing too close to the teeter totter, falling off the slide to lie unconscious for half an hour, and spraining my neck after falling off the monkey bars. All of these incidents left me a little bruised and feeling stupid for being such a klutz, but nothing a trip to the hospital couldn't fix. Unfortunately, not all children are as lucky as I was.[7]*

Patricia's personal illustration establishes her involvement with the topic and reminds audience members of their own "near-misses" on playgrounds. In short, it effectively opens her speech and gains the attention of her audience.

Not all topics lend themselves to personal illustrations, but illustrations drawn from secondary sources can also be used effectively. Former First Lady Barbara Bush opened her 1990 Wellesley College commencement address with this secondary illustration:

> *Wellesley, you see, is not just a place, but an idea, an experiment in excellence in which diversity is not just tolerated, but is embraced.*
>
> *The essence of this spirit was captured in a moving speech about tolerance given last year by the student body president of one of your sister colleges. She related the story by Robert Fulghum about a young pastor who, finding himself in charge of some very energetic children, hit upon a game called "Giants, Wizards, and Dwarfs." "You have to decide now," the pastor instructed the children, "Which you are . . . a giant, a wizard, or a dwarf?" At that, a small girl tugging on his pants leg asked, "But where do the mermaids stand?"*
>
> *The pastor told her there are no mermaids. "Oh yes there are," she said. "I am a mermaid."*
>
> *This little girl knew what she was and she was not about to give up on either her identity or the game. She intended to take her place wherever mermaids fit into the scheme of things.[8]*

Mrs. Bush's story both introduced the theme of her address and captured the attention of her audience.

STARTLING FACTS OR STATISTICS

A second method of introducing a speech is the use of a startling fact or statistic. Startling an audience with the extent of a situation or problem will invariably catch their attention as well as motivate them to listen further to what you have to say.

This speech opening must have caused the audience to sit up and take notice:

> *It has claimed more lives than the Gulf, Korean, and Vietnam wars combined. According to a 1994 Centers for Disease Control Report, AIDS has become the third leading cause of death for Americans between the ages of 25 and 44, and the sixth leading killer of 15-to 24-year-olds.[9]*

The statistics on AIDS are indeed startling. In addition, the speaker employs the technique of suspense, not naming the killer until after she relays the shocking fact of the first sentence. Almost in spite of themselves, audience members will mentally guess the cause of such an alarming fact. And because they will invest mental energy in thinking about the answer, the speaker will have their attention.

Like the methods of organization discussed in Chapter 9, the methods of introduction are not mutually exclusive. Very often, two or three are effectively combined in a single introduction. For example, the following speaker combined illustrations and startling statistics for this effective introduction to a speech on geriatric medicine:

> *Although my grandfather continued to struggle against dying, he did not go gentle into that good night. He died in an Arkansas hospital of what doctors officially termed as "old age."*
>
> *My grandfather was a member of one of the fastest growing groups in America: those over 65. Between the years 1990 and 1980, the number of people over 65 has tripled. By the year 2040, most of us will not be short of companions our age, because by then the elderly population will be at least 45 percent.[10]*

QUOTATIONS

Using an appropriate quotation to introduce a speech is a common practice. Often a past writer or speaker has expressed an opinion on your topic that is more authoritative, comprehensive, or better stated than what you can say. Kimberly opened her speech on accident prevention with a quotation from newspaper columnist and poet Don Marquis:

> *Now and then*
> *There is a person born*
> *Who is so unlucky*
> *That he runs into accidents*
> *Which started out to happen*
> *To somebody else[11]*

A different kind of quotation, this one from an expert, was chosen by another speaker to introduce the topic of the disappearance of childhood in America:

"As a distinctive childhood culture wastes away, we watch with fascination and dismay." This insight of Neil Postman, author of DISAPPEARANCE OF CHILDHOOD, *raised a poignant point. Childhood in America is vanishing.*[12]

Because the expert was not widely recognized, the speaker included a brief statement of his qualifications. This authority "said it in a nutshell"—expressed in concise language the central idea of the speech.

Although a quote can effectively introduce a speech, do not fall into the lazy habit of turning to a collection of quotations every time you need an introduction. There are so many other interesting, and sometimes better, ways to introduce a speech that quotes should be used only if they are extremely interesting, compelling, or very much to the point.

 ● HUMOR

Humor, handled well, can be a wonderful attention getter. It can help relax your audience and win their good will for the rest of the speech. The following anecdote, for example, could be used to open a speech on the importance of adequate life insurance:

"If you were to lose your husband," the insurance salesman asked the young wife, "what would you get?"

She thought for a moment, then ventured: "A parakeet."[13]

Another speaker used humor to express appreciation for being invited to speak to a group by beginning his speech with this story:

Three corporate executives were trying to define the word fame.

One said, "Fame is getting invited to the White House to see the President."

The second one said, "Fame is being invited to the White House and while you are visiting, the phone rings and he doesn't answer it."

The third executive said, "You're both wrong. Fame is being invited to the White House to visit with the President when his Hot Line rings. He answers it, listens a minute, and then says, 'Here, it's for you!' "

Being asked to speak today is like being in the White House and the call's for me.[14]

Humor need not always be the stuff of Donald O'Connor's classic "Make 'Em Laugh" routine or the Three Stooges' slapstick comedy. It does not even have to be a joke. It may take more subtle forms, such as irony or incredulity. When General Douglas MacArthur, an honor graduate of the United States Military Academy at West Point, returned to West Point in 1962 to receive the Sylvanus Thayer award for service to his nation, he delivered his now-famous "Farewell to the Cadets." He opened that speech with this humorous illustration:

As I was leaving the hotel this morning, a doorman asked me, "Where are you bound for, General?" And when I replied, "West Point," he remarked, "Beautiful place. Have you ever been there before?"[15]

MacArthur's brief illustration caught the audience's attention and made them laugh—in short, it was an effective way to open the speech.

Certain subjects of course do not lend themselves to a humorous introduction. It would hardly be appropriate to open a speech on teenage suicide, for example, with a funny story. Nor would it be appropriate to use humor in a talk on certain serious crimes. Used with discretion, however, humor can provide a lively, interesting, and appropriate introduction for many speeches.

● QUESTIONS

When using a question to open a speech, you will generally use a *rhetorical* question, the kind you don't expect an answer to. Nevertheless, your listeners will probably try to answer mentally. Questions prompt the audience's mental participation in your introduction. Such participation is an excellent way to ensure their continuing attention to your speech.

Lisa opened her speech on geographical illiteracy with a series of questions:

Can you name the states that border the Pacific Ocean? What country lies between Panama and Nicaragua? Can you name the Great Lakes?[16]

And Richard opened his speech on teenage suicide with this simple question: "Have you ever been alone in the dark?"[17]

To turn questions into an effective introduction, the speaker must do more than just think of good questions to ask. He or she must also deliver the questions effectively. Effective delivery includes pausing briefly after each question, so that audience members have time to try to formulate a mental answer. After all, the main advantage of questions as an introductory technique is to "hook" the audience by getting them to engage in a mental dialogue with you. The speaker who delivers questions most effectively is also one who may look down at notes while he or she asks the question, but who then reestablishes eye contact with listeners. As we will discuss in more detail in Chapter 13, eye contact signals that the communication channel is open. Establishing eye contact with your audience following a question provides additional motivation for them to think of an answer.

Questions are commonly combined with another method of introduction. For example, Beth opened her speech on the inadequacies of the current U.S. driver's license renewal system with three startling brief examples followed by a question:

In 31 states a blind man can be licensed to drive. In 5 states, just send in your check and they will send back your renewed license, no questions asked.

In 1916 my grandfather got his license for the first time. No exam was required; no exam has been required since. Ever wonder why our highways seem a bit unsafe today?[18]

Either by themselves or in tandem with another method of introduction, questions can provide effective openings for speeches.

REFERENCES TO HISTORICAL EVENTS

What American is not familiar with the opening line of Lincoln's classic Gettysburg Address: "Four score and seven years ago, our fathers brought forth on this continent a new nation, conceived in liberty, and dedicated to the proposition that all men are created equal"? Note that this opening sentence refers to the historical context of the speech. You, too, may find a way to begin a speech by making a reference to a historical event.

Every day is the anniversary of something. Perhaps you could begin a speech by drawing a relationship between a historical event that happened on this day and your speech objective. How do you discover anniversaries of historical events? You could consult Jane M. Hatch's *The American Book of Days;* this resource lists key events for every day of the year and also provides details of what occurred.[19] Another source, *Anniversaries and Holidays,* by Ruth W. Gregory, identifies and describes key holidays.[20] Finally, many newspapers have a section that identifies key events that occurred on "this day in history." If, for example, you know you are going to be speaking on April 6, you could consult a copy of a newspaper from April 6 of last year to discover the key commemorative events for that day.

We are not recommending that you arbitrarily flip through one of these sources to crank up your speech; your reference to a historical event should be linked clearly to the purpose of your speech. Note how National Education Association President Keith Geiger opened his keynote address delivered on July 4, 1991, at the opening of the NEA conference in Miami Beach, Florida:

> . . . *on this 4th of July, as we celebrate independence, I'd like to talk about dependence, because that is the natural state of childhood. And, on this day when we note freedoms to be enjoyed, I'd also like to talk about rights guaranteed. In this year 1991, the year marking the 200th anniversary of our Bill of Rights, I want to talk about the rights and protections required by America's children.*[21]

Geiger not only referred to the July 4 holiday, but to the significance of the year 1991 as the anniversary of the Bill of Rights.

REFERENCES TO RECENT EVENTS

If your topic is timely, a reference to a recent event can be a good way to open your speech. An opening taken from a recent news story can take the form of an illustration, a startling statistic, or even a quotation, gaining the additional advantages discussed under each of those methods of introduction. Moreover, referring to a recent event will increase your credibility by showing that you are knowledgeable about current affairs.

"Recent" does not necessarily mean a story that broke just last week or even last month. An occurrence that has taken place within the past year or so can be considered recent. Even a particularly significant event that is slightly older than that, such as the breakup of the Soviet Union, can qualify. Andra opened her speech, "Censorship of the Media by the Media," with a reference to just such an event:

On December 21, 1988, one of the most media-covered tragedies in aviation history occurred. I'm sure you all remember the tragic story of Pan Am's flight 103 which blew up over Lockerbie, Scotland, killing 259 people . . . . The media reported that the plane had carried a bomb planted by the Popular Front for the Liberation of Palestine. But today as I speak there is a file in Ohio Representative James A. Traficant's office that tells a different story . . . .

This is not a speech about the CIA or the hostages in Lebanon or, for that matter, Pan Am 103. This is a speech about why nobody wanted to print that report that is in Representative Traficant's office and why even though the freedom of the press is protected from government censorship by law, there doesn't seem to be anything to protect us from censorship of the press by the press.[22]

● PERSONAL REFERENCES

A reference to yourself can take several forms. You may reveal your authority on the subject of your speech, as did the speaker whose introduction to the speech on Boy Scouting was quoted earlier in this chapter. You may express appreciation at having been asked to speak, as did the late Texas congresswoman Barbara Jordan when she opened her speech to the 1992 Democratic National Convention:

At this time; at this place; at this event sixteen years ago—I presented a keynote address. I thank you for the return engagement . . . .[23]

Or you may share a personal experience, such as this one offered by Vice President of the United States and Harvard alumnus Al Gore, at the opening of his address to the 1994 Harvard graduating class:

Throughout our four years at Harvard the nation's spirits sank. The race riot in Watts was fresh in our minds when we registered as freshmen. Though our hopes were briefly raised by the passage of civil-rights legislation and the promise of a war on poverty, the war in Vietnam grew steadily more ominous and consumed the resources that were needed to make good on the extravagant promises for dramatic progress here at home . . . . All of this cast a shadow over each of our personal futures.[24]

Although personal references take a variety of forms, what they do best, in all circumstances, is to establish a bond between you and your audience.

● REFERENCES TO THE OCCASION

Instead of referring in your introduction to a historical event, you can refer to the occasion at hand. For example, when a neighborhood elementary school celebrates its twenty-fifth anniversary, its first principal might open her remarks this way:

It is a special joy for me to be here this afternoon to help celebrate the twenty-fifth anniversary of Crockett Elementary School. How well I remember the excitement and anticipation of that opening day so many years ago.

How well I remember the children who came to school that first day. Some of them are now your parents. It was a good beginning to a successful twenty-five years.

References to the occasion are often used at weddings, birthday parties, dedication ceremonies, and other such events. It is customary to make a personal reference as well, placing oneself in the occasion. The audience at the school probably expected the principal to do just that. The reference to the occasion can also be combined with other methods of introduction, such as an illustration or an opening question.

REFERENCES TO PRECEDING SPEECHES

If your speech is one of several being presented on the same occasion, such as a speech class, a symposium, or a lecture series, you will usually not know until shortly before your own speech what other speakers will say. Few experiences will make your stomach sink faster than hearing a speaker just ahead of you speak on your topic. Worse still, that speaker may even use some of the same supporting materials you had planned to use. When this happens, you must decide on the spot whether referring to one of these previous speeches will be better than using the introduction you originally prepared. It may be wise to refer to a preceding speech when another speaker has spoken on a topic so related to your own that you can draw an analogy. In a sense, your introduction becomes a transition from that earlier speech to yours. Here is an example of an introduction delivered by a fast-thinking student speaker under those circumstances:

When Juli talked to us about her experiences as a lifeguard, she stressed that the job was not as glamorous as many of us imagine. Today I want to tell you about another job that appears to be more glamorous than it is—a job that I have held for two years. I am a bartender at the Rathskeller.[25]

In summary, as you plan your introduction, remember that any combination of the methods just discussed is possible. With a little practice, you may find yourself choosing from several good possibilities as you prepare your introduction.

Purposes of conclusions

Your introduction creates an important first impression; your conclusion leaves an equally important final impression. Long after you finish speaking, your audience is likely to remember the effect, if not the content, of your closing remarks.

Unfortunately, many speakers pay less attention to their conclusions than to any other part of their speeches. They believe that if they can get through the first 90 percent of a speech, they can think of some way to conclude it. Perhaps you have had the experience of listening to a speaker who failed to plan the conclusion. Awkward final seconds of stumbling for words may be followed by hesitant applause from an audience that is not even sure the speech is over. It is hardly the best way to leave people who came to listen to you.

An effective conclusion has four purposes:

- Summarize the speech.

- Reemphasize the main idea in a memorable way.

- Motivate the audience to respond.

- Provide closure.

Just as you learned ways to introduce a speech, you can learn how to conclude one. We will begin by considering the purposes of conclusions and will go on to study methods that will help you achieve those purposes.

● SUMMARIZE THE SPEECH

Remember the golden rule of public speaking: "Tell them what you're going to tell them; tell them; then tell them what you've told them." Conclusions fulfill the final third of that prescription. They are a speaker's last chance to repeat his or her main ideas for the audience. Most speakers summarize their speech as the first part of the conclusion or perhaps even as the transition between the body of the speech and its end. The summary is to the conclusion what the preview statement is to the introduction.

John summarized his speech on emissions tampering in an effective way, casting the summary as an expression of his fears about the problem and the actions that could solve his fears:

I'm frightened. Frightened that nothing I could say would encourage the 25 percent of emissions-tampering Americans to change their ways and correct the factors that cause their autos to pollute disproportionately. Frightened that the American public will not respond to a crucial issue unless the harms are both immediate and observable. Frightened that the EPA will once again prove very sympathetic to industry. Three simple steps will alleviate my fear: inspection, reduction in lead content, and, most importantly, awareness.[26]

Many speakers end their speeches with a summary alone. Many others, though, combine a summary with one of the other methods of conclusion to be discussed later in this chapter.

● REEMPHASIZE THE MAIN IDEA IN A MEMORABLE WAY

Another purpose of a conclusion is to restate the main idea of the speech in a memorable way. The conclusions of a number of famous speeches are among the most memorable statements we have. For example, General Douglas MacArthur's farewell to the nation at the end of his career concluded with these memorable words:

"Old soldiers never die; they just fade away." And like the old soldier of that ballad, I now close my military career and just fade away—an old soldier who tried to do his duty as God gave him the light to see that duty. Good-bye.[27]

But memorable endings are not the exclusive property of great orators. With practice, most people can prepare similarly effective conclusions. Chapter 12, will offer you ideas for using language to make your statements more memorable. As a preliminary example of the memorable use of language, here is how John concluded his speech on lobbying:

Mr. Lincoln, . . . you once told us government was "by the people." I don't think you could have imagined who is now doing the "buying" for us.[28]

This speaker's clever play on Lincoln's phrase helped his audience remember the central idea of his speech.

Another way to reach a memorable conclusion is to borrow the words of someone else. Jay drew on two quotations to help make a final memorable point in a speech on book deterioration:

One person described such an experience (a book deteriorating in her hands) this way: "The front part of the book I took from the shelf was in my left hand, the back was in my right hand, and in between was this yellow snow drifting to the floor." That yellow snow is an idea that has been destroyed, not debunked, but destroyed. As Gilbert Highet asserts, "Books are not lumps of lifeless paper, but minds alive on the shelves . . . so by taking one down and opening it up, we (hear) the voice of a person far distant from us in time and space, and hear him speaking to us. Mind to mind, heart to heart." Unless, of course, that voice falls fractured to the library floor in a flurry of yellow snow.[29]

The end of your speech is your last chance to impress the central idea upon your audience. Do it in such a way that they cannot help but remember it.

MOTIVATE THE AUDIENCE TO RESPOND

One of your tasks in an effective introduction is to motivate your audience to listen to your speech. Motivation is also a necessary component of an effective conclusion—not motivation to listen, but motivation to respond to the speech in some way. If your speech is informative, you may want the audience to think about the topic or to research it further. If your speech is persuasive, you may want your audience to take some sort of appropriate action—write a letter, buy a product, make a telephone call, or get involved in a cause. In fact, an *action* step is essential to the persuasive organizational strategy called the motivated sequence, which will be discussed in detail in Chapter 17.

In a speech on auto mechanic fraud, Kristen motivated her audience to wield their consumer power to stop the abuse:

> *. . . with every dollar we spend, we're telling Mr. Badwrench that it's good to be bad. If we close our wallets and start spending some common sense, we can say good-bye to Mr. Badwrench . . . and get the monkey wrench out of our lives.*[30]

Another speaker ended a speech on campus crime with this conclusion:

> *The vast majority of crimes that take place on college and university campuses are completely avoidable. By simply remembering that more and more people are falling victim to campus crime because many times they feel too safe and don't take necessary precautions, you can keep yourself from becoming another in the growing list of victims of campus crime.*[31]

In both of the preceding examples, the speakers draw on the principle of proximity, discussed earlier in this chapter, to motivate their audiences. If audience members feel that they are or could easily be personally involved or affected, they are more likely to respond to your message.

PROVIDE CLOSURE

Probably the most obvious purpose of a conclusion is to let the audience know that the speech has ended. Speeches have to "sound finished."

You can attain closure both verbally and nonverbally. Verbal techniques include using such transitions as "finally," "for my last point," and "in conclusion." As noted in Chapter 9, you should use care in signaling your conclusion. For one thing, such a cue gives an audience unspoken permission to tune out. Notice what students do when their professor signals the end of the class session. Books and notebooks slam shut, pens are stowed, and the class generally stops listening. A concluding transition needs to be followed quickly by the final statement of the speech. We will discuss another verbal technique for closure—referring to the introduction—later in this chapter.

You can also signal closure with nonverbal cues. You may want to pause between the body of your speech and its conclusion, slow your speaking rate, move out from behind a podium to make a final impassioned plea to your audience, or signal with falling vocal inflection that you are making your final statement.

PURPOSES OF YOUR SPEECH CONCLUSION

PURPOSE	TECHNIQUE
Summarize your speech.	Tell the audience what you told them.
Reemphasize the main idea in a memorable way.	Use a well-worded closing phrase. Provide a final example.
Motivate the audience to respond.	Urge the audience to think about the topic or to research it further. Suggest appropriate action.
Provide closure.	Use verbal and nonverbal transitions. Refer to your introduction.

Effective conclusions

Any of the methods of introduction discussed earlier can help you conclude your speech. Quotations, for example, are frequently used in conclusions, as in this speech on geographical illiteracy:

For in the words of Gilbert Grosvener, President of the National Geographic Society, "A knowledge of geography—where you are in relation to the rest of the world—is essential for an understanding of history, economics, and politics. Without it, the prospects of world peace and cooperation, as well as a grasp of human events is beyond our reach. With it, we not only understand others, but we can better understand ourselves."[32]

You may also turn to illustrations, personal references, or any of the other methods of introduction to conclude your speech. In addition, there are at least three other distinct methods of conclusion. These include references to the introduction, inspirational appeals or challenges, and appeals to action.

REFERENCES TO THE INTRODUCTION

In our discussion of closure, we mentioned referring to the introduction as a way to end a speech. Finishing a story, answering a rhetorical question, or reminding the audience of the startling fact or statistic you presented in the introduction are excellent ways to provide closure. Like bookends at either side of a group of books on your desk, a related introduction and conclusion provide unified support for the ideas in the middle.

Lori's topic dealt with personal problems caused by the current farm crisis. She had opened her speech with an illustration of an Iowan named Dale Burr, whose anguish had led to a murder-suicide. Her conclusion was this:

Just think . . . if someone had helped Dale Burr cope with the stress he was facing, maybe he and three others might not have died on that cold December day.[33]

John had begun his speech on the need for catastrophic health insurance by quoting Robert Browning:

> *Grow old along with me!*
> *The best is yet to be,*
> *The last of life, for which the first was made.*[34]

He concluded his speech by referring to that Browning quotation:

Robert Browning tells us the last of life is as precious as the first. While the future will always hold uncertainty, with catastrophic health insurance we can more fully prepare for whatever is yet to be.[35]

Benjamin had introduced his speech by talking about the downfalls inevitably suffered by the heroes of Greek mythology. He drew an analogy between the risks they faced and the risks inherent in the use of antibiotics—the dangers of overuse. Here is how that speaker ended his speech:

The demise of Medusa carries with it one final message. With her death, Perseus received two drops of blood. One drop had the power to kill and spread evil; the other, to heal and restore well-being. Similarly, antibiotics offer us two opposite paths. As we painfully take stock in our hubris, in assuming that we can control the transformation of nature, we may ponder these two paths. We can either let antibiotics do the work of our immune systems and proper farm management, which may return us to the times when deathly plagues spread across the world, or we can save these miracle drugs for the times when miracles are truly needed.[36]

Each of the three examples just given is quite different. In the first, the speech opened and closed with an illustration; in the second, both introduction and conclusion centered on a quotation; and in the third, beginning and ending relied on an analogy between mythology and modern medicine. What the three speeches had in common was that the conclusion of each harked back to the introduction to make the speech memorable.

● INSPIRATIONAL APPEALS OR CHALLENGES

Another way to end your speech is to issue an inspirational appeal or challenge to your listeners, rousing them to a high emotional pitch at the conclusion of the speech. The conclusion becomes the climax. One famous example comes from the "I Have a Dream" speech of Martin Luther King, Jr.:

From every mountainside, let freedom ring, and when this happens . . . when we allow freedom to ring, when we let it ring from every village and every hamlet, from every state and every city, we will be able to speed up that day when all of God's children, black men and white men, Jews and Gentiles, Protestants and Catholics, will be able to join hands and sing in

the words of the old Negro spiritual, "Free at last! Thank God Almighty, we are free at last!"[37]

That King's conclusion was both inspiring and memorable has been affirmed by the growing fame of that passage through the years since he delivered the speech.

Toward the end of his presidency Ronald Reagan delivered a poignant farewell address to the Republican National Convention. Answering assertions that he was entering the twilight of his life, he concluded his speech with these words:

Twilight, you say?

Listen to H. G. Wells: "The past is but the beginning of a beginning, and all that is and has been is but the twilight of the dawn."

That's a new day—a sunlit new day—to keep alive the fire so that when we look back at the time of choosing, we can say that we did all that could be done.

Never less.[38]

● APPEALS TO ACTION

As we noted earlier in the section on motivating an audience to respond, persuasive speeches often include an appeal to action in their conclusions. Note how Mark combined a call to action with a reference to his introduction, as he urged his audience to act on the issue of pesticide control:

The Pied Piper fooled his prey. We are also being fooled. Fooled by the Federal Government and fooled by chemical lawn spray companies. There is no reason that 800 people should die or 800,000 people be injured every year as a result of these chemical poisonings. One brief letter. One small action. These can help better insure that we are not led to our unsuspecting injuries or deaths. Meagan Connelley recovered from her chemical poisoning. But now she must hide from the Pied Piper of Pesticides as he plays on. She can only hope that legislation will be enacted to provide better control over the use of these pesticides in our lawns. For Meagan's sake, and for our own personal safety, can't we be that hope?[39]

Summary

In this chapter, we explored the purposes and methods of introductions and conclusions. We stressed the importance of beginning and ending your speech in a way that is memorable and that also provides the repetition audiences need.

A good introduction gets the audience's attention, introduces your subject, gives the audience a reason to listen, establishes your credibility, and previews your main ideas.

Introducing your subject and previewing the body of your speech can be accomplished by including your central idea and preview statement in the introduction. You can gain favorable attention and provide a motivation for listening by using one or a combination of the following: illustrations, startling facts or statistics, quotations, humor, questions, references to historical events, references to recent events, personal references, references to the occasion, or references to preceding speeches, if there are any.

Concluding your speech is just as important as introducing it, for it is the conclusion that leaves the final impression. Specifically, a conclusion should summarize your speech, reemphasize your main idea in a memorable way, motivate the audience to respond, and provide closure.

Conclusions may take any one of the forms used for introductions. In addition, you can refer to the introduction, make inspirational appeals or challenges, or make appeals to action.

Once you have planned the introduction and the conclusion, you have completed the final organizational step of the speech preparation process.

● CRITICAL THINKING QUESTIONS

1. Nakai is planning to give his informative speech on Native American music, displaying and demonstrating the use of such instruments as the flute, the Taos drum, and the Yaqui rain stick. He asks you to suggest a good introduction for the speech. How do you think he might best introduce his speech?

2. Knowing that you have recently visited the Vietnam Veterans Memorial, your American history professor asks you to make a brief presentation to the class about the Wall: its history, its symbolic meaning, and its impact on the families, comrades, and friends of those memorialized there. Write both an introduction and a conclusion for this speech.

3. How could you establish a motivation for your classroom audience to listen to you on each of the following topics?

Cholesterol

Prison reform

Speed traps

The history of greeting cards

Elvis Presley

Ozone depletion

● ETHICAL QUESTIONS

1. Marty and Shanna, who are in the same section of a public speaking class, are discussing their upcoming speeches. Marty has discovered an illustration that she thinks will make an effective introduction. When she tells Shanna about it, Shanna is genuinely enthusiastic. In fact, she thinks it would make a great introduction for her own speech, which is on a different topic, but still relevant

to Marty's illustration. When the students are assigned their speaking days, Shanna realizes that she will speak before Marty. She badly wants to use the introductory illustration that Marty has discovered. Can she ethically do so, assuming she cites in her speech the original source of the illustration?

● SUGGESTED ACTIVITIES

1. Using one of the suggested topics in Critical Thinking Question 3, write a complete introduction and conclusion for a speech. Then write a brief paragraph in which you identify and explain the principles you followed in preparing your introduction and conclusion.

2. Examine the sample speeches in Appendix C. Identify the approach each speaker uses to begin and conclude the speech.

3. Go to the library and find a book of quotations, such as *Bartlett's Familiar Quotations*. Find interesting quotations that could be used to begin speeches on the following topics:

   The joys of raising children

   The value of an education

   We watch too much TV

   Everyone should take a geography course

● USING TECHNOLOGY AND MEDIA

1. If you are developing your speeches on a word processor, begin a file of possible introductions and conclusions. Over the next few weeks, as you hear or read compelling stories or illustrations, startling facts or statistics, or humorous anecdotes, enter them into this file, with source citations. Then, when it comes time to work on the introduction of an upcoming speech—or even to choose a topic—peruse this file for ideas. Keeping such a file is a strategy used by many who speak frequently in public.

"Painted Wood Sculpture of a Dog."
Guatemalan/SuperStock

Outlining Your Speech

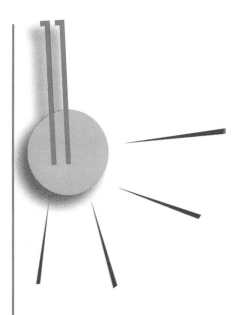

*Every discourse ought
to be a living creature;
having a body of its own
and head and feet; there
should be a middle, a
beginning, and end,
adapted to one another
and to the whole.*
—Plato

● OBJECTIVES

**After studying this chapter you
should be able to do the following:**

1. *Describe the purposes of a preparation
   outline and a delivery outline.*

2. *Identify and explain guidelines for
   preparing a preparation outline and a
   delivery outline.*

3. *Demonstrate standard outline form.*

4. *Prepare a preparation outline and a
   delivery outline for a speech you are
   working on.*

5. *Deliver a speech from speaking notes.*

while ago, a family decided to spend a weekend near the Texas Gulf Coast. Soon after they left home on a hot, cloudless June morning, the air conditioning in their car broke down. By late afternoon, the car was *very* hot, the family was *very* tired, and the prospect of an air-conditioned motel room was *very* welcome. The husband was driving and the wife navigating as they approached their destination. Only a few more minutes, they thought, and they would relax in the cool quiet of their room. Imagine their frustration when, a half hour later, they were still searching for the motel. "Let *me* see the map," demanded the exasperated husband.

"Here, if you think you can do better," snapped the wife. "This map is useless!"

Trying to remain cool and collected (no easy task with the temperature approaching 100 degrees), the husband studied the map. Sure enough, it looked as though they should be at the motel by now. In sweaty desperation, he finally stopped to ask for directions.

"Oh, you should've turned right four blocks back," explained a store clerk. The wife had been right. The map *was* useless because it had not shown the necessary turn in the road.

This actually happened—to our family! We experienced directly the frustration of having an inaccurate map. Just as we rely on maps to find our way on unfamiliar roads, so do we rely on outlines to be "speech maps." In Chapter 9, you learned approaches to organizing your ideas and supporting materials. In Chapter 10 you learned how to introduce and conclude your speech effectively and memorably. Now, in this chapter, we will discuss how to map, or outline, the organization you have developed.

Actually, most speakers find that they need to prepare two types of outline: (1) a preparation outline and (2) a delivery outline. Let's examine the purposes and requirements of each of these outlines in turn.

Preparation outline

Although few speeches are written in paragraph form, most speakers develop a detailed preparation outline that includes main ideas, subpoints, and supporting materials. It also includes the specific purpose, central idea, introduction, conclusion, and signposts.

DEVELOPING A PREPARATION OUTLINE

To begin your outlining task, you might try a technique known as "mapping" or "clustering." Write on a sheet of paper all the main ideas, subpoints, and supporting materials for the speech. Then use geometric shapes and lines to indicate the logical relationships among them, as shown in Figure 11.1.[1]

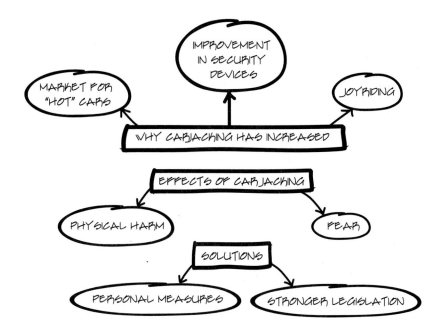

FIGURE 11.1
A map that shows the relationships between each of three main ideas and their subpoints.[1] Main ideas are enclosed by rectangles; subpoints, by ovals. Supporting materials could be indicated by another shape and connected to the appropriate subpoints.

Nationwide Insurance speechwriter Charles Parnell favors yet another technique for beginning a preparation outline:

> *I often start by jotting down a few ideas on the (computer) screen, then move them around as necessary to build some sort of coherent pattern. I then fill in the details as they occur to me.*

> *What that means is that you can really start anywhere and eventually come up with an entire speech, just as you can start with any piece of a puzzle and eventually put it together.[2]*

Whatever technique you choose to begin your outline, your ultimate goal is to produce a plan that allows you to judge the unity and coherence of your speechto see how well the parts fit together and how smoothly the speech flows. Your completed preparation outline will help you ensure that all points and subpoints are clearly and logically related and adequately supported. The following suggestions will help you complete your preparation outline.

- *Write your preparation outline in complete sentences, like those you will use when delivering your speech.* Unless you write complete sentences, you will have trouble judging the coherence of the speech. Moreover, complete sentences will help during your first rehearsals. If you write cryptic phrases, you may not remember what they mean.

■ *Use standard outline form.* Although you did not have to use standard outline form when you generated the kind of preliminary outline discussed in Chapter 6, you will need to do so now. This form lets you see at a glance the exact relationships among various points, subpoints, and supporting materials in your speech. It is an important tool for evaluating your speech, as well as a requirement in many public speaking courses. To produce a correct outline, follow the instructions given here.

1. *Use standard outline numbering.* Logical and fairly easy to learn, outline numbering follows this sequence:

   I. First main point

      A. First subpoint of *I*

      B. Second subpoint of *I*

         1. First subpoint of *B*

         2. Second subpoint of *B*

            a. First supporting material of 2

            b. Second supporting material of 2

   II. Second main point

   It is unlikely that you will subdivide beyond the level of lowercase letters (*a, b,* etc.) in most speech outlines.

2. *Use at least two subdivisions, if any, for each point.* Logic dictates that you cannot divide anything into one part. If, for example, you have only one piece of supporting material, incorporate it into the subpoint or point that it supports. If you have only one subpoint, incorporate it into the main point above it. Although there is no limit to the number of subpoints you may have, if you have more than five or six, you may want to place several of them under another main point. An audience will remember your ideas more easily if they are divided into blocks of three or four.

3. *Indent points, subpoints, and supporting material properly.* Main points, indicated by Roman numerals, are written closest to the left margin. Notice that the *periods* following the Roman numerals line up, so that the first *words* of the main points also line up.

   I. First main point

   II. Second main point

   III. Third main point

   Subpoints and supporting materials begin directly underneath the first *word* of the point above.

I. First main point

   A. First subpoint of *I*

If a sentence takes up more than one line, the second line begins under the first *word* of the preceding line:

I. Every speech has three parts.

   A. The first part, both in our discussion and in actual delivery, is the introduction.

The same rules of indentation apply at all levels of the outline.

RE CAP

SUMMARY OF CORRECT OUTLINE FORM

Rule	Example
1. Use standard outline numbering.	I. A. 1. a. (1) (a)
2. Use at least two subpoints, if any, for each main point.	I. A. B.
3. Properly indent main points, subpoints, and supporting material.	I. First main point A. First subpoint of *I* 1. First supporting material for *A* 2. Second supporting material for *A* B. Second subpoint of *I* II. Second main point

■ *Write and label your purpose and central idea at the top of your preparation outline.* Unless your instructor directs you to do otherwise, do not work the purpose statement and central idea into the outline itself. Instead, label them and place them separately at the top of the outline. Your purpose statement and central idea can serve as yardsticks by which to measure the relevance of each main point, subpoint, and piece of supporting material. Everything in the speech should contribute to your purpose and directly support your central idea.

■ *Add key transitions, previews, summaries, and an introduction and conclusion to your outline.* Write the introduction and preview statement before the outline, the conclusion after the outline, and the signposts within the outline. Follow your instructor's guidelines as to whether you should incorporate these elements into your numbering system.

The sample outline that follows is for a ten-minute persuasive speech by student speaker Mark Culkins.[3] Notice that in this example the specific purpose, central idea, introduction, preview statement, transitions, and conclusion are separated from the numbered points in the body of the speech. Be sure to learn and follow your own instructor's requirements for how to incorporate these elements.

SAMPLE PREPARATION OUTLINE

Purpose: By the end of my speech, the audience will use caution when driving near tandem trucks.

Central Idea: Tandem trucks are a hazard to drivers on the nation's highways.

Introduction: The mood was festive; the participants were very happy, as children usually are on a bus that's taking them home from school. But their happiness soon turned to tragedy. The bus had come to a stop. Within seconds, it was struck from behind by a large tandem truck. A boy in the back of the bus was killed instantly. The bus driver and the remaining children were all injured. The truck driver saw the bus but he couldn't stop. The brakes that he'd been meaning to have repaired failed. It was this failure that shocked the small town of Tuba City, Arizona, last April. It was a failure that could have been and should have been prevented.

Preview Statement: Today I'd like to discuss the hazards of tandem trucks on our nation's highways. The first thing I want to tell you about is how Congress and the trucking industry lobbyists have seriously compromised our safety on our nation's roads and highways. The next thing I will explain is the federal government's ability, or rather inability, to deal with these unsafe trucks. Finally, I will make some suggestions as to how you and I, the public at large, can take action against and protect ourselves from these large, safety-violating trucking firms.

I. Our safety is seriously jeopardized by the presence of these trucks on our nation's roads and highways.
   A. Accidents involving tandem trucks are frequent and fatal. The Knight-Ridder newspapers, after finishing an extensive probe into the issue of truck safety, concluded that tandem trucks are involved in twice as many fatal accidents as automobiles.
   B. Thanks to legislation passed by Congress and promoted by the trucking industry lobbyists, you'll be seeing more of those wider, longer, and heavier trucks taking to our nation's roads and highways.
   C. These concessions will make injuries and fatalities increase.
      1. According to the 1985 *Statistical Abstract of the United States,* 30,360 persons were killed in truck-related accidents in 1982.
      2. There were 1,056,000 debilitating injuries such as paralysis; 957,000 temporary disabilities such as broken limbs; and over 99,000 permanent impairments such as loss of hearing or eyesight due to head, neck, and spinal injuries.
      3. Wage loss, medical expenses, and insurance costs were estimated to be well over $26 billion a year.

Transition: But why is it that these statistics are so high in comparison to automobiles?

Writing the purpose statement and central idea at the top of the outline helps the speaker keep them foremost in mind.

As Mark prepared his speech outline, he knew he wanted to begin by making the audience vividly aware of the problem. Strategies for introductions were discussed in detail in Chapter 10.

The preview statement introduces the topic and links the introduction to the body of the speech. Like the rest of the introduction, it usually appears before the numbered elements of the outline.

The first main idea of the speech is indicated here by the Roman numeral I. Notice the format of the second line, which begins under the first word of the first line.

Mark introduces a reason to support his first main point. Subpoints B and C supply additional reasons in support of point I.

Subpoints 1, 2, and 3 provide evidence to support subpoint C.

Mark adds a one-sentence transition to his second main point: that these big trucks represent an ever-present danger.

Once you have completed your preparation outline, you should use it to help analyze and possibly revise the speech. The following questions can help you in this critical thinking task.

▧ *Does the speech as outlined fulfill the purpose you have specified?* If not, you need to revise the specific purpose or change the direction and content of the speech itself.

II. Trucks are an accident waiting to happen.
   A. According to Knight-Ridder, on April 22, 1985, "The Motor Carrier Bureau is unable to inspect most trucking companies and is rarely able to follow up on inspections because of manpower shortages. Three out of four trucking companies have never been audited for safety."

Transition: Well, one would at least hope that the firms that had been audited would thus be safe. This hope is unrealistic.
   B. Even when trucks are found to be in violation of the federal standards, the average fine per truck is only $19.
   C. Weigh stations, which are supposed to monitor truck loads and truck safety, are inadequate.
      1. There are only 144 safety inspectors to staff over 500 weigh stations and audit nearly 1,000 trucking companies every year.
      2. An Associated Press article stated in April 1985, "Nearly one out of three trucks stopped by safety inspectors in 1983 were ordered out of service immediately because of safety defects that could cause an accident."

Transition: The problem is clear. We have been taken advantage of by these large trucking firms.
   D. Examples abound of accidents occurring because of unsafe trucks.
      1. *U.S. News and World Report,* May 1984, reports: "The failure of a rear spring on a tanker rig carrying 8,600 gallons of gasoline on a Philadelphia freeway caused an accident that killed two persons and engulfed the truck and three other vehicles in flames."
      2. In April 1984, a tractor-semitrailer carrying a full load of propane gas exploded, killing two persons and seriously injuring four others.
   E. The federal government has made little progress.
      1. According to the General Accounting Office, "Nevertheless, the Department of Transportation has not taken action to obtain the necessary budgeting increases to hire additional safety inspectors."
      2. Again, according to the GAO, "The Carrier Safety Bureau has been very hesitant to issue fines to unsafe truck companies."
III. A solution needs to be found.
   A. Write letters to Congress.
   B. Steer clear of those large trucks.
      1. Be especially cautious when passing one.
      2. Be especially cautious when one is passing you.
   C. Always wear your seat belt.

Conclusion: Safety, that's all we're asking for. To feel secure in knowing that the truck that's coming up behind you is going to stop. The bus driver in Tuba City must have surely thought that the truck coming up behind him was going to stop. This issue is especially important to you and me, as drivers who spend countless hours on our nation's roads and highways—our nation's unsafe roads and highways. How many more people must die before we, as responsible citizens, will take action?

Mark presents his second main point.

Mark offers supporting material for his second point.

Transition indicates Mark's awareness of possible rebuttal to subpoint A. In subpoints B and C, Mark gives two reasons current measures to protect the public don't work effectively.

Mark offers evidence to support subpoint C.

Having presented the problem and documented its causes, Mark moves next to a discussion of the significance of the problem.

Two examples document how serious the problem is.

Subpoint E returns to a discussion of the causes of the problem.

Point III suggests the need for a solution; subpoints A, B, and C suggest three possible solutions that individuals can implement.

Mark refers to his opening example as he concludes his speech. Other methods of concluding a speech were discussed in Chapter 10. Like the introduction, the conclusion should be carefully planned in the preparation outline.

- *Are the main ideas logical extensions (natural divisions, reasons, or steps) of the central idea?* If not, revise either the central idea or the main ideas. Like the first question, this one relates to the unity of the speech and is critical to making certain the speech "fits together" as a whole.

- *Do the preview and transitions enhance the comfortable flow of each idea into the next?* If not, change or add the preview or transitions. If they are not adequate, the speech will lack coherence.

- *Does each subpoint provide support for the point under which it falls?* If not, then either move or delete the subpoint.

- *Is your outline form correct?* For a quick reference, check the earlier Recap box, "Summary of Correct Outline Form."

Once you have considered these five questions, you are ready to rehearse your speech, using the preparation outline as your first set of notes. See Chapter 13 for additional tips on effective rehearsal.

Delivery outline

As you rehearse your speech, you will find that you need your preparation outline less and less. Both the structure and the content of your speech are pretty well set in your mind. At this point, you are ready to prepare a delivery outline.

● DEVELOPING A DELIVERY OUTLINE

Delivery outlines, as the name implies, are meant to give you all you will need to present your speech in the way you have planned and rehearsed. A delivery outline should not be so detailed that it encourages you to read it rather than speak to your audience. Here are a few tips:

- *Make the outline as brief as possible, and write in single words or short phrases rather than complete sentences.*

- *Include the introduction and conclusion in much shortened form.* You may feel more comfortable if you have the first and last sentences written in full in front of you. Writing out the first sentence eliminates any fear of a mental block at the outset of your speech. And writing a complete last sentence ensures a smooth ending to your speech and a good final impression.

- *Include supporting materials and signposts.* Write out statistics, direct quotations, and key transitions. Notice the transitions between points I and II, between IIA and IIB, and between IIC and IID in the sample delivery outline in the next section. Writing key transitions in full ensures that you will not grope awkwardly for a way to move from one point to the next. After you

Experienced college lecturers are experts at preparing delivery outlines. Before preparing your own outline, you might ask instructors in your other courses to show you the notes they use. [Photo: Con/Alon Reinnger/ Woodfin Camp & Associates]

have rehearsed the speech several times, you will know where you are most likely to falter and can add or omit written transitions as needed.

■ *Do not include a purpose statement or a written central idea in your delivery unless it is part of the introduction or preview.*

■ *Use a standard outline form so that you can easily find the exact point or piece of supporting material you are seeking when you glance down at your notes.*

RECAP

TWO TYPES OF SPEECH OUTLINES

TYPE	PURPOSE
Preparation outline	Allows speaker to examine speech for completeness, unity, coherence, and overall effectiveness. Serves as first rehearsal outline.
Delivery outline	Can serve as speaking notes.

● SAMPLE DELIVERY OUTLINE

The delivery outline for the speech on the hazards of tandem trucks is given next. Note that the specific purpose and central idea are not included, and that the introduction and conclusion are in shortened form.

As you rehearse the speech, you will probably continue to revise the delivery outline. You may decide to cut further or to add or delete transitions. Your outline should provide just enough information to ensure smooth delivery. It should not burden you with unnecessary notes or compel you to look down too often during the speech.

SAMPLE DELIVERY OUTLINE

Intro.: The mood was festive; the participants were very happy. Tragedy—struck by tandem truck. Boy killed; others injured. Brake failure. Tuba City, Arizona, shocked.

Preview: Hazards of tandem trucks:

1. Congress and lobbyists have compromised safety
2. Federal govt's inability to deal with trucks
3. Action and protection

I. Danger

    A. Frequent and fatal accidents

    B. More trucks

    C. Increase in injuries and casualties

        1. 1985 *Stat. Abstract*—30,360 killed in 1982

        2. 1,056,000 debilitating injuries; 957,000 temporary injuries; 99,000 permanent impairments (hearing, eyesight)

        3. Cost—$26 billion

Trans.: But why is it that these statistics are so high in comparison to automobiles?

II. Accident waiting to happen

    A. Rare inspections—Knight-Ridder, April 22, 1985—"The Motor Carrier Bureau is unable to inspect most trucking companies and is rarely able to follow up on inspections because of manpower shortages. Three out of four trucking companies have never been audited for safety."

Trans.: Well, one would at least hope that the firms that had been audited would thus be safe. This hope is unrealistic.

    B. Average fine—$19

    C. Inadequate weigh stations

        1. 144 inspectors, 500 stations, 1,000 trucking cos.

        2. AP, April 1985—"Nearly one out of three trucks stopped by safety inspectors in 1983 was ordered out of service immediately because of safety defects that could cause an accident."

Trans.: The problem is quite clear. We, the American people, have been taken advantage of by these large trucking firms.

    D. Examples of accidents

        1. *U.S. News,* May 1984—"The failure of a rear spring on a tanker rig carrying 8,600 gallons of gasoline on a Philadelphia freeway caused an accident that killed two persons and engulfed the truck and three other vehicles in flames."

        2. April 1984—semi carrying propane exploded, killing 2 and injuring 4

    E. Little progress

        1. GAO—"Nevertheless, the Department of Transportation has not taken action to obtain the necessary budgeting increases to hire additional safety inspectors."

        2. "The Carrier Safety Bureau has been very hesitant to issue fines to unsafe truck companies."

III. Solutions

    A. Letters to Congress

    B. Caution

        1. When passing

        2. When being passed

    C. Seat belts

Concl.: Safety, that's all we're asking for. Tuba City. We spend countless hours on roads. How many more people must die before we, as responsible citizens, will take action?

Note both shortened version of, and use of phrases in, the introduction.

The preview statement is in list form to make it easy for the speaker to glance down and pick up major points to be previewed.

Both main points and subpoints are single words and short phrases. Note that statistics are written down to ensure accuracy.

Transitions are labeled so that the speaker can find them quickly. The label itself is likely to be abbreviated, as it is here.

Direct quotations are written out word for word.

Like the introduction, the conclusion is written in abbreviated form. The final sentence is written out to ensure a fluent finish.

Many speakers find paper difficult to handle quietly, so they transfer their delivery outlines to note cards. Note cards are small enough to hold in one hand, if necessary, and stiff enough not to rustle. Two or three 4-by-6 or 5-by-8-inch note cards will give you enough space for a delivery outline; the exact number of cards you use will depend on the length of your speech. Type or print your outline neatly on one side, making sure that the letters and words are large enough to read easily. You may find it helpful to plan your note cards according to logical blocks of material, using one note card for the introduction, one or two for the body, and one for the conclusion. At any rate, plan so that you do not have to shuffle note cards midsentence. Number the note cards to prevent fiascoes if your notes get out of order.

Whether you decide to use note cards or regular sheets of paper, you can use an alternative format for your speaking notes. For example, you could use a map, such as the one illustrated in Figure 11.1. Or you could use a combination of words, pictures, and symbols, as in the notes reproduced in Figure 11.2.[4] What is important is that the speaking notes make sense to *you*.

F IGURE 11.2
Speaking notes used by Mark Twain for a lecture on Roughing It *delivered in Liverpool, England, in 1874.*[4]

FIGURE 11.3
Your speaking notes can include delivery cues and reminders.

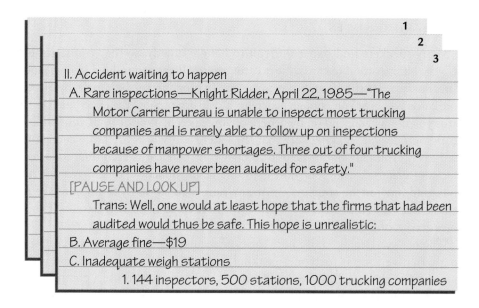

II. Accident waiting to happen
  A. Rare inspections—Knight Ridder, April 22, 1985—"The
      Motor Carrier Bureau is unable to inspect most trucking
      companies and is rarely able to follow up on inspections
      because of manpower shortages. Three out of four trucking
      companies have never been audited for safety."
[PAUSE AND LOOK UP]
      Trans: Well, one would at least hope that the firms that had been
      audited would thus be safe. This hope is unrealistic:
  B. Average fine—$19
  C. Inadequate weigh stations
          1. 144 inspectors, 500 stations, 1000 trucking companies

A final addition to your speaking notes will be delivery cues and reminders, such as "Louder," "Pause," or "Move in front of podium." (See Figure 11.3.) Delivery cues should be written in the margins by hand, or if the entire outline is handwritten, in ink of a different color. Several years ago, former President Gerald Ford accidentally read the delivery cue "Look into the right camera" during an address. Clearly differentiating delivery cues from speech content will help prevent such mistakes.

If you are using slides or other visual aids to support your speech, be sure to write delivery cues in the margins of your notes. [Photo: Tom Main/Tony Stone Images]

Summary

I n this chapter, we examined the purposes and processes of developing two types of outlines. Most public speakers prepare: the preparation outline and the delivery outline.

A preparation outline includes all the elements of your speech: purpose statement and central idea; introduction; carefully organized main points, subpoints, and supporting materials; previews, summaries, and transitions necessary for coherence; and conclusion. Write each of these elements in complete sentences and standard outline form. Use the preparation outline to begin rehearsing your speech.

After you have rehearsed several times from the preparation outline, prepare a delivery outline. This, with slight adjustments, will become your final speaking notes. You need not include the purpose statement or central idea. Note all other ideas and materials in as much detail as you will need when delivering the speech. You may eventually transfer the delivery outline to note cards and add delivery cues.

CRITICAL THINKING QUESTIONS

1. The following delivery outline for the body of a speech contains a number of errors in form. Find five of those errors.

The College Work-Study Program

I.   Program eligibility

    A. four initial requirements for work-study students

        1. Have need for employment

        2. Good grades

        3. Be a full-time student

        4. Be a citizen or permanent resident of the U.S.

    B. Application

        a. Submit financial aid form to Central State

II. Job assignments

    A. Jobs related to your major field of study

    B. Jobs using your special interests and skills

2. Myorka thinks it is silly to worry about using correct outline form for either her preparation or delivery outline. Do you agree with her? Develop at least two reasons you do or do not.

3. Geoff plans to deliver his speech from some hastily scrawled notes on a sheet of notebook paper torn from his class notebook. What advice would you offer him for preparing more effective and efficient speaking notes?

ETHICAL QUESTIONS

1. Can a speaker legitimately claim that a speech is extemporaneous if he or she has constructed a detailed preparation outline? Explain your answer.

SUGGESTED ACTIVITIES

1. Select a speech from Appendix D. Prepare a delivery outline of that speech.

2. Discuss the pros and cons of having a speaker's outline in front of you while you are listening to the speech.

USING TECHNOLOGY AND MEDIA

1. Take notes as you listen to an audio or videotape of a speech. Then, using either a map or a cut-and-paste method, organize your notes into an outline that you think clearly and accurately reflects both the speaker's organization and the intended relationship among ideas and supporting materials.

2. If your word processing program has an outlining function, experiment with it. Do you find it easier or more difficult to use than manually assigning Roman numerals, letters, and numbers?

"Stranger in Paradise."
Christian Pierre/SuperStock

Using Words Well: Speaker Language and Style

*A speech is poetry;
cadence, rhythm,
imagery, sweep!
A speech reminds us
that words, like children,
have the power to make
dance the dullest
beanbag of a heart.*
—Peggy Noonan

OUTLINE

Oral versus written language style
*Oral Style Is More Personal · Oral Style Is
Less Formal · Oral Style Is More Repetitious*

Using words effectively
*Use Concrete Words · Use Unbiased Words ·
Use Vivid Words · Use Simple Words ·
Use Words Correctly*

Crafting memorable word structures
Creating Drama · Creating Cadence

A second look at memorable word structures

Creating arresting images
Metaphors and Similes · Personification

Tips for using language effectively

Summary

OBJECTIVES

**After studying this chapter you
should be able to do the following:**

1. *Describe three differences between oral
   and written language styles.*

2. *List and explain five ways to use words
   effectively.*

3. *List and explain seven techniques for creating drama and cadence through word
   structures.*

4. *List and define three common figures of
   speech.*

5. *Offer tips for using language effectively
   in public speeches.*

eople lazily scanning the classified ads and headlines of their local newspapers must have rubbed their eyes in disbelief when they read the following:[1]

FORECLOSURE LISTINGS
Entire state of NJ available. Deal directly with owners. 5–8 months before auction. Call 201-286-1156.

BABYSITTER
Looking for infant to babysit in my home. Excellent references.

NEED Plain Clothes Security. Must have shoplifting experience. Apply between 8 A.M.–3 P.M. Mon.–Fri., at suite 207.

Mayor Says D.C. Is Safe Except for Murders

IOWA CEMETERIES ARE DEATH TRAPS

FAMILY CATCHES FIRE JUST IN TIME, CHIEF SAYS . . .
The Richard Harder family Sunday returned home from church just in time, Lindsey Fire Chief Tom Overmyer said. The family . . . got back from church about 11:15 A.M. to find their kitchen table on fire and . . .

These ads and headlines from the "Headlines" files of comedian Jay Leno are, as he notes, funny "because they were never intended to be funny in the first place. That they're checked and rechecked by a proofreader makes them funnier still." Certainly they illustrate that using language accurately, clearly, and effectively can be a challenge, even for professional wordsmiths!

For public speakers, the task is double challenging. One must speak clearly and communicate ideas accurately. At the same time, it is important to present those ideas in such a way that your audience will listen to, remember, and perhaps act on what you have to say.

In this chapter we will focus on the power of language. We will suggest ways to communicate your ideas and feelings to others accurately and effectively. We will also discuss how the choice of words and word structures can help make your message memorable.

Oral versus written language style

When you think of someone as having "style," you probably first think of the way he or she dresses. Language is very much like clothing. You dress your ideas in the words you choose. And just as your wardrobe can give you a distinctive and attractive style, so your choice of words can give your thoughts a distinctive and attractive form of expression. In the last analysis, style—whether in clothing or language—is a way of expressing yourself.

Your speech has memorable style when you use words and phrases that are distinctive. Most everyday speech lacks a distinctive style. Most sentences consist of a subject-verb or subject-verb-object form of construction. Sometimes, though, you, like most of us, may say something in a way that is different from the normal phrasing of a sentence. You use a word or phrase in a way that is unique and original with you. That is speaking with a distinctive style. Before identifying some techniques to add style to your speeches, let's note some general differences in style between the way you talk and the way you write.

Your instructor has probably told you not to write your speech out word for word. The professor has said this because of the differences between writing and talking. There are at least three major differences between a written style and an oral style of language.

● ORAL STYLE IS MORE PERSONAL

When speaking, you can look your listeners in the eye and talk to them directly. If you see that they don't like or don't understand what you are saying, you can adjust your statements and explanations to gain greater acceptance. In other words, you and your audience can interact, something a writer and reader cannot do. This interaction provides you, the public speaker, with personal contact and exchange of warmth with your audience, an experience not available to the writer working in seclusion. That warmth and personal contact affects your speech and your verbal style. As a speaker, you are likely to use more pronouns (*I, you*) than you would in writing. You are also more likely to address specific audience members by name.

● ORAL STYLE IS LESS FORMAL

Written communication often uses a somewhat formal language and structure. It should be noted that memorized speeches usually sound like they were written because the words and phrases are longer, more complex, and more formal than those used by most speakers. Spoken communication, by contrast, is usually less formal, characterized by shorter words and phrases and less complex sentence structures. Speakers generally use many more contractions and colloquialisms than writers. Oral language is also much less varied than written language, with only fifty words accounting for almost 50 percent of what we say. Finally, spoken language is often less precise than written language. Speakers are more likely than writers to use somewhat vague quantifying terms, such as *many, much,* and *a lot.* The use of such terms may, in fact, be an asset to a speaker who wants to be thought of by his audience as "personal" and "connected." Walter Weintraub, a clinical professor of psychiatry at the University of Maryland Medical Center, has dubbed Bill Clinton a "mainstream" speaker, due in part to his "theatrical . . . use of such adverbial intensifiers as 'really,' 'very,' 'so,' and 'such.' "[2]

Of course, there are great variations in both oral and written styles. Spoken language may sometimes be quite formal, and written language may at times be informal, so that the demarcation between the two verbal styles is not always pronounced. You have only to compare the speaking styles of Ronald Reagan and Jimmy Carter to glimpse a small part of the variations that are possible. Note the use of personal pronouns, contractions, and relatively short sentences in this excerpt from a 1984 speech by Ronald Reagan:

> *We've also offered to increase significantly the amount of U.S. grain for purchase by the Soviets, and to provide the Soviets a direct fishing allocation off U.S. coasts. But there's much more we could do together. I feel particularly strongly about breaking down the barriers between the peoples of the United States and the Soviet Union, and between our political, military, and other leaders.[3]*

In contrast, the style of Jimmy Carter's announcement of the 1980 Russian grain embargo conforms more closely to what we have described as a typical written style: fewer personal pronouns and longer and more complex sentences.

> *These actions will require some sacrifice on the part of all Americans, but there is absolutely no doubt that these actions are in the interest of world peace and in the interest of the security of our own nation, and are also compatible with actions being taken by our own major trading partners and others who share our deep concern about this new Soviet threat to world stability.[4]*

The personality of the speaker or writer, the subject of the discourse, the audience, and the occasion all affect the style of the language used.

● ORAL STYLE IS MORE REPETITIOUS

When you don't understand something you are reading in a book or an article, you can stop and reread a passage, look up unfamiliar words in the dictionary, or ask someone for help. When you're listening to a speech, those opportunities usually aren't available. For this reason, an oral style is and should be more redundant.

When you study how to organize a speech, you learn to provide an overview of major ideas in your introduction, develop your ideas in the body of the speech, and summarize key ideas in the conclusion. You build in repetition to make sure that your listener will grasp your message. Even during the process of developing an idea, it is sometimes necessary to state it first, restate it in a different way, provide an example, and finally, summarize it.

ORAL STYLE	More personal, facilitating interaction between speaker and audience
	Less formal
	More repetitious
WRITTEN STYLE	Less personal, with no immediate interaction between writer and reader
	More formal
	Less repetitious

Using words effectively

As a speaker, your challenge is to use words well so that you can communicate your intended message. Ideally, language should be concrete, unbiased, vivid, simple, and used correctly. We shall discuss each of these factors.

USE CONCRETE WORDS

A concrete word refers to an object or describes an action or characteristic in the most specific way possible. An abstract word is more general. A linguistic theory known as general semantics holds that the more concrete your words, the clearer your communication. Semanticists use a "ladder of abstraction" to illustrate how a concept, an idea, or a thing can be described in either concrete or abstract terms. Figure 12.1 is an example. The words are most abstract at the top of the ladder and become more concrete as you move down the ladder. For maximum clarity in your communication, you should use more concrete words than abstract ones in your speeches.

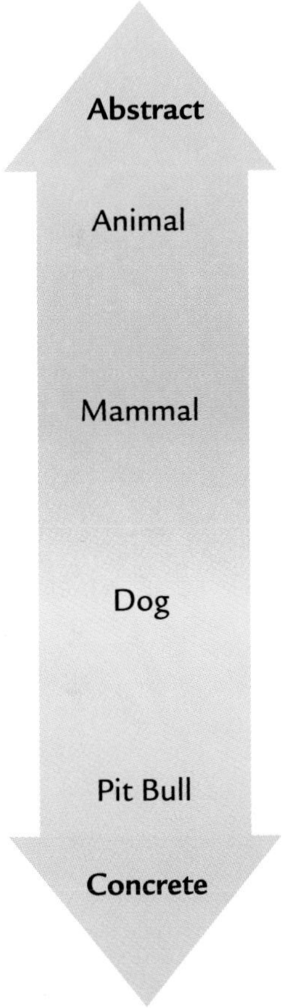

USE UNBIASED WORDS

During the O. J. Simpson murder trial, the testimony of Los Angeles police detective Mark Fuhrman was discredited in large part because of his injudicious use of racially demeaning slurs. Criticizing Fuhrman's language as both inappropriate and inaccurate, essayist Patricia Raybon observes,

> *There are offensive individuals, even criminal individuals. But groups aren't guilty. Certainly not by label. These terms, so sadly familiar to all of us, don't fit now in America and never did. In a multiracial world like ours, racial and cultural shorthand is societal suicide in more ways than one.*[5]

Abstract

Animal

Mammal

Dog

Pit Bull

Concrete

FIGURE 12.1
A "ladder of abstraction" is used by semanticists to show how a concept, idea, or thing can be described in either concrete or abstract terms.

Describing this object in the broadest terms—as a stringed musical instrument—would hardly do it justice. Instead, what concrete details would you include in a verbal description to create an image of this object for your audience? [Photo: Tom Main/Tony Stone Images]

Certainly a speaker whose language insults any sexual, racial, cultural, or religious group runs a great risk of committing "societal suicide" by offending his or her audience members. And even speakers who would never dream of using overly offensive language may find it difficult to avoid language that more subtly stereotypes or discriminates. Sexist language falls largely into this second category.

For example, not many years ago, a singular masculine pronoun (*he, him, his*) was the accepted way to refer to a person of unspecified sex:

Everyone should bring *his* book to class tomorrow.

This usage is now considered sexist and unacceptable. Instead, you may include both a masculine and a feminine pronoun:

Everyone should bring *his* or *her* book to class tomorrow.

Or you may reword the sentence so that it is plural and the pronoun can be gender neutral:

All students should bring *their* books to class tomorrow.

Another usage now considered sexist is the use of a masculine noun to refer generically to all people. The word *man* is the primary offender, but as a speaker you should also monitor your use of such masculine nouns as *mankind, chairman, fireman,* and *congressman.* When possible, you should choose instead such gender-neutral alternatives as *humanity, chairperson* or *chair, firefighter,* and *member of congress.*

In addition to avoiding masculine nouns and pronouns to refer to all people, speakers need to avoid sexist language that patronizes or stereotypes people:

SEXIST	UNBIASED
President Bill Clinton and Hillary send their daughter to a private school in Washington.	President and Mrs. Clinton send their daughter to a private school in Washington.
	or
	Bill and Hillary Clinton send their daughter to a private school in Washington.

The policeman is an underpaid professional who risks his life daily.	Police are underpaid professionals who risk their lives daily.
The male nurse took good care of his patients. (Note: The term *male nurse* implies that nursing is a typically female role. The pronoun *his* clarifies the sex of the nurse.)	The nurse took good care of his patients.

As noted earlier, it is not always easy to avoid biased language. Even with good intentions and deliberate forethought, you can find yourself at times caught in a double bind. For example, say that Dr. Pierce is a young black female M.D. If you don't mention her age, race, and gender when you refer to her, you may reinforce your listeners' stereotypical image of a middle-aged white male physician. But if you *do* mention these factors, you may be suspected of implying that Dr. Pierce's achievement is unusual. There is no easy answer to this dilemma or others like it. You will have to consider your audience, purpose, and the occasion in deciding how best to identify Dr. Pierce.

As women and racial and ethnic minorities have become increasingly visible in such professions as medicine, law, engineering, and politics, the public has grown to expect unbiased, inclusive language from news commentators, teachers, textbooks, and magazines—and from public speakers. Language that does not reflect these changes will disrupt your ability to communicate your message to your audience, which may well include members of the minority group to which you are referring.

USE VIVID WORDS

If you were to describe your pet snake to your audience, you would need to do more than say it is a three-foot-long serpent approximately two inches in diameter. Instead, you would want to use as much sensual imagery as you can. Think of the colors and patterns on your snake. What would your listeners feel if they touched it? Would it feel cold, clammy, soft? What does the snake sound like? Describe its hiss. Describe your snake in terms that would appeal to your listeners' senses.

In his speech honoring the signing of the Jewish-Palestinian peace agreement in 1993, President Bill Clinton described the bitterness that

> *has* robbed *the entire region of its resources, its potential, and too many of its sons and daughters. The land has been so* drenched *in warfare and hatred, the conflicting claims of history* etched *so deeply in the souls of the combatants . . . . [emphasis added]*[6]

Note Clinton's use of such vivid verbs as *robbed, drenched,* and *etched,* all of which create bold, forceful, and memorable sensual images.

When searching for the right word to make your language vivid, consult a thesaurus—a book that lists synonyms. But in searching for an alternative word, do not feel that you have to choose the most obscure or unusual term to vary your description. Language that is both animated and simple can very effectively evoke an image for your listeners.

USE SIMPLE WORDS

John F. Kennedy's inaugural address on January 20, 1961, was both eloquent and memorable. Although we will analyze some of the many stylistic features of that speech later in this chapter, perhaps its most significant attribute was its simplicity:

> Theodore Sorensen, special counsel to the president and his principal speechwriter, has recorded that Kennedy specifically asked him to look into the "secret" of Lincoln's "Gettysburg Address," which he hoped to emulate. Sorensen reported that "Lincoln never used a two- or three-syllable word where a one-syllable word would do, and never used two or three words where one word would do." Thus, the guidelines for style emerged.[7]

The best language is often the simplest. Your words and sentences should be immediately understandable to your listeners. Don't try to impress them with jargon and complicated sentences. Instead, as linguist Paul Roberts advises, "Decide what you want to say and say it as vigorously as possible . . . and in plain words."[8]

In his essay "Politics and the English Language," George Orwell lists rules for clear writing. Several are worth remembering.

> Never use a long word where a short one will do. If it is possible to cut a word out, always cut it out. Never use a foreign phrase, a scientific word, or a jargon word if you can think of an everyday English equivalent.[9]

Tape-record your practice sessions. As you play the tape back, listen for chances to say what you want with fewer words. Used wisely, simple words and simple phrases communicate with great power and precision. But don't restrict yourself to simple phrases and sentences, or your speech will be choppy. A few carefully worded complex or compound sentences will add variety to your speech.

USE WORDS CORRECTLY

> I was listening to the car radio one day when a woman reading the news referred to someone as a suede-o-intellectual. I pondered through three traffic lights until I realized she wasn't talking about shoes, but a pseudointellectual.[10]

A public speech is not the place to demonstrate your lack of familiarity with English vocabulary and grammar. In fact, your effectiveness as a public speaker depends in part on your ability to use the English language correctly. If you are unsure of the way to apply a grammatical rule, seek assistance from a good English usage handbook. If you are unsure of a word's meaning, use a dictionary.

Perhaps the greatest challenge to using words correctly is awareness of **connotations** as well as **denotations**. Language operates on two levels. The denotation of a word is its literal meaning, the definition you find in a dictionary. For example, the denotation of the word *notorious* is "famous." The connotation of a word is not usually found in a dictionary, but consists of the meaning we associate with the word, based on our past experiences. *Notorious* connotes fame for

connotation
The meaning we associate with a word, based on our past experiences.

denotation
The literal meaning of a word.

As you plan and deliver your speech, be mindful of different connotations the same word might carry for different audience members. The word pharmacist, for example, might conjure up dramatically different images for listeners from distinct cultures. [Photo: Con/Alon Reinnger/ Woodfin Camp & Associates]

some dire deed. *Notorious* and *famous* are not really interchangeable. It is just as important to consider the connotations of the words you use, as it is to consider the denotations.

Frank Luntz, the pollster who helped construct the GOP "Contract with America," demonstrates his awareness of the importance of connotations in his advice for politicians speaking to the American people:

> *Say you are cutting "bureaucrats," who have no friends, not "programs," which have lots. Repeat whenever you can that "it's time to put the government on a diet," and never say "orphanage."*[11]

Luntz based his advice on responses from actual audiences. For example, test audiences agreed by a three-to-one margin that welfare children who have been abused would be better off in an orphanage. But when Luntz used the phrase *foster home* instead of *orphanage*, the approval rating increased to five-to-one. Luntz's findings support the notion that a word may be denotatively correct but still not the right word for the speaker's purpose.

Sometimes connotations are private. For example, the word *table* is defined denotatively as a piece of furniture consisting of a smooth flat slab affixed on legs. But when you think of the word *table*, you may think of the old oak table your grandparents used to have. *Table* may evoke for you an image of playing checkers with your grandmother. This is a private connotation of the word, a unique meaning based on your own past experiences. Private meanings are difficult to predict, but as a public speaker you should be aware as you speak, of the possibility of audience members' private connotations. This awareness is particularly important when you are discussing highly emotional or controversial topics.

And finally, if your audience includes non-native speakers, to whom the nuances of connotation may not be readily apparent, it may be necessary to explain your intentions in more detail, rather than relying on word associations.

Crafting memorable word structures

The President of the United States is scheduled to make an important speech in your hometown. You decide to attend the speech. You find his thirty-minute presentation both interesting and informative. In the evening, you turn on the news to see how the networks cover his address. All three major networks excerpt the same ten-second portion of his speech. Why? What is it that makes certain portions of a speech quotable or memorable? Presidential speechwriter Peggy Noonan has said.

> *Great speeches have always had great soundbites . . . .They sum up a point, or make a point in language that is pithy or profound.*[12]

In other words, memorable speeches are stylistically distinctive. Earlier in this chapter, we discussed the importance of using words that are concrete, unbiased, vivid, simple, and used correctly. In this section we will turn our attention to groups of words, or word structures—phrases and sentences that create the unique drama and cadences needed to make a speech memorable.[13]

CREATING DRAMA

One way in which you can make phrases and sentences memorable is to utilize the potential of such structures to create drama in your speech—to keep the audience in suspense or to catch them slightly off guard by saying something in a way that differs from the way they expected you to say it. Three stylistic devices that can help you achieve such drama are omission, inversion, and suspension.

■ When you leave out a word or phrase that the audience expects to hear, you are using **omission**. Telegrams often use an economy of words, since you are charged by the word, and the more you can leave out, the cheaper will be your cost. But, of course, the words you leave out must be understood by

omission
Leaving out a word or phrase the listener expects to hear.

your listeners or readers. For example, a captain of a World War II Navy destroyer used omission to inform headquarters of his successful efforts at sighting and sinking an enemy submarine. He spared all details when he cabled back to headquarters: "Sighted sub–sank same." Using as few words as possible, he communicated his message in a memorable way. About 2,000 years earlier, another military commander informed his superiors in Rome of his conquest of Gaul with the economical message: "I came, I saw, I conquered." That commander was Julius Caesar.

■ The technique of reversing the normal word order of a phrase or sentence is **inversion.** It is commonly used in poetry. Within a few lines of *Paradise Lost,* Milton refers to "Spirits damn'd" and "Creatures rational,"[14] inverting the usual English adjective-noun pattern to a less common noun-adjective pattern. Speakers, too, use inversion to make their remarks memorable. In his 1852 eulogy for Daniel Webster, clergyman Theodore Parker infused a question with drama by using inversion: "Do men now mourn for him, the great man eloquent?"[15] And John F. Kennedy inverted the usual subject-verb-object sentence pattern to object-subject-verb in this brief declaration from his 1961 inaugural address: "This much we pledge . . . ."[16]

inversion
Reversing the normal word order of a phrase or sentence.

■ When you read a mystery novel, you are held in suspense until you reach the end and learn "who done it." The stylistic technique of verbal **suspension** does something similar. It occurs when you use a key word at the end of a sentence, rather than at the beginning. When Abraham Lincoln left Springfield, Illinois, for Washington, D.C., in the winter of 1861, he told his friends, "To this place, and the kindness of these people, I owe everything." [17] The more usual, but less memorable, structure would have been, "I owe everything to this place and the kindness of these people."

suspension
Withholding a key word or phrase until the end of a sentence.

Advertisers use the technique of suspension frequently. A few years ago, the Coca-Cola Company used suspension as the cornerstone of its worldwide advertising campaign. Rather than saying, "Coke goes better with everything," the copywriter decided to stylize the message by making *Coke* the last word in the sentence. The slogan became "Things go better with Coke." Again, the stylized version was more memorable because it used language in an unexpected way.

● CREATING CADENCE

Even very small children can memorize nursery rhymes and commercial jingles with relative ease. As we grow older, we may make up rhythms and rhymes to help us remember such facts as "Thirty days hath September, April, June, and November," and "Red sky at night/A sailor's delight." Why? Rhythms are memorable. The public speaker can take advantage of language rhythms, not by speaking in singsong patterns, but by using such stylistic devices as parallelism, antithesis, repetition, and alliteration.

■ **Parallelism** occurs when two or more clauses or sentences have the same grammatical pattern. When he delivered the Phi Beta Kappa oration at Harvard in 1837, Ralph Waldo Emerson cast these simple expressions in parallel structures:

parallelism
Using the same grammatical pattern for two or more clauses or sentences.

We will walk on our feet; we will work with our own hands; we will speak our own minds.[18]

Speaking to the people of Berlin in July 1994, Bill Clinton made a series of paradoxes more memorable by casting them in parallel structures:

We stand together where Europe's heart was cut in half and we celebrate unity. We stand where crude walls of concrete separated mother from child, and we meet as one family. We stand where those who sought a new life instead found death. And we rejoice in renewal.[19]

▪ The word **antithesis** means "opposition." In language style, antithesis is a sentence having a parallel structure, but with the two parts contrasting each other. Speakers have long realized the dramatic potential of antithesis. In Franklin Roosevelt's first inaugural address, he declared, "Our true destiny is not to be ministered unto but to minister to ourselves and to our fellow men."[20] Both in meaning and structure, his words foreshadowed the more famous remark of John F. Kennedy nearly thirty years later: "Ask not what your country can do for you; ask what you can do for your country."[21] We will examine Kennedy's statement in greater detail later in this chapter.

Antithesis is not restricted to politicians. When William Faulkner accepted the Nobel prize for literature in 1950, he spoke the now famous antithetical phrase: "I believe that *man will not merely endure: he will prevail.*"[22] An antithetical statement is a good way to end a speech. The cadence it creates will make the statement memorable.

▪ **Repetition** of a key word or phrase gives rhythm, power, and memorability to your message. At the climax of Patrick Henry's "Liberty or Death" speech in 1775 was this passionate use of repetition: "The war is inevitable—and let it come! I repeat it, sir, let it come!"[23] Twentieth-century speakers, too, recognize the power of repetition as a memorable stylistic device. In 1993, veteran reporter and CBS news anchor Dan Rather delivered the following eloquent and impassioned challenge to his colleagues:

In the constant scratching and scrambling for ever better ratings and money and the boss' praise and a better job, it is worth pausing to ask: how goes the real war, the really important battle of our professional lives? How goes the battle for quality, for truth, and justice, for programs worthy of the best within ourselves and the audience? How goes the battle against "ignorance, intolerance, and indifference?" The battle not to be merely "wires and lights in a box," the battle to make television not just entertaining but also, at least some little of the time, useful for higher, better things? How goes the battle?[24]

The repeated question, "How goes the battle?" rings in one's mind long after hearing or reading the passage.

▪ **Alliteration** is the repetition of a consonant sound (usually an initial consonant) several times in a phrase, clause, or sentence. Alliteration adds cadence to a thought. Two mid-twentieth-century orators who favored alliteration

---

antithesis
A two-part parallel structure in which the second part contrasts with the first.

alliteration
The repetition of a consonant sound (usually the first consonant) several times in a phrase, clause, or sentence.

were Franklin Roosevelt and Winston Churchill. Roosevelt called for "discipline and direction" in his first inaugural address;[25] little more than a week later, in his first fireside chat, he urged weary listeners to have "confidence and courage."[26] Churchill, rousing Englishmen to resist the Nazi onslaught in 1940, used the alliterative phrase "disaster and disappointment."[27] Addressing the Congress of the United States a year later, he praised "virility, valour and civic virtue."[28] Used sparingly, alliteration can add cadence to your rhetoric.

RECAP

CRAFTING MEMORABLE WORD STRUCTURES

Word Structures with Drama

OMISSION	Boil an idea down to its essence by leaving out understood words.
INVERSION	Reverse the expected order of words and phrases.
SUSPENSION	Place a key word at the end of a phrase or sentence.

Word Structures with Cadence

PARALLELISM	Use the same pattern to begin several sentences or phrases.
ANTITHESIS	In parallel structures, oppose one part of a sentence to another.
REPETITION	Repeat a key word or phrase several times for emphasis.
ALLITERATION	Use the same initial consonant sound several times in a phrase or sentence.

A second look at memorable word structures

We'd like to illustrate all seven techniques of creating memorable word structures with one final example.[29] If you asked almost anyone for the most quoted line from President Kennedy's speeches, that quote would probably be "Ask not what your country can do for you; ask what you can do for your country." Besides expressing a noble thought, a prime reason this line is so quotable is that it uses all seven stylistic techniques.

"Ask not . . ." is an example of omission. The subject, *you,* is not stated. "Ask not" is also an example of inversion. In casual everyday conversation, we would usually say "do not ask" rather than "ask not." The inversion makes the opening powerful and attention-grabbing.

The sentence also employs the technique of suspension. The key message of the phrase is suspended or delayed until the end of the sentence: "ask what you can do for your country." If the sentence structure had been reversed, the impact would not have been as dramatic. Consider: "Ask what you can do for your country rather than what your country can do for you."

Kennedy uses parallelism and antithesis. The sentence is a parallel construction of two clauses, one in opposition to the other.

He also uses the technique of repetition. He uses a form of the word *you* four times in a sentence of seventeen words. In fact, he uses only eight different words in his seventeen-word sentence. Only one word, *not* occurs only once in the entire sentence.

Finally, Kennedy adds alliteration to the sentence with the words *ask, can,* and *country.* The alliterative *k* sound is repeated at more or less even intervals.

Creating arresting images

In addition to using effective and memorable words and word structures, you can add style to your message by using figures of speech to create arresting and memorable images. A **figure of speech** deviates from the ordinary, expected meanings of words, to make a description or comparison unique, vivid, and memorable. Common figures of speech include metaphors, similes, and personification.

METAPHORS AND SIMILES

A **metaphor** is an implied comparison. Actor Edward Olmos, who portrayed Los Angeles teacher Jaime Escalante in the 1988 film *Stand and Deliver,* recently told a group of high school students that "Education is the vaccine for violence."[30] Olmos's comparison between education and vaccine is consistent with other health metaphors often used to identify social problems as "ills" and their solutions as "cures." The vaccine metaphor is particularly effective in this context, because it emphasizes the power of education to *prevent* a serious social problem, rather than *solve* an existing one.

A **simile** is a more overt comparison that includes the word *like* or *as.* In his 1995 "State of the World" diplomatic address, Pope John Paul II called the war in Bosnia a tragedy "which in a way seems like the shipwreck of the whole of Europe."[31] A shipwreck, which suggests indiscriminate, violent death and total devastation, is a particularly powerful simile for the Bosnian conflict.

PERSONIFICATION

Personification is the attribution of human qualities to inanimate things or ideas. Franklin Roosevelt personified nature as a generous provider in this state-

figure of speech
Language that deviates from the expected meaning of words to make a description or comparison unique, vivid, and memorable.

metaphor
An implied comparison between two things.

simile
An overt comparison between two things, that uses the word like *or* as.

personification
The attribution of human qualities to inanimate things or ideas.

ment from his first inaugural: "Nature still offers her bounty and human efforts have multiplied it. Plenty is at our doorstep."[32]

Stylistic devices should not be used to camouflage lack of content. Nor should your speech be so stylized that it sounds like flowery poetry rather than a speech. But using the stylistic techniques we have discussed can have important benefits for you as a public speaker.

RECAP

CREATING ARRESTING IMAGES

Figures of Speech	Examples
Metaphors are implied comparisons.	This exam was a real bear.
Similes compare by using the word *like* or *as*.	Life is like a river.
Personification is the attribution of human qualities to inanimate things or ideas.	Mother Earth

---

Tips for using language effectively

Having reviewed ways to add style and interest to the language of your speech, we must now consider how best to put those techniques into practice.

- Even though we have made great claims for the value of style, do not overdo it. Including too much highly stylized language can put the focus on your language rather than on your content. Use distinctive stylistic devices sparingly.

- Save your use of stylistic devices for times during your speech when you want your audience to remember your key ideas or when you wish to capture their attention. Some kitchen mixers have a "burst of power" switch to help churn through difficult mixing chores with extra force. Think of the stylistic devices that we have reviewed as opportunities to provide a burst of power to your thoughts and ideas. Use them in your opening sentences, statements of key ideas, and conclusion.

- Short words are more forceful than long ones. Think of those monosyllabic commands—Sit! March! Stop! When a technical term is too unusual or cumbersome, find a way to describe the concept with another word, or use a simile or a metaphor. To talk about the process of floccinaucinihilipilification (the action or habit of estimating something as worthless) may make an interesting speech, but the word itself probably will not add to your audience's ability to remember it.

■ Use stylistic devices to economize. When sentences become too long or complex, see if you can recast them with antitheses or suspensions. Also remember the possibility of omission.

Summary

In this chapter we suggested ways to use words to give your ideas maximum impact. We noted that there is a difference between the way people talk and the way they write when it comes to the use of language. In general, oral style is more personal, less formal, and more repetitious than is written style.

Words should be concrete, vivid, unbiased, simple, and used correctly. We explored the importance of understanding the connotations of words, as well as their denotations.

We also focused on how to create drama and cadence with word structures. We provided definitions and examples of the techniques of omission, inversion, suspension, parallelism, antithesis, repetition, and alliteration. We also made suggestions for creating arresting images through such figures of speech as metaphors, similes, and personification.

Effective speakers take great care in wording their speeches. Time invested in using words and word structures well can help you gain and maintain the attention of your audience, and can help your audience understand your message and remember what you say.

CRITICAL THINKING QUESTIONS

1. Toni practices her speech for you and asks for advice on polishing the speech, including polishing the style of her language. Offer Toni at least three general suggestions for using language effectively.

2. Not long ago, a reader wrote in a letter to "Dear Abby":

   > *. . . a woman does not have a maiden name until she takes a married name. What she has is a* surname. *"Maiden" refers to a former name that was given up in favor of her husband's name. Women who retain their own names (or their surnames) after marriage do not have a maiden name.*
   >
   > *This may sound picky to some, but for women (and their husbands) who choose this option, the term* maiden name *is offensive.*[33]

   Analyze the reader's point in light of the discussion of sexist language in this chapter. Do you agree or disagree that the term maiden name is sexist? Why or why not?

3. The following are five memorable metaphors from historical speeches:[34]

> an iron curtain

> I have but one lamp by which my feet are guided, and that is the lamp of experience.

> Speak softly and carry a big stick.

> You shall not crucify mankind upon a cross of gold.

> snake pit of racial hatred

First, explain what each metaphor means. Now express the same idea in ordinary language. What do you gain or lose by doing so?

● ETHICAL QUESTIONS

1. A high school salutatorian who was raped when she was a 14-year-old sopho-more, wanted to mention the experience in her salutatory speech, thanking the people who had helped her, and assuring her classmates that they could overcome even the most devastating experiences in life.[35] The principal, how-ever, edited her speech, changing the word *rape* to the phrase *a terrible thing*. The student claimed she needed to use the concrete word to emphasize con-fronting such experiences head-on. The principal said he was simply suggest-ing ways to make the language of the speech more appropriate. Discuss the ethical implications of this debate over language style. Did the student have the right to call the attack "rape"? Or was the principal correct in censoring the term, out of consideration for the occasion and audience?

● SUGGESTED ACTIVITIES

1. One of the challenges in coining metaphors and similes is to avoid clichés. For example, we all know such simile clichés as "hungry as a bear," "smooth as glass," and "pretty as a picture." But similes can be quite effective as atten-tion-getting devices if they deviate from the expected. Try to invent at least three new endings for each of the following similes:

hungry as _____

_____

_____

smooth as _____

_____

_____

pretty as _____

_____

_____

mean as _____

_____

_____

smart as _____

_____

_____

2. Consult *Roget's Thesaurus,* or the thesaurus on your word processing computer program, and find a more concrete or vivid word to express each of the following:

cry	rich
clumsy	love
error	smooth
cold	surprise
frightened	restore
great	full
little	increase

3. Find examples of omission, inversion, suspension, parallelism, antithesis, repetition, and alliteration in one or more of the speeches in Appendix C.

USING TECHNOLOGY AND MEDIA

1. Readability indexes can help you determine how easily your writing can be understood. The number of sentences per paragraph, words per sentence, and characters per word are all factors that affect readability. Some word processing programs will evaluate readability for you. If your word processing program offers this feature, write out the introduction or conclusion, or a main idea with subpoints and supporting materials, for your next speech. Run a readability test to determine how easily understandable your style is.

"Five Faces."
Diana Ong/SuperStock

Delivering Your Speech

Speak the speech, I pray you, as I pronounced it to you, trippingly on the tongue.
—*William Shakespeare*

● OBJECTIVES

After studying this chapter you should be able to do the following:

1. Identify three reasons delivery is important to a public speaker.

2. Identify and describe four types of delivery.

3. Identify and illustrate physical characteristics of effective delivery.

4. Describe the steps to follow when you rehearse your speech.

5. List four suggestions for enhancing the final delivery of your speech.

hat's more important: what you say or how you say it? Delivery has long been considered an important part of public speaking. But is the delivery of your speech more important than the content of your message? Since ancient Greece, people have argued about the role delivery plays in public speaking.

More than 2,000 years ago, some thinkers held that delivery was not an "elevated" topic of study. In his classic treatise *The Rhetoric,* written in 333 B.C., Aristotle claimed that "the battle should be fought out on the facts of the case alone; and therefore everything outside the direct proof is really superfluous." Writing in the first century, Quintilian, Roman rhetorician and author of the first book on speech training, acknowledged the importance of delivery when he said that the beginning speaker should strive for an "extempore" or conversational delivery style. His countryman, the great orator Cicero, claimed that without effective delivery, "a speaker of the highest mental capacity can be held in no esteem, while one of moderate abilities, with this qualification, may surpass even those of the highest talent." Sixteen centuries later, the elocution movement carried the emphasis on delivery to an extreme. For elocutionists, speech training consisted largely of techniques and exercises for improving posture, movement, and vocal quality.

Today speech communication teachers believe that both content and delivery contribute to speaking effectiveness. A recent survey suggested that "developing effective delivery" is a primary goal of most speech teachers.[1] Considerable research supports the claim that delivery plays an important role in influencing how audiences react to a speaker and his or her message. It is your audience who will determine whether you are successful. Delivery counts.

Although some courses on public speaking are offered in various countries throughout the world, most of the formal instruction on how to deliver a speech is found in the United States. Our advice about speech delivery, therefore, is closely related to the discipline of speech communication here in the United States. It's not possible for us to provide a comprehensive compendium of each cultural expectation you may face as you give speeches in a variety of educational and professional settings, but we will try to sample conventions and preferences of other cultures as we discuss the topics related to delivery throughout this chapter.

Rehearsing your speech

n previous chapters we have discussed how to develop an audience-centered message. We have guided you through the process of preparing a speech, from selecting a topic through organizing your speech. As shown in Figure 13.1, your next step is to rehearse your speech in preparation for your speech performance. This chapter reviews key principles and techniques that can help you maximize your rehearsal efficiency as you prepare to deliver your speech.

F **IGURE 13.1**
*Rehearsing your speech
delivery will help you
present your speech with
confidence.*

Consider
the
Audience

Deliver
Speech

Select and
Narrow
Topic

Rehearse
Speech

Determine
Purpose

Organize
Speech

Develop
Central
Idea

Gather
Supporting
Material

Generate
Main
Ideas

Importance of delivery

THE ROLE OF NONVERBAL BEHAVIOR IN DELIVERY

The way you hold your notes, your gestures and stance, and your impatient adjustment of your glasses all contribute to the overall effect of your speech. Nonverbal factors such as body language play a major role in the communication process. As much as 65 percent of the *social meaning* of messages is based on nonverbal signals.[2]

In a public speaking situation, nonverbal elements have an influence on the audience's perceptions about a speaker's effectiveness. A classic study by Alan H. Monroe suggests that audience members equate effective public speaking with effective delivery.[3] In comparing good and bad speakers, Monroe found that the first six characteristics student audiences associated with an ineffective speaker were related to the speaker's delivery. A monotonous voice was rated as the most distracting, followed by stiffness, lack of eye contact with the audience, fidgeting, lack of enthusiasm, and a weak voice. In keeping with these negative findings, he also observed that audiences liked direct eye contact, alertness, enthusiasm, a pleasant voice, and animated gestures.

Examining the "general effectiveness" of student speeches, another researcher concluded that delivery was almost twice as important as content when students gave self-introduction speeches and three times as important when students gave persuasive speeches.[4] The way you deliver a speech does influence the way listeners will respond to your message.

COMMUNICATING EMOTIONS AND ATTITUDES

Nonverbal behavior is particularly important in communicating feelings, emotions, attitudes, likes, and dislikes to an audience. One researcher found that as little as 7 percent of the emotional impact of a message is communicated by the words we use.[5] About 38 percent hinges on such qualities of voice as inflection, intensity, or loudness, and 55 percent hinges on our facial expressions. Generalizing from these findings, we may say that approximately 93 percent of emotional meaning is communicated nonverbally. Although some scholars question whether these findings can be applied to all communication settings, the research does suggest that the manner of delivery provides important information about the speaker's feelings and emotions. Audience expectations can help you match the amount of emotional expression you exhibit to your listeners. For example, when speaking to predominantly African American listeners, some African American preachers and politicians use a more emotional delivery style than when speaking to non–African American listeners.

In addition, your delivery will affect your listeners' emotional responses to you. A recent study found that when a speaker's delivery was effective, the audience felt greater pleasure and had a more positive emotional response than when the same speaker had poor delivery.[6] In addition to these stronger emotional responses, listeners seemed to understand speakers better and believe them more when their delivery was good. Clearly, if you want your audience to respond positively to both you and your message, it pays to polish your delivery techniques.

AUDIENCES BELIEVE WHAT THEY SEE

"I'm very glad to speak with you tonight," drones the speaker in a monotone, eyes glued to his notes. His audience probably does not believe him. When our nonverbal delivery contradicts what we say, people generally believe the nonverbal message. In this case, the speaker is communicating that he's *not* glad to be talking to this audience.

We usually believe nonverbal messages because they are more difficult to fake. Although we can monitor certain parts of our nonverbal behavior, it is difficult to control all of it consciously. Research suggests that a person trying to deceive someone may speak in a higher vocal pitch, at a slower rate, and with more pronunciation mistakes than normal.[7] Blushing, sweating, and changed breathing patterns also often belie our stated meaning. As the saying goes, "What you do speaks so loud, I can't hear what you say."

Methods of delivery

The style of delivery you choose will influence your nonverbal behaviors. There are four basic methods of delivery from which a speaker can choose: manuscript reading, speaking from memory, impromptu speaking, and extemporaneous speaking. Let's consider each in some detail.

● MANUSCRIPT READING

You have a speech to present and are afraid you will forget what you have prepared to say. So you write your speech and then read it to your audience.

Speech teachers frown on this approach, particularly for public speaking students. Reading is usually a poor way to deliver a speech. Although it may provide some assurance of not forgetting the speech, reading from a manuscript is rarely done well enough to be interesting. You have probably attended a lecture that was read and wondered, "Why doesn't he just make a copy of the speech for everyone in the audience rather than reading it to us?"

However, some speeches should be read. One advantage of reading from a manuscript is that you can choose words very carefully when dealing with a sensitive and critical issue. The President of the United States, for example, often finds it useful to have his remarks carefully scripted. An awkward statement could result in serious consequences, not only for his political career but also for the security of our nation. Statements to the press by the chief executive officers of corporations under fire should be delivered from carefully crafted papers rather than tossed off casually.

Roger Ailes, a media consultant to Republican presidents and governors, suggests that if you do have to read from a manuscript, to ensure maximum eye contact, you should type your speech in short, easy-to-scan phrases on the upper two thirds of the paper so that you do not have to look too far down into your notes.[8] You should try to have eye contact at the end of a sentence by scooping up an entire line of a speech. He also recommends that you do not read a speech too quickly. Use your index finger to keep your place in the manuscript so you don't lose your place.

The key to giving an effective manuscript speech is to sound as though you are *not* giving a manuscript speech. Speak with vocal variation—vary the rhythm, inflection, and pace of your delivery. Be familiar enough with your manuscript that you can have as much eye contact with your audience as possible. Use gestures and movement to add interest and emphasis to your message.

SPEAKING FROM MEMORY

"All right," you think, "since reading a speech is hard to pull off, I'll write my speech out word for word and then memorize it." You're pretty sure that no one will be able to tell, since you won't be using notes. Memorizing your speech also has the advantage of allowing you to have maximum eye contact with the audience. But most memorized speeches *sound* stiff, stilted, and overrehearsed. The inherent differences between speaking and writing will be evident in a memorized speech, just as they can be heard in a manuscript speech. You also run the risk of forgetting parts of your speech and awkwardly searching for words in front of your audience. For these reasons, speech teachers do not encourage their students to memorize speeches for class presentation.

If you are accepting an award, introducing a speaker, making announcements, or delivering other brief remarks, however, a memorized delivery style is sometimes acceptable. But as with manuscript speaking, you must take care to make your presentation sound lively and interesting.

IMPROMPTU SPEAKING

You have undoubtedly already delivered many impromptu presentations. Your response to a question posed by a teacher in class, or an unrehearsed rebuttal to a comment made by a colleague during a meeting, are examples of impromptu presentations. The impromptu method is often described as "thinking on your feet" or "speaking off the cuff." The advantage of impromptu speaking is that you can speak informally, maintaining direct eye contact with the audience. But unless a speaker is extremely talented or has learned and practiced the techniques of impromptu speaking, the speech itself will be unimpressive. An impromptu speech usually lacks logical organization and thorough research. There are times, of course, when you may be called on to speak without advance knowledge of the invitation or when something goes awry in your efforts to deliver your planned message. This was the case when Harvard University president Neil Rudenstine discovered pages missing from his procedural guide during the 1994 commencement. He improvised the conferring of degrees on a group of candidates, "Since I have no text, I will make it up," he told his laughing audience, and proceeded to do so:

> *By virtue of every last single bit and ounce of authority delegated to me, and recognizing every single achievement that you may or not have made, I wish to confer on you the degrees of master of arts, master of science, master of engineering, and master of forest science. May you do your work well, live your lives well, and take your degrees properly with you.*[9]

Rudenstine's efforts were somewhat more successful than was the performance given some years earlier by a friend of your authors, who is a Fellow at Cambridge University in England. Given the responsibility of conferring degrees upon the graduates of his college, he had carefully memorized his Latin text, but found to his horror that his mind went blank when the moment arrived. Sheepishly, he admits, "I got through it by mumbling some bits of Latin I could remember, but I think I said something like, 'Blessed be the fruit of thy womb.'"

What is the lesson from these examples? If you know you will be giving a speech, prepare and rehearse it. For the times when you may be called on to deliver an improvised or impromptu speech, the following guidelines can help ease you through it.

- *Consider your audience.* Just as you have learned to do in other speaking situations, when you are called on for impromptu remarks, think first of your audience. Who are the members of your audience? What are their common characteristics and interests? What do they know about your topic? What do they expect you to say? What is the occasion of your speech? A quick mental check of these questions will help ensure that even impromptu remarks are audience-centered.

- *Be brief.* When you are asked to deliver an off-the-cuff speech, your audience knows the circumstances and will not expect or even want a lengthy discourse. One to three minutes is a realistic time frame for most impromptu situations. Some spur-of-the-moment remarks, such as press statements, may be even shorter.

- *Speak honestly, but with reserve, from personal experience and knowledge.* Because there is no opportunity to conduct any kind of research before delivering an impromptu speech, you will have to speak from your own experience and knowledge. Remember, audiences almost always respond favorably to personal illustrations, so use any appropriate and relevant ones that come to mind. Of course, the more knowledge you have about the subject to be discussed, the easier it will be to speak about it off the cuff. But do *not* make up information or provide facts or figures about which you are not certain. An honest "I don't know" or a very brief statement is more appropriate.

- *Be cautious.* No matter how much knowledge you have, if your subject is at all sensitive or your information is classified, be careful when discussing it during your impromptu speech. If asked about a controversial topic, give an honest but noncommittal answer. You can always elaborate later, but you can never take back something rash you have already said. It is better to be cautious than sorry!

- *Organize!* Off-the-cuff remarks need not falter or ramble. Effective impromptu speakers still organize their ideas into an introduction, body, and conclusion. Consider organizing your points using a simple organizational strategy such as chronological order or a topical pattern. A variation on the chronological pattern is to use the past, present, future model of addressing an issue. This pattern is well known to students who compete in impromptu speaking contests. The speaker organizes the impromptu speech by discussing (1) what has happened in the past, (2) what is happening now, and (3) what may happen in the future.

If you are not reading from a manuscript, reciting from memory, or speaking impromptu, what's left? Extemporaneous speaking is the approach most speech communication teachers recommend for most situations. When delivering a speech extemporaneously, you speak from a written or memorized general outline, but you do not have the exact wording in front of you or in memory. You have rehearsed the speech so that you know key ideas and their organization, but not to the degree that the speech sounds memorized. An extemporaneous style is conversational; it gives your audience the impression that the speech is being created as they listen to it, and to some extent it is. Audiences prefer to hear something live rather than something canned. Even though you can't tell the difference between a performance that is taped or live when it is broadcast on TV, you would probably prefer seeing it live. There is added interest and excitement associated with seeing something happening now. An extemporaneous speech sounds live rather than as though it were prepared yesterday or weeks ago. The extemporaneous method reflects the advantages of a well-organized speech delivered in an interesting and vivid manner.

When giving his first State of the Union address, President Clinton walked to the lectern with his speech manuscript ready to roll on the TelePrompTer. But according to the *New Yorker,* rather than reading his speech as most presidents do (he only spoke four consecutive words of his prepared text), he used his text like a jazz musician uses music. He used an extemporaneous style to embellish his prepared remarks as a musician embellishes key themes when improvising.

You develop an extemporaneous style by first rehearsing your speech, using many notes or perhaps looking at your full-content outline. As you continue to rehearse, you try to rely less on your notes, but you don't try to memorize your message word for word. After going over your speech a few times, you find that you have internalized the overall structure of the speech, although the exact way you express your ideas may vary. You rely less on your notes and focus more on adapting your message to your listeners. The final draft of your speaking notes may be an abbreviated outline or a few key words and essential facts or statistics that you want to remember.

RECAP

METHODS OF DELIVERY

MANUSCRIPT	Reading your speech from a prepared text
MEMORIZED	Giving a speech from memory without using notes
IMPROMPTU	Delivering a speech without preparing
EXTEMPORANEOUS	Knowing the major ideas, which have been outlined; the exact wording has not been memorized

SPEAKERS AT WORK

Soon after he retired, John Reinhardt, former Foreign Service officer and ambassador to Nigeria, former director of the National African Art Museum of the Smithsonian Institution, and professor emeritus at the University of Vermont, was asked by the Woodrow Wilson National Fellowship Foundation to share some of his experiences with college students. This narrative describes a speaking situation that called for quick thinking on his part to adapt to his audience's expectations. Reinhardt's successful strategy illustrates one of the suggestions you will find in chapter 15: Present new information by relating it to things that are familiar to your audience.

Several years ago, I was invited for a five-day visit to a lovely small college in a rural community, where I was to speak on foreign policy—how it is made, who makes it, and what principles guide the making. Approximately 250 people were expected to attend my 45-minute lecture, including townspeople who were disturbed about recent trends in foreign affairs. I was told to be prepared to field questions from an eager audience.

This scenario seemed worthy of my best efforts. Before I left on my trip, I prepared a written text containing a wealth of details about the roles of the president, the secretary of state, self-determination, national interest, public opinion, and other factors in shaping foreign policy.

When I arrived on campus and began meeting informally with faculty and students, however, I started to suspect that my prepared text might extend beyond my prospective audience's interests and level of political sophistication. These suspicions were confirmed the evening of my lecture as I sat on stage listening to the person introducing me: The audience was being promised a talk on the trappings, not the substance, of foreign policy.

Instead of panicking, I quickly shifted gears by seizing upon several observations I had made during my first days on campus: First, although the college library subscribed to *The Economist,* it was read by only a handful of professors; second, although the exhibit room at the library contained several pieces of rather good African art, they attracted scant attention from the campus population; and third, although an excellent reproduction of a Woodrow Wilson portrait was prominently displayed in the foyer of one of the college's main buildings, the only people who gave it a second glance were art students accompanied by their instructors.

I used these observations to organize an extemporaneous speech around a three-part thesis: First, that the table of contents for each issue of *The Economist* constitutes a brief "tour" of the principal concerns affecting relations among nations; second, that art can buttress our understanding of the radical differences between the cultures of different nations and thereby foster good relations between the peoples of those nations; and third, that Wilson's portrait depicts a man pleading for the citizens of the United States to understand and support his foreign policy—a plea made by every President in our history.

By focusing on familiar, concrete objects, I managed to capture my audience's interest and lead them to an understanding of some basic but critical concepts about foreign policy.

My speech enjoyed a rousing reception. It was followed by more than an hour of questions and answers as well as animated informal "sidebar" conversations later in the evening. And I learned in the months that followed that *The Economist* was in great demand in the library, and that both the African art exhibit and the Wilson foyer were attracting unprecedented numbers of visitors.

Characteristics of effective delivery

You have learned the importance of effective delivery and have identified four methods of delivery. You now know that for most speaking situations, you should strive for a conversational style. But you still may have a number of specific questions about enhancing the effectiveness of your delivery. Typical concerns include these: "What do I do with my hands?" "Is it all right to move around while I speak?" "How can I make my voice sound interesting?" While these concerns may seem overwhelming, presenting a well-prepared and well-rehearsed speech is the best antidote to jitters about delivery. Practice and focus on communicating your message to your audience are vital for effective communication and great for your confidence. To help answer specific questions about presenting a speech, we will consider five major categories of nonverbal behavior that affect delivery: body language, eye contact, facial expression, vocal delivery, and personal appearance.

● BODY LANGUAGE

body language
A person's gestures, movement, and posture, which influence how a message is interpreted.

Gesture, movement, and posture are the three key attributes of physical delivery, or **body language.** Your body language will influence whether your audience sees you as credible and competent. It also helps determine whether you successfully gain and hold audience interest. A good public speaker knows how to use effective gestures and maintain an appropriate posture while speaking to an audience.

● GESTURES   The next time you have a conversation with someone, notice how both of you use your hands and bodies to communicate. Important points are emphasized with gestures. You also gesture to indicate places, to enumerate items, and to describe objects. Gestures have the same functions for public speakers. Yet many people who gesture easily and appropriately in the course of everyday conversations aren't sure what to do with their hands when they find themselves in front of an audience.

There is evidence that the gestures we use when speaking vary from culture to culture. When he was mayor of New York City during the 1930s and 1940s, Mayor Fiorello La Guardia, fluent in Yiddish and Italian as well as English, would speak the language appropriate for his audience. One researcher studied old newsreels of the mayor and discovered that with the sound turned off viewers could still identify the language spoken by the mayor. How? When speaking English, he used minimal gestures. When speaking Italian, he used broad, sweeping gestures. And when speaking Yiddish, he used short and choppy hand movements.

Cultural expectations can help you make decisions about your approach to using gestures. Listeners from Japan and China, for example, prefer a quieter, less flamboyant use of gestures. When one of your authors spoke in England, several listeners noted the use of "typical American gestures and movement." British listeners seemed to prefer that the speaker stay behind a lectern and use relatively few gestures. Other Europeans agree they can spot an American speaker because

Americans typically are more animated in their use of gestures, movement, and facial expressions than are European speakers.

Public speaking teachers often observe several unusual, inappropriate, and unnatural gestures among their students. Common problems include keeping your hands behind your back in a "parade rest" pose. We are not suggesting that you never put your hands behind your back, only that standing at parade rest during an entire speech looks awkward and unnatural and may distract your audience.

Another common position is standing with one hand on the hip in a "broken wing" pose. Worse than the "broken wing" is both hands resting on the hips in a "double broken wing." The speaker looks as though he or she might burst into a rendition of "I'm a Little Teapot." Again, we are not suggesting that you should never place your hands on your hips, only that to hold that one pose throughout a speech looks unnatural and will keep you from using other gestures.

Few poses are more awkward-looking than when a speaker clutches one arm, as if grazed by a bullet. The audience half expects the speaker to call out reassuringly, "Don't worry, Ma; it's only a flesh wound." Similarly, keeping your hands in your pockets can make you look as if you were afraid to let go of your change or your keys.

Some students clasp their hands and let them drop in front of them in a distracting "fig leaf clutch." Gestures can distract your audience in various other ways as well. Grasping the lectern until your knuckles turn white or just letting your hands flop around without purpose or control does little to help you communicate your message.

If you don't know what to do with your hands, think about the message you want to communicate. As in ordinary conversation, your hands should simply help emphasize or reinforce your verbal message. Specifically, note the following ways in which your gestures can lend strength to what you have to say: (1) repeating, (2) contradicting, (3) substituting, (4) complementing, (5) emphasizing, and (6) regulating.

- *Repeating.* Gestures can help you repeat your verbal message. For example, you can say, "I have three major points to talk about today," while holding up three fingers. Or you can describe an object as twelve inches long while holding your hands about a foot apart. Repeating what you say through nonverbal means can reinforce your message.

- *Contradicting.* Since your audience will sooner believe what you communicate nonverbally than verbally, you need to monitor your gestures to make sure that you are not contradicting what you say. It is difficult to convey an image of control and confidence by using flailing gestures and awkward poses. You don't want to display behavior that will conflict with your intended image or message, nor do you want to appear stiff and self-conscious. So the crucial thing to keep in mind while monitoring your own behavior is to *stay relaxed.*

- *Substituting.* Not only can your behavior reinforce or contradict what you say, but your gestures can also substitute for your message. Without uttering a word, you can hold up the palm of your hand to calm a noisy crowd. Flashing two fingers to form a *V* for victory or raising a clenched fist are other common examples of how gestures can substitute for a verbal message.

- *Complementing.* Gestures can also add further meaning to your verbal message. A politician who declines to comment on a reporter's question while holding up her hands to augment her verbal refusal, uses her gesture to complement or provide further meaning to her verbal message.

- *Emphasizing.* You can give emphasis to what you say by using an appropriate gesture. A shaking fist or a slicing gesture with one or both hands help emphasize a message. So does pounding your fist into the palm of your hand. Other gestures can be less dramatic but still lend emphasis to what you say. You should try to allow your gestures to arise from the content of your speech and your emotions.

- *Regulating.* Gestures can also regulate the exchange between you and your audience. If you want the audience to respond to a question, you can extend both palms to invite a response. During a question-and-answer session, your gestures can signal when you want to talk and when you want to invite others to do so.

● USING GESTURES EFFECTIVELY Turn-of-the-century elocutionists taught their students how to gesture to communicate specific emotions or messages. Today teachers of speech act differently. Rather than prescribe gestures for specific situations, they feel that it is more useful to offer suitable criteria (standards) by which to judge effective gestures, regardless of what is being said. Here are some guidelines that you can think about when working on your delivery.

- *Stay natural.* Gestures should be *relaxed,* not tense or rigid. Your gestures should flow with your message. Avoid sawing or slashing through the air with your hands unless you are trying to emphasize a particularly dramatic point. The pounding fist or raised forefinger in hectoring style will not necessarily enhance the quality of your performance.

- *Be definite.* Gestures should appear *definite* rather than as accidental brief jerks of your hands or arms. If you want to gesture, go ahead and gesture. Avoid minor hand movements that will be masked by the lectern.

- *Use gestures that are consistent with your message.* Gestures should be *appropriate* for the verbal content of your speech. If you are excited, gesture more vigorously. But remember that prerehearsed gestures that do not naturally arise from what you are trying to say are likely to appear awkward and stilted.

- *Vary your gestures.* Strive for *variety* and versatility in your use of gesture. Try not to use just one hand or one all-purpose gesture. Gestures can be used for a variety of purposes, such as enumerating, pointing, describing, and symbolizing an idea or concept (such as clasping your hands together to suggest agreement or a coming-together process).

- *Don't overdo it.* Gestures should be *unobtrusive;* your audience should focus not on the beauty or appropriateness of your gestures but on your message. Your purpose is to communicate a message to your audience, not to perform for your listeners in such a way that your delivery receives more attention than your message.

- *Coordinate gestures with what you say.* Gestures should be *well timed* to coincide with your verbal message. When you announce that you have three major points, your gesture of enumeration should occur simultaneously with your utterance of the word *three*. It would be poor timing to announce that you have three points, pause for a second or two, and then hold up three fingers.

- *Make your gestures appropriate to your audience and situation.* Gestures must be *adapted to the audience*. In more formal speaking situations, particularly when speaking to a large audience, bolder, more sweeping, and more dramatic gestures are appropriate. A small audience in a less formal setting calls for less formal gestures.

In summary, keep one important principle in mind: Use gestures that work best for you. Don't try to be someone that you are not. Jesse Jackson's style may work for him, but you are not Jesse Jackson. Your gestures should fit your personality. We believe it is better to use no gestures than to try to counterfeit someone else's gestures. Your nonverbal delivery should flow from *your* message.

RECAP

EFFECTIVE GESTURES

THE MOST EFFECTIVE GESTURES ARE . . .

Natural and relaxed	Unobtrusive
Definite	Coordinated with what you say
Consistent with your message	Appropriate to your audience and situation
Varied	

● MOVEMENT Should you walk around during your speech, or should you stay in one place? If there is a lectern, should you stand behind it, or would it be acceptable to stand in front of it or to the side? Is it all right to sit down while you speak? Can you move among the audience, as Oprah Winfrey does on her TV talk show? You may well find yourself pondering one or more of these questions while preparing for your speeches. The following discussion may help you answer them.

You may want to move about while delivering your speech, but you should take care that your movement does not detract from your message. If the audience focuses on your movement rather than on what you are saying, it is better to stand still. In short, your movement should be consistent with the verbal content of your message. It should make sense rather than appear as aimless wandering.

As you consider incorporating movement into your speech, you should also be mindful of the physical barriers that exist between you and your audience. Barriers such as a lectern, rows of chairs, a chalkboard, an overhead projector, or other audio-visual aids may act as obstacles between you and your audience. If physical barriers make you feel too far removed from your audience, move closer. Several studies suggest that in North America the most effective classroom teachers stand closer to their students.[10] They move out from behind their desks so they can have more eye contact with their students. Apparently, this physical proximity enhances learning.

You may also signal the beginning of a new idea or major point in your speech with movement. As you move into a transition statement or change from

Proximity conventions vary widely from culture to culture. Within cultures, certain occasions may also demand specific distance relationships between speaker and audience. Here, an audience in American Samoa assumes a seating arrangement appropriate for listening to a speech by a Talking Chief. [Photo: Don Smetzer/Tony Stone Images]

a serious subject to a more humorous one, movement can be a good way to signal that your approach to the speaking situation is changing.

Your use of movement during your speech should make sense to your listeners. Avoid random pacing and overly dramatic gestures. Our advice about proximity and other delivery variables should be tempered by the cultural expectations of an audience. British listeners have commented to us that American teachers often tend to stand too close to an audience when speaking. British educators prefer more formal styles of oratory, in which the speaker is separated from the audience.

● POSTURE   Although few formal studies of posture in relation to public speaking have been conducted, there is evidence that the way you carry your body communicates significant information. One study even suggests that your stance can reflect on your credibility as a speaker.[11] Slouching across the lectern, for example, does not project an image of vitality and interest in your audience.

Whereas your face and voice play the major role in communicating a specific emotion, your posture communicates the *intensity* of that emotion. If you are happy, your face and voice will reflect your happiness; your posture will communicate the intensity of your joy.

Since the days of the elocutionists, few speech teachers or public speaking texts have advocated specific postures for public speakers. Today we believe that the specific stance you adopt should come about naturally, as a result of what you have to say, the environment, and the formality or informality of the occasion. For example, it may be perfectly appropriate as well as comfortable and natural to sit on the edge of a desk during a very informal presentation. Most speech teachers, however, do not encourage students to sit while delivering classroom speeches. In general, avoid slouched shoulders, shifting from foot to foot, or drooping your head. Your posture should not call attention to itself. It should instead reflect your interest in the speaking event and your attention to the task at hand.

● EYE CONTACT

Of all of the delivery features discussed in this chapter, the most important one in a public speaking situation is eye contact. Eye contact with your audience opens communication, makes you more believable, and keeps your audience interested. Each of these functions contributes to the success of your delivery. Eye contact also provides you with feedback about how your speech is coming across.

Making eye contact with your listeners clearly shows that you are ready to talk to them. Most people start a conversation by looking at the person they are going to talk to. The same process occurs in public speaking.

Once you've started talking, continued eye contact lets you know how your audience is responding to your speech. You don't need to look at your listeners continuously. As the need arises, you should certainly look at your notes, but also look at your listeners frequently, just to see what they're doing.

Most listeners will think you are capable and trustworthy if you look them in the eye. Several studies document a relationship between eye contact and increased speaker credibility.[12] Speakers with less than 50 percent eye contact are considered unfriendly, uninformed, inexperienced, and even dishonest by their listeners.

Another study showed that those audience members who had more than 50 percent eye contact with their speaker performed better in postspeech tests than did those who had less than 50 percent eye contact.[13] However, not all people from all cultures prefer the same amount of direct eye contact when listening to someone talk. In interpersonal contexts, people from Asian cultures, for example, prefer less direct eye contact when communicating with others.

Most audiences in the United States prefer that you establish eye contact with them even before you open your speech with your attention-catching introduction. When it's your time to speak, walk to the lectern (or the front of the audience if you're not using a lectern), pause, and look at your audience before you say anything. Eye contact nonverbally sends the message, "I am interested in you; tune me in; I have something I want to share with you." You should have your opening sentence well enough in mind that you can deliver it without looking at your notes or away from your listeners.

Try to establish eye contact with the entire audience, not just with the front row or only one or two people. Look to the back and front and from side to side of your audience, selecting an individual to focus on and then moving on to someone else. You need not rhythmically move your head back and forth like a lighthouse beacon. It's best not to establish a predictable pattern for your eye contact. Look at individuals, establishing person-to-person contact with them—not so long that it will make a listener feel uncomfortable, but long enough to establish the feeling that you are talking directly to that individual. *Don't* look over your listeners' heads; establish eye-to-eye contact.

FACIAL EXPRESSION

Media experts today doubt that Abraham Lincoln would have survived as a politician in our appearance-conscious age of telegenic politicians. His facial expression, according to those who saw him, seemed wooden and unvaried.

Your face plays a key role in expressing your thoughts, and especially your emotions and attitudes.[14] Your audience sees your face before they hear what you are going to say. Thus, you have an opportunity to set the emotional tone for your message before you start speaking. We are not advocating that you adopt a phony smile that looks insincere and plastered on your face, but a pleasant facial expression helps establish a positive emotional climate. Your facial expression should naturally vary to be consistent with your message. Present somber news with a more serious expression. To communicate interest in your listeners, keep your expression alert and friendly.

Although we are technically capable of producing over 250,000 different facial expressions, we most often express only six primary emotions: happiness, anger, surprise, sadness, disgust, and fear. According to cross-cultural studies by psychologist Paul Ekman, the facial expressions of these emotions are virtually universal, so even a culturally diverse audience will be able to read your emotional expressions clearly. When you rehearse your speech, consider standing in front of a mirror or, better yet, videotape yourself practicing your speech. Note whether you are allowing your face to help communicate the emotional tone of your thoughts.

VOCAL DELIVERY

Have you ever listened to a DJ on the radio and imagined what he or she looked like, only later to see a picture and have your image of the announcer drastically altered? Vocal clues play an important part in creating the impression we have of a speaker. Based on vocal clues alone, you make inferences about a person's age, status, occupation, ethnic origin, income, and a variety of other matters. As a public speaker, your voice is one of your most important delivery tools in conveying your ideas to your audience. Your credibility as a speaker and your ability to communicate your ideas clearly to your listeners will in large part depend on your vocal delivery.

Vocal delivery includes pitch, rate, volume, pronunciation, articulation, pauses, and general variation of the voice. A speaker has at least two key vocal obligations to an audience: Speak to be understood, and speak with vocal variety to maintain interest.

● SPEAKING TO BE UNDERSTOOD   To be understood, you need to control three aspects of vocal delivery: volume, articulation, and pronunciation.

■ *Volume*   The fundamental purpose of your vocal delivery is to speak loudly enough so that your audience can hear you. The **volume** of your speech is determined by the amount of air projected through your larynx, or voice box. More air equals more volume of sound. Your diaphragm, a muscle in your upper abdomen, helps control the volume of sound by increasing the flow of air from your lungs through your voice box. If you put your hands on your diaphragm and say, "Ho-ho-ho," you will feel the muscles contract and the air being forced out of your lungs. Breathing from your diaphragm rather than increasing air flow through your lungs alone can increase the volume of sound as well as enhance the quality of your voice.

volume
The softness or loudness of a speaker's voice.

■ *Articulation*   The ability to make speech sounds clearly and distinctly is **articulation.** In addition to speaking loudly enough, you need to say your words so that your audience can understand them. Without distinct enunciation or articulation of the sounds that make up words, your listeners may not understand you or may fault you for simply not knowing how to speak clearly and fluently. Here are some commonly misarticulated words[15]

articulation
The ability to make speech sounds clearly and distinctly.

whadayado	*instead of*	what do you do
wanna	*instead of*	want to
seeya	*instead of*	see you
dint	*instead of*	didn't
lemme	*instead of*	let me
mornin	*instead of*	morning
wep	*instead of*	wept
soun	*instead of*	sound

■ Many errors in articulation result from a simple flaw: laziness. It takes effort to articulate speech sounds clearly. We often get in a hurry to express our idea, or we just get into the habit of mumbling, slurring, and abbreviating. Such speech flaws may not keep your audience from understanding you, but poor enunciation does reflect on your credibility as a speaker.

■ The best way to improve your articulation of sounds is first to identify words or phrases that you have a tendency to slur or chop. Once you have identified them, practice saying the words correctly. Make sure that you can hear the difference between the improper and proper pronunciation. Your speech teacher can help you check your articulation.

■ *Pronunciation.*   Whereas articulation is concerned with the production of sounds, **pronunciation** refers to the sounds that form words in standard English. Mispronouncing words can also detract from a speaker's credibility. Often, however, we are not aware that we are not using standard pronunciation unless someone points it out.

Some speakers reverse a speech sound by saying "aks" instead of "ask." Some allow an *r* sound to intrude into some words, saying "warsh" instead of "wash," or leaving out sounds in the middle of a word by saying "actchally" instead of "actually" or "Febuary" instead of "February." Some speakers also accent syllables in nonstandard ways; they say "po´ lice" instead of "police" or "Um´ brella" rather than "Umbrella."

If English is not your native language, you may have to spend extra time working on your pronunciation and articulation. Here are two useful tips to help you. First, make an effort to prolong your vowel sounds. Speeeeak tooooo prooooolooooong eeeeeeach voooooowel soooooound yooooooooou maaaaaaaake. Second, to reduce choppy-sounding word pronunciation, blend the end of one word into the beginning of the next phrase. Make your speech flow from one word to the next, instead of separating it into individual, bite-size chunks of sound.[16]

Most speech teachers encourage students to develop a standard American dialect when delivering a speech, much like the dialect most national news broadcasters have when delivering the evening news. Yet many listeners may prefer to hear a message in a dialect similar to their own. Whereas many Americans found President Kennedy's pronunciation of "Cuba" as "Cuber" peculiar, New Englanders thought it sounded natural and familiar. If you have the ability to switch back and forth between a standard and nonstandard dialect, consider your audience. Ultimately, they will determine the effectiveness of your choice.

● SPEAKING WITH VARIETY   To speak with variety is to vary your pitch, rate, and pauses. It is primarily through the quality of our voices, as well as our facial expressions, that we communicate whether we are happy, sad, bored, or excited. If your vocal clues suggest that you are bored with your topic, your audience will probably be bored also. Appropriate variation in vocal pitch and rate as well as appropriate use of pauses can add zest to your speech and help maintain audience attention.

■ *Pitch.*   Vocal **pitch** is how high or low your voice sounds. You are able to sing because you can change the pitch of your voice to produce a melody. Lack of variation in pitch has been consistently identified as one of the most distracting characteristics of ineffective speakers. A monotone is boring.

Everyone has a habitual pitch. This is the range of your voice during normal conversation. Some people have a habitually high pitch, while others have a low pitch. The pitch of your voice is determined by how fast the folds in your vocal cords vibrate. The faster the vibration, the higher the pitch. Male vocal folds open and close approximately 100 to 150 times each second; female vocal cords vibrate about 200 times per second, thus giving them a higher vocal pitch.

Your voice has **inflection** when you raise or lower the pitch as you pronounce words or sounds. Your inflection is what helps determine the meaning of your utterances. A surprised "ah!" sounds different from a disappointed "ah." Different, too, would be "ah?" Your vocal inflection is thus an important indicator of your emotions and helps give clues as to how to interpret your speech.

inflection
The variation of the pitch of your voice.

The best public speakers vary their inflection considerably. We're not suggesting that you need to imitate a top-forty radio disc jockey when you speak. But variation in your vocal inflection and overall pitch helps you communicate the subtlety of your ideas.

Record your speech as you rehearse, and evaluate your use of pitch and inflection critically. If you are not satisfied with your inflection, consider practicing your speech with exaggerated variations in vocal pitch. Although you would not deliver your speech this way, it may help you explore the expressive options available to you.

■ *Rate*   How fast do you talk? Most speakers average between 120 and 180 words per minute. There is no "best" speaking rate. Great speakers use no standard rate of speech that can account for their speaking skill. Daniel Webster purportedly spoke at about 90 words per minute, Franklin Roosevelt 110, President Kennedy a quick-paced 180. Martin Luther King, Jr., started his "I Have a Dream" speech at 92 words a minute and was speaking at 145 during his conclusion.[17] The best rate depends on two factors: your speaking style and the content of your message.

A common fault of many beginning speakers is to deliver a speech too quickly. One symptom of speech anxiety is that you tend to rush through your speech to get it over with. Relying on feedback from others can help you determine whether your rate is too rapid. Tape-recording your message and listening critically to your speaking rate can help you assess whether you are speaking at the proper speed. Fewer speakers have the problem of speaking too slowly, but a turtle-paced speech will almost certainly make it more difficult for your audience to maintain interest. Remember, your listeners can grasp information much faster than you can give it to them.

You need not deliver your entire speech at the same pace. It is normal for you to speak more rapidly when talking about something that excites you. You slow your speaking rate to emphasize key points or ideas. Speaking rate is another tool you can use to add variety and interest to your vocal delivery. The pace of your delivery, however, should make sense in terms of the ideas you are sharing with your listeners.

■ *Pauses*   An appropriate pause can often do more to accent your message than any other vocal characteristic. President Kennedy's famous line, "Ask not what your country can do for you; ask what you can do for your country," was effective not only because of its language but also because it was delivered with a pause dividing the two thoughts. Try delivering that line without the pause; it just doesn't have the same power without it.

Effective use of pauses, also known as effective timing, can greatly enhance the impact of your message. Whether you are trying to tell a joke, a serious tale, or a dramatic story, your use of a pause can determine the effectiveness of your anecdote. Jay Leno, David Letterman, and Roseanne are masters at timing a punch line. Radio commentator Paul Harvey is known for his flair for vocal delivery. His dramatic pauses serve as meaningful punctuation in his talks.

Beware of the vocalized pause. Many beginning public speakers are uncomfortable with silence and so, rather than pausing where it seems natural and normal, they vocalize sounds such as "umm," "er," "you know," and "ah." We think you will agree that "Ask not ah what your er country can do ah for you; ask you know what you umm can do er for your uh country" just doesn't have the same impact as the unadorned original statement. Vocalized pauses will annoy your audience and detract from your credibility; eliminate them.

Silence can be an effective tool in emphasizing a particular word or sentence. A well-timed pause coupled with eye contact can powerfully accent your thought. Asking a rhetorical question of your audience such as "How many of you would like to improve your communication skills?" will be more effective if you pause after asking the question rather than rushing into the next thought. Silence is a way of saying to your audience: Think about this for a moment. Pianist Arthur Schnabel said this about silence and music, "The notes I handle not better than many pianists. But the pauses between the notes, ah, that is where the art resides."[18] In speech, too, an effective use of a pause can add emphasis and interest.

● **USING A MICROPHONE**   "Testing. Testing. One . . . two . . . three. Is this on?" These are not effective, attention-catching opening remarks. Yet countless public speakers have found themselves trying to begin their speech, only to be upstaged by an uncooperative public address system. No matter how polished your gestures or well intoned your vocal cues, if you are inaudible or use a microphone awkwardly, your speech will not have the desired effect.

There are three kinds of microphones, only one of which demands much technique. The **lavaliere microphone** is the clip-on type often used by newspeople and interviewees. Worn on the front of a shirt or dress, it requires no particular care other than not thumping it or accidently knocking it off. The **boom microphone** is used by makers of movies and TV shows. It hangs over the heads of the speakers and is remote-controlled, so the speaker need not be particularly concerned with it. The third kind of microphone, and the most common, is the **stationary microphone.** This is the type that is most often attached to a lectern, sitting on a desk, or standing on the floor. Generally, the stationary microphones used today are multidirectional. You do not have to remain frozen in front of a stationary mike while delivering your speech. However, you do need to take some other precautions when using one.

First, if you have a fully stationary microphone, rather than one that converts to a hand mike, you will have to remain behind the microphone, with your mouth about the same distance from the mike at all times to avoid distracting fluctuations in the volume of sound. You can turn your head from side to side and use gestures, but you will have to limit other movements.

lavaliere microphone
A microphone that can be clipped on an article of clothing to amplify your voice; may also be worn on a string around your neck.

boom microphone
A microphone that is suspended from a bar and moved to follow the speaker; often used in movies and TV.

stationary microphone
A microphone attached to a podium or at the end of a rod that is usually located within twelve inches of a speaker's mouth.

Second, microphones amplify sloppy habits of pronunciation and enunciation. Therefore, you need to speak clearly and crisply when using a mike.

Third, if you must test a microphone, count or ask the audience whether they can hear you. Blowing on a microphone produces an irritating noise! Do not tap, pound, or shuffle anything near the microphone. These noises, too, will be heard by the audience loudly and clearly. If your notes are on cards, quietly slide them aside as you progress through your speech. Notes on paper are more difficult to handle quietly, but do so with as little shuffling as you can manage.

Finally, when you are delivering your speech, speak directly into the microphone, making sure that your words are appropriately amplified. Some speakers, because they have a microphone in front of them, lower their volume and become inaudible.

Under ideal circumstances, you will be able to practice with the type of microphone you will use before you speak. If you have the chance, figure out where to stand for the best sound quality and how sensitive the mike is to extraneous noise. Practice will accustom you to any voice distortion or echo that might occur so that these sound qualities do not surprise you during your speech.

 RECAP

CHARACTERISTICS OF GOOD VOCAL DELIVERY

GOOD SPEAKERS	POOR SPEAKERS
Have adequate volume	Speak too softly to be heard
Articulate speech sounds clearly and distinctly	Slur speech sounds
Pronounce words accurately	Mispronounce words
Have varied pitch	Have a monotonous pitch
Vary speaking rate	Consistently speak too fast or too slow
Pause to emphasize ideas	Rarely pause or pause too long

● PERSONAL APPEARANCE

Most people have certain expectations about the way a speaker should look. One of your audience analysis tasks is to identify what those audience expectations are. This can be trickier than it might at first seem. John T. Molloy has written two books, *Dress for Success* and *Dress for Success for Women,* in an effort to identify what the well-dressed businessperson should wear. But as some of his own research points out, appropriate wardrobe varies, depending on climate, custom, culture, and audience expectations. It may be improper to wear blue jeans to a business meeting, but it would be just as inappropriate to wear a business suit to a rodeo or grade school picnic.

There is considerable evidence that your personal appearance affects how your audience will respond to you and your message, particularly during the opening moments of your presentation. If you violate their expectations about appearance, you will be less successful in achieving your purpose.

Styles and audience expectations change and are sometimes unpredictable. Therefore, a general rule of thumb to follow is this: When in doubt about what to wear, select something conservative. Also take your cue from your audience. You need not always mirror their appearance, but if you know that the males in your audience wear suits and ties and the females wear dresses, you would be wise to avoid dressing more casually.

Audience diversity and delivery

Most of the suggestions we have offered in this chapter assume that your listeners will be expecting a typical North American approach to delivery. However, these assumptions are based on research responses from United States college students who are mostly white and college-aged, so our suggestions are not applicable to every audience. As we have stressed throughout the book, you will need to adapt your presentation to the expectations of your listeners, especially those from different cultural backgrounds. Consider the following suggestions to help you develop strategies for adapting both your verbal and nonverbal messages for a culturally diverse audience.

- *Avoid an ethnocentric mind set.* **Ethnocentrism** is an attitude that your own cultural approaches are superior to those from other cultures. As we suggested in Chapter 5, culture is learned, and each culture has specific approaches for communicating with others. When considering how to adapt your delivery style to your audience, try to view different approaches and preferences not as right or wrong but merely as different from your own.

- *Consider using a less dramatic delivery style for predominantly high-context listeners.* As you recall from Chapter 5, a high-context culture places considerable emphasis on unspoken messages. Therefore, you need not be overly expressive for a high-context audience. For example, for many Japanese people, a delivery style that included exuberant gestures, overly dramatic facial expressions, and frequent movements might seem overdone. A more subtle, less demonstrative approach would create less "noise" and be more effective.

- *If you know that you will be speaking to a group of people from a cultural background different from your own, try to observe other speakers presenting to that audience.* Talk with people you may know who are familiar with the cultural expectations. Ask specific questions. When speaking in Poland, one of your authors expected the speech to start promptly at 11:00 A.M. as announced in the program and on posters. By 11:20 it was clear the speech would not begin on time. In Poland, it turns out, all students know

ethnocentrism
The attitude that your own cultural approaches are superior to those from other cultures.

about the "academic quarter." This means that most lectures and speeches begin at least 15 minutes, or a quarter hour, after the announced starting time. If your author had asked another professor about the audience's expectations, he would have known this custom in advance. As you observe or talk with speakers who have addressed your target audience, ask the following questions:

What are audience expectations about where I should stand while speaking?
Do listeners like direct eye contact?
When will the audience expect me to start and stop my talk?
Will listeners find movement and gestures distracting or welcome?

■ *Know the code.* Communication occurs when both speaker and listener share the same code system—both verbal and nonverbal. One of your authors became very embarrassed after speaking to a Caribbean audience because he used a circled thumb and finger gesture to signal "OK." Later he discovered that this was an obscene gesture—like extending a middle finger to a North American audience. Even subtle nonverbal messages communicate feelings, attitudes, and cues about the nature of the relationship between you and your audience, so it is important to avoid gestures or expressions that would offend your listeners.

Although we cannot provide a comprehensive description of each cultural expectation you may face in every educational and professional setting, we can remind you to keep cultural expectations in mind when you rehearse and deliver a speech. We are not suggesting that you totally abandon your own cultural expectations about speech delivery. Rather, we urge you to become sensitive and responsive to cultural differences. Since there is no universal dictionary of nonverbal meaning, try to spend some time asking people who are from the same culture as your prospective audience about what gestures and expressions your audience will appreciate.

Rehearsing your speech: some final tips

Just knowing some of the effective characteristics of speech delivery will not make you a better speaker unless you can put these principles into practice. Effective public speaking is a skill that takes practice. Practicing takes the form of rehearsing. The following suggestions will help you make the most of your rehearsal time.

■ Finish drafting your speech outline at least two days before your speech performance. The more time you have to work on putting it all together, the better.

■ Before you prepare the speaking notes to take with you in front of your audience, rehearse your speech aloud to help determine where you will need notes to prompt yourself.

■ Revise your speech as necessary to keep it within the time limits set by your instructor or whoever invited you to speak.

- Prepare your speaking notes. Use whatever system works best for you. Some speakers use pictorial symbols to remind them of a story or an idea. Others use complete sentences or just words or phrases in an outline pattern to prompt them. Most teachers advocate note cards for speaking notes.

- Rehearse your speech standing up so that you can get a feeling for your use of gestures as well as your vocal delivery. Do not try to memorize your speech or choreograph specific gestures. As you rehearse, you may want to modify your speaking notes to reflect changes that seem appropriate.

- If you can, present your speech to someone else so you can practice establishing eye contact. Seek feedback from your captive audience about both your delivery and your speech content.

- If possible, tape-record or videotape your speech during the rehearsal stage so that you can observe your vocal and physical mannerisms and make changes necessary. If you don't have a video camera, you may find it useful to practice before a mirror so that you can observe your body language.

- Rehearse using all of your visual aids. As we will discuss in the next chapter, don't wait until the last minute to plan, prepare and rehearse with flipcharts, slides, overhead transparencies or other visual aids that you will need to manipulate as you speak.

- Your final rehearsals should try as much as possible to re-create the speaking situation you will face. If you will be speaking in a large classroom, try to find a large classroom in which to rehearse your speech. If your audience will be informally seated in chairs in a semicircle, then this should be the context in which you rehearse your speech. The more realistic the rehearsal, the more confidence you will gain.

- Practice good delivery skills while rehearsing. Remember this maxim: Practice *makes* perfect if practice *is* perfect.

Delivering your speech

The day arrives and you are ready. Using information about your audience as an anchor, you have developed a speech with an interesting topic and a fine-tuned purpose. Your central idea is clearly identified. You have gathered interesting and relevant supporting material (examples, illustrations, statistics) and organized it well. Your speech has an appropriate introduction, a logically arranged body, and a clear conclusion that nicely summarizes your key theme. You have rehearsed your speech several times; it is not memorized, but you are comfortable with the way you express the major ideas. Your last task is calmly and confidently to communicate with your audience. You are ready to deliver your speech.

As you approach the time for presenting your speech to your audience, consider the following suggestions to help you prepare for your successful performance.

■ At the risk of sounding like your mother, we suggest that you get plenty of rest before your speech. Last-minute, late-night final preparations can take the edge off your performance. Many professional public speakers also advocate that you watch what you eat before you speak; a heavy meal or too much caffeine can have a negative effect on your performance.

■ Review the suggestions in Chapter 2 for becoming a confident speaker. It is normal to have prespeech jitters. But if you have developed a well-organized, audience-centered message on a topic of genuine interest to you, you're doing all the right things to make your speech a success. Remember some of the other tips for developing confidence. Re-create the speech environment when you rehearse. Use deep breathing techniques to help you relax. Also make sure you are especially familiar with your introduction and conclusion. Act calm to feel calm.

■ Arrive early for your speaking engagement. If your room is in an unfamiliar location, give yourself plenty of time to find it. As we suggested in Chapter 5, you may want to rearrange the furniture or make other changes in the speaking environment. If you are using audiovisual equipment, check to see that it is working properly and set up your graphic support material carefully. You might even project a slide or two to make sure they are in the tray right side up. Relax before you deliver your message; budget your time so you do not spend your moments before you speak harriedly looking for a parking place or frantically trying to attend to last-minute details.

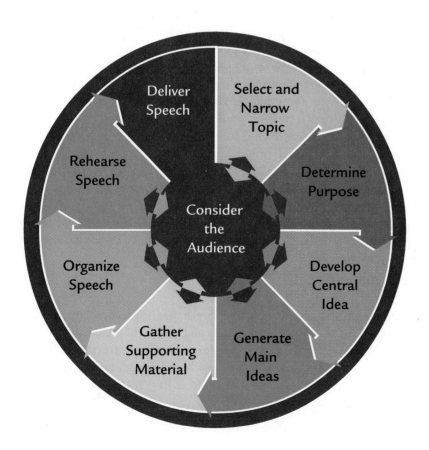

FIGURE 13.2
You need to be audience-centered during the final step of the speechmaking process—delivering the speech.

■ Visualize success. Picture yourself delivering your speech in an effective way. Also, remind yourself of the effort you have spent preparing for your speech. A final mental rehearsal can boost your confidence and help ensure success.

Even though we have identified many time-tested methods for enhancing your speech delivery, keep in mind that speech delivery is an art rather than a science. The manner of your delivery should reflect your personality and individual style.

Summary

In this chapter, we discussed the importance of effective speech delivery and identified suggestions for enhancing your delivery. The way you deliver your speech is the primary way in which you communicate your thoughts and emotions to an audience. Audiences will believe what they see more readily than what they hear.

Of the four methods of delivery—manuscript, memorized, impromptu, and extemporaneous—the extemporaneous method is most desirable in most situations. Speak from an outline without memorizing the exact words.

We have offered several suggestions for enhancing your delivery. Your gestures and movements should appear natural and relaxed, definite, consistent with your message, varied, unobtrusive, and coordinated with what you say. They should also be appropriate to your audience and situation. Eye contact is the single most important delivery variable; looking at your audience helps control communication, establishes your credibility, maintains audience interest, and provides feedback about how your speech is coming across. Your facial expressions and vocal cues are the primary ways in which you communicate your feelings and emotions to an audience. How loudly you speak, how clearly you articulate, and how correctly you pronounce the words you use determine how well your audience will understand your thoughts; your vocal pitch, rate, and use of pauses help provide variation to add interest to your talk.

The chapter concluded with several final suggestions for rehearsing and delivering your speech. We suggested that you leave at least two days to focus on your speech delivery and develop your speaking notes. As much as possible, re-create the speech environment when you rehearse. You will be rewarded with a smoother delivery style and more confidence when you deliver your message.

● CRITICAL THINKING QUESTIONS

1. Roger was so nervous about his first speech that he practiced his speech on the evolution of the television sitcom again and again. He could have given the speech in his sleep. He had some great examples; his instructor had praised his outline; but as he gave his speech, he saw his classmates tuning out. What might he have done wrong and how could he have rescued his speech?

2. Monique has difficulty knowing what to do with her hands when she speaks. Because she is self-conscious about her gestures, she often just puts her hands

behind her back. What advice would you give Monique to help her use gestures more effectively?

3. Professor Murray speaks slowly and with a monotone; consequently, many of her students do not like to listen to her music history lectures. What can she do to give her voice some variety?

ETHICAL QUESTIONS

1. Most politicians at the state or national level hire image consultants to help them project the most positive impression of their skills and abilities. Is it ethical to use such consultants, especially if the sole objective is to manipulate constituents into thinking the speaker is more credible than he or she really is?

2. What can listeners do to be less distracted by the delivery and emotional elements of a speaker's message and focus more on the substance or content of the message?

SUGGESTED ACTIVITIES

1. Attend a political campaign speech presented by a politician. Pay particular attention to his or her delivery. Provide a written critique of the speaker's use of posture, gesture, eye contact, vocal clues, and appearance. If you were a campaign consultant, what advice would you give this politician?

2. While you are rehearsing your next class speech, experiment with using a new delivery style. If you seldom, if ever, use gestures, practice using more gestures than normal to experience a different, more effective delivery approach. Make a conscious effort to change your vocal delivery style; if you normally have little vocal variation, try delivering your speech with considerable variation or changes in pitch, rate, volume, and intensity. After your experiment with a new delivery style, write a brief report describing what the advantages or disadvantages of the different delivery strategies were.

3. To develop greater vocal variety, read a passage from one of your favorite novels or a poem that you have studied in one of your English classes. Read your selection, giving special attention to making it interesting, exciting, or lively. Try to communicate the emotional meaning of the piece with your voice. Experiment with using your voice by varying your pitch and rate. Even though it may seem odd or overly dramatic, experience how it feels to use a greater variety of your vocal tools.

4. Most dictionaries will show you how to pronounce words, in addition to defining them. Look up the following words and practice saying them correctly out loud:

library
nuclear
athlete
hundred

recognize
mischievous
comparable
picture
perspiration

USING TECHNOLOGY AND MEDIA

1. Videotape one of your speeches, either when you present it in front of your class or during your rehearsal. Critique your tape, focusing on your delivery. Write a 200- to 400-word analysis of your delivery strengths and weaknesses based on the principles and suggestions presented in the chapter.

2. Use a tape recorder to record your speech as you rehearse. Note whether your vocal rate, pitch, quality, and intensity communicate the emotions and feelings you wish to express to your listeners. Also note whether your pronunciation and articulation of words is clear and appropriate.

3. Watch a video or a film featuring public speakers from a culture different from your own. Note differences and similarities in the use of gestures and other nonverbal delivery cues.

4. Listen to well-known TV or radio broadcasters, such as Paul Harvey, Dan Rather, Diane Sawyer, Peter Jennings, and Jane Pauley, noting how they pronounce words. If you are watching the announcer on TV, observe his or her eye contact and facial expression as well. Note whether the nonverbal message is consistent with the verbal message.

"Stupa Wall Detail."
Asian/SuperStock

Visual Aids

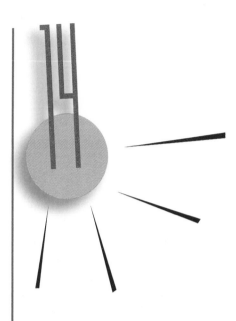

Seeing . . . , most of all the senses, makes us know and brings to light many differences between things.
—Aristotle

● OBJECTIVES

After studying this chapter you should be able to do the following:

1. Discuss five ways in which visual aids help communicate ideas to an audience.

2. Describe the use of three-dimensional visual aids.

3. Identify ways of producing and using two-dimensional visual aids.

4. Discuss the uses of audiovisual aids.

5. Identify guidelines for developing visual aids.

6. Identify guidelines for using visual aids.

razier walked to the front of the class and dramatically pulled a two-foot papier-mâché model of a cockroach out of a sack. He attached a string to the "bug" and suspended it from the ceiling. Then he began his speech about how to rid a home of pests. The trouble was, no one listened to Frazier's message. His audience was obsessed with the creature dangling in midair.

The intention was good, but the execution was bad. Frazier had failed to use visual aids effectively. Visual aids are powerful tools. They can help communicate your ideas with greater clarity and impact than can words alone, but they can also overwhelm your speech. For maximum effectiveness, you need to follow the guidelines described in this chapter.

A visual aid is any object that calls on sight to help your audience understand your point. Charts, photographs, posters, drawings, graphs, slides, movies, and videos are just some of the types of visual aids that we will discuss. Some of these, such as movies and videos, call on sound as well as sight to help you make your point.

When you are first required to give a speech using visual aids, you may scratch your head, wondering, "How can I use visual aids in an informative or persuasive speech? Those kinds of speeches don't lend themselves to visuals." As it happens, almost any speech can benefit from visual aids. An assignment that requires you to use visual aids is not as different from other types of speeches as you might at first think. Your general objective will still be to inform, persuade, or entertain. The key difference is that you will be using supporting material that can be seen, rather than only heard by an audience.

In this chapter, we will look at visual aids as an important communication tool and will also examine several kinds. Toward the end of the chapter, we will suggest guidelines for using visual aids in your speeches. Appendix C provides additional tips and strategies for preparing visual aids for presentations.

Why use visual aids?

Visual aids are invaluable to you as an audience-centered speaker. They help your audience *understand* and *remember* your message, communicate your *organization* of ideas, gain and maintain *attention,* and illustrate a *sequence* of events or procedures.[1]

■ *Visual aids enhance understanding.* Of your five senses, you learn more from sight than from all of the others combined. In fact, it has been estimated that over 80 percent of all information comes to you through sight. To many people, seeing is believing. We are a visually oriented society. For example, most of us learn the news by seeing it on TV. Because your audience is accustomed to visual reinforcement, it is wise to consider how you can increase their understanding of your speech by using visual aids. For example, a picture of Maui will help your listeners understand the beauty of Hawaii better than just a verbal description. As the old cliché has it, a picture is indeed worth a thousand words.

■ *Visual aids enhance memory.*   Not only will your audience improve their understanding of your speech, but they will also better remember what you say as a result of visual reinforcement. It is well known that you remember most what you understand best. Researchers estimate that you remember 10 percent of what you read, 20 percent of what you hear, 30 percent of what you see, and 50 percent of what you simultaneously hear and see. In your speech about the languages spoken in Africa, your audience will be more likely to remember Arabic, Swahili, and Hausa if you have the words displayed visually, rather than just saying them.

■ *Visual aids help listeners organize ideas.*   Most listeners need help understanding the structure of your speech. Even if you clearly lay out your major point, use effective internal summaries, and make clear transition statements, your listeners will welcome additional help. Listing major ideas on a chart, a poster, or an overhead transparency will add clarity to your talk and help your audience grasp your main ideas. Visually presenting your major ideas during your introduction, for example, can help your audience follow them as you bring them into the body of your speech. Key ideas can be displayed during your conclusion to help you summarize your message succinctly.

■ *Visual aids help gain and maintain attention.*   Keshia began her speech about poverty in America by showing the face of an undernourished child. She immediately had the attention of her audience. Chuck began his speech with the flash of his camera to introduce his photography lecture. He certainly alerted his audience at that point. Midway through her speech about the lyrics in rock music, Tomoko not only spoke the words but also displayed a giant poster of the song lyrics so that her audience could read the words and sing along. Visual aids not only grab the attention of your listeners, but they also keep their interest when words alone might not.

■ *Visual aids help illustrate a sequence of events or procedures.*   If your purpose is to inform an audience about a process—how to do something or how something functions—you can do this best through actual demonstrations or with a series of visuals. Whether your objective is instructing people to make a soufflé or to build a greenhouse, demonstrating the step-by-step procedures will help your audience understand the processes. If you wish to explain how hydroelectric power is generated, a series of diagrams can help your listeners understand and visualize the process.

When demonstrating how to make something, such as your prize-winning cinnamon rolls, you can have each step of the process prepared ahead of time and show your audience how you go through the steps of preparing your rolls. You could have the dough already mixed and ready to demonstrate how you sprinkle on the cinnamon. A climax to your speech could be to unveil a finished pan of rolls still warm from the oven. If time does not permit you to demonstrate how to prepare your rolls, you could have at hand a series of diagrams and photographs to illustrate each step of the procedure.

WHY USE VISUAL AIDS?

1. They help your audience understand your message.

2. They help your audience remember your message.

3. They communicate the organization of your message.

4. They gain and maintain audience attention.

5. They illustrate a sequence of events or procedures.

Types of visual aids

The first question many students ask when they learn they are required to use visual aids is, "What type of visual aid should I use?" We will discuss various kinds, grouped into three classifications: three-dimensional visual aids, two-dimensional visual aids, and audiovisual aids.

● THREE-DIMENSIONAL VISUAL AIDS

● OBJECTS   You have played the trombone since you were in fifth grade, so now you decide to give an informative speech about the history and function of this instrument. Your trombone is an obvious visual aid, which you could show to your audience as you talk about how it works. Perhaps you might play a few measures to demonstrate its sound and your talent.

Or you are an art major and have just finished a watercolor painting. Why not bring your picture to class to illustrate your talk about watercolor techniques?

Objects add interest because they are tangible. They can be touched, smelled, heard, and even tasted, as well as seen. Objects are real, and audiences like the real thing.

If you use an object as a visual aid, make sure that it can be handled with ease. If an object is too large, it can be unwieldy and difficult to show to your audience. Tiny objects can only be seen close up. It will be impossible for your listeners to see the detail on your antique thimble, the intricate needlework on your cross-stitch sampler, or the attention to detail in your miniature log cabin. Other objects can be dangerous to handle. One speaker, for example, attempted a demonstration of how to string an archery bow. He made his audience extremely uncomfortable when his almost-strung bow flew over the heads of his listeners. He certainly got their attention, but he lost his credibility.

● MODELS   If it is not possible to bring to the classroom the object you would like to show your audience, consider showing them a model. Since you cannot bring a World War II fighter plane to class, buy or build a scale model instead. To illustrate her lecture about human anatomy, one student brought a plastic model of a skeleton. An actual human skeleton would have been difficult to get and carry to class.

Most colleges and universities do not allow firearms on campus. A drawing that shows the features of a gun is much safer than using a real gun as a visual aid. If you need to show the movable parts of a gun, perhaps a papier-mâché, plastic, or wood model would serve.

● PEOPLE In addition to inanimate objects, people can serve as visual aids for a speech. Delia wanted to show some of her own dress designs, so she asked several women to model her clothes during her speech. Paul wanted to illustrate several wrestling holds, so he used a friend to help demonstrate how he won the district wrestling championship. Amelia, a choreographer for Folklorico Mexicano, wanted to illustrate an intricate Latin folk dance, so she arranged to have one of the troupe's dancers attend her speech to demonstrate the dance.

Using people to illustrate your message can be tricky, however. It is usually unwise to ask for spur-of-the-moment volunteers for help while you are delivering your speech. Instead, choose a trusted friend or colleague before your presentation so that you can fully inform him or her about what needs to be done. Rehearse your speech using your living visual aid.

Also, it is distracting to have your support person stand beside you doing nothing. If you don't need the person to demonstrate something during your opening remarks, wait and introduce the person to your audience when needed.

Generally, *you* can serve as a visual aid to demonstrate or illustrate major points. If you are talking about the game of tennis, you might bring your favorite racquet to class so that you can illustrate your superb backhand or simply show novices the proper way to hold this device. If you are a nurse or an emergency room technician giving a talk about medical procedures, by all means wear your uniform to establish your credibility.

Finally, do not allow your assistants to run away with the show. For example, don't let your dance student perform the *pas de bourre* longer than necessary to illustrate your technique. Nor should you permit your models to prance about too provocatively while displaying your dress designs. And don't allow your buddy to throw you when you demonstrate the wrestling hold that made you champ. Remember, your visual aids are always subordinate to your speech. You must remain in control.

● TWO-DIMENSIONAL VISUAL AIDS

Although tangible, three-dimensional objects, models, and people can be used to illustrate a talk, the most common visual aids are two-dimensional: drawings, photographs, maps, graphs, charts, slides, flip charts, overhead transparencies, and the chalkboard. Today, you can use computer software to generate many of these forms, as we will discuss a little later in the chapter.

● DRAWINGS A drawing is a popular and often-used visual aid because it is easy and inexpensive to make. Drawings can be tailored to your specific needs. To illustrate the functions of the human brain, for example, one student traced

If you were to use it for a speech, this remarkable photograph would have to be enlarged so that the back row of your audience could distinguish clearly between the katydid and the rosebud. [Photo: Frank Oberle/Tony Stone Images]

an outline of the brain and labeled it with large block letters to indicate where brain functions are located. Another student wanted to show the different sizes and shapes of leaves for trees in the area, so she drew enlarged pictures of the leaves, using appropriate shades of green.

You don't have to be a master artist to develop effective drawings. As a rule, large and simple line drawings are more effective for stage presentations than are detailed images. If you have absolutely no faith in your artistic skill, you can probably find a friend or relative who can help you prepare a useful drawing, or you may be able to use computer software which generate simple line drawings or icous.

To see how simple drawings can help clarify ideas, you may want to take another look at the sample speech in Chapter 2 on pages 30 and 31, which incorporated visual aids.

● PHOTOGRAPHS Photographs can be used to show objects or places that cannot be illustrated with drawings or that an audience cannot view directly. The problems with photos, however, is that they are usually too small to be seen clearly from a distance. If your listeners occupy only two or three rows, it might be possible to hold a photograph close enough for them to see a key feature of the picture. The details will not be visible, however, beyond the first row. Passing a photograph among your listeners is not a good idea either; it creates competition for your audience's attention.

The only sure way to use a printed photograph as a visual aid for a large audience is to enlarge it. Some photo shops will produce poster-size color laser photocopies at a modest cost. Or you can also take a picture of your photograph with slide film and project the image onto a large screen with a slide projector.

● SLIDES Slides can help illustrate your talk if you have access to a screen and a slide projector. A photograph of your recent vacation might be too small to be seen, but a slide can be projected so that all can see the picture clearly. Automatic programming and remote-control features on many modern projectors help you change from one slide to the next without relying on anyone else for help. And audiences generally enjoy slides, which have an inherent attention factor that a speaker can use to his or her advantage.

Working with slides can also present problems. Projector bulbs can burn out, and slides can jam in the projector. Moreover, with the lights out, you are less able to receive nonverbal feedback, and you cannot maintain eye contact with your audience.

Giving a slide lecture, therefore, requires considerable preparation. First, be sure that the slides are right side up and in the order in which you want to show them during your speech. Second, you must know in which direction the slide carousel moves as it feeds the projector so that you will know how to load it. Third, you must know how to operate the programming feature or the remote-control switch so that you can move back and forth among your slides, if you wish.

● **MAPS**   Most maps are designed to be read from a distance of no more than two feet. As with photographs, the details on most maps won't be visible to your audience. You could use a large map, however, to show general features of an area. Or you can use a magnified version of your map. Certain copiers are able to enlarge images as much as 200 percent. It is possible, using a color laser copier, to enlarge a standard map of Europe enough for listeners in the last row to see the general features of the continent. Using a dark marker, one speaker highlighted the borders on a map of Europe to indicate the countries she had visited the previous summer (see below). She used a red marker to show the general path of her journey.

To use a map effectively, you will probably need to modify it so that your listeners can both see it and read it. Many computer graphics programs include maps that can be enlarged or customized for your speech.

● **GRAPHS**   A graph is a pictorial representation of statistical data in an easy-to-understand format. Since statistics are abstract summaries of many examples, most listeners find graphs an effective way to make the data more concrete. Graphs are particularly effective in showing overall trends and relationships among data. The four most common types of graphs are bar graphs, pie graphs, line graphs, and picture graphs. Many of today's computer programs can easily convert statistics into visual form.

F IGURE 14.1
Bar graphs can help summa-
rize statistics clearly.

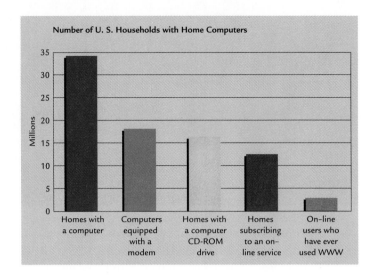

F IGURE 14.2
Bar graphs make information
clear and immediately visible
to your audience.

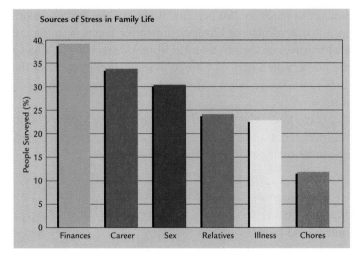

- *Bar Graphs*   A bar graph consists of flat areas—bars—of various lengths to represent information. The bar graph in Figure 14.1 clearly shows the number of U.S. households equipped with computer technology. Figure 14.2 illustrates the sources of stress in family life. These two graphs make the information clear and immediately visible to the listeners. By comparison, words and numbers are more difficult to assimilate, especially in something as ephemeral as a speech.

- *Pie Graphs*   A pie graph shows the general distribution of data. The pie graph in Figure 14.3 shows how working mothers in the United States would use an extra hour of free time. Pie graphs are especially useful in helping your listeners to see quickly how data is distributed in a given category or area.

- *Line Graphs*   Line graphs show relationships between two or more variables. Like bar graphs, line graphs plot a course through statistical data to show overall trends (Figure 14.4). A line graph can cover a greater span of time or numbers than a bar graph without looking cluttered or confusing.

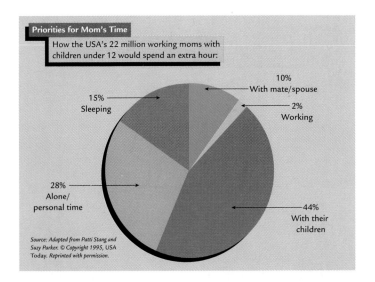

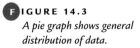
FIGURE 14.3
A pie graph shows general distribution of data.

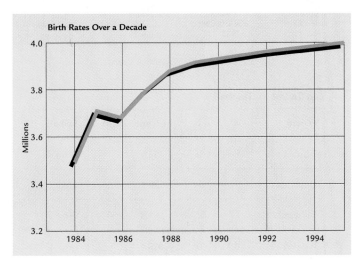

FIGURE 14.4
Line graphs show relationships between two or more variables

As with other types of visual aids, a simple line graph communicates better than a cluttered one.

■ *Picture Graphs* In place of either a line or a bar, you can use pictures to supplement the data you are summarizing (Figure 14.5). Picture graphs look somewhat less formal and less intimidating than other kinds of graphs. One of the advantages of picture graphs is that few words or labels need to be used, which makes them easier for your audience to read.

● **CHARTS** Charts summarize and present a great deal of information in a small amount of space (Figure 14.6). As visual aids, charts have several advantages. They are easy to use, reuse, and enlarge. They can also be displayed in a variety of ways. You can use a flip chart, a poster, or an overhead projector, which you can use to show a giant image of your chart on a screen. As with all other visual aids, charts must be simple. Do not try to put too much information on one chart.

FIGURE 14.5

Consider adding visual symbols to enhance your presentation of statistics. (Adapted from October 16, 1995 U.S. News and World Report.)

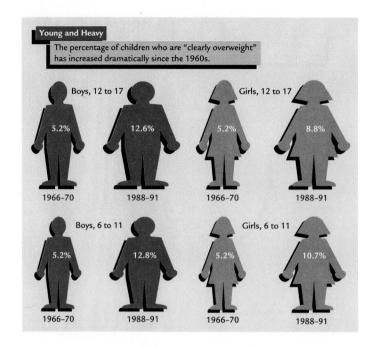

Young and Heavy

The percentage of children who are "clearly overweight" has increased dramatically since the 1960s.

Boys, 12 to 17

5.2%   12.6%

1966–70   1988–91

Girls, 12 to 17

5.2%   8.8%

1966–70   1988–91

Boys, 6 to 11

5.2%   12.8%

1966–70   1988–91

Girls, 6 to 11

5.2%   10.7%

1966–70   1988–91

FIGURE 14.6

Charts summarize and present a great deal of information in a small amount of space.

Top Teams in Baseball

Team	W	L	Percent	GB	Streak
Toronto	84	69	.583	— —	Won 2
Baltimore	78	64	.549	5	Lost 2
Milwaukee	77	65	.542	6	Won 2
New York	69	74	.483	14	Lost 1

The key to developing effective charts is to prepare very carefully the lettering of the words and phrases you use. If the chart contains too much information, audience members may feel it is too complicated to understand, and ignore it. If your chart looks at all cramped or crowded, divide the information into several charts and display each as needed. Print your letters instead of writing them in longhand. If a computer is available, consider using one that has the software capability to prepare large charts or graphs. Make sure that your letters are large enough to be seen clearly in the back row. Use simple words or phrases, and eliminate unnecessary words.

● **FLIP CHARTS**   Flip charts are commonly used in business presentations and training sessions. They consist of a large pad of paper resting on an easel. You can either prepare your visuals on the paper before your speech or draw on the paper while speaking. Flip charts are easy to use. During your presentation, you need only flip the page to reveal your next visual.

Most experienced flip chart users recommend that you use lined paper to keep your words and drawings neat and well organized. Another suggestion is to make penciled-in speaking notes on the chart that only you can see. Brief notes on a flip chart are less cumbersome than using note cards or carrying a clipboard with notes. If you do use crib notes, however, be sure that your notes are few and brief; using too many notes will tempt you to read rather than have eye contact with your audience.

● OVERHEAD TRANSPARENCIES   As a student, you may be familiar with what an overhead projector looks like, but you probably have had little experience in using one yourself. This instrument projects an image drawn on clear sheets of plastic, called transparencies, onto a screen so that the image can be seen by a large group.

Overhead projectors are popular because they have several advantages. They allow you to maintain eye contact with your audience, yet still see your visual. Unlike other projectors, the overhead doesn't require that you turn off the lights in the room to see the projected image. You may wish to dim the lights a bit, but most images can be seen clearly in normal room light. Overheads also permit you to prepare your transparency ahead of time and to make marks on it during your presentation. If you do write during your speech, limit your markings to a few short words or to underlining key phrases.

Consider the following suggestions when using an overhead projector.

■ If possible, practice with the overhead projector in the room in which you will be delivering your speech. That way you can be certain that the projector is the proper distance from the screen and that your image will be large enough to be seen.

■ Turn the overhead projector off when you are not showing a visual, so that it will not detract from your speech.

■ Do not put too much information on one transparency. Use no more than seven lines on one sheet. Do not use a full page of typewritten material in an overhead projection.

■ Align the overhead so the projector head beams the image directly onto the screen. If the image is too low, it will get projected up and suffer distortion from a keystone effect (see Figure 14.7), which makes the image seem larger at the top and smaller at the bottom. Besides making sure that the projector is properly aligned, you can tilt the projector screen forward if it is mounted high on a wall.

■ You may need to increase the volume of your voice when you use an overhead projector. The fan's motor, which keeps the high-intensity projector bulb cool, can be noisy.

●FIGURE 14.7
Note the difference between an overhead projector image that produces a keystone effect and an image made by a projector that is properly adjusted.

- Reveal one line of text at a time by blocking out the text below it with a sheet of paper. This helps hold the audience's interest.

- If possible, try leaving the bottom fourth of your transparency blank. Images that are projected low on the screen often are not visible to audience members in the back.

- Consider using the overhead projector without a transparency as a spotlight to highlight something you have written on a poster or chalkboard. With a large audience, an accent light can add emphasis to other visuals.

- Consider using color. Colored acetate sheets are available from most bookstores. You can also use different-colored markers to highlight key points.

- For ease of handling, place the transparency in a cardboard frame, available wherever acetate sheets are sold. A frame lessens the likelihood that the transparencies will stick together or become torn along the edges.

● COMPUTER-GENERATED GRAPHICS   It is becoming easier and more practical to generate high-quality charts, posters, banners, and graphs with a personal computer. Even if you don't own a personal computer, or one with graphics capability, most copy stores and many campuses have computers and computer labs for student use. There are several software programs that permit you to develop professional-looking graphics.

Using programs such as PowerPoint® or Persuasion®, you can design color graphics on your computer and directly project them to an audience, using a special large-screen projector or a liquid crystal display (LCD) panel that fits on top of an overhead projector. Although this technology may not be available for speeches you deliver in your classroom, many businesses now use it for sales and training presentations. During the presentation, a speaker can retrieve the graphs and charts by simply clicking a key on the keyboard or using the mouse. If it is not practical to carry a computer and other hardware to a speaking engagement, some programs allow you to create slides or to print the computer images onto transparencies for an overhead projector. Or you can print the images on paper and develop dazzling posters to display on an easel.

Many programs can also incorporate color pictures that you store in the computer using a special piece of hardware called a scanner. You can incorporate video and audio into your presentation as well. Images and sound are recorded digitally in your computer and can be displayed on command with the click of your mouse. For example, when your authors teach students principles of speech delivery, we use computer-generated graphics to illustrate the lecture and include video clips that illustrate appropriate and inappropriate delivery methods. If you're using a computer to develop your visual aids, consider the following suggestions.

- Allow yourself plenty of time to produce the graphics. Don't wait until the night before your speech to learn a computer program to produce your words or images. Your final hours should be focused on rehearsing, not on learning a computer program.

■ Charts, graphs, and outlines produced on a computer were probably not designed to be seen by an audience several feet away. Most photocopy stores can assist you in transforming a graph or chart into a transparency that can be used on an overhead projector. Or you could have your graphic enlarged for a modest fee. Again, allow plenty of time for these processes.

■ As with other visual aids, simple computer graphics are often better than busy, complicated visuals. Using a computer may tempt you to add extra information and use multiple fonts. Using too many type styles and more than seven lines of text makes a visual too distracting. The focus should remain on the speech; the visual is to provide emphasis. Appendix C offers additional tips for using computer-generated graphics.

● THE CHALKBOARD   For people in college, the most readily accessible visual aid is a chalkboard. A chalkboard has several advantages: It costs little; it is simple to use; it's low-tech, so you need not worry about extension cords or special techniques.

Chalkboards, however, have serious disadvantages as well. When you write on the board, you have your back to your audience; you do not have eye contact! Some speakers try to avoid that problem by having their visual on the board before their speech starts. But then listeners often look at the visual rather than listening to the introductory remarks. Moreover, chalkboards are probably the least novel visual aid, so they are not particularly effective at getting or holding audience attention.

A chalkboard is best used only for brief phrases, or very simple line diagrams that can be drawn in just a few seconds. It is usually better to prepare a chart, graph, or drawing on a poster or an overhead transparency than to use a chalkboard.

● AUDIOVISUAL AIDS

Perhaps the most exciting presentational aids are those that join sound to sight in communicating ideas. You are probably familiar with all of these: movies, videotapes, and CD-ROM, as well as audio aids such as tapes and compact discs. Now you can consider these familiar media in a new context. Instead of being passively entertained or instructed by them, you may use them actively to support your ideas.

● VIDEOTAPES AND MOVIES   Now that videocassette recorders (VCRs) and cameras are widely available, more public speakers are using videotapes to help communicate their ideas. A VCR can be hooked up to a regular TV to show brief scenes from a rented movie, an excerpt from a training film, or a video that you made yourself. VCRs permit stop-action freeze-frame viewing, and some have a slow-motion function. You can also play and replay a scene several times if you want your audience to watch subtle movement or action.

A twenty-five-inch screen is generally visible to an audience of twenty-five or thirty people. For larger audiences, you will need several TV monitors or a large projection TV system. As noted earlier, you can use a large-screen video projector to display your video. Or, if it is available, you could use a liquid crystal display (LCD) panel connected to an overhead projector to project your image. Before you decide to use a videotape, however, think about whether it will really enhance your speech. Although movies can dramatically capture and hold your audience's attention, they are not really designed as supporting material for a speech. Usually, they are conceived as self-contained packages, and unless you show only short excerpts, they can quickly overwhelm your speech. Of course, if you are a skilled moviemaker, you will probably have enough control over your medium to tame it and make it serve your purpose. Be sure to rehearse with the equipment you will be using until you can handle it smoothly.

● CD-ROM   One of the newest technologies finding its way into classrooms, corporate meetings, training sessions, and lecture halls is the CD-ROM. These compact discs include words, photos, and video clips. They are played back in special CD-ROM-equipped computers which can be used in combination with a large-screen video projector or an LCD panel connected to an overhead projector. All of the information can be retrieved instantly because it is stored digitally; one disc can contain hundreds of moves or books, or an entire encyclopedia. While giving a lecture about Elizabeth Cady Stanton, you could click the computer mouse a couple of times to project her picture or hear an actress read one of her speeches. Or, if you want your audience to hear the dramatic opening four notes of Beethoven's 5th symphony, you can click the mouse to retrieve his famous dit, dit, dit, daaaaah. CD-ROM's key advantage is the ease and speed with which a speaker can retrieve audio or visual information.

● AUDIO AIDS   Tapes, or compact audio discs can either complement a visual display or music, you might play a few measures of Bach's Toccata and Fugue in D Minor on tape, CD, or portable electronic keyboard to illustrate a point. While showing slides of her recent Caribbean vacation, a student used a recording of steel drum music as a soft background for her talk. Another student interviewed students on campus about local parking problems. Rather than reading quotes from irate drivers who couldn't find a place to park, he played a few excerpts of taped interviews.

As with movies and videos, use audio aids sparingly. You do not want your speech's electronic soundtrack to interfere with your message. Probably the easiest and least expensive audio aid to use is a tape recorder that uses cassettes. It is small enough to handle easily, can be held up to a microphone to amplify the sound to a large audience, and can be cued to start exactly where you want it to.

A compact disc has excellent fidelity, and it can be cued to start at a certain passage. Some CD players need a separate amplifier and speakers to take full advantage of the improved sound quality.

Guidelines for developing visual aids

MAKE IT EASY TO SEE

Without a doubt, the most violated principle of using visual aids in public speaking is "Make it big!" Countless speeches have been accompanied by writing on a chart or graph that is too small to read, an overhead projector image that is not large enough to be legible, or a graph on a flip chart that simply can't be deciphered from the back row. If the only principle you carry away from this chapter is to make your visual aid large enough to be seen by all in your audience, you will have gained more skill than a majority of speakers who use visual aids in speeches. *Write big!*

KEEP IT SIMPLE

Simple visuals usually communicate best. Some students think that the visuals accompanying a speech have to be as complicated as a Broadway production, complete with lights and costumes. Resist trying to make your visuals complicated. Indeed, *any* complexity is too much. Words should be limited to key words or phrases. Lengthy dissertations on poster board or an overhead usually do more harm than good. Don't cram too much information on one visual aid. If you have a great deal of information, it is better to use two or three simple charts or overhead transparencies than to attempt to put all your words on one visual.

SELECT THE RIGHT VISUAL AIDS

Because there are so many choices among visual aids, you may wonder, "How do I decide which visual aid to use?" Here are some suggestions.

- *Consider your audience.* Factors such as audience size will dictate the size of the visual you select. If you have a large audience, do not choose a visual aid unless it can be seen clearly by all. The age, interests, and attitudes of your audience will also affect your selection of audiovisual support.

- *Think of your speech objective.* Don't select a visual aid until you have decided on the purpose of your speech.

- *Take into account your own skill and experience.* Use only equipment with which you are comfortable or have had practical experience.

- *Know the room in which you will speak.* If the room has large windows with no shades and no other way to dim the lights, do not consider using visuals that require a darkened room.

● PREPARE POLISHED VISUAL AIDS

Prepare your visual aid well in advance of your speaking date, and try to make it as attractive and polished looking as possible. Avoid late-night, last-minute visual aid construction. A sloppy, amateurish visual will convey the impression that you are not a credible speaker, even if you have spent many hours preparing the verbal part of your speech. Appendix C offers several suggestions for giving your visuals eye-catching appeal.

● DO NOT USE DANGEROUS OR ILLEGAL VISUAL AIDS

Earlier we described a speech in which the speaker accidentally caused an archery bow to shoot over the heads of his startled audience. Not only did he lose credibility because he was not able to string the bow successfully, but he also endangered his audience by turning his visual aid into a flying missile. Dangerous or illegal visual aids may either shock your audience or physically endanger them. This type of visual aid will also detract from your message. They are never worth the risk of a ruined speech or an injured audience member.

If your speech seems to call for a dangerous or illegal object or substance, substitute a model, picture, chart, or other representational device.

Guidelines for using visual aids

REHEARSE WITH YOUR VISUAL AIDS

Jane nervously approached her speech teacher ten minutes before class. She wondered whether class could start immediately because her visual aid was melting. She had planned to explain how to get various stains out of clothing, and her first demonstration would show how to remove chewing gum. But she had forgotten the gum, so she had to ask for a volunteer from the audience to spit out his gum so she could use it in her demonstration. The ice that she had brought to rub on the sticky gum had by this time melted. All she could do was dribble some lukewarm water on the gummed-up cloth in a valiant but unsuccessful effort to demonstrate her cleaning method. It didn't work. To make matters worse, when she tried to set her poster in the chalkboard tray, it kept falling to the floor. She was left embarrassed and on the edge of tears. It was obvious that she had not rehearsed with her visual aids.

Your appearance before your audience should not be the first time you deliver your speech while holding up your chart, turning on the overhead projector, operating the slide projector, or using the flip chart. Practice with your visual aids until you feel at ease with them.

HAVE EYE CONTACT WITH YOUR AUDIENCE, NOT YOUR VISUAL AIDS

You may be tempted to talk to your visual aid rather than to your audience. Your focus, however, should remain on your audience. Of course, you will need to glance at your visual to make sure that it isn't upside down or that it is the proper visual. But do not face it while giving your talk. Keep looking your audience in the eye.

EXPLAIN YOUR VISUAL AIDS

Some speakers believe that they need not explain a visual aid. They think it's enough just to show it to their audience. Resist this approach. When you exhibit your chart showing the overall decline in the stock market, tell your audience what point you are trying to make. Visual support performs the same function as verbal support. It helps you communicate an idea. Make sure that your audience knows what that idea is. Don't just unceremoniously announce, "Here are the recent statistics on birthrates in the United States" and hold up your visual without further explanation. Tell them how to interpret the data. Always set your visuals in a verbal context.

DO NOT PASS OBJECTS AMONG YOUR AUDIENCE

You realize that your marble collection will be too small to see, so you decide to pass some of your most stunning marbles around while you talk. Bad idea. While you are excitedly describing some of your cat's-eye marbles, you have provided a distraction for your audience. People will be more interested in seeing and touching your marbles than in hearing you talk about them.

What can you do if your object is too small to see without passing it around? If no other speaker follows your speech, you can invite audience members to come up and see your object when your speech is over. If your audience is only two or three rows deep, you can even hold up the object and move in close to the audience to show it while you maintain control.

USE ANIMALS WITH CAUTION

Most actors are unwilling to work with animals—and for good reason. At best, they may steal the show. And most often, they are unpredictable. You may *think* you have the smartest, best-trained dog in the world, but you really do not know how your dog will react to a strange environment and an unfamiliar audience. The risk of having an animal detract from your speech may be too great to make planning a speech around one worthwhile.

A zealous midwestern university student a few years ago decided to give a speech on cattle. What better visual aid, he thought, than a cow? He brought the cow to campus and led her up several flights of stairs to his classroom. The speech in fact went well. But the student had neglected to consider one significant problem: Cows will go up stairs but not down them.

Another student had a handsome, well-trained German shepherd guard dog. The class was enjoying his speech and his demonstrations of the dog's prowess until the professor from the next classroom poked his head in the door to ask for some chalk. The dog lunged, snarling and with teeth bared, at the unsuspecting professor. Fortunately, he missed—but the speech was concluded prematurely.

These and other examples emphasize our point: use animals with care, if at all.

USE HANDOUTS EFFECTIVELY

Many speech instructors feel that you should not distribute handouts during a speech. Handing out papers during your presentation will only distract your audience. However, many audiences in business and other types of organizations expect a summary of your key ideas in written form. If you do find it necessary to use written material to reinforce your presentation, keep the following suggestions in mind.

- Don't distribute your handout during the presentation unless your listeners must refer to the material while you're talking about it. Do not distribute handouts that have only a marginal relevance to your verbal message. They will defeat your purpose.

- If you do need to distribute a handout and you see that your listeners are giving the written material more attention than they are giving you, tell them where in the handout you want them to focus. For example, you could say, "I see that many of you are interested in the second and third pages of the report. I'll discuss those items in just a few moments. I'd like to talk about a few examples before we get to page two."

- If your listeners do not need the information during your presentation, tell them that you will distribute a summary of the key ideas at the end of your talk. Your handout might refer to the specific action you want your audience to take, as well as summarize the key information you have discussed.

TIME YOUR VISUALS TO CONTROL YOUR AUDIENCE'S ATTENTION

A skillful speaker knows when to show a supporting visual and when to put it away. For example, it's not wise to begin your speech with all of your charts, graphs, and drawings in full view unless you are going to refer to them in your opening remarks. Time the display of your visuals to coincide with your discussion of the information contained in them.

Jessica was extremely proud of the huge replica of the human mouth that she had constructed to illustrate her talk on the proper way to brush one's teeth. It stood over two feet tall and was painted pink and white. It was a true work of art. As she began her speech, she set her mouth model in full view of the audience. She opened her speech with a brief history of dentistry in America. But her listeners never heard a word. Instead, they were fascinated by the model. Jessica would have done better to cover her visual with a cloth and then dramatically reveal it when she wanted to illustrate proper tooth brushing.

Here are a few more suggestions for timing your visual aids.

- Remove your visual aid when you move to your next point, unless the information it contains will also help you communicate your next idea.

- Have your overhead transparency already in place on the projector. When you are ready to show your visual, simply turn on the projector to reveal your drawing. Change to a new visual as you make your next point. Turn the projector off when you are finished with your visual support.

- Consider asking someone beforehand to help you hold your visual aid, turn the pages of your flip chart, or change the slides on the projector. Make sure that you rehearse with your assistant so that all goes smoothly during your presentation.

USE TECHNOLOGY EFFECTIVELY

You may be tempted to use some of the new technologies we have described because of their novelty rather than because of their value in helping you communicate your message. Most of them, however, are expensive. And many classrooms and lecture rooms are not equipped with the necessary hardware. Also, in order to project images from large-screen projectors or LCD panels, the lights must be very dim or completely off in the room. As we have noted, when you use audiovisual equipment that requires a dark room, you lose vital visual contact with your listeners.

Despite these drawbacks, CD-ROMs and computer-generated graphics are destined to play a growing role in public speaking. If your college or university is equipped for them, be sure to observe the basic cautions we have offered for other, less glitzy visual aids. Keep your visuals simple. Make sure the words or images are large enough to be seen by your listeners. Integrate the words and images into your talk. Time your visuals to coincide with information you are presenting. And don't forget to rehearse with these visuals. It is especially important to learn in advance of your speech how to operate the hardware efficiently.

REMEMBER MURPHY'S LAW

According to Murphy's Law, if something can go wrong, it will. When you use visual aids, you increase the chances that problems or snags will develop when you present your speech. The chart may fall off the easel, you may not find any chalk, the bulb in the overhead projector may burn out. We are not saying that you should be a pessimist, just that you should have backup supplies and a backup plan in case your best-laid plans go awry.

If something doesn't go as you planned, do your best to keep your speech on track. If the chart falls over, simply pick it up and keep talking; don't offer lengthy apologies. If you can't find the chalk you will need and it is your turn to speak, quietly ask a friend to go on a chalk hunt in another room. A thorough rehearsal, a double check of your equipment, and extra supplies such as extension cords, projector bulbs, or masking tape can help repeal Murphy's Law.

RECAP

CHECKLIST FOR USING VISUAL AIDS

WHEN DEVELOPING VISUAL AIDS

Are your visual aids easy to see?

Are they simple and uncluttered?

Do they suit your audience, speech objectives, and speech environment?

Are they attractive and carefully prepared?

Are your visual aids legal and nonthreatening to your audience?

WHEN USING YOUR VISUAL AID DURING YOUR SPEECH

Have you rehearsed with your visual aids?

Do you look at your audience when you talk, rather than at your visual aids?

Do you explain your visual aids, rather than just show them?

Can you avoid having to pass around your visual aids?

Have you used well-timed handouts?

Do your visual aids keep your audience's attention focused on your speech?

Can you operate the hardware you have chosen, and do you have backup supplies?

Summary

Visual aids are tools to help you communicate your ideas more dramatically than can words alone. In this chapter, we looked at different types of visual aids and reviewed general guidelines for their use.

Visual aids help influence your listeners' understanding and recollection of your ideas. They also help you communicate the organization of your ideas, gain and maintain the audience's attention, and illustrate a sequence of events or procedures.

Three-dimensional visual aids include objects, models, and people. Two-dimensional visual aids include drawings, photographs, slides, maps, graphs, charts, flip charts, projected transparencies, and the chalkboard. Software graphics packages can be used to produce many of these options inexpensively and efficiently. Audiovisual aids include movies and videotapes. Audio aids such as tapes and compact discs can also be used to help communicate ideas to your listeners.

When you prepare your visual aids, make sure your visuals are large enough to be seen clearly by all of your listeners. Adapt your visual aids to your audience, the speaking environment, and the objectives of your speech. Prepare your visuals well in advance, and make sure they are not illegal or dangerous to use.

As you present your speech, remember these suggestions: be sure to look at your audience, not your visual aid; talk about your visual, don't just show it; avoid passing objects among your audience; use handouts to reinforce the main points in your speech; time your visuals carefully; and be sure to have backup supplies and a contingency plan.

CRITICAL THINKING QUESTIONS

1. Nikki plans to give a talk to the Rotary Club in an effort to encourage the club members to support a local bond issue for a new library. She wants to make sure they understand how cramped and inadequate the current library is. What type of visual support could she use to make her point?

2. Professor Chou uses only the chalkboard to illustrate her anthropology lectures. Occasionally, she will write a word or two on the board. What other types of visual or auditory aids could Professor Chou use to help in teaching her lessons?

3. Mayor Bryan will address the board of directors of a large microchip firm, hoping to lure them to his community. He plans to use handouts, several charts, a short video clip and an overhead projector to show several transparencies. What advice would you give the mayor to make sure his presentation is effective?

ETHICAL QUESTIONS

1. Masha found the perfect pie chart in *USA Today* to illustrate her talk on U.S. census figures for population trends. If she tells her audience that the source of her visual is *USA Today,* does she also need to cite the U.S. census bureau?

2. Ceally wants to educate his college classmates about the increased use of profanity in contemporary music. He would like to play sound clips of some of the most offensive lyrics to illustrate his point. Would you advise Ceally to play these songs, even though doing so might offend several members of the audience?

3. Derrick is planning to give a speech about emergency first aid. His brother is a paramedic and licensed nurse. Is it ethical for Derrick to wear his brother's paramedic uniform without telling his listeners that the outfit belongs to his brother?

1. You will need the following materials to complete this assignment:

A piece of paper or poster board measuring at least fifteen by twenty inches

At least two felt-tipped markers or a set of marking pens

A ruler or straightedge

A pencil with an eraser

Five speech topics are given here, with a brief description of each (as needed), and a group of statistics or other content that could be communicated with the help of a visual aid. Design and complete a visual aid for *two* of the following speech descriptions.

a. A speech about drug use in the United States that incorporates the following statistics:

In 1993, 2.1 million Americans were hard-core cocaine users.

In 1993, about half a million Americans were hard-core heroin users.

In 1993, 9 million Americans reported they had used marijuana at least once in the month before the survey was conducted.

In 1988, 2.5 million Americans were hard-core cocaine users.

In 1988, 590,000 Americans were hard-core heroin users.

In 1988, 11.6 million Americans reported they had used marijuana at least once in the month before the survey was conducted.

b. A speech about how third-party candidates have fared in presidential elections. Note the following statistics:

Candidate	Highest Rating in Polls	Percentage of Popular Vote
1948 Henry Wallace	2%	2.4%
1968 George Wallace	20%	13.5%
1980 John Anderson	13%	6.6%
1992 Ross Perot	39%	19.0%

c. A speech on the importance of nonverbal communication. During a discussion of how we communicate emotion nonverbally, the speaker wants to present the figures that about 55 percent of emotion is communicated facially, about 38 percent is communicated vocally, and only about 7 percent is communicated verbally.

d. A speech on career counseling. During the speech, statistics are quoted from *Parents* magazine, in which a woman undergoing career counseling is asked to lay out her ideal plan of time allotment. She hopes to spend 35 percent of her time at a part-time job, 10 percent doing housework, 20 percent in activities with her children, 12 percent cooking, 7 percent socializing, 6 percent watching TV, and 10 percent reading and working on hobbies.

e. A speech on the importance of calcium in the diet. *Good Housekeeping* reports on the calcium contents of certain common foods: 1 cup of 2 percent milk has 352 mg, 1 cup of lowfat yogurt has 294 mg, 1 ounce of cheddar cheese has 213 mg, 1 cup of ice cream has 194 mg, and 1 cup of broccoli has 136 mg.

USING TECHNOLOGY AND MEDIA

1. If your school has a media resources center, make an appointment to visit it and review the electronic audio and video equipment that is available for your use. While you will undoubtedly be familiar with such AV equipment as overhead projectors and videotape machines, ask about the availability of newer technology such as CD-ROM, personal computers for generating and displaying graphics, and liquid crystal display panels.

2. Review recent issues of magazines or journals that advertise the latest presentation technology. Journals such as *Training* or *Training and Development*, published by the American Society for Training and Development, are good magazines to peruse. Note the new technology that is being advertised and be prepared to discuss how the new AV resources could enhance speech presentations.

3. Watch a national or local broadcast of the evening news and pay particular attention to the use of visuals and graphics used to help communicate the news stories. Evaluate the effectiveness of the news program's use of visuals, using the criteria that were discussed in this chapter.

"Men Exist for the Sake of One Another. Teach Them or Bear with Them."
Lawrence Jacob/National Museum of American Art/Art Resource

Speaking to Inform

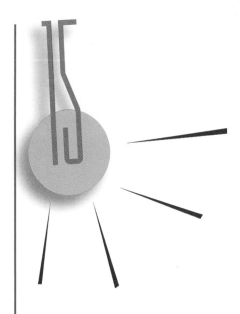

Not only is there an art in knowing a thing, but also a certain art in teaching it.
—Cicero

● OBJECTIVES

After studying this chapter you should be able to do the following:

1. *Identify four goals of speaking to inform.*

2. *Describe five different types of informative speeches.*

3. *Identify strategies to use when your goal is to explain new ideas, clarify complex processes, or change an inaccurate perception or idea.*

4. *List and explain eight principles for making an informative speech memorable.*

As you are walking home, a car pulls over, the driver leans across the car, rolls down the window, and asks, "How do you get to Interstate 70?"

Your history professor has asked each student to give an oral report describing one battle from the Civil War. You decide to review the Battle of Gettysburg.

Each Thanksgiving you send your aunt a fruitcake made from your unique prize-winning recipe. This Thanksgiving, when she comes for her annual visit, she asks you to tell her how to make your special cake.

In each of these situations, your task is to give information to someone. Whether you are having spontaneous conversation or delivering a rehearsed speech, you will often find that your speaking purpose is to inform, or teach someone something you know. A recent survey of both speech teachers and students who had taken a speech course found that the single most important skill taught in a public speaking class is how to give an informative speech.[1]

Conveying information to others is a useful skill in most walks of life. You may find that informing others will be an important part of your job. As a regional manager of a national corporation, you may have to report sales figures every fiscal quarter; as an accountant, you may have to teach your secretary how to organize your files. Other activities, such as teaching a Chinese cooking class or chairing monthly meetings of the Baker Street Irregulars, can also require you to provide information.

In this chapter, we will suggest ways to build on your experience and enhance your skill in informing others. We will discuss goals of informative speaking, examine different types of informative tasks, and discuss specific ways to inform others. Finally, we will present some general principles for making your informative presentations memorable.

Goals of informative speaking

Speaking to inform others is a challenging task. The information you communicate to someone else is rarely, if ever, understood completely as you intended it. As we discussed in Chapter 4, one day after hearing your presentation, most audiences will remember only about half of what you told them. And they will recall only about 25 percent two weeks later. Your job is to ensure as much retention of what you have conveyed as possible, by presenting the information as effectively as you can.

In Chapter 12, we discussed the importance of using concrete and vivid words to make your ideas clear, and using simple words in standard English sentences to keep your message accurate. But as an informative speaker, you have another major challenge: to make your message interesting. The best way to achieve this goal is to remain audience-centered. Keep your listeners in mind as you select and narrow a topic, fine-tune your purpose, and complete each speech preparation and presentation task. As we noted in Chapter 10, your listeners may be interested in your topic for a variety of reasons. It may affect them directly, it may add to their knowledge, it may satisfy their curiosity, or it may entertain them. These reasons are not mutually exclusive, of course. For example, if you were talking to a group of businesspeople about the latest changes in local tax policies, you would be discussing something that would affect them directly, add to their knowledge, *and* satisfy their curiosity. But your listeners' primary interest would be in how taxes would affect them. By contrast, if you were giving a lecture on fifteenth-century Benin sculpture to a middle-class audience at a YMCA, your listeners would be interested because your talk would add to their knowledge, satisfy their curiosity, and entertain them. Such a talk can also affect your listeners directly by making *them* more interesting to others. If your audience feels that they will benefit from your speech in some way, your speech will interest them. And an interesting speech commands attention, as well as respect.

If your audience consists of adult listeners, you will need to ensure that you deliver your message in the way that adults learn best. Adult learners prefer the following:[2]

- To be given information they can use immediately

- To be actively involved in the learning process

- To connect their life experiences with the new information they learn

- To know how the new information is relevant to their busy lives

- To receive information that is relevant to their needs

Most people who work in business have an in-basket on their desk to receive letters that must be read and work that must be done. Each of us also has a kind of mental in-basket, an agenda for what we want or need to accomplish. As we noted in Chapter 5, you will hold your audience's interest, and also have more success in informing them, if you tailor your information to address your audience's agenda.

Types of informative speeches

Informative speeches can be classified according to the subject areas they cover. Classifying your speech can help you decide how to organize the information you want to present. As you will see in the following discussion, the demands of your purpose will often dictate a structure for your speech. As you look at these suggestions about structure, however, remember that good organization is only one factor in your audience's ability to process your message. In the next section, we will discuss additional strategies for ensuring that your listeners will *understand* the information in your speech.

SPEECHES ABOUT IDEAS

Speeches about ideas are usually more abstract than the other types of speeches. The following principles, concepts, and theories might be topics of idea speeches:

Principles of communication

Freedom of speech
Evolution
Theories of aging
Hinduism
Communal living
Trickle-down theory of economics

Most speeches about ideas are organized topically (by logical subdivisions of the central idea) or according to complexity (from simple ideas to more complex ones). The following example illustrates how one student organized an idea topic into an informative speech:

TOPIC: Liberation theology

GENERAL PURPOSE: To inform

SPECIFIC PURPOSE: At the end of my speech, the audience should be able to discuss the definition and origin of liberation theology in Latin America.

I. Definition of liberation theology

   A. Theological concepts

   B. Sacramental innovations and explanations

   C. Social theories

II. Intellectual origins of liberation theology

   A. In Christian tradition and thought

   B. In Marxism minus atheism

Luisa decided that the most logical way to explain liberation theology was to talk first about the definition of liberation theology and second, about its origins. She chose a topical organization—a logical division of available information about liberation theology. (See Chapter 9 for more information on topical organization.)

● SPEECHES ABOUT OBJECTS

A speech about an object might be about anything tangible—anything you can see or touch. You may or may not show the actual object to your audience while you are talking about it. (Chapter 14 provides suggestions for using objects as visual aids to illustrate your ideas.)

Objects that could form the basis of an interesting speech might include these:

A collection of yours (rocks, compact discs, baseball cards, and so on)
Sports cars
Violins
Personal computers
8mm video cameras
Vietnam Memorial
Toys

An "object" may be something as complex and fascinating as this Native American cliff dwelling in Mesa Verde National Park. An informative speech might discuss the dwelling's structure along with its practical and ceremonial uses, the material culture of the Anasazi people, the park's efforts to preserve the dwelling, and other related topics. [Photo: Gavin Heller/ Tony Stone Images]

The time limit for your speech will determine the amount of detail you can share with your listeners. Even in a thirty- to forty-five-minute presentation, you cannot talk about every aspect of any of the objects listed. So you will need to focus on a specific purpose. Here's a sample outline for a speech about an object:

TOPIC: Pipe organs

GENERAL PURPOSE: To inform

SPECIFIC PURPOSE: At the end of my speech, the audience should be able to describe the three major parts and functions of a tracker pipe organ.

  I. The console

    A. The keyboards

      1. Great organ

      2. Swell organ

      3. Positive organ

    B. The pedal boards

    C. The stops

 II. The pipes

    A. Flue pipes

    B. Reed pipes

III. The air system

    A. Air reservoir

B. Motor

C. Fan

Speeches about objects may be organized topically (the speech about pipe organs is practically self-organizing, according to the three parts of the instrument). This type of speech may also be organized chronologically. A speaker might, for example, focus on the history and development of the organ. That speech would probably be organized chronologically. Or, the speech could be organized spatially, noting the physical layout of a pipe organ.

If a how-to discussion becomes the central focus of a speech, it then becomes a speech about a procedure.

● SPEECHES ABOUT PROCEDURES

A speech about a procedure discusses how something works (for example, the human circulatory system), or describes a process that produces a particular outcome (such as how grapes become wine). At the close of such a speech, your audience should be able to describe, understand, or perform the procedure you have described. Here are some examples of procedures that could make effective informative presentations:

How state laws are made
How the U.S. patent system works
How a rotary engine works
How to refinish furniture
How to select an inexpensive stereo system
How to plant an organic garden
How to avoid long lines at registration

Notice that all these examples start with the word *how*. A speech about a procedure usually focuses on how a process is completed or how something can be accomplished. Speeches about procedures are often presented in workshops or other training situations in which people learn skills.

Anita, describing how to develop a new training curriculum in teamwork skills, used an organizational strategy that grouped some of her steps together like this:

I. Conduct a needs assessment of your department.

A. Identify the method of assessing department needs.

1. Consider using questionnaires.

2. Consider using interviews.

3. Consider using focus groups.

B. Implement the needs assessment.

II. Identify the topics that should be presented in the training.

A. Specify topics that all members of the department need.

B. Specify topics that only some members of the department need.

III. Write training objectives.

A. Write objectives that are measurable.

B. Write objectives that are specific.

C. Write objectives that are attainable.

IV. Develop lesson plans for the training.

A. Identify the training methods you will use.

B. Identify the materials you will need.

Her audience will remember the four general steps much more easily than they could have hoped to recall if each aspect of the curriculum development process were listed as a separate step.

Many speeches about procedures include visual aids (see Chapter 14). Whether you are teaching people how to hang wallpaper or how to give a speech, showing them how to do something is almost always more effective than just telling them how to do it.

● SPEECHES ABOUT PEOPLE

A biographical speech could be about someone famous or about someone you know personally. Most of us enjoy hearing about the lives of real people, whether famous or not, living or dead, who had some special quality about them. The key to presenting an effective biographical speech is to be selective. Don't try to cover every detail of your subject's life. Relate the key elements in the person's career, personality, or other significant life features so that you are building to a particular point rather than just reciting facts about an individual. Perhaps your grandfather was known for his generosity, for example. Mention some notable examples of his philanthropy. If you are talking about a well-known personality, pick information or a period that is not widely known, such as the person's childhood or private hobby.

One speaker gave a memorable speech about his neighbor:

> To enter Hazel's house is to enter a combination greenhouse and zoo. Plants are everywhere; it looks and feels like a tropical jungle. Her home is always warm and humid. Her dog Peppy, her cat Bones, a bird named Elmer, and a fish called Frank can be seen through the philodendron, ferns, and pansies. While Hazel loves her plants and animals, she loves people even more. Her finest hours are spent serving coffee to her friends and neighbors, playing Uno with family until late in the evening, and just visiting about the good old days. Hazel is one of a kind.

Note how the speech captures Hazel's personality and charm. Speeches about people should give your listeners the feeling that the person is a unique, authentic individual.

One way to talk about a person's life is in chronological order—birth, school, career, marriage, achievements, death. However, if you are interested in presenting a specific theme, such as, "Winston Churchill, master of English prose," you may decide instead to organize those key experiences topically. First you would discuss Churchill's achievements as a brilliant orator whose words defied German steel in 1940, and then trace the origins of his skill to his work as a cub reporter in South Africa during the Boer War of 1899 to 1902.

SPEECHES ABOUT EVENTS

Where were you on January 28, 1986—the day the *Challenger* space shuttle exploded and killed all seven astronauts on board? Chances are that you clearly remember where you were and what you were doing on that and other similarly fateful days. Major events punctuate our lives and mark the passage of time.

A major event can form the basis of a fascinating informative speech. You can choose to talk about an event that you have either witnessed or researched. Your goal is to describe the event in concrete, tangible terms and to bring the experience to life for your audience. Were you living in Miami when Hurricane Andrew struck? Have you witnessed the inauguration of a president, governor, or senator? Did you experience the ravages of the midwest floods of 1993 or 1995? Or you may want to re-create an event that your parents or grandparents lived through. What was it like to be in Pearl Harbor on December 7, 1941?

You may have heard a recording of the famous radio broadcast of the explosion and crash of the dirigible *Hindenburg*. The announcer's ability to describe both the scene and the incredible emotion of the moment has made that broadcast a classic. As that broadcaster was able to do, your purpose as an informative speaker describing an event is to make that event come alive for your listeners and to help them visualize the scene.

An event such as the funeral of Yitzhak Rabin, the Israeli Prime Minister who was assassinated in 1995, offers a rich array of speech possibilities. In addition to describing the extraordinary gathering of world leaders on that day (Jordan's King Hussein is the speaker in this photograph), you could discuss both the background and the implications of incidents that took place before and during the event. [Photo: AP Photo/ Michel Lipchitz]

Most speeches built around an event follow a chronological arrangement. But a speech about an event might also describe the complex issues or causes behind the event and be organized topically. For example, if you were to talk about the Civil War, you might choose to focus on the three causes of the war:

I. Political

II. Economic

III. Social

Although these main points are topical, specific subpoints may be organized chronologically. However you choose to organize your speech about an event, your audience should be enthralled by your vivid description.

 RECAP

TYPES OF INFORMATIVE SPEECHES

Speech Type	Description	Typical Organizational Patterns	Sample Topics
Speeches about ideas	Present abstract information or information about principles, concepts, theories, or issues	Topical Complexity	Communism Contract with America Buddhism
Speeches about objects	Present information about tangible things	Topical Spatial Chronological	The Rosetta Stone Museums Space shuttle The U.S. Capitol building
Speeches about procedures	Review how something works or describe a process	Chronological Topical Complexity	How to . . . Fix a carburetor Operate a nuclear power plant Use a computer Trap lobsters
Speeches about people	Describe either famous people or personal acquaintances	Chronological Topical	Bill Clinton Nelson Mandela Indira Gandhi Your granddad Your favorite teacher
Speeches about events	Describe an actual event that either has happened or will happen	Chronological Topical Complexity Spatial	Oklahoma City bombing Inauguration Day Cinco de Mayo

Strategies for informing your listeners

We have discussed the kinds of topics that are appropriate for an informative speech and linked them to specific organizational strategies. But selecting the organizational pattern for your talk is only one of the decisions you make when you seek to inform. You should also consider the specific method or strategy you will use to present new information and ideas to your audience. Recent educational research suggests that certain types of informing strategies work best for certain types of informative goals and audience backgrounds. One researcher identifies three sets of approaches and strategies, which we will examine next.[3]

STRATEGIES TO EXPLAIN NEW IDEAS

With swift changes occurring in every area of life, new words and concepts appear almost daily. The second edition of the unabridged *Random House Dictionary of the English Language,* published in 1987, contains 50,000 more words and 75,000 more definitions than did the first edition, published in 1966.[4] *RAM, CD-ROM, cyberspace,* and *new world order* are just a few of the concepts that have recently come into use. As a public speaker, you are responsible for ensuring that your listeners understand the words and phrases you use, particularly if the primary goal of your speech is to explain a new idea.

In Chapter 8, we discussed the use of definition as a type of supporting material. *Defining a term in words* can be particularly helpful in informative speeches, whether you quote words directly from a standard dictionary or use your own. In addition, you can use definitions by example and operational definitions.

A **definition by example** uses concrete examples to show the audience what the term or concept means. One student speaker, for example, defined the term *advertising* by pointing to the numerous advertisements for magazine subscriptions and credit card applications that were posted on the bulletin board at the front of the classroom. Another speaker who wanted to define *primitive antiques* displayed several examples of kitchen utensils and photographs of furniture to show her audience the defining characteristics of a primitive antique. In addition, she brought photographs of nonprimitive antiques and noted differences between the two classes of antiques to further clarify her definition. Using *negative examples* coupled with positive examples can be an effective strategy for teaching defining characteristics.

As we discussed in Chapter 8 an **operational definition** focuses on a particular procedure for observing or measuring the concept that is being defined. For example, if you are giving an informative speech about intelligence, you may choose to define intelligence by describing the procedures used in an IQ test and explaining how the test measures intelligence.

definition by example
Uses concrete examples to show the audience what the term or concept means.

operational definition
Focuses on a particular procedure for observing or measuring the concept that is being defined.

What is the best way to explain new ideas or concepts? It depends on the knowledge and experiences of your audience. If you are presenting completely new information to listeners, you may want to use simple, familiar examples. As a general rule of thumb, more sophisticated listeners will understand technical or operational definitions; less sophisticated listeners will appreciate clear, easy-to-understand definitions, coupled, if possible, with a vivid example.

⬤ STRATEGIES TO CLARIFY COMPLEX PROCESSES

If you are trying to tell your listeners about a complex process, you will need more than definitions to explain what you mean. Research suggests that you can demystify a complex process if you first provide a simple overview of the process with an analogy, model, picture, or vivid description.[5]

Before going into great detail, first give listeners the "big picture" or convey the gist of what the process is about.[6] *Analogies* (comparisons) are often a good way to do this. For example, if you are describing how a personal computer works, you could say that it stores information like a filing cabinet or that computer software works like a piano roll on an old-fashioned player piano. In addition to using an analogy, consider using a *model* or other visual aid to show relationships among the parts of a complex process, following the guidelines we presented in Chapter 14.

You can also *describe* the process, providing more detail than you do when you just define something. Descriptions answer questions about the who, what, where, why, and when of the process. Who is involved in the process? What is the process, idea, or event that you want to describe? Where and when does the process take place? Why does it occur, or why is it important to the audience? (Of course, not all of these questions apply to every description.)

Or, you could clarify the process with a *word picture*. As you learned in Chapter 8, word pictures are lively descriptions that help your listeners form a mental image by appealing to their senses of sight, taste, smell, sound, and touch. The following suggestions will help you construct effective word pictures.

- Form a clear mental image of the person, place, or object before you try to describe it.

- Describe the appearance of the person, place, or object. What would your listeners see if they were looking at it? Use lively language to describe the flaws and foibles, bumps and beauties of the people, places, and things you want your audience to see. Make your description an invitation to the imagination—a stately pleasure dome into which your listeners can enter and view its treasures with you.

- Describe what your listeners would hear. Use colorful, onomatopoetic words, such as *buzz, snort, bum, crackle,* or *hiss.* These words are much more descriptive than the more general term *noise.* Imitate the sound you want your listeners to hear with their "mental ear." For example, instead of saying, "When I walked in the woods, I heard the sound of twigs breaking beneath my feet and wind moving the leaves above me in the trees," you might say, "As I walked in the woods, I heard the crackle of twigs underfoot and the rustle of leaves overhead."

- Describe smells, if appropriate. What fragrance or aroma do you want your audience to recall? Such diverse subjects as Thanksgiving, nighttime in the tropics, and the first day of school all lend themselves to olfactory imagery. No Thanksgiving would be complete without the rich aroma of roast turkey and the pungent, tangy odor of cranberries. A warm, humid evening in Miami smells of salt air and gardenia blossoms. And the first day of school evokes for many the scents of new shoe leather, unused crayons, and freshly painted classrooms. In each case, the associated smells greatly enhance the overall word picture.

- Describe how an object feels when touched. Use words that are as clear and vivid as possible. Rather than saying that something is rough or smooth, use a simile, such as "the rock was rough as sandpaper" or "the pebble was as smooth as a baby's skin." These descriptions appeal to both the visual and tactile senses.

- Describe taste, one of the most powerful sensory cues, if appropriate. Thinking about your grandmother may evoke for you memories of her rich homemade noodles; her sweet, fudgy, nut brownies; and her light, flaky, buttery pie crust. Descriptions of these taste sensations would be welcome to almost any audience, particularly your fellow college students subsisting mainly on dormitory food or their own cooking! More important, such description can help you paint an accurate, vivid image of your grand-mother.

- Describe the emotion that a listener might feel if he or she were to experience the situation you relate. If you experienced the situation, describe your own emotions. Use specific adjectives rather than general terms such as *happy* or *sad*. One speaker, talking about receiving her first speech assignment, described her reaction with these words: "My heart stopped. Panic began to rise up inside. Me? . . . For the next five days I lived in dreaded anticipation of the forthcoming event."[7]

Note how effectively her choice of such words and phrases as "my heart stopped," "panic," and "dreaded anticipation" describe her terror at the prospect of making a speech—much more so than if she had said simply, "I was scared."

The more vividly and accurately you can describe emotion, the more intimately involved in your description the audience will become.

Sometimes your audience may think they understand the terms and concepts you use, or how a process works. The problem is that their understanding is wrong. But simply telling your listeners that their current understanding of facts is off base may not be the most effective strategy for correcting their thinking. You may first have to convince people that their ideas are wrong. Your general speech objective is still to inform or teach, yet you will first have to challenge their current understanding of an idea or concept before you present the accurate information. For example, if your listeners think that AIDS is transferred through kissing or other casual contact rather than through unprotected sexual contact, you may have to acknowledge their beliefs and then construct a sound argument to show how inaccurate they are. Experienced speakers use a four-part strategy for this purpose.[8]

■ *Summarize the common misconceptions about the issue or idea you are discussing.* "Many people think that AIDS can be transmitted through casual contact such as kissing or that it can easily be transmitted by your dentist or physician."

■ *State why these misconceptions may seem reasonable.* Tell your listeners why it is logical for them to hold that view or identify "facts" that they may have heard that would lead them to their current conclusion. "Since AIDS is such a highly contagious disease, it seems reasonable to think that it can be transmitted through such casual contact."

■ *Dismiss the misconceptions and provide evidence to support your point.* Here you need sound and credible data to be persuasive. "In fact, countless medical studies have shown that it is virtually impossible to be infected with the AIDS virus unless you have unprotected sexual contact or use infected and unsterilized hypodermic needles from someone who has AIDS." In this instance, you would probably cite specific results from two or three studies to lend credibility to your claim.

■ *State the accurate information that you want your audience to remember.* Reinforce the conclusion you want your listeners to draw from the information you presented, with a clear summary statement such as, "According to recent research, the most common factor contributing to the spread of AIDS is unprotected sex. This is true for individuals of all sexes and sexual orientations."

As a final word in this discussion of strategies for informing your listeners, we want to emphasize again that you as a speaker are responsible for ensuring that your audience understands your message. As you learned in Chapter 5, monitoring nonverbal cues and adapting your speech to your audience's responses are critical activities during your delivery. Even the most perfectly structured informative speech will be a failure if your audience cannot understand or remember the information. Watch for puzzled or vacant expressions as you progress through your speech, and don't hesitate to backtrack or try another informative strategy if necessary.

RECAP

STRATEGIES FOR INFORMING LISTENERS

Informative Purpose	Strategy	Appropriate Uses
Explain new ideas	Define with words Define by example Define with negative examples Define by operation	When the audience does not understand key terms, concepts or ideas
Clarify complex process	Provide the "big picture" or an overview of the process Use an analogy or comparison Use a model or visual aid Use a detailed description Use a word picture	When you are describing a complex procedure or a set of interrelated principles
Change a common misconception	First, state the common misconception Second, state why it seems reasonable Third, refute it with evidence Fourth, state the accurate information you want the listener to remember	When your listeners share a common misconception about a problem or issue and you want to correct their misunderstanding

Making your informative speech memorable

Think of the best teacher you ever had. He or she was most probably a good lecturer with a special talent for making information interesting and memorable. Like teachers, some speakers are better than others at presenting information in an interesting and memorable way. In this section, we will review some of the principles that can help you become this kind of speaker.

PRESENT INFORMATION THAT RELATES TO YOUR LISTENERS

Throughout this book, we have encouraged you to develop an audience-centered approach to public speaking. Being an audience-centered informative speaker means that you are aware of information that your audience can use. If, for example, you are going to teach your audience pointers about trash recycling, be sure to talk about specific recycling efforts on your campus or in your own community. Adapt your message to the people who will be in your audience.

In Chapter 7, we introduced the concept of *proximity*—choosing supporting materials that might influence or be familiar to your listeners. Proximity, or close-ness, is basic to informative speaking, as it is to all public speaking, and helps explain why one of the first steps in preparing a speech is to analyze the audience. Once you know their needs and interests, you will be able to choose a relevant topic or adapt the one you have.

Another basis for adapting your topic to your audience is to find out why *you* are interested in the topic. Using your own interests and background as a start, you can then find ways to establish common bonds with your audience. This will help make your topic relevant to your listeners.

Most audiences will probably not be waiting breathlessly for you to talk to them. You will need to motivate them to listen to you.

Some situations have built-in motivations for listeners. A teacher can say, "There will be a test covering my lecture tomorrow. It will count toward 50 percent of your semester grade." Such threatening methods may not make the teacher popular, but they certainly will motivate the class to listen. Similarly, a boss might say, "Your ability to use these sales principles will determine whether you keep your job." As with the teacher, your boss's statement will probably motivate you to learn the company's sales principles. By contrast, you will rarely have the power to motivate your listeners with such strong-arm tactics, and you will therefore need to find more creative ways to get your audience to listen to you.

One way to arouse the interest of your listeners is to ask them a question. Speaking on the high cost of tuition, you might ask, "How many of you are interested in saving tuition dollars this year?" You'll probably have their attention. Then proceed to tell them that you will talk about several approaches to seeking low-cost loans and grants.

"Who would like to save money on their income taxes?" "How many of you would like to have a happier home life?" "How many of you would like to learn an effective way of preparing your next speech?" There are other examples of questions that could stimulate your listeners' interest and motivate them to give you their attention. Besides using rhetorical questions, you can begin with an anecdote, a startling statistic, or some other attention-grabbing device.

Don't assume that your listeners will be automatically interested in what you have to say. Pique their interest with a question. Capture their attention. Motivate them to listen to you. Tell them how the information you present will be of value to them. As the British writer G. K. Chesterton once said, "There is no such thing as an uninteresting topic; there are only uninterested people."[9]

● BUILD IN REDUNDANCY

It is seldom necessary for writers to repeat themselves. If readers don't quite understand a passage, they can go back and read it again. When you speak, however, it is useful to repeat key points. As we have noted before, audience members generally cannot stop you if a point in your speech is unclear or if their minds wander; you need to build in redundancy to make sure that the information you want to communicate will get across. As noted in Chapter 9, most speech teachers advise their students to structure their speeches as follows:

1. Tell them what you're going to tell them. In the introduction of your speech, provide a broad overview of the purpose of your message. Identify the major points you will present.

2. Tell them. In the body of your speech, develop each of the main points mentioned during your introduction.

3. Tell them what you've told them. Finally, in your conclusion, summarize the key ideas discussed in the body.

USE SIMPLE IDEAS RATHER THAN COMPLEX ONES

Your job as a public speaker is to get your ideas over to your audience, not to see how much information you can cram in. The simpler your ideas and phrases, the greater the chance that your audience will remember them.

Let's say you decide to talk about state-of-the-art personal computer hardware. Fine—just don't try to make your audience as sophisticated as you are about computers in a five-minute speech. Discuss only major features and name one or two leaders in the field. Don't load your speech with details. Edit severely your own material.

As we noted in Chapter 9 and earlier in this chapter, your audience will more readily understand your information if you organize your major points logically. Regardless of the length or complexity of your speech, you must always follow a logical pattern in order to be understood.

REINFORCE KEY IDEAS VERBALLY

You can reinforce an idea by using such phrases as "This is the most important point" or "Be sure to remember this next point; it's the most compelling one." Suppose you have four suggestions for helping your listeners avoid a serious sunburn, and your last suggestion is the most important. How can you make sure your audience knows that? Just tell them. "Of all the suggestions I've given you, this last tip is the most important one. Here it is: The higher the PABA level on your sunscreen, the better." Be careful not to overuse this technique. If you claim that every other point is a key point, soon your audience will not believe you.

REINFORCE KEY IDEAS NONVERBALLY

You can also signal the importance of a point with nonverbal emphasis. Gestures serve the purpose of accenting or emphasizing key phrases, as italics do in written communication.

A well-placed pause can provide emphasis and reinforcement to set off a point. Pausing just before or just after making an important point will focus attention on your thought. Raising or lowering your voice can also reinforce a key idea.

Movement can help emphasize major ideas. Moving from behind the lectern to tell a personal anecdote can signal that something special and more intimate is about to be said. As we discussed in Chapter 13, your movement and gestures should be meaningful and natural, rather than seemingly arbitrary or forced. Your need to emphasize an idea can provide the motivation to make a meaningful movement.

SAMPLE INFORMATIVE SPEECH

"Sleeping with the Enemy: House Dust Mites"[9]

Maria Ereni Ciach, West Chester University

As children, we all read and loved the classic Dr. Seuss tale, *Horton Hears a Who*. I'm sure you remember Horton the elephant who loved nothing more than playing in the great outdoors. One day, while splashing around in a stream, Horton heard someone quietly crying for help. The sound was coming from a tiny piece of dust that was blowing around in the wind. After the bit of dust landed, Horton realized that an entire colony of creatures called Whos lived inside that single particle. But as adults, we know better than to believe in Whos; the idea of an entire colony of creatures living in a single piece of dust is silly, right? Well, not exactly. Try to explain that one to the house dust mites.

They don't sting or bite. They don't transmit diseases to humans, and they don't make your pets itch. However, according to Dr. Claude Frazier, house dust mites are the major allergenic agent known among all insects, and as a result, are responsible for making many of us miserable. These invaders are invisible to the naked eye, and you'd never know you were sharing quarters with them unless someone you know, or perhaps you yourself, happens to be allergic. I received a publication from Dr. George Kern, a member of the American Board of Allergy and Immunology, that states that over 20 million Americans are allergic to house dust mites, and those are just the reported cases.

So now that maybe you're beginning to wonder if you are part of that 20 million, let me tell you a little more about these interesting little whatevers that live wherever they want. First, we'll see what house dust mites are, and where they live; next, how they affect our lives; and finally, we'll venture into the world of the toxically allergic, to see how they cope with the allergens that never die.

Let's begin by focusing in on our subject. This is a picture of the average house dust mite under a scanning electron microscope. Cute little bugger, isn't he? These science-fiction type horror insects were first discovered in 1964 by two Dutch scientists, Drs. Spiaksma and Voorhoorst. The April 1990 edition of *Prevention* magazine tells us that house dust mites are actually tiny members of the arachnid, or spider family, that are known by the scientific world as Dermatophagoides farinae. I was lucky enough to have five years of lessons in the Greek language, so I can tell you what this long, fancy scientific word means. Basically, "derma" means skin, and "phagoide" means, well, eating. If you put the two words together, you get a skin-eating insect. So, where do house dust mites live? According to Dr. Claude Frazier, not only do house dust mites live in dust, but also in particles of human and animal dander, kapok, and cotton lint commonly found in rugs, furniture, box springs, mattresses, draperies, and any other place where a large number of dead human skin cells can be found. Additionally, dust mites are also considered a form of harmless parasite, as they also enjoy eating dead skin cells right off of your body. But they are not just eating there. According to Biotech Allergy Systems, each mite lives between two and four months, and the average female lays between 20 and 50 eggs every three weeks. As a result, there are over 2 million mites in every bed, hundreds of millions in every home, billions in every school, and countless entities of them in dormitories.

We now know our enemy, and in more ways than one, he is ours. As I've already mentioned, house dust mites affect the lives of over 20 million Americans through allergies. The April 1990 edition of *Prevention* magazine included an interesting article about the author's son. This young man had very few symptoms of any type of allergy while living at home, but after moving into his college dormitory, he immediately devel-

To effectively get attention and introduce her topic, Maria begins with a story from a classic children's book.

Citing an expert helps establish both her credibility as a knowledgeable speaker and the importance of her topic.

The statistic from Dr. Kern establishes the significance of her topic to her audience. She follows this statistic with a direct reference to her audience.

Maria explicitly tells her audience the key ideas she will discuss. This clear overview will help her listeners remain focused on her message. Her use of a visual aid (an enlarged picture of a dust mite) helps her audience visualize exactly what she is talking about; the visual helps hold listeners' attention. Maria skillfully defines important terms by discussing the origin of the words. The definition of a dust mite as a skin-eating insect helps her make her first point, describing what dust mites are, before she goes on to her second point, identifying where dust mites live.

oped symptoms including a terrible cough, wheezing and sneezing attacks, and being constantly short of breath. After having a series of skin-prick allergy tests done, this young man found that he was seriously allergic to dust mites.

In fact, one out of every twelve people is allergic to dust mites, and those are just the reported cases. Let me ask you a few questions about your past medical history. Do you often experience watery eyes, runny nose, and sneezing or coughing attacks? Do these attacks often occur first thing in the morning? Do symptoms start or get worse while making your bed? Do you have frequent recurrent bouts of sinusitis? According to Dr. Claude Frazier in his book, *Insects and Allergy,* these are the symptoms of house dust mite allergies.

But in actuality, it's not the mite itself that causes the watery eyes and runny nose. Instead, a protein found in the waste products of house dust mites causes the allergic symptoms I described earlier. Therefore, just killing the mites does not solve the problem. Research from Biotech Allergy Systems has shown that mite waste products continue to cause allergic reaction in people long after the particular mite that produced them has died.

According to a brochure from the Acarosan company, cleanliness is not the answer, either. Spic 'n Span and elbow grease may be a psychological help, and will certainly please your mother, but in fact will do nothing to solve the problem at hand. You could clean until you wear away every piece of furniture in your house, and they would still exist. Dust mites are a part of every home, and unless you take specific measures against them, they're there for good.

Therefore, for many allergy sufferers, the answer lies in their dust, or rather, in its removal. According to Biotech Allergy Systems, each person spends one-third or more of each day in his or her bedroom, so obviously, the mightiest mite problem would exist in there. Consider this picture supplied by the Allergy Control Products, Inc., which illustrates the ideal mite-free bedroom. This may look a little drastic for most people, but for those who are toxically allergic, as well as for many severe asthmatics, researchers have found that these living conditions can make all the difference. First of all, the more your living quarters resemble a hospital room, the closer you are to living mite-free. Notice that the ideal mite-free bedroom contains no pictures, posters, carpeting, draperies, or upholstered furniture. If carpeting cannot be removed, using a dust mite allergy control product such as Acarosan can effectively deactivate the allergens in the rug. Secondly, by using a high-quality HEPA air cleaner you can purify the air you breathe and also decrease the number of airborne "Whos" looking for a Horton to land on. Thirdly, by using air conditioners in the summer and humidifiers in the winter, you can effectively prevent the increased growth of new mites in the home. Finally, to sleep snug as a bug in a rug, encase all pillows, box springs, and mattresses in specially designed allergy-proof cases. According to Dr. Kern, these cases trap the existing mites underneath a high-quality casing, and prevent future mites from congregating on top.

Now the dust mite allergy control products I just told you about can't be found in stores, but through two main mail order agencies that you can contact. You can call Biotech Allergy Systems at their number 1-800-422-DUST, and ask them for their free brochure. Or if you are interested in the Acarosan mite deactivator, you can call Fissions, Inc., at their number, 1-800-999-MITE. Catchy numbers, aren't they? All these products have been researched, tested, and proven very effective. Often, simply by using these products, future illness and allergy shots can be prevented.

Horton heard the Who and responded. Now that we know a little bit more about the inhabitants on the dust around us, we have yet another explanation as to our wheezing and sneezing. House dust mites are a part of our lives, and for better or for worse, we'll be co-existing for many years to come. So sleep tight, and, well, you know.

This brief internal summary helps clarify her overall organization of ideas and enhances audience comprehension of her message. She now moves on to her third major idea—-how dust mites affect our lives.

Using rhetorical questions is a technique that can help keep listeners interested and involved in your message.

Throughout the speech Maria has drawn facts and statistics from credible, unbiased sources to help clarify her ideas.

She now moves into her last point, how allergy sufferers cope with allergies caused by dust mites.

Showing a picture of what the ideal mite-free bedroom looks like lets her efficiently describe one way allergy sufferers could deal with dust mites.

She uses signposts to clarify her organization by explicitly enumerating her ideas.

She gives her audience sources of extra information.

Her conclusion makes a nice reference to the story she used to begin her speech; she also has an effective, well thought out way of ending her speech.

PACE YOUR INFORMATION FLOW

Organize your speech so that you present an even flow of information, rather than bunch up a number of significant details around one point. If you present too much new information too quickly, you may overwhelm your audience. Their ability to understand may falter.

You should be especially sensitive to the flow of information if your topic is new or unfamiliar to your listeners. Make sure that your audience has time to process any new information you present. Use supporting materials both to help clarify new information and to slow down the pace of your presentation.

Again, do not try to see how much detail and content you can cram into a speech. Your job is to present information so that the audience can grasp it, not to show off how much you know.

RELATE NEW INFORMATION TO OLD

Most of us learn by building on what we already know. We try to make sense out of our world by associating the old with the new. Your understanding of calculus is based on your knowledge of algebra. Even when you meet someone for the first time, you may be reminded of someone you already know.

When presenting new information to a group, help your audience associate your new idea with something that is familiar to them. Use an analogy or a word picture. Tell bewildered college freshmen how their new academic life will be similar to high school and how it will be different. Describe how your raising cattle over the summer was similar to taking care of any animal; they all need food, water, and shelter. By building on the familiar, you help your listeners understand how your new concept or information relates to their experience.

CREATE MEMORABLE VISUAL AIDS

Research about learning styles suggests that many of your listeners are more likely to remember your ideas if you can reinforce them with visual aids. As we noted in Chapter 14, pictures, graphs, posters, and computer-generated graphics can help you gain and maintain audience members' attention, as well as increase their retention. Today's audiences are exposed daily to a barrage of messages conveyed through highly visual electronic media—CD-ROM, the World Wide Web, and video. They have grown to depend on more than words alone to help them remember ideas and information. When you present summaries of data, a well-crafted line graph or colorful pie chart can quickly and memorably reinforce the words and numbers you cite.

Summary

To inform is to teach someone something you know. In this chapter, you have studied the goals, principles, and strategies that public speakers use to inform others.

There are four goals of informative speeches. First, your message should be clear. Use words and phrases that the listener can understand. Second, your message should be accurate. Don't rely solely on your memory of the facts. Consult dictionaries and other resource materials to ensure an accurate presentation. Third, your message should be vivid. By making your message lively, you help your listeners remember your key ideas. Fourth, your message should be interesting to your listeners. Consider your audience's interests, needs, likes, and dislikes.

In this chapter, we examined the five basic types of informative speeches. Speeches about *ideas* are often abstract and generally discuss principles, concepts, or theories. Speeches about *objects* discuss tangible things. Speeches about *procedures* explain a process or describe how something works. Speeches about *people* can be about either the famous or the little known. Speeches about *events* describe major occurrences or personal experiences.

We also presented several strategies for informing others. When you are seeking to explain new ideas, use clear definitions, examples, negative examples, or operational definitions. When your goal is to explain a complex process, give an overview of the process, use visual aids, or use word pictures to clarify the process. When your goal is to change a common misconception, first acknowledge the misconception, and then use evidence to support the more accurate idea or conclusion you want to teach your listeners.

The chapter concluded with a discussion of nine principles that will help you prepare and present a memorable informative speech.

CRITICAL THINKING QUESTIONS

1. You have been asked to speak to a kindergarten class about your chosen profession. Identify approaches to this task that would help make your message clear, interesting, and memorable to your audience.

2. Hillary Webster, M.D., will be addressing a medical convention of other physicians to discuss the recent weight loss technique she has successfully used with her patients. What advice would you give to help her present an effective talk?

3. Ken's boss has given him the task of presenting a report to a group of potential investors about his company's recent productivity trends. The presentation includes many statistics. What suggestions would you offer to help Ken give an interesting and effective informative presentation?

ETHICAL QUESTIONS

1. Before giving a speech to your class in which you share personal information about a friend of yours, should you ask permission from your friend?

2. You are a chemistry major, and you are considering whether you should give a speech to your public speaking class about how pipe bombs are made. Is this an appropriate topic for your audience?

3. In order to give your five-minute speech about nuclear energy, you are going to have to make the presentation very simple, even though the process you describe is complex. How can you avoid misrepresenting your topic? Should you let your audience know that you are oversimplifying the process?

SUGGESTED ACTIVITIES

1. From the following list of suggested topics for an informative speech, select five and develop a specific-purpose sentence for each. For one of those topics, identify two to four major ideas. Organize them topically, chronologically, or according to some other logical pattern of organization.

   How to get a better grade in public speaking
   The spread of terrorism in the Middle East
   How the U.S. Constitution was written
   A historical person I wish I could meet

What makes a good teacher
The best way to lose weight
How to buy a color TV
Surrogate parenthood
Safe-driving principles
How the stock market works
CB radios

2. Replace each of the following words with a livelier one:

cat	airplane	house
work	light	eat
walk		

3. Look up the origin of the following words in a comprehensive dictionary, such as the *Oxford English Dictionary* or the *Etymological Dictionary of Modern English*.

logic	pillow
communication	teacher
dance	

4. Write a word picture—a vivid, colorful description that appeals to the senses—for one of the following scenes:

Christmas morning when you were six
A visit to your grandparents' house
Your first day at college
Your most frightening experience
Your most memorable Fourth of July celebration

USING TECHNOLOGY AND MEDIA

1. Use the key word thesaurus of an electronic database such as Educational Resources Information Center (ERIC) or the Index to the Humanities to help you select and explore a topic for an informative speech.

2. If your word processing software includes an electronic dictionary, use it to define key terms and concepts in your informative speech. Use the thesaurus to help you make your language vivid.

3. You might find useful video or photo images to help you describe complex processes by consulting one of the many CD-ROM encyclopedias. Although many electronic encyclopedias use fewer words to describe a process than print encyclopedias, they often include effective moving images or graphics. Use these for inspiration to develop your own visual aids.

"The Propagandist."
Diego Rivera/Art Resource

Principles of Persuasive Speaking

. . . the power of speech,
to stir men's blood.
—William Shakespeare

● OBJECTIVES

After studying this chapter you
should be able to do the following:

1. *Define persuasion.*

2. *Describe cognitive dissonance.*

3. *Identify Maslow's five levels of needs,*
   which explain how behavior is motivated.

4. *Select and develop an appropriate topic*
   for a persuasive speech.

5. *Identify four principles of persuasive*
   speaking.

t happens over six hundred times each day. It appears as commercials on TV and radio; as advertisements in magazines, newspapers, and billboards; and as fund-raising letters from politicians and charities. It also occurs when you are asked to give money to a worthy cause or to donate blood. "It" is persuasion. Efforts to persuade you occur at an average rate of once every two and a half minutes each day.[1] Because persuasion is such an ever-present part of your life, it is important for you to understand how it works. What are the principles of an activity that can shape your attitudes and behavior? What do car salespersons, advertising copywriters, and politicians know about how to change your thinking and behavior, that you don't?

In this chapter, we are going to discuss how persuasion works. Such information can help you sharpen your own persuasive skills and can also help you become a more informed receiver of the persuasive messages that come your way. In this chapter, we will define persuasion and discuss the psychological principles underlying all or most efforts at persuading others. We will also discuss some tips for choosing a persuasive speech topic and developing arguments for your speeches. In Chapter 17, we will examine some of the specific strategies for crafting a persuasive speech.

What is persuasion?

persuasion
The process of changing or reinforcing attitudes, beliefs, values, or behavior.

Persuasion is the process of changing or reinforcing attitudes, beliefs, values, or behavior. Trying to get a person to sign up for a new class, to exercise more, to eat less, to stop smoking, to oppose abortions, and to favor legalizing marijuana are all examples of efforts to persuade. You are trying to get your listener to think, feel, or behave in a predetermined manner. Note that our definition of persuasion is not limited to changing ideas or behavior. You can also reinforce or strengthen existing attitudes or behaviors persuasively. A minister who encourages his or her congregation to continue to contribute to the church knows that they have given before; the minister wants them to keep on giving. He wants to reinforce their existing behavior.

PERSUASIVE AND INFORMATIVE SPEAKING

In Chapter 15, we discussed several strategies for informative speaking—the oral presentation of new information to listeners so that they will understand and remember what is communicated. The purposes of informing and persuading are interrelated. Why inform an audience? Why give new information to others? We often provide information to give listeners new insights that may affect their attitudes and behavior. Information alone has the potential to convince others, but if information is coupled with strategies to persuade, the chances of success increase. Persuasive speakers try to influence the listener's points of view or behavior. If you want your listeners to respond to your persuasive appeal, you will need to think carefully about the way you structure your message to achieve your specific purpose.

Because of the interrelationship between persuasive speaking and informative speaking, you will build on the principles of informative speaking that you studied in Chapter 15. Your speech will still need to be well organized, with interesting supporting material, well-chosen language, smooth transitions, and fluent delivery. But now your speech purpose will target change or reinforcement of your audience's attitudes, beliefs, values, or behavior. As a persuasive speaker, you will need to develop arguments and evidence to support your speech's objective.

In this context, the word *argument* does not mean "quarrel" or "disagreement." Rather, it means "reason for believing something," and *evidence* is the proof that supports the reason. Arguments and evidence always go together, just as they do in a court of law.

Your credibility as a speaker is even more important when your objective is to persuade than when you are interested only in giving information. Your audience is more likely to be persuaded if they believe, trust, and like you. To be fully persuasive, you will also need to appeal to your listeners' emotions as you try to change or reinforce their ideas and behavior. In short, the art of persuading others involves appeals to reason and emotion.

In persuasive speeches, the speaker asks the audience to make an explicit choice, rather than just informing them of the options. As a persuasive speaker, you will do more than teach; you will ask the listeners to respond to the information you share. Audience analysis is crucial to achieving your goal. To advocate a particular view or position successfully, you must understand your listeners' attitudes, beliefs, values, and behavior.

Goals of persuasive speaking

Look at our definition of *persuasion* once again: the process of changing or reinforcing attitudes, beliefs, values, or behavior. We can classify the different types of persuasive speeches by examining the goals of persuasion. As a speaker, you could attempt to change *attitudes* of your listeners by discussing what they like and dislike, such as their feelings about a proposed shopping mall. You may also want to change or reinforce what your audience *believes* to be true or false, factual or nonfactual. You may want to change their belief that the mall will lower unemployment in their community. If you change or reinforce your listeners' *values*, you will speak about enduring principles of goodness or what is right and what is wrong. In the case of the proposed mall, you may want your audience to re-examine the idea that development always is good for the economy. Finally, changing or reinforcing *behavior* may be your objective. For salespersons, politicians, and safety officers, changing or reinforcing what people do is often a goal. Or, of course, your speech could have a combination of these goals. Knowing your speech goal can help you make appropriate choices in achieving your persuasive objective. Let's examine each of these persuasive speech goals more closely.

● INFLUENCING ATTITUDES

attitude
A learned predisposition to respond favorably or unfavorably toward something; like or dislike.

An **attitude** is a learned predisposition to respond favorably or unfavorably toward something. What does this mean? It refers to the way you have learned to respond to your world, based on your past associations and experiences. For example, what is your attitude toward snakes? What would happen if a friend of yours sneaked up behind you right now while you were reading this book and without warning thrust a snake in your face? Given the fear most people have of the slithering reptiles, you would probably recoil in horror. In this case, you have a learned predisposition to dislike snakes. As a persuasive speaker, you will need to know your listeners' attitudes toward your speech topic so that you can anticipate their responses and develop strategies to change or reinforce those attitudes.

Attitudes reflect or express your likes and dislikes. What's your attitude toward chocolate cake? If you like it, you have a positive attitude toward it. If you hate it and it makes you break out in a rash, you have a negative attitude toward it. Or perhaps you have no strong feelings about chocolate cake; you can take it or leave it. You are neutral toward it; your attitude is one of indifference.

Your attitudes toward persons, places, and things, then, can be classified as positive, negative, or indifferent. If you want to persuade a listener to buy a set of encyclopedias, you would be wise to know what his or her existing attitudes are about encyclopedias, books, salespersons, and education. The more you know about your listeners' attitudes and how they developed those attitudes, the better able you will be to adopt your message to them.

Suppose you did a prespeech analysis of your audience and discovered that most of your listeners are opposed to increasing the state sales tax to enhance education. If you wanted to change this attitude, your speech outline might look like this:

SPECIFIC PURPOSE: At the end of my speech, the audience should be able to respond favorably to current legislation that would increase the state sales tax to support education.

CENTRAL IDEA SENTENCE: Increasing the state sales tax would result in dramatic improvement in our state's ability to provide quality education for all citizens.

I. An increase in the state sales tax is needed.

A. Our tax rate is among the lowest in the country.

B. Our state does not have the resources to adequately meet our educational needs.

II. An increase in the state sales tax would enhance education in our state.

A. Elementary education would be enhanced.

B. Secondary education would be enhanced.

C. Higher education would be enhanced.

A speech may also be designed to reinforce or strengthen attitudes currently held by the audience. Speaking to a local service organization such as the Kiwanis or Rotary Club about the importance of volunteering would reinforce listeners' attitudes and encourage them to continue their community service activities.

INFLUENCING BELIEFS

A **belief** is the way in which a person structures reality to accept something as either true or false. If you believe in something, you are convinced it exists. You have structured your sense of what is real and what is unreal to account for the existence of whatever you believe in. If you believe in God, you have structured your sense of what is real and unreal to recognize the existence of God. Undoubtedly, you believe that the sun will rise again in the morning and set in the evening. Based on your experience, this is what you believe to be true. You believe something to be true or false depending on your past experience or the evidence you have available. As a public speaker, it is very important to understand the key beliefs of your audience, especially if your goal is to change or reinforce listener beliefs.

Since beliefs are founded on people's conceptions of what is true or false, speeches that attempt to change or reinforce beliefs often focus on issues of fact. Is nuclear power safe? Does fluoridated water help prevent tooth decay? These issues hinge on whether or not something is true or false, effective or not effective. Here's a sample outline of a speech on the topic "Does taking a course in public speaking enhance your chances of getting a good job?"

belief
The way a person structures reality to accept something as either true or false.

SPECIFIC PURPOSE:	At the end of my speech, the audience will agree that successfully completing a course in public speaking can enhance a person's chances of getting a good job.
CENTRAL IDEA SENTENCE:	A public speaking course builds skills in research, organizing ideas, and delivering messages effectively, all of which are valued by employers.

I. The skills taught in a public speaking course are valued in the workplace.

A. Several surveys of directors of personnel indicate that public speaking skills are valuable.

B. Several surveys of chief executive officers of Fortune 500 companies indicate that public speaking skills are valuable.

II. The skills taught in a public speaking course have direct application to many careers.

A. Research skills are important for careers in which gathering and using information is critical.

B. Organizational skills are important for careers that require managing large amounts of information.

C. Delivery skills are important to any career in which an individual presents ideas to others.

● INFLUENCING VALUES

value
An enduring concept of good and bad, right and wrong.

A **value** is a concept of intrinsic good and bad, right and wrong. Helping those in need, for example, is intrinsically good—that is, it is good in and of itself, without reference to anything else. What do you value? For most Americans, it would be such things as honesty, trustworthiness, freedom, loyalty, marriage, family, and money. If you value something, you classify it as good or desirable. If you do not value something, you think of it as bad or wrong. Values form the basis of your life goals and the motivating force behind your behavior. Understanding what your listeners value can help you refine your analysis of them and adopt the content of your speech to those values.

Why is it useful to make distinctions among attitudes, beliefs, and values? Since the essence of persuasion is to change or reinforce these three qualities, it is very useful to know exactly which one you are targeting. Of the three qualities, audience values are the most stable. Most of us acquired our values when we were very young and have held on to them into adulthood. Our values, therefore, are generally deeply ingrained. It is not impossible to change the values of your listeners, but it is much more difficult than trying to change a belief or an attitude. Political and religious points of view, which are usually based on long-held values, are especially difficult to modify.

A belief is more susceptible to change than a value, but it is still difficult to alter. Beliefs are changed by evidence. You might have a difficult time, for example, trying to change someone's belief that the world is flat; you would need to show that existing evidence supports a different conclusion. Usually it takes a great deal of evidence to change a belief and alter the way your audience structures reality.

Attitudes (likes and dislikes) are much easier to change than either beliefs or values. Today we may approve of the president of the United States; tomorrow we may disapprove because of a recent action he has taken. We may still *believe* that the country is financially stable, and we may still value a democratic form of government, but our *attitude* toward the President has changed because of his recent policy decision.

As Figure 16.1 shows, values are the most deeply ingrained; they change least frequently. Beliefs change, but not as much as attitudes. Trying to change an audience's attitudes is easier than attempting to change their values. We suggest that you think carefully about your purpose in making a persuasive speech. Know with certainty whether your objective is to change or reinforce an attitude, a belief, or a value. Then decide what you have to do to achieve your objective.

Speeches that focus on changing or reinforcing audience values emphasize how and why something is better than something else. Persuasive speeches that discuss abortion rights, animal rights, euthanasia, and Republican party policies versus Democratic party policies are examples of speech topics that typically touch on listener's values. In the following outline for a speech to a group of middle-aged adults, observe how the speaker identifies reasons grown children should take an active role in ensuring that the needs of their elderly parents are met.

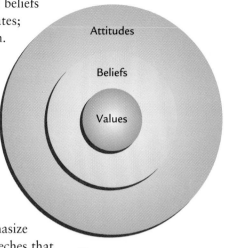

FIGURE 16.1
Attitudes—our likes and dislikes— are more likely to change than are our beliefs or values. Our sense of what is right and wrong—our values—are least likely to change over time.

SPECIFIC PURPOSE:
> At the end of my speech, the audience will be able to state why children should assume responsibility for caring for their elderly parents.

CENTRAL IDEA SENTENCE:
> Mature children of aging parents have a moral, civic, and ethical responsibility to care for their elderly parents who are unable to care for themselves.

> I. Children have a moral responsibility to care for their elderly parents.
>
> II. Children have a civic responsibility to care for their elderly parents.
>
> III. Children have an ethical responsibility to care for their elderly parents.

INFLUENCING BEHAVIOR

Although the objective of many speeches you give will be simply to change or reinforce listeners' attitudes, beliefs, or values, sometimes you will also want to translate how your listeners think or feel about an issue into some sort of action. You may want your speech to motivate people to sign a petition, vote a certain way, or buy your product. Or you may want someone to continue to do what he or she is already doing—perhaps working hard on a project or contributing to your organization.

Note how the following example of a speech delivered to parents of elementary school students identifies positive benefits of becoming a school volunteer. The speech reinforces the value listeners place on a quality education, but it also tries to motivate audience members to take action.

SPECIFIC PURPOSE: At the end of my speech, audience members will commit to spending at least one hour per week as school volunteers.

CENTRAL IDEA SENTENCE: Becoming a regular school volunteer will result in greater satisfaction with the quality of education children receive, lower taxes, improved academic success, and improved classroom discipline.

   I. Parents who volunteer to work in their children's school report being more satisfied with the quality of education that their children receive.

   II. Becoming a school volunteer will help keep taxes lower, because volunteers can help with tasks that paid staff would otherwise have to perform.

   III. Schools with an active cadre of volunteers report improved academic success for children enrolled in the school.

   IV. Schools with an active volunteer program report less violence and better classroom discipline than schools without an active volunteer program.

Motivating listeners

It's late at night, and you're watching your favorite talk show before going to bed. The program is interrupted by a commercial extolling the virtues of ice cream. Suddenly, you remember that you have the flavor advertised, royal rocky road. You apparently hadn't realized how hungry you were for ice cream until the ad reminded you of the lip-smacking goodness of the cool, creamy, smooth treat. Before you know it, you are at the freezer, doling out a couple of scoops of ice cream.

If the sponsor of that commercial knew how effective it had been, he or she would be overjoyed. The ad was persuasive and changed your behavior. How does persuasion work? What principles explain why you were motivated to dig through the freezer at twelve o'clock at night for a carton of ice cream? Let's look at several approaches that explain why we respond to efforts at persuasion.

Dissonance theory is based on the principle that people strive to act in a way that is consistent with their attitudes, beliefs, and values.[2] According to the theory, whenever you are presented with information that is inconsistent with your current attitudes, beliefs, values, or behavior, you experience a kind of discomfort called **cognitive dissonance.** If you smoke, for example, but learn that smoking greatly increases your chances of lung cancer, you will experience cognitive dissonance. The word *cognitive* has to do with our thoughts. *Dissonance* means "lack of harmony or agreement." When you think of a dissonant chord in music, you probably think of a series of sounds that are unpleasant or not in tune with the melody or other chords. Cognitive dissonance, then, means that you are experiencing a way of thinking that is inconsistent and uncomfortable. Your discomfort with your incompatible thoughts often prompts you to change your attitudes, beliefs, values, or behavior so that you can restore your sense of balance.

The need to restore balance is common. We have all experienced it at one time or another. If you are walking down a flight of stairs too fast and start to lose your balance, you will probably grab for the handrail so you won't fall. This is similar to the process that, according to dissonance theory, occurs psychologically when information you hear causes you discomfort.

Creating dissonance in a persuasive speech can be an effective way to change attitudes and behavior. The first tactic in such a speech is to identify an existing problem or need. For example, a speaker seeking to ban aerosol sprays could begin her speech by focusing on a need we all generally share, such as the need for a well-preserved environment. The speaker could then point out that the continued use of aerosol sprays depletes the ozone layer, which protects us from the sun's harmful rays. By doing so, the speaker is deliberately creating dissonance. She knows that people in her audience appreciate the convenience of aerosol sprays, so their attitudes about protecting the environment *conflict with* their feelings about getting housework done easily or styling their hair effectively. So her next move would aim at restoring the audience's sense of balance. She could

■
cognitive dissonance
The sense of disorganization that prompts a person to change when new information conflicts with previously organized thought patterns.

The message on this billboard is designed to create dissonance for women living with violent men, urging them to take action before the violence escalates out of control. Such messages counteract our human tendency to avoid confronting our personal and societal problems head on. [Photo: Bob Daemmrich/ Stock Boston]

claim that her solution—using nonaerosol sprays—can resolve the conflict. Using this strategy, the speaker may motivate the audience to change their behavior. The change itself is her objective.

Political candidates use a similar strategy. A mayoral candidate usually tries first to make his or her audience aware of problems in the community, then blames the current mayor for most of the problems. Once dissonance has been created, the candidate then suggests that these problems would be solved, or at least managed better, if he or she were to be elected as the city's next mayor. Using the principles of dissonance theory, the mayoral candidate first upsets the audience, then restores their balance and feeling of comfort by providing a solution to the city's problem: his or her selection as mayor.

Vonda Ramey, calling for more attention to children who cannot read, created dissonance in the minds of her listeners when she documented the widespread problem of illiteracy in her prize-winning oration "Can You Read This?"

> Approximately two-thirds of U.S. colleges and universities have to provide remedial reading and writing courses for students. The University of California at Berkeley, which gets the top one-eighth of all high school students, has to put almost half of the freshmen in remedial composition classes.

> Instructional materials used by the armed forces look like comic books, with pictures and simple language to help new recruits who have a problem reading. One manual has five pages of just pictures to show a soldier how to open the hood of a truck.[3]

Listeners are likely to experience some dissonance upon learning how many people cannot read.

 ● HOW LISTENERS COPE WITH DISSONANCE   Effective persuasion requires more than simply creating dissonance and then suggesting a solution to the problem. When your listeners are confronted with dissonant information, there are a number of options available to them besides following your suggestions.[4] You need to be aware of other ways your audience may react before you can reduce their cognitive dissonance.

■ *Listeners discredit the source.*   Instead of believing everything you say, your listeners could choose to discredit you. Suppose you drive a German-made BMW and you hear a speaker whose father owns a Chevrolet dealership advocate that all Americans should drive cars made in America. You could agree with him, or you could decide that the speaker is biased because of his father's occupation. Instead of selling your BMW and buying an American-made car, you could simply suspect the speaker's credibility and ignore the suggestion to buy American automobiles. When you seek to be a persuasive speaker, you need to ensure that your audience will perceive you as competent and trustworthy so that they will accept your message.

■ *Listeners reinterpret the message.*   A second way in which your listeners may overcome cognitive dissonance and restore balance is to hear what they want to hear. They may choose to focus on the parts of your message that are consistent with what they already believe and ignore the unfamiliar or controversial parts. Your job as an effective public speaker is to make your message as clear as possible so that your audience will not reinterpret your message. If you tell a customer looking at a new kind of computer that it takes ten steps to get into the word-processing program, but that the program is easy to use, the customer might focus on those first ten things and decide the computer is hard to use. Choose your words carefully, and use simple, vivid examples to keep listeners focused on what's most important.

■ *Listeners seek new information.* Another way that listeners cope with cognitive dissonance when confronted with a distressing argument is to seek more information on the subject. Your audience members may look for additional information to negate your position and to refute your well-created arguments. As the owner of a minivan, you would experience dissonance if you hear a speaker describe the recent rash of safety problems with minivans. You might turn to your friend and whisper, "Is this true? Are minivans really dangerous? I've always heard they were safe." You would request new information to validate your ownership of a minivan. Similarly, when listeners hear a political speech that tries to change their view, they may seek new information to help justify their own stand on the issues.

■ *Listeners stop listening.* Some messages are so much at odds with listeners' attitudes, beliefs, and values that the audience may decide to stop listening. Most of us do not seek opportunities to hear or read messages that oppose our opinions. It is unlikely that a staunch Democrat would attend a fundraiser for the state Republican party. The principle of selective exposure suggests that we tend to pay attention to messages that are consistent with our points of view and to avoid those that are not. When we do find ourselves trapped in a situation in which we are forced to hear a message that doesn't support our beliefs, we tend to tune the speaker out. We stop listening to avoid the dissonance. Being aware of the existing thoughts and feelings of the audience can help ensure that they won't tune you out.

■ *Listeners do change their attitudes, beliefs, values, or behavior.* A fifth way an audience may respond to dissonant information is to do as the speaker wishes them to. As we have noted, if listeners change their attitudes, they can reduce the dissonance that they experience. You listen to a life insurance salesperson tell you that when you die, your family will have no financial support. This creates dissonance; you think of your family as happy and secure. So you decide to take out a $100,000 policy to protect your family. This action restores your sense of balance. The salesperson has persuaded you successfully. The goals of advertising copywriters, salespeople, and political candidates are similar: They want you to experience dissonance so that you will change your attitudes, beliefs, values, or behavior.

USING NEEDS TO MOTIVATE LISTENERS

Need is one of the best motivators. The person who is looking at a new car because he or she needs one right now is more likely to buy one than the person who is just thinking about how nice it would be to drive the latest model. The more you understand what your listeners need, the greater the chances are that you can gain and hold their attention and ultimately get them to do what you want. The classic theory that outlines our basic needs was developed by Abraham Maslow.[5] Maslow suggests that there is a hierarchy of needs that motivates the behavior of all of us. Basic needs (such as food, water, and air) have to be satisfied before we can be motivated to respond to higher-level needs. Figure 16.2 illustrates Maslow's five levels of needs, with the most basic at the bottom. When attempting to persuade an audience, a public speaker attempts to stimulate these needs in order to change or reinforce attitudes, beliefs, values, or behavior. Let's examine these needs in some detail.

● PHYSIOLOGICAL NEEDS   The most basic needs for all humans are physiological: air, water, and food. According to Maslow's theory, unless those needs are met, it will be difficult to motivate a listener to satisfy other needs. If your listeners are hot, tired, and thirsty, it will be more difficult to persuade them to vote for your candidate, buy your insurance policy, or sign your petition in support of local pet leash laws. As a public speaker, you should be sensitive to the basic physiological needs of your audience so that your appeals to higher-level needs will be heard.

● SAFETY NEEDS   Once basic physiological needs are met, your listeners are concerned about their safety. We have a need to feel safe, secure, and protected, and we need to be able to predict that the need for safety of ourselves and our loved ones will be met. The classic sales presentation from insurance salespersons includes appeals to our need for safety and security. Many insurance sales efforts include photos of wrecked cars, anecdotes of people who were in ill health and could not

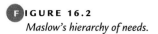

FIGURE 16.2
Maslow's hierarchy of needs.

 is labeled top to bottom: Self-actualization needs, Self-esteem needs, Social needs, Safety needs, Physiological needs.

pay their bills, or tales of the head of a household who passed away, leaving the basic needs of his or her family unmet. Appeals to use seat belts, stop smoking, start exercising, and use condoms all play to our need for safety and security.

In a speech titled "Emissions Tampering: Get the Lead Out," John appealed to his listeners' need for safety and security when he began his speech with these observations:

> A major American producer is currently dumping over 8,000 tons of lead into our air each year, which in turn adversely affects human health. The producers of this waste are tampering with pollution control devices in order to cut costs. This tampering escalates the amount of noxious gases you and I inhale by 300 to 800%. That producer is the American motorist.[6]

● SOCIAL NEEDS   We all need to feel loved and valued. We need contact and reassurance from others that they care about us. According to Maslow, these social needs translate into our need for a sense of belonging to a group (fraternity, religious organization, friends). Powerful persuasive appeals are based on our need for social contact. We are encouraged to buy a product or support a particular issue because others are buying the product or supporting the issue. The message is, to be liked and respected by others, you must buy the same things they do or support the same position they support.

● SELF-ESTEEM NEEDS   The need for self-esteem reflects our desire to think well of ourselves. Jesse Jackson is known for appealing often to the self-worth of his listeners by inviting them to chant, "I am somebody." This is a direct appeal to his listeners' need for self-esteem. Advertisers also appeal to our need for self-esteem when they encourage us to believe that we can be noticed by others or stand out in the crowd if we purchase their product. Commercials promoting luxury cars usually invite you to picture yourself in the driver's seat with a beautiful person next to you while you receive looks of envy from those you pass on the road. The powerful need for self-esteem fuels many persuasive messages.

● SELF-ACTUALIZATION NEEDS   At the top of Maslow's hierarchy is the need for **self-actualization.** This is the need to achieve our highest potential. The U.S. Army uses the slogan "Be all that you can be" to tap into the need for self-actualization. Calls to be the best and the brightest are appeals to self-actualization. According to the assumption that our needs are organized into a hierarchy, the other four need levels must be satisfied before we can be motivated to achieve the ultimate in personal satisfaction.

self-actualization
The need to achieve our highest potential; to be "all that we can be."

● USING POSITIVE MOTIVATION

"A chicken in every pot" was the positive motivational appeal of a depression-era politician claiming that a vote for him would result in a return to prosperity. Positive motivational appeals are statements made by a speaker suggesting that good things will happen if the speaker's advice is heeded. A key to using positive motivational appeals effectively is to know what your listeners value. Knowing what audience members view as desirable, good, and virtuous can help you select the benefits of your persuasive proposal that best appeal to them.

SPEAKERS AT WORK

As the Southeast Region Coordinator for American Forests, a national non-profit organization dedicated to protecting and planting trees, Nancy S. Masterson is often invited to speak at civic and professional gatherings. Here she describes how one audience member gently reminded her that dramatic delivery is only one component of a successful persuasive speech.

A couple of years after I joined American Forests, I became responsible for educating the public about a research project on urban tree planting for energy conservation. My job was not just to inform; we needed funds to purchase trees for this project. Accordingly, I sought expert advice about how to motivate people, and organized a standard speech using a classical persuasive sequence: (1) Get the audience's attention, (2) define and examine the problem, (3) propose a solution, (4) get the audience to visualize the outcome, (5) call for action.

My first opportunity to try out this speech was at a conference center in a city I didn't know very well, addressing a group I had never heard of. When I arrived, however, I discovered a stunning building in a natural setting and was warmly greeted at the door. It only got better from there. Attendance was double what I'd expected, we started on time, and I received an accurate, glowing introduction.

During my speech, everything continued to click. The audience hung on my every word. I found myself relaxing, feeling in control, and playing with my timing. First I'd hold them with a whisper, then startle them with a loud flourish. When I painted for them a vision of a cooler, greener world of beautiful tree-lined cities, they nodded and smiled in rapt attention. When I ended, they broke into a hearty round of applause.

As I opened the floor for questions, the magic seemed to continue when I called on a man in the back and heard his first words: "This was the best talk we have had since I started coming to this club," he said. But then he added, "Except, you did one thing really *wrong.*"

He paused while I withered at the lectern. Had I totally misread this group's response? What had I said to offend them? Then, to my relief, he explained with a smile, "You never told us how we can help."

He was right. I had gotten so caught up in the effect of my words that I had totally forgotten to give the last and most critical part of my talk: a specific call to action. American Forests relies on me to recruit new members and raise funds for planting trees and protecting forests, not to cast spells over my audience. Ever since this first experience with dramatic persuasion, I never forget to ask my audience to donate money for trees we must plant today in order to create the forests I urge them to envision for tomorrow.

What do most people value? A comfortable, prosperous life; stimulating, exciting activity; a sense of accomplishment; world, community, and personal peace; and happiness are some of the many things people value.

How can you use these values in a persuasive speech? When identifying reasons for your audience to think, feel, or behave as you want them to, review the values just listed to determine what benefits would accrue to your listeners. If, for example, you advocate that your listeners enroll in a sign language course, what are the benefits to the audience? You could stress the sense of accomplishment, contribution to society, or increased opportunities for friendship that would develop if they learned this new skill. A speech advocating that recording companies print the lyrics of all songs on the label of the recording could appeal to family values.

Most salespersons know that it is not enough just to identify, in general terms, the features of their product. They must translate those features into an obvious benefit that enhances the customer's quality of life. It is not enough for the real estate salesperson to say, "This floor is the new no-wax vinyl." It is more effective to add, "And this means that you will never have to get down on your hands and knees to scrub another floor." The car salesperson who recommends purchasing the extra maintenance agreement and says, "By purchasing this extra maintenance coverage, you will never have to worry about repair bills for as long as you own this car," also makes a positive feature a readily identifiable benefit for the listener. When using positive motivational appeals, be sure your listeners know how the benefits of your proposal can improve their quality of life or the lives of their loved ones.

● USING NEGATIVE MOTIVATION

"If you don't stop what you're doing, I'm going to tell Mom!" Whether that sibling realized it or not, he was using a persuasive technique called *fear appeal*. One of the oldest methods of trying to change someone's attitude or behavior, the use of a threat is also one of the most effective. In essence, the appeal to fear takes the form of an "if-then" statement. If you don't do X, awful things will happen to you. A persuader builds an argument on the assertion that a need will not be met unless the desired behavior or attitude change occurs. The principal reason that appeals to fear continue to be made in persuasive messages is that they work. A variety of research studies support the following principles for using fear appeals.[7]

- A strong threat to a loved one tends to be more successful than a fear appeal directed at the audience members themselves. A speaker using this principle might say, "Unless you are able to get your children to wear seat belts, they could easily be injured or killed in an auto accident."

- The more competent, trustworthy, or respected the speaker, the greater the likelihood that an appeal to fear will be successful. A speaker with less credibility will be more successful with moderate threats. The surgeon general of the United States will be more successful in convincing people to use condoms to lessen the risk of AIDS than you will.

- Fear appeals are more successful if you can convince your listeners that the threat is real and will probably occur unless they take the action you are advocating. For example, you could dramatically announce, "Last year, thousands of smokers developed lung cancer and eventually died. Unless you stop smoking, there is a high probability that you could develop lung cancer, too."

The effectiveness of fear appeals is based on the theories of cognitive dissonance and Maslow's hierarchy of needs. The fear aroused creates dissonance, which can be reduced by following the recommendation of the persuader. Appeals to fear are also based on targeting an unmet need. Fear appeals depend on a convincing insistence that a need will go unmet unless a particular action or attitude change occurs.

USING FEAR APPEALS TO PERSUADE

1. Fear appeals involving loved ones are often more effective than appeals directed to audience members themselves.

2. The greater your credibility, the more likely your fear appeal will be effective.

3. You must convince your audience that the threat is real and could actually happen.

Cognitive dissonance, needs, and appeals to the emotions, both positive and negative, can all persuade listeners to change their attitudes, beliefs, values, and behavior. Realize, however, that persuasion is not as simple as these approaches may lead you to believe. There is no precise formula for motivating and convincing an audience. Attitude change occurs differently in each individual; there are no magic words, phrases, or appeals. Persuasion is an art that draws on science. Cultivating a sensitivity to listeners' emotions and needs, and using public speaking strategies you have learned, will help you make your persuasive messages effective.

Developing your persuasive speech

Now that you understand what persuasion is and how it works, let's turn our attention to the task of preparing a persuasive speech. After you analyze your audience, one of your first challenges when asked to present a persuasive speech is to choose an appropriate topic.

CHOOSING A PERSUASIVE SPEECH TOPIC

The best persuasive speech topic is one about which you feel strongly. What attitudes, beliefs, values, and behaviors do you hold dear? If your listeners sense that you are not committed or excited about your topic, they won't be, either. Many of the mechanics of delivery and presentation can be defined more readily if you are speaking about a topic with passion and conviction. So the first step in choosing a persuasive topic is to look to your own attitudes, beliefs, and values. Use the brainstorming method that we have discussed in other chapters in your effort to identify your interests and convictions. We offer some thought-starting suggestions in Appendix B.

Controversial issues make excellent sources for persuasive topics. A controversial issue is a question about which people disagree. Here are several: Should the university increase tuition so that faculty members can have a salary increase? Should public schools distribute condoms to students? Should the government provide health insurance to all citizens? You need to be audience-centered—know the local, state, national, or international issues that interest your listeners.

We recommend that you, as a student of public speaking, pay attention to the media to help keep you current on the important issues of the day. If you're not already doing so, you should read at least one newspaper every day. Take a look at a national news magazine such as *Time, Newsweek,* or *U.S. News and World Report* to keep in touch with issues and topics of interest. The editorial page of the newspaper is also a good place to see what issues are of interest to people. Another interesting source of controversial issues is talk radio programs. Both national and local radio call-in programs may give you some ideas that are appropriate for a persuasive speech. Even if you already have a clear idea of your speech topic, keeping up with the media can give you additional ideas to help narrow your topic or find interesting and appropriate supporting material.

● DEVELOPING YOUR PURPOSE

Once you have decided on a broad topic for your persuasive speech, your next step is to focus on a specific idea within that topic. In Chapter 6, we discussed techniques for narrowing your topic to fit your time limit. Those same strategies will be helpful as you try to give your persuasive speech focus.

Most persuasive speakers find it useful to formulate a **proposition,** or the basic statement with which you want your audience to agree. For persuasive speeches, a proposition statement is a component of the specific-purpose statement we discussed in earlier chapters. Here are examples of propositions:

proposition
a statement which summarizes the ideas with which you want your audience to agree.

All students should be required to take a foreign language.

Our jury system is unfair.

Organic gardening is better for the environment than gardening with chemicals.

There are three categories of propositions: fact, value, and policy. Determining which category your persuasive proposition fits into can help clarify your objective and help you select specific persuasive strategies. Let's examine each of these types of propositions in more detail.

● PROPOSITION OF FACT   A **proposition of fact** focuses on whether
something is true or false, on whether it did or did not happen. Bill Clinton was elected president by a majority of Americans in 1992. The Kansas City Royals won the 1983 World Series. Texas is bigger than Poland. Each of these statements is a proposition of fact that can be verified simply by looking the answer up in the encyclopedia. Other propositions of fact will take more time and skill—perhaps an entire persuasive speech to prove. Here are examples of more controversial propositions of fact:

proposition of fact
Focuses on whether something is true or false; on whether it did or did not happen.

Talk radio is directly responsible for violence against U.S. government agencies.

When women joined the military the quality of the military improved.

Children who were abused by their parents are more likely to abuse their own children.

Past tax increases have not reduced the federal deficit.

The gasoline engine is the prime culprit in the deterioration of the ozone layer.

There is no general deterioration of our environment.

In order to prove each of these propositions, a speaker would need to provide specific supporting evidence. To persuade listeners to agree with a proposition of fact, the speaker must focus on changing or reinforcing their beliefs. A belief, as you recall, is the way in which a person structures reality to accept something as either true of false. Most persuasive speeches that focus on a proposition of fact begin by identifying one or more reasons that the proposition is true.

Tabitha's persuasive speech on the topic of fluorocarbons was based on a proposition of fact:

TOPIC:	Fluorocarbons from air conditioning systems
GENERAL PURPOSE:	To persuade
PROPOSITION:	Fluorocarbons deplete the earth's ozone layer.
SPECIFIC PURPOSE:	At the end of my speech, audience members should be able to state that fluorocarbons deplete the ozone layer and are therefore harmful to the environment.
MAJOR IDEAS:	I. Fluorocarbons are prevalent in old air conditioning systems.
	II. Fluorocarbons are a prime cause of ozone depletion.
	A. Scientists have evidence that fluorocarbons deplete the ozone layer.
	B. Congress has passed legislation limiting the use of fluorocarbons.

proposition of value
Calls for the listener to make a judgment about the worth or importance of something.

● PROPOSITION OF VALUE   A **proposition of value** is a statement that calls for the listener to make a judgment about the worth or importance of something. Values, as you recall, are enduring concepts of good and bad, right and wrong. Value propositions are based on something being either good or bad. Note these examples:

It is wrong to turn away immigrants who want to come to the United States.

Democracy is a better form of government than Communism.

Speech communication is a better major than home economics.

A private school education is more valuable than a public school education.

Capital punishment is good for the country.

It is better for citizens to carry concealed weapons than to let criminals rule society.

Each of these propositions either implies or directly states that something is better than something else. Value propositions often directly compare two things and suggest that one of the options is better than the other.

Manny's speech was designed to convince his audience that contemporary rock music is better than classical music.

TOPIC:	Rock music
GENERAL PURPOSE:	To persuade
PROPOSITION:	Rock music is better than classical music for three reasons.
SPECIFIC PURPOSE:	After listening to my speech, the audience should listen to rock music more often than they listen to classical music.
MAJOR IDEAS:	I. More people listen to rock music than to classical music.
	II. Rock music can increase worker productivity, whereas classical music is more likely to put people to sleep.
	III. Rock music is more sophisticated than classical music.

● PROPOSITION OF POLICY The third type of proposition, a **proposition of policy,** advocates a specific action—changing a policy, procedure, or behavior. Note how all of the following propositions of policy include the word "should"; this is a tip-off that the speaker is advocating a change in policy or procedure.

> The Gifted and Talented Program in our school district should have a full-time coordinator.
>
> Our community should set aside one day each month as "Community Cleanup Day."
>
> Senior citizens should pay for more of their medical costs.
>
> Our state should seek more block grants from the federal government.

In a speech based on a proposition of policy, Paul decided to convince his audience that academic tenure for college professors should be abolished. He organized his speech topically, identifying reasons academic tenure is no longer a sound policy for most colleges and universities. To support his proposition of policy, he used several propositions of fact. Note, too, that Paul's specific purpose involved specific action on the part of his audience.

TOPIC:	Academic tenure
GENERAL PURPOSE:	To persuade
PROPOSITION:	Our college, along with other colleges and universities, should abolish academic tenure.

proposition of policy
Advocates a specific action—a changing a policy, procedure, or behavior.

SPECIFIC PURPOSE:	After listening to my speech, audience members should sign a petition calling for the abolition of academic tenure.
MAJOR IDEAS:	I. Academic tenure is outdated.
	II. Academic tenure is abused.
	III. Academic tenure contributes to ineffective education.

Here's another example of a persuasive speech based on a proposition of policy. Again, note how the major ideas are propositions of fact used to support the proposition of policy.

TOPIC:	Computer education
GENERAL PURPOSE:	To persuade
PROPOSITION:	Every person in our society should know how to use a personal computer.
SPECIFIC PURPOSE:	After listening to my speech, all audience members who have not had a computer course should sign up for one.
MAJOR IDEAS:	I. Most people who own a personal computer do not know how to use most of the features.
	II. Computer skills will help you with your academic studies.
	III. Computer skills will help you get a good job, regardless of your major or chosen profession.

RECAP

PERSUASIVE PROPOSITIONS

Type	Definition	Examples
Proposition of fact	A statement that focuses on whether something is true or false.	The state legislature has raised tuition 10 percent during the last three years.
		More people are burning U.S. flags today than during the 1960s.
Proposition of value	A statement that either asserts something is better than something else or presumes what is right and what is wrong, or what is good and what is bad.	The electoral college is a better way to elect presidents than is direct popular vote.

Type	Definition	Examples
		It is better to keep your financial records on a personal computer than to make the calculations by hand.
Proposition of policy	A statement that advocates a change in policy or procedures.	Our community should adopt a curfew for all citizens under eighteen.
		All handguns should be abolished.

Putting persuasive principles into practice

We have identified some of the factors that can motivate an audience and provided some clues for formulating a proposition for your speech. We conclude this chapter by discussing some general principles to help you link the theory of persuasion with the practice of persuasion.

■ *Persuasion will be more likely to occur if you try to change the listener's point of view gradually rather than suddenly.* Rarely does a listener hear a single thirty-second commercial and then purchase the product advertised. Dramatic changes of attitudes, beliefs, values, or behavior can occur after a brief exposure to a persuasive message, but it usually takes time and repeated exposure to bring about permanent attitude changes in your listeners. Political candidates and advertisers typically develop prolonged campaigns to achieve their ultimate goal of getting your vote or your dollar.

■ *Put your goal in terms that are consistent, rather than dissonant, with the attitudes, beliefs, values, and behavior of your audience.* You will be a more successful advocate if your audience thinks your proposition is compatible with the existing views. Again, we remind you to be audience-centered.

One theory suggests that when confronted with a persuasive message, listeners' responses can be classified into one of three categories: latitude of acceptance (they generally agree with the speaker), latitude of rejection (they disagree), and latitude of noncommitment (they're not sure how to respond).[8] As a persuasive speaker, it is in your interest to gain as much latitude of acceptance as you can while you are trying to change your audience's views. Your goal, of course, is to have your message fully accepted by your listeners. To do that, you will need to know where they stand on the issues before you craft your message so that you can adapt to their position.

■ *Persuasion will be more likely to occur if the advantages of your proposition are greater than the disadvantages.* Whenever you make a decision to buy something, you do a brief cost-benefit analysis. You consider the cost of the item (a new computer at $1,500), and you also think of the benefits the purchase will bring (better grades, less time spent typing because editing is so easy). If the benefits of purchasing the new computer outweigh the costs, you decide to make the purchase.

In a similar way, your job as a speaker is to convince your listeners that the benefits or advantages of adopting your point of view will outweigh whatever costs or disadvantages are associated with your proposal. Most salespersons are taught not to reveal what an item will cost until they are sure you understand the benefits of whatever they are selling. They want you to visualize owning and enjoying the product first. If you conclude that the benefits outweigh the costs, you will probably buy the product.

■ *Persuasion will be more likely to occur if your proposal meets your listeners' needs.* We have already described Maslow's hierarchy of needs and how people are motivated to satisfy more basic needs first and then satisfy higher-level needs such as self-esteem and self-actualization. In the early stages of developing your persuasive message, identify how your proposal or viewpoint will satisfy the needs of your audience. What do your listeners need that they currently do not have? How can you adapt your message to tie into their unmet needs? Answering these questions can give you some useful and powerful strategies for developing your persuasive objective and speech.

The principles described in this chapter should give you some insight into the way persuasion works. Our overview of the approaches to persuasion should help you choose a persuasive topic and formulate a specific speech purpose. In Chapter 17, we will build on the principles reviewed here and suggest specific strategies for developing your persuasive message.

Summary

In this chapter, we discussed some general theories that explain how persuasion works to change or reinforce attitudes, beliefs, and values, which are the determinants of behavior. We then described how you can build this theoretical knowledge into your speech preparation to deliver a persuasive message.

Persuasion is the process of changing or reinforcing attitudes, beliefs, values, or behavior. Attitudes are learned predispositions to respond favorably or unfavorably toward something. A belief is the way a person structures what is true and what is false. A value is a conception of right and wrong.

We examined several perspectives that explain how persuasion works. First, we discussed the concept of cognitive dissonance, which holds that we all strive for balance or consistency in our thoughts. When a persuasive message invites us to change our attitudes, beliefs, values, or behavior, we respond by trying to maintain intellectual balance or cognitive consistency.

A second theory explains why we are motivated to respond to persuasion by proposing that we wish to satisfy our needs. Abraham Maslow identified a five-level hierarchy of needs: physiological, safety, social, self-esteem, and self-actualization.

Third, we noted how positive motivational appeals can help you develop a persuasive message.

A fourth theoretical approach that helps us understand how persuasion works is the use of negative motivational appeals—notably, appeals to fear. Fear can motivate us to respond favorably to a persuasive suggestion. To avoid pain or discomfort, we may follow the recommendation of a persuasive speaker.

Preparing and presenting a persuasive speech requires the same approach as preparing any other kind of speech. A key first concern is choosing an appropriate topic. We discussed some tips for choosing a persuasive speech topic and formulating a proposition of fact, value, or policy.

The chapter concluded by describing the application of the broad principles of persuasion to preparing a persuasive speech.

● CRITICAL THINKING QUESTIONS

1. Your local chamber of commerce has asked for your advice in developing a speakers' bureau that would address public safety issues in your community. What suggestions would you offer to motivate citizens to behave in ways that would protect them from AIDS, traffic, and severe weather?

2. Martha has been asked to speak to the Association for the Preservation of the Environment. What are possible persuasive topics and propositions that would be appropriate for her audience?

3. If you were attempting to sell a new computer system to the administration of your school, what persuasive principles would you draw on to develop your message?

● ETHICAL QUESTIONS

1. Zeta plans to give a persuasive speech to convince her classmates that term limits should be imposed for senators and members of congress—even though she is personally against term limits. Is it ethical to develop a persuasive message based on a proposition with which you personally disagree?

2. Tom plans to begin his speech on driver safety using a graphic picture showing traffic accident victims who were maimed and killed because they did not use seat belts. Is such graphic use of fear appeals ethical?

1. Collect four or five magazine advertisements for various products. Analyze the persuasive strategies in each ad. Look for applications of cognitive dissonance, Maslow's hierarchy of needs, or fear appeals. Which theory do you see being illustrated most often?

2. Write a short essay noting similarities and differences in preparing and presenting an informative speech and a persuasive speech.

3. Select a controversial topic such as abortion, gun control, multilingualism, or use of contraceptives by teenagers. For the topic you select, analyze your own attitudes, beliefs, and values. What do you like and dislike about the issue? What do you believe is true or not true? What key values do you hold that lead you to your point of view?

   After you have analyzed your attitudes, beliefs, and values on the topic, do a similar analysis projecting attitudes, beliefs, and values that your classmates may hold toward the issue. You could also analyze the attitudes, beliefs, and values of your parents.

4. Identify fear appeals that have been successful in motivating you to change your attitudes, beliefs, values, or behavior.

5. Prepare and deliver a five-minute persuasive speech in which you argue against one of your own attitudes, beliefs, or values. Did your audience believe you?

● USING TECHNOLOGY AND MEDIA

1. Spend an evening watching TV, paying particular attention to the motivational appeals used in the commercials. Note whether the ad uses negative motivational strategies to convince you that you need the product. If you have a VCR, tape some of the commercials and bring them to class for discussion.

2. Listen to a tape recording of a motivational speaker attempting to help his or her listeners stop smoking, lose weight, or gain financial independence. Many are available at video stores for rent, or some can be checked out of your school or public library. Analyze the persuasive strategies the speaker uses to achieve his or her goal.

3. If you have access to cable TV, watch a C-SPAN broadcast of a member of congress attempting to argue for or against a particular proposition. Note whether it is a proposition of fact, value, or policy. Identify the persuasive strategies and organizational pattern the speaker uses.

"Freedom March"
Anna Belle Lee Washington

Strategies for Speaking Persuasively

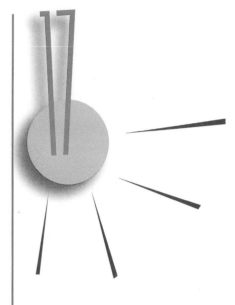

*Speech is power:
Speech is to persuade, to
convert, to compel.*
—Ralph Waldo Emerson

● OBJECTIVES

**After studying this chapter you
should be able to do the following:**

1. *Identify strategies to improve your initial,
derived, and terminal credibility.*

2. *Use principles of effective reasoning to
develop a persuasive message.*

3. *Employ effective techniques of using
emotional appeal in a persuasive
speech.*

4. *Adapt your persuasive message to
receptive, neutral, and unreceptive
audiences.*

5. *Identify strategies for effectively organizing a persuasive speech.*

he ancient Greek philosopher Aristotle defined *rhetoric* as the process of discovering the "available means of persuasion." What are these "available means" that can help you persuade an audience? In Chapter 16, we focused on the principles of persuasion to give you a general understanding of how persuasion works. In this chapter, we will discuss methods that can help you prepare your persuasive speech. Specifically, we will suggest how to gain credibility, develop well-reasoned arguments, and move your audience with emotion. We will also discuss how to adapt your specific message to your audience, and we will end with some suggestions for organizing your persuasive message.

Establishing credibility

f you were going to buy a new car, to whom would you turn for advice? Perhaps you would ask a trusted family member, or you might seek advice from *Consumer Reports,* a monthly publication that reports studies of various products on the market, among them automobiles. In other words, you would probably turn to a source that you consider knowledgeable, competent, and trustworthy—a source you think is credible.

Credibility is the audience's perception of a speaker's competence, trustworthiness, and dynamism. As a public speaker, especially one who wishes to persuade an audience, you hope that your listeners will have a favorable attitude toward you. Current research points clearly to a relationship between credibility and speech effectiveness: The more believable you are to your listener, the more effective you will be as a persuasive communicator. Whom do most people find credible? Even though he left the "CBS News" anchor desk in 1981, a 1995 survey found that Walter Cronkite is the most trusted person in the United States. He is highly credible.

Aristotle used the term *ethos* to refer to a speaker's credibility. He thought that a public speaker should be ethical, possess good character, have common sense, and be concerned for the well-being of the audience. Quintilian, a Roman teacher of public speaking, also felt that an effective public speaker should be a person of good character. Quintilian's advice was that a speaker should be "a good man speaking well." The importance to a speaker of a positive public image has been recognized for centuries. But don't get the idea that credibility is something that a speaker literally possesses or lacks. Credibility is based on the listeners' mind-set regarding the speaker. Your listeners, not you, determine whether you have credibility or lack it.

Credibility is not just a single factor or a single view of you by your audience. It is many factors and many views. Aristotle's speculations as to the factors that influence a speaker's ethical character have been generally supported by modern experimental studies.

credibility
The audience's perception of a speaker's competence, trustworthiness, and dynamism.

One clear factor in credibility is **competence**—the speaker should be considered informed, skilled, or knowledgeable about the subject he or she is talking about. If a used-car salesman sings the virtues of a car on his lot, you want to know what qualifies him to give believable information about the car.

When you give a speech, you will be more persuasive if you convince your listeners that you are knowledgeable about your topic. If, for example, you say it would be a good idea if everyone had a medical checkup each year, your listeners might mentally ask, "Why? What are your qualifications to make such a proposal?" But if you support your conclusion with medical statistics showing how having a physical exam each year dramatically leads to a prolonged life, you enhance the credibility of your suggestion. Thus, one way to enhance your competence is to cite credible evidence to support your point.

A second major factor that influences your audience's response to you is **trustworthiness.** You trust people whom you believe to be honest. While delivering your speech, you have to convey to your audience your honesty and sincerity. Your audience will be looking for evidence that they can trust you, that you are believable.

Earning an audience's trust is not something that you can do simply by saying, "Trust me." Trust is earned by demonstrating that you have had experience dealing with the issues you talk about. Your listeners would be more likely to trust your advice about how to travel around Europe on $50 a day if you had been there, than they would if you took your information from a tour book you bought from the bargain table at the bookstore. Your trustworthiness may be suspect if you advocate something that will result in a direct benefit to you. That's why salespersons and politicians are often stereotyped as being untrustworthy; if you do what they say, they will clearly benefit from a sales commission if you buy a product, or gain power and position if you give your vote.

A third factor in credibility is the speaker's **dynamism** or energy. Dynamism is often projected through delivery. **Charisma** is a form of dynamism. A charismatic person possesses charm, talent, magnetism, and other qualities that make the person attractive and energetic. Presidents Franklin Roosevelt and Ronald Reagan were considered to be charismatic speakers.

● ENHANCING YOUR CREDIBILITY

Speakers build their credibility in three phases, the first of which is **initial credibility.** This is the impression of your credibility your listeners have even before you speak. Giving careful thought to your appearance and establishing eye contact before you begin your talk will enhance both your confidence and your credibility. It is also wise to prepare a brief description of your credentials and accomplishments so that the person who introduces you can use it in his or her introductory remarks. Even if you are not asked for a statement beforehand, be prepared with one.

Derived credibility is the perception of your credibility your audience forms as you present yourself and your message. Most of this book presents principles and skills that help establish your credibility as a speaker. Several specific

competence
The factor in a speaker's credibility that refers to being perceived as informed, skilled, or knowledgeable.

trustworthiness
The factor in a speaker's credibility that refers to being perceived as believable and honest.

dynamism
The factor in a speaker's credibility that refers to being perceived as energetic.

charisma
Characteristic of a talented, charming, attractive speaker.

initial credibility
The impression of a speaker's credibility that listeners have before the speaker starts a speech.

derived credibility
The perception of a speaker's competence, trustworthiness, and dynamism based on what the speaker says and does during a speech.

Ana Lopez, a junior high school principal in San Marcos, Texas, uses her public speaking skills frequently to address student, faculty, parent, and community groups. In this narrative she describes some of the techniques she has developed to establish her credibility when she welcomes the diverse parent group in her district at the first school event of the season.

One of the highlights of each year for me is hosting an annual Open House at my school. This is the first opportunity for many of the parents to meet me and hear me speak. We all congregate in the school's cafeteria, where I give them a welcome address, introduce the faculty and staff, and then provide a general overview of the school.

Our community is very diverse. My school district is 60 to 65 percent Hispanic, 38 percent Anglo, and 2 percent Black. Within all of these populations, about one third are professionals and two thirds are blue-collar workers. So whenever I speak to all of the parents, I am conscious of being closely scrutinized for various qualities.

You see, I am not only female, but also Hispanic. So some people in the group are checking to see if I am competent to serve as a principal: Am I intelligent enough? Do I seem to know what I'm doing? Others in the group are gauging how "Hispanic" I really am. Will I be fair to their children and treat everyone equally, they wonder, or will I show special favor to my own kind?

Although knowing what all of these people are thinking makes me nervous at the beginning of every speech, once I get going, I have fun. My love for people and my love for my job always make public speaking easy for me in the end.

I'm not a person who writes formal speeches. Instead, I jot down notes or key words to trigger my thoughts, then speak extemporaneously. I also use a couple of special techniques to address all of the segments of my audience at their own level of understanding and interest. First, when I give my welcome, I do it first in English and then in Spanish. This technique is very effective in earning trust from the Hispanic portion of my audience, and everyone else appreciates what it means to them.

Second, I try to explain things in a way that the whole audience can understand—not too simple and not too difficult. I begin by explaining the general concept; then I use a concrete example and "down to earth" language to illustrate it. For example, if I'm explaining the modified block scheduling that we use at school, I'll say that it involves dividing the entire week up into segments. Then I'll say, "For example, a student will go to classes 1, 2, 3, and 4 on one day, and classes 5, 6, 7, and 8 on the next day."

I maintain a lot of eye contact to be sure that all of the various groups in my audience seem to be grasping my explanation; I'm always sensing whether the group is with me. By the end of a presentation, I can feel the warmth and responsiveness from my audience. When people come up, introduce themselves, and compliment my speech, then I know I've done a good job.

research-supported skills for enhancing your credibility as you speak include establishing common ground with your audience, supporting your key arguments with evidence, and presenting a well-organized message.

You establish common ground by indicating in your opening remarks that you share the values and concerns of your audience. Politicians might speak of their own children to begin to persuade an audience that they understand why the budget cuts they have enacted upset parents. If you are a student persuading classmates to enroll in an economics class, you could stress that an understanding of economic issues will be useful for them as they face the process of interviewing for a career. Of course, you have an ethical responsibility to be truthful when announcing how you and your audience share common goals.

Having evidence to support your persuasive conclusions strengthens your credibility. Margo was baffled as to why her plea for donations for the homeless fell flat. No one offered any financial support for her cause when she concluded her speech. Why? She offered no proof that there really were impoverished people in the community. If she had provided well-documented evidence that there was a problem and that the organization she supported could effectively solve the problem, she would have been more likely to have her position supported.

Presenting a well-organized message also enhances your credibility as a competent and rational advocate. Rambling, emotional requests rarely change or reinforce listeners' opinions or behavior. We will present specific organizational strategies for persuasive messages later in the chapter. Regardless of the organizational pattern you use, it is crucial to ensure that your message is logically structured with appropriate use of internal summaries, signposts, and enumeration of key ideas.

The last phase of credibility, called **terminal credibility** or final credibility, is the perception of your credibility your listeners have when you finish your speech. Again we emphasize the value of eye contact. Don't start leaving the lectern or the speaking area until you finish your closing sentence. Also, after your speech, be prepared to answer questions. Even if there is no planned question-and-answer period following your speech, be ready to respond to questions from interested listeners.

terminal credibility
The final impression listeners have of a speaker's credibility after the speech has been concluded.

RECAP

HOW TO ENHANCE YOUR CREDIBILITY

INITIAL CREDIBILITY: *Improving Your Image before You Speak*

Give careful consideration to your appearance.

Establish eye contact with the audience before you begin speaking.

Prepare a brief description of your credentials and accomplishments that can be read to the audience.

DERIVED CREDIBILITY: *Improving Your Image during Your Speech*

Establish common ground with your audience.

Support your arguments with evidence.

Present a well-organized speech.

TERMINAL OR FINAL CREDIBILITY: *Developing a Lasting Positive Image*

End with eye contact.

Be prepared for questions.

Using logic and evidence to persuade

he reason we need higher taxes for a new school is simple," claimed the school board member. "We don't have enough room for our students. It just makes sense." In an effort to persuade fellow board members to vote for higher taxes, this board member was using a logical argument supported with the evidence of overcrowded classrooms. **Logic** is a formal system of rules for making inferences. Aristotle called it *logos*, which literally means "the word." Learning how to develop logical arguments can make your persuasive efforts more convincing. It can also clarify your own thinking and help make your points clear to your listeners. Logic is central to all persuasive speeches.

Reasoning is the process of drawing a conclusion from evidence. Our school board member reached the conclusion that a new school was needed because of the evidence of crowded classrooms. Evidence consists of the facts, examples, statistics, and expert opinions that you use to support the points you wish to make. It is your task when advancing an argument to prove your point. **Proof** consists of evidence plus the conclusion you draw from it. The evidence in the claim made by our board member is the overcrowded classrooms. The conclusion: New taxes are needed to build new classrooms. Let's consider the two key elements of proof in greater detail. Specifically, we will look at types of reasoning and tests of evidence.

● TYPES OF REASONING

Developing well-reasoned arguments for persuasive messages has been important since antiquity. If your arguments are structured in a rational way, you have a greater chance of persuading your listeners. There are three major ways to structure an argument to reach a logical conclusion: inductively, deductively, and causally.

● INDUCTIVE REASONING
Reasoning that arrives at a general conclusion from specific instances or examples is known as **inductive reasoning.** Using this reasoning approach, you reach a general conclusion based on specific examples, facts, statistics, and opinions. For example, if you were giving a speech attempting to convince your audience that foreign cars are unreliable, you might use inductive reasoning to make your point. You could announce that you recently bought a foreign car that gave you trouble. Your cousin also bought a foreign car that kept stalling on the freeway. Finally, your English professor told you that her foreign car has broken down several times in the past few weeks. Based on these specific examples, you ask your audience to agree with your general conclusion: Foreign cars are unreliable.

As a persuasive speaker, your job is to construct a sound argument. That means basing your generalization on evidence that you can find. When you listen to a persuasive message, notice how the speaker tries to support his or her conclusion. To judge the validity of a generalization arrived at inductively, keep the following questions in mind.

logic
The formal system of using rules to make an inference.

reasoning
The process of drawing a conclusion from evidence.

proof
Evidence that establishes the validity of a conclusion or assertion.

inductive reasoning
A process of reasoning using specific instances or examples to reach a general conclusion.

- *Are there enough specific instances to support the conclusion?* Are three examples of problems with foreign cars enough to prove your point that all foreign cars are unreliable? Of the several million foreign cars that are manufactured, three cars, especially if they are different makes, are not a large sample. If those examples were supported by additional statistical evidence that over 50 percent of foreign car owners complained of serious engine malfunctions, the evidence would be more convincing.

- *Are the specific instances typical?* Are the three examples that you cite representative of all foreign cars manufactured? How do you know? What are the data on the performance of foreign cars? Also, are you, your cousin, and your professor typical of most car owners? The three of you may be careless about routine maintenance of your autos.

- *Are the instances recent?* If the foreign cars that you are using as examples of poor reliability are more than three years old, you cannot reasonably conclude that today's foreign cars are unreliable products. Age alone may explain the poor performance of your sample.

The logic in this example, therefore, is not particularly sound. The speaker would need considerably more evidence to prove his or her point.

Reasoning by analogy is a special type of inductive reasoning. An **analogy** is a comparison. This form of reasoning compares one thing, person, or process with another, to predict how something will perform and respond. When you observe that two things have a number of characteristics in common and that a certain fact about one is likely to be true of the other, you have drawn an analogy and reasoned from one example to reach a conclusion about the other. If you try to convince an audience that mandatory seat belt laws in Texas and Florida have reduced highway deaths and therefore should be instituted in Kansas, you are reasoning by analogy. You would also be reasoning by analogy if you claimed that capital punishment reduced crime in Brazil and therefore should be used in the United States as well. But as with reasoning by generalization, there are questions that you should ask to check the validity of your conclusions.

analogy
A special type of inductive reasoning in which you compare one thing, person, or process with another to predict how something will perform and respond.

- *Do the ways in which the two things are alike outweigh those in which they are different?* Can you compare the crime statistics of Brazil to those of the United States and claim to make a valid comparison? Are the data collected in the same way in both countries? Are there other factors besides the seat belt laws in Texas and Florida that could account for the lower automobile accident death rate? Maybe differences in the speed limit or the types of roads in those states can account for the difference.

- *Is the assertion true?* Is it really true that capital punishment has served as a deterrent to crime in Brazil? Is it really true that mandatory seat belt laws in Florida and Texas have reduced auto highway deaths? You will need to give reasons the comparison you are making is valid, and evidence that will prove your conclusion to be true.

deductive reasoning
A process of reasoning from a general statement or principle to reach a specific conclusion.

syllogism
A three-part way of developing an argument; it has a major premise, a minor premise, and a conclusion

major premise
A general statement that is the first element of a syllogism.

minor premise
A specific statement about an example that is linked to the major premise; it is the second element of a syllogism.

conclusion
The logical outcome of an argument which stems from the major premise and the minor premise.

● **DEDUCTIVE REASONING**   Reasoning from a general statement or principle to reach a specific conclusion is **deductive reasoning**. This is just the reverse of inductive reasoning. Deductive reasoning can be structured in the form of a syllogism. A **syllogism** is a way of organizing an argument. It has three elements: a major premise, a minor premise, and a conclusion. To reach a conclusion deductively, you start with a general statement that serves as the **major premise.** In a speech attempting to convince your audience that the communication professor teaching your public speaking class is a top-notch teacher, you might use a deductive reasoning process. Your major premise is "All communication professors have excellent teaching skills." The **minor premise** is a more specific statement about an example that is linked to the major premise. Here's the minor premise in the argument you are advancing: "John Smith, our teacher, is a communication professor." The **conclusion** is based on the major premise and the more specific minor premise. In reasoning deductively, you need to ensure that the major and minor premises are true and can be supported with evidence. The conclusion to our syllogism is "John Smith has excellent teaching skills." The persuasive power of deductive reasoning derives from the fact that the conclusion cannot be questioned if the premises are accepted as true.

To test the truth of an argument organized deductively, consider the following questions.

■ *Is the major premise (general statement) true?* Is it really true that *all* communication professors have excellent teaching skills? What evidence do you have to support this statement? The power of deductive reasoning hinges in part on whether your generalization is true.

■ *Is the minor premise (the particular statement) also true?* If your minor premise is false, your syllogism can collapse right there. In our example, it is easy enough to verify that John Smith is a communication professor. But not all minor premises can be verified as easily. For example, it would be difficult to prove the minor premise in this example:

All gods are immortal.

Zeus is a god.

Therefore, Zeus is immortal.

■ We can accept the major premise as true because immortality is part of the definition of *god.* But proving that Zeus is a god would be very difficult. In this case, the truth of the conclusion hinges on the truth of the minor premise.

causal reasoning
A process of reasoning in which two or more events are related in such a way as to conclude that one or more of the events caused the others.

● **CAUSAL REASONING**   A third type of reasoning is called **causal reasoning.** When you reason by cause, you relate two or more events in such a way as to conclude that one or more of the events caused the others. For example, you might argue that having unprotected sex causes the spread of AIDS.

There are two ways to structure a causal argument. First, you can reason from cause to effect, moving from a known fact to a predicted result. You know, for example, that interest rates have increased in the past week. Therefore, you might argue that *because* the rates are increasing, the Dow Jones Industrial Average will decrease. In this case, you move from something that has occurred (rising interest rates) to something that has not yet occurred (decrease in the stock market). Weather forecasters use the same method of reasoning when they predict the weather. They base a conclusion about tomorrow's weather on what they know about today's meteorological conditions.

A second way to frame a causal argument is to reason backward, from known effect to unknown cause. You know, for example, that a major earthquake has occurred (known effect). To explain this event, you propose that the cause of the earthquake is a shift in the fault line (unknown cause). You cannot be sure of the cause, but you are certain of the effect. A candidate for President may claim that the cause of current high unemployment (known effect) is mismanagement by the present administration (unknown cause). He then constructs an argument to prove that his assertion is accurate. To prove his case, he needs to have evidence that the present administration mismanaged the economy. The key to developing strong causal arguments is in the use of evidence to link something known with something unknown. An understanding of the appropriate use of evidence can enhance inductive, deductive, and causal reasoning.

RECAP

TYPES OF REASONING

Type	Definition	Example
Inductive reasoning	Thought pattern that moves from specific information to a general conclusion	When tougher drug laws went into effect in Kansas City and St. Louis, drug traffic was reduced. The United States should therefore institute tougher drug laws.
Deductive reasoning	Thought pattern that moves from a general statement to a specific conclusion	All bachelors are unmarried men. Frank is a bachelor. Therefore, Frank is an unmarried man.
Causal reasoning	Thought pattern that relates two or more events to prove that one or more of the events caused the others	Since the 65-mile-per-hour speed limit went into effect, traffic deaths have increased. The increased highway speed has caused an increase in highway deaths.

AUDIENCE DIVERSITY AND REASONING

As we have stressed, effective strategies for developing your persuasive objective will vary depending on the background and cultural expectations of your listeners. Most of the logical, rational methods of reasoning discussed in the preceding sections evolved from Greek and Roman traditions of argument (see Appendix A). Rhetoricians from the United States typically use a straightforward factual-inductive method of supporting ideas and reaching conclusions.[1] First, they identify facts and directly link them to support a specific proposition or conclusion. For example, in a speech to prove that the government spends more money than it receives, the speaker could cite year-by-year statistics on income and expenditures to document the point. North Americans also like debates involving a direct clash of ideas and opinions. Our low-context culture encourages people to be more direct and forthright in dealing with issues and disagreement than do high-context cultures.

Not all cultures assume a direct, linear, methodical approach to supporting ideas and proving a point.[2] People from high-context cultures, for example, may expect that participants will establish a personal relationship before debating issues. Some cultures use a deductive pattern of reasons, rather than an inductive pattern. They begin with a general premise and then link it to a specific situation when they attempt to persuade listeners. During several recent trips to Russia, your authors have noticed that to argue that Communism was ineffective, Russians often start with a general assumption: Communism didn't work. Then they use this assumption to explain specific current problems in areas such as transportation and education.

Middle Eastern cultures usually do not use standard inductive or deductive structures. They are more likely to use narrative methods to persuade an audience. They tell stories that evoke feelings and emotions, allowing their listeners to draw their own conclusions by inductive association.[3]

Although this text stresses the kind of inductive reasoning that will be persuasive to most North Americans, if your audience is from another cultural tradition, you may need to use alternative strategies. If you are uncertain about which approach will be most effective, consider using a variety of methods and strategies to make your point. Use facts supported with analysis, but also make sure you provide illustrative stories and examples. Also, try to observe and talk with other speakers who are experienced at addressing your target audience.

In Middle Eastern cultures, speakers use narrative techniques to educate and persuade listeners. [Photo: Ilene Perluman/Stock Boston]

● SUPPORTING YOUR REASONING WITH EVIDENCE

You cannot simply state a conclusion without proving it with evidence. Evidence in persuasive speeches consists of facts, examples, statistics, and expert opinions.

In Chapter 8 we discussed the essential details of using these types of supporting material in speeches. When attempting to persuade listeners, it is useful to make sure that your evidence logically supports the inductive, deductive, or causal reasoning you are using to reach your conclusion.

When using facts to persuade, make sure your fact is really a fact. A **fact** is something that has been directly observed to be true or can be proved to be true. The shape of the earth, the number of women CEO's, who won the 1992 presidential election have all been directly observed or measured. Without direct observation or measurement, we can only make an inference. An **inference** is a conclusion based on available evidence.

Examples are illustrations that are used to dramatize or clarify a fact. Only valid true examples can be used to help prove a point. For example, one speaker, in an effort to document the increased violence in children's television programs,

fact
Something that has been directly observed to be true or can be proved to be true.

inference
A conclusion based on available evidence.

example
An illustration used to dramatize or clarify a fact.

told her audience, "Last Saturday morning as I watched cartoons with my daughter, I was shocked by the countless times we saw examples of beatings and even the death of the cartoon characters in one half-hour program." The conclusion she wanted her audience to reach: Put an end to senseless violence in children's television programs.

A hypothetical example, one that is fabricated to illustrate a point, should not be used to reach a conclusion. It should be used only to clarify. David encouraged his listeners to join him in an effort to clean up the San Marcos River. He wanted to motivate his audience to help by asking them to "Imagine bringing your children to the river ten years from now. You see the river bottom littered with cans and bottles." His example, while effective in helping the audience to visualize what might happen in the future, does not prove that the river ecosystem will deteriorate. It only illustrates what might happen if action isn't taken.

Opinions can serve as evidence if they are made by an expert, someone who can add credibility to your conclusion. The best opinions are made by someone known to be unbiased, fair, and accurate. If the surgeon general has expressed an opinion regarding drug testing, his or her opinion would be helpful evidence. Even so, opinions are usually most persuasive if they are combined with other evidence, such as facts or statistics, that supports the expert's position.

A **statistic** is a number used to summarize several facts or samples. In the speech included at the end of this chapter, Jeffrey Jamison uses statistics effectively to document the serious problem of alkali batteries polluting the environment. He cites evidence from the *New York Times* which documents ". . . each year we are adding 150 tons of mercury, 130 tons of lead, and 170 tons of cadmium to the environment."[4] Without these statistics Jeffrey's claim that alkali batteries are detrimental to the environment would not be as potent. Again, you may want to review the discussion on the appropriate use of statistics in Chapter 8.

If you are reasoning using an inductive strategy (from specific examples to a general conclusion), you need to make sure you have enough facts, examples, statistics, and credible opinions to support your conclusion. If you reason deductively (from a generalization to a specific conclusion), you will need evidence to document the truth of your initial generalization. When developing an argument using causal reasoning, evidence is again vital when you attempt to establish that one or more events caused something to happen.

● AVOIDING FAULTY REASONING: ETHICAL ISSUES

We have emphasized the importance of developing sound, logical arguments supported with appropriate evidence. You have an ethical responsibility to use your skill in constructing well-supported arguments with logical reasoning and sound evidence. Not all people who try to persuade you will use sound arguments to get you to vote for them, buy their product, or donate money to their cause. Many persuaders use inappropriate techniques called fallacies. A **fallacy** is false reasoning that occurs when someone attempts to persuade without adequate evidence or with arguments that are irrelevant or inappropriate. You will be both a better and more ethical speaker and a better listener if you are aware of the following fallacies.

opinion
Testimony or quotation that expresses attitudes, beliefs, or values of someone else.

statistic
Numerical data that summarizes facts and examples.

fallacy
False reasoning that occurs when someone attempts to persuade without adequate evidence or with arguments that are irrelevant or inappropriate.

● CAUSAL FALLACY   The Latin term for this fallacy is *post hoc, ergo propter hoc,* which translates as "after this, therefore, because of this." It refers to making a faulty causal connection. Simply because one event follows another does not mean that the two are related. If you declared that your school's football team won this time because you sang your school song before the game, you would be guilty of a causal fallacy. There are undoubtedly other factors that explain why your team won, such as good preparation or facing a weaker opposing team. For something to be a cause, it has to have the power to bring about a result. "That howling storm last night knocked down the tree in our backyard" is a logical causal explanation.

Here are more examples of causal fallacies:

The increased earthquake and hurricane activity is caused by the increase in violence and war in our society.

As long as you wear this lucky rabbit's foot, you will never have an automobile accident.

The decline of morals in this country is caused by excessive government spending.

In each instance, there is not enough evidence to support the cause–effect conclusion.

● BANDWAGON FALLACY   Someone who argues that "everybody thinks it's a good idea, so you should too" is using the bandwagon fallacy. Simply because someone says that "everyone" is "jumping on the bandwagon" or supporting a particular point of view does not make the point of view correct. Sometimes speakers use the bandwagon fallacy in a more subtle way in their efforts to persuade:

Everybody knows that talk radio is our primary link to a free and democratic society.

Most people agree that we spend too much time worrying about Medicare.

Everybody agrees with me that we need a change in Congress.

Beware of sweeping statements that include you and others without offering any evidence that the speaker has solicited opinions.

● EITHER–OR   Someone who argues that there are only two approaches to a problem is trying to oversimplify the issues. "It's either vote for higher property taxes or close the library," asserts Daryl at a public hearing on tax increases. Such a statement ignores a variety of other solutions to a complex problem. The following are additional examples of inappropriate either–or simplistic reasoning:

Mothers should either stay home and spend less time at work, or we will have an increase in juvenile delinquency.

Either television violence is reduced, or we will have an increase in child and spouse abuse.

Either more people should start volunteering their time to work for their community or your taxes will increase.

● HASTY GENERALIZATION   A person who reaches a conclusion from too little evidence or nonexistent evidence is making a hasty generalization. For example, simply because one person became ill after eating the meat loaf in the cafeteria does not mean that everyone eating in the cafeteria will contract serious health problems because of food poisoning. Here are some additional hasty generalizations:

It's clear that our schools can't educate children well, because my niece went to school for six years and she still can't read at her grade level.

The city does a terrible job of taking care of the elderly, because my grandmother lives in a city-owned nursing home and the floors there are always filthy.

We don't need mandatory lawn watering rules in our city, because the people I know do their best to conserve water.

● ATTACKING THE PERSON   Also known as *ad hominem*, Latin for "to the man," this involves attacking irrelevant personal characteristics about the person who is proposing an idea rather than attacking the idea itself. A statement such as "We know Janice's idea won't work because she has never had a good idea yet" does not really deal with the idea, which may be perfectly valid. Don't dismiss an idea solely because you have been turned against the person who presented it. Here are some more examples of ad hominem attacks:

Anyone who is a talk-radio host certainly has no idea how to develop a plan to reduce the deficit.

She was educated in a foreign country and could not possibly have good ideas for improving education in our community.

Tony is an awful musician and is not sensitive enough to chair such an important committee.

● RED HERRING   The red herring fallacy takes place when someone attacks an issue by using irrelevant facts or arguments as distractions. This fallacy gets its name from an old trick of dragging a red herring across a trail to divert the dogs who may be following. Speakers use a red herring when they want to distract an audience from the real issues. For example, a politician who had been accused of taking bribes while in office calls a press conference. During the press conference, he talks about the evils of child pornography, rather than addressing the charge against him; he is using the red herring technique to divert attention from the real issue—did he or did he not take the bribe? Here's an additional example of a fallacious argument using the red herring method:

From a speech against gun control: The real problem is not eliminating handguns from Americans; the real problem is that pawnshops that sell guns are controlled by the Mafia.

● APPEAL TO MISPLACED AUTHORITY   When ads use baseball catchers to endorse automobiles and TV heroes to sell political candidates or an airline or hotel, we are faced with the fallacious appeal to misplaced authority. Although we have great respect for these people in their own fields, they are no more expert than we are in the areas they are advertising. As both a public speaker and a listener, you must recognize what is valid expert testimony and what is not. For example, a physicist who speaks on the laws of nature or the structure of matter could reasonably be accepted as an expert. But if the physicist speaks on politics, the opinion expressed is not that of an expert and is no more significant than your own. The following examples are appeals to misplaced authority:

> Former Congressman Smith endorses the new art museum, so every business should get behind it, too.

> Our history professor recommended that we stay at the Frontier Place in Orlando, so it must be good.

> Tipper Gore thinks this cookie recipe is the best, so you should try it too.

● NON SEQUITUR   If you argue that a new parking garage should not be built on campus because the grass has not been mowed on the football field for three weeks, you are guilty of a non sequitur (Latin for "it does not follow"). Grass growing on the football field has nothing to do with the parking problem. Your conclusion simply does not follow from your statement. The following are examples of non-sequitur conclusions:

> We should not give students condoms, because TV has such a pervasive influence on our youth today.

> You should endorse me for Congress, because I have three children.

> We need more parking on our campus, because we are the national football champions.

> You should help pick up trash in our community, since our new cable TV studio is now in operation.

Using emotion to persuade

Roger Ailes, political communication consultant, has nominated several memorable moments as outstanding illustrations of speakers using emotional messages powerfully and effectively:[5]

> *Martin Luther King, announcing his vision of brotherhood and equality at the Lincoln Memorial in 1963, extolled, "I have a dream!"*

General Douglas MacArthur, in announcing his retirement before a joint session of Congress, April 19, 1951, closed his speech with "Old soldiers never die; they just fade away. And like the old soldier of that ballad, I now close my military career and just fade away."

British Prime Minister Winston Churchill in his 1940 speech to the House of Commons in preparing his people for war intoned, "Let us therefore brace ourselves to our duties, and so bear ourselves that, if the British Empire and its Commonwealth last for a thousand years, men will still say, 'This was their finest hour.' "

Emotion is a powerful way to move an audience and support your persuasive purpose. Aristotle used the term *pathos* to refer to the use of appeals to emotion. An appeal to emotion can be an effective way to achieve a desired response from an audience. Whereas logical arguments may appeal to our reason, emotional arguments generally appeal to nonrational sentiments. Often we make decisions based not on logic, but on emotion.

One theory suggests that emotional responses can be classified along three dimensions.[6] First, you respond with varying degrees of *pleasure or displeasure*. Pleasurable stimuli consist of such things as smiling, healthy babies, or daydreams about winning $1 million in a sweepstakes. Stimuli causing displeasure may be TV images of the beating of Rodney King by police or news stories of child abuse.

A second dimension of emotional responses exists on a continuum of *arousal–nonarousal*. You become aroused emotionally at such things as seeing a snake in your driveway, or you may be lulled into a state of nonarousal by a boring lecture.

The third dimension of emotional responses is one's feeling of *power or powerlessness* when confronted with some stimulus. When thinking about the destructive force of nuclear weapons or the omnipotence of God, you may feel insignificant and powerless. Or perhaps you feel a sense of power when you imagine yourself conducting a symphony or winning an election.

These three dimensions—pleasure, arousal, and power—are believed to form the bases of all our emotional responses. The theory predicts that if listeners feel pleasure and are also aroused by something, such as a political candidate or a product, they will tend to form a favorable view of the candidate or product. A listener's feeling of being powerful or powerless has to do with being in control and having permission to behave as he or she wishes. A listener who feels powerful is more likely to respond to the message.

As a public speaker trying to sway your listeners to your viewpoint, your job is to use emotional appeals to achieve your goal. If you wanted to persuade your listeners that capital punishment should be banned, you would try to arouse feelings of displeasure and turn them against capital punishment. Advertisers selling soft drinks typically strive to arouse feelings of pleasure when you think of their product. Smiling people, upbeat music, and good times are usually part of the formula for selling soda pop.

Though the underlying theory of emotions may help you understand how emotions work, as a public speaker your key concern is "How can I ethically use emotional appeals to achieve my persuasive purpose?" Let's consider several methods.

■ *Use concrete examples that help your listeners visualize what you describe.* Using a concrete example of an emotionally moving scene can create a powerful response in your audience. Describing what it was like after a tornado destroyed the town of Saragosa, Texas, can evoke strong emotions in your listeners. The images used to evoke the emotions can also help communicate the power of nature and the value of taking proper precautions when a storm warning is sounded.

> *The town is no more. No homes in the western Texas town remain standing. The church where twenty-one people perished looks like a heap of twisted metal and mortar. A child's doll can be seen in the street. The owner, four-year-old Maria, will no longer play with her favorite toy; she was killed along with five of her playmates when the twister roared through the elementary school.*

■ *Use emotion-arousing words.* Words and phrases can trigger emotional responses in your listeners. *Mother, flag, freedom,* and *slavery* are among a large number of emotionally loaded words. Patriotic slogans, such as "Remember the Alamo" or "Remember Pearl Harbor," can produce strong emotional responses.

■ *Use nonverbal behavior to communicate your emotional response.* The great Roman orator Cicero believed that if you want your listeners to experience a certain emotion, you should first model that emotion for them. If you want an audience to feel anger at a particular law or event, you must display anger and indignation in your voice, movement, and gesture. As we have already noted, delivery plays the key role in communicating your emotional responses. If you want your audience to become excited about and interested in your message, you must communicate that excitement and interest through your delivery.

■ *Use visual images to evoke emotions.* In addition to nonverbal expressions, pictures or images of emotion-arousing scenes can amplify your speech. As you know from reading the newspaper, a photograph of the bombed-out Alfred P. Murrah building in Oklahoma City can arouse anger and sadness about the meaningless loss of life at the hands of those who wanted to inflict pain. An image of a lonely farmer looking out over his waterlogged field following a ravaging flood can communicate his sense of despair. A picture of children in war-torn Bosnia can communicate the devastating effects of violence with greater impact than can mere words alone. In contrast, a photo of a Bosnian mother and child reunited after an enforced separation can communicate the true meaning of joy. You can use similar images as visual aids to evoke your audience's emotions, both positive and negative. Remember, however, that when you use visual images, you have the same ethical responsibilities as you do when you use verbal forms of support: make sure your image is from a credible source and that it has not been altered or taken out of context.

■ *Use selected appeals to fear.* The threat that harm will come to your listeners unless they follow your advice is an appeal to fear. As discussed in Chapter 16, listeners can be motivated to change their behavior if appeals to fear are used appropriately. Research suggests that high fear arousal ("You will be killed in an auto accident unless you wear a seat belt") is more effective than moderate or low appeals, if you are a highly credible speaker.[7] However, you may be taking a risk in arousing too much anxiety in your listeners. They may find what you have to say so exaggerated that they stop listening to you. Hence, unless you are a highly credible speaker, moderate fear appeals directed toward your listeners or their loved ones seem to work best.

■ *Consider using appeals to several emotions.* Appealing to the fears and anxieties of your listeners is one of the most common types of emotional appeals used to persuade, but you could also elicit several other emotions to help achieve your persuasive goal.

Hope. Listeners could be motivated to respond to the prospect of a brighter tomorrow. When Franklin Roosevelt said, "The only thing we have to fear is fear itself," he was invoking hope for the future. Bill Clinton used this technique very effectively during his campaign by focusing on his roots in Hope, Arkansas.

Pride. "The pride is back" is a slogan used to sell cars. An appeal to pride can also be used to motivate listeners in a persuasive speech. The appeal to achieve a persuasive objective based on pride in oneself or one's country, state, or hometown can be very powerful.

Nation of Islam leader Louis Farrakhan's emotion-laden appeals to African-American racial pride have elicited a storm of controversy. Here Farrakhan punctuates a lengthy oration with expansive gestures to sway his audience at the Million Man March, held in Washington, D.C. in October, 1995. [Photo: Greg Pearc/Tony Stone Images]

Courage. Challenging your audience to take a bold stand or to step away from the crowd can emotionally change your listeners to take action. Referring to courageous men and women as role models can help motivate your listeners to take similar actions. Patrick Henry's famous "Give me liberty, or give me death!" speech appealed to his audience to take a courageous stand on the issues before the people.

Reverence. The appeal to the sacred and the revered can be an effective way to motivate. Sacred traditions, revered institutions, or cherished and celebrated individuals can be used to help inspire your audience to change or reinforce attitudes, beliefs, values, or behavior. Mother Teresa, holy writings, and the Congress of the United States are examples of revered people or things that may be perceived as sacred by your listeners. As an audience-centered speaker, however, you need to remember that what may be sacred to one individual or audience may not be sacred to another.

USING EMOTIONAL APPEALS: ETHICAL ISSUES

Regardless of which emotions you use to motivate your audience, you have an obligation to be ethical and forthright. Making false claims, misusing evidence to arouse emotions, or relying only on emotions without any evidence to support a conclusion violates ethical standards of effective public speaking.

A **demagogue** is a speaker who attempts to gain power or control over others by using impassioned emotional pleas and appealing to the prejudices of listeners. The word *demagogue* comes from the Greek term *demagogos*, meaning "popular leader." Speakers who become popular by substituting emotion and fallacies in place of well-supported reasoning are guilty of demagoguery. During the late 1940s and early 1950s, Wisconsin Senator Joseph McCarthy sought to convince the nation that closet Communists had infiltrated government, education, and the entertainment industry. Since this was at the height of the Cold War, anything or anyone remotely connected to communism elicited an immediate negative emotional response. For a time, McCarthy was successful in his effort to expose the unpatriotic Communists among us. His evidence, however, was scanty, and he relied primarily on scaring his listeners about the potential evil of alleged Communists. His trumped-up evidence and unethical use of fear appeals eventually undermined his credibility and earned him a reputation as a demagogue. You have an ethical responsibility not to misuse emotional appeals when persuading others.

Your credibility, reasoning, and emotional appeals are the chief ways to persuade an audience. Now you need to refine your technique. Your use of these persuasive strategies depends on the composition of your audience. As we have observed several times before, an early task in the public speaking process is to analyze your audience. This is particularly important in persuasion. Audience members are not just sitting there waiting to respond to every suggestion a speaker makes.

demagogue
A speaker who gains control over others by using unethical emotional pleas and appeals to listeners' prejudices.

RECAP

TIPS FOR USING EMOTION TO PERSUADE

Use concrete examples.

Use emotion-arousing words.

Use nonverbal behavior to communicate your emotional response.

Use visual images.

Use selected appeals to fear.

Use appeals to a variety of emotions such as hope, pride, courage, or reverence.

Strategies for adapting ideas to people and people to ideas

One definition of persuasive communication nicely summarizes the importance of adapting your message to your audience. "Rhetoric," suggests Donald C. Bryant, "is the process of adjusting ideas to people and people to ideas."[7] Your appeals to reason, emotion, and your own credibility are all dependent on the attitudes, beliefs, and values of your listeners.

Audience members may hold differing views of you and your subject. Your task is to find out if there is a prevailing viewpoint held by a majority of your listeners. If they are generally friendly toward you and your ideas, you need to design your speech differently than if your listeners are neutral, apathetic, or hostile. Research studies as well as seasoned public speakers can offer some useful suggestions to help you adapt your approach to your audience. We will discuss three general responses your audience may have to you: receptive, neutral, and unreceptive.

PERSUADING THE RECEPTIVE AUDIENCE

It is always a pleasure when the audience you face already supports you and your message. In speaking to a receptive group, you can explore your ideas in greater depth than otherwise. Here are some suggestions that may help you make the most of your speaking opportunity.

- *Identify with your audience.* To establish common ground with her audience, Rita told her audience of fellow students, "Just like most of you, I struggle to pay my way through college. That's why I support expanding the campus work-study program." Like Rita, if you are a college student speaking to other college students with similar backgrounds and pressures, point to your similar backgrounds and struggles. Emphasize the similarities between you and your audience. What other common interests do you have? The introductory portion of your speech is a good place to mention your common interests and background.

- *Clearly state your speaking objective.* When speaking to a group of her campaign workers, mayoral candidate Maria Hernandez clearly stated early in her speech, "My reason for coming here today is to ask each of you to volunteer three hours a week to help me become the next mayor of our city." We have stressed several times how important it is to provide an overview of your major point or purpose. This is particularly so when speaking to a group who will support your point of view.

- *Tell your audience exactly what you want them to do.* Besides telling your listeners what your speaking objective is, you can also tell them how you expect them to respond to your message. Be explicit in directing your listeners' behavior.

- *Ask listeners for an immediate show of support.* Evangelists usually speak to favorable audiences. Evangelist Billy Graham, for example, always asks those who support his Christian message to come forward at the end of his sermon. Asking for an immediate show of support helps to cement the positive response that you have developed during your speech.

- *Use emotional appeals effectively.* You can usually move a favorable audience to action with strong emotional appeals while also reminding them of the evidence that supports your conclusion. If the audience already supports your position, you need not spend a great deal of time on lengthy, detailed explanations or factual information. You can usually assume that your listeners are already in possession of much of that material.

● PERSUADING THE NEUTRAL AUDIENCE

Think how many lectures you go to with an attitude of indifference. Probably quite a few. Many audiences will fall somewhere between wildly enthusiastic and unreceptive; they will simply be neutral or indifferent. They may be neutral because they don't know much about your topic or because they just can't make up their minds whether to support your point of view. They may also be indifferent because they don't see how the topic or issue affects them. Regardless of the reason for your listeners' indifference, your challenge is to make them interested in your message. Let's look at some approaches to gaining their attention and keeping their interest.

- *Capture your listeners' attention early in your speech.* "One day the Energizer bunny will die."[9] In the sample speech about alkali batteries that concludes this chapter, Jeffrey Jamison's provocative opening statement effectively captures the attention of his listeners. All introductions should try to get your audience's attention, but this is particularly important when speaking to an audience that is indifferent.

- *Refer to beliefs that many listeners share.* When speaking to a neutral audience, identify common concerns and values that you plan to address. Martin Luther King's "I Have a Dream" speech (Appendix D) illustrates a reference to his listeners' common beliefs.

- *Relate your topic not only to your listeners but also to their families, friends, and loved ones.* You can capture the interest of your listeners by appealing to the needs of people they care about. Parents will be interested in ideas and policies that affect their children. People are generally interested in matters that may affect their friends, neighbors, and others with whom they identify, such as members of their own religion or economic or social class.

- *Be realistic in what you can accomplish.* Don't overestimate the response you may receive from a neutral audience. People who start with an attitude of indifference are probably not going to become as enthusiastic as you are after hearing just one speech. Persuasion does not occur all at once or at a first hearing of arguments.

PERSUADING THE UNRECEPTIVE AUDIENCE

One of the biggest challenges is to persuade audience members who are against you or your message. If they are hostile toward you personally, your job is to seek ways to enhance your acceptability and persuade them to listen to you. If they are unreceptive to your point of view, there are several approaches that you can use to help them listen to you.

- *Don't immediately announce that you plan to change their minds.* Paul wondered why his opening sales pitch ("Good morning. I plan to convince you to purchase this fine set of knives at a cost to you of only $250") was not greeted enthusiastically. If you immediately and bluntly tell your listeners that you plan to change their opinions, it can make them defensive. It is usually better to take a more subtle approach when announcing your persuasive intent.

- *Begin your speech by noting areas of agreement before you discuss areas of disagreement.* In addressing the school board, one community member began his persuasive effort to convince board members they should not raise taxes by stating, "I think each of us here can agree with one common goal: We want the best education for our children." Once you help your audience understand that there are issues on which you agree (such as agreeing that the topic you will discuss is controversial), your listeners may be more attentive when you explain your position.

- *Don't expect a major shift in attitude from a hostile audience.* Set a realistic limit on what you can achieve. A realistic goal might be to have your listeners hear you out and at least consider some of your points.

- *Acknowledge the opposing points of view that members of your audience may hold.* Summarize the reasons individuals may oppose your point of view. Doing this communicates that you at least understand the issues. Your listeners will be more likely to listen to you if they know that you understand their viewpoint. Of course, after you acknowledge the opposing point of view, you will need to cite evidence and use arguments to refute the opposition and support your conclusion. In speaking to a neighborhood community group about the possibility of building a new airport near their homes, City Manager

Anderson early in his talk acknowledged, "I am aware that a new airport brings unwanted changes to a neighborhood. Noise and increased traffic are not the type of challenges you want near your homes." He went on to identify the actions the city would take to minimize the problems a new airport would cause.

■ *Establish your credibility.* Being thought credible is always an important goal of a public speaker, and it is especially important when talking to a hostile audience. Let your audience know about the experience, interest, knowledge, and skill that give you special insight into the issues at hand.

Strategies for organizing persuasive messages

Is there one best way to organize a persuasive speech? The answer is no. Specific approaches to organizing speeches depend on audience, message, and desired objective. But how you organize your speech does have a major effect on your listeners' response to your message.

Research suggests that there are some general principles to keep in mind when preparing your persuasive message.[10] If you feel that your audience may be hostile to your point of view, advance your strongest arguments first. If you save your best argument for last, your audience may have already stopped listening. Do not bury key arguments and evidence in the middle of your message. Information presented first and last is more likely to be remembered by your listeners. In speaking to his fraternity about the evils of drunk driving, Frank wisely began his speech with his most powerful evidence: The leading cause of death among college-age males is alcohol-related automobile accidents. He got their attention with his sobering fact.

Another key suggestion: If you want your listeners to take some action, it is best to tell them what you want them to do at the end of your speech. If you call for action in the middle of your speech, it won't have the same power as including it in your conclusion.

It is also usually better to present both sides of an issue, rather than just the advantages of the position you advocate. If you don't acknowledge arguments that your listeners have heard, they will probably think about them anyway.

Yet another sound strategy: Make some reference to the counter-arguments and then refute them with evidence and logic. It may be wise to compare the proposal you are making with an alternate proposal, perhaps one that is offered by someone else. By comparing and contrasting your solution with another recommendation, you can show how your proposal is better.

Even though we have discussed ways of organizing speeches in Chapter 9, there are special ways to organize persuasive speeches. Here we present four organizational patterns: problem–solution, refutation, cause and effect, and the motivated sequence.

PERSUASIVE ORGANIZATIONAL STRATEGIES

Place your strongest arguments first, especially if your audience may be hostile.

At the end of your speech, tell your audience what you want them to do.

Present both sides of an issue, rather than just the advantages of the position you advocate.

Compare your proposal with a proposal offered by someone else, showing how your recommendation is superior.

PROBLEM–SOLUTION

The most basic organizational pattern for a persuasive speech is to make the audience aware of the problem, then present a solution that clearly solves it. Almost any problem can be phrased in terms of something you want more of or less of. The problem–solution pattern works best when a clearly evident problem can be documented and a solution can be proposed to deal with the evils of the well-documented problem.

If you are speaking to an apathetic audience or the listeners are not aware that a problem exists, a problem–solution pattern works nicely. Your challenge will be to provide ample evidence to document that your perception of the problem is accurate. You'll also need to convince your listeners that the solution you advocate is the most appropriate one to resolve the problem.

Many political candidates use a problem–solution approach. Problem: The government wastes your tax dollars. Solution: Vote for me and I'll see to it that government waste is eliminated. Problem: We need more and better jobs. Solution: Vote for me and I'll institute a program to put people back to work.

Note how the following arguments used in Jason Fruit's speech, "The Dangers of Electromagnetic Fields," first document a clear problem and then recommend strategies for managing the problem.

Problem:

I. Power lines and power stations around the country emit radiation and are now being shown to increase the risk of cancer.

   A. Childhood leukemia rates are higher in children who live near large power lines.

   B. The International Cancer Research Institute in Lyon, France, published a report linking electromagnetic fields and childhood cancer.

Solution:

II. Steps can be taken to minimize our risk of health hazards caused by electromagnetic energy.

A. The federal government should establish enforceable safety standards for exposure to electromagnetic energy.

B. Contact your local power company to make sure their lines are operated safely.

C. Stop using electric blankets.

D. Use protective screens for computer display terminals.

The problem–solution arrangement of ideas applies what we learned about cognitive dissonance in Chapter 16. Identify and document a concern that calls for change, and then suggest specific behaviors that can restore cognitive balance.

● REFUTATION

Another way to persuade an audience to your point of view is to prove that the arguments against your position are false, to refute them. To use refutation as a strategy for persuasion, you first identify objections to your position that your listeners may hold and then refute or overcome those objections with arguments and evidence. You would be most likely to use refutation as your organizational strategy when your position is being attacked. Or, if you know what your listeners' chief objections are to your persuasive proposal, you could organize your speech around the arguments your listeners hold.

As we noted earlier, research suggests that in most cases it is better to present both sides of an issue rather than just the advantages of the position you advocate. Even if you don't acknowledge arguments that your listeners have heard, they will probably think about them anyway.

Suppose, for example, you plan to speak to a group of real estate developers advocating a new zoning ordinance that would reduce the number of building permits granted in your community. Your listeners will undoubtedly have some concerns over how the ordinance will affect new housing starts and the overall economic forecast. You could organize your presentation to this group using those two obvious concerns as major issues to refute. Your major points could be:

I. The new zoning ordinance will not cause an overall decrease in the number of new homes built in our community.

II. The new zoning ordinance will have a positive effect on the economic growth in our community.

After your persuasive presentation with a refutation strategy, if there is a question-and-answer forum, you should be prepared to answer questions. Credible evidence, facts, and data will be more effective than emotional arguments alone when you face an audience that you know is not in favor of your persuasive objective. In your postspeech session, you can use your refutation skills to maintain a favorable audience response to your message in the face of criticism or attacks on the soundness of your logic.

CAUSE AND EFFECT

Like the problem–solution pattern to which it is closely related, the cause and effect approach was introduced in Chapter 9 as a useful organizational strategy. One way to use the cause–effect method is to begin with an effect or problem, and then identify the causes of the problem in an effort to convince your listeners that the problem is significant. A speech on the growing problem of gangs might focus on poverty, drugs, and a financially crippled school system.

You could also organize a message by noting the problem and then spelling out the effects the problem has. If you identify the problem as too many unsupervised teenagers roaming your community's streets after 11:00 P.M., you could organize a speech noting the effects this problem is having on your fellow citizens.

THE MOTIVATED SEQUENCE

The motivated sequence is a five-step organizational plan that has proved successful for several decades. Developed by Alan Monroe, this simple yet effective strategy for organizing speeches incorporates principles that have been confirmed by research and practical experience.[11] Based on the problem–solution pattern, it also uses the cognitive dissonance approach, which we discussed in Chapter 16: First disturb your listeners, and then point them toward the specific change you want them to adopt. The five steps are attention, need, satisfaction, visualization, and action.

1. *Attention.* Your first goal is to get your listeners' attention. In Chapter 10, we discussed specific attention-catching methods of beginning a speech. Remember the particular benefits of using a personal or hypothetical example, a startling statement, an unusual statistic, a rhetorical question, or a well-worded analogy. The attention step is, in essence, the introduction to your speech.

   Vic Vieth began his prize-winning speech titled "Prisoners of Conscience" with this dramatic, attention-catching description:

   Tenzin Chodrak lived on nine ounces of grain a day as he was forced to work a rock-hard soil beneath a beating sun. In time, his hair fell out and his eyebrows fell off. Tortured by his hunger, he ate rats and worms and, eventually, his leather jacket.[12]

2. *Need.* After getting the attention of your audience, now establish why your topic, problem, or issue should concern your listeners. Arouse dissonance. Tell your audience why the current program, politician, or whatever you're attempting to change is not working. Convince them there is a need for a change. You must also convince your listeners that this need for a change affects them directly. During the need step, you should develop logical arguments backed by ample evidence to support your position.

   To document the need for greater involvement in human rights issues around the world, Vic established the need for concern in his "Prisoners of Conscience" speech with the following:

There is no accurate estimation of the number of the world's prisoners of conscience. (Prisoners of conscience are people who have been jailed for beliefs and convictions that challenge their government.) Human rights organizations are overburdened and understaffed, and what estimates they do provide us are only the roundest of guesses. Still, Amnesty International says there are perhaps 10,000 in the former Soviet Union and 2,000 in Poland, 15,000 in Turkey, and 10,000 spread across Africa, 5,000 in South America, and some 100,000 are strung across Pakistan, Afghanistan, Iran, Iraq, South Korea, and the Philippines. . . . In its most recent state of the world report, the United Nations conceded (that) our planet is still racked with "political liquidations, mass killings and torture."[13]

3. *Satisfaction.* After you present the problem or need for concern, you next briefly identify how your plan will satisfy the need. What is your solution to the problem? At this point in the speech, you need not go into great detail. Present enough information so that your listeners have a general understanding of how the problem may be solved.

Vic established the satisfaction step in his speech when he noted: "First, we must recognize that human rights is a worthy objective. . . . Second, once we recognize human rights as a worthy objective, we can move to make it once again a part of our foreign policy."[14]

4. *Visualization.* Now you need to give your audience a sense of what it would be like if your solution were or were not adopted. You could take a *positive visualization* approach: Paint a picture with words to communicate how wonderful the future will be if your solution is adopted. You could take a *negative visualization* approach: Tell your listeners how awful things will be if your solution is not adopted. If they think things are bad now, just wait; things will get worse. Or you could present both a positive and negative visualization of the future: The problem will be solved if your solution is adopted, and the world will be a much worse place if your solution is not adopted.

In moving to this step for his "Prisoners of Conscience" speech, Vic used a positive visualization approach when he said, "If we can muster the moral decency to defend political freedom, we may one day achieve political freedom for everyone, everywhere."[15]

He could have had an even stronger visualization step by noting the specific benefits of supporting his solution. He could have helped his audience visualize the specific joy men and women will have once they are set free. Martin Luther King's moving "I Have a Dream" speech (Appendix D) provided strong positive visualization:

I have a dream that one day this nation will rise up and live out the true meaning of its creed, "We hold these truths to be self-evident, that all men are created equal."

I have a dream that one day on the red hills of Georgia the sons of former slaves and the sons of former slaveowners will be able to sit down together at the table of brotherhood.

I have a dream that one day even the state of Mississippi, a state sweltering with the heat of injustice, sweltering with the heat of oppression, will be transformed into an oasis of freedom and justice.

I have a dream that my four little children will one day live in a nation where they will not be judged by the color of their skin but by the content of their character. I have a dream today.

I have a dream that one day, down in Alabama, with its vicious racists, with its governor having his lips dripping with the words of interposition and nullification, one day right there in Alabama little black boys and black girls will be able to join hands with little white boys and white girls as sisters and brothers. I have a dream today.

I have a dream that one day every valley shall be exalted, every hill and mountain shall be made low, the rough places will be made plane and the crooked places will be made straight, and the glory of the Lord shall be revealed, and all flesh shall see it together.[16]

5. *Action.* This last step forms the basis of your conclusion. You tell your audience the specific action they can take to implement your solution. Identify exactly what you want your listeners to do. Give them simple, clear, easy-to-follow steps to achieve your goal. For example, you could give them a phone number to call for more information, provide an address so that they can write a letter of support, hand them a petition to sign at the end of your speech, or tell them for whom to vote. Outline the specific action you want them to take.

In the "Prisoners of Conscience" speech, Vic identified some specific actions his audience could take:

It's up to us to support the work of organizations such as America's Watch and Amnesty International, chapters of which are on almost every campus, and it's up to us to elect, this election year, a government which places high on its list of priorities the defense of human rights.[17]

You can modify the motivated sequence to suit the needs of your topic and audience. If, for example, you are speaking to a receptive audience, you do not have to spend a great deal of time on the need step. They already agree that the need is serious. They may, however, want to learn about some specific actions that they can take to implement a solution to the problem. Therefore, you would be wise to emphasize the satisfaction and action steps.

Conversely, if you are speaking to a hostile audience, you should spend considerable time on the need step. Convince your audience that the problem is significant and that they should be concerned about the problem. You would probably not propose a lengthy, detailed action.

If your audience is neutral or indifferent, spend time getting their attention and inviting their interest in the problem. The attention and need steps should be emphasized.

The motivated sequence is a guide, not an absolute formula. Use it and the other suggestions about speech organization to help you achieve your specific objective. Be audience-centered; adapt your message to your listeners.

Aristotle defined *rhetoric* as "the process of gathering the available means of persuasion." In this chapter, we have described some of the means that are available to you.

 RECAP

ORGANIZATIONAL PATTERNS FOR PERSUASIVE SPEECHES

Type	Definition	Example
Problem–solution	Present the problem; then present the solution.	I. The national debt is too high. II. We need to raise taxes to lower the debt.
Refutation	Anticipate your listeners' key objections to your proposal and then address them.	I. Even though you may think we pay too much tax, we are really undertaxed. II. Even though you may think the national debt will not go down, tax revenue will lower the deficit.
Cause–effect	First present the cause of the problem; then note how the problem affects the listeners. Or, identify a known effect; then document what causes the effect.	I. The high national debt is caused by too little tax revenue and too much government spending. II. The high national debt will cause both inflation and unemployment to increase.
Motivated sequence	A five-step pattern of organizing a speech, consisting of these steps: attention, need, satisfaction, visualization, action.	I. Attention: Imagine a pile of one-thousand-dollar bills 67 miles high. That's our national debt. II. Need: The increasing national debt will cause hardships for our children and grandchildren. III. Satisfaction: We need higher taxes to reduce our debt. IV. Visualization: Imagine our country in the year 2050; it could have low inflation and full employment or be stuck with a debt ten times our debt today. V. Action: If you want to lower the debt by increasing tax revenue, sign my petition that I will send to our senators.

SAMPLE PERSUASIVE SPEECH

Alkali Batteries: Powering Electronics and Polluting the Environment[18]

Jeffrey E. Jamison, Emerson College, Massachusetts

One day the Energizer bunny will die. Since its inception in 1989 the lovable little pink bunny has not only interrupted television commercials and movie previews, but also has significantly helped to increase sales of Energizer batteries. Unfortunately, the creative people at Chiat, Day and Mojo may have hit closer to home than they realized when they developed the "it's still going" campaign. For we all know that one day the batteries inside the bunny will run out, and when they do, we just throw them out. Unfortunately, these batteries are still going—going into landfills and incinerators, where the dangerous chemicals they contain are still going—going into the air we breathe, the water we drink, and the food we eat. Michael Fisher, Executive Director of the Sierra Club, warns in a personal interview that unsafe disposal of alkali batteries will become one of America's most serious environmental threats during the next three to five years.

In order to understand how truly devastating the threat from batteries is to our environment and to ourselves, we need to first identify what it is about the batteries themselves that makes them so dangerous to the environment; then focus in on the problems with our current disposal methods; finally, consider the steps we must take to insure that our health and the environment are still going far into the future.

The threat to our health and to the environment that batteries present begins with the batteries themselves. In short, batteries are composed of very dangerous elements. David Macaulay explains in his book *The Way Things Work* that common alkali batteries are composed of three different elements: cadmium, mercury, and lead. Cadmium, which forms the core of the battery, acts as the energy source. Mercury, which circulates around the cadmium, stabilizes the reaction, producing a steady energy flow. Lead forms the protective casing of the battery. Unfortunately, as the *Wall Street Journal* pointed out on June 4, 1990, these same three elements are among the most dangerous substances in our environment. According to the JAMA, lead in the environment causes damage to both our immune system and neurological systems; cadmium is responsible for cancer as well as liver and kidney disease; and mercury can cause kidney and lung disease, neurological, and genetic disorders. The *Boston Globe* warned on March 19, 1990, that mercury, lead, and cadmium can enter our respiratory system through the air we breathe or by ingestion of contaminated food and/or water. Unlike other elements that our bodies can naturally flush out, these heavy metals only accumulate in our systems. When the toxicity levels of these elements reach a certain point, the effects are fatal.

While the batteries are inherently dangerous, when they are in your Walkman, flashlight, fire detectors, or toys they really pose no serious health or environmental threat. For batteries were designed with a lead casing to contain the hazardous materials during their use. However, it is when you dispose of these batteries that the dangerous substances they contain are being released into our environment.

In his 1990 book, *The Green Consumer,* John Elkington, from the United Nations Environment Programme, explains that we currently dispose of batteries in two ways: they are either buried in landfills or they are incinerated. And here is where the problem begins. Those batteries that are buried in landfills corrode, allowing the mercury, lead, and cadmium to seep into nearby groundwater, which contaminates our drinking water as well as the food chain. Even supposedly safe landfills, which

Jeffrey's opening statement is designed to catch the attention of the listeners.

Jeffrey immediately launches into the problem by stating how alkali batteries negatively affect our quality of life. He makes a connection between his problem and, according to Maslow's hierarchy, our most basic need: the need for air and water to survive.

He clearly identifies his purpose by previewing the major points he will make in his speech.

In this portion of his message, Jeffrey draws on research from credible sources to educate his listeners about the problem.

Having laid out the risks these chemicals pose to humans, he begins to focus his audience's attention by defining the problem more precisely.

Here he gets to the heart of the problem by noting how batteries are being dumped in landfills.

are lined to prevent substances buried there from entering the ecosphere, are not safe. The *Boston Globe* warned in its March 19, 1990 edition that mercury simply eats through the protective lining into the environment. In addition, the hole that mercury creates can allow other dangerous substances to enter the environment.

While disposal in landfills is dangerous. *The Green Consumer* adds that the second disposal method, incineration, is even more dangerous. Ironically, the battery industry recognizes the potential harm of incinerated batteries, and prints a warning label on batteries that reads: "Do not dispose in fire." When batteries are incinerated, the heavy metals they contain gasify and escape into the atmosphere, providing a more direct path into our bodies.

> *He explicitly states how the problem has a direct effect on his listeners' quality of life.*

Now how much damage can one alkali battery do? Not much. However, *Seventh Generation Magazine,* June of 1990, says considering that we throw away three billion house batteries each year, the consequences are disastrous. The *New York Times* warns that each year we are adding 150 tons of mercury, 130 tons of lead, and 170 tons of cadmium to the environment. Sean Hect, from the Environmental Action Coalition, explained in a personal interview that . . . we have not had one battery death (reported) because it is impossible to trace the path of the mercury, lead, and cadmium back to the batteries. However, he adds, considering that 50 percent of the mercury and 25 percent of the cadmium dumped into the environment each year comes from alkali batteries, this is a problem that clearly affects all of us.

> *Jeffrey uses statistics to document the significance of the problem.*

We have to realize that everything we throw away is recycled into the environment, through our air and water. We can no longer believe that once something is out of sight it is out of mind. It is this philosophy that has placed us in the environmental bind we are in today. We need to realize that these batteries are like time bombs, and they are activated once they are thrown into the garbage. The February 25, 1989 issue of the *New York Times* claims that one of the primary reasons we are oblivious to the situation is that we are "dependent on them to power scores of modern devices, from talking dolls and Walkmans to camcorders and laptop computers." *Business Japan,* March of 1990, claims that recent technology has invigorated the battery industry to the tune of $5 billion a year. And with more technology on its way, that figure is expected to triple within the next three to five years. On top of the fact that we are becoming increasingly dependent on these batteries, we think nothing of throwing them away, for they are referred to as disposable batteries. This is a contradiction; while we can throw the batteries away, we can never dispose of the mercury, lead, and cadmium. For they are still active in the environment years after we throw the batteries away. What is almost as shocking as the battery problem itself is that a few simple steps can make a significant difference.

> *He makes the issue he is discussing more urgent by describing the way the problem is growing.*

> *After spending most of his effort documenting the significance of the problem, he turns his attention to solutions.*

Summary

Means of persuasion are techniques that can help you convince your listeners to follow your recommendations. In this chapter, we emphasized how to persuade with credibility, logic, and emotion. Credibility is the view that a listener has of a speaker. The three factors of credibility are competence, trustworthiness, and dynamism. We also identified specific strategies for enhancing your credibility before, while, and after you speak.

Rhode Island, Florida, and New York have banned the incineration of household batteries. In addition, New York State is currently considering a battery bill, similar to the bottle bill of the 1980s. The battery bill would require that we pay a deposit, which is returned to us once we turn in our used batteries. While these are steps in the right direction, we cannot wait for our legislatures to act. We can all take steps individually to solve the problem. The *Recycler's Handbook* advocates recycling. We recycle paper and plastic, why not batteries? Recycling is simple. Collect your used batteries in a plastic container. Once the container is full, contact your local household hazard waste facility. Every municipality has one, and you can find this number in your local phone book. Then place the container on the curb, and the batteries will be picked up; the mercury, lead, and cadmium will be extracted and recycled. This is important considering that 50 percent of all the mercury and 25 percent of all the cadmium used in the United States goes into the production of alkali batteries. The elements will be reused and not just dumped into the environment. While recycling is a step in the right direction, we must also take steps to cut down on our dependency on alkali batteries.

His concluding line makes a direct reference to his introduction and provides closure to his message.

The 1991 book *Ecologue* explains that the most economically and environmentally sound solution is to use rechargeable batteries. One rechargeable battery will last as long as a hundred alkali batteries. So you're getting more bang for your buck, and at the same time, you are not shocking the environment. Rechargers and rechargeable batteries can be purchased in most hardware, appliance, and department stores. The batteries cost around $2 apiece and the rechargers will run around $20. The initial cost may seem high, but the return is invaluable both economically and environmentally.

Here he provides a specific action for the audience to take that will have a direct impact on the problem he has documented.

Every day millions of batteries are dumped into landfills and incinerators; in turn, every year, hundreds of thousands of tons of mercury, cadmium, and lead needlessly enter our air, water, and food supplies. We can no longer continue to consume these heavy metals. And the longer we wait to act, the worse the situation will become, because the elements will continue to build up in the environment and our bodies.

Now he is beginning to conclude his speech by summarizing the problem that he has documented.

These batteries can be very useful and valuable as long as we are responsible with them. As we've seen today, the batteries themselves are inherently dangerous; however, the real problem lies in the unsafe disposal of these batteries. After you walk out of the room today and the batteries of your Walkman, flashlight, or Nintendo Gameboy run out, don't throw them out; save them for a recycling day. When you go to replace these batteries, make sure you use rechargeable batteries. By recycling and recharging, we can make sure that not only the Energizer bunny but also our health and the environment are still going.

He explicitly gives his listeners two specific actions to take: recycle and recharge batteries. He makes a direct connection between his suggested actions and the problem he identified.

Using effective logical arguments hinges on the proof you employ. Proof consists of evidence plus the reasoning that you use to draw conclusions from evidence. The three types of reasoning discussed were inductive reasoning from specific instances or examples to reach a general conclusion, deductive reasoning from a general statement to reach a specific conclusion, and causal reasoning relating two or more events in such a way as to conclude that one or more of the events caused the others. We also presented suggestions for using four types of evidence: facts, examples, opinions, and statistics. We concluded our section on developing logical arguments by identifying several fallacies that you should avoid.

We noted that emotion theory has identified three dimensions of emotional response to a message: pleasure–displeasure, arousal–nonarousal, and power–powerlessness. Specific suggestions for appealing to audience emotions included examples; emotion-arousing words; nonverbal behavior; selected appeals to fear; and using appeals to several emotions such as hope, pride, courage, or the revered.

To persuade skillfully, you need to adapt your message to your audience. We reviewed strategies for adapting to receptive, neutral, and unreceptive audiences.

The chapter ended with specific strategies for organizing a persuasive speech. We discussed four patterns for organizing a persuasive speech: problem–solution, refutation, cause–effect, and the motivated sequence. The five steps of the motivated sequence are attention, need, satisfaction, visualization, and action. We suggested that you adapt the motivated sequence to your specific audience and persuasive objective.

● CRITICAL THINKING QUESTIONS

1. Imagine that you are delivering your final speech of the semester in your public speaking class. What specific strategies can you implement to enhance your initial, derived, and final credibility as a public speaker in the minds of your classmates?

2. Josh McCoy is speaking to his neighborhood homeowners' association, attempting to persuade his neighbors that a crime-watch program should be organized. What logical arguments and emotional strategies would help him ethically achieve his persuasive objective?

3. Janice Hakawa is pondering options for organizing her persuasive speech, which has the following purpose: "The audience should be able to support the establishment of a wellness program for our company." Using this purpose, draft the main ideas for a speech organized according to each of the following organizational patterns: problem–solution, refutation, cause–effect, the motivated sequence.

● ETHICAL QUESTIONS

1. Karl has a strong belief that the tragedy of the holocaust could occur again. He plans to show exceptionally graphic photographs of holocaust victims during his speech to his public speaking class. Is it ethical to show graphic, emotional photos to a captive audience?

2. Tony was surfing the Internet and found just the statistics that he needs for his persuasive speech. Yet he does not know the original source of the statistics—just the Internet address. Is that sufficient documentation for the statistics?

3. Martika wants to convince her classmates, a captive audience, that they should join her in a twenty-four-hour sit-in at the university president's office to protest the recent increase in tuition and fees. The president has made it

clear that any attempt to occupy his office after normal university closing hours will result in arrests. Is it appropriate for Martika to use a classroom speech to encourage her classmates to participate in the sit-in?

SUGGESTED ACTIVITIES

1. Identify three nationally known credible speakers. Identify methods and strategies that the speakers use to establish their credibility in a speaking situation.

2. Listen to a talk-radio program, and attempt to identify the types of reasoning used to develop a persuasive argument. Also, identify reasoning fallacies that you hear on call-in talk-radio programs.

3. Identify a speaking situation during which the speaker effectively used emotional appeals. Describe the strategies that were used effectively to obtain an emotional response from the audience.

4. Develop strategies for presenting the same persuasive speech objective to three different audiences: an unreceptive audience, a neutral audience, and a receptive audience. Note the different strategies that you used in attempting to adapt your message to different listeners.

5. Identify the faulty reasoning in the following arguments:

   A. We have to do something about the quality of life in our state. Either we should build more prisons or build more schools.

   B. Everyone knows we need to spend more money on the environment.

   C. As soon as the Republicans took control of Congress, the stock market in Mexico had trouble. The Republicans are to blame for the problems in Mexico.

   D. Baseball hall-of-famer Joe Dimaggio uses this coffee machine, so it must be good.

   E. It is obvious that anyone who switched from one political party to another party can have no credible options for balancing the federal budget.

USING TECHNOLOGY AND MEDIA

1. Listen to a talk-radio call-in program and analyze the appropriateness or inappropriateness of the logic, reasoning, and evidence people use to make persuasive points. Note whether the callers and the talk-show host use any reasoning fallacies.

2. As you listen to TV or radio commercials, try to identify the steps of the motivated sequence. Note which of the five steps the commercials emphasize most or least.

3. Discuss the appropriateness of unsolicited telephone sales pitches. What are their advantages and disadvantages as a means of persuasion?

"The Dinner Quilt."
Faith Ringgold

Special-Occasion Speaking

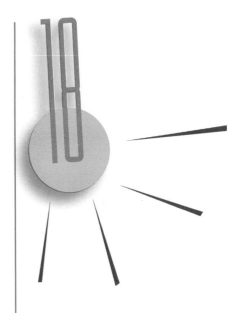

Historians agree that
the greatest banquet
speech in history was the
one by the ancient
Greek philosopher
Socrates moments after
he drank hemlock.
"Gack," he said, falling
face-first into his chicken.
The other Greeks
applauded like crazy.
—Dave Barry

● OBJECTIVES

**After studying this chapter you
should be able to do the following:**

1. *Identify and explain the requirements
   for two types of speaking
   situations likely to arise in the
   workplace.*

2. *List and describe seven types of
   ceremonial speeches.*

3. *Explain the purpose and characteristics
   of an after-dinner speech.*

here is money in public speaking. The ex-presidents, generals, athletes, and entertainment personalities who speak at the extravagant rallies orchestrated by motivational consultant Peter Lowe receive at least $30,000 for a single talk. In fact, before he became ill, former President Ronald Reagan was rumored to earn as much as $75,000 for a Lowe appearance.[1]

Although most of us will never be rewarded with such lucrative contracts for our public speaking efforts, it *is* likely that we will at some time be asked to make a business or professional presentation or to speak on some occasion that calls for celebration, commemoration, inspiration, or entertainment. Special occasions are important enough and frequent enough to merit study, regardless of the likelihood of resulting wealth or fame for the speaker.

In this chapter, we will discuss the various types of speeches that may be called for on special occasions, and examine the specific and unique audience expectations for each. First, we will discuss two speaking situations that are likely to occur in the workplace. We will then turn our attention to several types of ceremonial speeches and the after-dinner speech. We will end this chapter by annotating a successful special-occasion speech, a keynote address.

Public speaking in the workplace

Nearly every job involves the use of some public speaking skills. In many careers and professions, public speaking is a daily part of the job. Workplace audiences may range from a group of three managers to a huge auditorium filled with company employees. Presentations may take the form of routine meeting management, reports to company executives, training seminars within the company, or public relations speeches to people outside the company. The occasions and opportunities are many, and chances are good that you will be asked or expected to do some on-the-job public speaking in the course of your career. In addition to the information below, this text's Appendix C, on preparing visual aids for presentations, will help you succeed on these occasions.

● REPORTS

One of the most common types of on-the-job presentations is the report. You may be asked to report on how to increase sales in the next quarter or to present a market survey your division has conducted in the past several months. Whatever the specific objective of the report, the general purpose is to communicate information or policy, sometimes ending with a persuasive appeal to try some new course of action.

Most successful reports are structured in a manner similar to the following:

■ When you are presenting your report, keep in mind that your audience is there to hear you address a particular need or problem. Begin by briefly acknowledging that situation.

- If you are reporting on a particular project or study, explain how the information was gathered. Discuss what the research group decided to do to explore the problem.

- Finally, present the possible solutions you have come up with. For some reports, the most important part is this outline of new courses of action or changes in present policy. In addition, tell your audience what's in it for them—what benefits will accrue to them directly as a result of the new proposal. One business consultant suggests:

> Tune your audience into radio station WIIFM— What's In It For Me. Tell your listeners where the benefits are for them, and they'll listen to everything you have to say.[2]

In addition to listening to the presentation, audience members usually receive a written copy of the report.

● PUBLIC RELATIONS SPEECHES

People who work for professional associations, blood banks, utility companies, government agencies, universities, churches, or charitable institutions, as well as commercial enterprises, are often called on to speak to an audience about what their organization does or about a special project the organization has taken on. These speeches can be termed public relations speeches. They are designed to inform the public and improve relations with them—either in general, or because a particular program or situation has raised some questions.

As in presenting reports, the public relations speaker first discusses the need or problem that has prompted the speech. Then he or she goes on to explain how the company or organization is working to meet the need or solve the problem, or why it feels there is no problem.

It is important in public relations speaking to anticipate objections. The speaker may suggest and counter potential problems or criticisms, especially if past presentations have encountered some opposition to the policy or program. The speaker should emphasize the positive aspects of the policy or program and take care not to become unpleasantly defensive. He or she wants to leave the impression that the company or organization has carefully worked through potential pitfalls and drawbacks. It should be noted that not all reports make policy recommendations. Many simply summarize information for those who need to know. For example, local developer Jack Brooks is very aware that many of those present at the City Council meeting are opposed to his developing an area of land within the popular Smythson Creek greenbelt. Rather than ignore the objections, he deliberately and carefully addresses them:

> Many of you here tonight played in the Smythson Creek greenbelt as children. It was there that you learned to swim and that you hiked with your friends. I, too, share memories of those experiences.
> I want to assure you that my proposed development will actually help to preserve the greenbelt. We will dedicate in perpetuity an acre of unspoiled greenbelt

for each acre we develop. Further, we will actively seek to preserve that unspoiled land by hiring an environmental specialist to oversee its protection.

As things stand now, we risk losing the entire greenbelt to pollution and unmanaged use. I can promise a desirable residential development, plus the preservation of at least half the natural environment.

Chapter 19 will address other workplace communication challenges, such as meeting management and various forums for group presentations.

Ceremonial speaking

Ceremonial speeches make up a broad class of speeches delivered on many kinds of occasions. In this chapter, we will explore seven types of ceremonial speeches: introductions, award presentations and nominations, acceptances, keynote addresses, commencement addresses, commemorative addresses, and eulogies.

INTRODUCTIONS

Most of us have heard poor introductions. A nervous speaker making an introduction stands up and mispronounces the main speaker's name. Or the introducer speaks for five or ten minutes him- or herself.

An introductory speech is much like an informative speech. The speaker delivering the introduction provides information about the main speaker to the audience. The ultimate purpose of an introduction, however, is to arouse interest in the speaker and his or her topic. When you are asked to give a speech of introduction for a featured speaker or an honored guest, your purposes are similar to those of a good opening to a speech: You need to get the attention of the audience, build the speaker's credibility, and introduce the speaker's general subject. You also need to make the speaker feel welcome while revealing some personal qualities to the audience so that they can feel they know the speaker more intimately. There are two cardinal rules of introductory speeches: be brief and be accurate.

■ *Be brief.* The audience has come to hear the main speaker or honor the guest, not to listen to you.

■ *Be accurate.* Nothing so disturbs a speaker as having to begin by correcting the introducer. If you are going to introduce someone at a meeting or dinner, ask that person to supply you with relevant biographical data beforehand. If someone else provides you with the speaker's background, make sure that the information is accurate. Be certain that you know how to pronounce the speaker's name and any other names or terms you will need to use.

This short speech of introduction adheres to the two criteria we have just suggested: it's brief and it's accurate.

This evening, friends, we have the opportunity to hear one of the most innovative mayors in the history of our community. Mary Norris's experience in running her own real estate business gave her an opportunity to pilot a new approach to attracting new businesses to our community, even before she was elected mayor in last year's landslide victory. She was recently recognized as the most successful mayor in our state by the Good Government League. Not only is she a skilled manager and spokesperson for our city, but she is also a warm and caring person. I am pleased to introduce my friend, Mary Norris.

Finally, keep the needs of your audience in mind at all times. If the person you are introducing truly needs no introduction to the group, do not give one! Just welcome the speaker and step aside. "Friends" (or "Ladies and gentlemen"), "please join me in welcoming our guest speaker for tonight, the former chairman of this club, Mr. Daniel Jones." Note that the President of the United States is always introduced simply: "Ladies and gentlemen, the President of the United States."

● AWARD PRESENTATIONS AND NOMINATIONS

Presenting an award is somewhat like introducing a speaker or a guest: You need to remember that the audience did not come to hear you but to see and hear the winner of the award. Nevertheless, presenting an award is an important responsibility, one that has several distinct components.

First, when presenting an award, you should refer to the occasion of the presentation. Awards are often given to mark the anniversary of a special event, the completion of a long-range task, the accomplishments of a lifetime, or high achievement in some field.

Next, you should talk about the history and significance of the award. This section of the speech may be fairly long if the audience knows little about the award; it will be brief if the audience is already familiar with the history and purpose of the award. Whatever the award, a discussion of its significance will add to its meaning for the person who receives it.

The final section of the award presentation will be naming the person to whom it has been given. The longest part of this segment is the description of the achievements that contributed to receiving the award. That description should be in glowing terms. Hyperbole is appropriate here. If the name of the person getting the award has already been made public, you may refer to him or her by name throughout your description. If you are going to announce the individual's name for the first time, you will probably want to recite the achievements first and leave the person's name for last. Even though some members of the audience may recognize from your description the person about whom you are talking, you should still save the drama of the actual announcement until the last moment.

Nominating speeches are similar to award presentations. They, too, involve noting the occasion and describing the purpose and significance of, in this case, the office to be filled. The person making the nomination should explain clearly why the nominee's skills, talents, and past achievements serve as qualifications for the position. And the actual nomination should come at the end of the speech. When Senate minority leader Everett Dirksen nominated Barry Goldwater for the Republican presidential candidacy in 1964, he emphasized those personal qualities of the admittedly controversial candidate that he thought would appeal to the audience:

> *Whether in commerce or finance, in business or industry, in private or public service, there is such a thing as* COMPETENCE. *What is it but the right vision, the right touch, in the right way, at the right time? What man could be a jet pilot without this touch? But Barry Goldwater has demonstrated it over and over in his every activity. As Chief of Staff of his state National Guard, he brought about its desegregation shortly after World War II and long before Civil Rights became a burning issue. He brought integration to his own retail enterprises. For his own employees he established the 5-day week and a health and life insurance plan. All this was done without fanfare or the marching of bands.*[3]

And Dirksen ended his speech with the nomination itself:

> *. . . I nominate my friend and colleague, Barry Goldwater of Arizona, to be the Republican candidate for President of the United States.*

● ACCEPTANCES

For every award, there is usually at least a brief acceptance speech. Acceptance speeches have received something of a bad name because of the lengthy, emotional, rambling, and generally boring speeches delivered annually on prime-time TV by the winners of the film industry's Oscars. As the late humorist Erma Bombeck once wryly noted,

> *People exchange wedding vows in under thirty seconds. Clinton pledged to be President in less than thirty seconds. You only get thirty seconds to come up with the final "Jeopardy" answer. My kids can demolish a pizza in thirty seconds. So how long does it take to say, "Thank you?"*[4]

The same audience who may resent a lengthy oration will readily appreciate a brief, heartfelt expression of thinks. In fact, brief acceptance speeches can actually be quite insightful, even inspiring, and leave the audience feeling no doubt that the right person won the award.

Chances are that if you ever have to give an acceptance speech, it will be impromptu, since you will probably not know that you have won until the award is presented. A fairly simple three-part formula should help you compose a good acceptance speech on the spur of the moment.

First, you should thank the person for making the presentation and the organization that he or she represents. It is also gracious to thank a few people who have contributed greatly to your success—but not a long list of everyone you have ever known, down to the family dog.

Next, you should comment on the meaning or significance of the award to you. PLO leader Yasi Arafat interpreted his 1994 Nobel peace prize as a catalyst for continuing efforts toward peace in the Middle East:

I realize that this award, which is of ultimate significance and gesture, was not granted to me and to my two partners ... to crown an endeavor that we have completed but rather to encourage us to continue a road which we have started, continue in wider steps and deeper consciousness in order to convert the option of peace—the peace of the brave—from mere theory to a practice in reality.[5]

You may also wish to reflect on the larger significance of the award to the people and ideals it honors. In an eloquent acceptance speech, Elie Wiesel, Holocaust survivor, author, and lifelong advocate of human rights, began his acceptance speech for the 1986 Nobel peace prize with these words:

It is with a profound sense of humility that I accept the honor you have chosen to bestow upon me. I know your choice transcends me. This both frightens and pleases me.

It frightens me because I wonder: Do I have the right to represent the multitudes who have perished? Do I have the right to accept this great honor on their behalf? I do not. That would be presumptuous. No one may speak for the dead, no one may interpret their mutilated dreams and visions.

It pleases me because I may say that this honor belongs to all the survivors and their children, and through us, to the Jewish people with whose destiny I have always been identified.[6]

Finally, try to find some meaning the award may have for your audience—people who respect your accomplishments and who may themselves aspire to similar achievements. In what has become one of the most often quoted acceptance speeches ever made, novelist William Faulkner dedicated his 1950 Nobel prize for literature to "the young men and women already dedicated to the same anguish and travail, among whom is already that one who will some day stand here where I am standing."[7]

KEYNOTE ADDRESSES

A keynote address is usually presented at or near the beginning of a meeting or conference. The keynote emphasizes the importance of the topic or purpose of the meeting, motivates the audience to learn more or work harder, and sets the theme and tone for other speakers and events.

The hardest task the keynote speaker faces is being specific enough to arouse interest and inspire the audience. One way in which a keynote speaker can succeed in his or her task is to incorporate examples and illustrations to which the audience can relate. The late Texas congresswoman Barbara Jordan delivered two Democratic National Convention keynote addresses, one in 1976 and the most recent in 1992. Note how she used examples in this excerpt from the 1992 keynote:

> *The American dream is not dead. True, it is gasping for breath, but it is not dead. However, there is no time to waste because the American dream is slipping away from too many. It is slipping away from too many black and brown mothers and their children; from the homeless of every color and sex; from the immigrants living in communities without water and sewer systems. The American dream is slipping away from the workers whose jobs are no longer there because we are better at building war equipment that sits in warehouses than we are at building decent housing....*[8]

A complete keynote address is annotated at the end of this chapter.

COMMENCEMENT ADDRESSES

Every graduation must have a speech—sometimes several. This unwritten but binding law means that the commencement address should take its place among other types of special-occasion speeches. Sometimes the commencement speaker is an outstanding member of the faculty or administrative staff of the school; often the speaker is someone invited from outside the school. However he or she is selected, the commencement speaker must fulfill two important functions.

First, a commencement speaker should praise the graduating class. Since the audience includes the families and friends of the graduates, the commencement speaker can gain their good will (as well as that of the graduates themselves) by pointing up the significance of the graduates' accomplishments. Beverly Chiodo of Southwest Texas State University congratulated the graduates of that university in the opening remarks of her 1987 commencement address: "This is a [historic] day. Graduates, we, your family, friends, and professors, are glad we are here; and we rejoice in your accomplishments."[9]

The second function of the commencement speaker is to turn graduates toward the future. A commencement address is not the proper forum in which to bemoan the world's inevitable destruction or the certain gloomy future of today's graduates. Few could get away with the comments made some years ago by political satirist Art Buchwald to the graduates of Georgetown University:

I have examined your grades. Your collective entry into the world of business marks the end of the free enterprise system as we know it. Thank you.[10]

Rather than attempting sarcastic humor, most commencement speakers offer new, bright goals and try to inspire the graduates to reach for them. Heritage Foundation President Edwin J. Feulner, Jr., offered these words to the 1994 graduates of Grove City College, Grove City, Pennsylvania:

You are leaving this college with an education and an unmatched freedom of opportunity. Do not fear. Certainly, you have anxieties about your career and your future. But your degree and the philosophy of the school awarding it are a potent combination. You have been given the freedom that knowledge bestows and an understanding of the personal responsibility that freedom demands. What a preparation for an accomplished, noble life![11]

● COMMEMORATIVE ADDRESSES AND TRIBUTES

Commemorative addresses—those delivered during special ceremonies held to celebrate some past event—are often combined with tributes to the person or persons involved. For example, a speech given on the Fourth of July both commemorates the signing of the Declaration of Independence and pays tribute to those who signed it. Your town's sesquicentennial celebrates both the founding and the founders of the town. And if you were asked to speak at the reception for your grandparents' fiftieth wedding anniversary, you would probably relate the stories they've told you of their wedding day and then go on to praise their accomplishments during their fifty years together.

The speaker who commemorates or pays tribute is, in part, an informative speaker. He or she needs to present some facts about the event and/or people being celebrated. Then the speaker builds on those facts, urging the audience to let past accomplishments inspire them to achieve new goals. "Remember the Alamo!" the famous battle cry that inspired the Texans who fought for independence at San Jacinto, at once commemorated those massacred at the mission in San Antonio and drew upon their heroism for inspiration. Speaking at Pointe du Hoc, France, during June 1994 ceremonies to commemorate the fifty-year anniversary of D-Day, President Bill Clinton paid tribute to the assembled veterans:

We are the children of your sacrifice. We are the sons and daughters you saved from tyranny's reach. We grew up behind the shield of the strong alliances you forged in blood upon these beaches, on the shores of the Pacific and in the skies above us. We flourished in the nation you came home to build. The most difficult days of your lives bought us fifty years of freedom.[12]

His tribute completed, Clinton added this challenge: "Let us carry on the work you began here. You completed your mission here, but the mission of freedom goes on, the battle continues."

● EULOGIES

Speeches of tribute delivered when someone has died are an especially difficult form of commemorative address. When you deliver a eulogy, you should mention—indeed, linger over—the unique achievements of the person to whom you are paying tribute and, of course, express a sense of loss. At the funeral of former First Lady Jacqueline Kennedy in 1994, Senator Edward Kennedy remembered his sister-in-law in this way:

> *She was a blessing to us and to the nation, and a lesson to the world on how to do things right, how to be a mother, how to appreciate history, how to be courageous.*
>
> *No one else looked like her, spoke like her, wrote like her, or was so original in the way she did things.*[13]

It is also proper in a eulogy to include personal, even tasteful humorous recollections of the person who has died. In his April 27, 1994, eulogy for Former President Richard M. Nixon, Senator Robert Dole related this incident:

> *In her marvelous biography of her mother, Julie [Nixon Eisenhower] recalls an occasion where Pat Nixon expressed amazement at her husband's ability to persevere in the face of criticism. To which the President replied, "I just get up every morning to confound my enemies."*[14]

Finally, turn to the living, and encourage them to transcend their sorrow and sense of loss and feel instead gratitude that the dead person had once been alive among them. In eulogizing Winston Churchill, Adlai Stevenson assured his audience,

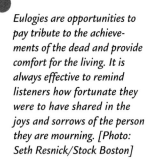

Eulogies are opportunities to pay tribute to the achievements of the dead and provide comfort for the living. It is always effective to remind listeners how fortunate they were to have shared in the joys and sorrows of the person they are mourning. [Photo: Seth Resnick/Stock Boston]

We are right to mourn. Yet in contemplating the life and the spirit of Winston Churchill, regrets for the past seem singularly insufficient. One rather feels a sense of thankfulness and of encouragement that throughout so long a life, such a full measure of power, virtuosity, mystery, and zest played over our human scene.[15]

After-Dinner Speaking

f you are a human being or even a reasonably alert shrub, chances are that sooner or later a club or organization will ask you to give a speech. The United States is infested with clubs and organizations, constantly engaging in a variety of worthwhile group activities such as (1) eating lunch; (2) eating dinner; (3) eating breakfast; and of course (4) holding banquets. The result is that there is a constant demand for post-meal speakers, because otherwise all you'd hear would be the sounds of digestion.[16]

With typically irreverent wit, columnist Dave Barry thus begins his observations of the activity known as after-dinner speaking. Certainly he is right about one thing: the popularity of mealtime meetings and banquets with business and professional organizations and service clubs. And with such meetings inevitably comes the requirement for an after-dinner speech.

Interestingly, not only is the after-dinner speech not always after *dinner* (as Barry points out, the meal is just as likely to be breakfast or lunch), but it is also not always *after* anything. The after-dinner speech may also be delivered before the meal or even between courses. Former First Lady Barbara Bush preferred to schedule speeches first and dinner later during state dinners. In another variation, Librarian of Congress James Billington, at a dinner in honor of philosopher Alexis de Tocqueville, served up one speech between each course, "so that one had to earn the next course by listening to the speech preceding it."[17] Regardless of the variation, the after-dinner speech is something of an institution, and one with which a public speaker should be prepared to cope.

After-dinner speeches may present information or persuade, but their primary purpose is to entertain. The theme of the meeting may suggest or even dictate the speaker's central idea, but he or she will usually avoid "heavy" subjects, such as diseases or social ills. The best after-dinner speech is one that makes a thought-provoking point with humor.

For most speakers, humor is the challenge of the after-dinner speech. Even the speaker who knows how to gather and organize information and deliver it effectively may be at a loss when it comes to techniques and strategies for creating humor. The Comedy Gym, an Austin, Texas–based school for aspiring stand-up comedians, advocates that one of the best ways to create humor is to start with what speakers know— "themselves, their lives, what makes *them* laugh."[18] Notice how student Chris O'Keefe, first-place winner in After-Dinner Speaking at the 1987 American Forensic Association National Individual Events Tournament, uses a personal anecdote (and some well-timed props) to open his speech on reading Shakespeare:

At a certain point in my life, I came to the realization that I wanted to spend my life's effort to become a great playwright. (Looks at watch) It has been about an hour and a half now and the feeling is still going strong. As a matter of fact, I have already written my first play. (Pulls out play) I wrote it out in the hall, or really wherever I could find a place to sit down. (Pulls out toilet paper) I hope that a hundred years from now people still admire, appreciate, and respect my work.[19]

If you do not have an endless supply of original funny stories, you may be comforted to learn that sourcebooks of humor are available.

It is true that some people seem to be "naturally" funny. Nonverbal comic devices such as timing and facial expression are their usual style. If you are not a funny person—if, for example, you cannot get a laugh from even the funniest joke—you may choose to prepare and deliver an after-dinner speech that is lighthearted and clever rather than uproariously funny. Such a speech can still be a success.

SAMPLE KEYNOTE ADDRESS
Opportunities for Hispanic Women: It's Up to Us[20]
Janice Payan

Thank you. I felt as if you were introducing someone else because my mind was racing back 10 years, when I was sitting out there in the audience at the Adelante Mujer conference. Anonymous. *Comfortable.* Trying hard to relate to our "successful" speaker, but mostly feeling like Janice Payan, working mother, *glad for a chance to sit down.*

I'll let you in on a little secret. I *still am* Janice Payan, working mother. The only difference is that I have a longer job title, and that I've made a few discoveries these past 10 years that I'm eager to share with you.

The first is that keynote speakers at conferences like this are *not* some sort of alien creatures. Nor were they born under a lucky star. They are ordinary *Hispanic women* who have stumbled onto an extraordinary discovery.

And that is: *Society lied to us.* We *do* have something up here! We *can* have not only a happy family but also a fulfilling career. We *can* succeed in school and *work* and *community life,* because the key is not supernatural powers, it is *perseverance.* Also known as *hard work! And God knows Hispanic women can do hard work!!!* We've been working hard for centuries, from sun-up 'til daughter-down!

One of the biggest secrets around is that successful Anglos were not born under lucky stars, either. The chairman of my company, Jack MacAllister, grew up in a small town in eastern Iowa. His dad was a teacher; his mom was a mom. Jack worked, after school, sorting potatoes in the basement of a grocery store. Of course I realize, *he could have been hoeing them,* like our migrant workers. Nevertheless, Jack came from humble beginnings. And so did virtually every other corporate officer I work with. The major advantage they had was living in a culture that allowed them to *believe* they would get ahead. So more of them did.

It's time for *Hispanic women* to believe we can get ahead, *because we can.* And because *we must.* Our families and workplaces and communities and nation need us to reach our full potential. There are jobs to be done, children to be raised, opportunities to be seized. We must look at those opportunities, choose the ones we will respond to, and *do something about them.* We must do so, for others. And we must do so, for ourselves. *Yes,* there are barriers. You're up

In her introduction, Payan identifies herself with her audience.

In the following four paragraphs, Payan develops her central idea and the theme (key note) of the conference: Hispanic women can succeed.

Sample Keynote Address

As noted earlier in this chapter, the keynote address is one kind of special-occasion speech. The keynote speaker's role is to open a conference or convention by establishing the theme, motivating and inspiring the audience, and setting the tone for other speakers and events to follow.

Janice Payan, vice president of U.S. West Communications, was asked to deliver the keynote address to the Adelante Mujer (Onward Women) conference in May of 1990. Her speech is noteworthy in part because she so successfully incorporated examples and illustrations to which the audience could relate. The text of her speech follows, with annotations.

against racism, sexism, and too much month at the end of the money. *But so was any role model you choose.*

Look at Patricia Diaz-Denis. Patricia was one of nine or ten children in a Mexican-American family that had low means, but high hopes. Her parents said that Patricia should go to college. But they had no money. So, little by little, Patricia scraped up the money to send herself. Her boyfriend was going to be a lawyer. And he told Patricia, "You should be a lawyer, too, because *nobody can argue like you do!*" Well, Patricia didn't even know what a lawyer was, but she became one—so successfully that she eventually was appointed to the Federal Communications Commission in Washington, D.C.

> *Payan supports her claim with a narrative example.*

Or look at Toni Pantcha, a Puerto Rican who grew up in a shack with dirt floors, no father, and often no food. But through looking and listening, she realized the power of *community*—the fact that people with very little, when working together, can create much. Dr. Pantcha has created several successful institutions in Puerto Rico, and to me, *she* is an institution. I can see the wisdom in her eyes, hear it in her voice, wisdom far beyond herself, like Mother Teresa.

> *A second and third example waylay any audience suspicions that the first example was an exception and strengthen the audience members' confidence in their own abilities to succeed.*

Or look at Ada Kirby, a Cuban girl whose parents put her on a boat for Miami. Mom and Dad were to follow on the next boat, but they never arrived. So Ada grew up in an orphanage in Pueblo, and set some goals, and today is an executive director at U.S. WEST's research laboratories.

Each of these women was Hispanic, physically deprived, but *mentally awakened to the possibilities of building a better world,* both for others and for themselves. Virtually every Hispanic woman in America started with a similar slate. In fact, let's do a quick survey. If you were born into a home whose economic status was something *less* than rich . . . please raise your hand. It's a good thing I didn't ask the *rich* to raise their hands. I wouldn't have known if anyone was listening. All right. So you were not born rich. As Patricia, Toni, and Ada have shown us, it doesn't matter. It's the choices we make from there on, that make the difference.

> *Payan synthesizes the common theme of the three examples, which reiterates the stated central idea of her speech.*

If you're thinking, "that's easy for *you* to say, Payan," then I'm thinking: "little do you know . . . ." If you think I got where I am because I'm smarter than you, or have more energy than you, you're wrong. If I'm so smart, why can't I parallel park? If I'm so energetic, why do I still need eight hours of sleep a night? And I mean *need.* If I hadn't had my eight hours last night, you wouldn't even want to *hear* what I'd be saying this morning!

> *Payan tells her own story in an extended personal narrative.*

[sample keynote address continued]

I am more like you and you are more like me than you would guess. I'm a third-generation Mexican-American . . . born into a lower middle-class family right here in Denver. My parents married young; she was pregnant. My father worked only about half the time during my growing-up years. He was short on education, skills, and confidence. There were drug and alcohol problems in the family. My parents finally sent my older brother to a Catholic high school, in hopes that would help him. They sent me to the same school, to *watch* him. That was okay.

In public school I never could choose between the "Greasers" and the "Soshes." I wanted desperately to feel that I "belonged." *But did not like feeling that I had to deny my past to have a future.* Anybody here ever feel that way?

Anyway, the more troubles my brother had, the more I vowed to avoid them. So, in a way, he was my inspiration. As Victor Frankl says, there is meaning in every life. By the way, that brother later died after returning from Vietnam.

I was raised with typical Hispanic female expectations. In other words: If you want to *do* well in life, you'd better . . . can anybody finish that sentence? Right! *Marry* well. I liked the idea of loving and marrying someone, but I felt like he should be more than a "meal ticket." And I felt like *I* should be more than a leech. I didn't want to feel so dependent. So I set my goals on having a marriage, a family, *and* a career. I didn't talk too much about those goals, so nobody told me they bordered on *insanity* for a Hispanic woman in the 1960s.

At one point, I even planned to become a doctor. But Mom and Dad said, "wait a minute. That takes something like 12 years of college." I had no idea how I was going to pay for *four* years of college, let alone *12.* But what scared me more than the cost was the *time:* In 12 years I'd be an *old woman.* Time certainly changes your perspective on that. My advice to you is, if you want to be a doctor, go for it! It doesn't take 12 years, anyway. If your dreams include a career that requires college . . . go for it! You may be several years older when you finish, but by that time you'd be several years older if you *don't* finish college, too.

For all my suffering in high school, I finished near the top of my graduating class. I dreamed of attending the University of Colorado at Boulder. You want to know what my counselor said? You already know. That I should go to a business college for secretaries, at most. But I went to the University of Colorado, anyway. I arranged my own financial aid: a small grant, a low-paying job, and a *big* loan. I just thank God that this was the era when jeans and sweatshirts were getting popular. That was all I had!

I'm going to spare you any description of my class work, except to say that it was difficult—and worth every painful minute. What I want to share with you is three of my strongest memories—and strongest learning experiences—which have nothing to do with books.

One concerns a philosophy professor who, I was sure, was a genius. What I liked best about this man was not the answers he had—but the questions. He asked questions about the Bible, about classic literature, about our place in the universe. He would even jot questions in the margins of our papers. And I give him a lot of credit for helping me examine my own life. I'm telling you about him because I think each of us encounter people who make us think—sometimes painfully. And I feel, very strongly, that we should listen to their questions and suffer through that thinking. We may decide everything in our lives is just like we want it. But we may also decide to change something.

My second big "non-book" experience was in UMAS—the United Mexican American Students. Lost in what seemed like a rich Anglo campus, UMAS was an island of familiarity: people who looked like me, talked like me, and *felt* like me. We shared our fears and hopes and hurts—and did something about them. We worked

Here the speaker ends her chronological autobiography and draws from it three of her most valuable learning experiences.

Notice the speaker's use of ordinals (first, second, third) as signposts.

hard to deal with racism on campus, persuading the university to offer Chicano studies classes. But the more racism we experienced, the angrier we became. Some members made bombs. Two of those members died. And I remember asking myself: "Am I willing to go up in smoke over my anger? Or is there another way to make a difference?" We talked a lot about this, and concluded that two wrongs don't make a right. Most of us agreed that working *within* the system was the thing to do. We also agreed not to deny our Hispanic heritage: not to become "coconuts"—brown on the outside and white on the inside—but to look for every opportunity to bring *our* culture to a table of many cultures. That outlook has helped me a great deal as a manager, because it opened me to listening to all points of view. And when a group is open to all points of view, it usually chooses the right course.

The third experience I wanted to share from my college days was the time they came nearest to ending prematurely. During my freshman year, I received a call that my mother had been seriously injured in a traffic accident. Both of her legs were broken. So was her pelvis. My younger brother and sister were still at home. My father was unemployed at the time, and I was off at college. So who do you think was elected to take on the housework? Raise your hand if you think it was my father. No??? Does anybody think it was *me?* I am truly amazed at your guessing ability. Or is there something in our Hispanic culture that says the women do the housework? Of course there is. So I drove home from Boulder every weekend; shopped, cleaned, cooked, froze meals for the next week, did the laundry, you know the list. And the truth is, it did not occur to me until some time later that my father could have done some of that. I had a problem, but I was part of the problem. I *did* resist when my parents suggested I should quit school. It seemed better to try doing everything, than to give up my dream. And it was the better choice. But it was also very difficult.

Which reminds me of another experience. Would it be too much like a soap opera if I told you about a personal crisis? Anybody want to hear a story about myself that I've never before told in public? While still in college, I married my high school sweetheart. We were both completing our college degrees. My husband's family could not figure out why I was pursuing college instead of kids, but I was. However, it seemed like my schoolwork always came last.

One Saturday night I had come home from helping my Mom, dragged into our tiny married-student apartment, cooked a big dinner for my husband, and as I stood there washing the dishes, I felt a teardrop trickle down my face. Followed by a flood. Followed by sobbing. *Heaving.* If you ranked crying on a scale of 1 to 10, this was an 11. My husband came rushing in with that . . . you know . . . that "puzzled-husband" look. He asked what was wrong. Well, it took me awhile to figure it out, to be able to put it into words. When I did, they were 12 words: "I just realized I'll be doing dishes the rest of my life."

Now, if I thought you'd believe me, I'd tell you *my* husband finished the *dishes.* He did not. But we both did some thinking and talking about roles and expectations, and, over the years, have learned to share the domestic responsibilities. We realized that we were both carrying a lot of old, cultural "baggage" through life. *And so are you.*

I'm not going to tell you what to do about it. But I am going to urge you to realize it, think about it, and even to cry over the dishes, if you need to. You may be glad you did. As for me, *What have I learned from all this?* I've learned, as I suggested earlier, that Hispanic women have bought into a lot of myths, through the years. Or at least *I* did. And I want to tell you now, especially you younger women, the "five things I wish I had known" when I was 20, 25, even 30. In fact, some of these things I'm *still* learning—at 37. Now for that list of "five things I wish I had known."

First: I wish I had known that I—like most Hispanic women—was underestimating my capabilities. When I first went to work for Mountain Bell, which has since

From her three learning experiences, Payan extracts a significant personal crisis. She captures the audience's attention by telling them they will be privy to an intimate experience "I've never before told in public."

The conclusion that Payan draws from her personal crisis about carrying "old, cultural 'baggage'" provides a transition into the next part of her speech, an enumeration and explanation of five things she wishes she had known earlier in life. The next section of her speech deals with these five points.

[sample keynote address continued]

become U.S. WEST Communications, I thought the "ultimate" job I could aspire to would be district manager. So I signed up for the courses I knew would help me achieve and handle that kind of responsibility. I watched various district managers, forming my own ideas of who was most effective—and why. I accepted whatever responsibilities and opportunities were thrown my way, generally preparing myself to be district manager.

My dream came true. But then it almost became a nightmare. After only 18 months on the job, the president of the company called me and asked me to go interview with *his* boss—the president of our parent company. And the next thing I knew, I had been promoted to a job *above* that of district manager. Suddenly, I was stranded in unfamiliar territory. They gave me a big office at U.S. WEST headquarters down in Englewood, where I pulled all the furniture into one corner. In fact, I sort of made a little "fort." From this direction, I could hide behind the computer. From that direction, the plants. From over here, the file cabinet. Safe at last. *Until,* a friend from downtown came to visit me. She walked in, looked around, and demanded to know: "*What is going on here?* Why was your door closed? Why are you all scrunched up in the corner?" I had all kinds of excuses. But she said: "You know what I think? I think you're afraid you don't deserve this office!"

As she spoke, she started dragging the plants away from my desk. For a moment, I was angry. Then afraid. Then we started laughing, and I helped her stretch my furnishings—and my confidence. And it occurred to me that had I pictured, from the beginning, that I could become an executive director, I would have been better prepared. I would have pictured myself in that big office. I would have spent more time learning executive public speaking. I would have done a lot of things. And I began to do them with my new, expanded vision of becoming an officer—which subsequently happened.

I just wish that I had known, in those early years, how I was underestimating my capabilities. I suspect that *you are, too.* And I wonder: *What are you going to do about it?*

Second: I wish I had known that power is not something others give you. It is something that comes from *within yourself* . . . and which you can then share with others.

In 1984, a group of minority women at U.S. WEST got together and did some arithmetic to confirm what we already knew. Minority women were woefully underrepresented in the ranks of middle and upper management. We had a better chance of winning the lottery! So we gathered our courage and took our case to the top. Fortunately, we found a sympathetic ear. The top man told us to take our case to *all* the officers. We did. But we were scared. And it showed. We sort of "begged" for time on their calendars. We apologized for interrupting their work. Asked for a little more recognition of our plight. And the first few interviews went terribly. Then we realized: we deserve to be on their calendars as much as anyone else does. We realized that under-utilizing a group of employees is not an interruption of the officers' work—it *is* the officers' work. We realized that we should not be asking for help—we should be *telling* how *we could help.* So we did.

And it worked. The company implemented a special program to help minority women achieve their full potential. Since then, several of us have moved into middle and upper management, and more are on the way. I just wish we had realized, in the beginning, where power really comes from. It comes from within yourself . . . and which you can then share with others. I suspect *you* need to be reminded of that, too. And I wonder: *What are you going to do about it?*

Third: I wish I had known that when I feel envious of others, I'm really just showing my lack of confidence in myself. A few years ago, I worked closely with one of my

Payan continues to develop her points with personal illustrations.

Again, she uses ordinal numbers as signposts.

co-workers in an employee organization. She is Hispanic. Confident. Outgoing. In fact, she's so likeable I could hardly stand her! But as we worked together, I finally realized: She has those attributes; I have others. And I had to ask myself: do I want to spend the time it would take to develop her attributes, or enjoy what we can accomplish by teaming-up our different skills? I realized that is the better way. I suspect that you may encounter envy from time to time. And I wonder: *What are you going to do about it?*

Fourth: I wish I had realized that true success is never something you earn single-handedly. We hear people talk about "networking" and "community" and "team-building." What they mean is an extension of my previous idea: We can be a lot more effective working in a group than working alone.

This was brought home to me when I was president of our Hispanic employees' organization at U.S. WEST Communications. I wanted my administration to be the best. So I tried to do everything myself, to be sure it was done right. I wrote the newsletter, planned the fund-raiser, scheduled the meetings, booked the speakers, everything. For our big annual meeting, I got the chairman of the company to speak. By then, the other officers of the group were feeling left out. Come to think of it, they *were* left out. Anyway, we were haggling over who got to introduce our big speaker. I was determined it should be me, since I so "obviously" had done all the work.

As it turned out, I missed the big meeting altogether. My older brother died. And I did a lot of painful thinking. For one thing: I was glad my team was there to keep things going while I dealt with my family crisis. But more important: I thought about life and death and what people would be saying if *I* had died. Would I prefer they remember that "good ol' Janice sure did a terrific job of arranging every last detail of the meeting?" Or that "we really enjoyed working with her"? "Together, we did a lot." All of us need to ask ourselves that question from time to time. And I wonder: *What are you going to do about it?*

Hispanic women in America have been victims of racism, sexism, and poverty for a long, long time. I know, because I was one of them. I also know that when you stop being a victim is largely up to you. I don't mean you should run out of here, quit your job, divorce your husband, farm out your kids, or run for president of the United States.

But I *do* mean that "whatever" you can dream, you can become. A couple of years ago, I came across a poem by an Augsburg College student, Devoney K. Looser, which I want to share with you now.

> "I wish someone had taught me long ago
> "How to touch mountains
> "Instead of watching them from breathtakingly safe distances.
> "I wish someone had told me sooner
> "That cliffs were neither so sharp nor so distant nor so solid as they seemed.
> "I wish someone had told me years ago
> "That only through touching mountains can we reach peaks called beginnings, endings or exhilarating points of no return.
> "I wish I had learned earlier that ten fingers and the world shout more brightly from the tops of mountains
> "While life below only sighs with echoing cries.
> "I wish I had realized before today
> "That I can touch mountains
> "But now that I know, my fingers will never cease the climb."

> Please, my sisters, never, ever, cease the climb.
> Adelante Mujer!

Payan concludes her final point and her speech with a poem. Her conclusion fulfills the duty of the keynote speaker to inspire and motivate the audience, and to set the tone for the rest of the conference.

Summary

Chances are that at some time most of us will be called on to speak in a business or professional setting, or for some occasion that calls for celebration, commemoration, inspiration, or entertainment. These *special-occasion speeches* are critical thinking activities that require the speaker to synthesize and apply his or her speaking skills to unique situations.

Public speaking skills are used frequently in the workplace, from making report presentations, to representing your company or profession before the public. In this chapter we discussed the unique requirements of these two professional speaking challenges.

We next explored guidelines for and offered examples of several types of ceremonial speeches, including introductions, award presentations and nominations, acceptances, keynote addresses, commencement addresses, commemorative addresses, and tributes and eulogies.

We discussed after-dinner speaking, an established institution that at its best makes a thought-provoking point with humor. We offered a number of guidelines for impromptu speaking, which may be required by many special occasions, and we ended the chapter with an annotated special-occasion speech, a keynote address.

● CRITICAL THINKING QUESTIONS

1. Having just completed her degree, Maya has a job interview for a position she really wants. You and she became friends when you took public speaking as sophomores, and she has asked your advice in preparing for the interview. Explain to Maya how she can apply to her interview some of the principles and skills the two of you learned in public speaking class.

2. A well-known author and poet is coming to campus for a series of lectures. Because you are president of the English Club, you have been asked to introduce this guest for her opening lecture. What will you do to ensure that you follow the two "cardinal rules" of introductory speeches?

3. Now that she has been elected student body president, Rita knows that she will be called on to deliver impromptu remarks on a number of occasions. Offer Rita pointers that she can apply to any impromptu speaking situation.

ETHICAL QUESTIONS

1. You have been a member of the jury during a highly publicized and controversial murder trial in your community. After the verdict is delivered, you find yourself in great demand as a keynote speaker for meetings of local organizations. Several offer to pay you well. Is it ethical to "cash in" on your experiences in this way?

2. Even during times of intense personal crisis—for example, the death of a family member—the press relentlessly pursues celebrities to try to elicit impromptu statements. Is this an ethical practice? Does the public's right to know justify the invasion of privacy?

SUGGESTED ACTIVITIES

1. Each student should place a common object in a large grocery bag and bring it to class. Your instructor will gather the bags and redistribute them at random. When it is your turn to speak, remove the item from the bag you received and deliver a short impromptu speech in which you try to sell the object to your audience, following the steps of the motivated sequence.

2. Attend a special-occasion speaking event, such as a school commencement, an award ceremony, or a luncheon for the retiring editor of your school newspaper. Write a critique of the speeches given, and evaluate the speeches based on the criteria presented in this chapter.

3. Pair up with another student in the class to discuss your common interests, vocational goals, and hobbies. Discover something your partner does well, and invent an award that you could give your colleague. Deliver a short presentation speech in which you bestow your award (e.g., "Best Short Story Written in English Class," "Best Piano Player in the Community"). The recipient of the award should then deliver a short acceptance speech.

USING TECHNOLOGY AND MEDIA

1. Videotape several of the acceptance speeches during some televised awards ceremony—the Oscars, the Tony Awards, the Country Music Awards, or the Peoples' Choice Awards, for example. Analyze the success of these speeches, based on the suggestions offered in this chapter.

"Conference Room."
Diana Ong/SuperStock

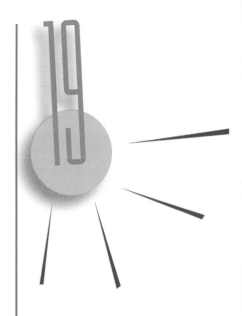

Speaking in Small Groups

Never doubt that a small group of thoughtful concerned citizens can change the world. Indeed, it's the only thing that ever has.
—Margaret Mead

● OBJECTIVES

After studying this chapter you should be able to do the following:

1. Define small group communication.

2. Organize group problem solving, using the steps of reflective thinking.

3. Participate effectively in a small group as a member or leader.

4. Make effective contributions to a group meeting.

5. Present group conclusions in a symposium, forum, panel presentation, or written report.

6. Develop a plan for coordinating a group project.

t has been estimated that more than 11 million meetings are held every day in the United States. Groups are an integral part of our lives. Work groups, family groups, therapy groups, committees, and group projects for classes are just a few of the groups in which we may participate at one time or another. Chances are that you have had considerable experience in communicating in small groups.

Why learn about group communication in a public speaking class? Aristotle identified the link between public speaking and group discussion over two thousand years ago when he wrote, "Rhetoric is the counterpart of dialectic." By this he meant that our efforts to persuade are closely linked to own group efforts to search for truth.

In his time, people gathered to discuss and decide public issues in a democratic manner. Today we still turn to a committee, jury, or task force to get facts and make recommendations. We still "search for truth," in groups. And, as in ancient Athens, once we believe we have found the truth, we still present the message to others in speeches and lectures.

This chapter concentrates on group problem solving and decision making for at least two main reasons.[1] First, you will spend a major part of your work time in small groups. Up to 15 percent of a typical organization's total personnel budget is spent on group work. Middle managers generally spend up to 35 percent of their time working in groups. Most senior managers work in groups up to 60 percent of their working day.[2] A second reason to learn about groups is that it can help reduce some of the uncertainty and anxiety you may have about group deliberations. If you know more about group processes, you can improve your skill at working in groups and therefore your enjoyment of it as well.

In this chapter, you will learn some key communication principles and skills to help you work as a productive member of a team. Specifically, you will discover what small group communication is, and you will learn to identify the advantages and disadvantages of working in groups, describe ways to improve group problem solving, recognize leadership skills, and become an effective group participant or group leader. You will also learn some tips for planning and executing a group project. By the end of the chapter, you will be able to use various formats for reporting group findings to others.

What is small group communication? It occurs when a group of three to around a dozen people interact who share a common purpose, feel a sense of belonging to the group, and influence one another. When groups are larger than twelve people, communication usually resembles public speaking more than group interaction.

Solving problems in groups

A central purpose of many groups is solving problems. Problem solving is a means of finding ways of overcoming obstacles to achieve a desired goal. How can we raise money for the new library? What should be done to improve the local economy? How can we make higher education affordable for everyone in our state? Each of these questions implies that there is an obstacle (lack of money) blocking the achievement of a desired goal (new library, more local income, affordable education).

Imagine that you have been assigned to suggest ways to make a college education more affordable. The problem: The high cost of higher education keeps many people from their goal of attending college. How would you begin to organize a group to solve this problem? In 1910 John Dewey, a philosopher and educator, identified the way most individuals tackle a problem. He called his method of problem solving **reflective thinking.** His multistep method has been adapted by groups as a way to organize the process of solving problems. Here are his suggestions: (1) Identify and define the problem, (2) analyze the problem, (3) generate possible solutions, (4) select the best solution, and (5) test and implement the solution. Although not every problem-solving discussion has to follow these steps, reflective thinking does provide a helpful blueprint that can relieve some of the uncertainty that exists when groups try to solve problems.

reflective thinking
A method of structuring a problem-solving discussion that includes the following steps: (1) identify and define problem, (2) analyze the problem,(3) generate possible solutions, (4) select the best solution, and (5) test and implement the solution.

1. IDENTIFY AND DEFINE THE PROBLEM

Groups work best when they define their problem clearly and early in their problem-solving process. To reach a clear definition, the group should consider the following questions:

- What is the specific problem that concerns us?

- What terms, concepts, or ideas do we need to understand in order to solve the problem?

- Who is harmed by the problem?

- When do the harmful effects occur?

Policy questions can help define a problem and also identify the course of action that should be taken to solve it. As you recall from chapter 16, policy questions begin with the words, "What should be done about " or "What could be done to improve . . . " Here are some examples:

- What should be done to improve security on our campus?

- What should be done to improve the tax base in our state?

- What steps can be taken to improve the United States' trade balance with other countries?

If your group were investigating the high cost of pursuing a college education, for example, after defining key terms, such as "higher education" and "college," and gathering statistics about the magnitude of the problem, you could phrase your policy question this way: "What could be done to reduce the high student cost of attending college?"

2. ANALYZE THE PROBLEM

■
analyze
To examine the causes, effects, and history of a problem to better understand it.

Ray Kroc, founder of McDonald's, said, "Nothing is particularly hard if you divide it into small jobs." Once the group understands the problem and has a well-worded question, the next step is to analyze the problem. **Analysis** is a process of examining the causes, effects, symptoms, history, and other background information that will help a group eventually reach a solution. When analyzing a problem, a group should consider the following questions:

■ What is the history of the problem?

■ How extensive is the problem?

■ What are the causes, effects, and symptoms of the problem?

■ Can the problem be subdivided for further definition and analysis?

■ What methods do we already have for solving the problem, and what are their limitations?

■ What new methods can we devise to solve the problem?

■ What obstacles might keep us from reaching a solution?

To analyze the problem of the high cost of attending college, your discussion group will have to use the library to research the history of the problem and existing methods of solving it (see Chapter 7).

Then, besides discussing these questions, the group should also develop practical criteria for evaluating an acceptable solution. Criteria are standards for making judgments. They help you recognize a good solution when you encounter one; criteria also help the group stay focused on a goal. Typical criteria for an acceptable solution specify that the solution should be implemented on schedule, should be attainable within a given budget, should be agreed to by all group members, and should remove the problem.

3. GENERATE POSSIBLE SOLUTIONS

When your discussion group has identified, defined, and analyzed the problem, you will be ready to generate possible solutions using group brainstorming (see Chapter 6). Use the following guidelines:

■ *Set aside judgment and criticism.* Criticism and faultfinding stifle creativity. If group members find withholding judgment difficult, have the individual members write suggestions on paper first and then share the ideas with the group.

■ *Think of as many possible solutions to the problem as you can.* All ideas are acceptable, even wild and crazy ones. Piggyback off one another's ideas. All members must come up with at least one idea.

■ *Have a member of the group record all the ideas that are mentioned.* Use a flip chart or chalkboard, if possible, so that all ideas can be seen and responded to.

■ *After a set time has elapsed, evaluate the ideas, using criteria the group has established.* Approach the solutions positively. Do not be quick to dismiss an idea, but do voice any concerns or questions you might have. The group can use brainstorming again later if it needs more creative ideas.

4. SELECT THE BEST SOLUTION

Next, the group needs to select the solution that best meets the criteria and solves the problem. At this point, the group may need to modify its criteria or even its definition of the problem. To help the group evaluate the solution, consider the following questions:

■ Which of the suggested solutions deals best with the obstacles?

■ Does the suggestion solve the problem in both the short and the long term?

■ What are the advantages and disadvantages of the suggested solution?

■ Does the solution meet the established criteria?

■ Should the group revise its criteria?

■ What is required to implement the solution?

- When can the group implement the solution?

- What result will indicate success?

To reach group agreement on a solution, some group members will need to abandon their attachment to their individual ideas for the overall good of the group. Experts who have studied how to achieve **consensus**—all members supporting the final decision—suggest that it helps to summarize frequently and keep the group oriented toward its goal. Emphasizing where group members agree, clarifying misunderstandings, writing down known facts for all members to see, and keeping the discussion focused on issues rather than emotions are also strategies that facilitate group consensus.

consensus
All group members support and are committed to the decision of the group.

5. TEST AND IMPLEMENT THE SOLUTION

The group's work is not finished when it has identified a solution. "How can we put the solution into practice?" and "How can we evaluate the quality of the solution?" have yet to be addressed. The group may want to develop a step-by-step plan that describes how the solution will be implemented, a time frame for implementation, and a list of individuals who will be responsible for carrying out specific tasks.

RECAP

STEPS IN PROBLEM SOLVING: REFLECTIVE THINKING

1. Identify and clearly define the problem.

2. Analyze the problem.

3. Generate possible solutions.

4. Select the best solution.

5. Test and implement the solution.

Tips for participating in small groups

To be an effective group participant, you have to understand how to manage the problem-solving process. But knowing the steps is not enough; you also need to prepare for meetings, evaluate evidence, effectively summarize the group's progress, listen courteously, and be sensitive to conflict.

COME PREPARED FOR GROUP DISCUSSIONS

To make a contribution at group meetings, you need to be informed about the issues. Prepare for group discussions by researching the issues. If the issue before your group is the use of asbestos in school buildings, for example, research the most recent scientific findings about the risks of this hazardous material. Chapter 7 described how to use the library and the resources of the Internet to gather information for your speeches. Use those research techniques to prepare for group deliberations as well. Bring your research notes to the group; don't just rely on your memory or your personal opinion to carry you through the discussion. Without research, you will not be able to analyze the problem adequately.

DO NOT SUGGEST SOLUTIONS BEFORE ANALYZING THE PROBLEM

Research suggests that you should analyze a problem thoroughly before trying to zero in on a solution.[3] Resist the temptation to settle quickly on one solution until your group has systematically examined the causes, effects, history, and symptoms of a problem.

EVALUATE EVIDENCE

One study found that a key difference between groups that make successful decisions and those that don't, lies in the ability of the group members to examine and evaluate evidence.[4] Ineffective groups are more likely to reach decisions quickly without considering the validity of evidence (or sometimes without any evidence at all). Such groups usually reach flawed conclusions.

HELP SUMMARIZE THE GROUP'S PROGRESS

Because it is easy for groups to get off the subject, group members need to summarize frequently what has been achieved and to point the group toward the goal or task at hand. One research study suggests that periodic overviews of the discussion's progress can help the group stay on target.[5] Ask questions about the discussion process rather than the topic under consideration: "Where are we now?" "Could someone summarize what we have accomplished?" and "Aren't we getting off the subject?"

LISTEN AND RESPOND COURTEOUSLY TO OTHERS

Chapter 4's suggestions for improving listening skills are useful when you work in groups, but understanding what others say is not enough. You also need to respect their points of view. Even if you disagree with someone's ideas, keep your emotions in check and respond courteously. Being closed-minded and defensive usually breeds group conflict.

HELP MANAGE DISAGREEMENT

In the course of exchanging ideas and opinions about controversial issues, disagreements are bound to occur. You can help prevent conflicts from derailing the problem-solving process by doing the following:

Group leaders do not have all the answers. The most effective groups divide leadership responsibilities, first assessing the tasks that need to be accomplished. [Photo: Greg Pearc/Tony Stone Images]

- Keep the discussion focused on issues, not personalities.
- Rely on facts rather than on personal opinions for evidence.
- Seek ways to compromise; don't assume that there must be a winner and a loser.
- Try to clarify misunderstandings in meaning.
- Be descriptive rather than evaluative and judgmental.
- Keep emotions in check.

If you can apply these basic principles, you can help make your group an effective problem-solving team.

Leadership in small groups

To lead is to influence others. Some see a leader as one individual empowered to delegate work and direct the group. In reality, however, group leadership is often shared.

LEADERSHIP RESPONSIBILITIES

causal reasoning
A process of reasoning in which two or more events are related in such a way as to conclude that one or more of the events caused the others.

Leaders are needed to help get tasks accomplished and maintain a healthy social climate for the group. Rarely does one person perform all of these leadership responsibilities, even if a leader is formally appointed or elected. Most often a number of individual group members assume some specific leadership task, based on their personalities, skills, sensitivity, and the group's needs. If you determine that the group needs a clearer focus on the task or that maintenance roles are needed, be ready to influence the group appropriately to help get the job done in a positive, productive way. Figure 19.1 shows the specific roles for both *task* and *maintenance* functions.[6]

FIGURE 19.1
Leadership roles in groups and teams

LEADERSHIP ROLES IN GROUPS AND TEAMS

Leaders Help Get Tasks Accomplished

TASK LEADERSHIP ROLES

Agenda setter: helps establish the group's agenda

Secretary: takes notes during meetings and distributes handouts before and during the meeting

Initiator: proposes new ideas or approaches to group problem solving

Information seeker: asks for facts or other information that helps the group deal with the issues and may also ask for clarification of ideas or obscure facts

Opinion seeker: asks for clarification of the values and opinions expressed by group members

Information giver: provides facts, examples, statistics, and other evidence that help the group achieve its task

Opinion giver: offers opinions about the ideas under discussion

Elaborator: provides examples to show how ideas or suggestions would work

Evaluator: makes an effort to judge the evidence and the conclusion the group reaches

Energizer: tries to spur the group to further action and productivity

Leaders Help Maintain a Healthy Social Climate

GROUP MAINTENANCE LEADERSHIP ROLES

Encourager: offers praise, understanding, and acceptance of others' ideas

Harmonizer: mediates disagreements that occur between group members

Compromiser: attempts to resolve conflicts by trying to find an acceptable middle ground between disagreeing group members

Gatekeeper: encourages the participation of less talkative group members and tries to limit lengthy contributions of other group members

Leaders can be described by the types of behavior, or leadership styles, that they exhibit as they influence the group to help achieve its goal. When you are called upon to lead, do you give orders and expect others to follow you? Or do you ask the group to vote on the course of action to follow? Or maybe you don't try to influence the group at all. Perhaps you prefer to hang back and let the group work out its own problems.

These strategies describe three general leadership styles: *authoritarian, democratic,* and *passive.*[7] Authoritarian leaders assume positions of superiority, giving orders and assuming control of the group's activity. Although authoritarian leaders can usually organize group activities with a high degree of efficiency and virtually eliminate uncertainty about who should do what, most problem-solving groups prefer democratic leaders.

Having more faith in their groups than do authoritarian leaders, democratic leaders involve their groups in the decision-making process rather than dictating what should be done. Democratic leaders focus more on guiding discussion than on issuing commands.

Passive leaders allow a group complete freedom in all aspects of the decision-making process. They do little to help the group achieve its goal. This style of leadership (or nonleadership) often leaves a group frustrated because it lacks guidance and has to struggle with organizing the work. Figure 19.2 compares the three styles.

What is the most effective leadership style? Research suggests that no single style is most effective in all group situations. Sometimes a group needs a strong authoritarian leader to make decisions quickly so that the group can achieve its goal. Although most groups prefer a democratic leadership style, leaders sometimes need to assert their authority to get the job done. The best leadership style depends on the nature of the group task, the power of the leader, and the relationship between the leader and his or her followers.

Managing meetings

Even though millions of meetings take place each day, most people don't like them. President John Kennedy was quoted as saying, "Most committee meetings consist of twelve people to do the work of one." Others agree with humorist Dave Barry's analogy in which he compared a modern business meeting to a funeral, noting that in a meeting " . . . you have a gathering of people who are wearing uncomfortable clothing and would rather be somewhere else. The major difference is that most funerals have a definite purpose. Also, nothing is ever really buried in a meeting."[8]

What bothers meeting attendees most? Here is a list of the most cited meeting sins:

Getting off the subject

No goals or agenda

FIGURE 19.2
Leadership Styles

LEADERSHIP STYLES

Authoritarian	Democratic	Passive
1. All determination of policy made by leader.	1. All policies are a matter of group discussion and decision, encouraged and assigned by the leader.	1. Complete freedom for group or individual decisions; minimum leader participation.
2. Techniques and activity steps dictated by the authority, one at a time; future steps are always largely uncertain.	2. Discussion period yields broad perspectives; general steps to group goal are sketched out; when technical advice is needed, leader suggests alternative procedures.	2. Leader supplies various materials, making it clear that he or she can supply information when asked but taking no other part in the discussion.
3. Leader dictates specific work tasks and teams.	3. Members are free to work with anyone; group decides on division of tasks.	3. Complete nonparticipation of leader.
4. Leader tends to be personal in praise or criticism of each member; remains aloof from active group participation except when directing activities.	4. Leader is objective or fact-minded in praise and criticism, trying to be a regular group member in spirit without doing too much of the work.	4. Leader offers infrequent spontaneous comments on member activities and makes no attempt to appraise or control the course of events.

Too long

Poor or inadequate preparation

Inconclusive

Disorganized

Ineffective leadership/lack of control

Irrelevance of information discussed

Time wasted during meetings

Starting late

Not effective for making decisions

Interruptions from within and without

Certain individuals dominate the discussion

Rambling, redundant, or digressive discussion

No published results or follow-up actions[9]

If these are the key meeting problems, what are the solutions? The short answer to this question is a simple one: Don't do these things. You may, however, need more direction than that, so here are a few suggestions to help you manage group meetings with skill.

To be effective, a meeting should have a balance between two characteristics: *structure* and *interaction*. Structure refers to such attributes as an organized agenda and a logical, rational approach to discussing the issues. A meeting with too much structure resembles a speech. When there is a minimum of interaction and only one or two people do all the talking, participants may wonder why there is a need for a meeting; the information could have been distributed by memo. Interaction includes the dynamic process of managing the talk and group discussion. A meeting with too much interaction and not enough structure rambles and digresses and has no clear purpose. The key to managing a meeting is to strike a proper balance between structure and interaction.

● HOW TO GIVE MEETINGS STRUCTURE

As a leader, the most powerful tool you have to give a meeting structure is an **agenda,** a brief list or description of what you will discuss, arranged in chronological order. Develop an agenda by determining your overall goal. Most meetings have one or more of the following goals: to share information, to discuss issues, to make decisions, and to solve problems.

Some experts suggest that if sharing information is one goal, it should be done early in the meeting, especially if the information is related to decisions and actions the group will take later in the meeting.[10] Often groups spend too much time on early agenda items and give less attention to those scheduled for late in the meeting (when most people want to leave). Therefore, do not schedule important items for the end of the meeting. Instead, cover vital issues early, and use the end of the meeting to determine what needs to happen at the next meeting, to summarize the action that needs to be taken, and to determine who will do what.

If you are a meeting leader, keep your eye on two things: the clock and the agenda. Think of your agenda as the map—where you want to go. Think of the clock as your gas gauge—the amount of fuel you have to get where you want to go. If you are running low on fuel (time), you will either need to budget more or recognize that you will not get where you want to go.

● HOW TO FOSTER GROUP INTERACTION

In addition to giving a meeting structure, leaders should ensure that a meeting is interactive. A meeting is not a speech during which the leader talks and the rest of the group listens. Draw out quiet members by calling them by name and asking for their opinions. You may need to ask more talkative members to hold their comments until all have contributed to the discussion. Another strategy for encouraging participation and keeping the discussion on track is periodically to summarize group members' contributions.

agenda
A written description of the items and issues that a group will discuss during a meeting.

Even if you are not the designated leader or meeting facilitator, you can use strategies to enhance the quality of discussion. One research team made the following recommendations for meeting participants:[11]

■ Organize your contributions, and make one point at a time. Rambling and disorganized comments increase the likelihood that the meeting will stray from the agenda.

■ Speak only if your contribution is relevant, and support your ideas with evidence. Facts, statistics, and well-selected examples help keep the group focused on the task.

■ Listen actively and monitor your nonverbal messages. Check your understanding of group member comments by summarizing or paraphrasing, and watch your own body language.

As you have undoubtedly noticed, the skills of being a good meeting participant mirror the skills of being a good communicator when giving a speech. Presenting organized, thoughtful, well-supported, and well-presented ideas will enhance the overall quality of meeting deliberations.

Reporting group recommendations

Most problem-solving groups report the results of their deliberations to others in one of the following oral or written forms: symposium presentations, forum presentations, panel discussions, and written reports. We will discuss these forms in the following sections.

● SYMPOSIUM PRESENTATION

A **symposium** is a public discussion in which a series of short speeches is presented to an audience. The members of the group share the responsibility of presenting information to a larger group. Usually a moderator and the group members are seated in front of the audience, each prepared to deliver a brief report. Each speaker should know what the others will present so that the same ground is not covered twice. At the end of the speeches, the moderator can summarize the key points that were presented. The audience can then participate in a question-and-answer session or a forum presentation.

■ **symposium**
A public discussion in which a series of short speeches is presented to an audience.

● FORUM PRESENTATION

A **forum presentation** consists of an audience directing questions to a group, and group members responding with short impromptu speeches. In ancient Rome, the forum was a marketplace where citizens went to shop and discuss the hot issues of the day. It later became a public meeting place where political speeches were often delivered.

■ **forum presentation**
A discussion that usually follows a group discussion or symposium, which allows audience members to respond to ideas.

A forum often follows a more structured presentation, such as a symposium or a prepared speech by one group member. Forum presentations work best when all group members know the issues and are prepared to respond unhesitatingly to questioners.

● PANEL DISCUSSION

panel discussion
A group discussion designed to inform an audience about issues or a problem or to make recommendations.

A **panel discussion** is an informative group presentation. Individuals on the panel may use notes containing key facts or statistics, but they do not present formal speeches. Usually a panel discussion is organized and led by an appointed chairperson or moderator.

An effective moderator gets all the panelists to participate, summarizes their statements, and serves as a gatekeeper to make sure that no member of the panel dominates the discussion. Often, panel discussions are followed by a question-and-answer period.

● WRITTEN REPORT

Written reports summarize a group's key deliberations and final recommendations. Such reports often accompany a symposium, forum, or panel discussion.

The steps of reflective thinking can provide a way to organize a report. Begin by describing the group members; then present the definition of the problem the group discussed. Next, include the problem analysis, criteria that were established, possible solutions, the best solution, and suggestions for implementing the solution. For the sake of clarity, use headings and subheadings liberally throughout the report. The length of the report will vary with the significance of the problem and the length of time the group has spent together. Include a bibliography of the sources used to reach the group's conclusion.

The original Roman Forum was a lively marketplace, where acrobats as well as speakers commanded public attention. [Photo: North Wind Pictures]

Tips for planning a group presentation

Working in groups takes a coordinated team effort. If you are used to developing reports and speeches on your own, it may be a challenge to work with others on a group assignment. Consider these suggestions to enhance teamwork:

■ *Make sure each group member understands the task or assignment, and work together to identify a topic.* Take a few moments to verbalize the goals and objectives of the assignment. Don't immediately plunge in and try to start dividing up the work just so you can hurry off to your next class or responsibility.

■ *If your group assignment is to solve a problem or to inform the audience about a specific issue, try brainstorming to develop a topic or problem question (see Chapter 6).* Then assess your audience's interests as well as group members' interests and talents to help you choose among your ideas.

■ *Give group members individual assignments.* After you decide on your group's presentation topic, divvy up the tasks involved in investigating the issues. Also devise a plan for keeping in touch with one another frequently to share information and ideas.

■ *Develop a group outline and decide on an approach.* After group members have researched key issues, begin drafting an outline of your group presentation, following the steps of the reflective thinking process we presented earlier in this chapter.

■ *Decide on your presentation approach.* Determine whether you will use a symposium, forum, or panel presentation, or some combination of these approaches. Make decisions about who will present which portions of your outline and how to integrate them. Your presentation should have an introduction and a definite ending that reflect your group's work as an integrated problem-solving unit.

■ *Rehearse the presentation.* Just as you would for an individual speech, rehearse the presentation. If you are using visual aids, be sure to incorporate them in your rehearsal. Also, be sure to time your presentation when you rehearse.

■ *Incorporate principles and skills of effective audience-centered public speaking when giving the group presentation.*

■ *Armed with a well-planned outline, present your findings to your audience, incorporating the skills and principles of effective public speaking.* If you are using a symposium format, each group presentation is essentially a mini-speech. A panel or forum presentation is more extemporaneous and may even have an impromptu quality, but your delivery and comments should still be well organized. In addition, your visual aids should enhance your presentation by being clear and attractive.

Summary

R esearch has shown that effective group members prepare for meetings, evaluate evidence, summarize the group's progress, listen well, and help manage group conflict.

Leaders perform the useful functions of organizing the work, helping to achieve the task, and maintaining the social climate of the group. Leaders of small groups adopt one or more of three styles: authoritarian, democratic, or passive. The best style depends on the group task, the leader's authority, and the leader's relationship with other group members.

Meeting leaders are responsible for preparing and distributing an agenda, keeping the meeting on track, and making sure there is balanced participation by meeting members. Other group members make sure their contributions are well - organized, relevant, and understood by others. Listening and monitoring the nonverbal messages of others can also promote effectiveness.

● CRITICAL THINKING QUESTIONS

1. Imagine that you are a member of a school board in a small, economically depressed community. The board is trying to decide whether to build new schools to relieve the severe student overcrowding problem. To build new schools would result in a hefty, unpopular tax increase for community property owners. What procedures should the board use to systematically analyze the problem?

2. Ken is the manager of a shoe store. Each week he presides over a team meeting of all employees in the store. The employees are having difficulty reaching consensus about a new work schedule. What communication behaviors would help Ken facilitate consensus and manage group conflict?

3. Your group, which has attempted to suggest ways of reducing the high cost of attending college, is ready to make its report to the college president. What are some possible methods or group formats of sharing the group's findings with the administration?

● ETHICAL QUESTIONS

1. Karen is working in a group with four other people. One group member, Ed, seems to have taken charge and is making assignments for other group members. Although Ed's leadership skills are helping to get a lot accomplished, Karen resents his overly zealous efforts to take charge. Should Karen keep quiet and just go along with Ed, or should she speak up and express her concerns about his actions?

2. Cheryl has found an article in the *National Review* that summarizes the problem and identifies several solutions for the group project she is working on. Should she urge the group to base its decisions on this one article, or should the group keep looking for more information?

3. Kim Lee is a member of the Right to Life Organization on campus. Her position in the club calls for her to do research for other club members about abortion issues. For her class group project, she has talked other group members into discussing the abortion issue. Afterwards, she plans to distribute the research of other group members to members of her Right to Life Organization. Is it ethical for her to do so without telling them of her plan?

● SUGGESTED ACTIVITIES

1. Identify five groups to which you belong, and indicate how each group engages in small group communication as defined in this chapter.

2. For each of the problems listed, cite possible criteria for a solution.

   Violence on TV

   Child abuse

   Increase in domestic U.S. terrorism

   Teenage smoking

   Health care for the poor

3. Working with a group of other students, use the brainstorming method of generating possible solutions for the following problems:

   Lack of parking space on campus

   High college tuition costs

   Declining reading scores in elementary grades

   Student apathy on campus

4. Compare the advantages and disadvantages of using the following methods for reporting group recommendations:

   Symposium presentation

   Forum presentation

   Panel discussion

   Written report

5. Select one of the following policy questions and, working with other group members, brainstorm possible solutions.

A. What could be done to decrease illegal drug use in the United States?

B. What strategies would improve communication between parents and teenagers?

C. What strategies could lower the crime rate on your campus?

D. What could be done to eliminate overcrowding in some of America's most popular national parks?

USING TECHNOLOGY AND MEDIA

1. While working on a group project, videotape one of your meetings. After the meeting, watch the video, noting your own use of group communication skills. Describe the various leadership roles that you assumed during the meeting. Describe how effectively your group developed and followed an agenda.

2. If you have access to the Internet and have participated in an interactive discussion with someone on a bulletin board or other electronic forum, describe the differences between electronically mediated discussions and live, face-to-face interaction with others. Note advantages and disadvantages of discussion in cyberspace compared with face-to-face discussion.

3. Based on the discussion about using technology for visual aids in Chapter 14, describe various types of media and electronic visual aids (for example, computer graphics, videos, CD-ROM) that you could use to present group recommendations to an audience. Discuss ways that your team could manipulate these media effectively. For example, while one group member is giving an oral presentation, other group members might operate the VCR or overhead projector. Brainstorm other ways electronic resources might enhance a team presentation.

Epilogue

Now that you are about to complete your public speaking course, you may barely be able to resist the temptation to pat yourself on the back. Before taking this course, you, like the survey population we mentioned in Chapter 2, may have feared public speaking more than death! But you have survived and perhaps even excelled. Now you can file away your notes and will never have to give another speech, right? Wrong!

There is indeed life after public speaking class—a life that will demand frequent practice and sharpening of the skills to which you have been introduced in this course. Your classroom experience has taught you how to become a better public speaker. We hope that it has also taught you to become your own best critic—able to say, "I need more eye contact," or "I need a statistic to prove this point," or "I need a transition here." But one course cannot make you a polished speaker. Learning to speak in public is an ongoing process rather than a static goal.

In the years to come, both in college and beyond, you will use and continue to develop your public speaking skills in many areas of your professional and personal life. In Chapter 2 of this text, we discussed some of the skills you would learn and practice as a public speaker: organization, audience analysis and adaptation, research, effective presentation, and critical listening. Certainly you will find yourself applying these skills to numerous situations—to speaking opportunities, of course, but also to other situations that require critical listening and analytical thinking. As you take other courses, apply for a job, prepare a report for your company, attend city council meetings, and go about your day-to-day personal business, you will find yourself using the skills you learned in your public speaking class.

Of course, chances are that you will also find yourself in a number of actual public speaking situations. Perhaps you will give few "laboratory" speeches like those you have given in your speech class. But you will undoubtedly deliver one or more of the types of special-occasion speeches that we discussed in Chapter 18. You will introduce a speaker, present or receive an award, deliver a speech to commemorate a person or an occasion, give a book review, or make a sales pitch. And you will look back to this course for guidance.

Realistically, you will not remember every detail of the course or of this text. But we hope that you will remember the bottom line: that to be effective, public

Your completion of this course is the commencement of your continuing development as a public speaker. [Photo: Charles Gupton/Stock Boston]

speaking must be *audience-centered*. Every step of the public speaking process, from selecting and narrowing the topic, to preparing the speech, to final delivery, must be approached with the audience in mind. If the audience does not understand your message or does not respond as you had hoped, your speech cannot be a success, regardless of the hours of research or rehearsal you may have dedicated to the task.

One final note about the audience-centered approach is in order here: Being audience-centered is not the same as being manipulative. As we discussed in Chapter 2, if you adapt to your audience to the extent that you abandon your own values and sense of truth, you have become an unethical speaker rather than an audience-centered one. An audience-centered speaker does not tell an audience only what they want to hear.

One of the types of special-occasion speeches we discussed in Chapter 18 was the commencement address. Your completion of this course is also the commencement—the beginning—of your continuing development as a public speaker. The traditional theme of the commencement speaker is "Go forth. You have been prepared for the future." With what better thought can we leave you? Go forth. You have been prepared for the future.

Appendix A: The Classical Tradition of Rhetoric*

BY THOMAS R. BURKHOLDER

Preparing and delivering a speech always seems to be a very personal task. You must research your own topic. You must analyze and attempt to adapt to the particular audience you will face. You must find a way to cope with your own nervousness. When you confront those problems, it is sometimes helpful to remember that countless others have done so before you. And for as long as people have been giving speeches, they have been looking for ways to make them better. In fact, the study of speeches and speechmaking, or the study of rhetoric, dates back to the earliest years of Western civilization, hundreds of years before the birth of Christ. So in a way, your own efforts are a continuation of that classical tradition.

Speechmaking is probably as old as language itself. And speech criticism is probably as old as listening! But perhaps the earliest recorded evidence of "rhetorical consciousness," the awareness of excellence in speechmaking, appears in the writing of Homer, the ancient Greek poet. His *Iliad*, written before 700 B.C., contains numerous well-organized, well-written speeches or orations. They appear in scenes depicting debates between humans and gods, in councils of military leaders, and so forth. And they demonstrate that the ancient Greeks had a clear sense of rhetorical excellence.

The earliest teachers of rhetoric

We will probably never know who first offered advice to another person who was preparing to deliver an oration. But many ancient writers credit a teacher named Corax with the "invention" of rhetoric sometime around 476 B.C. Corax was a resident of the city of Syracuse on the island of Sicily. He developed a "doctrine of general probability," to be used by speakers in the courts. Imagine a small man being brought into court and accused of beating a much larger, stronger man. According to the doctrine of general probability, the small man should defend himself by saying something like: "It is surely unlikely (not probable) that I would beat this man. After all, he is much larger and stronger than I. I would be crazy to risk making him angry by hitting him." But the larger man could

*Published by permission of Thomas R. Burkholder.

resort to the same doctrine in response: "Of course people would think it unlikely that he would hit me. That is exactly why he felt safe in doing it!"

Another similar exchange was the basis of the most famous story about Corax and his student, Tisias. Tisias refused to pay Corax for his lessons in rhetoric, so Corax sued him in court. Corax addressed the judges: "Tisias must pay me regardless of your decision. If he wins the case, that proves the lessons I taught him were valuable and I deserve payment. And if he loses, the court will force him to pay. So either way, he must pay." But Tisias responded: "I shall pay nothing. If I lose the case, that will prove the training I received from Corax was worthless and he does not deserve payment. But if I win the case, the court will decree that I owe him nothing. So either way, I shall not pay." The judges quickly tired of such banter and threw the case out of court with the admonition, *"Mali corvi malum ovum,"* or "A bad egg from a bad crow!" Legend has it that Tisias promptly left Syracuse and opened his own school of rhetoric in Greece.

Beginning of the Greek tradition: The Sophists

Whether Tisias actually went to Greece is unknown. But by the middle of the fifth century B.C., schools of rhetoric flourished in the Greek city states. Citizens often spoke in the assemblies or legislatures, and because there were no lawyers, they presented their own cases in the courts. It was soon apparent that the most skilled speakers prevailed in the assembly and won in court. Speech teachers were in great demand. The Greeks called these teachers "Sophists," a term which literally means "wisdom bearer." The rhetorical training offered by these teachers varied greatly. Some, such as Antiphon (480–411 B.C.) and Lysias (459–380 B.C.), were actually logographers. They merely wrote speeches to be delivered by their clients and made no effort to provide training in rhetoric. Others, like Protagoras (481–411 B.C.) and Gorgias (485–380 B.C.), advertised themselves as teachers of eloquence, or the art of effective speaking.

Protagoras is often considered to be the originator of academic debating, because he required his students to argue opposing sides of issues. He believed that each side of important questions had merit, and that humans could never be certain of the "truth." Thus, he encouraged his students to build the strongest possible case for the side of the issue they were assigned to debate. Such training, he felt, would best prepare his students to conduct their affairs in the assembly and the courts. Gorgias was perhaps the first teacher of rhetoric to encourage careful use of language. He believed that speakers would be more persuasive if their speaking style was embellished. He encouraged the use of stylistic devices familiar to modern writers, such as assonance, alliteration, antithesis, and parallelism.

One of the most famous Sophists was Isocrates (436–338 B.C.). Unlike Protagoras and Gorgias, who taught only rhetoric, Isocrates claimed to train citizens to be statesmen. He made rhetoric the center of a more fully developed course of study designed to make his students wise as well as eloquent. Isocrates believed that three qualities were necessary for a person to be a great orator and statesman. First, that person must possess natural ability. Second, that ability must be developed and refined through practice and experience. Finally, to be a great orator and statesman, a person must be well educated, not just in rhetoric, but in philosophy as well. While no one can teach natural ability, Isocrates endeavored to provide his students with practice, experience, and philosophical education.

Although the Sophists attracted many students, and many Sophists became wealthy from their teaching efforts, they were not without their critics. Many felt that the training provided by the Sophists was worthless, if not dangerous. Teachers like Gorgias were accused of providing worthless training by emphasizing florid language with no regard for substance. Teachers like Protagoras were accused of training speakers to "make the worse case appear the better" by urging speakers to develop strong speeches on both sides of any issue. And Sophists in general were often criticized for failing to make their students better, more virtuous people. Without question, the most severe critic of the Sophists was the great Greek philosopher, Plato (427–347 B.C.).

Plato

Plato was the student of Socrates (469–399 B.C.), and he went on to become one of the most profound and influential thinkers in history. In 385 B.C., Plato founded the famous Academy in Athens. The Academy attracted the best and brightest students and teachers in all of Greece, and remained in operation for almost nine hundred years. Plato's writings were a major influence in the development of Western philosophy and culture. His *Republic* was a blueprint for the ideal political state ruled over by a philosopher-king. His other writings covered a wide variety of subjects, including psychology, logic, and rhetoric. Most of his writings were "dialogues," which resembled plays in which the characters discussed important issues. In many of Plato's dialogues, Socrates was the chief character.

In a typical dialogue, Plato had Socrates attempt to determine the truth relevant to the issue at hand by engaging other characters in a series of questions and answers. That approach is now frequently called the "Socratic method" or the "Platonic method." It illustrated the process of "dialectic," which Plato believed was the means of discovering truth. The dialogues were often named after the characters who opposed Socrates in the discussion. Two of the dialogues, *Gorgias* and *Phaedrus,* named after those Sophists, dealt explicitly with rhetoric.

Plato's dialogues are complicated and often difficult to understand fully. Scholars have debated their meaning for centuries. Some have argued that *Gorgias* and *Phaedrus* presented inconsistent and conflicting views of rhetoric; that Plato condemned rhetoric in *Gorgias* and then praised it in *Phaedrus*. In fact, when taken together, the two dialogues presented Plato's clear and coherent view of the nature and function of rhetoric.

In *Gorgias*, Plato, through the character of Socrates, condemned rhetoric *as practiced* by many Sophists of his day. He said that the rhetoric of the Sophists was merely a "knack" or a form of flattery, intended only to please the ears of listeners much like cookery pleases the palate. He condemned the Sophists for using florid language, pleasant to the ear, to "make the worse case appear the better." And he accused them of first claiming to impart wisdom and thus to make their students more just and virtuous, and then of failing to do so. But these charges were leveled at rhetoric as the Sophists practiced it, not at rhetoric itself.

In *Phaedrus*, once again through the character of Socrates, Plato praised rhetoric as it *ought to be practiced*, The Sophists focused their attention on speaking in assemblies and courts. But Plato saw the true rhetoric as a means of using language to influence the minds of listeners, wherever they might be. Going further, he saw rhetoric as a means of influencing the very souls of listeners, thus making them more virtuous. The difference between the Sophistic and Platonic ideas of rhetoric grew from Plato's understanding of "truth."

In Plato's view, truth, or knowledge, existed on several levels. The lowest, least reliable, yet most common level was called *doxa*. This sort of knowledge was the product of the human senses, of what people observed. It was least reliable because it was so easily corrupted; the senses were easily misled. Thus, Plato's condemnation of the rhetoric of the Sophists grew from its aim of pleasing (and often, he felt, misleading) the senses of listeners. On the other end of Plato's scale was *episteme*, or true knowledge. It was the product not of sensory observation, but rather of philosophical inquiry. For Plato, rhetoric as it ought to be practiced was grounded in *episteme*. Only this "true" rhetoric could be trusted to influence the souls of listeners.

The idea of rhetoric based on truth is appealing. But before we award too much praise to Plato, we must know also that he thought most people were not capable of achieving true knowledge. Only philosophers could attain true knowledge, and thus, in the ideal political state described in his *Republic*, only the philosopher-king was allowed to use rhetoric, for the good of the state. Such uses of rhetoric are frightening. Seen in that light, the Sophists' idea that both sides of important issues should be debated in public seems preferable indeed.

Aristotle

Plato's most famous student was Aristotle (384–322 B.C.). Of all ancient scholars, including Plato, no other was more influential than Aristotle. He wrote extensively on subjects as diverse as philosophy, drama, natural science, and rhetoric. Like his teacher, Aristotle had a profound effect on the development of Western culture.

Throughout his life, Aristotle was directly associated with the most brilliant and important people of his time. His father, Nicomachus, was physician in the court of Amyntas II, king of Macedon and father of Philip the Great. When Aristotle was seventeen, he was sent to Athens to study in the Academy. There he remained until Plato's death. In 343 B.C., he was summoned back to Macedon to become tutor to Philip's son, Alexander the Great. Aristotle returned to Athens in 335 B.C. and eventually founded his own school, the Lyceum. After the death of Alexander in 323 B.C., he came under suspicion in Athens because of his prior close association with Macedon. Aristotle fled to the city of Chalcis where he died the next year.

Aristotle's *Rhetoric* is the earliest systematic discussion of speechmaking of which we have record. It probably existed first as his own notes for lectures he gave to students in the Lyceum. Legend has it that his students edited and published those notes after Aristotle's death. His approach to rhetoric was influenced by the philosophy of Plato. But his practical suggestions for speakers demonstrate that Aristotle was influenced by the Sophists as well. In effect, he was able to transcend both Plato and the Sophists and form a distinctive theory of rhetoric. The impact of his work continues today. Indeed, much of what appears earlier in this textbook originated with Aristotle.

Like Plato, Aristotle believed in true or ultimate knowledge. Also like Plato, he believed that only through philosophical inquiry, which was beyond the ability of most people, could true knowledge be attained. But Plato viewed rhetoric as a means through which, for the good of the state, philosopher-kings might manipulate those incapable of gaining true knowledge. Aristotle took a very different position. He believed that even those who could not attain true knowledge could, nevertheless, be persuaded to the good. Thus, persuasion was an acceptable, although inferior, substitute for true knowledge. In Plato's ideal state, only the philosopher-king could employ rhetoric because in the hands of the unenlightened, rhetoric could do great harm. In contrast, Aristotle believed that rhetoric was a morally neutral art. He did not restrict the use of rhetoric to rulers alone because he believed that, in any dispute, good would prevail provided both sides were equally well prepared; that is, provided both sides were equally well trained in rhetoric.

Aristotle envisioned rhetoric as an art, as a system which could be taught. He defined rhetoric as "the faculty of discovering, in any given case, the available means of persuasion." These means of persuasion he classified into three types: *ethos,* or ethical appeals, based on the degree of credibility awarded to a speaker by listeners; *logos,* or logical appeals; and *pathos,* or appeals to listeners' emotions. The *Rhetoric* offered speakers extremely detailed suggestions for discovering, understanding, and implementing each means of persuasion.

Aristotle also classified the different situations, or "given cases," in which speeches might be given. Those were: deliberative, or legislative speaking; forensic, or speaking in the courts; and epideictic, or what he called the "ceremonial oratory of display." Today, we would call that last type "special-occasion" speaking. According to Aristotle, those types were determined by the role listeners must play in each case; by the sort of "decision" they must make after hearing a particular speech. In that regard, Aristotle, like this textbook, took an "audience-centered approach" to speechmaking.

In Aristotle's system of classification, those who hear deliberative speeches were asked to render a decision regarding the most expedient course for future action. Those who heard forensic speeches were asked to judge the justice or injustice of a person's past action. And those who heard epideictic speeches were asked to award either praise or blame to the subject (usually a person) of the speech, and to judge the orator's skill as well. The *Rhetoric* offered speakers detailed suggestions for demonstrating the expedience or inexpediency of proposed courses of action, the justice or injustice of a person's deeds, and those qualities worthy of praise or blame. Aristotle also allowed for considerable overlap between the three types, indicating that while one type would predominate, elements of all three might appear in a single speech.

His discussions of expediency, justice, and qualities worthy of praise or blame, made Aristotle's *Rhetoric* more than a simple "handbook" for speakers. Those discussions provided a philosophical or ethical foundation for speechmaking. But its practical suggestions made the *Rhetoric* an extremely useful manual for public speaking as well.

The Roman tradition

The Greek tradition of rhetoric had its most immediate, and perhaps its greatest, influence in the Roman educational system. In the second century B.C., Rome's military might extended the Republic to the east. There, Romans became familiar with Greek culture and the Greek educational system. Much of what they discovered was incorporated into Roman society, and that included training in rhetoric. In fact, rhetorical training eventually became the center of Roman education.

The Roman education system was designed to prepare citizens to participate in the affairs of the state. Primarily, that meant citizens must be prepared to speak in the legislatures and the courts. Rhetorical instruction began in the Roman grammar schools. There, students engaged in a progressive series of written and spoken exercises called the *Progymnasmata*. The lessons built on each other, with each more difficult than the one which preceded it. Near the end of the program of instruction, students were assigned a thesis which required them to develop arguments on a given theme, such as whether it was more noble to be a soldier or a lawyer. The series of lessons culminated in exercises in which students were required to speak for and against an existing law.

With grammar school instruction completed, most students moved on to schools of rhetoric. Instruction there was more broad in scope, but it continued to focus on preparing students to be productive citizens of Rome; that is, to be effective speakers. Students were required to learn a vast body of rhetorical theories and concepts based on centuries of oratorical study. They were taught that the art of rhetoric consisted of five separate arts: *invention,* which involved gathering and analyzing facts and physical evidence; *arrangement,* or organization; *style,* or the eloquent and effective use of language; *memory,* or recollection of the speech for presentation; and *delivery.* These five classical "canons" of rhetoric are familiar to today's students of public speaking. The exercises in which students in Roman times participated were of two types, *suasoria* and *controversia.* Suasoria were exercises in legislative speaking. Students debated hypothetical questions of public policy, laws, and so forth. *Controversia* were exercises in forensic or legal speaking. Students argued opposing sides of hypothetical court cases, much as present-day law students do in "moot court" contests.

Following their training in schools of rhetoric, Roman students were often apprenticed to practicing rhetoricians, such as legislators or lawyers. There the students were given opportunities to learn by observing other speakers in legislative and judicial situations. Thus, the entire Roman educational system was designed to prepare citizens to assume roles as orators in the society. Rome produced many scholars who contributed to the rhetorical tradition. Two of the most important were Cicero (106–43 B.C.) and Quintilian (A.D. 35–95).

Marcus Tullius Cicero was the child of an upper middle-class family from central Italy. Social custom dictated that he pursue his education in Rome, where he studied with the leading rhetoricians of his day. According to many, he became the greatest orator in all of Rome. His most famous works on the theory and practice of rhetoric were *De Inventione,* written when he was approximately twenty years old; *De Oratore,* published in 55 B.C; and *Brutus* and *Orator,* both written in approximately 46 B.C. Cicero's aim in these works was to gather, synthesize, and expand upon the greatest teachings of previous Greek and Roman rhetoricians. He was appalled by the emphasis given to style and delivery in some schools of rhetoric, and felt the true orator should be a fully educated person. Cicero saw rhetoric as far more than courtroom pleading. Rather, he believed that the ideal orator was the learned philosopher-statesman, who used his talent for the good of the state. In his view, the true orator should be able to speak with eloquence and wisdom on any important subject.

Marcus Fabius Quintilianus was born in the part of the Roman Empire which is now Spain. Like Cicero, he was the product of a traditional Roman education. But unlike Cicero, Quintilian lived in a time when oratory began to be repressed. Tyrants ruled the Roman Empire; the legislative speaking, and even the legal speaking, which characterized Cicero's time, were greatly restricted. Despite that fact, or perhaps because of it, Quintilian's aim as a teacher of rhetoric was to educate the perfect orator. His most famous rhetorical treatise was *Institutio Oratoria,* which emphasized the moral and ethical uses of rhetoric. For Quintilian, the ideal orator was "a good man speaking well." Unfortunately, that dictum has been much abused by many modern rhetorical scholars, often to justify the study of the speaking and speeches of only highly successful political figures who were usually white and male. In fact, Quintilian urged those who would become great orators to pursue not only eloquence, but excellence in morality and ethical character as well—qualities which are certainly not limited to, or perhaps even characteristic of, successful politicians!

Conclusion

The rhetorical tradition which began with the ancient Greeks and Romans has been a significant influence in Western civilization. Their theories and guidelines for successful rhetorical practice have been analyzed, refined, and extended by countless scholars for thousands of years. This textbook is a part of that tradition. Many of the rhetorical principles and suggestions for effective speechmaking which appear in this book can be traced through the ages back to such classical rhetoricians as Isocrates, Plato, Aristotle, Cicero, and Quintilian. Throughout history, other rhetorical scholars have made important contributions as well. But as you work to prepare your own speeches, to be delivered in class or in other settings, it is interesting and perhaps even comforting to know that your efforts are a continuation of a classical tradition of rhetoric which is as old as our Western culture.

THE CLASSICAL TRADITION OF RHETORIC

Rhetoricians	Dates	Contributions
The First Teachers		
Corax and Tisias	476 B.C.	Doctrine of general probability
The Greek Tradition		
The Sophists		
Protagoras	481–411 B.C.	Originator of academic debate
Gorgias	485–380 B.C.	Effective language use
Isocrates	436–338 B.C.	The orator-statesman
Plato	427–347 B.C.	*Gorgias* and *Phaedrus*; philosopher-king as orator
Aristotle	384–322 B.C.	*Rhetoric*; philosophical and practical guide for orators; rhetoric as a teachable art
The Roman Tradition		
Cicero	106–43 B.C.	*De Inventione, De Oratore, Brutus,* and *Orator*; Rome's greatest orator; philosopher-statesman as the ideal orator
Quintilian	A.D. 35–95	*Institutio Oratoria*; eloquence combined with moral and ethical excellence; the good man speaking well

● REFERENCES

Aristotle, *Rhetoric and Poetics*. W. Rhys Roberts and Ingram Bywater, trans. New York: The Modern Library, 1954.

Black, Edwin, "Plato's View of Rhetoric." *Quarterly Journal of Speech* 44 (December 1958): 361—374.

Clark, Donald Lemen, *Rhetoric in Greco-Roman Education*. New York: Columbia University Press, 1957.

Guthrie, W.K.C., *The Sophists*. Cambridge: Cambridge University Press, 1971.

Hamilton, Edith, and Huntington Cairns, eds., *The Collected Dialogues of Plato*. Princeton: Princeton University Press, 1961.

Kauffman, Charles, "The Axiological Foundations of Plato's Theory of Rhetoric," *Central States Speech Journal* 33 (Summer 1982): 353—366.

Kennedy, George, *The Art of Persuasion in Greece*. Princeton: Princeton University Press, 1963.

Murphy, James J., ed., *A Synoptic History of Classical Rhetoric*. Davis, CA: Hermagoras Press, 1983.

————, ed., *Quintilian on the Teaching of Speaking and Writing*. Translations from Books 1, 2, and 10 of *Institutio Oratoria*. Carbondale: Southern Illinois University Press, 1987.

Watson, J. S., trans., *Cicero on Oratory and Orators*. Carbondale: Southern Illinois University Press, 1970.

Appendix B: Suggested Speech Topics

One of the more challenging tasks for beginning speakers is deciding what to talk about. We identified several suggestions in Chapter 6 to help you select and narrow your topic. Specifically, we suggested you should:

1. Consider the audience.

2. Consider the demands of the occasion.

3. Consider yourself.

We also described three techniques to help you with your topic selection hunt:

1. Brainstorm—free associate topics until you have a long list before you start to critique your topics.

2. Listen to the media and read; keep current on the news of the day.

3. Scan lists and indexes.

To help prime your creative pump, we have included the following list of topics.* As presented here, most of the topics are appropriate for an informative speech. Depending on your point of view, they could also be adapted for persuasive speech topics.

● INFORMATIVE SPEECH TOPICS

Why go to graduate school?
The history and significance of the Panama Canal
What's happening in Honduras? (or another country?)
Why are so many farmers going broke?
What exactly happened on Black Monday?
What's the current role of health education?
What's going on with nuclear energy?
What is the privacy act?
Is censorship going on in the U.S.?
What's involved in being an organ donor?

*We thank Professor Russell Wittrup, Southwest Texas State University, for sharing his speech topic ideas with us.

What are the standards used to get credit cards?

The history of the Bosnian situation

The evolution of the musician as a popular hero

What are the facts on world hunger?

What are the facts on the homeless in the U.S.?

Who is a powerful contemporary writer?

What is subliminal advertising?

The social/economic problems in Mexico

What the experts say about choosing a career

Present trends in animal conservation

What goes into making a compact disc?

Whatever happened to Laetrile?

What's the U.S. doing about littering?

How is technology affecting education?

Which diets really work?

What is socialized medicine?

What do primary elections tell us?

What are the goals of General Studies courses?

The facts on child abuse

What the experts say about apartment vs. dorm life

New discoveries in health care

What's the current status on finances for U.S. education?

What's happening with solar energy?

The facts on religious cults

What's happening with the draft?

What are the rights of adopted children?

The facts about legalized prostitution

How happy are marriages without children?

What is involved in being a blood donor?

What has the 55 mph speed limit done for safety?

What's being done to save national parks?

Who gets guaranteed student loans and why?

What are new methods in waste disposal?

Why people become vegetarians

Tips on bicycle safety and protection

How can you adopt animals from zoos?

Whatever happened to UFOs?

Is there life on other planets?

What exactly are money market funds?

What the experts say about crime prevention

The previous decade in Russia

How do we choose a president in the U.S.?

How does the stock market work?

What's being done to find a cure for AIDS?

What's being done to make reparations to Native Americans?

Rap music as cultural expression

Do we have any ecological crises?

What are the job forecasts for the future?

What's the background to the problems in Ireland?

What's the media's role in shaping the news?

What's the New Age movement?

The latest in genetic engineering

Technology in the twentieth century

The changing job market

What is "sexist" language?

New trends in advertising

What does English as an official language mean?

How are movie ratings determined?

What are the facts about legalized gambling?

Are there any new concepts in mass transportation?

What is the role of the A.C.L.U.?

The impact of the instant replay in sports

How are maps made?

What is the latest in stereophonic technology?

How is the rate of inflation determined?

The effect of the falling rate of the peso

How is a loudspeaker made?

The effect of telephone deregulation

The history of the ___ river

The history of the ____ building

What's the future for real estate?

The history of blue laws

How can you test yourself for blood/alcohol level?

What's being done about TV violence?

What can/cannot a chiropractor do for you?

What is the foreign exchange student program?

What kinds of work do volunteers do?

Tips on fire prevention

The facts about diet pills

What happens in drug therapy clinics?

The history of jazz music (or select another type of music.)

What is electroshock therapy?

The history of cable TV

How do unions work?

Living together

Success of designated smoking area laws

The history of cremation customs

How does cloning work?

What are the current child custody laws?

Test tube baby births

The facts about teenage alcoholism

New breakthroughs for the handicapped

What is the Consumer Protection Agency?

How are scholarships awarded?

What is the "Sunset Law" for government agencies?
What is the impact of the new immigration laws?
What has been the impact of recycling centers?
Why the change in marriage and divorce rates?
Sexual harassment: what it is and how to deal with it if it happens to you
Is there a "glass ceiling" for working women?

● PERSUASIVE SPEECH TOPICS

We should reduce our fat intake.
We should reduce our body weight.
Spend more leisure time doing [something].
Volunteer for [something].
The electoral college system for electing presidents should be changed.
Every U.S. citizen should spend two years in mandatory community service.
State drug laws should be changed.
The income tax system should be changed.
All undergraduate courses should be graded on a pass–fail basis only.
Everyone should take a foreign language.
Everyone should read a weekly news magazine regularly.
Couples should (or should not) live together before marriage.
We devote too much attention to college athletics.
Don't invest in the stock market.
The U.S. should have a tougher trade policy.
All farmers should be given low-interest loans.
The government should provide health care for all.
Divorce laws should be changed.
Spend less time watching TV.
Casino gambling should (or should not) be legalized in this state.
Birth control pills should (or should not) be dispensed by state-supported schools.
The federal court system needs to be changed.
A college education should be available to all citizens at no cost.
Teachers should be paid more.
Nuclear power plants should (or should not) be phased out.
Developing alternative energy sources must become a national priority.
School choice should (or should not) be promoted.
Affirmative action is the best way to overcome discrimination.
What working mothers and fathers need from their employers.
Why a national health care system will (or won't) work.
College students should (or shouldn't) be given the opportunity to pay off
    their tuition through public service.
The use of animals in research should be fully regulated.
It's time to put an end to violence on television.

Appendix C: Preparing Visual Aids for Presentations

BY DAN CAVANAUGH

No matter what career path you pursue after you graduate from college, chances are that sooner or later you will be asked to give a work-related presentation in front of an audience. Typically, the oral reports and public relations speeches described in the section "Public Speaking in the Workplace" in Chapter 18 rely more heavily upon visual support than do traditional speeches. This Appendix is designed to help you prepare the materials you need for such presentations. It supplements the information on Visual Aids in Chapter 14, introducing more specific planning and design techniques for creating effective graphics.

We will begin with a discussion of storyboarding, a visual planning technique used widely in advertising and other industries. Storyboarding encourages speaking to treat visual aids as an integral part of a presentation rather than as an afterthought. Next we will introduce you to basic principles of layout and design that will help you produce attractive visuals in any medium, touching upon considerations such as choosing typefaces, point sizes and colors. Finally, we will provide a brief introduction to using graphic software, including the popular PowerPoint™ program. For users who can apply basic design principles, these programs make it easy to produce polished, professional-looking presentations for a wide variety of audiences and settings.

STORYBOARDING

Storyboarding is a planning technique that combines words and pictures to create an outline. Each page in the storyboard focuses on the support for a single point, described in sentences, phrases, or key words, and then illustrated with rough sketches of visuals. The verbal support might include facts, statistics, anecdotes, quotes, references to sources, or transition statements to move your presentation from one point to the next.

Experienced public speakers may use storyboards as a substitute for a detailed formal outline when they are preparing a presentation. But until you have logged in hours of successful public presentations, you should probably consider storyboarding as a way to coordinate your visual ideas with your words. Either begin with a storyboard and then construct a more polished outline, or begin with a preparation outline and then transform it into a storyboard.

To get a sense of how storyboarding might work for you, imagine that you have been asked by your supervisor to prepare a 20-minute public relations presentation for a town planning committee on a proposed addition to your company's building. There was some resistance when the company announced its plans, so you know you must make your presentation persuasive.

First, consider your audience and fine tune your persuasive objective. Then you can make a list of the main points you'd like to cover, knowing that each one will become a page of your storyboard:

1. Over the years, Nortco has established strong bonds with the community;

2. Nortco's expansion will increase economic benefits to the community;

3. Nortco's addition has been carefully planned and thoughtfully designed to create minimal disturbance during the construction phase and to beautify and enhance the surrounding neighborhood.

Once you have your main points, you can begin creating your storyboards. Divide a piece of paper into two columns and label it "Storyboard #1." In the leftcolumn, write the main idea, then notes about supporting points, as shown in Figure C1.

Storyboard #1—
Town Planning Presentation

Point: Over the years, Nortco has established strong bonds with the community.

Support:

- Employs 150 local workers with combined annual wages of 3,750,000.

- Sponsors local organizations with donations totaling more than $500K annually.

- Scholarships totaling more than $300K annually.

- Summer music series, winter festival, Run-for-Fun Fest.

- Key player in the fight against airport development.

Transition: Now let's see how we plan to sustain and increase this community commitment with the planned expansion.

OR

Storyboard #2—
Town Planning Presentation

Point: Nortco's expansion will increase economic benefits to the community.

Support:

- New facility will extend 50 more skilled job opportunities to the community.

- The increase in workers will mean growth in revenues for local retailers.

- The expansion will also increase tax revenues for the town.

- Nortco is planning a PR campaign in conjunction with the expansion that will boost the town's image and attract more businesses.

Transition: By now you're probably wondering what the new facility will look like.

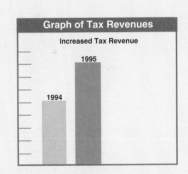

FIGURES C1
Storyboards for a Persuasive Presentation

Next, as shown in Figure C1, sketch the visuals you plan to include in the right column. Don't worry if you are not a fabulous artist. These sketches are placeholders for the finished visual aids that you will learn to prepare later in this Appendix.

When you do your sketches, be conservative about the number of visuals you plan. Select key supporting points to illustrate with a few memorable words or images. No matter what medium you plan to use, you should give your audience enough time to absorb what you place in front of their eyes and to listen carefully to your verbal information before they must shift their attention to another image.

Converting a simple main point and support outline like the ones in our sample storyboards into a more formal outline is a relatively simple task. Figure C2 shows an outline mode from the storyboard for the second main point listed above.

FIGURES C2
Translating a Storyboard into a Formal Outline

> **Town Planning Presentation Outline**
> Purpose: To persuade the audience that they should support Nortco's
>   expansion.
> I. Over the years, Nortco has established strong bonds with the community.
>   A. Nortco employs 150 local workers with combined annual wages of
> $3,7500,000
>   B. Nortco sponsors local organizations with donations totaling more than
> $500K annually
>   C. Nortco's endowed scholarships total more than $300K annually
>   D. Nortco sponsors community events:
>   1. music series
>   2. winter festival
>   3. Run-for-Fun Fest
>   E. Nortco has been a key player in the fight against airport development
>
> II. Nortco's expansion will increase economic benefits to the community.
>   A. The new facility will extend 50 more skilled job opportunities to the
>   community
>   1. 15 will be managerial positions paying $30K plus
>   2. 25 will be administrative paying $15K plus
>   3. The remainder will be clerical and maintenance paying 12K plus
>   B. The increase in workers will mean growth in revenues for local retailers
>   1. Restaurants, dry cleaners, shoe repairs, clothing and gift shops,
>   etc., will get more robust lunch-hour and after-five trade
>   2. A higher overall wage base will result in higher spending across all local
>   retail categories
>   C. The expansion will also increase tax revenues for the town
>   1. Overall projections show a $50K plus increase in annual taxes over
>   5 years
>   2. Employees will also purchase and upgrade homes, boosting the revenue
>   base
>   D. Nortco is planning a regional PR campaign in conjunction with the exspan-
>   sion that will boost the town's image and attract more business
>   1. There is promised coverage from local newspapers, cable TV, and radio
>   2. We are placing articles in regional business publications and planning a
>   regional marketing/advertising campaign
>   3. Governor and state officials are coming for the ribbon-cutting ceremony

After you do your storyboard and select an appropriate graphic medium for your audience, topic, and setting (see Chapter 14), you can begin designing your visual aids. Even if you are paying a professional to execute graphics from your rough sketches, it is helpful to know the basic principles that govern good design so that you can specify what you want in the final product. The strategies below apply to graphic preparation in any medium. Keeping these in mind as you design will enable you to produce visual aids that are attractive, instructive, and memorable.

● KEEP YOUR GRAPHICS SIMPLE
Presentation graphics should be simple and uncluttered. This principle, introduced in Chapter 14, bears repeating. As you begin to work with sophisticated layout and design tools, you may be tempted to load up your graphics with fancy fonts, clip art, and outlandish colors. Resist that temptation. Such visuals can quickly become hard to read and distracting. Instead of supporting your presentation, they will actually confuse your audience and detract from your message.

Remember that your visual aids are meant to clarify and amplify, not merely decorate, your presentation. Each element in your visual aid should serve a clear and specific purpose that is appropriate to your audience, topic, and setting. A decorative background using clip art of a desert island, for example (see Figure C3), would not be appropriate for an instructional presentation on how to surf the Internet. However colorful and attention-getting it might be, the background would not relate to the subject matter, so it would do nothing to enhance your audience's understanding of cyberspace.

● INCLUDE A MANAGEABLE AMOUNT OF INFORMATION
Your visual aids should enhance your message, not deliver it for you. The text on each visual should convey a sufficient amount of information to tell your audience what you think is most important, but your speech should fill in the blanks. Each visual aid should also make sense on its own. The slide in Figure C4, for example, does not provide enough infor-

FIGURE C3
An Inappropriate Use of Clip Art

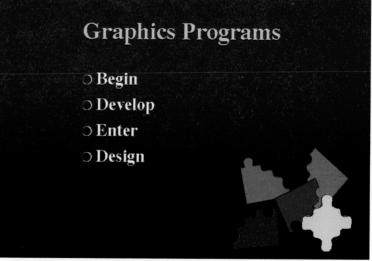

FIGURE C4
Not Enough Information

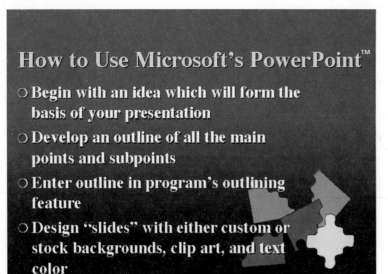

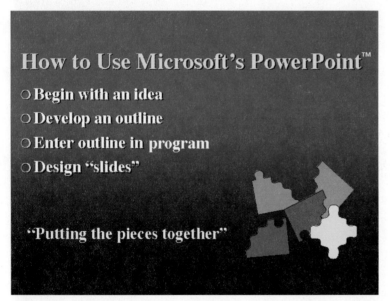

mation to give audience members much of a handle on the topic. They might grasp that the presentation will be about how to develop graphics programs and that it will cover four steps. But it does not have enough specific information for readers to understand the nature of those steps.

In contrast, the slide in Figure C5 is overloaded with information; the key words in each step are obscured by the extra words that surround them. Slides like these create interference during a presentation. Instead of focusing on the speaker's words, audience members have to struggle to read and absorb this information, which makes them stop listening. In addition, audience members who take notes have a tendency to write down whatever appears on the screen. If there are too many words for them to jot down quickly, they tune out and concentrate on writing.

The slide in Figure C6 achieves a happy medium; each step is stated succinctly so that the key words receive proper emphasis; readers can easily follow along and listen without distraction as the speaker provides more verbal information about each step. Note-takers can use the key words as headings, and then fill in as they listen. In addition, note that the caption "putting the pieces together" explains why the puzzle art is in the slide; it serves as a visual metaphor for the PowerPoint™ design process.

● GROUP RELATED ELEMENTS INTO VISUAL UNITS   By grouping related points, you can help your audience grasp key concepts and understand relationships as you convey information. In Figure C7, for example, it is immediately obvious that the elements on the left relate to text concerns, whereas those grouped on the right relate to visual concerns. As the text in the figure states, grouping points frees up space. This space, in turn, highlights the text blocks and also provides a resting place for the eye.

The alignment you choose for your type and images also affects the open space on the page and directs the reader's gaze. Alignment can be flush left (initial letters line up at the left margin), flush right (final letters line up at the right margin), or centered. Centered alignment is often effective for titles, but cen-

body text can look ragged and disorderly. As Figure C7 shows, a flush left alignment (top text grouping) or flush right alignment (bottom text grouping) makes the text look crisp and allows the eye to flow easily from point to point.

● REPEAT ELEMENTS TO UNIFY YOUR PRESENTATION   If you are designing a series of graphics, try to repeat a word, symbol, style, or font to convey a sense of unity in your presentation. Figure C8 shows a number of ways you can accomplish this repetition, such as choosing a different symbol to use instead of a bullet, a consistent color scheme, or consistent spacing. Repetition can be boring, so you may want to vary your visuals a bit more than the ones shown here, but keep in mind that consistency will help your audience process and remember complex information.

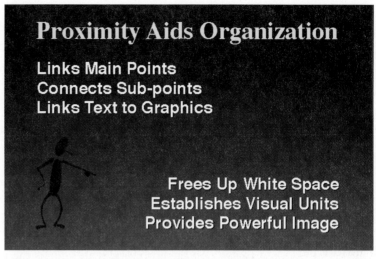

Proximity Aids Organization

Links Main Points
Connects Sub-points
Links Text to Graphics

Frees Up White Space
Establishes Visual Units
Provides Powerful Image

FIGURE C7
Use of Grouping and Alignment

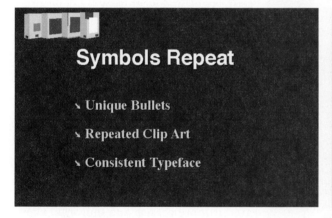

Symbols Repeat

↘ **Unique Bullets**

↘ **Repeated Clip Art**

↘ **Consistent Typeface**

Colors Repeat

↘ **Color of Titles**

↘ **Color of Text**

↘ **Color of Background**

● VARY YOUR TYPEFACES AND POINT SIZES JUDICIOUSLY   Today's personal computers offer thousands of options for designers when it comes to choosing typefaces and varying the size of the type. It is easy to get carried away by all of the possibilities, but if you combine typefaces carelessly, you will soon discover that your choices will conflict instead of complementing one another. The strategies below should help you avoid conflict in your designs.

● CHOOSING A TYPEFACE   A single typeface includes a collection of all upper and lowercase letters, numbers, symbols, and punctuation which have a consistent structure and form. Each typeface has a name. It may also have variations that have an

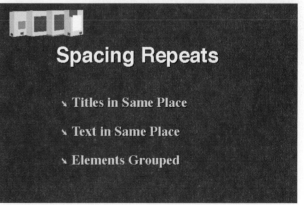

Spacing Repeats

↘ **Titles in Same Place**

↘ **Text in Same Place**

↘ **Elements Grouped**

FIGURES C8
Options For Designing with Repetitive elements

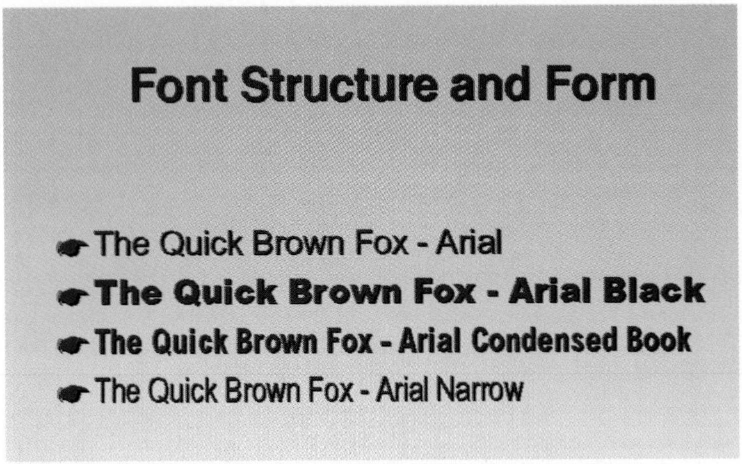

Font Structure and Form

☞ The Quick Brown Fox - Arial

☞ **The Quick Brown Fox - Arial Black**

☞ **The Quick Brown Fox - Arial Condensed Book**

☞ The Quick Brown Fox - Arial Narrow

FIGURE C9
Variations of a Typeface

Serif
Bodoni Book
New Century Schoolbook
Garamond
Poster
Vanguard

Sans Serif
Denmark
Ergoe
Garrison Sans
Herald
Phinster Fine

Script
Cotillion
Kauflinn
Mariah
Palace Script
Sheer Beauty

Decorative
bobby pin
(decorative text)
Cow Spots
PAGE CLIPS
Stars & Stripes

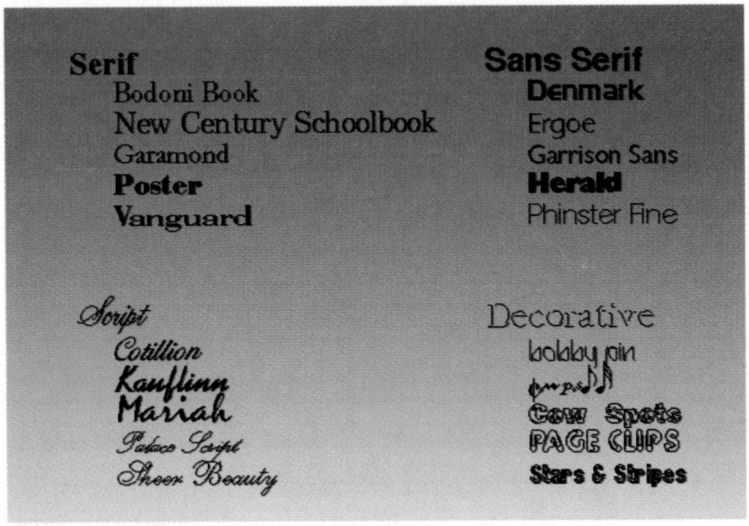

FIGURE C10
*Typefaces Grouped by
Font Type*

identical structure but a different form. The difference between structure and form is illustrated in Figure C9. Each of the lines in the box is a variation of the typeface Arial. The letters for each variation have the same structure. They have a vertical orientation, the transitions between their vertical and horizontal lines are smooth, and the lines that make up the letters do not vary much in thickness. The form for each variation, however, is quite different. If we consider Arial as the standard form, then Arial Black is a stronger, bolder, thicker variation. Arial Narrow is reduced on the horizontal scale and, as the name implies, it looks narrower. The differences in the form give each variation its own personality, conveying a heavier more solid feeling, or a lighter, more delicate feeling.

Designers usually divide typefaces into four different types of fonts: serif, sans serif, script, and what we will call decorative. Serif fonts are those like the one you are reading. They have little lines at the tops and bottoms of the letters (serifs) which are a remnant of the finishing strokes on letters when they were handwritten. San serif fonts do not have extra lines, and all the lines in the letters are of uniform thickness. Serif fonts are easier to read for longer passages because the serifs guide the eye from one letter to the next. Script fonts mimic handwriting, but they are far more precise and uniform. They can be very fancy and complicated. They can also be hard to read, so be cautious about using them in your visual aids. Finally, there are ornamental fonts. Decorative fonts are designed not so much to be easily read, but to convey a feeling or tone. The letters in decorative fonts may look like trains, flowers, small people, cow spots, bobby pins, strange symbols, and even playing cards. Use these fonts sparingly, for emphasis. Figure C10 shows a few examples of each font type. Notice how much easier it is to read some of them than others.

Most designers agree that you should not use more than two typefaces on a single visual aid and that they should be from two different font categories. The most common combination is a sans serif font for a title and a serif font for a subtitle or text. This choice is driven by considerations of readability and clarity. A sans serif font is clean and clear; it can convey a feeling of strength as long as there is not too much text. Serif fonts are more readable, so they are a better choice for body text or subtitles. Of course, designers do sometimes violate these guidelines to achieve special effects. There is no law that says you cannot use a serif font in a title and a sans serif font in the text. Just be sure that your audience will be able to read and understand your message.

● CHOOSING TYPE SIZES   You also need to think about readability when you decide what sizes of type to use for the various elements in your graphics. Of course, all of your type must be big enough to be seen by people in the back row of your audience. How big is big enough? The people at Microsoft who designed the templates for the PowerPoint™ graphics presentation program have specified general guidelines for visual aids. They recommend 44 point type for titles, 32 point type for subtitles or text if there is no subtitle, and 28 point type if there is a subtitle. These are somewhat larger point sizes than you might have seen elsewhere, but they reason that it is better to be too big than too small. The minimum point sizes you should consider for visuals other than slides are 36 point for titles, 24 point for subtitles, and 18 point for text. For slides, you could go somewhat smaller, since projection enlarges the image. You might use 24 point for titles, 18 point for subtitles, and 14 point for text. Figure C11 shows how these points look in print.

In any medium, avoid using all upper case letters for emphasis. except in short titles. Longer stretches of text in all caps is hard to read, because our eyes are used to seeing contrasting letter sizes. When we read, we not only recognize the shapes of individual letters, but also the shapes of words. When you drive on a highway, you can probably recognize the sign for your exit far before you are close enough to make out the individual letters because you recognize the shape of the words.

● USE COLOR TO CREATE A MOOD
AND SUSTAIN ATTENTION

Graphic design people have long known that warm colors (oranges, reds) appear to come forward and have an exciting effect, whereas cool colors (greens, blues) seem to recede and have a more calming effect. So when you choose colors, think about how you want your audience to react to your visual aid. Your topic, setting, personality, and purpose should influence your choice of colors. For example, if you are in a business setting, you might use cool colors to convey news which is not particularly good and warm colors to convey news that is. In the first instance you might want to calm your listeners, and in the second you might want to excite them.

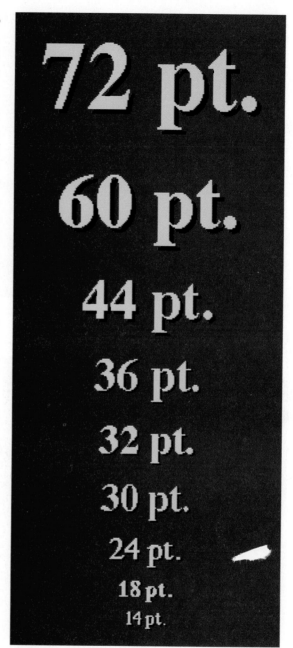

● FIGURE C11
A Range of Point Sizes

FIGURE C12
*Effective and Ineffective Color
Combinations*

It is also important to choose colors for backgrounds and text or graphics that contrast with one another but do not conflict. Figure C12 provides examples of an effective and ineffective color combination. The use of purple against a blue background is not effective because both colors are dark and the purple does not stand out from the background.

Be cautious about using green and red combinations in your visual aids. Some of your audience members may have a type of color blindness that makes these two colors indistinguishable from one another. Moreover, even for those without red-green color blindness, this combination is not effective. As you can see in Figure C13, the red type against the green background is difficult to read. The colors are not harmonious and do not contrast effectively, and the text and graph are hard on the eyes. For those with red-green color blindness, Figure C13 would appear to be an almost solid box with few or no distinctive features.

If your visual aids will be overheads, you should consider dark text on a light background. You might use black, dark blue, or dark red text that would stand out crisply from a white, light gray, or light yellow background. Each color would be distinctive and would provide excellent contrast for high readability. If your visual aids will be computer generated and projected using 35 millimeter slides, an LCD, or other projection system, light text on a dark background will

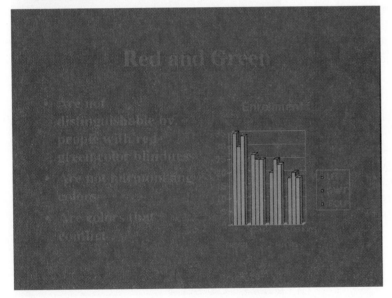

FIGURE C13
*Red-Green Color
Combinations Are
Not Effective*

produce better results. Yellow and white text on black, dark blue, or dark green backgrounds will provide the contrast you will need for an attention-getting presentation. Attractive and harmonious color combinations will get and hold your listeners' attentions longer than combinations which are neither. Don't use too many colors. Two different colors of text on one background color should be sufficient. To unify your presentation, consider using the same color for all of your backgrounds, then vary the complementary colors you use for the text. For example, if you choose a dark green for your background color, you could use white, yellow, and a very light gray for text. Save your most dramatic color contrasts for the most important point.

● USING BLACK AND WHITE EFFECTIVELY If your budget or lack of equipment limits your color choice to black and white, you can still use contrast to create attractive graphics. By choosing contrasting typefaces, spacing text widely or more compactly, using larger or smaller text, and using both bold and normal text, you can create differences in textual color. The different groups of text in Figure C14 contrast dramatically with one another and show the interesting "coloring" that you can achieve with black and white.

● USING POWERPOINT™ AND OTHER GRAPHICS PROGRAMS

Bodoni Black
Along with close spacing, bolding, and large type size appears dense and heavy.

Fifth Avenue
Along with wide spacing, bolding, and smaller type size appears lighter and airier.

Relief-Serif
Along with wide spacing, no bolding, and smaller type size appears even lighter and less substantial.

● FIGURE C14
Using Contrasts to Create "Color" with Black and White

So far, this Appendix has attempted to suggest guidelines for the production of effective and visually appealing graphics. You have learned guidelines for layout and design, selecting fonts and type size, and the use of color. Although these guidelines are very useful, it may be difficult for you to translate them into effective graphics unless you have the proper equipment.

One of the best tools for producing graphics today is a graphics presentation program like PowerPoint™ by Microsoft , Persuasion by Adobe, or Freelance Graphics by Lotus. These programs can assist you in making extremely professional looking visual aids, including transparencies, 35 millimeter slides, handouts, and even posters. You can also show the visual aids you produce with these programs right on a computer screen to show a small audience (6-12) or project them onto a large screen using a projection system. These programs allow you to adapt your designs to suit a wide variety of settings without actually redoing them each time.

Although you need to have some computer skills to use these programs, the skills you need are really quite basic. If you are reasonably adept at word processing, for example, then using a graphics presentation program should not be very difficult. In fact, most of the programs make the learning relatively easy and provide professionally designed templates to guide your efforts. Using these templates, you can input your text in outline form, and the program will automatically format it into a presentation. The real strength of these programs, then, is that they make getting started a simple matter. As you become more expert, you can alter, improve, adapt, and refine your presentations to a greater extent.

There are many powerful and user-friendly graphics presentation programs available for use on both Windows© and Macintosh© computers. PowerPoint™ is the industry leader, and you will probably encounter it when you enter the business world, so we have chosen it for our demonstration. Let's now walk through a visual display preparation using PowerPoint™ to see how this programs works. We will work from the outline of the speech on the proposed

Nortco addition that we developed earlier (see page A–15).Keep in mind that we will cover only a few basic functions of this powerful, versatile program.

● WALKTHROUGH: PREPARING A VISUAL DISPLAY WITH POWERPOINT™

After we load the PowerPoint™ program into our computer and double-click on the PowerPoint™ icon on our desktop, we see a screen that looks like Figure C15. Notice that we have several choices. The "Auto Content Wizard"

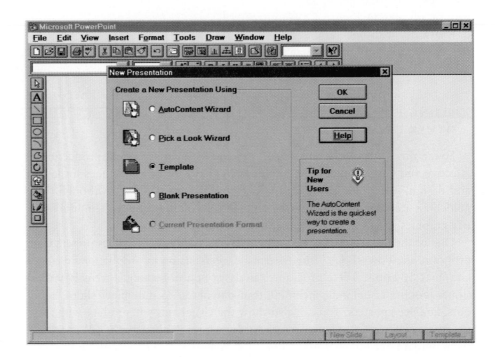
FIGURE **C15**
*PowerPoint™ Main Menu
[Screen shot reprinted with permission from Microsoft Corporation.]*

would guide us through the design and layout process by asking specific questions about our presentation. The "wizard" would simply plug the information we give it into an appropriate presentation format. "Pick a Look Wizard" formats the screen to fit the type of presentation we're giving. For example, if we're giving a computer-generated slide show, the "Pick a Look Wizard" will automatically create a slide with dark backgrounds and light text. Or, if we are creating transparencies, it will create slides with light backgrounds and dark text. The "Template" option would offer us a variety of presentation formats and designs from which to choose. To start from scratch and create an original presentation format, we would choose "Blank Presentation." Finally, if we wanted to access a format we had previously created, we would click on "Current Presentation Format."

For now we will just open a template. So we click on the Template button and then the OK button. Next we see a menu screen which looks like Figure C16. The center box tells us that we are in the PowerPoint™ templates slideshow

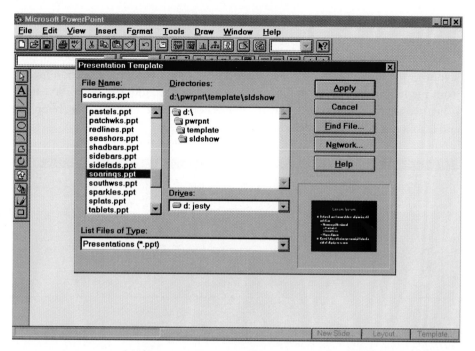

F IGURE C16
PowerPoint™ Template Menu
[Screen shot reprinted with
permission from Microsoft
Corporation.]

directory. The left box provides the name of 55* templates available to us. We can preview each template by clicking on it once and seeing it in the preview box on the lower right. When we find one we like, we simply highlight it and click on the "Apply" button. You can see that we have chosen the template "soarings.ppt" and it is highlighted in the preview box.

Having selected a template for the color and background design of our presentation and clicked "Apply," we are presented with the AutoLayout menu screen (Figure C17). We have a choice of twenty-one AutoLayouts for our text and

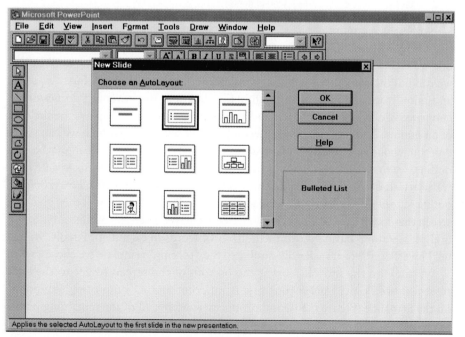

F IGURE C17
PowerPoint™ AutoLayout
Menu [Screen shot reprinted
with permission from
Microsoft Corporation.]

*Number may vary for different versions of PowerPoint™

graphics. No matter which template we had chosen, we would still see these same choices for layouts. The templates determine the style and colors for the background and text; the AutoLayout menu allows us to choose the design and layout of the text and graphics on the template. We'll choose the second layout from the left at the top. It will provide us with a title and a bulleted text box. When we click on the "OK" button, PowerPoint™ will combine our template and layout choices and display the results (Figure C18).

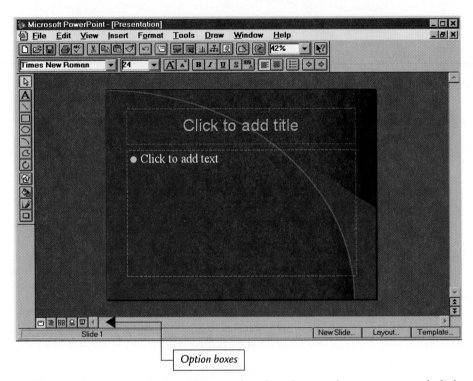

FIGURE C18
PowerPoint™ Soarings.ppt Template and Auto-layout [Screen shot reprinted with permission from Microsoft Corporation.]

Now we have more choices. We can do what the template suggests and click anywhere in either box to enter our text. However, since we have saved the outline we created from our Nortco storyboard in our word processing application, we can use the copy and paste functions to insert our outline here. First, we select an option from one of the five small option boxes at the lower left corner of the template slide. We click on the second box from the left which displays the skeleton of an outline. The computer then gives us a blank screen onto which we can either type a new outline or paste the one we have already saved. To paste in our Nortco outline, we first open up the word processing file where our outline is saved. Then we select all of the text, copy it, and exit the file. When the blank PowerPoint™ outline screen reappears, we can paste in the text. PowerPoint™ will then give us a screen that looks like Figure C19. Note that we have edited the outline a bit for an oral presentation, paring down the number of words in each item. Finally, we can tell PowerPoint™ to transfer the outline to the "soaring" template we chose earlier.

We click on the far left icon at the bottom of the screen to get to the slide screen. PowerPoint™ places our first main point and its supporting sub-points on the first slide (Figure C20), and produces slides for all of the remaining points in the outline.

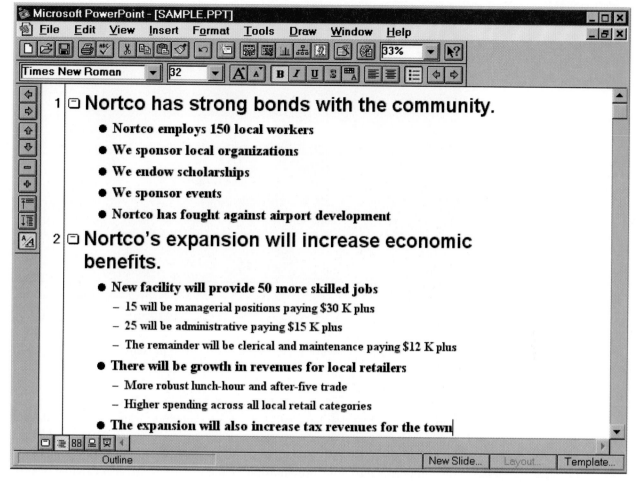

FIGURE C19
PowerPoint™ Outline Screen [Screen shot reprinted with permission from Microsoft Corporation.]

Once we have completed this step, we are ready to show the visual displays on the computer screen for a small number of people, project them onto a large screen using a projection system, or print them as a series of transparencies, notes, slides, or handouts.

Note that these visual displays follow the design principles we learned in this Appendix: the text color contrasts well with the background color but is complementary; the text is left justified and spaced in a way that suggests a relationship among the elements; there is enough but not too much information; the background and bullets are repetitive elements that tie the slides together; the title is a 44 point sans serif font and the body text is a 32 point serif font for greater readability; and we have avoided using reds and greens. PowerPoint™ made it easy for us, because these design principles are built into the templates.

We have briefly described the ease with which you can develop an effective presentation in PowerPoint™, but you should know that most computer graphics programs are extremely powerful and can produce very sophisticated results.

F IGURE C20

*PowerPoint™ Final Screen
[Screen shot reprinted with
permission from Microsoft
Corporation.]*

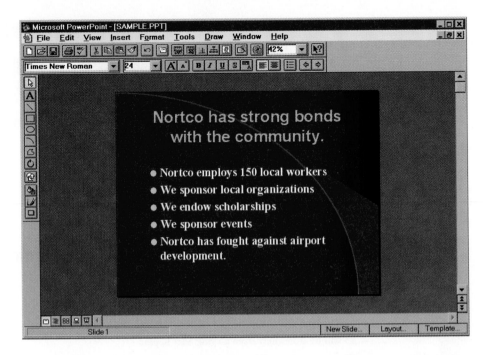

For example, if you were giving a PowerPoint™ presentation in which you needed to display a graph, you could either create it within PowerPoint™ or import the graph from another program. PowerPoint™ would automatically alter the colors to match your color scheme. In addition, PowerPoint™ can also import images that you have entered in your computer using a scanning device. So if you were giving the speech in our earlier Nortco example, you could take a picture of the finish line at the Run-For-Fun, digitize it using your scanner, and then import it into your presentation. Some programs are also capable of producing a quick series of images that look like animation, integrating sound clips, and even displaying short film clips to make your presentations even more exciting and attention-grabbing. For more details, see the user's manual of the program you are using to see how it can help you prepare the kinds of presentations that are becoming an increasingly important requirement for many careers.

The suggestions in this Appendix about storyboarding, layout and design, and using graphics software provide only a glimpse of the thousands of available options for producing effective graphics. We encourage you to experiment with different techniques, programs, and visual elements before you are up against a tight deadline for a course or workplace presentation. Then, when you have a specific task to complete, you will have the facility to produce efficiently the kinds of visual aids that are appropriate for your particular audience, topic and setting.

Appendix D: Speeches for Analysis and Discussion

● I HAVE A DREAM*

by Martin Luther King, Jr., Washington, D.C., August 28, 1963

I am happy to join with you today in what will go down in history as the greatest demonstration for freedom in the history of our nation.

Five score years ago, a great American, in whose symbolic shadow we stand today, signed the Emancipation Proclamation. This momentous decree came as a great beacon light of hope to millions of Negro slaves, who had been seared in the flames of withering injustice. It came as a joyous daybreak to end the long night of their captivity.

But one hundred years later, the Negro is still not free. One hundred years later, the life of the Negro is still sadly crippled by the manacles of segregation and the chains of discrimination. One hundred years later, the Negro lives on a lonely island of poverty in the midst of a vast ocean of material prosperity. One hundred years later, the Negro is still languished in the corners of American society and finds himself an exile in his own land. And so we've come here today to dramatize a shameful condition.

In a sense we've come to our nation's Capitol to cash a check. When the architects of our republic wrote the magnificent words of the Constitution and the Declaration of Independence, they were signing a promissory note to which every American was to fall heir. This note was a promise that all men—yes, black men as well as white men—would be guaranteed the unalienable rights of life, liberty, and the pursuit of happiness.

It is obvious today that America has defaulted on this promissory note insofar as her citizens of color are concerned. Instead of honoring this sacred obligation, America has given the Negro people a bad check—a check which has come back marked "insufficient funds."

But we refuse to believe that the bank of justice is bankrupt. We refuse to believe that there are insufficient funds in the great vaults of opportunity of this nation. And so we've come to cash this check—a check that will give us upon demand the riches of freedom and the security of justice.

We have also come to this hallowed spot to remind America of the fierce urgency of now. This is no time to engage in the luxury of cooling off or to take the tranquilizing drug of gradualism. Now is the time to make the real promises of democracy. Now is the time to rise from the dark and desolate valley of segregation to the sunlit path of racial justice. Now is the time to lift our nation from the quicksands of racial injustice to the solid rock of brotherhood. Now is the time to make justice a reality for all of God's children.

It would be fatal for the nation to overlook the urgency of the moment. This sweltering summer of the Negro's legitimate discontent will not pass until there is an invigorating autumn of freedom and equality. Nineteen sixty-three is not an end, but a beginning. Those who hope that the Negro needed to blow off steam and will now be content will have a rude awakening if the nation returns to business as usual. There will be neither rest nor tranquility in America until the Negro is granted his citizenship rights. The whirlwinds of revolt will continue to shake the foundations of our nation until the bright day of justice emerges.

But there is something that I must say to my people, who stand on the warm threshold which leads into the palace of justice. In the process of gaining our rightful place, we must not be guilty of wrongful deeds. Let us not seek to satisfy our thirst for freedom by drinking from the cup of bitterness and hatred.

We must forever conduct our struggle on the high plane of dignity and discipline. We must not allow our creative protest to degenerate into physical violence. Again and again we must rise to the majestic heights of meeting physical force with soul force.

The marvelous new militance which has engulfed the Negro community must not lead us to a distrust of all white people. For many of our white brothers, as evidenced by their presence here today, have come to realize that their destiny is tied up with our destiny. They have come to realize that their freedom is inextricably bound to our freedom. We cannot walk alone.

As we walk, we must make the pledge that we shall always march ahead. We cannot turn back. There are those who are asking the devotees of civil rights, "When will you be satisfied?" We can never be satisfied as long as the Negro is the victim of the unspeakable horrors of police brutality. We can never be satisfied as long as our bodies, heavy with the fatigue of travel, cannot gain lodging in the motels of the highways and hotels of the cities. We cannot be satisfied as long as the Negro's basic mobility is from a smaller ghetto to a larger one. We can never be satisfied as long as our children are stripped of their selfhood and robbed of their dignity by signs stating "For Whites Only." We cannot be satisfied as long as a Negro in Mississippi cannot vote and a Negro in New York believes he has nothing for which to vote. No, no, we are not satisfied, and we will not be satisfied until justice rolls down like waters, and righteousness like a mighty stream.

I am not unmindful that some of you have come here out of great trials and tribulations. Some of you have come fresh from narrow jail cells. Some of you have come from areas where your quest for freedom left you battered by the storms of persecution and staggered by the winds of police brutality. You have been the veterans of creative suffering. Continue to work with the faith that unearned suffering is redemptive.

Go back to Mississippi, go back to Alabama, go back to South Carolina, go back to Georgia, go back to Louisiana, go back to the slums and ghettos of our Northern cities, knowing that somehow this situation can and will be changed. Let us not wallow in the valley of despair.

I say to you today, my friends, so even though we face the difficulties of today and tomorrow, I still have a dream. It is a dream deeply rooted in the American dream.

I have a dream that one day this nation will rise up and live out the true meaning of its creed, "We hold these truths to be self-evident, that all men are created equal."

I have a dream that one day on the red hills of Georgia the sons of former slaves and the sons of former slaveowners will be able to sit down together at the table of brotherhood.

I have a dream that one day even the state of Mississippi, a state sweltering with the heat of injustice, sweltering with the heat of oppression, will be transformed into an oasis of freedom and justice.

I have a dream that my four little children will one day live in a nation where they will not be judged by the color of their skin but by the content of their character. I have a dream today.

I have a dream that one day, down in Alabama, with its vicious racists, with its governor having his lips dripping with the words of interposition and nullification, one day right there in Alabama little black boys and black girls will be able to join hands with little white boys and white girls as sisters and brothers. I have a dream today.

I have a dream that one day every valley shall be exalted, every hill and mountain shall be made low, the rough places will be made plane and the crooked places will be made straight, and the glory of the Lord shall be revealed, and all flesh shall see it together.

This is our hope. This is the faith that I go back to the South with. With this faith we will be able to hew out of the mountain of despair a stone of hope. With this faith we will be able to transform the jangling discords of our nation into a beautiful symphony of brotherhood. With this faith we will be able to work together, to pray together, to struggle together, to go to jail together, to stand up for freedom together knowing that we will be free one day.

This will be the day—this will be the day when all of God's children will be able to sing with new meaning, "My country 'tis of thee, sweet land of liberty, of thee I sing. Land where my fathers died, land of the Pilgrims' pride, from every mountainside, let freedom ring." And if America is to be a great nation, this must become true.

So let freedom ring from the prodigious hilltops of New Hampshire. Let freedom ring from the mighty mountains of New York. Let freedom ring from the heightening Alleghenies of Pennsylvania!

Let freedom ring from the snowcapped Rockies of Colorado! Let freedom ring from the curvaceous slopes of California!

But not only that. Let freedom ring from Stone Mountain of Georgia!

Let freedom ring from Lookout Mountain of Tennessee!

Let freedom ring from every hill and molehill of Mississippi. From every mountainside, let freedom ring.

And when this happens, when we allow freedom to ring—when we let it ring from every village and every hamlet, from every state and every city—we will be able to speed up that day when all of God's children, black men and white men, Jews and Gentiles, Protestants and Catholics, will be able to join hands and sing, in the words of the old Negro spiritual, "Free at last! Free at last! Thank God almighty, we are free at last!"

● TECHNOLOGY STRATEGIES FOR 2005: GAZING INTO A CRYSTAL BALL

by Douglas E. Olesen, President and CEO, Battelle*

Good evening. It certainly feels good to be back home and to see so many familiar faces. I want to thank Mike McCormack and all the members of the Society for inviting me here today. You have a strong tradition of excellent lectures here, and I hope I can live up to it. I'd also like to thank Grady Auvil. A lot of people talk about improving science education. But you're really doing something about it.

Like many of you here this evening, I have some wonderful memories about growing up here in Wenatchee. I remember on cold winter mornings my father going out to start our Pontiac and putting a brick on the accelerator pedal to keep it going while it warmed up. As some of you may remember, my folks owned a store over on Springwater Street. One cold morning, the car was out in front of the store warming up with the brick on the accelerator. Well, my mother went out and got in the car, and, of course, she forgot about the brick. She calmly put it in gear, and then well you can imagine. The car shot forward like a bullet fight into the store.

That story pretty much sums up my early relationship with high technology. I think it's only fair that I warn you of my heritage before I start making predictions about the key technologies of the future.

Fortunately for me, I joined an organization like Battelle that has thousands of extremely bright and extremely talented scientists and engineers. Battelle is famous around the globe in science and technology circles and in the business community. It was founded back in 1929, and it's now one of the world's largest and most respected technology organizations. Our revenue will be around $1 billion this year. We have 8,000 scientists, engineers, and support staff. And our basic mission is to help industry and government put technology to work.

But, still, we have a fairly low name recognition in the general public. That's because we don't often manufacture and sell products. And all the things we've invented don't have our name on them.

But I'm sure all of you know many of our developments very well. You've probably used one today. And you may even be carrying one with you.

We're probably best known for developing xerography. We licensed and later sold this to a small company called Haloid, which then changed its name to Xerox.

*Delivered before The Institute for Science and Society, 2nd Annual Grady Auvil Lecture, Wenatchee, Washington, April 7, 1995

We also played a major role in developing tamper-proof packaging and the UPC bar code. You use this at almost every check-out counter. We developed some of the original technology for compact disks and holograms. You have a hologram on your credit cards as an anti-counterfeit device.

We also helped develop the sandwich coin. (That's why you may be carrying a little piece of Battelle around with you.) It was developed because the amount of silver in coins got to be more valuable than the face value of the coin. We developed a coating for Titleist that keeps golf balls from splitting. This came from our development of Sno-Pake, the fluid used to correct typing errors. And one of our developments quickly became a necessity in this part of the country — cruise control. We even invented a chocolate bar that won't melt out in the sun. Hershey manufactured these for our troops in Desert Storm. One of our latest is an electric toothbrush for Teledyne Water Pik. It operates five times faster than its competitors. That means it cleans better.

Today, our work ranges from the depths of the ocean to the heights of the space shuttle. From the factory floor to the farmer's fields.

We do a tremendous amount of work related to the environment. For instance, we're developing new ways to clean up hazardous waste. We led the country's largest alternative fuels program in California. And we do a lot of work developing, testing, and registering pesticides.

We work in the health care field, inventing and developing drugs and developing new health care products.

We develop defense-related technology.

We help industry develop new products and processes, and we help speed up their time to market.

And, of course, we manage and operate the Pacific Northwest Laboratory in Richland [Washington].

In addition to our technological work, we're also heavily involved in education. Just like your Institute for Science and Society, we're dedicated to increasing science literacy in the country. Hundreds of Battelle's employees in Richland, Columbus, and elsewhere volunteer in grade schools and high schools. And last year, we distributed more than $900,000 to schools and education programs.

Now that you know a little about the Battelle of today, let's take a look at the future.

Many of you may think it's difficult to predict technological advancements. But it's not always as hard as it seems. What's more difficult is predicting the technology that will really change our lives, and how it will affect us.

Back around the turn of the century (the previous turn of the century), there were many scientists and science writers who predicted we'd fly to the moon before the century was over. But none of them foresaw an even more amazing feat — that we would all be able to sit in our living room and watch those first men walking on the moon while it was happening. They didn't foresee television, which is arguably the technology that has changed our lives the most this century.

This type of practical technology is our focus at Battelle. We strive to work on technology that will genuinely improve the quality of life. So, that's the type of technology I'll be talking about this evening.

Earlier this year, we got together a group of Battelle's most visionary technology experts, and we asked them to gaze into their crystal balls and tell us what were going to be the biggest technologies in the business world 10 years from now.

We set three guidelines for them.

The first is fairly obvious: These technologies must provide a benefit and be of value to the end user.

Second, the companies that develop or own these technologies must gain a competitive advantage from them.

And finally, these technologies must support a company's business goals. In other words, these are the technologies that are going to make a lot of money for someone.

So, we weren't looking at government-sponsored technologies. Instead, we focused on the technologies that businesses would be wise to invest in right now. Our goal — and, by the way, this is always Battelle's goal — was to mesh technology advances with business and market realities.

Of course, none of these predictions are sure things. Back in the 1970s, when I was working at PNL, lots of people thought the big research push over the next 20 years would be in alternative energy sources. But 20 years later, we're still driving cars powered by gasoline, and most of the homes in the country still get their heat and electricity from oil, natural gas, and coal-burning power plants.

What happened? Well, more oil became available, energy prices fell, and the immediate need disappeared. Consequently, R&D investments in that area shrank significantly. Clearly, we still need new energy sources, so we still need that research. But since there's no immediate market for those products, there's no money for the research.

Of course, some of the technologies I'll talk about this evening could have the same fate. These aren't sure things; they're opportunities. If the right investments are made in these technologies, they'll likely produce some great results.

Before I start on my top-10 list, I'd like to tell you about a few of the more exciting technologies that did not make the list. These could also be important, money-making technologies in the next decade, but we had to limit our list to 10.

For one, global positing systems that will allow some prisoners to remain at home, because the police could monitor exactly where that person is at any time. We'll also be able to use the same technology to track our children wherever they are. That could be a big deterrent to kidnapping. We'll be using that technology to track stolen cars, and we could even use it to track our pets. So, you'll never lose your dog, no matter how hard you try.

We also foresee increased husbandry of the oceans. Within ten years, we'll be repopulating the oceans as a source for food.

We'll also have major products that are totally recyclable or reusable. Even products like automobiles and refrigerators will be designed to be completely recycled or reused.

And, we may even have robotic devices that will take care of cleaning your house or mowing your lawn.

Finally, I hope there will be some new technology that will help us avert a possible water crisis. Clean water is quickly becoming scarcer in many parts of the world, and within the next 15 years, a barrel of clean water could cost $20.

Those all could be important technologies by 2005, but like I said, we had to keep our list to the top 10.

Like David Letterman, I suppose I should start at the bottom of the list.

10. The number 10 technology on our list is computer software and other products related to "edutainment." These include educational games and computerized simulations.

All of you who have children know that students today are much more technologically sophisticated than we ever were. Whenever I go into someone's house and see that the VCR clock isn't blinking, then I'm pretty sure that a teenager lives there. They're usually the only ones in the family who know how to program the VCR.

But despite our technical shortcomings today, we were more comfortable with technology than our parents. And you can bet that tomorrow's students will be even more adept with technology than today's whiz kids. So, tomorrow's students will expect much more from education. And so will their parents.

That will mean a big payoff for companies that can develop products that put more education into entertainment and more entertainment into education. So, in five to 10 years, most textbook publishers will have software developers working alongside their authors. After all, when Steven Speilberg's son Max turns 12 and needs an exciting program to help him learn his math, then I'm sure someone's going to make one for Dad to buy.

We're going to see applications for these edutainment products at home, in school, and in the workplace, where retraining the work force will continue to be more and more important.

9. A lot of people ask us about the topic of the next item on our list. They want to know what kind of fuel our cars will be using in ten years or so. Is it going to still be gasoline, or reformulated gasoline? Is it going to be electricity? Or will cars be running on ethanol, methanol, or some other fuel?

Our answer? Yes.

In 10 years, the automobile in your driveway could be running on two different fuels — and they'll likely be reformulated gasoline and some other fuel. One fuel would be used for acceleration and the other for maintaining your speed. In this part of the country, that other fuel might be electricity (if we can improve battery technology). But in Iowa, the other fuel might be ethanol. And in Colorado, maybe it could be natural gas.

At Battelle, we recently completed the country's largest alternative fuels program. In the program, more than 100 FedEx delivery trucks in Southern California ran on five different fuels over two years.

And which fuel was the winner?

Actually, there was no clear-cut winner. We found that they all had lower emissions. But, none stood head and shoulders above the others. No single fuel would be able to meet all the needs of every fleet owner, for instance. Each business would have to look at the pros and cons of each fuel before deciding which way to go.

8. For the next item on our technology list, let's move from one of the few things that might be more precious than our cars — and that's our health.

Within the next 10 years, we'll see the development of a number of new and more effective ways to detect and treat diseases. We'll have new diagnostic tools that use highly accurate sensors to detect diseases at very early stages.

For example, at Battelle we now have a machine that can measure gases in parts per trillion.

Just for reference, how long is a trillion seconds? How many think it's more than a year? How many think it's more than 10 years? Does anyone think it's more than 100 years? Actually, it's about 315,000 years. So, detecting parts per trillion is comparable to being able to isolate one single second in a period of 315,000 years.

But what does that have to do with diagnosing diseases? Well, if someone has cirrhosis of the liver, or lung cancer, or a number of other diseases — even at very early stages — their breath contains small amounts of certain chemicals. If doctors could detect those chemicals, they might be able to detect a disease by just analyzing a person's breath.

(By the way, we're now using that machine — it's called a Trace Atmospheric Gas Analyzer — to analyze air pollutants over the North Pacific.)

In addition to detecting diseases earlier, we'll also be able to treat them more effectively with drug delivery systems that target specific parts of the body.

Imagine chemotherapy that could be better targeted just to cancer cells so you wouldn't lose your hair or experience other harmful side effects.

One of the biggest reasons for the importance of medical developments on this list is simple demographics. The oldest of the baby boomers will be 60 years old in just 10 years, so if any of the young people here tonight have the slightest inclination about going into medicine, now may be the time.

7. Given the general personality of the baby boom generation, we decided to list one other development ahead of these new medical treatments.

Number seven on our list is anti-aging products and services.

Unfortunately, there's no way we can prevent aging, but we will be able to make the process a little less traumatic. These new developments may range from aging creams that actually work to an effective cure for baldness.

6. Number six on our list is a development that links up shoppers directly to the factory floor. New, smart systems will be able to control manufacturing processes, and they'll be able to create individual products for individual consumers.

In 10 years, when you need a new suit or a new outfit, you might head down to your favorite store, but instead of trying on a lot of clothes, you'll just pick out a style and a fabric and then have all your measurements taken electronically. Those measurements, along with your order, will go immediately to the factory. And a few days later, your perfectly tailored suit will come straight to your home.

Just imagine the possibilities for a system like this. Imagine getting blue jeans that actually fit. Or, for all of you who have bunions, imagine getting shoes that actually fit. We may even buy our cars this way.

Factories will also be using these smart systems to gather information from sensors up and down the assembly line. And then the systems will automatically make decisions like slowing down or speeding up the line, fixing a piece of equipment, or ordering supplies.

5. The computer chip of course, is the big driver behind this type of development. And the same is true for the number-five item on our list.

In 10 years, it will be possible for you to carry around a laptop computer that's about the size of a pocket calculator. These new products will be interactive, wireless data centers. You might use it as a fax, a phone, a source for news or stock market reports, and as a tool for accessing more information than is in your library.

In addition to this super computer in your pocket, you'll also be carrying around smart cards that have the power of a computer and will perform a number of daily activities for you They might serve as the key for your car, or your personal calendar, or a record of your complete medical history — and they may even serve as your money. You won't hear pockets jingling anymore with keys and loose change.

We're working on a project right now that will put these smart cards to work on college campuses, so that students could pay for their tuition, sign up for their classes, download textbooks onto their computer, do their laundry, and order a pizza, all with one smart card.

In fact, we predict that in 15 years there will be a billion computers and smart cards in the United States.

4. Number four on my list is one that very well could be the next hot item in the entertainment industry. It's digital high-definition television. The important word to remember there is "digital."

I'm sure you've all probably heard of HDTV — how it will make the quality of your television picture approach the quality of a movie screen. For those of you like me who grew up with black-and-white television, the first time you see one of these digital HDTV sets will be like the first time you saw color TV. And they're going to do the same thing to old color TVs that compact disks did to the LP.

What many people might find especially surprising about this new technology is that American companies will likely be the leaders in the global HDTV market. For several years, Japanese companies have been working on analog high-definition television, and they've already come out with some products.

But a few American companies have taken the lead in digital HDTV, and that's really where the market is going to go.

Now, we need one manufacturer to step forward and set the standard for others to follow. We need one standard model — like the VHS became for the videotape industry.

This HDTV technology will also lead to better computer images for advanced computer modeling and imaging. But, looking just at the market for television sets, this is a multibillion dollar industry. After all, more homes in the United States have televisions than have telephones.

Eventually, within 20 years or so, your digital high-definition television will have a very large, but very thin screen, and you'll hang it on the wall like a picture. At Battelle, we've already developed that display screen technology for use in military aircraft.

3. Throughout this list, we've seen some incredible electronic products, but we'll need the third technology on this list to keep many of those electronic gadgets working. I'm talking about high-density energy sources.

We'll be developing amazing electronics, but we'll have to find ways to harness the energy to use them. We'll have to develop portable, inexpensive fuel sources so that we'll have energy available where and when we need it. Innovations in batteries and materials will pave the way for these new fuel sources. And this innovation will be driven, to a great extent, by the electric vehicle market.

These new batteries or fuel cells will greatly expand the market for electronics around the globe and into Third World countries. After all, you can't use a laptop if you don't have the energy to operate it.

2. A moment ago, I mentioned that advances in materials will help lead to these new fuel cells. And that's number two on our list — super materials.

Currently, to make new materials, we have to combine two or more other materials, maybe under intense heat, or pressure, or some other circumstance — and then we're able to alter the make-up of the material to make it fit our needs. It can be an extremely long and difficult process to develop a material with exactly the characteristics you're looking for. That's a lot of trial and error involved.

But within 10 years, we'll actually be designing new materials at the molecular level. We'll be able to manipulate the molecules in a material to make it lighter, stronger, more flexible, or whatever we need.

Here's an example of what we can do simply by manipulating a molecule. Polyethylene is a material that we use every day now. And we've been able to use it in a variety of forms, just by changing the structure of the molecule. At one end of the spectrum, we use it as paraffin oil. But we can make the molecule stronger and use it to make a wax. We can alter it again and use it to make sandwich bags. Or, making the molecule even stronger, we can make trash bags that won't puncture. Or, finally, we can make polyethylene so strong that we can weave polyethylene fibers into unbreakable sails for boats competing for the America's Cup.

Within 10 to 20 years, we'll be using hundreds of new, high-performance materials that we've developed by manipulating molecules. We'll be using these super materials in the transportation industry, computers, energy, and communications, to name just a few. And I'm sure they'll find a way into our pricier golf clubs and tennis rackets.

The potential for these new materials seems almost unlimited, because the number of molecules in the world is virtually unlimited.

1. The number one item in our top-10 list is somewhat similar to these new materials designed at the molecular level. But instead of manipulating molecules, we're talking about manipulating the human gene.

Right now, we're standing at the threshold of a golden age for biology. Over the next few decades, we're really going to begin to thoroughly understand biological processes and the causes of disease. In fact, if you look back at where the computer industry was 10 or 15 years ago, that's where biological and genetic research is now.

Today, there's a great deal of research going on to map the human genome. The genome is like the encyclopedia of all our genetic material. What we're doing right now is defining the volumes in that encyclopedia, and that should be finished by the year 2000. For instance, just last month, a group of scientists reported that they may have discovered the master control gene for the formation of the eye.

After this stage of defining the volumes in our genetic encyclopedia, then we'll likely isolate most of our efforts on defining problem areas. We're seeing the beginning of that type of research with discoveries of gene flaws that may be connected to kidney and breast cancer, leukemia, dyslexia, Alzheimer's, Lou Gehrig's disease — even alcoholism and obesity. We seem to read about a new one every week.

The result of this research will be an explosion in new medical treatments and cures over the next 20 years. This genetic research may in the next 10 years lead to cures for specific types of cancer — and possibly even AIDS.

And we're going to see many other new life-saving treatments. For instance, we predict that over the next quarter century, we'll prevent 13 million deaths from heart disease. That's about three times the entire population of the state of Washington. New medical advances will also prevent more than 2 million deaths from lung cancer, leukemia, and colo-rectal cancer. That's more than the population of Utah.

But along with these new medical treatments, our genetic advances will raise some of the most difficult ethical issues that we'll face in this period.

Say, for instance, that you find out that you carry the gene defect that makes you more susceptible to developing Alzheimer's Disease at an early age. Maybe that discovery will allow you to start monitoring for the disease and maybe even take some new treatment. But at some time down the road, will insurance companies and potential employers want to see your genetic make-up before deciding to cover or hire you? Before we decide to marry someone, will we want to see their genetic scorecard?

Obviously, these are going to be extremely complex issues. And we're going to be facing them very soon. Really, though, I think we'd all gladly take on these types of issues if we could find cures for some of the deadly diseases facing us today.

That's our list, from bottom to top. And as you can see, we're pretty excited about the future at Battelle. But we're also very realistic. We know that the right investments have to be made for any of these predictions to come true. As I mentioned earlier, they're really more "opportunities" than they are "predictions."

To close this evening, I want to talk briefly about two kinds of investments that will help us take advantage of these opportunities.

The first deals with the basic process of going from a technological idea — like one of the 10 I've talked about — to the finished product.

As you can imagine, research and development can be extremely expensive. And it's only going to grow more expensive as our technology grows more complex. Along with this trend toward more complex and more expensive research, businesses are facing stronger competition, more pressure to bring new products to the market faster than ever, and stricter environmental standards.

With all these pressures, businesses are increasingly demanding higher returns from their investments in new products and processes. And that makes any long-term research a very difficult proposition.

A lot of companies today are looking for help to deal with all these factors. And more and more, the step they're taking is to form alliances and partnerships with organizations such as Battelle to help with their long-term and near-term innovation. These partnerships can help reduce the companies' costs and give them access to new technologies and a world-class staff of scientists and engineers.

Over the next 10 to 15 years, I think we're going to see businesses going one step further. I propose that this movement toward more technology alliances and partnerships is really just a transition.

In the future, many companies will be outsourcing all their R&D — just like they might outsource their janitorial services, their printing services, or their advertising today. They'll maintain a vice president of technology to manage a network of R&D alliances with suppliers, universities, and R&D organizations. Maybe they'll have their own staff of scientists and engineers housed right in one of these other organizations. This type of setup could be the ultimate way to access the latest technology at the least cost.

That's one kind of investment that will help companies develop those top 10 technologies.

The second — and final — type of investment I wanted to mention is a little different. It's one that we're all going to have to make — businesses and the public alike. It's an investment in education — and particularly in science and math education.

One of our biggest obstacles that could keep us from developing some of these technologies is simply our inability to get our students excited about science and math.

The National Research Council estimates that 75 percent of all high school graduates in this country would flunk out of a college freshman math or engineering course. Less than half of our high school graduates have even taken chemistry or algebra II.

One result of this apathy toward science is that we may be facing a terrible shortage of scientists and engineers in the near future.

Currently, there are just over 1,500 high school students in Wenatchee. (That's up quite a bit from my graduation in 1957.) Anyway, if this is a typical group, only two of those 1,500 students will ultimately go on to receive a Ph.D. in science or engineering.

But even more important than this shortage is the fact that we're producing a society and a work force that, to a great extent, is scientifically illiterate. One recent study showed that:

—Half of all Americans don't believe that humans evolved from earlier species of animals.

—Two-thirds don't know how many planets there are in the solar system.

—And only one in every twelve adults can identify the causes of acid rain.

As Carl Sagan has said:

"We live in a society exquisitely dependent on science and technology, in which hardly anyone knows anything about science and technology."

And the fact is, as each year passes, we're all going to have to know a lot more about science and technology. The *Wall Street Journal* reported last year that Ford is now hiring more college-educated people to work on its assembly lines. In fact, they've more than doubled their hiring of assembly-line workers with college experience. Why? It's simple. They've found that these workers are better able to adapt to changing technology. And it's changing all the time, so I see that trend increasing in the years ahead.

With that kind of future in front of us, one of our most important challenges is to show students that science and technology are the best tools we have to create opportunities. They need to see that we can use science to save lives, create employment, and make a better life for us all.

I think we all share in that responsibility. As business leaders, educators, parents, grandparents, and taxpayers, we all need to work to spark our kids' interest in science.

Your own Institute for Science and Society is a great example of a group of people who've taken that responsibility to heart. I'm really impressed with your programs to promote science literacy to public officials, the general public, and especially to teachers.

More than ever before, education is going to be the key to our economic development — education in the school and education at home. It's the best blueprint we have for building better tomorrow — and for making all of my predictions tonight come true.

● SCHADENFREUDE

by Karon Bowers, Bradley University

It was a whirlwind romance of chicken McNuggets, sweaty smooches, and fumbling passes. It was my junior year. I was a cheerleader and dating the football team captain. It was my birthday, Thursday, 10:30 A.M., right after third period typing, in the locker bay. It happened to be the celebration of our one-month anniversary. Captain Cool decided to dump me for a really ugly freshman cheerleader, Thelma Valentine. I hated her. According to "Dear Diary" entry number 430, October 1, 1986: "Weren't you the one that tried to hurt me with good-by? Did you think I'd crumble? Did you think I'd lay down and die? Oh no. Not I. I will survive. Hey. Hey." After wishing for every possible disaster, from car crashes to a burning case of any venereal disease, I resigned myself to accepting fate and cheering on everyone, except him. "Go team go! Go all the way! Except for Shawn, I hope you die today!" My dreams came true. He broke his arm. Yes! Life was beautiful! There was to be no date! I was overcome by inner pleasure over his misfortune. What was I experiencing? The knowledge that I was Elizabeth Montgomery's bewitched TV child Tabitha. Okay, maybe not, but it was schadenfreude. Not Frugen Glazen or Farfigneuten, but Schadenfreude. That little twinge of pleasure we all feel when fate deals a bad hand—to someone else.

In order to understand this phenomenon, we must, first, learn how to spell it; second, examine what schadenfreude is; third, focus on why it exists; and finally, explore some ways we can learn to deal with schadenfreude.

Now first, schadenfreude—S-C-H-A-D-E-N-F-R-E-U-D-E—schadenfreude.

Second, what does this word mean? Schadenfreude is a German word with "schaden" meaning "damage" and "freude" meaning "joy." This is not to be confused with Sigmund Freud(e), who studied a different kind of joy all together.

Schadenfreudites live by the philosophy, "It's not enough that I succeed. Others must fail." You know, it's that feeling you get when you see someone getting a ticket on the side of the road. You're not thinking, "Oh gosh buddy, tough break." You're thinking, "Ha Ha, you got a ticket, not me."

In *Newsweek* of November 2, 1987, Michael O'Neill explains that schadenfreude is our way of asserting superiority over others and thus feeling better about ourselves. But have you ever been sitting there, mocking the fuchsia and pea green lavender fashion fiasco on the guy next to you, only to turn around and find your best friend laughing at your Farrah Fawcett, dippity-dooed, Aquanet hair-sprayed bouffant, velour v-neck, Hushpuppy sweater, and dirt-brown, wedged Bass loafers? I have. It's not funny.

Well, now that we know how to spell it and what schadenfreude is, we need to understand why it exists. One reason we experience schadenfreude is that we are, by nature, competitive. "Oh no, Karon, say it isn't so! Say that I have been doing this activity all of my life just for the camaraderie." Yeah, right, and Debbie did Dallas just for artistic integrity! The February edition of *Gentleman's Quarterly*—I read it for the Obsession ads—explains that schadenfreude breeds in environments where success and failure are measured. Take for example the Olympic finals of women's figure skating. Ya know, when I saw Kristi Yamaguchi fall, I thought, "Oh, Kristi. You sold the gold. It's Debi Thomas revisited." But then I sat and watched as every other skater fell on her sequined, cheesy, tutu pitooters, and I thought, "Hey, Kristi, way to go for the gold. You hexed 'em!" Schadenfreude. Now that's some ancient Japanese secret, huh? For many of us though, success is not always winning the big prize. It's just getting closer to it than our rivals do, which often pits us in a battle of one-upmanship. "You think you had it rough; my dad grounded me for three weeks!" "Well, my dad locked me in the garage for three days!" "Well, my dad used to stab me!" "Oh yeah? How hard and how many times?"

Well, another reason why we experience schadenfreude is that we are all afraid of failure. In her book, *The Impostor Phenomenon,* Dr. Pauline Rose Clance explains that the fear of failure invades our lives. So when we have an opportunity to laugh at someone else it gives us a sense of reprieve. The clown slipping on a banana peel and snapping his spine in twain assures us that there is justice in the world. However, if you see an old woman on a walker ambling down the street, and suddenly she slips on a banana peel and her life alert button is nowhere to be found . . . yeah, well, maybe it's not that healthy. But the point is, as long as it's not our butts getting busted, it's funny. These feelings are very natural. It's only when individuals allow themselves to become victims of schadenfreude that they tend to believe that they are supreme beings, that no one and nothing can touch them. Witness Leona Helmsley. Witness Leona Helmsley going off to jail. Witness Leon Helmsley being dragged around prison hooked to the belt loops of Carol, being traded for a carton of Newport Kings. In reality these individuals are merely avoiding any real world situation that would put them at risk, limiting their ability to learn and grow.

So far we've examined what schadenfreude is and why it exists, now it's time to learn how we can deal with it.

First, we need to learn to question our own behavior and actions rather than laughing at others' shortcomings. As Molly Douglas explains in her book, *Teen Girl Talk: A Guide to Beauty, Fashion, and Health,* "Unfortunately, today's society implies that only the beautiful succeed. Dismiss this theory now! It's rubbish! And for others, remember it is important to have inner beauty." Well, Douglas goes on to state, "Your first period can be worrisome, but it shouldn't be." Liar!

By focusing on improving our own behavior and actions rather than laughing at others' shortcomings, we can not only sincerely feel better about ourselves, but also be more likable, have friends, get picked first in kickball, get those nice, cute bunny Valentines instead of the rhino-snake-buzzard-circling-over-a-dead-carcass-on-a-highway variety which you used to give to all those schadenfreu-dites in the fourth grade.

Second, we need to realize that failures are as important as successes. As Michael O'Neill explains in his article, "Let's Hear It for the Losers," "Losing is a primal element of progress." You lose only to gain more later. This is also known as the Oprah Winfrey diet plan.

Finally, if you continue to feel little twinges of schadenfreude, remember the immortal words of Dire Straits: "Sometimes you're the windshield. Sometimes you're the bug." Sometimes you feel like a nut. Sometimes you don't . . . because schadenfreude is a question of perspective.

Well, after understanding what schadenfreude is, why it exists, and how we can learn to deal with it, it is clear that schadenfreude will continue to be a part of the human psyche. It's only after we understand the schadenfreude beast that we can tame it.

So, what happened when my latest beau dumped me? It was our fourth anniversary. It was the day before our wedding. It was while I was getting my new Toni perm. I said, "Stop right there. I gotta know right now. Do you love me? Will you love me forever?" Witness Dear Diary entry number 2786, March 27, 1992. "Dear Diary: I gave him Thelma's number. They deserve each other."

Notes

CHAPTER 1

1. Louis Nizer, *Reflections Without Mirrors,* quoted in Jack Valenti, *Speak Up With Confidence: How to Prepare, Learn, and Deliver Effective Speeches* (New York: William Morrow and Company, 1982), p. 34.

2. James C. Humes, *The Sir Winston Method: Five Secrets of Speaking the Language of Leadership* (New York: William Morrow and Company, 1991), p. 13–14.

3. As quoted in Brent Filson, *Executive Speeches: Tips on How to Write and Deliver Speeches From 51 CEO's* (New York: John Wiley and Sons, 1994), p. 1.

4. Dan B. Curtis, Jerry L. Winsor, and Ronald D. Stephens, "National Preferences in Business and Communication Education," *Communication Education* 38 (January 1989): 6–14.

5. National Archives and Records Administration, Kennedy's Inaugural Address of 1961 (1987), p. 6.

6. Sidney Blumenthal, "Rendezvousing with Destiny," *The New Yorker,* 8 March 1993, p. 44.

7. Ibid.

8. "Hecklers Disrupt Gingrich Book Stop," *Austin American-Statesman,* 6 June 1995, p. A3.

9. Herman Cohen, *The History of Speech Communication: The Emergence of a Discipline: 1914–1945* (Annandale, VA: Speech Communication Association, 1994), p. 2.

10. Randall A. Lake, "Enacting Red Power: The Consummatory Function in Native American Protest Rhetoric," in Christine Kelly et al., eds., *Diversity in Public Communication: A Reader* (Dubuque, IA: Kendall-Hunt, 1995), p. 204.

11. Adetokunbo F. Knowles-Borishade, "Paradigm for Classical African Orature," in Christine Kelly et al., eds., *Diversity in Public Communication: A Reader* (Dubuque, IA: Kendall-Hunt, 1995), p. 100.

CHAPTER 2

1. We thank Barbara Patton of Southwest Texas State University for sharing her speech outline with us.

2. Sample speech written by Christopher D. Therit, Millersville University, Department of Communication and Theatre, Millersville, Pennsylvania.

3. Survey conducted by R. H. Bruskin and Associates, *Spectra* 9 (December 1973) 4.

4. Steven Booth Butterfield, "Instructional Interventions for Situational Anxiety and Avoidance," *Communication Education* 37 (1988): 214–223.

5. Joe Ayres and Theodore S. Hopf, "The Long-Term Effect of Visualization in the Classroom: A Brief Research Report," *Communication Education* 39 (1990): 75–78.

6. Joe Ayers and Theodore S. Hopf, "Visualization: A Means of Reducing Speech Anxiety," *Communication Education* 34 (1985): 318–323.

CHAPTER 3

1. Richard Lacayo, "A Moment of Silence," *Time,* 8 May 1995, p. 45.

2. Ibid., p. 46.

3. Samuel Walker, *Hate Speech* (Lincoln, NE: University of Nebraska Press, 1994), p. 162.

4. "Three Decades Later, Free Speech Vets Return to UC Berkeley," *Sacramento Bee,* 3 December 1994, p. A1.

5. Walker, p. 2.

6. Edwin R. Bayley, *Joe McCarthy and the Press* (Madison, WI: Wisconsin University Press, 1981), p. 29.

7. Marc Gunther, "Campaign Sound Bites to Grow to at Least 30 Seconds on CBS," *Austin American-Statesman,* 11 July 1992, p. A1.

8. Tom Wicker, "Improving the Debates," *The New York Times,* 21 June 1991, p. A16.

9. Bill Bradley, "Race and the American City," address delivered in the U.S. Senate, March 26, 1992. Reprinted in Owen Peterson, ed., *Representative American Speeches, 1991–92* (New York: The H.W. Wilson Company, 1992), p. 139.

10. Serge F. Kovaleski, "Gingrich Gets the Facts Wrong in Some of His Recent Speeches," *Austin American-Statesman,* 4 March 1995, p. A8.

11. Dee Sellars, "College Thinking," in Jeffrey Gordon, ed., *The University and Your Life* (Southwest Texas State University: College of General Studies, 1995), p. 100.

12. Stephen H. Wildstrom, "Laptops for the Desktop," *Business Week,* 3 July 1995, p. 18.

13. Harold Barrett, *Rhetoric and Civility: Human Development, Narcissism, and the Good Audience* (Albany: State University of New York Press, 1991), p. 154.

14. Richard M. Weaver, "A Responsible Rhetoric," address delivered at Purdue University, March 29, 1955. Ed. by Thomas Clark and Richard Johannesen for *The Intercollegiate Review,* (Winter 1976–77): 82.

15. Waldo W. Braden, *Abraham Lincoln, Public Speaker* (Baton Rouge: Louisiana State University Press, 1988), p. 90.

16. Adapted from Richard L. Johannesen, "Perspectives on Ethics in Persuasion," in Charles U. Larson, ed., *Persuasion: Reception and Responsibility,* 2d. ed. (Belmont, CA: Wadsworth Publishing, 1979), p. 271.

● CHAPTER 4

1. Study conducted by Paul Cameron, as cited in Ronald B. Adler and Neil Town, *Looking Out/Looking In: Interpersonal Communications* (New York: Holt, Rinehart and Winston, 1981), p. 218.

2. Douglas Ehninger, Bruce E. Gronbeck, Ray E. McKerrow, and Alan H. Monroe, *Principles and Types of Speech Communication* (Glenview, IL Scott, Foresman, 1986), p. 43.

3. Albert Mehrabian, *Nonverbal Communication* (Hawthorne, NY: Aldine, 1972).

4. Paul Ekman and Wallace Friesen, "Head and Body Cues in the Judgement of Emotion: A Reformulation," *Perceptual and Motor Skills* 25 (1967): 711–724.

5. Ralph G. Nichols and Leonard A. Stevens, "Six Bad Listening Habits," in *Are You Listening?* (New York: McGraw-Hill, 1957).

6. Paul Rankin, "Listening Ability: Its Importance, Measurement and Development," *Chicago Schools Journal* 12 (January 1930): 177–179.

7. Nichols and Stevens.

8. John T. Masterson, Steven A. Beebe, and Norman H. Watson, *Invitation to Effective Speech Communication,* (Glenview, IL.: Scott, Foresman, 1989), p.5.

● CHAPTER 5

1. For an excellent review of gender and persuasability research see: Daniel J. O'Keefe, *Persuasion: Theory and Research* (Newbury Park, CA: Sage, 1990), p.176–177. Also see: James B. Stiff, *Persuasive Communication (New York: The Guilford Press, 1994) p. 133–136.*

2. Ibid.

3. Ibid.

4. The research summarized here is based on pioneering work by Geert Hofstede, *Culture's Consequences: International Differences in Work-Related Values* (Beverly Hills, CA: Sage, 1984). Also see: Edward T. Hall, *Beyond Culture* (New York: Doubleday, 1976).

5. John T. Masterson and Norman Watson, "The Effects of Culture on Preferred Speaking Style," paper presented at the Speech Communication Association Conference, November 1979.

6. See Devorah A. Lieberman, *Public Speaking in the Multicultural Environment* (Englewood Cliffs, NJ: Prentice Hall, 1994).

7. John Wait Bowers and John Courtwright, *Research Methods in Communication* (Glenview, IL.: Scott, Foresman, 1982.) 4. Abraham H. Maslow and N. L. Mintz, "Effect of Esthetic Surroundings," *Journal of Psychology* 41 (1956): 247–254.

8. For an excellent discussion of how to adapt to specific audience situations see: Jo Sprague and Douglas Stuart, *The Speaker's Handbook* (Fort Worth: Harcourt, Brace, Jovanovich College Publishers, 1992), p. 345.

9. Lieberman. Also see: Edward T. Hall, *The Silent Language* (Greenwich, CT: Fawcett, 1959); and Edward T. Hall, *The Hidden Dimension* (Garden City, NJ: Doubleday, 1966).

● CHAPTER 6

1. L.M. Boyd, syndicated column.

2. Bruce Gronbeck, from his presidential address, delivered at the annual conference of the Speech Communication Association, November 1994.

3. Alex F. Osborn, *Applied Imagination* (New York: Scribner's, 1962).

4. Marilyn Hernandez, "The Work-Study Program," student speech, University of Miami, 1983.

5. Monique Russo, "The 'Starving Disease' or Anorexia Nervosa," student speech, University of Miami, 1984.

6. Jennifer Travis, "The World Through a Child's Eyes," in *Winning Orations 1994* (Mankato, MN: Interstate Oratorical Association, 1994), p. 103.

7. Josh Wilson, "Sudden Infant Death Syndrome," student speech, Southwest Texas State University, 1987.

● CHAPTER 7

1. Debbie Graves, "The Libraries of Tomorrow Might Be Without Books," *Austin American-Statesman,* 10 June 1995, p. B6.

2. Richard J. Smith and Mark Gibbs, *Navigating the Internet* (Indianapolis: Sams Publishing, 1994), p.2.

3. Allen C. Benson, *The Complete Internet Companion for Librarians* (New York: Neal-Schuman Publishers, 1995), p. 298.

4. Ibid.

5. *The Lawyer,* November 1, 1994.

6. Steven Levy, "No Place for Kids?" *Newsweek,* 3 July 1995, p. 48.

CHAPTER 8

1. Bettijane Levine, "Fighting the Giant," *Los Angeles Times,* 10 August 1994, p. E-1.

2. Marilyn Hernandez, "The March of Dimes," student speech, University of Miami, 1981.

3. U.S. Newswire, "Transcript of President Clinton's Remarks at the Brady Law One-Year Anniversary Commemoration," 28 February 1995.

4. Glen Martin, "Tragic Trilogy," in *Winning Orations 1994* (Mankato, MN: Interstate Oratorical Association, 1994), p. 74.

5. Christopher M. Wanner, "May the Forests Be With Us," *Winning Orations 1993* (Interstate Oratorical Association), p. 73.

6. Professor Frazer White, University of Miami.

7. Heidi Wadeson, "Huffing: The Drugs of Choice?" in *Winning Orations 1994* (Interstate Oratorical Association), p. 92.

8. Amy Andrews-Henrickson, "Lessons Not Learned from History: Gulf War Syndrome," in *Winning Orations 1994,* p. 65.

9. Kelly McInerney, untitled speech, in *Winning Orations 1990* (Interstate Oratorical Association), p. 14.

10. Shannon Burger, "Will It Hurt?" in *Winning Orations 1994* (Interstate Oratorical Association), p. 89.

11. "Emotional Abuse," *Austin American-Statesman,* 14 January 1988, p. E2.

12. Barbara Bush, "Choices and Change" (1 June 1990), in Halford Ross Ryan, ed., *Contemporary American Public Discourse* (Prospect Heights, IL: Waveland Press, 1992), p. 382.

13. Percy Bysshe Shelly, "Ode to the West Wind."

14. Laial Dahr, "Schools: Learning Zone or Battle Zones?" in *Winning Orations 1994* (Interstate Oratorical Association), p. 61.

15. Elizabeth Cady Stanton, address to the first women's rights convention (1848), in Houston Peterson, ed., *A Treasury of the World's Great Speeches* (New York: Simon & Schuster, 1965), p. 388–392.

16. Eric B. Wolff, title unknown, in *Winning Orations 1994* (Interstate Oratorical Association), p. 67.

17. Richard D. Propes, "Alone in the Dark," in *Winning Orations 1985* (Interstate Oratorical Association), p. 23.

18. Ibid.

19. Kathryn Kasdorf, untitled speech, in *Winning Orations 1985,* p. 16.

20. Brenda Gerlach, "The Thickening Fog," in *Winning Orations 1985,* p. 73.

21. Joseph D. Stephens, "Corporate Sponsored Day Care," in *Winning Orations 1985,* p. 83.

22. Ann Landers, "To Understand a Trillion, Start Counting," *San Antonio Express-News,* 29 April 1995.

23. Garry Trudeau, "The Value of Impertinent Questions" (1986), in Owen Peterson, ed., *Representative American Speeches 1986–1987* (New York: H. W. Wilson, 1987), p. 133.

24. John J. Isaza, "The Phone Muggers," in *Winning Orations 1985* (Interstate Oratorical Association), p. 83.

25. Forrester Research, Inc., as appearing in Associated Press, "Net Players Change," *Austin American-Statesman,* 21 February 1996, p. D1.

26. Tara Trainor, "A Loyal Friend," in *Winning Orations 1990* (Interstate Oratorical Association), p. 52.

27. Jay W. Brown, "The Burning Question of Our Nation's Books," in *Winning Orations 1984* (Interstate Oratorical Association), p. 43.

28. Lester L. Tobias, letter to the editor, *Newsweek,* 22 February 1988, p. 4. Courtesy *Newsweek.*

29. Robert Rager, "Amusement Park Safety," in *Winning Orations 1985* (Interstate Oratorical Association), p. 38.

30. Ibid., p. 39.

31. Ibid., p. 40.

32. Ibid, p. 41.

33. Joseph K. Ott, "America's Internal Cold War," in *Winning Orations 1985,* p. 45.

34. Ibid.

35. Beth Wolff, "The Technological Twilight Zone," in *Winning Orations 1985,* p. 76.

CHAPTER 9

1. Adapted from Craig Scott, "The American Farm Crisis," in *Winning Orations 1986* (Mankato, MN: Interstate Oratorical Association, 1986), p. 15–18.

2. Adapted from John Kuehn, title unknown, *Winning Orations 1994* p. 83–85.

3. Adapted from Laurel Johnson, "Where There's a Will There's a Way," in *Winning Orations 1986,* p. 59–62.

4. Adapted from Vonda Ramey, "Can You Read This?" in *Winning Orations 1985* p. 32–35.

5. Adapted from Amy Stewart, title unknown, *Winning Orations 1994,* p. 47–49.

6. The following information is adapted from Devorah A. Lieberman, *Public Speaking in the Multicultural Environment* (Englewood Cliffs, N.J.: Prentice Hall, 1994).

7. Adapted from Andy Wood, "Superbugs: Scourge of the Post-Antibiotic Era," *Winning Orations 1994,* p. 23–25.

8. Richard C. Delancey, "About the Same Is Not the Same," *Winning Orations 1993* p. 95.

9. Loren Schwarzwalter, "An Answer for America's Future," in *Winning Orations 1987,* p. 86–87.

10. Chris Fleming, title unknown, in *Winning Orations 1994,* p. 50.

11. Athena Papachronis, title unknown, in *Winning Orations 1994*, p. 33.

12. Jo Leda Carpenter, "Sun Exposure and Cancer: A Cause and Effect," in *Winning Orations 1987*, p. 17.

13. Jamie Lee Wagner, "Sleep Deprivation: Our Nation's Other Deficit," in *Winning Orations 1994*, p.7.

14. Rachel F. Glickson, "Green Marketing," in *Winning Orations 1994*, p.15.

15. Kent Busek, "Farm Suicides," in *Winning Orations 1986*, p. 82.

16. Melody Hopkins, "Collegiate Athletes: A Contradiction in Terms," in *Winning Orations 1986*, p. 111.

17. Johnson, "Where There's a Will," p. 59.

18. Heather Green, "Radon in Our Homes," in *Winning Orations 1986*, p. 4.

19. Molly A. Lovell, "Hotel Security: The Hidden Crisis," in *Winning Orations 1994*, p. 18.

20. Neela Latey, "U.S. Customs Procedures: Danger to Americans' Health and Society," in *Winning Orations 1986*, p. 22.

21. Susan Stevens, "Teacher Shortage," in *Winning Orations 1986*, p. 27.

22. Green, "Radon in Our Homes," p. 5.

23. Terry O'Bryan Kiszka, "Your Last Gift to Life—Your Human Organs," in *Winning Orations 1986*, p. 35.

24. Lori Van Overbeke, "NutraSweet," in *Winning Orations 1986*, p. 58.

25. Adapted from Heath Honaker, "A New Brand of Homeless," in *Winning Orations 1986*, p. 108–111.

● CHAPTER 10

1. Kathryn Kasdorf, untitled speech, in *Winning Orations 1985* (Mankato, MN: Interstate Oratorical Association, 1985), p. 16.

2. Amy Gillespie, "Listen Up!" in *Winning Orations 1985*, p. 48.

3. Mary Tatum, "Silver Dental Fillings: The Toxic Poison," in *Winning Orations 1987*, p. 1.

4. Andy Wood, "Superbugs: Scourge of the Post-Antibiotic Era," in *Winning Orations 1994*, p. 23.

5. Loren Schwarzwalter, "An Answer for America's Future," in *Winning Orations 1987*, p. 85.

6. This illustration and all succeeding illustrations without reference numbers were written by the authors.

7. Patricia A. Cirucci, "Grounds for Disaster," in *Winning Orations 1991* (Interstate Oratorical Association), p. 102.

8. Barbara Bush, "Choices and Change," *Vital Speeches of the Day* (1 July 1990): 549.

9. Jen Siebels, "AZT: The 'Magic Bullet' That Missed," *Winning Orations 1994* (Interstate Oratorical Association), p. 20.

10. Kasdorf, title unknown, p. 16.

11. Kimberly Lewis, "Accident Prone," in *Winning Orations 1991*, p. 114.

12. Theresa Clinkenbeard, "The Loss of Childhood," in *Winning Orations 1984*, p. 4.

13. Adapted from Eleanor L. Doan, ed., *The Speaker's Sourcebook* (Grand Rapids, MI: Zondervan, 1960), p. 128.

14. Joe Griffith, *Speaker's Library of Business Stories, Anecdotes, and Humor* (Englewood Cliffs, NJ: Prentice Hall, 1990), p. 335.

15. Douglas MacArthur, "Farewell to the Cadets," address delivered at West Point, May 12, 1962. Reprinted in Richard L. Johannesen, R.R. Allen, and Wil A. Linkugel, eds., *Contemporary American Speeches*, 7th ed. (Dubuque, IA: Kendall/Hunt, 1992), p. 393.

16. Lisa M. Kralik, "Geographical Illiteracy," in *Winning Orations 1987* (Interstate Oratorical Association), p. 76.

17. Richard Propes, "Alone in the Dark," in *Winning Orations 1985*, p. 22.

18. Beth Moberg, "Licensed to Kill," in *Winning Orations 1985*, p. 89.

19. Jane M. Hatch, *The American Book of Days* (New York: Wilson, 1978).

20. Ruth W. Gregory, *Anniversaries and Holidays* (Chicago: American Library Association, 1975).

21. Keith Geiger, "A Bill of Rights for Children," address delivered to the NEA, July 4, 1991. Reprinted in Owen Peterson, ed., *Representative American Speeches, 1991–92* (New York: The H.W. Wilson Company, 1992), p. 99–100.

22. Andra Farthing, "Censorship of the Media by the Media," in *Winning Orations 1991* (Interstate Oratorical Association), p. 26.

23. Barbara Jordan, "Change: From What to What?" *Vital Speeches of the Day* (15 August 1992): 651.

24. Al Gore, "The Cynics Are Wrong," address delivered at Harvard, June 9, 1994. Abridged and reprinted in *Harvard magazine* (July-August 1994): 28.

25. Student speech, University of Miami, 1981.

26. John Ryan, "Emissions Tampering: Get the Lead Out," in *Winning Orations 1985* (Interstate Oratorical Association), p. 63.

27. MacArthur, "Farewell to the Cadets," p. 396.

28. John O'Connor, "Buy the People," in *Winning Orations 1984* (Interstate Oratorical Association), p. 27.

29. Jay W. Brown, "The Burning Question of Our Nation's Books," in *Winning Orations 1984*, p. 46.

30. Kristen Amondsen, "Outfoxing Mr. Badwrench," in *Winning Orations 1987*, p. 32.

31. Pam Crity, title unknown, in *Winning Orations 1994*, p. 40.

32. Kralik, "Geographical Illiteracy," p. 78.

33. Lori Spiczka, "Farming: It's a Matter of Life and Death," in *Winning Orations 1987*, p. 106.

34. Robert Browning, "Rabbi Ben Ezra," *Dramatis Personae* (1864). quoted by John Mietus, Jr., "The Best Is Yet to Be," in *Winning Orations 1987*, p. 54.

35. Mietus, "The Best Is Yet to Be," p. 57.

36. Benjamin P. Berlinger, "Health and the Hubris of Human Nature: The Tragic Myth of Antibiotics," in *Winning Orations 1987*, p. 35.

37. Martin Luther King, Jr., "I Have a Dream," in Johannesen et al., *Contemporary American Speeches*, p. 369.

38. Ronald Reagan, "Address to the Republican National Convention," address delivered to the Republican National Convention on August 15, 1988. Reprinted in the *Austin American-Statesman*, 16 August 1988, p. A7.

39. Mark Culkins, "Killer in the Grass," in *Winning Orations 1987* (Interstate Oratorical Association), p. 10.

● CHAPTER 11

1. Adapted from Michael Butterworth, "The Road to Security: How to Combat the Carjacking Crisis," *Winning Orations 1993* (Mankato, MN: Interstate Oratorical Society, 1993), p. 23–25.

2. Charles Parnell, "Speechwriting: The Profession and the Practice," *Vital Speeches of the Day* (15 January 1990): 56.

3. Both sample outlines in this chapter are adapted from Mark Culkins, "A Tisket, a Tasket, a Tandem Truck Casket," in *Winning Orations 1986* (Interstate Oratorical Society), p. 9–12.

4. From Milton Meltzer, *Mark Twain Himself* (New York: Wings Books, 1960), p. 121. Original in the New York Public Library.

● CHAPTER 12

1. Advertisements and headlines compiled by Jay Leno, *Headlines* (New York: Wing Books, 1992).

2. "President's Body Language Loud and Clear," *The Sun* (Baltimore), 10 August 1994, p. 1D.

3. Ronald Reagan, "Address to the United Nations," *Vital Speeches of the Day* (15 October 1984): 6.

4. Jimmy Carter, "Soviet Military Intervention in Afghanistan," *Vital Speeches of the Day* (15 June 1980): 195.

5. Patricia Raybon, quoted on National Public Radio's *Weekend Edition* (4 September 1995).

6. Bill Clinton, Speech delivered at the signing ceremony for the Jewish-Palestinian peace agreement, September 13, 1993. In Owen Peterson, ed., *Representative American Speeches 1993-94* (New York: H. W. Wilson, 1994), p. 101.

7. National Archives and Records Administration, *Kennedy's Inaugural Address of 1961* (1987), p. 1.

8. Paul Roberts, "How to Say Nothing in Five Hundred Words,"

in William H. Roberts and Gregoire Turgeson, eds., *About Language* (Boston: Houghton Mifflin, 1986), p. 28.

9. George Orwell, "Politics and the English Language," reprinted in William H. Roberts and Gregoire Turgeson, eds., *About Language* (Boston: Houghton Mifflin, 1986), p. 282.

10. Erma Bombeck, "Missing Grammar Genes Is, Like, the Problem," *Austin American-Statesman*, 3 March 1992.

11. Ann Devroy, "House Republicans Get Talking Points: GOP Pollster's Memo Offers Advice on How to Win With Words," *Washington Post*, 2 February 1995, p. A9.

12. Peggy Noonan, *What I Saw at the Revolution* (New York: Random House, 1990), p. 71.

13. We acknowledge the following source for several examples used in our discussion of language style: William Jordan, "Rhetorical Style," *Oral Communication Handbook* (Warrensburg, MO: Central Missouri State University, 1971–1972), p. 32–34.

14. John Milton, *Paradise Lost*, II. ll. 482, 498.

15. Theodore Parker, eulogy for Daniel Webster (October 31, 1852), in Houston Peterson, ed., *A Treasury of the World's Great Speeches* (New York: Simon & Schuster, 1965), p. 410–416.

16. John F. Kennedy, inaugural address (January 20, 1961), in Bower Aly and Lucille F. Aly, eds., *Speeches in English* (New York: Random House, 1968), p. 272.

17. Abraham Lincoln, farewell address, Springfield, IL (February 4, 1861), in Peterson, *A Treasury of the world's Great Speeches*, p. 508–509.

18. Ralph Waldo Emerson, "The American Scholar," delivered August 31, 1837, in Glenn R. Capp., ed., *Famous Speeches in American History* (Indianapolis: Bobbs-Merrill, 1963), p. 84.

19. Federal News Service, "President Clinton's Address to the People of Berlin," delivered at the Brandenburg Gate, 12 July 1994.

20. National Archives and Records Administration, *Franklin D. Roosevelt's Inaugural Address of 1933* (1988), p. 13–14.

21. Kennedy, inaugural address, in Aly and Aly, *Speeches in English*, p. 275.

22. William Faulkner, acceptance of the Nobel prize for literature, delivered December 10, 1950, in Peterson, *A Treasury of the World's Great Speeches*, p. 814–815.

23. Patrick Henry, "Liberty or Death," delivered March 23, 1775, in Capp, *Famous Speeches in American History*, p. 22.

24. Dan Rather, "Call It Courage," delivered at the annual international convention of the Radio-Television News Directors Association, Miami Beach, Florida, September 29, 1993, in Owen Peterson, ed., *Representative American Speeches 1993–94* (New York: H. W. Wilson, 1994), p. 127.

25. National Archives and Records Administration, *Franklin Roosevelt's Inaugural Address of 1933*, p. 22.

26. Franklin D. Roosevelt, first fireside chat on March 12, 1933, in Peterson, *Treasury*, p. 751–754.

27. Winston Churchill, "finest hour" address, delivered on June

18, 1940, in Peterson, *Treasury,* p. 754–760.

28. Winston Churchill, address to the Congress of the United States, delivered on December 26, 1941, in Aly and Aly, *Speeches in English,* p. 233.

29. Adapted from Jordan, *Oral Communication Handbook,* p. 34.

30. Osker Spicer, "Actor Olmos Tells Youth to Dig Down for Strength," *The Oregonian,* 12 October 1994, p. B1.

31. Reuters News Agency, "Pope Calls Bosnian War Europe's Shipwreck," 9 January 1995.

32. In National Archives and Records Administration, *Franklin Roosevelt's Inaugural Address of 1933,* p. 12.

33. "Dear Abby," *San Marcos Daily Record,* 5 January 1993, p. 7.

34. Activity developed by Loren Reid, *Speaking Well* (New York: McGraw-Hill, 1982), p. 96.

35. "Reference to Rape Edited From Graduation Speech," *The Kansas City Star,* 5 June 1995, p. B3.

⬤ CHAPTER 13

1. James W. Gibson, John A. Kline, and Charles R. Gruner, "A Reexamination of the First Course in Speech at U.S. Colleges and Universities," *Speech Teacher,* 23 (September 1974): 206–214.

2. Ray Birdwhistle, *Kinesics and Context* (Philadelphia: University of Pennsylvania Press, 1970).

3. Alan H. Monroe, "Measurement and Analysis of Audience Reaction to Student Speakers' Studies in Attitude Changes," *Bulletin of Purdue University Studies in Higher Education,* 22 (1937).

4. Paul Heinberg, "Relationship of Content and Delivery to General Effectiveness," *Speech Monographs,* 30 (June 1963): 105–107.

5. Albert Mehrabian, *Nonverbal Communication* (Hawthrone, NY: Aldine, 1972).

6. Steven A. Beebe and Thompson Biggers, "The Effect of Speaker Delivery upon Listener Emotional Response," paper presented at the International Communication Association, May 1989.

7. Paul Ekman, Wallace V. Friesen, and K. R. Schere, "Body Movement and Voice Pitch in Deception Interaction," *Semiotica* 16 (1976): 23–27; Mark Knapp, R. P. Hart, and H. S. Dennis, "An Exploration of Deception as a Communication Construct," *Human Communication Research* 1 (1974): 15–29.

8. Roger Ailes, *You Are the Message* (New York: Doubleday, 1989), p. 37–38.

9. Neil Rudenstien "John Harvard's Journal," *Harvard Magazine* July-August 1994, p. 43.

10. James C. McCroskey, Virginia P. Richmond, Aino Sallinen, Joan M. Fayer, and Robert A. Barraclough, "A Cross-Cultural and Multi-Behavioral Analysis of the Relationship Between Nonverbal Immediacy and Teacher Evaluation," *Communication Education* 44 (1995): 281–290.

11. Michael J. Beatty, "Some Effects of Posture on Speaker Credibility," library paper, Central Missouri State University, 1973.

12. Steven A. Beebe, "Eye Contact: A Nonverbal Determinant of Speaker Credibility," *Speech Teacher,* 23 (January 1974): 21–25; Steven A. Beebe, "Effects of Eye Contact, Posture and Vocal Inflection upon Credibility and Comprehension," *Australian Scan Journal of Nonverbal Communication,* 7–8 (1979–80): 57–70; Martin Cobin, "Response to Eye Contact," *Quarterly Journal of Speech,* 48 (1963): 415–419.

13. Beebe, "Eye Contact," 21–25.

14. Paul Ekman, Wallace V. Friesen, and S. S. Tomkins, "Facial Affect Scoring Technique: A First Validity Study," *Semiotica* 3 (1971).

15. Adapted from Lester Schilling, *Voice and Diction for the Speech Arts* (San Marcos: Southwest Texas State University, 1979).

16. These suggestions were made by Jo Sprague and Douglas Stuart, *The Speaker's Handbook* (Fort Worth, TX: Harcourt Brace Jovanovich, 1992), p. 331, and were based upon research by Patricia A. Porter, Margaret Grant, and Mary Draper, *Communicating Effectively in English: Oral Communication for Non-Native Speakers* (Belmont, CA: Wadsworth, 1985).

17. Stephen Lucas, *The Art of Public Speaking* (New York: Random House, 1986), p. 231.

18. "Comment" *The New Yorker* March 1, 1993.

⬤ CHAPTER 14

1. Emil Bohn and David Jabusch, "The Effect of Four Methods of Instruction on the Use of Visual Aids in Speeches," *The Western Journal of Speech Communication,* 46 (Summer 1982): 253–265.

⬤ CHAPTER 15

1. John R. Johnson and Nancy Szczupakiewicz, "The Public Speaking Course: Is It Preparing Students with Work-Related Public Speaking Skills?" *Communication Education,* 36 (April 1987): 131–137.

2. Malcom Knowles, *Self-Directed Learning* (Chicago: Follett Publishing, 1975).

3. This discussion is based on an excellent review of the literature found in Katherine E. Rowan, "A New Pedagogy for Explanatory Public Speaking: Why Arrangement Should Not Substitute for Invention," *Communication Education* 44 (1995): 236–250.

4. "Chocoholic? Look It Up," *Newsweek,* 14 September 1987, p. 69.

5. Rowan, "A New Pedagogy for Explanatory Public Speaking."

6. Ibid.

7. Marcie Groover, "Learning to Communicate: The Importance of Speech Education in Public Schools," in *Winning Orations, 1984* (Mankato, Minn.: Interstate Oratorical Association, 1984), p. 7.

8. Rowan.

9. Marie Ereni Ciach, "Sleeping with the Enemy: House Dust Mites," *Winning Orations, 1991* (Mankato, Minn.: Interstate Oratorical Association, 1991).

CHAPTER 16

1. Alvin Toffler, *Future Shock* (New York: Bantam Books, 1970), p. 3.

2. Leon Festinger, *A Theory of Cognitive Dissonance* (Evanston, Ill.: Row, Peterson, 1957).

3. Vonda Ramey, "Can You Read This?" in *Winning Orations, 1985* (Mankato, Minn.: Interstate Oratorical Association, 1985), p. 36.

4. For additional discussion, see Wayne C. Minnick, *The Art of Persuasion* (Boston: Houghton Mifflin, 1967).

5. Abraham H. Maslow, "A Theory of Human Motivation," in *Motivation and Personality* (New York: Harper & Row, 1954), chap. 5.

6. John Ryan, "Emissions Tampering: Get the Lead Out," in *Winning Orations, 1985*, p. 50.

7. For a discussion of fear appeal research, see Irving L. Janis and Seymour Feshback, "Effects of Fear Arousing Communications," *Journal of Abnormal and Social Psychology*, 48 (January 1953): 78–92; Frederick A. Powell and Gerald R. Miller, "Social Approval and Disapproval Cues in Anxiety-Arousing Situations," *Speech Monographs*, 34 (June 1967): 152–159; and Kenneth L. Higbee, "Fifteen Years of Fear Arousal: Research on Threat Appeals, 1953-68," *Psychological Bulletin*, 72 (December 1969): 426–444.

8. C. W. Sherif, M. Sherif, and R. E. Nebergall, *Attitudes and Attitude Change: The Social Judgment-Involvement Approach* (Philadelphia: Saunders, 1965).

CHAPTER 17

1. For an excellent discussion of the influence of culture on public speaking see: Devorah A. Lieberman, *Public Speaking in the Multicultural Environment* (Englewood Cliffs, NJ: Prentice Hall, 1994), p. 10.

2. Lieberman, G. Fisher, "International Negotiation," in Larry. A. Samovar and Richard. E. Porter, eds., *Intercultural Communication: A Reader* (Belmont, CA: Wadsworth, 1991), p. 193–200.

3. Ibid.

4. Jeffrey E. Jamison, "Alkali Batteries: Powering Electronics and Polluting the Environment," in *Winning Orations 1991* (Mankato, MN: Interstate Oratorical association, 1991), p. 43.

5. Roger Ailes, *You Are the Message* (New York: Doubleday, 1989).

6. Albert Mehrabian and J. A. Russell, *An Approach to Environmental Psychology* (Cambridge: MIT Press, 1974); T. Biggers and B. Pryor, "Attitude Change as a Function of Emotion Eliciting Qualities," *Personality and Social Psychology Bulletin*, 8 (1982): 94–99; Steven A. Beebe and T. Biggers, "Emotion-Eliciting Qualities of Speech Delivery and Their Effect on Credibility and Comprehension," paper presented at the annual meeting of the International Communication Association, New Orleans, May 1989.

7. See: Irving Janis and S. Feshback, "Effects of Fear-Arousing Communication," *Journal of Abnormal and Social Psychology*, 48 (1953): 78–92; Fredric A. Powell, "The Effects of Anxiety-Arousing Message When Related to Personal, Familial, and Impersonal Referents," *Speech Monographs*, 32 (1965): 102–106.

8. Donald C. Bryant, "Rhetoric: Its Functions and Its Scope," *Quarterly Journal of Speech*, 39 (December 1953): 26.

9. Jamison, "Alkali Batteries," p. 43.

10. Carl I. Hovland, Arthur A. Lunsdaine, and Fred D. Sheffield, "The Effects of Presenting 'One Side' versus 'Both Sides' in Changing Opinions on a Controversial Subject," in *Experiments on Mass Communication* (Princeton: Princeton University Press, 1949). Also see: Arthur Lunsdaine and Irving Janis, "Resistance to 'Counter-Propaganda' Produced by a One-Sided versus a Two-Sided 'Propaganda' Presentation." *Public Opinion Quarterly*, (1953): 311–318.

11. Douglas Ehninger, Bruce E. Gronbeck, Ray E. McKerrow, and Alan H. Monroe, *Principles and Types of Speech Communication* (Glenview, IL: Scott, Foresman, 1986), p. 15.

12. Vic Vieth, "Prisoners of Conscience," in *Winning Orations 1984* (Interstate Oratorical Association), p. 46.

13. Ibid., p. 47.

14. Ibid.

15. Ibid., p. 49.

16. Martin Luther King, Jr., "I Have a Dream" (August 28, 1963), in Houston Peterson, ed., *A Treasury of the World's Great Speeches* (New York: Simon & Schuster, 1965), p. 835–839.

17. Vieth, "Prisoners of Conscience," p. 49.

18. Jamison, "Alkali Batteries," p. 43–46.

CHAPTER 18

1. Jim Riley, "Motivational Event Preaches Success With Capital 'S,'" *The Tampa Tribune*, 11 December 1994, p. 1.

2. Roger E. Flax, "A Manner of Speaking," *Ambassador*, May-June 1991, p. 37.

3. Everett M. Dirksen, "Nominating Speech for Barry Goldwater" (July 15, 1964), in James R. Andrews and David Zarefsky, eds., *Contemporary American Voices* (New York: Simon & Schuster, 1965), p. 815.

4. Erma Bombeck, "Abbreviated Thank-you's Allow Us More Time to Study Danson's Head," *Austin American-Statesman*, 22 June 1993, p. F3.

5. "Arafat Calls for Speedier Peace in Nobel Speech," Reuter News Agency, 10 December 1994.

6. Elie Wiesel, "Acceptance of the 1986 Nobel Peace Prize," *The New York Times*, 11 December 1986, p. A8.

7. William Faulkner, acceptance of the Nobel prize for literature (December 10, 1950), in Houston Petersen, ed., *A Treasury of the World's Great Speeches* (New York: Simon & Schuster, 1965), p. 815.

8. Barbara Jordan, "Change: From What to What?" *Vital Speeches of the Day* (15 August 1992): 651.

9. Beverly Chiodo, "Choose Wisely: Establish a Good Name and Reputation," *Vital Speeches of the Day* (1 November 1987): 40.

10. Art Buchwald, as quoted by Win Borden in "Recommendations for Graduates: How You Play the Game of Life," *Vital Speeches of the Day* (15 April 1985): 400.

11. Edwin J. Feulner, Jr., "Fear and Freedom," *Vital Speeches of the Day* (1 July 1994): 571.

12. Bill Clinton, speech at Pointe du Hoc, France (June 1994), as quoted in David Shribman, "President, a Child of World War II, Thanks a Generation," *Boston Globe*, 7 June 1994, p. 1.

13. Edward Kennedy, eulogy for Jacqueline Kennedy Onassis (May 1994), as quoted in "The Texts of Personal Tributes and Poems at the Services for Mrs. Onassis," *The New York Times*, 24 May 1994, p. A10.

14. Robert Dole, "Eulogy for Former President Richard M. Nixon," *Vital Speeches of the Day* (1 June 1994): p. 483.

15. Adlai Stevenson, "Eulogy on Sir Winston Churchill" (January 28, 1965), in Halford Ross Ryan, *American Rhetoric from Roosevelt to Reagan*, 2d ed. (Prospect Heights, IL: Waveland Press, 1987), p. 178.

16. Dave Barry, "Speak! Speak!" *Austin American-Statesman*, 2 June 1991, p. C4.

17. Sarah Booth Conroy, "State Dinners Offer Speech as First Course," *Austin American-Statesman*, 10 November 1989.

18. Debi Martin, "Laugh Lines," *Austin American-Statesman*, 20 May 1988, p. D1.

19. Chris O'Keefe, untitled speech, in John K.Boaz and James Brey, eds., *1987 Championship Debates and Speeches* (Speech Communication Association and American Forensic Association, 1987), p.99.

20. Janice Payan, "Opportunities for Hispanic Women: It's Up to Us," *Vital Speeches of the Day* (1 September 1990): 697–700.

CHAPTER 19

1. Group communication principles presented in this chapter are adapted from Steven A. Beebe and John T. Masterson, *Communicating in Small Groups. Principles and Practices,* 3d ed. (New York: Harper Collins, 1977).

2. Roger K. Mosvick and Robert B. Nelson, *We've Got to Start Meeting Like This! A Guide to Successful Business Meeting Management* (Glenview, IL.: Scott, Foresman, 1987), p. 3.

3. Randy Y. Hirokawa and Roger Pace, "A Descriptive Investigation of the Possible Communication-Based Reasons for Effective and Ineffective Group Decision Making," *Communication Monographs,* 50 (December 1983): 363–379.

4. Randy Y. Hirokawa, "Group Communication and Problem-Solving Effectiveness: An Investigation of Group Phases," *Human Communication Research,* 9 (Summer 1983): 291–305.

5. Dennis S. Gouran, "Variables Related to Consensus in Group Discussion of Question of Policy," *Speech Monographs,* 36 (August 1969): 385–391.

6. Kenneth D. Benne and Paul Sheats, "Functional Roles of Groups Members," *Journal of Social Issues,* 4 (Spring 1948): 41–49.

7. Ralph White and Ronald Lippitt, "Leader Behavior and Member Reaction in Three 'Social Climates,'" in Darwin Cartwright and Alvin Zander, eds., *Group Dynamics,* 3d ed. (New York: Harper and Row, 1968), p. 319.

8. Dave Barry, *Dave Barry's Guide to Life* (New York: Wing Books, 1991), p. 311.

9. Mosvick and Nelson, *We've Got to Stop Meeting Like This!*

10. Thomas A. Kayser, *Mining Group Gold* (El Segundo, CA: Serif Publishing, 1990), p. 42.

11. Mosvick and Nelson, *We've Got to Stop Meeting Like This!*

Index

Narrowing a topic, 21, 113–115
Need for public speaking skills, 4–5
Needs as motivators, 364–365
Negative motivation, 367
Neutral audience, 88, 89, 398–399
Newspapers, 111, 143–145, 149, 155
Noise, 8, 10
Nominating speeches, 417–418
Non sequitur fallacy, 392
Nonverbal communication
    audience cues, 95–96
    in delivery, 277–278, 284–290, 295–296
    emotional appeals, 394
    listening skills, 60–61
    postspeech responses, 99
    reinforcing key ideas, 345
    responding to nonverbal cues, 96–98
    transitions, 205
Notes, speaking, 249–250
Note taking, 65–66, 138, 139, 156–158

Objects, speeches about, 332–334, 337
Objects as visual aids, 308, 321
Occasions
    introductory references to, 227–228
    special-occasion speeches, 413–431
    topic selection and, 20, 108–109
Omission, 264–265
Online services, 143
Open-ended questions, 93
Operational definitions, 171, 172
Opinions, 179–181, 202–203, 389
Oral citation, 47
Oral language style, 257–259
Organizations, finding, 140–141
Organizing speeches, 187–252
    conclusions, 229–234
    introductions, 216–229
    main points, 190–197
    outlines, 26–27, 126, 127, 197–198, 239–252
    overview, 25–28
    persuasive speeches, 400–407
    signposts, 203–208
    subdividing main points, 197–198

supporting material, 199–203
Outlines, 239–252
    delivery outline, 246–248
    format, 26–27, 242–243
    from main ideas, 126, 127
    preparation outline, 240–246
    subdividing main points, 197–198
Outside distractions, 58, 59
Overhead transparencies, 315–316
Overreaction, avoiding, 61

Pacing informative speeches, 348
Panel discussions, 446
Parallelism, 265–266
Passive leaders, 443
Pauses, 293–294
People, speeches about, 335–336, 337
People as visual aids, 309
Periodicals
    electronic indexes, 143–145
    library indexes, 148–149
    library resources, 148
    locating materials, 154–155
    newspapers, 111, 143–145, 149, 155
    topics from, 111–112
Personal appearance, 35, 139, 295–296
Personal concerns and listening, 57–59
Personification, 268–269
Persuasive speeches, 353–411
    adapting to the audience, 397–400
    defined, 22, 117
    developing, 369–373
    emotional appeals, 392–397
    establishing credibility, 380–383
    ethics of, 42–43, 389–392, 396
    goals of, 355–360
    informative speeches and, 354–355
    logic and evidence in, 384–392
    motivating listeners, 360–368
    organizing, 400–407
    overview, 21, 116–117
    principles of, 373–374
    sample, 407–409

Photographs as visual aids, 310
Physical activity and anxiety, 34, 35
Physiological needs, 364
Picture graphs, 313, 314
Pie graphs, 312, 313
Pitch, vocal, 292
Plagiarism, 45–46
Policy, proposition of, 371–372, 373
Positive motivation, 365–367
Postspeech analysis, 98–100
Posture, 288–289
Prejudice, 58–59
Premises, major and minor, 386
Preparation outline, 240–246
Presentations, 445–447
Previews, 204, 205–207, 220
Primacy principle, 192, 201–202
Problem-solution organization, 195–196, 401–402, 406
Procedures, speeches about, 334–335, 337, 339–340, 342
Pronunciation, 292
Proof, 384
Propositions, 369–373
Proximity, 183, 218–219, 343
Public relations speeches, 415–416
Purposes
    alternative purposes, 117
    central idea vs., 120–121, 123
    of conclusions, 229–232
    determining, 21–22, 115–119
    ethics and, 42–43
    general purposes, 21, 22, 116–117
    of informative speeches, 330–331
    of interviews, 136
    of introductions, 216–221
    of persuasive speeches, 355–360, 369–372
    specific purpose, 21–22, 117–119
    of visual aids, 306–307

Questionnaires, 92–94
Questions
    for interviews, 137–138, 139
    introducing speeches, 225
Quotations, 151, 180, 181, 223–224

Race, 82–84
Racist language, 259–261

Rate of speaking, 293
Reading for topic ideas, 111–112
Reading manuscript speeches, 279
Reasoning, 43–44, 125, 384–392
Receiver, 8, 10
Recency, 182, 192, 201
Recent events, referring to, 226–227
Receptive audience, 397–398
Recording interviews, 138, 139
Red herring fallacy, 391
Redundancy, need for, 56–57, 344–345
Reference materials, 112–113, 150–151
Reflective thinking, 435–438
Refutation, 402, 406
Rehearsal, 28–29, 33, 276, 297–298, 320
Reliability of statistics, 176–177
Religion of audience, 86
Remembering, listening stage, 56–57
Repetition, 258, 266, 285
Reports, 414–415, 446
Researching, 152–158
Resources for supporting material, 25
    electronic resources, 141–146
    interviews, 135–140
    library resources, 146–152
    locating materials, 154–155
    mail-order materials, 140–141
    personal resources, 135
    research organization, 152–158
Responsibilities of leadership, 440–442
Responsiveness of audience, 96

Safety needs, 364–365
Sample size for statistics, 176–177
Sedition Act, 41
Selecting
    listening stage, 55, 57
    supporting material, 182–183
    topic, 20–21, 33, 107–113, 368–369
    visual aids, 319
Self-actualization needs, 365
Self-critiquing, 70
Self-esteem needs, 365